TEXTILES

A CLASSIFICATION OF TECHNIQUES

TEXTILES

A CLASSIFICATION OF TECHNIQUES

ANNEMARIE
SEILER-BALDINGER

Smithsonian Institution Press
WASHINGTON, D.C.

**To the memory of Kristin and Alfred Bühler,
whose intellectual legacy it has been my privilege to continue**

Special thanks go to the **Stiftung zur Förderdung des Museums für Völkerkunde und Schweizerischen Museums für Volkskunde Basel** for funding the translation of the German text.

Published in the United States of America
by Smithsonian Institution Press

ISBN 1-56098-509-7

Library of Congress Catalog Number [still to come]

First published in Australia
by Crawford House Press, Bathurst, New South Wales

Cover: Design by Kylie Ledger
Woven blanket of the Mabo-Peul, brocade and tapestry with embroidered seam, Youvaru, Mali, III 20468
Sarong from the Philippines, dovetailed tapestry, IIc 20040

Printed in Hong Kong

00 99 98 97 96 95 94   5 4 3 2 1

The following drawings were prepared for earlier versions at the Museum für Völkerkunde Basel, using various sources: figs 8, 16, 19, 45, 64, 65d, 68, 70, 76, 85, 86, 120-128 (without 125a), 139, 143-151, 173, 174, 176, 179b, 181-183, 185, 186, 189, 190, 198a, 199b, 201, 203-220, 222, 223a, 225, 226, 230-238, 240, 242-245, 247, 249, 250, 253-265, 267-276, 278, 280-289.

Fig. 7 was drawn by Christina Schäublin, fig. 129 by Raphael Voléry; the remaining figures have been prepared by Susanna Gisin, Basel, using the following sources:
12d, 116, 132a-c, 202a-b from: P. Collingwood; Textile and Weaving Structures. London 1987
72b-c, 79, 80b-c, 81c, 82a-c, 83b, 84a-b, 93a-c, 134d-e from: Noémi Speiser; The Manual of Braiding. Basel 1983
94a-c, 96a-e, 98, 100a-b, 101, 202a+c-e from: P. Collingwood; The Techniques of Sprang. London 1974
136b-c, 137, 140 from: P. Collingwood; The Techniques of Tablet-Weaving. London 1982
262 from: P. Collingwood; The Techniques of Rug-Weaving. London 1968

Except where stated otherwise, the objects belong to the Museum of Ethnology, Basel, Switzerland, and were photographed by Peter Horner.

Contents

Index

Foreword

This book is a translation of the completely revised and expanded edition of Systematik der Textilen Techniken which appeared in 1991 (Basler Beiträge zur Ethnologie, vol. 32). It is based on the work Grundlagen zur Systematik der gesamten textilen Techniken produced by the pioneering efforts of my teachers Kristin and Alfred Bühler-Oppenheim (Denkschriften der Schweizerischen Naturforschenden Gesellschaft, Vol. LXXVIII, Tl. 2, Zurich 1948), and likewise focuses primarily on production processes and only secondarily on structures. As its title suggests, our classification is based essentially on techniques. It is therefore different in principle from Irene Emery's masterly work The Primary Structure of Fabrics (Washington D.C., 1966), which was discussed and expanded by Ann Rowe in 1984[1] and which is primarily concerned with the structures of finished fabrics. Both approaches have their pros and cons.[2] The "Washington" system has the great advantage that it can be applied to all textile products even if the process by which they are made is unknown or cannot be reconstructed. On the other hand, fabrics are likely to be grouped together even if they are produced by dissimilar methods.

The point is illustrated by the making of a simple piece of plaited fabric without the aid of any implements as opposed to the process of weaving which calls for sophisticated equipment. The structure of the finished material may be the same in both cases. Some intimation of the difficulties involved is given by the fact that, despite the rigour with which Emery adheres to her principle of classification, she cannot wholly dispense with some consideration of the methods of production.

Needless to say, our own system is open to equally pertinent criticism. Classification by methods of production has the great advantage of allowing the various techniques to be graded according to their level of sophistication. In the numerous cases where the working procedures are unknown it is often very hard to determine which method has been used without tedious and difficult investigations. Accordingly, the appendix to this book is intended to provide indications as to the criteria by which the technique used to obtain a given structure can be deduced.

It is undisputed that an exact description of a fabric must take both technique and structure into account, so that the two systems of classification are complementary and neither of them is complete without the other. On the other hand it must always be borne in mind that the number of structures is much smaller than the number of possible production techniques, i.e. there are many ways of obtaining one and the same structure. The terminology adopted in our classification therefore contains inevitable repetitions. The use of the term "weft wrapping" as opposed to "wrapping", for instance, is intended to make it clear that the former is purely a warp fabric technique while the latter is a plaiting method.

I am also aware of the difficulties involved in introducing new terminologies into a foreign language.[3] Robert Williamson and the late Dennis Stephenson have endeavoured to translate the German terms into English in as linguistically and technically correct a manner as possible. In this connection we followed the principle of ensuring that the employed term always expressed the number of thread systems, their relationship to each other and the structure. One exception in this respect is the terminology of knots, where more neutral and more precise designations based upon the mathematical theory of knots would have been desirable. In this case concessions have been made by retaining such customary but completely uninformative terms as (e.g.) "vertical granny knot".

In the case of some techniques notes on notation and theoretical aspects constitute a novel feature. Certain textile processes and structures have been found to display such striking regularities in their thread configurations that these can be handled mathematically.[4]

At all events it is quite conceivable that such an approach might also be instrumental in solving problems in systematics (particularly in the case of multiple-strand braiding and compound weaves).[5]

It is also to be expected that the future will produce "new" techniques.[6] Even the previously known processes are still far from having all been exhaustively investigated or systematised.

The terms given in foreign languages have been extended wherever possible. It is particularly unfortunate that French frequently lacks an appropriate vocabulary.[7]

In the bibliography, as in that of the German edition, works appearing up till 1990 have been included. Many new publications, mainly on the subject of weaving, have been produced since then. It is virtually impossible to include the whole of the world literature on textiles and no claims to completeness are made.

To make the literature easier to consult, the works have been arranged under various headings. Art historical studies dealing purely with stylistic rather than technical questions receive no or only marginal mention. Similarly, articles in technical journals intended for handicraft teachers or work instructors are omitted unless the studies are of a scientific nature.[8] Guidelines to the production of textiles (working instructions) are included only if they form part of a more extensive work.[9] Books or journals expressly devoted to carpets[10] have been omitted since carpet research forms a branch of its own within the field of textile science and would go beyond the compass of this work. The same also applies to the special field of lace.

Bark cloths, papyrus, felt and paper, i.e. fabrics which are not produced, or not solely produced, by mechanical means with the aid of interworking elements, have also been excluded. The "Basle" classification is thus narrower in its scope than Emery's work. In conclusion, an index facilitates reference to the various techniques and structures and to the equivalent terms in foreign languages.

I should like to express my thanks to those who have been instrumental in bringing out this English edition, in particular to the translators Robert Williamson and the late Dennis Q. Stephenson and to Norma Stephenson who carefully went over the manuscript and found time to discuss the terminological problems with me. My thanks also go to my former assistant Irene Reynolds, who helped me to read the proofs, and to my colleague Dr. Christian Kaufmann, who cooperated with Crawford House Press on my behalf whenever I was doing field work in South America.

Basle, December 1993

1. See her article "After Emery: Further Considerations of Fabric Classification and Terminology" (The Textile Museum Journal 23, Washington 1984:53-71).

2. For a neutral assessment of both systems consult Balfet and Desrosiers (1987:270ff.), Larsen (1986:34-36) and Barnes (Man 27,2,1992:418).

3. Particularly difficult problems present themselves in the field of primary textile techniques and warp fabrics (also see Rowe, 1984, 53ff.), whereas for (e.g.) weaving, a suitable vocabulary was available (Emery 1966, Rowe 1977, 1984; Burnham 1980, CIETA 1971).

4. cf. Seiler-Baldinger 1971, 1981, Frame 1984, Gibson 1977, Nordland 1966, Washburn-Crowe 1988 and Praeger 1986. I should like to thank Prof. Hans-Christoph Im Hof (Department of Mathematics, University of Basle), who provided me with the correct English terminology.

5. Nonmathematical approaches to the classification of multiple-strand braiding are to be found in Speiser (1983) whereas Larsen (1986), in spite of a promising chapter on "classification of interlacing", has scarcely anything new or even elucidatory to contribute.

6. As has been the case with ply-splitting (Quick/Stein 1982).

7. Romance languages are peculiarly inappropriate for a textile terminology. The vocabularies of the Centre International d'Etude des Textiles Anciens (CIETA) in Lyons, which have been translated into ten languages (German, English, Danish, Spanish, Finnish, Icelandic, Italian, Norwegian, Portuguese and Swedish), continue to concentrate on more advanced techniques of fabric production, especially on weaving, which accounts for only a small portion of the total number of textile techniques. In Portuguese Ribeiro (1988 inter alia) has taken the matter in hand whereas there is so far no definitive terminology in Spanish (Ann Rowe is presently collaborating with Peruvian colleagues in preparing a Spanish-English textile vocabulary, pers. comm. 1988).

8. e.g. Schweizerische Arbeitslehrerinnenzeitung (Basel, from 1917), Textilkunst (Hanover from 1973), Handwerken zonder Grenzen (Utrecht from 1982), The Bead Journal (Los Angeles from 1975) or Ornament (Los Angeles from 1985).

9. Further references to such books will be found in the relevant journals (see footnote 8), which are addressed to practicians, students and teachers.

10. e.g. Hali, the International Journal of Oriental Carpets and Textiles (London from 1978).

The Techniques of Element Production

For the elements or starting materials for the mechanical production of fabrics we also use the term threads. They may vary widely in material, appearance, strength,elasticity and fineness.

Piaroa woman plying cotton yarn, Majagua, Amazonas, Venezuela. Photo: A. Seiler-Baldinger

Production of Threads

Minimum Processing of the Raw Material

Threads of the simplest possible form are plant and animal products which need only the minimum of processing before use for the production of textiles. The main steps involve the collecting, cleaning, shredding, splitting and cutting of the material (e.g. roots, leaves and stalks), the extraction of fibres from stalks and leaves, and the cutting of skin, leather and metal foils. Elements obtained in this way, in contrast to those discussed below, are invariably rather short and are therefore not suitable for every kind of textile.

Reeling of Long Lengths of Threads

This method is used exclusively for certain types of silk, especially Chinese silk, which are obtained by reeling off the filament in its entire length from the cocoon.

Other terms used:

Abhaspeln von Fäden erheblicher Länge (Seiler-Baldinger 1991:8)
Haspeln, dévider, annaspare, innaspare, dobar, devanar, avhaspla (Burnham 1980:107)

Knotting of Short Elements

Pieces of leaf or bast fibres such as strips of bamboo, or bast of the banana tree or palm leaf, are tied together. After knotting, such threads can be twisted.

Other term used:

Verknüpfen kurzer Elemente (Seiler-Baldinger 1991:8)

Drawing of Metal Threads

Wire drawing is a special process in metal-working technology which is used occasionally to produce threads.

Other term used:

Ziehen von Metallfäden (Seiler-Baldinger 1991:8)

Twisting

Fibres or filaments of the same kind or of different origins are twisted between the hands or on a surface such as the thigh or calf, fresh material being continually added. This method is particularly suitable for long-fibred stem, bark and leaf bast.

Other terms used:

Twisting together two or more filaments (Emery 1966:8)
Throwing, torsion, torsione, torção, torsión, snodd (Burnham 1980:161)
Drillen (Seiler-Baldinger 1991:8)
Verdrillen (Burnham 1980:181)

Spinning

In this case the fibres are not twisted by hand only, but by the use of special implements such as the hand spindle or spinning wheel to which the rotary motion is imparted and at the same time augmented. These processes are particularly suitable for making threads from short fibres or hairs such as wool, cotton, flax or hemp, or from silk cocoons, or parts thereof which cannot be reeled. There are many transitional stages between twisting and spinning just as there are many different types of spinning implements and ways of using them.

Other terms used:

Single spun (Emery 1966:9)
Spinnen (Seiler-Baldinger 1991:8)
Filage, filature (Geijer/Hald 1974:80)
Filer (Burnham 1980:129)
Filare (CIETA 1971:58)
Hilar (CIETA 1971:58)
Fiação (Ribeiro 1988:91)
Spinna (Burnham 1981:129)

Strengthening and Ornamentation of Threads

These methods of thread formation are used to make elements of greater strength and thickness than can be achieved by twisting or spinning and they are also employed for thread ornamentation.

Plying

Two or more threads are twisted together, usually in a direction opposite to that of the spin of the original threads. The process can be repeated (2-ply, 3-ply etc.) and can be carried out manually or with the aid of ancillary equipment such as the ply spindle, gauge, or stick wheel (see direction of twist below).

Other terms used:
Zwirnen (Seiler-Baldinger 1991:9)
Retordre, mouliner (Geijer/Hald 1974:88)
Ritorto (CIETA 1971:74)
Retorcido conjunto simple/múltiple (Mirambell/Martínez 1986)
Tvinna (Geijer/Hald 1974:88)

Jaspé

Threads of different hues are twisted together. If the threads are woven, an "ikat-like" effect is produced in the finished fabric (see Ikat pp. 147-148).

Other terms used:
Jaspieren (Seiler-Baldinger 1991:9)
Screziato (CIETA 1971:28)
Jaspeado (CIETA 1971:28)
Melerad (CIETA 1971:28)

Gimping

A thread which is called a "core thread" is wrapped round with any desired material, which may often be of great fineness. The hue often changes from place to place. Drawn metal threads (gold, silver) are frequently used for this purpose.

Other terms used:
Winding, whipping (Sylwan 1941:102
Gimpen (Seiler-Baldinger 1991:9)
Filé (Geijer/Hald 1974:81)
Fil guipé, laminato, vergolinato (CIETA 1971:22)
Hilo entorchado (CIETA 1971:22)
Spunnen metalltråd (Geijer/Hald 1974:81)

Braiding

Three or more threads are interlaced to form a flat or three-dimensional braid. These are special forms of a technique for fabric production, like crocheting and knitting (see Plaiting, p. 38).

Other term used:
Flechten (Seiler-Baldinger 1991:9)

Crocheting and Knitting

Solid elastic threads can be formed by crocheting or tubular knitting thin strings. These operations can be performed with the fingers alone, but needles, sticks or forks are often employed (see Crocheting, p. 23 and Knitting p. 24).

Other term used:
Häkeln und Stricken (Seiler-Baldinger 1991:9)

Direction and Angle of Twist

Direction of Twist

The direction of twist of the fibres or individual fibre is important for twisted, spun or plied threads. The direction of twist is designated S or Z, depending on whether the spiral of the thread when held vertically follows the slant of the central portion of the one or other letter. The following symbols are in use:
Single threads:
S-twist of fibres or hairs \
Z-twist of fibres or hairs /
Two-ply thread:
S-twisted or spun, Z-plied V
Z-twisted or spun, S-plied Λ
The same symbols can be used for ply-yarns from more than two single threads, e.g. $_{V}^{3}$ to designate a 3-ply thread, S-twisted and Z-plied.

The direction of twist depends on the working method used for twisting or spinning and plying. If the fibres are twisted together by being rolled with the right hand on the thigh away from the body towards the knee, an S-twist is obtained. A Z-twist results from rolling in the opposite direction.
In spinning, the thread is Z-twisted if the spindle is rotated clockwise and the drawing out done in the opposite direction, whereas an S-twist is obtained by reversing the process.

Other terms used:
Direction of twist: S or Z spun or twist (Geijer/Hald 1974:82, 101)
Drehrichtung S und Z (Seiler-Baldinger 1991:9)
Torsion: tors, tordu S ou Z (Geijer/Hald 1974:82, 101)
Torsione(Burnham 1980:161)
Torção em Z/S (Ribeiro 1988:93)
Snodd: Z-(S-)spunnet, tvinnet (Geijer/Hald 1974: 82, 101)
Z- og S-spinding/tvinding (Bender-Jørgensen 1986:13)

Fig 1: Direction of twist S and Z

Angle of Twist

The angle of twist is important in comparative technical studies. In the case of single spun or twisted threads, the angle of twist refers to the acute angle the slant of the twist forms with the vertical axis of the fibres whereas in plied threads the angle is formed by the relationship of the individual threads to each other.

Other terms used:
Tightness or angle of twist (Emery 1966:11)
Drehwinkel (Seiler-Baldinger 1991:9)

References to Element Production: see pp. 156-157.

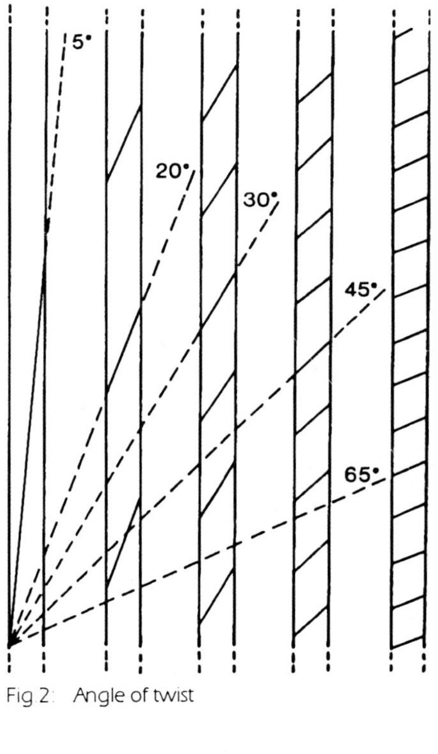

Fig.2: Angle of twist

The Techniques of Fabric Production

As used here, the term "fabric" comprises all the products of textile techniques that consist of basic elements (thread or groups of threads) which have been interworked by mechanical means to obtain the necessary coherence. The fineness and quality of the threads are of only secondary importance. The ordering of the threads in the fabric, for instance the crossing of the threads or thread groups, is known as interlacing. Manufacturing methods and forms of interworking and interlacing provide the basis of the present classification of fabric production.

To start with, we can distinguish between primary processes, i.e. methods using no or very simple implements, and more sophisticated techniques which invariably require equipment and have in their compass weaving and all its preparatory stages. From the technical point of view the second group is more homogeneous than the group of primary processes. It is often impossible to make any rigid classification or assign individual processes to sharply defined groups because of transitional stages between the individual processes. Moreover, even when seen in purely theoretical terms, the technical evolution from primary to more advanced techniques does not follow a single continuous line. The possibilities open to exploration are so diverse that they often lead to side branches or special forms which preclude further development. On the other hand there are many variations which are theoretically possible but remain unexploited.

Because of all these factors it is impossible to avoid overlapping in the classification. One of the results is that identical structures of interworking are repeated within the main groups of processes. In such cases it is the method of manufacture that is decisive.

Nivaclé woman's carrying net, hourglass looping, Gran Chaco, Paraguay, collection A. Seiler-Baldinger

Primary Textile Techniques

Methods of this type must be placed prior to weaving on technical (not historical) grounds. Such fabrics can be made by hand or with the aid of very simple implements. Primary textiles comprise mesh fabrics and plaiting.

Headband of a mummy, overhand knot, Paracas Necropolis, 500 B.C., Peru, IVc 9968

Fabric Production with a Single Continuous Element: Production of Mesh Fabrics

The fabric is produced with one single continuous thread or element (at least in theory) which is worked into meshes at definite and repeated intervals. Depending on the working method and the structure of the fabric, the thread may be of limited or unlimited length, thereby affecting the working method and the fabric structure. Meshes form the interworking elements of single-thread fabrics and they are therefore called mesh fabrics.

Definition of mesh:

The mesh comprises the run of the thread until it is repeated in a course or row, or until there is conformity of pattern in relationship to the adjacent courses or rows (= repeat). The signs "+" and "-" in the run of the thread indicate that the thread is passed over (+) or under (-) a portion of thread.

Definition of course and row:

In contrast to row, which is worked back-and-forth, the course consists of a linear, periodic sequence of meshes which is worked round-and-round.

The feature common to all the groups is that they can be executed in three ways: back-and-forth in the same plane, spiral or circular.

Mesh Formation with a Continuous Element of Limited Length

The meshes are formed by the leading end of the thread, the entire thread being drawn through the mesh last formed. The thread should therefore be of limited length and must be continually extended by attaching new pieces. Longer threads can be used only with an appropriate mesh width; such lengths are normally wound on needles or shuttles. For fine fabrics, and especially for complicated interworkings, an eyed needle is required. Strips of leaf or narrow boards are often used as mesh gauges to ensure uniformity of structure. Makeshift frames are often employed as an aid in the initial stages of making large fabrics. In many cases fingers alone are used.

Meshwork structures with elements of limited length can be classified into three main groups:

1. Linking
2. Looping
3. Knotting

Linking

1. Simple Linking

The thread is stretched over a length corresponding to the desired fabric width or length and loosely wrapped round itself in such a fashion that regularly spaced meshes of the simplest shape are formed. The second row of linking is formed at the lowermost point of the first row (vertical axes A and B). These structures are net-like and very elastic, the meshes being elongated and of diamond shape.

Linking can also be vertical instead of horizontal. Technically, this form approximates very closely to hourglass looping and its linked variants (see pp. 14-16).

Notation and theoretical observations:

The thread passes over 2 linking positions (= links) from A_1-A' and under 2 linking positions (from A'-A_2). This pattern can be written in abbreviated form as 2/2, the sign / representing the vertical axis. (Fig. 3a-b).

There are other possibilities of thread arrangement: 11/11 (Fig. 3c), 2/11 and 11/2 (Fig. 3d). The two latter forms are scarcely ever encountered in practice since an asymmetrical arrangement of threads in relation to the vertical axes would be a serious hindrance to a uniform movement sequence in production.

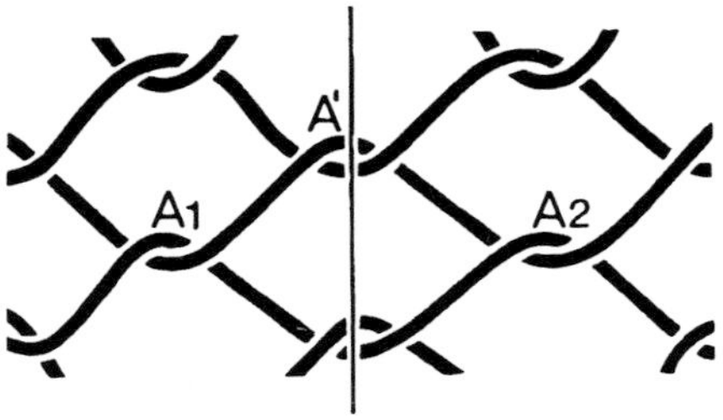

Fig. 3a: Thread configuration of a mesh in simple linking 2/2

Fig. 3b: Simple linking

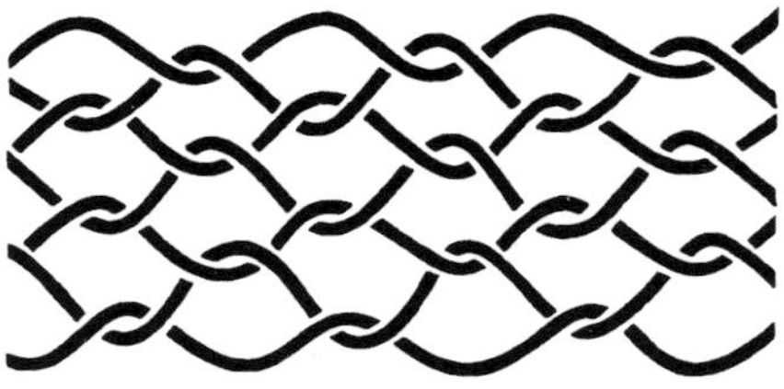

Fig. 3c: Simple linking 11/11

Fig. 3d: Simple linking 2/11 - 11/2

Other terms used:

Needle coiling, plaiting (Siewertsz v. Reesema 1926:63)
Spiralling (Singer 1953:9)
Simple interlacing (Dickey 1964:25)
Spiral interlinking (Emery 1966: 30, 60)
Mesh technique (Cardale-Schrimpff 1972:87)
Einfaches Einhängen (Seiler-Baldinger 1991:13)
Einfache Schlingentechnik (Feick 1917:542)
Spires enfilées les unes dans les autres (D'Harcourt 1934:87)
Reticolo (Mariotti 1982:28)
Acoplamento simple (Ribeiro 1986c:353)
Red sin nudo (Mora de Jaramillo 1974:34)
Enganchar (Vreeland/Muelle 1977:11)
Inhangen (Keppel 1984:30)

2. Linking on a Foundation

On completion of a row of meshes, the thread is passed back under this row before a new series of meshes is made. Alternatively, the thread is stretched out and wrapped round with its free end.

If the added element is not the continuous thread but another thread or even a set of elements, the process must be classified as coiling (see pp. 32-36). The same applies to all other methods of making mesh fabrics on a foundation.

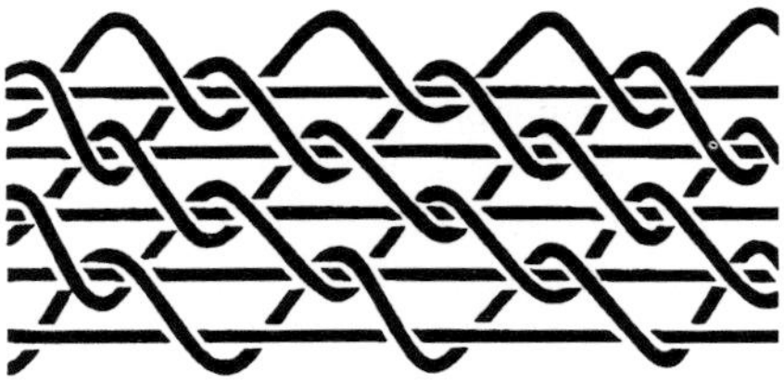

Fig. 4: Linking on a foundation

Other term used:

Einhängen mit Einlage (Seiler-Baldinger 1991:14)

3. Linking and Twisting (Twisted Linking)

Double or multiple linking or linking with one or more twists is obtained if the thread, instead of being simply linked to the meshes, is coiled one or more times around the lowermost points of the previous row. This method increases the fabric strength.

Theoretical observations:

Linking and twisting might also be regarded as linking with skipped meshes.

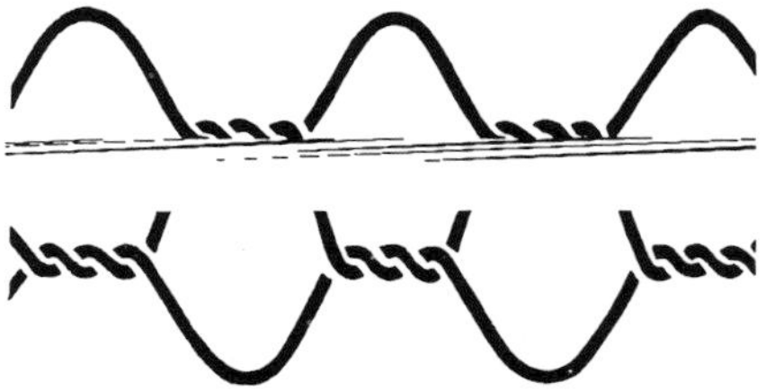

Fig. 5: Triple linking or twisted linking

Other terms used:

Link and twist, twisted link, interlinking with an added twist (Emery 1966:9, 62)
Mehrfaches Einhängen (Seiler-Baldinger 1991:14)
Enganchar y torcer (Vreeland/Muelle 1977:11)

4. Linking with Skipping of Rows

Linking with skipped rows is derived from the continuous skipping of individual meshes. In this method, the meshes that have been skipped over in one row are fixed in the next or one of the following sequences of operation. The skipping of rows produces thread intercrossings or interlacings which are reminiscent of plaiting and sprang (see pp. 37, 51ff.). Fabrics produced in this way have an extremely high extensibility in the direction transverse to the meshes and also a higher density than can be obtained with simple linking (Fig. 6).

Notation and theoretical observations:

We distinguish between skipping one (Fig. 6a), two (Fig. 6b), three, four (Fig. 7) five and up to n rows. A mesh thus consists of three links and 1-n thread intercrossings. The number of possible ways (P) in which the run of the element can be arranged increases geometrically with the number of skipped rows (crossings).

The over-under movements of the elements in the links are mutually dependent, thus yielding only one possible way of thread arrangement whereas there are two such possibilities in the skipped rows: up to the half mesh repeat A_1-A' is $P = 2^{n+1}$, in the whole repeat of A_1-A_2 $P = 2^{2(n+1)}$.

Thus for every type of linking with skipped rows, the number of possible variations can be calculated with precision. This is determined by the number of skipped rows (n; in our example n = 4) and by the links (A_1,A',A_2 or B_1,B',B_2). If n rows are skipped, the number is $P = 2^{2(n+1)}$ per mesh repeat (A_1-A_2 or B_1-B_2). Hence in our example (Fig. 7a-b) $2^{2(4+1)} = 2^{10} = 1024$ possibilities.

Just as in simple linking, the notation of the thread arrangement produces in our example for Fig. 6b linking with skipping of two rows $2^{22/22}$ (or 2:22/22) and for Fig. 7a linking with skipping of rows $4^{33/33}$ (or 4:33/33) and means that, between links A_1 and A', the element passes under (-) 3, over (+) 3 threads (or vice versa) up to the vertical axis AB' and then similarly from BA' (or A'-A_2). The A meshes (mesh repeat = A_1-A_2) are differentiated from the B meshes (mesh repeat = B_1-B_2) solely by reversal of the signs (Fig. 7b).

In this process, just as in simple linking, only the variant forms symmetrical to the vertical mesh axis are used. Logically, these correspond to the number of possibilities in a half mesh repeat (A_1-A' or B_1-B'), hence $P = 2^{n+1}$, in our example $P = 2^5 = 32$ axially symmetrical variants.

The axially symmetric arrangement of elements in the A and B meshes causes the latter to be reciprocally modified (i.e. 1/4 of the A-mesh repeat modifies 1/4 of the B-mesh repeat) and consequently the quadrants are related in the following manner: 1A to 4B, 2A to 3B, 3A to 2B, 4A to 1B (Fig. 7b).

In this way the number of possible variations is again reduced to $2^{(n/2)+1}$, which in our example yields $2^3=8$. There are also similar reductions in complex forms of interconnected looping (see pp. 13-14). These variant forms are limited for practical reasons and which ones are selected depends on the working method, i.e. the cultural background of the producer. If the rows are counted serially during production, the meshes of the uneven rows (1,3,5 etc.) are superimposed on each other (A meshes in the thread arrangement A_1 A_2), and with a slight upward shift, the meshes of the even rows (2,4,6, etc. B meshes, in the thread arrangement B_1 B_2). Thus in the completed fabric the A and B meshes alternate with each other in a slightly staggered pattern (see Fig. 7).

Fig. 6a: Linking with skipping of one row 1:3/3

Fig. 6b: Linking with skipping of rows 2:22/22

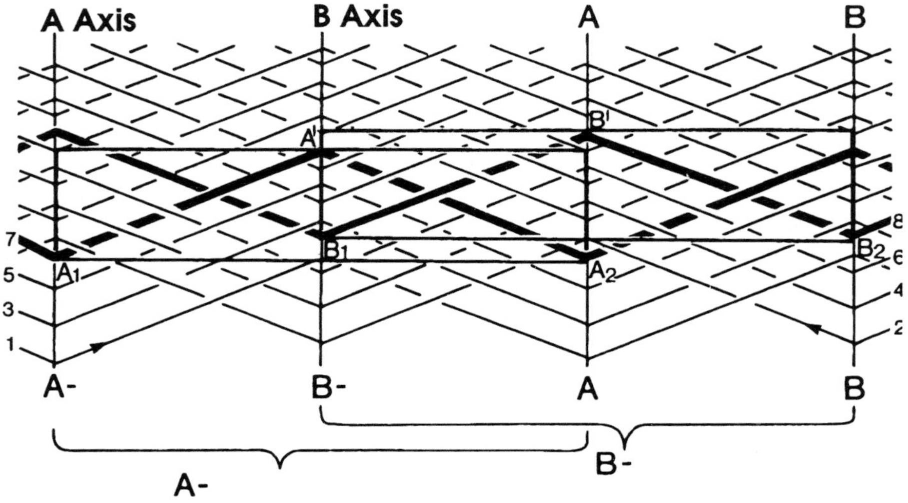

Fig. 7a: Linking with skipping of rows 4:33/33

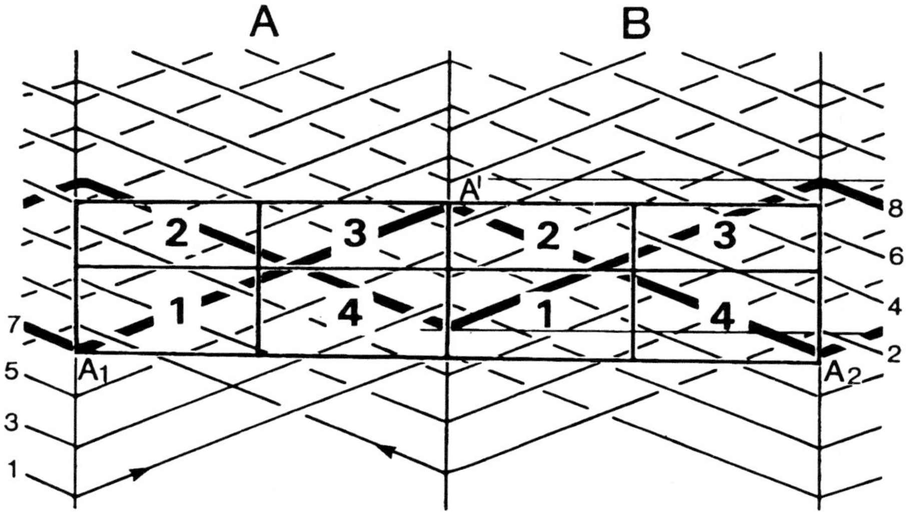

Fig. 7b: Linking with skipping of rows 4:33/33, with quadrants

Other terms used:

Einhängen mit Überspringen von Reihen (Seiler-Baldinger 1991:15)

Enmallado, urdido (Littlefield 1976:97)

Acoplamento com malha saltada (Ribeiro 1986c: 353)

Looping

In all fabrics of this type, the element is formed into loops. Coarser fabrics are made with the fingers and sometimes a gauge is used. Finer fabrics, for instance the so-called needle laces, require eyed needles. Depending on the loop size and the fineness of the yarn, fabrics of widely different appearance and variable extensibility are obtained.

There are numerous variations of looping which are distinguishable by:

- the basic loop form, which can be single, twisted or double, the latter being possible with one or more added twists,
- the relationship to the adjacent rows, e.g. by lateral interlinking (interconnected looping), with the possibility of skipping loops,
- the relationship to the adjacent rows by the linking of the continuous thread into the meshes of the preceding row (row skipping still possible) by piercing or encircling the loops of the next rows (pierced or encircled looping).

Other forms can be obtained by returning the thread on the completion of a row and encircling it with the loops of the next row (looping on a foundation, Fig. 8). If two sets of elements are used, the technique must be classified as coiling (see pp. 32-36).

To produce coloured patterns, parts of the continuous thread are dyed during the work process, replaced by threads of a different colour, or several threads of different colour are used together, the thread not required at any time often being hidden as an inlay or foundation (Fig. 8, looping with inlay).

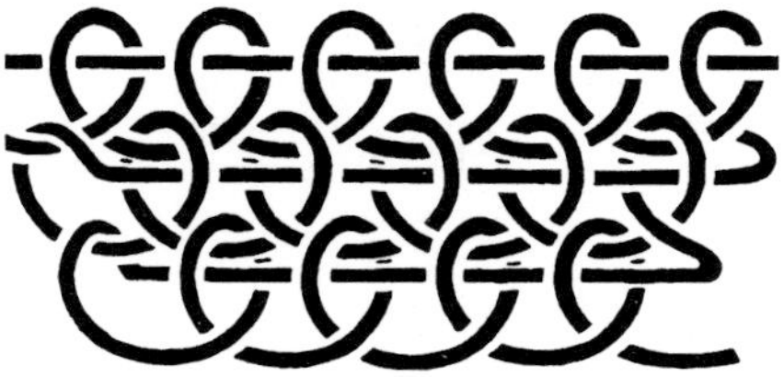

Fig. 8: Simple looping on a foundation

Other terms used:

Buttonhole over a thread (Bird/Bellinger 1954:100)
Simple loop over transverse yarns (Dickey 1964:14)
Einfaches Verschlingen mit Einlage (Seiler-Baldinger 1991:17)
Point de Venise (D'Harcourt 1934:89)
Enlace simple com embutimento (Ribeiro 1986c:365)

- the loop forms (linking the element of the next row into the meshes of the preceding row without lateral interlinking of the loops).

1. Simple Looping

This basic method differs from linking in that the yarn is linked with a mesh of the previous row and laid in the form of a loop crossed with itself in S- or Z-direction (left-over-right or right-over-left crossing) (Fig. 9a-b).

If the work is done in a circular fashion, i.e. in circular rows, or in back-and-forth rows with reversal of the workpiece, both faces are identical and show the same crossing of loops. With back-and-forth working in rows without reversal of the workpiece, on the other hand, one row exhibits S- and the other Z-crossed loops, both faces again being identical. Depending on mesh width, very firm or very elastic fabrics can be made.

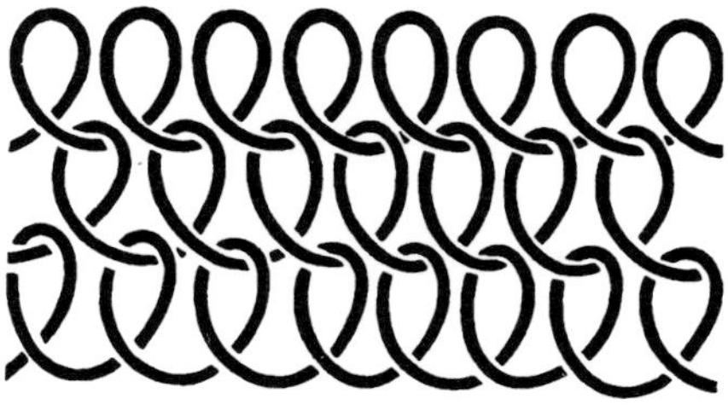

Fig. 9a: Simple looping with S crossing

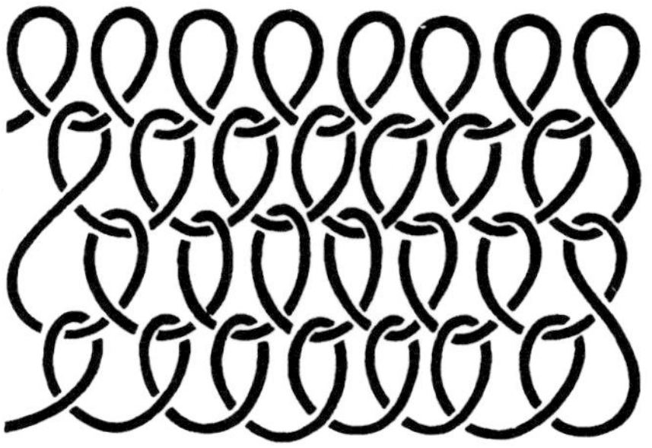

Fig. 9b: Simple looping with counter crossing S and Z

Other terms used:

Most primitive style of coiled netting (Mason 1890:264)
Coiled without foundation (Mason 1902:532)
Simple loop (Davidson 1935:120)
Plain looping (Miner 1935/36:182)
Half-hitch loop (Engel 1963:38)
Simple looping, buttonhole looping (Emery 1966:31)
Plain coiling (Weitlaner-Johnson 1966/67:196)
Simple knotless netting (Cardale-Schrimpff 1972:172)
Einfaches Verschlingen (Seiler-Baldinger 1991:17)
Gewöhnlicher Tüllstich (De Dillmont 1902:483)
Einfache Schlingentechnik (Radin 1906:936)
Point de tulle simple (D'Harcourt 1934:88)
Vannerie spiralée à une seule nappe (Leroi-Gourhan 1943:228)
Enlazado sencillo (Weitlaner-Johnson 1977:93)
Red de lazos (Alfaro Giner 1984:149)

Enlazado simple (Rolandi 1971:89)
Enlace simple (Ulloa 1985:16)
Cestería en espiral sin armazón (Mora de Jaramillo 1974:342)
Enlace simple (Ribeiro 1986c:353)
Inhanged lussen (Keppel 1984:30)

2. Double Looping

Instead of one loop as in the case of simple looping, two loops in opposite direction are formed. The method is practically never used for fabric production. This is the case only with interlinking with adjacent meshes (Fig. 13).

The method is theoretically interesting because many of its laterally interconnected variations are similar to those of linked hourglass looping. The loops can be all with S-crossing or alternately with S and Z crossing (counter-crossing).

Fig. 10a: Double looping with S crossing

Fig. 10b: Double looping with Z crossing

Fig. 10c: Double looping with counter crossing S and Z

Other terms used:

Fagoting (Birrell 1959:315)
Doppelschlaufiges Verschlingen (Seiler-Baldinger 1991:18)
Einfacher russischer Stich (De Dillmont 1902:606)

3. Twisted Looping

The loop is formed by the addition of one or more turns of the element about itself (Fig. 11a) which results in double or multiple-twisted loops (Fig. 11b). Twisting can be combined with single or double looping (Fig. 11c).

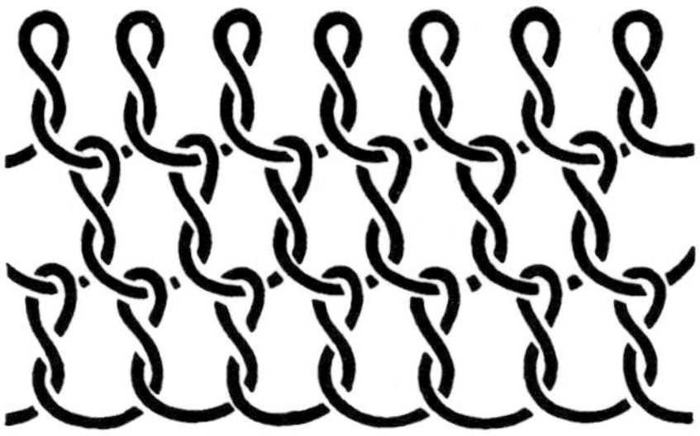

Fig. 11a: Twisted looping with S crossing

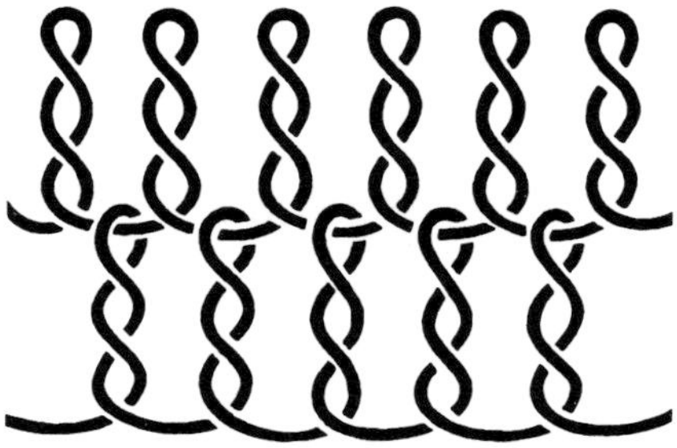

Fig. 11b: Triple twisted with S crossing

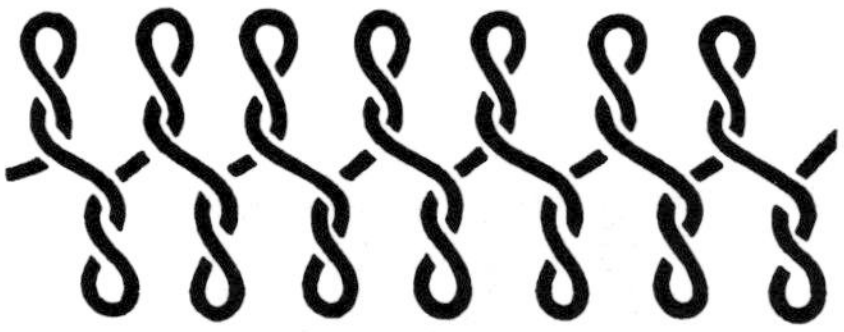

Fig. 11c: Twisted double looping with S crossing

Other terms used:

Loop and twist(s) (Davidson 1935:122)
Loop and double, triple, quadruple...twist (Singer 1935:13)
Lace stitch (Hald 1950: 289)
Buttonhole plain (Bird/Bellinger 1954:100)
Twisted half-hitch looping (Birrell 1959:316)
Twisted loop (Engel 1963:38)
Loop and twist, twisted buttonhole stitch (Emery 1966:31)
Full turn looping (Weitlaner-Johnson 1966/67:196)
Mehrfaches Verschlingen (Seiler-Baldinger 1991:18)
Point de tulle compliqué (D'Harcourt 1934:88)
Técnica de gaza con torsión (Weitlaner-Johnson 1977:111)
Lazos cerrados con torsión (Nardi 1978:40)
Red de lazos doble (Alfaro Giner 1984:149)

Twisted double looping:
Fagoting (Birrell 1959:315)
Loop and twist(s) in which adjacent units are oriented in opposite directions and introduced into adjacent rows to form a compound loop and twist pattern (Dickey 1964:19)
Mehrfaches doppelschlaufiges Verschlingen (Seiler-Baldinger 1991:19)
Gedrehter russischer Stich, Säulenstich (De Dillmont 1902:606f.)

- the relationship to adjacent meshes: interconnected or laterally linked looping:

4. Simple Interconnected or Laterally Linked Looping

The individual loops in each row are laterally linked. A loop can be linked with the preceding one, i.e. in the second mesh formation, in the second turn (Fig. 12a), or with one that is further separated (Fig. 12b-d). This process can also be designated as skipping of meshes.

Notation and theoretical observations:

For an accurate description of complex forms of interconnected looping, numerical symbols must be used to reproduce the thread arrangement. Just as in linking with skipping of rows, the thread arrangement for connecting to the second to nth turn is in axial symmetry to the vertices of the meshes (again with reversed signs). So the crossing pattern of the element in one half of the mesh is sufficient indication. Thus interconnected looping 3:212 means "interconnected in the third turn with the thread pattern $\pm 2 \mp 1 \pm 2$ (Fig. 12b). The number of crossings alters according to the number of turns whereas the number of links remains constant. In the nth turn the crossings amount to $C_a = n-1$ up to the link and $C_b = n-2$ after the link. The number of theoretically possible thread arrangements is thus
$P = 2^{Ca+Cb}$ or $2^{(n-1)+(n-2)} = 2^{2n-3}$

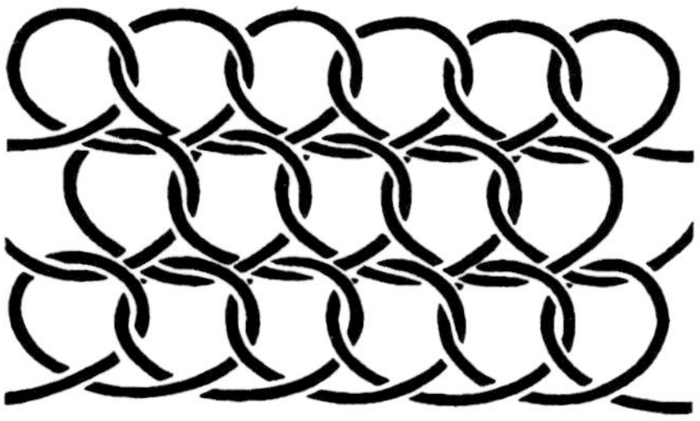

Fig. 12a: Simple interconnected looping in the second turn

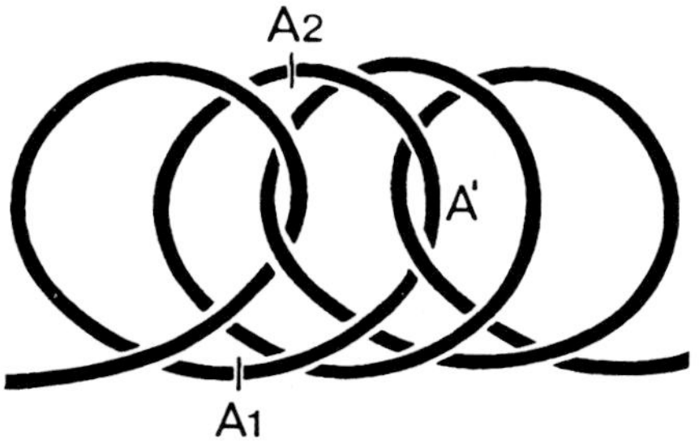

Fig. 12b: Interconnected looping in the third turn (A_1-A'-A_2: thread movement 3:212)

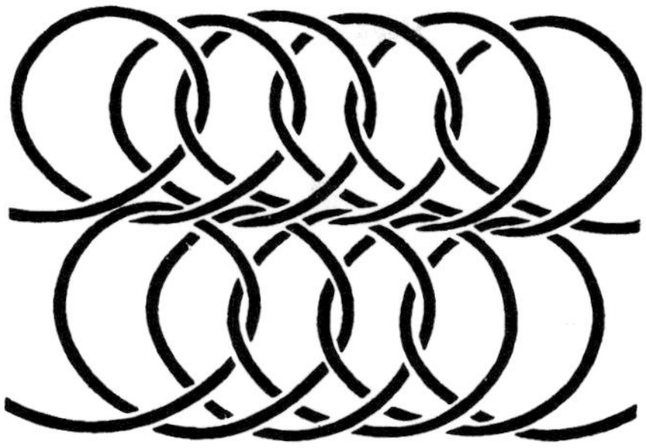

Fig. 12c: Looping interconnected in the third turn: thread movement 212

Fig. 12d: Looping interconnected in the sixth turn (6:2441)

Other terms used:

Cycloidal curling of a single element (Mason 1908:36)
Simple loop interlocking with one loop on all sides (Davidson 1935:120)
Interlocking simple loops (Singer 1935:12)
Interlocked half-hitch looping, circular looping (Birrell 1959:316)
Simple loop interlocking with the second loop on each side (Dickey 1964:17)
Einfaches verhängtes Verschlingen (Seiler-Baldinger 1991:19)
Geflochtener Türkischer Bogen (Mooi 1977:116)
Enlace interconectado lateral/terminal (Ribeiro 1986c:365)
Zijdelings lussen (Keppel 1984:30)
Nålbindning (Nylén 1969:316)

5. Double Interconnected Looping

As a means of fabric production, double looping is used only in its interlinked forms. Here again the loops can be connected with those of the adjacent or further situated meshes (in the second to nth turn), this being performed in the two loops either uniformly (Fig. 13a) or in different ways (Fig. 13b). Twisted double interconnected looping can also be linked laterally. However, these forms are identical with those of twisted interconnected loopings of the type of "linked" and "linked interconnected hourglass looping" (see pp. 14-16, Fig. 17-18).

Notation and theoretical observations:

As in the processes already referred to, the thread pattern of double interconnected looping can also be stated in numerals up to the apex of the mesh. Fig. 13a diagrams the type "connected in 2nd turn with thread pattern -1+2-2+1" whereas Fig. 13b shows the type "connected in the 2nd and 3rd turn with the thread pattern -2+3-2+1".

If the number of turns in both loops is the same, there will be thread crossings $C = 4(n-1)$. Consequently the number of theoretically possible thread arrangements is $P = 2^{c-1} = 2^{4n-5}$. If the number of turns of the two loops, n_a and n_b, are different, the number of thread crossings $C = 2(n_a+n_b-2)$ and that of the theoretical possibilities $P = 2^{2(n_a+n_b)-5}$.

The process has been continually confused with interconnected hourglass looping.

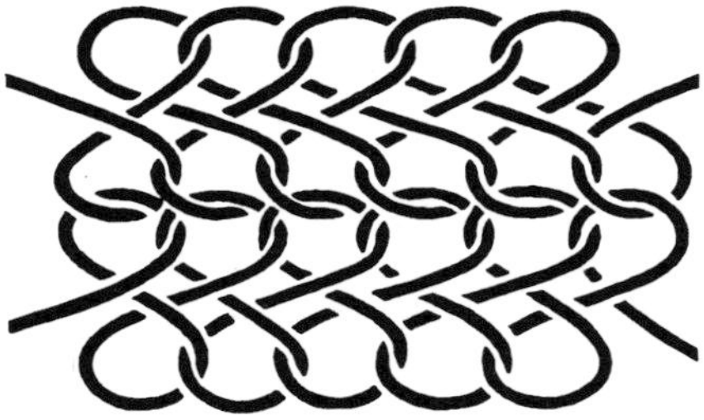

Fig. 13a: Double interconnected looping in the second turn

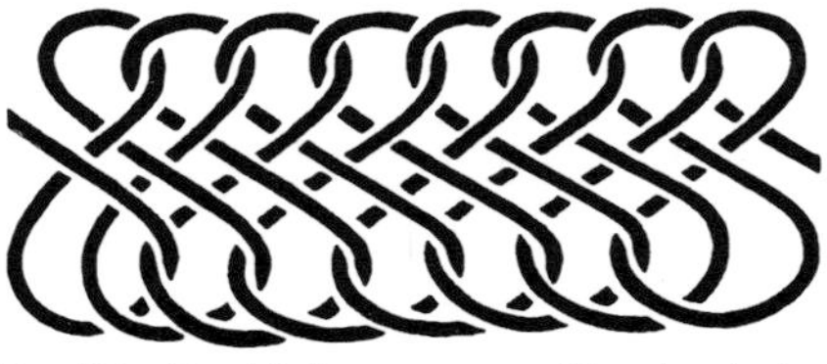

Fig. 13b: Double interconnected looping in the second and third turns

Other terms used:

The loop of the units does not interlock (connect), but hangs pendant as simple loop from the preceding row. Staggered hourglass, the cross-bar extends to lock with the two adjacent units forming a slightly staggered effect (Dickey 1964:24)
Figure eight looping (overlapping and interlaced) (Emery 1966:33)
Doppelschlaufiges verhängtes Verschlingen (Seiler-Baldinger 1991:20)
Enges Sanduhrverschlingen (Bühler-Oppenheim 1948:100)
Verhängter Hexenstich (Hinderling 1959:37)
Enlace interconectado com malha-ampulheta (Ribeiro 1986c: 365)

6. Twisted Interconnected Looping:

As in simple looping, loops can also be laterally linked in twisted looping. There are innumerable variations possible by altering the number of connecting points between the loops (base, final loop or intervening twists) and changing the span of the interconnections (number of turns) which can be varied or uniform throughout (Fig. 14a-b).

These factors must be taken into account when describing processes which are not featured separately. Fig. 14a shows a "triple-twisted looping connected in the middle twist" and in Fig. 14b a "quintuple-twisted looping connected in the fourth twist".

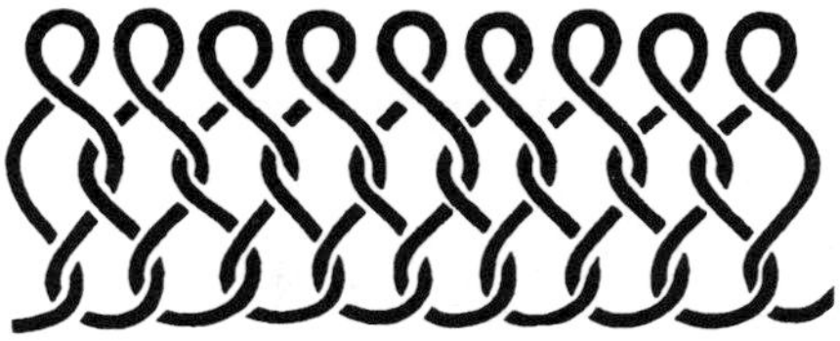

Fig. 14a: Twisted looping connected in the middle twist

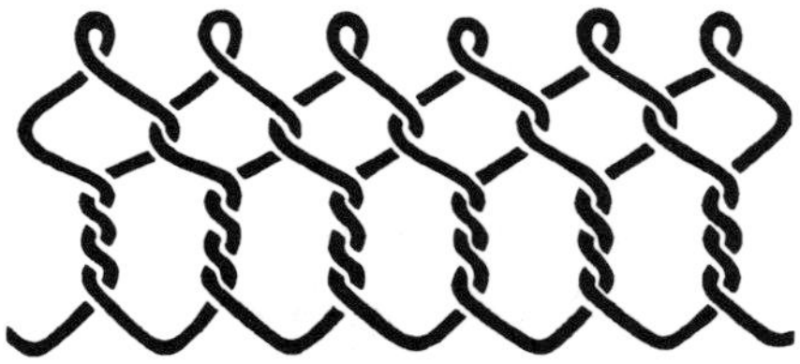

Fig. 14b: Twisted looping connected in the fourth twist

Other terms used:

Loop and twist with an interlocking with adjacent loops. This is merely another variation of the loop and twist technique (Singer 1934:19)
Twisted eight looped = TW/L (Engel 1963:38)
Mehrfaches verhängtes Verschlingen (Seiler-Baldinger 1991:21)

6.1. Hourglass Looping

Hourglass looping is in fact a twice-twisted looping interconnected in the second turn. It is one of the most popular and widely distributed processes of twisted looping.

Notation and theoretical observations:

There are only two possible thread configurations for hourglass looping, and these are $\pm 1 \mp 2 \pm 1$ and $\pm 1 \mp 1 \pm 1 \mp 1$. If thread configuration -2 is chosen for the first variant, Z-oriented (Fig. 15a) loops are obtained whereas S-oriented loops are obtained with +2 (Fig. 15b) and a herringbone structure results from thread arrangement 1111 (Fig. 15c).

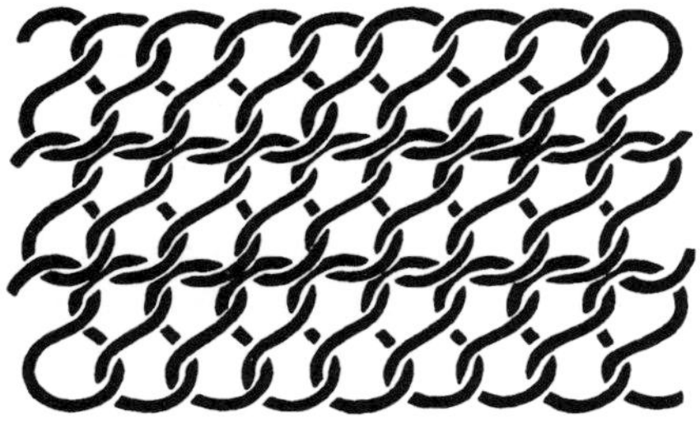

Fig. 15a: Hourglass looping with Z crossing

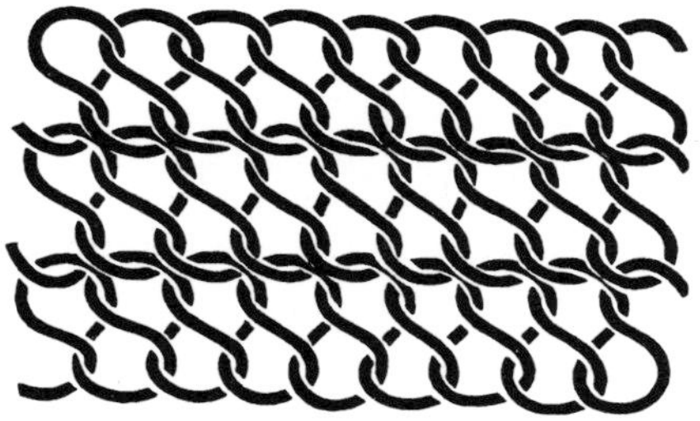

Fig. 15b: Hourglass looping with S crossing

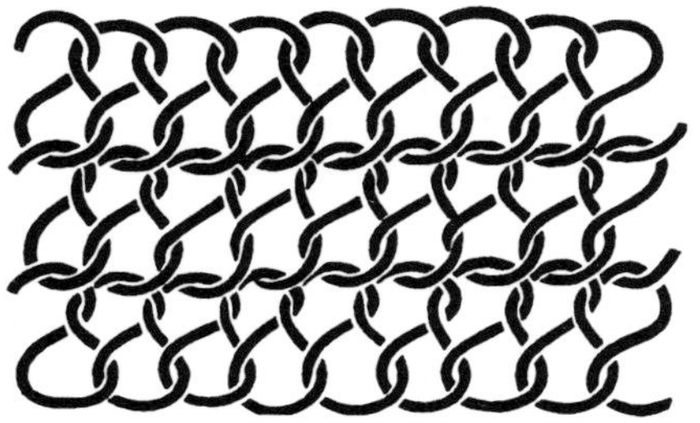

Fig. 15c: Hourglass looping with counter crossing

Other terms used:

Figure eight stitch (van Reesema 1926:65)
Type III hourglass pattern (Davidson 1935:122)
Type I: the loops of one mesh are directly and simply inserted into the loops of the next mesh (Engel 1963:37)
Double interconnected looping, figure eight or hourglass (Emery 1966:33)
Sanduhrverschlingen (Seiler-Baldinger 1991:21)
Doppelte Schlingtechnik (Radin 1906:931)
Doppelschlingtechnik (von Bayern 1908:145)
Enlace interconectado com malha-figura de 8 (Ribeiro 1986c:365)

6.2. Interconnected Hourglass Looping

If the loops of the hourglass configuration are interconnected not with the next mesh but with one of the following meshes of a row, the result is interconnected hourglass looping. Again the span of the links may be equal in both twist and loop or different. The structure is deceptively similar to that of double interconnected looping but never identical with it.

Notation and theoretical observations:

If the twists and the loops are linked at equal distances in the nth turn, i.e. if $n_a = n_b$, the number of thread crossings $C = 2(2n-3)$ and there are $2^{2(2n-3)-1}$ possible thread arrangements. If the turn numbers in a and b are different, $C = 2+2(n_a-2)+2(n_b-2) = 2(n_a+n_b-3)$ and there are $2^{2(n_a+n_b-3)-1}$ possible thread arrangements.
The formula thus also shows the differences between double interconnected looping and interconnected hourglass looping.

Fig. 16a: Interconnected hourglass looping with equal spacing 3^{242}

Fig. 16b: Interconnected hourglass looping with equal spacing 3^{2222}

Fig. 16c: Interconnected hourglass looping with unequal spacing

6.3. Linked Hourglass Looping

Linked hourglass looping is a multiple-twisted looping which is uniformly linked in all twists and the final loop, the number of twists, n, being an even number. Fabrics made by this method are simil[illegible] in appearance to simple linking, i.e. if $n > 20$, simple linking is the appropriate term. Depending on the thread configuration, the mesh structure can be S- or Z-twisted.

Notation and theoretical observations:

Instead of "n-fold interconnected looping", the variations of the process are described as "n-fold linked hourglass looping", with n denoting the number of connecting points (links) between the reversing mesh loops. Thus our example (Fig. 17) is not a "quadruple-twisted looping linked in all twists" but "twofold linked hourglass looping". With n-fold linked hourglass looping, the number of crossings is $C = 2n$, the number of possible variations $P = 2^{2n-1}$.

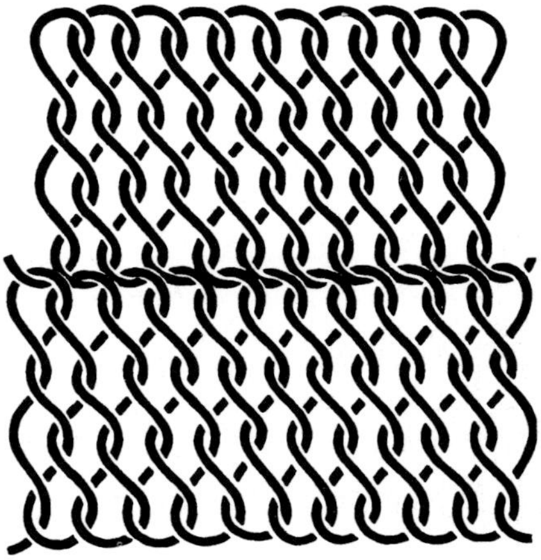

Fig. 17: Linked hourglass looping

Other terms used:

Simple looped over bind (Kroeber/Wallace 1954:132)
Eingehängtes Sanduhrverschlingen (Seiler-Baldinger 1991:22)
Überlanges Sanduhrverschlingen (Hinderling 1959:36)
Réseau à spires enfilées les unes dans les autres (D'Harcourt 1934:87)
Enlace de ampulhetas acopladas (Ribeiro 1986d:391)

6.4. Interconnected Linked Hourglass Looping

Like the ordinary figure-eight looping, linked hourglass looping can be connected laterally. Variations are obtained from the uniformity or disuniformity of the connection in the base and final loop as well as from the different ways in which the twists are linked. Here again it is appropriate to speak of linking with skipping of rows (see pp. 9-10) if the twists are $n > 20$, providing all the interconnections have received equal treatment.

Notation and theoretical observations:

In theory interconnected linked hourglass looping can also be derived from double interconnected and twisted looping.

The difference between simple and double looping is therefore removed if quadruple and more twisted looping and twofold to n-twisted double looping are connected laterally.

Just as in the preceding processes, we obtain from n-fold linked hourglass looping connected in n_a and n_b the formula $C = 2(n_a+n_b+n-1)$ for the number of thread crossings and the formula $P = 2^{2(n_a+n_b+n-1)-1}$ for the number of possible thread configurations.

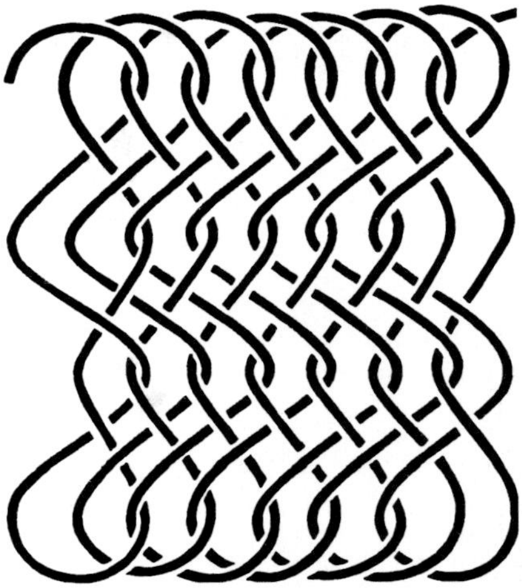

Fig. 18: Interconnected linked hourglass looping

Other terms used:

Figure of eight (Davidson 1935:122)
Complex interlocked hourglass looping (Birrell 1959:317)
When the eight looped fabric forms a chevron pattern we have called it the M-type (Engel 1963:36,38)
Figure of eight pattern in which the working strand crosses from the top of the completed unit over the full breadth of the unit to begin to the far side of that unit to start; figure of eight pattern which connects with two adjacent units to each side with the same row (Dickey 1964:22)
Linking with 2/2-2/2 interlacing (Grieder 1986:27)
Laced interlocking double hourglass (Dickey 1964:24)
Eingehänges verhängtes Sanduhrverschlingen (Seiler-Baldinger 1991:23)
Eigentliches Achterverschlingen; enges Sanduhrverschlingen (Hinderling 1959:35 and 37f.)
Fischgratverschlingen (Hinderling 1959:29ff.)

PLATE 1. Adornment of an Abelam warrior, linking with skipping of rows with nassa shells, Ilahine, Maprik, Papua-New Guinea, Vb 12607

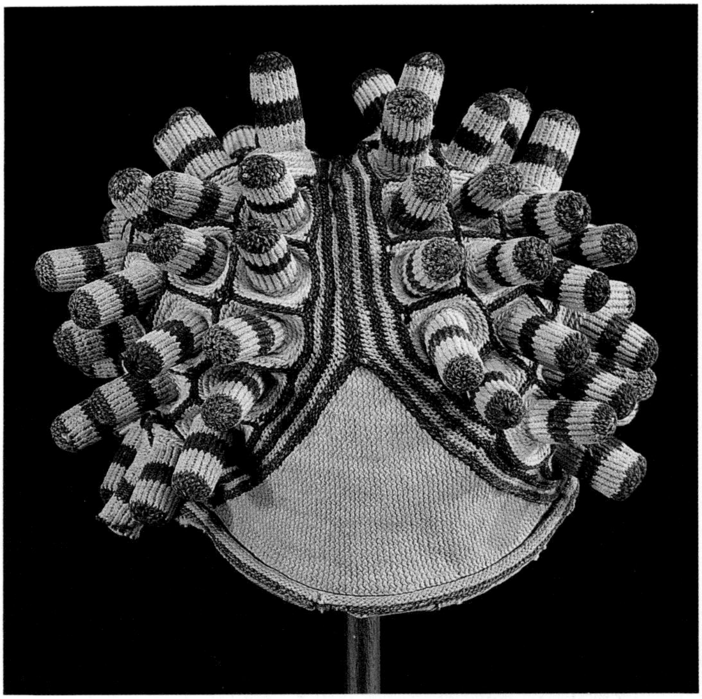

PLATE 2. Hat from Bamum, Cameroon, simple and encircled looping, III 26293

PLATE 3. Mask of the Chokwe, pierced looping and plaiting, Angola, III 19446

6.5. Cord Looping

Cord looping represents a special form of twisted interconnected looping with unequal spacing. Fabrics produced by this method are ribbed on one side (Fig. 19a) and smooth on the other side (Fig. 19b). Depending on the working direction the ribbed side has S- or Z-twisted wales or "cords".

Fig. 19a: Cord looping: face

Fig. 19b: Cord looping: reverse

Other term used:

Kordelverschlingen (Seiler-Baldinger 1991:24)

The relationship to the meshes of the adjacent row:

7. Simple Pierced Looping

In pierced looping the element is not linked into the mesh but through the loop of the preceding row. Double looping is rarely worked by piercing.

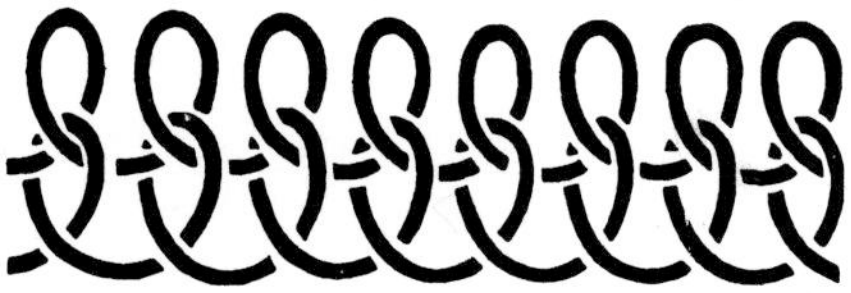

Fig. 20: Simple pierced looping

Other terms used:

Half-hitch through half-hitch (Davidson 1935:121)
Intra half-hitch looping (Birell 1959:317)
Looping into loops (Dendel 1974:86)
Einfaches durchstechendes Verschlingen (Seiler-Baldinger 1991:24)
Doorstekend lussen (Keppel 1984:30)

8. Pierced Interconnected Looping

As in simple pierced looping the thread is also drawn through the loop of the preceding row in the interconnected version. The more distant the loops which are interconnected, the more complex the structure becomes.

These methods are known collectively as "Vantsöm".

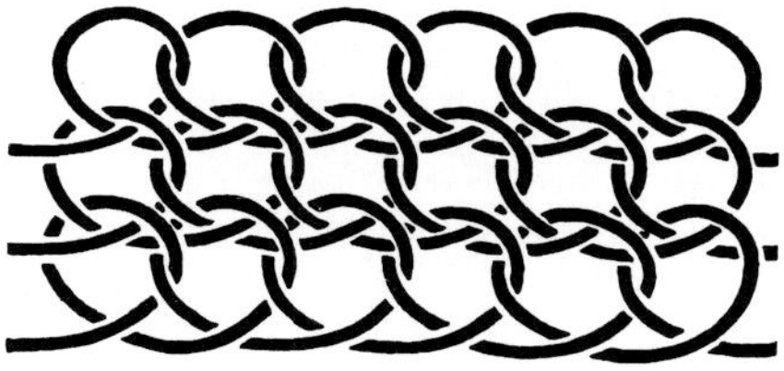

Fig. 21: Pierced interconnected looping

Other terms used:

Simple loop interlocking with each adjacent loop of its own row and with two loops of the adjacent rows (Davidson 1935:120)
Interlaced weave (Belen 1952:48)
Durchstechendes verhängtes Verschlingen (Seiler-Baldinger 1991:24)
Doppelt durchstechendes Verschlingen (Bühler-Oppenheim 1948:101)
Réseau à boucles imbriquées (D'Harcourt 1934:90)
Enlace interconectado lateral-terminal (Ribeiro 1988:120)
Nålebinding technique (Walton 1989:343)

9. Encircled Looping

The thread is taken behind the ascending and descending portions of the loops in the previous row and then simply looped. The structure obtained is similar to that produced by crossed knitting. If the working is circular and differently coloured elements are used, which do not float on the back side but also serve as the basis, the technique should be strictly classified as ornamental (cf. Embroidery). Such borderline cases are known mostly from pre-Columbian Peru.

Needless to say, encircling is a process which can also be used with interconnected looping (Fig. 23) and with twisted as well as double looping.

Fig. 22a: Encircled looping: face

Fig. 22b: Encircled looping: reverse

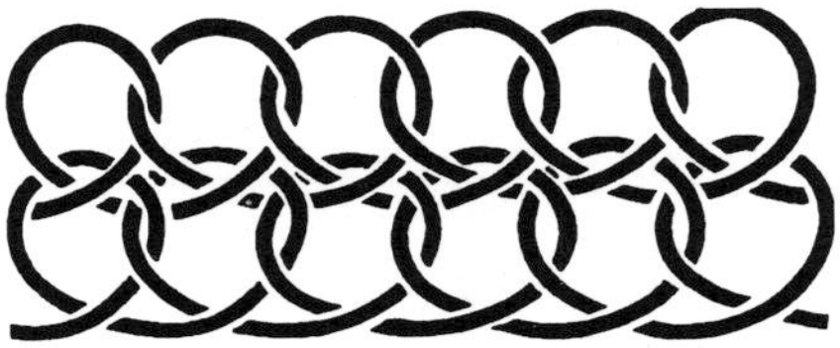

Fig. 23: Encircled interconnected looping

Other terms used:

Three dimensional knitting, needle knitting (O'Neale/Kroeber 1930:32, 37ff.)
Half-hitch around half-hitch (Davidson 1935:121)
Knit stem stitch (Bird/Bellinger 1954:100ff.)
Pseudo knit looping, Ceylonstitch (Birrell 1959:315)
Cross-knit loop (Emery 1966:48)
Umfassendes Verschlingen (Seiler-Baldinger 1991:24)
Point de tricot à l'aiguille à chas (D'Harcourt 1930:208)
Point de boucle (apparence de tricot) (D'Harcourt 1934:91)
Enlace circumscrito (Ribeiro 1986d:390)
Omvattend lussen (Keppel 1984:30)

Knotting

Knots are made by tightly drawing loops and thus securing the meshes. They are used for a wide variety of purposes. Here we are concerned only with their use in textile manufacture. For fabric production knots must be formed sequentially (i.e. the individual knots consist of two parts) either to and fro over a given width or in a circular fashion. In the first case the appearance of the knot changes from row to row and the two fabric sides are identical. In the second case the back side of the fabric differs in appearance from the front. Fabric-forming knots usually comprise two elements: the loop of the preceding row and the knot-forming thread. If knots consist of multiple threads, the technique must be designated interknotting (e.g. macramé, see p. 47). Unlike loops or meshes knots can be moved only with difficulty or not at all. The fabrics have therefore only a limited elasticity. Knots can be formed by hand alone although generally mesh gauges are employed for this purpose. Lace is an example of a particularly fine form of knotted fabric. Knots can be classified into two groups: suspended knots and fixed knots. In suspended knots, the knot-forming thread is simply linked to the mesh of the preceding row; in fixed knots, the mesh is fixed more rigidly in an appropriate manner by the running thread. There are several gradations between the two forms. In contrast to linking and looping, the number of variations theoretically possible in knotted fabrics can hardly be calculated because knots are "incalculable" in the truest sense of the word. Increased tension or even minimal displacement of its parts can transform a certain knot into one completely different in structure, a suspended knot even taking the place of a fixed one.

Unfortunately the rules of mathematical knot theory can be applied to our problem to only a limited extent since a knot, in the mathematical sense, is an embedding of a circle into Euclidean 3-space in which the relationship to the next row, so important for us, is irrelevant.

All knots can be ultimately derived from looping, and, as in the looping process, distinctions must be made regarding:

- the knot form itself, i.e. the type of thread intercrossing,
- the relationship to the next row (an important criterion in fabric-producing knots),
- the relationship to the adjacent knot of the same row (secondary in fabric-producing knots) and
- the tension exercised on the knot.
- knot forms:

The number of possible ways in which a thread or an element can be tied with itself is almost infinite (Ashley lists 3000) but the number that can be used in several rows for producing fabrics are derived, probably for practical reasons (rational working), from the various forms of looping. Hence we can omit from our study those knots consisting of a single element crossing itself in forms of interlacing and arranged in a plane or three-dimensional space.

the relationship to the adjacent rows and meshes:

1. Suspended Knots

Characteristic of the suspended knot is that the running thread is pulled through the meshes of the preceding row before securing the mesh by knotting. The working thread is therefore active and the loop of the adjacent row passive.

Suspended knots are the simplest netting knots from a technical point of view. The most important form is the simple knot or the overhand knot which is the basis for all the other knots in the group.

1.1. Simple Knot

Simple knots are formed from simple loops by pulling the running thread in from outside (Fig. 24).

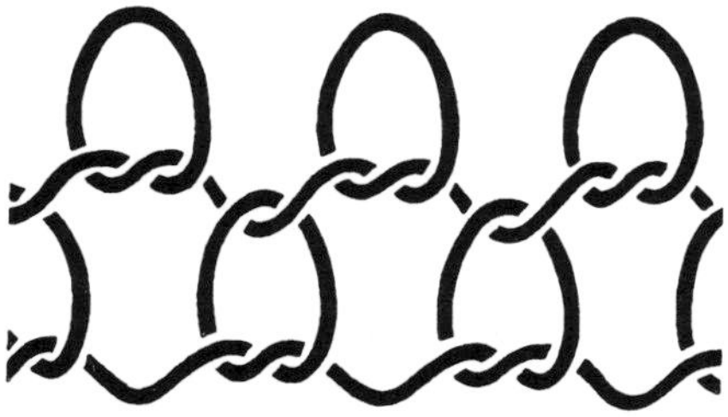

Fig. 24: Simple knot

Other terms used:

Fisherman's knot (Singer 1935:16)
Finger knot (O'Neale 1942:188)
Half knot, thumb knot (Wollard 1953:15,19)
Fingerknoten (Seiler-Baldinger 1991:26)
Flachknoten (Mooi 1977:36)
Fischerknoten (Hartung 1963:29)
Einfacher Knoten (Burgess 1981:21)
Noeud simple (D'Harcourt 1934:92)
Nó simple (Ribeiro 1986d:391)
Medio nudo o nudo sencillo (Weitlaner-Johnson 1977:33)

1.2. Overhand Knot

The path of the thread is identical with that in the simple knot but its positioning on the loop of the preceding row is different in that the thread passes over the side and not the crown of the loop in a half hitch.

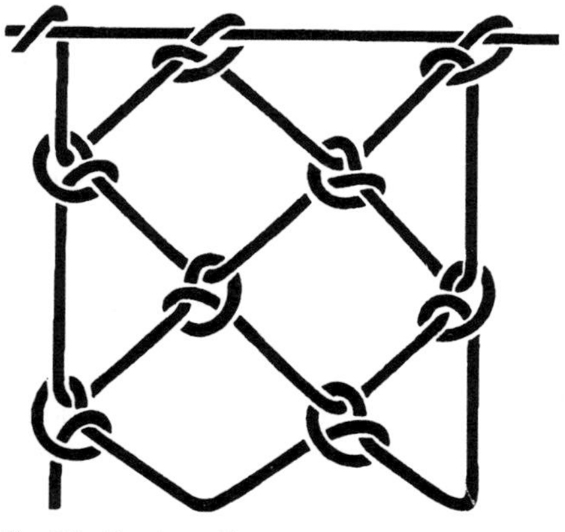

Fig. 25: Overhand knot

Other terms used:

Simple netting knot (Gayton 1948:84)
Knotted buttonhole stitch (Bird/Bellinger 1954:100)
Overhand knot, half-hitch appearance (Emery 1966:34)
Pfahlbauknoten (Seiler-Baldinger 1991:26)
Fischerknoten (Zechlin 1966:125)
Puncetto (Textile Museum St. Gallen 1988: no page given)
Nudo de vuelto de cabo (single half-hitch) (Weitlaner-Johnson 1977:33)

1.3. Slip Knot

The characteristic feature of the slip knot is that the yarn is laid in the form of a long loop on the preceding row before knotting is done. Different arrangements are possible (Fig. 26a-b); the loops may also be laterally connected (interconnected slip knot Fig. 27).

Fig. 26a: Slip knot

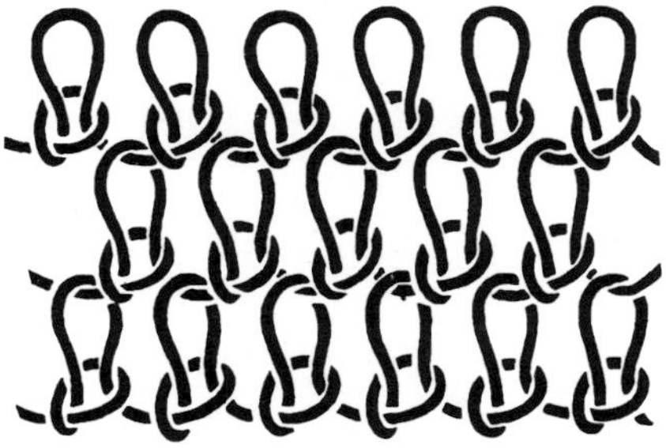

Fig. 26b: Slip knot

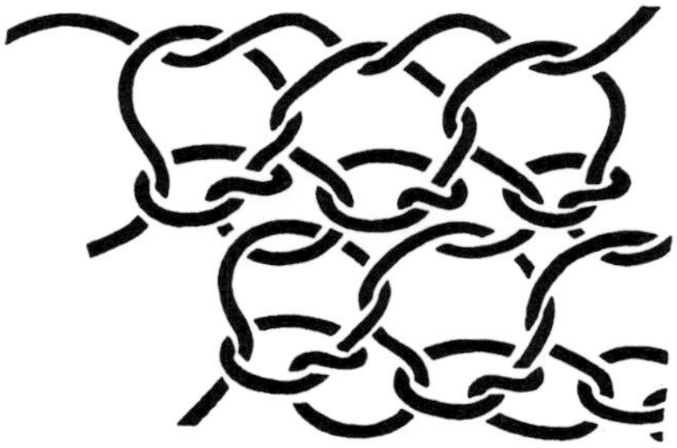

Fig. 27: Interconnected slip knot

Other terms used:

Knotted weave without foundation (Lothrop 1928:138)
Halter knot (Loud/Harrington 1929:83ff.)
Simple noose, true slip knot (Wollard 1953:21)

Slip knot, loop and overhand knot, knotted buttonhole (Emery 1966:35,36)
Overhand-slip knot, overhand running knot (Day 1967: 83,112)
Slip overhand knot (Collingwood 1968:77)
Schlüpfknoten (Seiler-Baldinger 1991:26)
Einfacher Schlaufenknoten (Burgess 1981:23)
Flüchtiger Schlaufenknoten (Hartung 1963:29)

2. Transition Forms from Suspended to Fixed Knots

In the transition forms, the "passive" pendant loop is fixed by the running thread through two loops. The basic method is the simple looping in which every alternate pendant loop is engaged by two closely drawn stitches. These may be symmetrical or asymmetrical.

2.1. Clove Hitch and Cow Hitch

The knot is asymmetrical to a vertical axis if the stitches are in the same direction (Fig. 28) and symmetrical if they are in opposite directions (Fig. 29). The latter differs from the square knot only in the position of the active element on the pendant loop (cf. fixed knots).

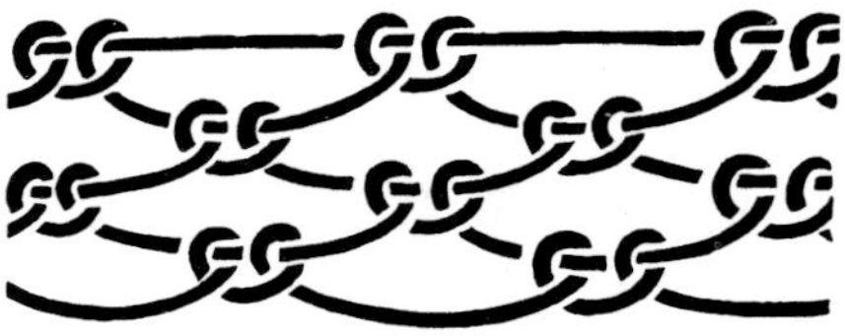

Fig. 28: Clove hitch (asymmetrical)

Fig. 29: Cow hitch (symmetrical)

Other terms used:

Clove hitch (asymmetrical):
Double simple loop (Davidson 1935:120)
Multiple half-hitch looping (Birrell 1958:315)
Clove hitch, two half-hitches, double simple looping, double Brussels stitch or double buttonhole stitch (Emery 1966:36)
Halber asymmetrischer Knoten (Seiler-Baldinger 1991:27)
Halber Knoten, halber Schlag (Hartung 1963:26)
Doble nudo de vuelto de cabo (double half-hitch) (Weitlaner-Johnson 1977:33)
Nó de cabeça de calhandra (Ribeiro 1986d:391)

Cow hitch (symmetrical):
Sailor's knot (Singer 1935:17)
Two half-hitches facing one another (Birrell 1959:315)
Knotted half-hitch loop (Engel 1963:38)
Cow hitch, lark's head knot, reversed half-hitches (Emery 1966:37)
Halber symmetrischer Knoten (Seiler-Baldinger 1991:27)
Doppelknoten (Liebert 1916:10)
Verschobener Kreuzknoten (Von Brandt 1957:42)
Smyrnaknoten (Hartung 1963:34)
Rauschknoten (Burgess 1981:38)
Nudo de presillo de alondra (Weitlaner-Johnson 1977:33)

2.2. Double Hitch Crossed Knot

In this knot the ascending portion of the first stitch and the descending portion of the second stitch cross each other.

Fig. 30: Double hitch crossed knot

Other terms used:

Zweischlaufiger gekreuzter Knoten (Seiler-Baldinger 1991:28)
Variante des Kreuzknotens (Von Brandt 1957:44)

3. Fixed Knots

The "active" knot-forming element is taken round the pendant loop of the previous row in such a way that the pendant loop is also engaged in the knot formation. The basis for all fixed knots is looping in its simple, pierced and encircled form.

3.1. Square Knot

This very simple knot is formed by connecting two adjacent rows of loops in such a way that they are symmetrically interknotted. Pulling makes a cow hitch into a square knot.

Fig. 31a:
Square knot: face

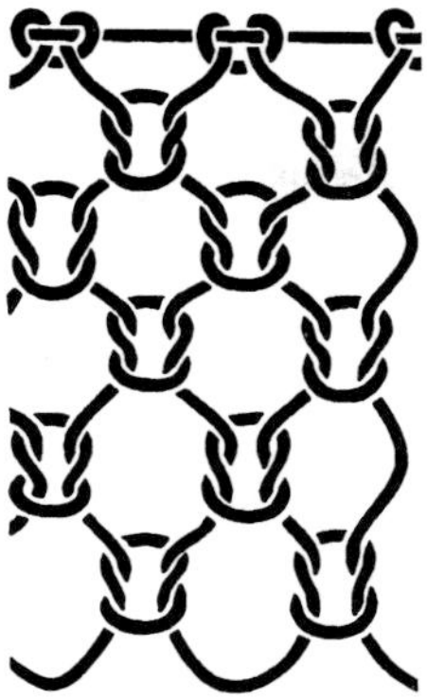

Fig. 31b:
Square knot: reverse

Other terms used:
Flat knot (Loud/Harrington 1929:85)
Reef knot, square knot (Wollard 1953:15)
Symmetrischer Knoten (Seiler-Baldinger 1991:28)
Echter Kreuzknoten (Von Brandt 1957:42)
Filet chinois, formé de deux demi-clefs (D'Harcourt 1934:94)
Noeud plat (Leroi-Gourhan 1943:271)
Nudo de hombre (Venegas 1956:232)
Nudo simple (Hammel/Haase 1962:221)
Nudo cuadrado (Rolandi 1985:36)
Nudo de envergue o nudo recto (Weitlaner-Johnson 1977:33)
Nudo de doble enlace (Millán de Palavecino 1960: Lam. 1 fig. 1)
Nó quadrado (Ribeiro 1986c:366)

3.2. Interlocking Symmetrical Knot

The running thread wraps round the descending portion of the pendant loop of the previous row. The latter in turn forms a loop and fixes the descending portion of the knot-forming element. This form is closely related to the square knot since in spite of its different structure, it can be converted into a square knot through simple twisting without altering the position of the loop limbs.

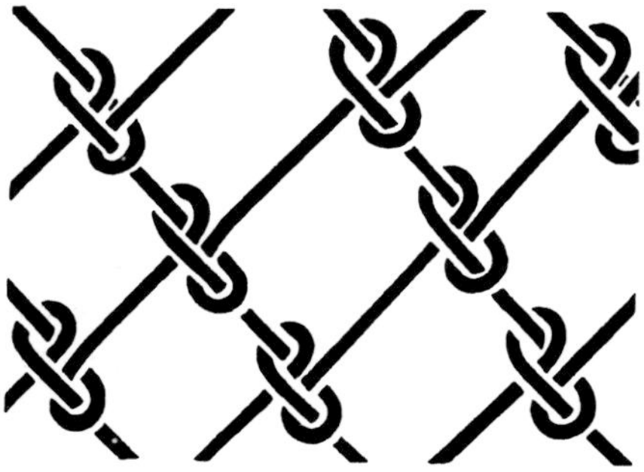

Fig. 32: Interlocking symmetrical knot

Other terms used:
Interlocking half-hitches with two cords (Singer 1935:18)
Verschobener symmetrischer Knoten (Seiler-Baldinger 1991:28)
Verschobener Kreuzknoten (Von Brandt 1957:45)

3.3. Vertical Granny Knot

This knot is formed in a manner similar to the square knot, but the second twining is in the same direction as the first and the knot is asymmetrical.

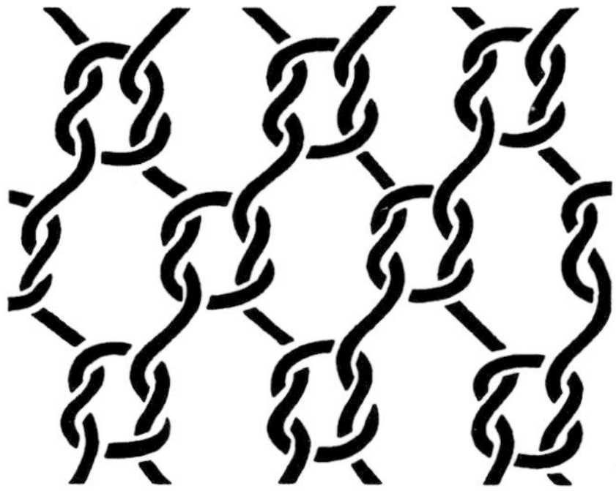

Fig. 33: Vertical granny knot

Other terms used:
Altweiberknoten (Seiler-Baldinger 1991:29)
Kreuzknoten (Niedner 1924:5)
Scheinbar symmetrischer Knoten (Müller 1967:224)
Nudo de costurera (Weitlaner-Johnson 1977:33)

3.4. Sheet Bend Knot

The working thread passes through the pendant loop in the previous row, wraps round its two ends and crosses over its ascending portion before leaving the loop. The knot is asymmetrical with dissimilar faces (34a and b).

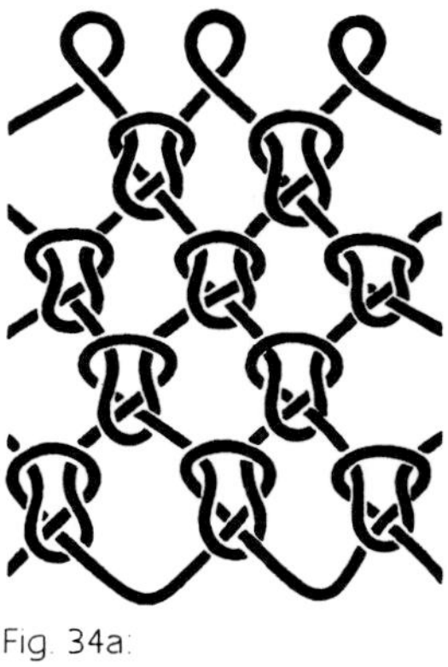

Fig. 34a:
Sheet bend knot: face

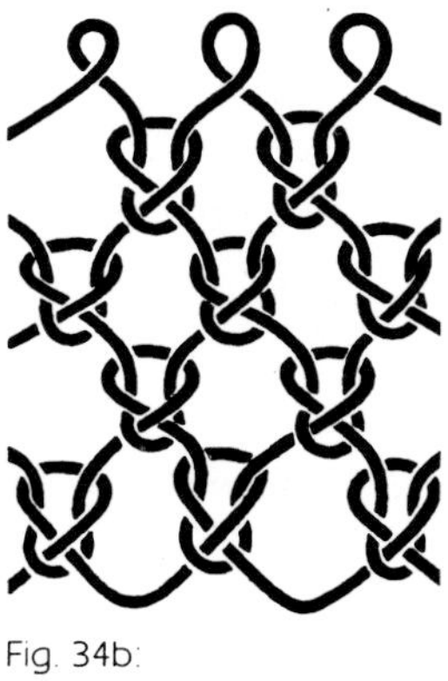

Fig. 34b:
Sheet bend knot: reverse

Other terms used:

Mesh knot, hawser bend (Loud/Harrington 1929:84)
Weaver's knot (Wollard 1953:19)
Thief's knot, netting knot (Peck Kent 1957:591)
Becket bend, swab hitch, simple bend, signal halyard bend (Day 1967:99)
Weberknoten (Seiler-Baldinger 1991:29)
Noeud plat (Leroi-Gourhan 1943:271)
Noeud de filet ordinaire (Guiart 1945:83)
Nudo de vuelta de escota o nudo de tejedor (Weitlaner-Johnson 1977:33)
Nó d'escota (Ribeiro 1986c:366)
Weversknop (Keppel 1984:39)

3.5. Fishnet Knot

The knot-forming element is passed through the crown of the pendant loop of the previous row and round its two ends. The fishnet knot is basically a variation of the sheet bend knot and can be converted into the sheet bend knot by tightening the crossing ends.

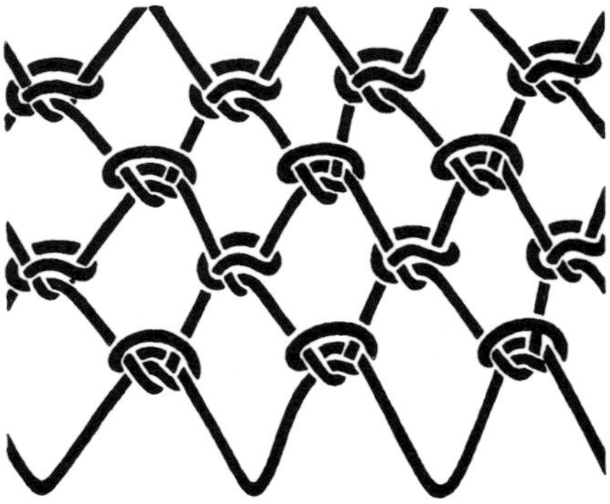

Fig. 35: Fishnet knot

Other terms used:

Sheet bend knot slightly modified (Singer 1935:22)
Weaver's knot (Rogers 1967:85)
Filetknoten (Seiler-Baldinger 1991:29)
Gewöhnlicher Fischnetzknoten, Schoetenstek (Bühler-Oppenheim 1947:105)
Filierknoten (Hartung 1963:60)
Nudo de filete (Venegas 1956:232)
Nudo simple (Hammel/Haase 1962:221)
Nó rede de pesca (Ribeiro 1986c:366)

3.6. Two- and Three-loop Flat Knot

The running thread and the loop of the preceding row interlace with each other. As a result a structure similar to braiding is obtained. Knots so formed cannot be displaced in any direction.

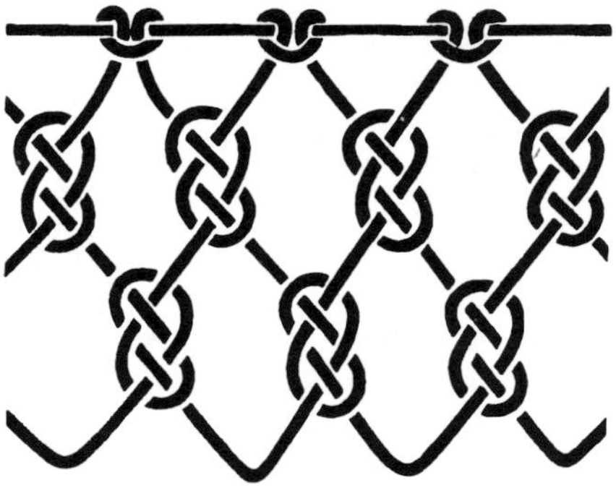

Fig. 36: Two-loop flat knot

Other terms used:

Carrick bend (Wollard 1953:68)
Zweischlaufiger Flachknoten (Seiler-Baldinger 1991:30)
Josefinen-Knoten (Mooi 1977:24)
Isabellenknoten (Textile Museum St. Gallen 1988: without page number)
Achterförmiger Zierknoten (Geijer 1938:102)
Trossenstek (Burgess 1981:43)

The three-loop flat knot consists of three loops which are intercrossed and linked, one passing under and the other over. The knot can be used for fabric production only if the loops of every third row interlace as two-loop flat knots. If the individual knots were to be simply linked with the loops of the preceding row, the result would be a variant type of the slip knot. The three-loop flat knot is generally found as an ornamental knot in trimming.

Fig. 37: Three-loop flat knot

Other terms used:

Carrick knot (Larsen 1986:74)
Dreischlaufiger Flachknoten (Seiler-Baldinger 1991:30)
Victoria-Knoten (Mooi 1977:24)

Meshwork Lace

Meshwork laces are a combination of looping and knotting. They have, however, developed into a special class and are generally denoted by the implements used in their manufacture (e.g. needle laces).

1. Tatting

Tatting is made with the aid of one or, rarely, more hand-shuttles on which the thread is wound. The technique is based on the cow hitch with loops of different lengths alternating and simple looping on a foundation. Tatting is often produced in combination with crocheting.

Other terms used:
Schiffchenarbeiten ("Frivolitäten") (Seiler-Baldinger 1991:30)
Occhi, Makuk (Liebert 1916:6)

2. Needle-point Laces

Needle-point laces are closely akin to looping. They are based on simple, double and twisted looping, with or without a foundation. In addition square knots, slip knots and cow hitches are employed. Eyed and sewing needles are used for working.

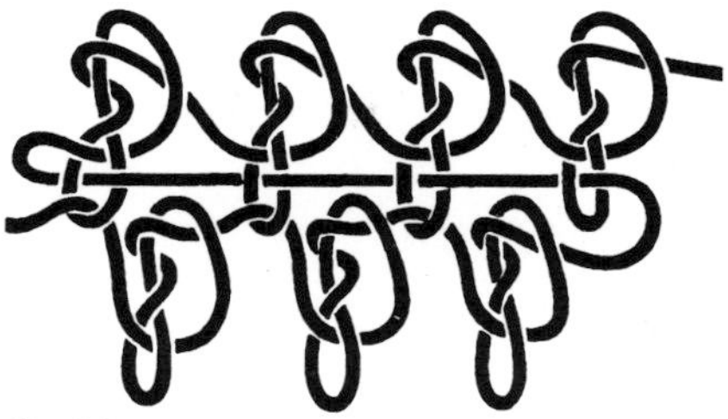

Fig. 38: Needle-point lace

Other terms used:
Needle-point laces are frequently named after the place where they are manufactured, e.g. Point de Venise, Point de France, Bibilla, Smyrna, etc.
Nadelspitzen (Seiler-Baldinger 1991:30)

Mesh Formation with a Continuous Element of Unlimited Length

Unlike techniques that use an element of limited length, the new mesh is formed by that portion of the thread nearest to the loop last formed.
Since it is not necessary to draw the element in its entire length through the previous mesh, it can be of any extent ("unlimited"). Mechanical aids, generally needles, are required except for the simplest forms of this group (simple crocheting). At least in this respect these techniques belong among the technically advanced primary methods. A distinction is made between crocheting and knitting depending on the nature of the production process.

Crocheting (vertical and lateral interlooping)

New meshes are formed by drawing the portion of the working element through one or more of the preceding meshes. Hence the new meshes are linked not only to the meshes of the previous row but also laterally to the meshes in the same row. Thus crocheting should better be called vertical and lateral interlooping. As such there is a similarity to certain forms of interconnected looping (see p. 13). Crocheting can be circular, to and fro, or in spirals. A crocheting needle is used as an accessory. The different mesh forms can be varied and combined at will in crocheting. Only a few of the basic forms are discussed here.

1. Simple Crochet Stitch

This is the simplest form and basic to all crochet stitches. Each new stitch is drawn through the previous one, thus forming a chain, which is the starting point in all crocheting.

Notation and theoretical observations:
A simple crochet stitch is comparable in structure to looping which is interconnected in the second turn with the thread configuration 2:111. In mathematical terms a chain of simple crochet stitches is a wild knot.

Fig. 39a: Simple crochet stitch: face

Fig. 39b: Simple crochet stitch: reverse

Other terms used:
Chain stitch (Birrell 1959:309)
Luftmasche (Seiler-Baldinger 1991:31)

2. Plain Crochet Stitch

The thread is drawn through an upper stitch of the previous row and through the stitch last formed.

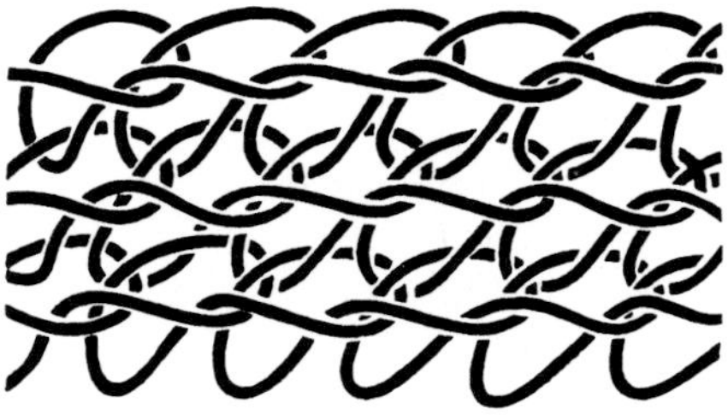

Fig. 40: Plain crochet stitch

Other terms used:
Single crochet (Birrell:309)
Kettenmasche (Seiler-Baldinger 1991:31)

3. Double Crochet Stitch

The thread is first drawn through the upper stitch of the previous row, then through the loop so formed and through the previous stitch. As in the case of plain crochet stitches, different variations are possible.

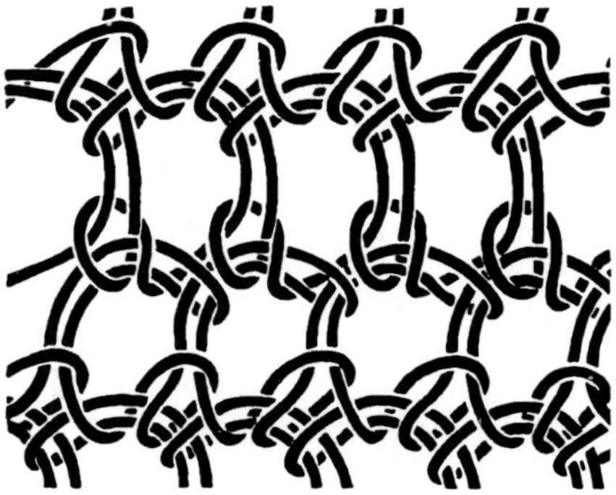

Fig. 41: Double crochet stitch

Other terms used:
Single stitch (Orr 1922:4)
Feste Masche (Seiler-Baldinger 1991:32)
These types of variation have a number of names in German, such as "Rosenstich", "Piquéstich" etc. (De Dillmont 1902:291ff.)

4. Treble Crochet Stitch

Treble crocheting produces small chains of stitches. The chains can be "half", "complete", "simple", "double" or "multiple", depending on how often the thread is laid on the needle prior to stitching.
Treble and simple crocheting are used in combination to produce openwork structures.

Fig. 42: Treble crochet stitch

Other terms used:
Treble crochet, double treble crochet, triple treble crochet, etc. (Orr 1922:4)
If simple crochet stitches are crocheted between the chains: Filet crochet, open spaces (Orr 1922:4)
Stäbchenmasche (Seiler-Baldinger 1991:32)

Knitting (vertical interlooping)

In knitting, the loops are arranged in a horizontal row (not interlooped) and connected to the corresponding meshes of the preceding row. This means that each loop has to be individually fixed, e.g. on forks, sticks or needles or that all loops of a row must be stored with the aid of an accessory (usually needles of different forms) till the next row is formed. Knitting can be to and fro or circular; in both cases horizontal and vertical rows of stitches are formed. Only the simplest forms are described here which, as in crocheting, can be modified and combined at will.

1. Plain Knitting

A loop is drawn through a previously formed stitch and fixed so that it cannot slip. The process is repeated with the next portion of thread.

Fig. 43a: Plain knitting: right

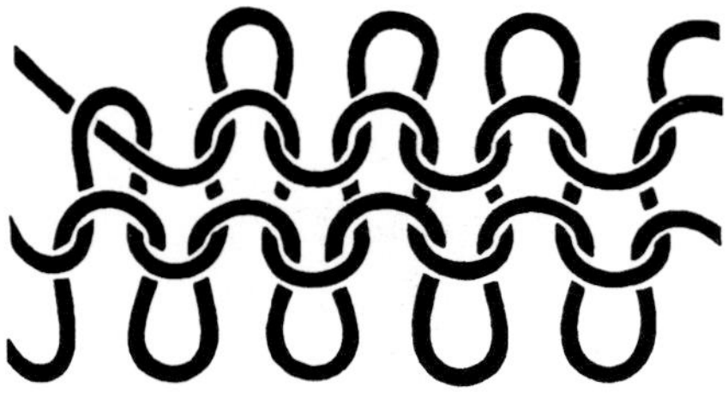

Fig. 43b: Plain knitting: left

Other terms used:
Stockinette stitch (Birrell 1959:306)
Plain knitting stocking stitch (Emery 1966:40)

Right and left rows alternating:
Plain knitting "garter stitch" (Emery 1966:40)
Rechte und linke Masche (Seiler-Baldinger 1991:32)

2. Crossed Knitting

The thread is crossed with itself while being drawn through a previously formed stitch. The structure is identical with encircled looping (see p. 17).

Fig. 44a: Crossed knitting: face

Fig. 44b: Crossed knitting: reverse

Other terms used:
Crossed knitting: right-over-left: stocking stitch,
Left-over-right: garter stitch (Emery 1966:41)
Verschränkte Masche (Seiler-Baldinger 1991:33)
Rechts verdrehte Masche (Lammèr 1975:98)

3. Cordage ("French ") Knitting

The loops are not arranged on needles but, depending on their number, fixed on fingers, forks or sticks. New stitches are formed by pulling the previously formed stitches over the working thread. This method is mainly used to produce knitted cordage; however, with the help of the appropriate mechanical aids, it should be possible to obtain tubular knitted fabrics as in the case of the modern mechanical refinements of knitting.

Fig. 45a:
French knitting on a fork

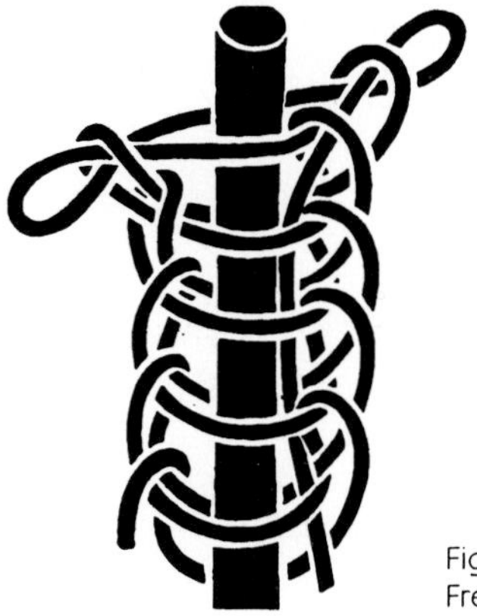

Fig. 45b:
French knitting on a stick

Other terms used:
Loop plaiting (Cardale-Schrimpff 1972:89)
Schnurstricken (Seiler-Baldinger 1991:33)
Nullestok eller Snoregaffel (Hald 1975:42)

References to the production of meshwork: see pp. 157-158.

Fabric Production with Two or More Sets of Elements (Thread Systems)

At least two elements are employed in making a fabric. Depending on how these are interrelated, i.e. the method of working (the systems are interchangeable in that both are active or one system is active and the other passive) and the structure of interworking, two main groups can be differentiated; namely, plaiting with a passive and an active system and plaiting with active systems.

Plaiting with a Passive and an Active System

Two or more groups of elements are used in such a fashion that one set of elements is always the active one. These active elements are used to fix the other group which remain passive throughout the process. An interchange of the two sets is not possible.

The structures are to some extent identical with the basic forms in methods employing a single element (e.g. linking and looping on a foundation). In such cases, the difference between the two methods is only in the use of two or more elements or thread groups, i.e. in the technique.

There is a large number of very diverse forms of plaiting with an active and a passive system which are very often used for basketry. The most important subgroups are splitting, wrapping, coiling and twining.

Twined basket of the Haida, Queen Charlotte Islands, Canada, c. 1890, IVa 59

Splitting

Relatively broad or thick elements placed parallel to one another form the passive group and are pierced through at the appropriate places by the running active elements. This very simple technique is closely similar to sewing.

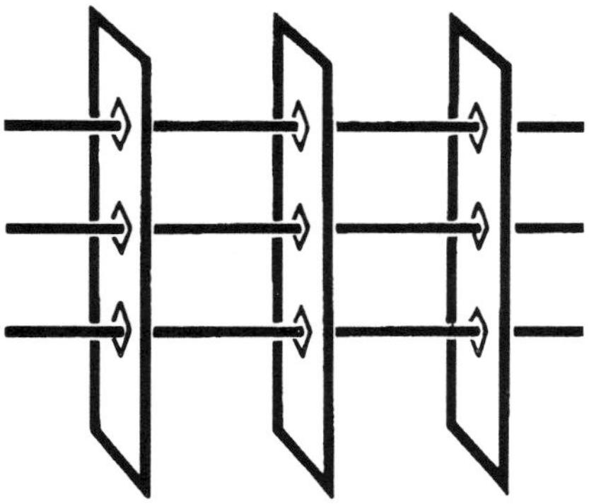

Fig. 46: Splitting

Other terms used:
Durchstechen des einen Systems (Seiler-Baldinger 1991:35)
Doorsteken (Keppel 1984:42)

Wrapping

Passive elements arranged parallel to one another are fixed through wrapping round them one or more active threads running perpendicular or oblique to the first set. Variations are obtained by skipping individual elements of the passive set or by bringing together a number of passive elements or changing the way the active thread is wound, looped or knotted.
The structures are identical with certain structures of warp fabrics (see pp. 57-61).

1. Simple and Multiple Wrapping

The active thread is wrapped once or more round only one, or simultaneously around two or more, of the passive elements (Fig. 47a-b). The wrapping can be in accordance with an S- or Z-twist (Fig. 47a-b, 48a-b) or alternating S- and Z-twists (Fig. 49).

Notation and theoretical observations:
For a better description of the movement of the active element the number of passive elements over which the thread passes to and fro is ascertained. Thus Fig. 47a yields a thread configuration of f(orwards) 2 b(ackwards) / (under) 1 again, in abbreviated form f2 b/1. This reflects the thread pattern of a repeat or a translation. Similarly, Fig. 47c gives a diagram of the thread pattern f2b/1f1b/1, Fig. 48a of f4b/2 and 48b of f4b/2f2b/2, and Fig. 49 of f1b/1f/1bf1/1f1.

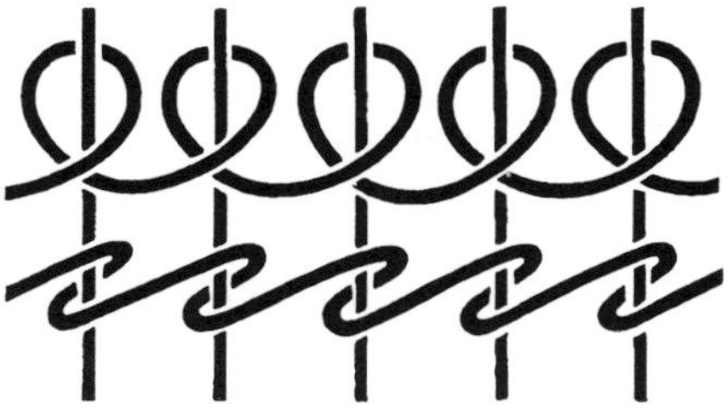

Fig. 47a: Simple wrapping of a passive element with Z slant

Fig. 47b: Simple wrapping of a passive element with S slant

Fig. 47c: Multiple or double wrapping of a passive element (with Z twist)

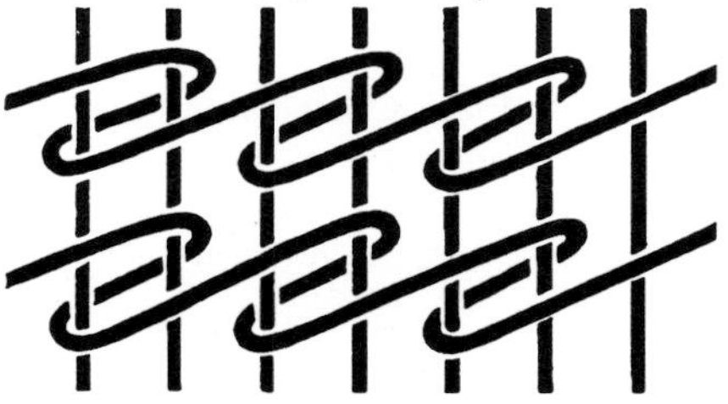

Fig. 48a: Simple wrapping of two passive elements (with Z twist)

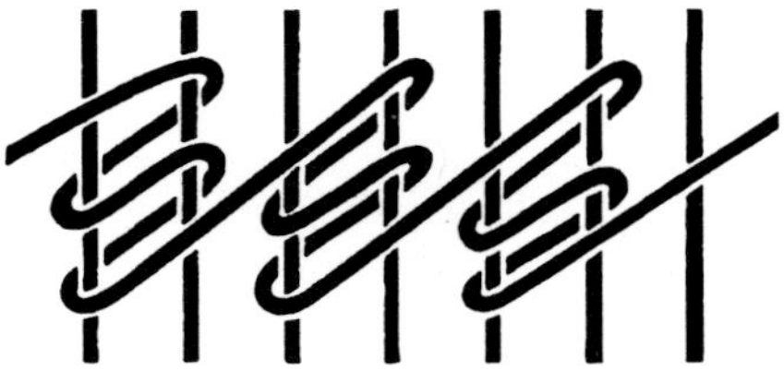

Fig. 48b: Multiple, i.e. double wrapping of two passive elements (with Z twist)

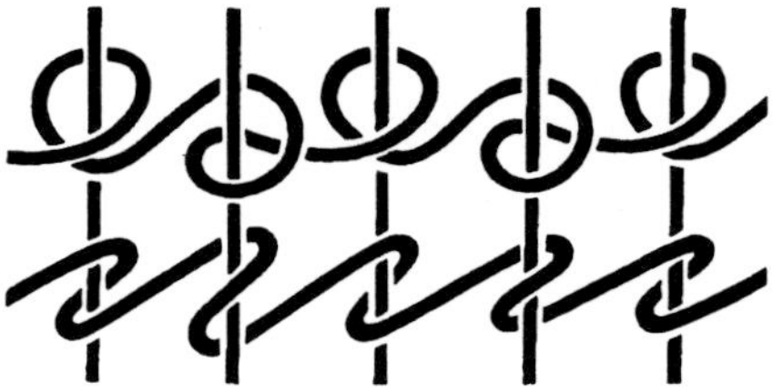

Fig. 49: Wrapping with alternating S and Z twist

Other terms used:

Wrapped weaving (Mason 1902:230)
Wrapped wicker weave (Tanner 1968:8)
Einfaches und mehrfaches Umwickeln (Seiler-Baldinger 1991:35)
Einfacher, eineinhalber und doppelter Rundschlag (Mooi 1977: 13)
Vannerie à brins spiralés (Leroi-Gourhan 1943:282)
Vannerie clayonnée à brins tournés (Balfet 1952:267)
Tressage soumak (Anquetil 1979:170)
Cestería espiral vertical simple con armadura simple (Barcelona 1976)
Cestería enrollada (Mora de Jaramillo 1974:340)
Wikkelen (Keppel 1984:45)

2. Looped Wrapping

The passive elements are held in place by the active elements in loops. These can be simple (Fig. 50), S- or Z-twisted, or even alternating S- and Z-twisted when the active element is wrapped in double loops (Fig. 51c). It is also possible for more than one passive element to be fixed at the same time (Fig. 52a). In the case of double-looped wrapping, the loops can also be staggered (Fig. 52b), i.e. one loop passes round element A, the other round passive element B. Similarly, two passive elements can be wrapped round so as to produce a staggered pattern (Fig. 52c). These structures are found especially in warp fabrics (see p. 60). Akin to looping, it is also possible to link the loops laterally (Fig. 53), thus affording scope for a large number of variations.

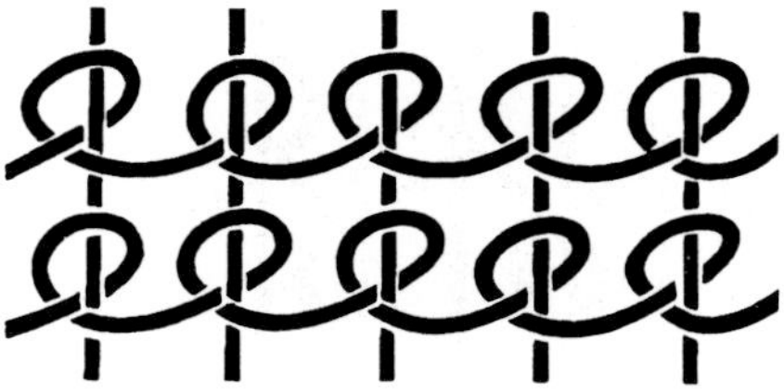

Fig. 50: Simple-looped wrapping with Z twist

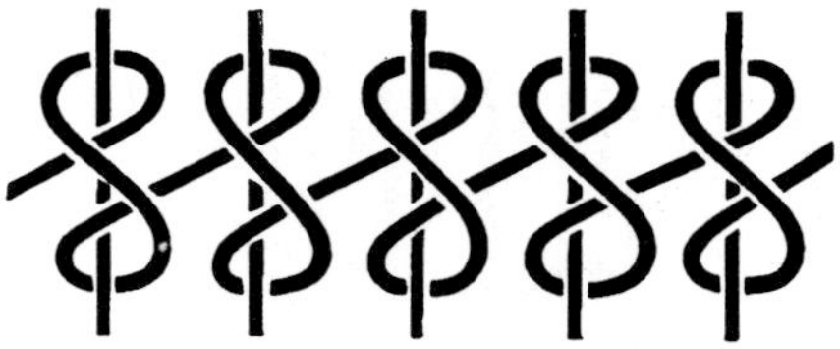

Fig. 51a: Double-looped wrapping with S twist

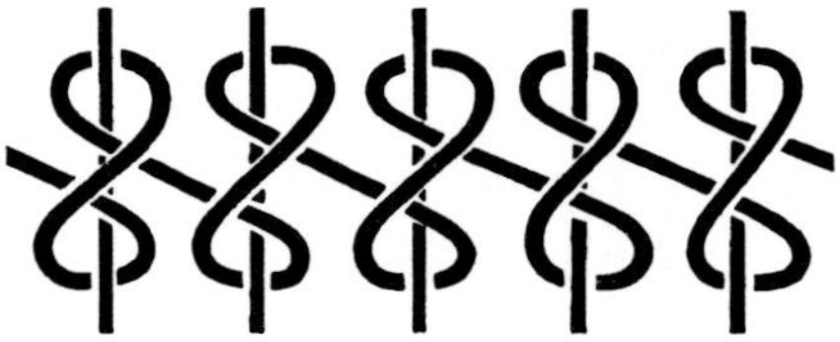

Fig. 51b: Double-looped wrapping with Z twist

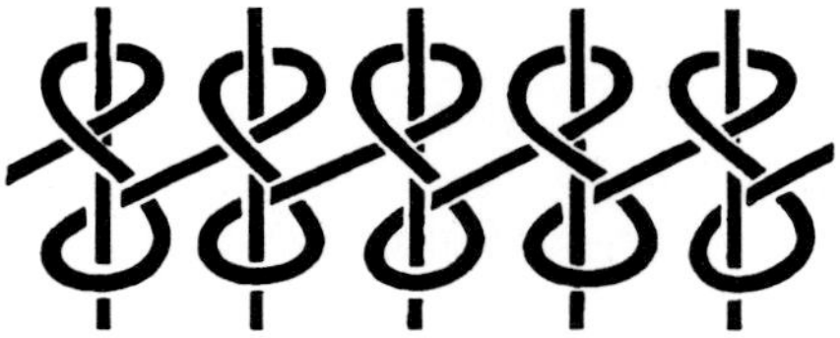

Fig. 51c: Double-looped wrapping with alternating S and Z twist

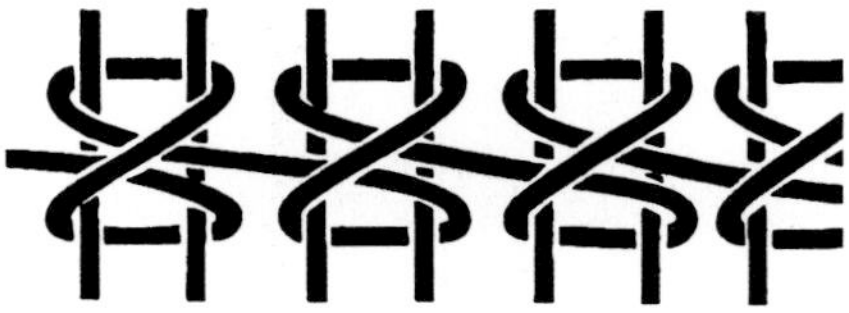

Fig. 52a: Double-looped wrapping around two passive elements

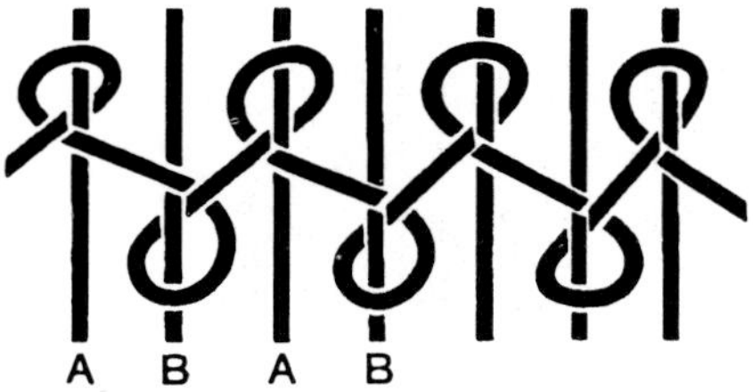

Fig. 52b: Staggered double-looped wrapping

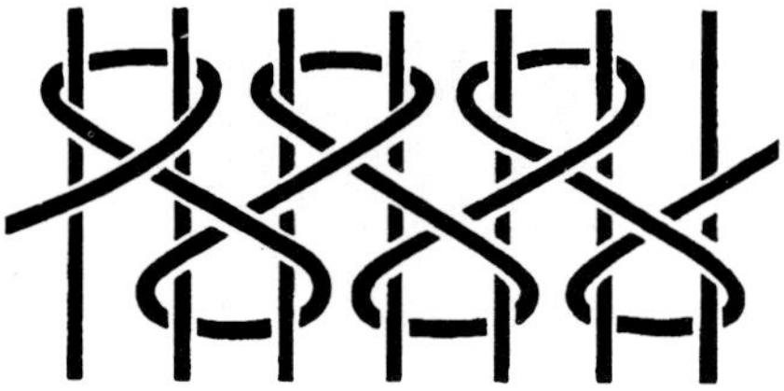

Fig. 52c: Staggered double-looped wrapping around two passive elements

Fig. 53: Interconnected looped wrapping

Other term used:
Umschlingendes Wickeln (Seiler-Baldinger 1991:36)

3. Knotted Wrapping

Knots are used instead of loops to fix the passive elements.

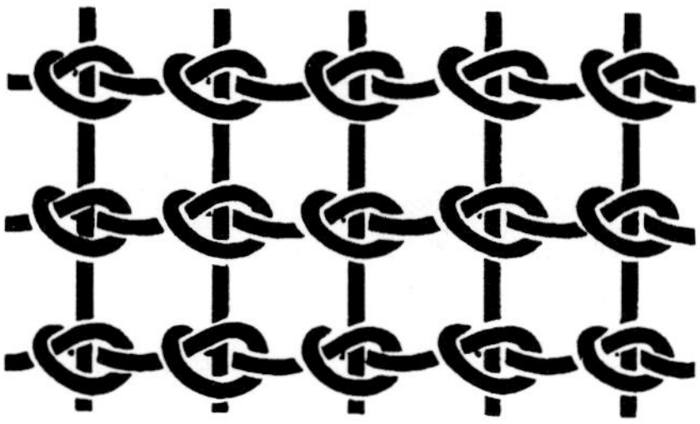

Fig. 54: Knotted wrapping

Other terms used:
Tie-twined matting technique (Massey/Osborne 1961:346)
Verknotendes Wickeln (Seiler-Baldinger 1991:37)
Cestería espiral vertical: cadeneta (Barcelona 1976)

Binding

Two or more passive sets of elements, usually consisting of stiff material, are laid crisscross one over the other. The crossings are fixed with the help of a running active thread, a set of elements or short thread pieces. Numerous variations are possible depending on the number and position of the passive systems (which should always be indicated) and on the type of interworking. These variant forms are related to those of wrapping.

1. Wrapped Binding

The crossing passive systems are fixed by wrapping (Fig. 55a), it also being possible to work diagonally to the passive systems (Fig. 55b).

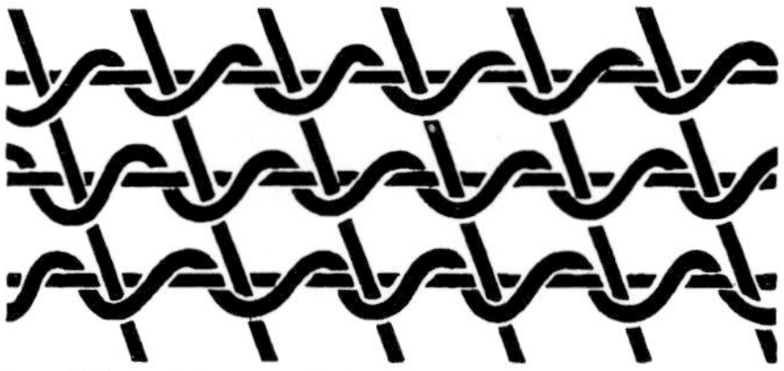

Fig. 55a: Wrapped binding parallel to one of the passive systems

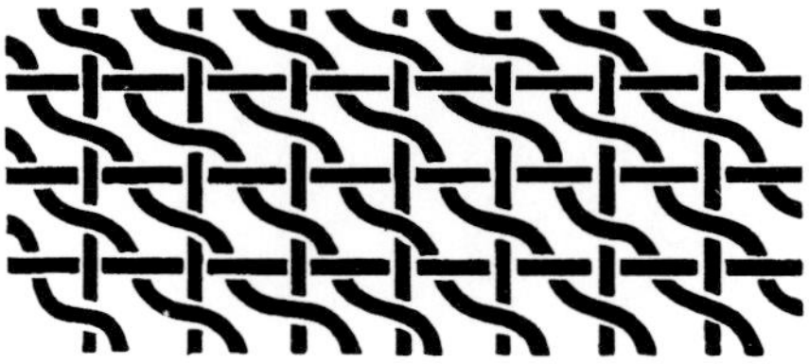

Fig. 55b: Wrapped binding diagonal to the passive systems

Other terms used:
Wrapped twined weaving (Mason 1902:235)
Wrapped twining (Nettinga-Arnheim 1977:47)
Plain bound weave (Cardale-Schrimpff 1972:417)
Weft-twined weave with stiff elements (Burnham 1981:8)
Umwickelndes Binden (Seiler-Baldinger 1991:37)
Vannerie spiralée à nappes superposées (Leroi-Gourhan 1943: 286)
Vannerie spiralée à nappes superposées liées (Balfet 1952:267)
Montants passifs superposés (Pellaton-Chable 1980:122)
Cestería superpuesta sin entrecruzamiento (Mora de Jaramillo 1974:337)
Cestería espiral horizontal simple (Barcelona 1976)
Cestería en espiral de madejas superpuestas (Alfaro Giner 1984: 167)
Trançado enlaçado com grade (Ribeiro 1986b: 319)

2. Looped Binding

The passive systems are fixed by simple loops with either an S- or Z-twist in single (Fig. 56a) or double loops (Fig. 56c), the active element being passed either parallel (Fig. 56a) or diagonal to the passive systems (Fig. 56b). With looped binding in double loops the same passive elements can be fixed by both loops (Fig. 56c) or in a staggered pattern (56d). If two active elements fix the passive elements in double loops, we speak of crisscross double-looped binding (Fig. 56e).

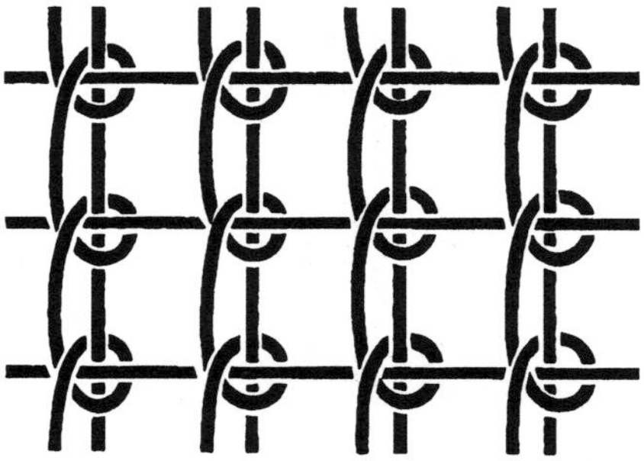

Fig. 56a: Looped binding parallel to one of the passive systems

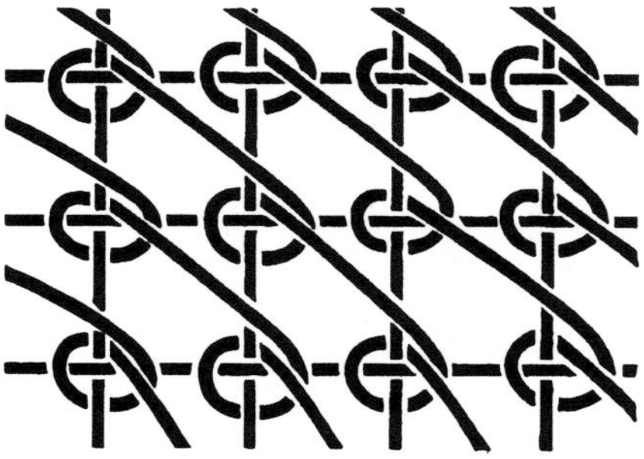

Fig. 56b: Looped binding diagonal to the passive systems

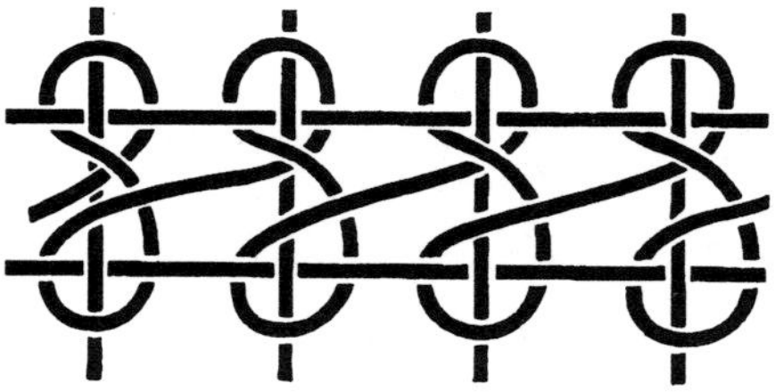

Fig. 56c: Double-looped binding

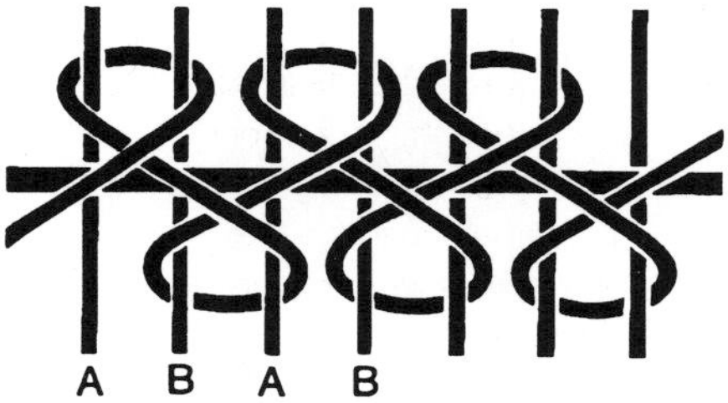

Fig. 56d: Staggered double-looped binding

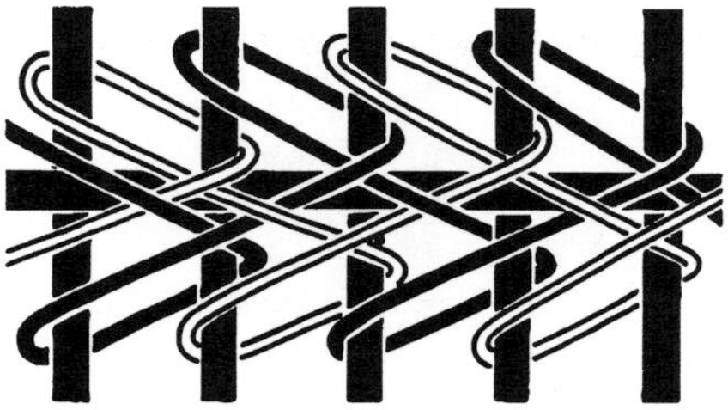

Fig. 56e: Crisscross double-looped binding

Other terms used:

Simple looped binding:
Einfaches umschlingendes Binden (Seiler-Baldinger 1991:38)
Clayonné à brins liés (Anquetil 1979:12)
Cestería espiral vertical con armadura compuesta (Barcelona 1976)

Double looped binding:
Complicated lattice twining (Barrett 1908:278)
Lattice wrapped weaving technique (Kissell 1915:141)
Doppelschlaufiges Binden (Seiler-Baldinger 1991:38)
Cestería espiral horizontal: espiral doble (Barcelona 1976)

3. Knotted Binding

The passive elements are fixed by knotting the active element.

Fig. 57: Knotted binding

Other term used:

Verknotendes Binden (Seiler-Baldinger 1991:39)

4. Twining

Two or more active elements are twined together in such a way that with every twist they fix one or more elements of the passive system.

This form of interlacement makes twining a transitional step to plaiting with active systems, since the individual threads (not thread pairs) of the active system cross the passive elements in an under one - over one structure. There are a number of variations of twining. These differ less from one another than the various types of coiling.

4.1. Two-strand Twining over a Passive System

Two active threads fix passive elements by twining. There are various forms depending on the direction of twist of the twine. In each passage this may be the same (Fig. 58a) or alternately in opposed directions (Fig. 58b). Another determining factor is the number of passive elements fixed per strand of twine (Fig. 58c), staggering also being possible (Fig. 58d).

Fig. 58a: Two-strand twining over a passive system with S twist

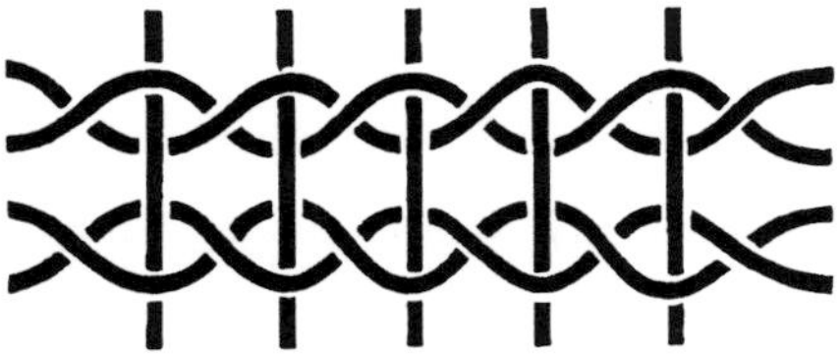

Fig. 58b: Two-strand twining over a passive system with S and Z twist (countered)

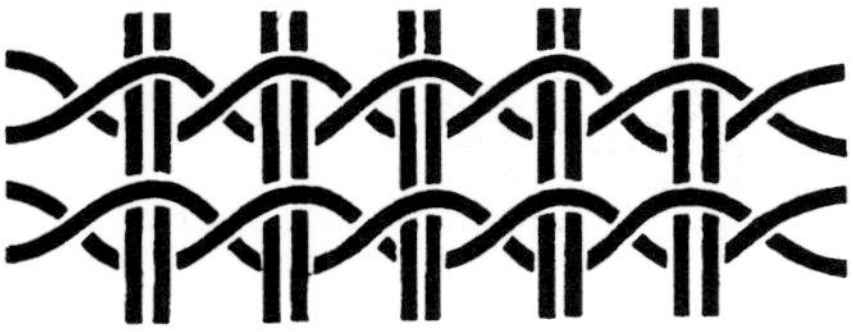

Fig. 58c: Two-strand twining over two passive elements

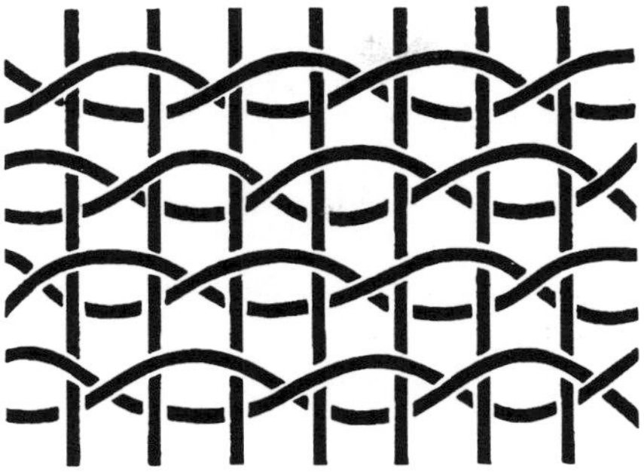

Fig. 58d: Staggered two-strand twining over a passive system

Other terms used:

Pairing or double pairing (Gallinger 1975:56)
Plain twining (Miner 1935/36:182)
Tied-twined basketry (Martin/Rinaldo et al. 1952:312)
Two-strand simple twining (Mohr/Sample 1954/55:347)
Twined wicker weave (Tanner 1968:12)
Simple twining (Green Gigli et al. 1974:131)
Paarweises Zwirnbinden über ein passives System (Seiler-Baldinger 1991:39)
Gittertechnik (Rohrer 1927:56)
Einfache Zwirnbindung (Vogt 1937:12)
Vannerie à brins spiralés cordés (Leroi-Gourhan 1943:286)
Vannerie cordée (Balfet 1952:261)
Torcitura (Mariotti 1982:28)
Cestería entrelazada (Saugy 1974:147)
Cestería espiral horizontal: espiral doble (Barcelona 1976)
Cestería atada o cordada (Alfaro Giner 1984:159)
Cestería romboidal atada (Alfaro Giner 1984:166)
Técnica enrolada (Melo Taveira 1980:22)
Torcido de trama simple (Rolandi 1981:159)
Trançado torcido (Ribeiro 1980:42)
Fitsen (Keppel 1984:55)

4.2. Two-strand Twining over Two Passive Systems

As in wrapped binding two passive thread systems are fixed by twining. The passive systems can be arranged either perpendicularly (Fig. 59a) or diagonally to each other (Fig. 59b).

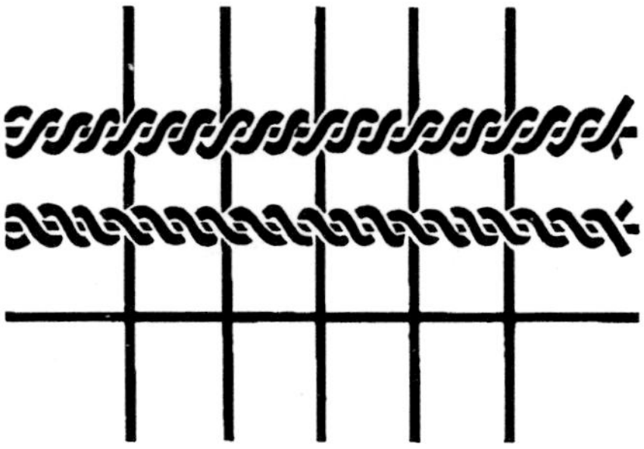

Fig. 59a: Two-strand twining over perpendicularly arranged passive systems

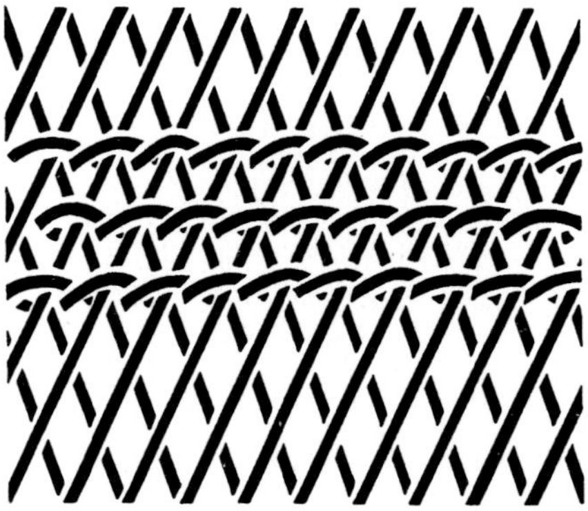

Fig. 59b: Two-strand twining over two diagonally arranged passive systems

Other terms used:
For all variations:
Lattice twining (Barrett 1908:146)
Twined lattice (Mason 1908:12)
Paarweises Zwirnbinden über zwei passive Systeme (Seiler-Baldinger 1991:40)
Cestería enrollada (Mora de Jaramillo 1974:340)

Passive systems arranged diagonally to each other:
Cross warp twined weaving (Mason 1902:13)
Torcido de trama diagonal (Rolandi 1981:157)

Passive systems arranged perpendicularly to each other:
Tee lattice or twined weaving (Mason 1902:16)

4.3. Twining with Three or More Active Elements (Waling)

Three or more active elements are so intertwined that two or more passive threads are invariably fixed in a twist of the active set. The same variations are possible here as with the two-strand twining.

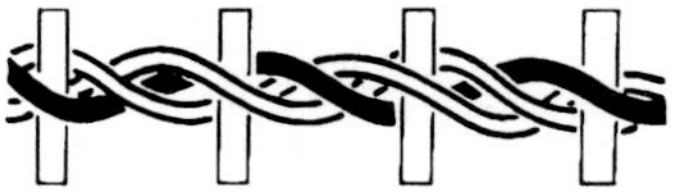

Fig. 60a: Waling (three-strand twining)

Fig. 60b: Waling: cross-section

Other terms used:
Three-strand twining (Barrett 1908:145ff.)
Triple-twist twined weave (Belen 1952:56f.)
Three-strand diagonal twining (Mohr/Sample 1954/55:347)
Three-ply twill twining (Buck 1957:142)
Waling (Hodges 1964:146)
Three-ply twined or braid weave (Navajo school 1972:86)
Triple pairing, four (five etc.)-rod coil (Gallinger 1975:56)
False embroidery: twining with three wefts (Underhill 1945:105)
Zwirnbinden mit zwei oder mehr aktiven Elementen (Kimmen) (Seiler-Baldinger 1991:40)

5. Braided Twining

Three or more elements are braided in such a way that they fix one or more passive threads.

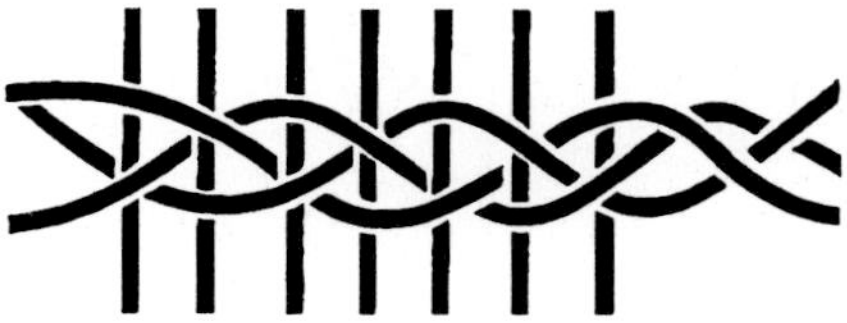

Fig. 61: Braided twining

Other terms used:
Three-ply braid and twined work (Mason 1902:16)
Three-strand braiding (Mason 1907:133)
Three-strand braided twining (Mohr/Sample 1954/55:347)
Braided three-strand twining (Emery 1966:203)
Flechtbinden (Seiler-Baldinger 1991:40)

Coiling

The elements of the passive systems, sometimes a bundle of threads, are fixed by an active element which usually runs in the same direction as the passive elements and not oblique to them as in wrapping. This technique is particularly rich in variations with widely different structures. There are two main groups. In the first group the active element is wrapped around the passive system: in the second it pierces the passive system. The first group is by far the more important and possesses innumerable variations. The course of the active element frequently

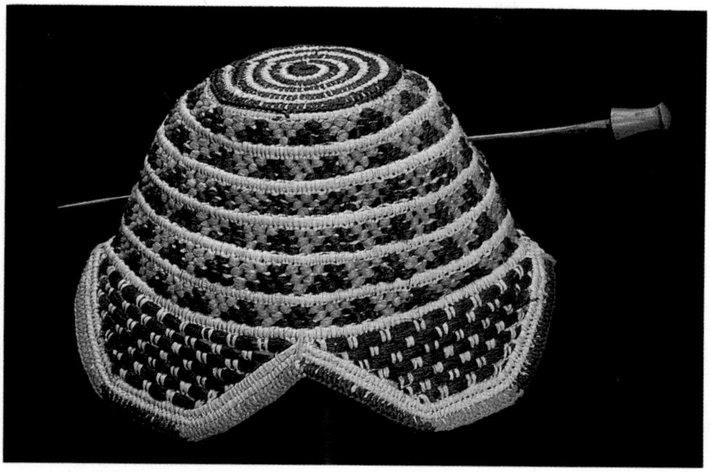

PLATE 4. Coiled hat of the Bakuba, Congo, III 11477

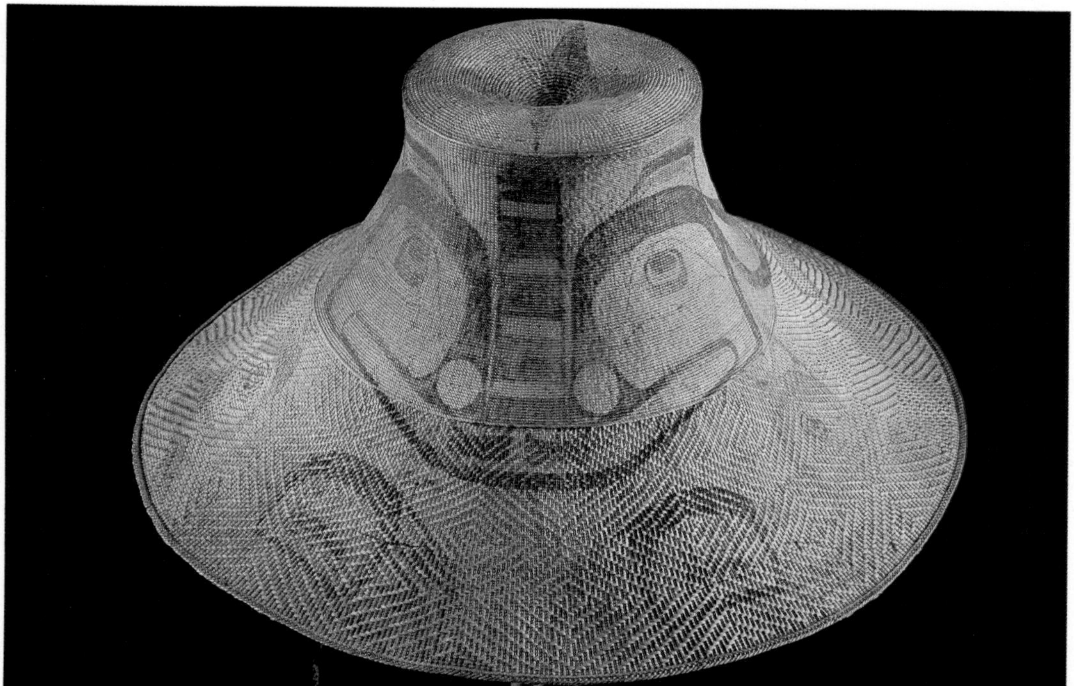

PLATE 5. Twined and wrapped hat of the Sitka, Alaska, IVa 147

Plate 6. Manioc trays of the Yek'uana, diagonal plaiting, Amazonas, Venezuela, IVc 9820-1, 15093-5

shows similarities to that in meshwork structures from elements of limited length. The pierced forms on the other hand are related to sewing.
By analogy the variations can be called linked, looped or knotted coiling. Structurally, meshwork on a foundation cannot be distinguished from the products of the first group. The close relationship between the two techniques is also apparent in a comparison of the manufacturing steps. For example, during the manufacturing stages a bag being made by simple looping over a strip serving as a template can be considered as coiled. On the other hand, once the bag is completed and the template removed, the product would be classified as meshwork.
The group of pierced coiling comprises forms in which the active thread splits the passive systems instead of wrapping round them. These variations accommodate exigencies of the material and are closely akin to sewing. The two main groups can also be combined with each other.
Coiling is often called "spiral coiling" because in its most familiar form (making of baskets, etc.) the passive system is wound in spirals.

Other terms used:
Wulsthalbflechten (Seiler-Baldinger 1991:41)
Un seul montant continu, spiralé (Pellaton-Chable 1980:122)
Cestería arollada o cosida (Saugy 1974:47)

1. Encircled Coiling

In this form of coiling the passive elements are never pierced but carefully wrapped round by the active element.
There are many variations and, as they do not differ basically from the pierced types in the thread configuration of the active element, they will not be dealt with again on a separate basis.

Other term used:
Umfassendes Wulsthalbflechten (Seiler-Baldinger 1991:41)

1.1. Wrapped Coiling

The fixing of the passive system is through wrapping, with the active element going round one or more passive units. A coherent structure is obtained either by having the active thread move over to the adjacent rows from time to time (Fig. 62a) or by having each row of the passive system wrapped twice (Fig. 62b). The wrapping can be in one or two directions (crossed wrapping). Further variations are obtained by arrangement of the active element during wrapping (Fig. 62c).

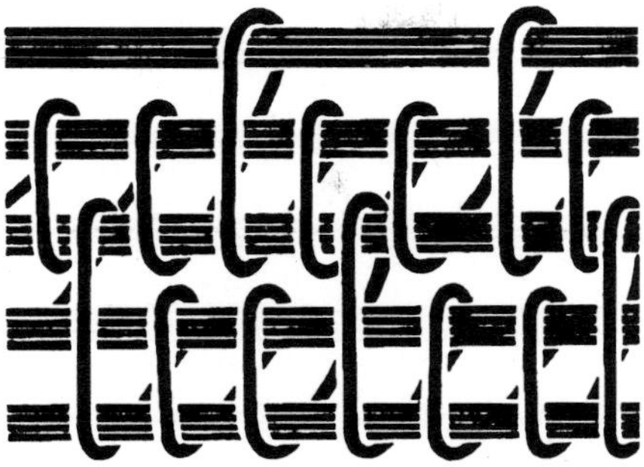

Fig. 62a: Encircled coiling, wrapping round adjacent elements

Fig. 62b: Wrapped coiling, active thread passing over two passive elements

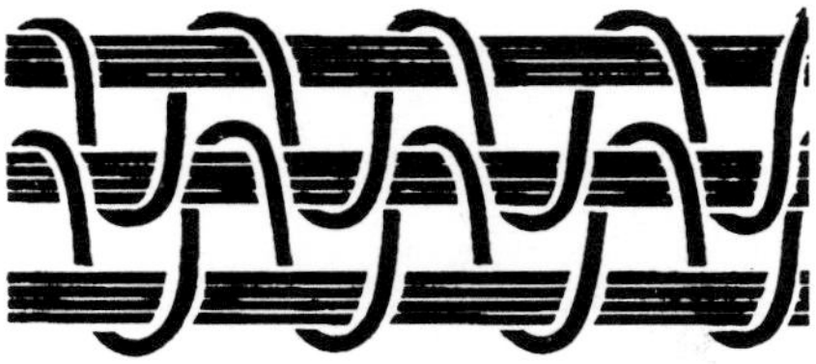

Fig. 62c: Wrapped coiling, active thread passing over one passive element and under another

Other terms used:
For the method illustrated in Fig. 62a:
Simple lacing coiling technique (Mason 1908:29)
Melanesian spiral coiling (Davidson 1919:169)
Coiled basketry whose sewing elements do not interlock (Kidder/Guernsey 1919:169)
Double couching stitches (VanStan 1959:192)
Non interlocking coiling (Lambert/Ambler 1961:64f.)
Coiled basketry plain wrapping; coiled basketry figure-of-eight (Navajo) wrapping (Hodges 1964:131)
Regular coiled weave (Tanner 1968:8)
Umfassendes umwickelndes Wulsthalbflechten, auf benachbarte Elemente übergreifend (Seiler-Baldinger 1991:41)

Achterstich (Zechlin 1966: 180)
Einfaches umwickelndes Wulsthalbflechten (Müller 1967: 248)
Vannerie spiralée à brins roulés (Balfet 1952: 29)
Point en huit (Anquetil 1979: 162)

For the method illustrated in Fig. 62b:
Coiled basketry long and short (lazy squaw) wrapping or Peruvian coil wrapping (Hodges 1964: 131)
Umwickelndes Wulsthalbflechten, Fadenführung aktiv über zwei passive Elemente (Seiler-Baldinger 1991: 42)

For the method illustrated in Fig. 62c:
Umwickelndes Wulsthalbflechten, Fadenführung aktiv über ein, unter ein passives Element (Seiler-Baldinger 1991: 42)
Cestería espiral horizontal: espiral alternante (Barcelona 1976)
Cestería en espiral verdadera (Alfaro Giner 1984: 167)

1.2. Linked Coiling

The passive elements are interconnected through simple linking. One or more units of the passive system can be engaged by the active thread. Linking can be only into the mesh loop of the active thread in the preceding row (Fig. 63a) or alternatively with an additional wrapping round the passive system (Fig. 63b). Different configurations of the active thread are possible.

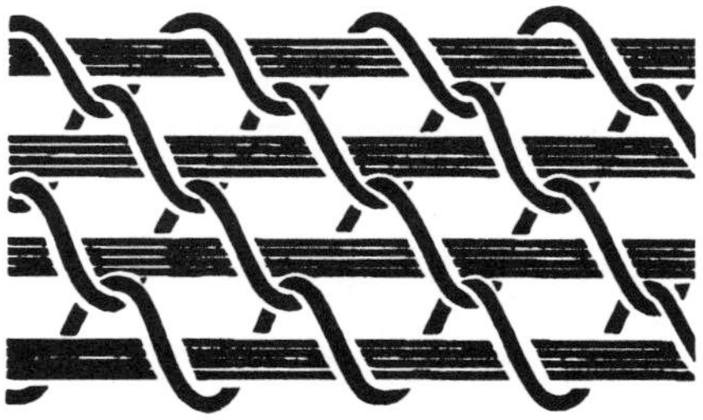

Fig. 63a: Linked coiling, through mesh of active element

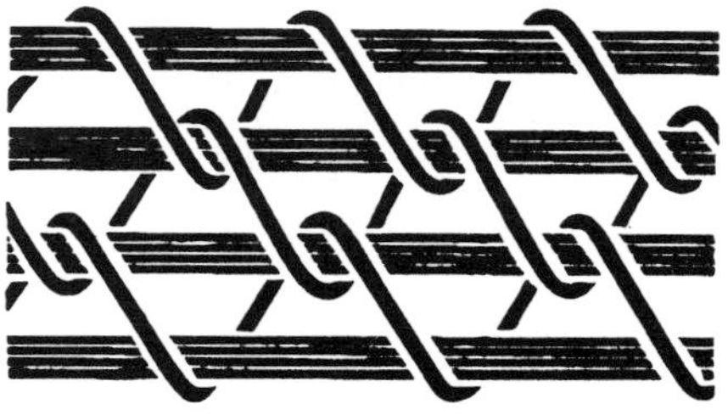

Fig. 63b: Linked coiling with additional wrapping round passive system

Other terms used:

Einhängendes Wulsthalbflechten (Seiler-Baldinger 1991: 42)
Cestería espiral de armadura libre (Barcelona 1976)

For the method illustrated in Fig. 63a:
Simple interlocking coils (Mason 1902: 21)
Einhängendes Wulsthalbflechten, in die Masche des aktiven Elementes (Seiler-Baldinger 1991: 42)
Vannerie spiralée à brins roulés (Balfet 1952: 268)

For the method illustrated in Fig. 63b:
Single lacing, interlocking variety (Mason 1908: 29)
Melanesian spiral coiling (Davidson 1919: 287)
Cross stitch coiled (Lambert/Ambler 1961: 64f.)
Simple linking on a foundation element, interlocked stitches (Emery 1966: 52)
Interlocked coiling stitch (Elsasser 1978: 626)
Einhängendes Wulsthalbflechten mit zusätzlicher Umfassung des passiven Elementes (Seiler-Baldinger 1991: 42)
Espiral de armadura libre entrelazada (Barcelona 1976)

1.3. Cross-linked Coiling

Two active elements hold the passive systems in position by means of crossed links. Depending on the thread configuration, this group provides the transition forms to plaiting with two active sets of elements.

Fig. 64a: Crisscrossed linked coiling with continuous wrapping

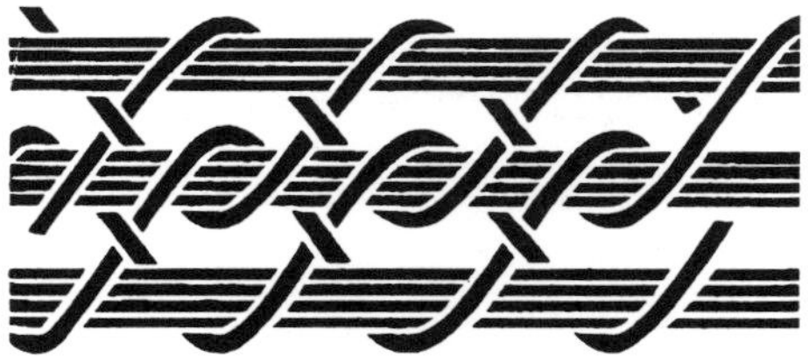

Fig. 64b: Cross-linked coiling, interlaced

Other terms used:

Double lacing (Mason 1908: 29)
Kreuzweise einhängendes Wulsthalbflechten (Seiler-Baldinger 1991: 42)
Espiral de armadura libre cruzada (Barcelona 1976)

1.4. Looped Coiling

The active thread fixes the passive system in all the variations of looping mentioned so far (cf. Meshwork), being interlocked either with the mesh of the active element (Fig. 65a-b) or with the passive elements (Fig. 65c). Simple (Fig. 65a and c), twisted (Fig. 65b) and double (Fig. 65d) looping are commonly used. Loops can be pierced, encircled or laterally interconnected, just as in the corresponding meshwork techniques.

Fig. 65a: Simple looped coiling, interlocked with mesh of active element

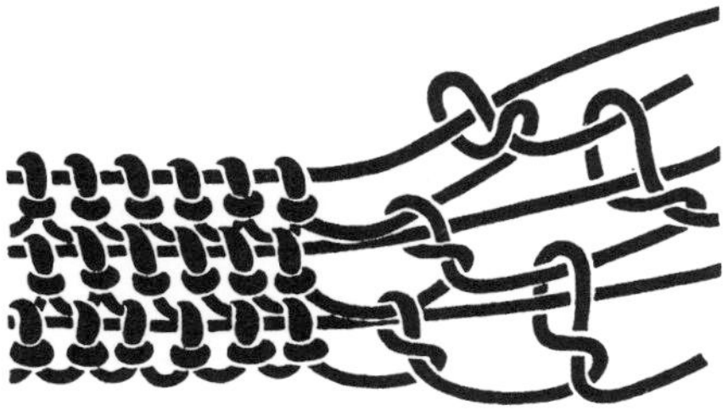

Fig. 65b: Loop and twist coiling, interlocked with mesh of active element

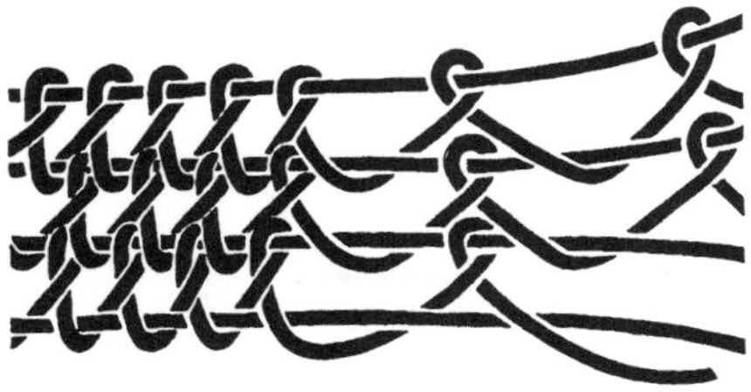

Fig. 65c: Simple looped coiling around the passive element

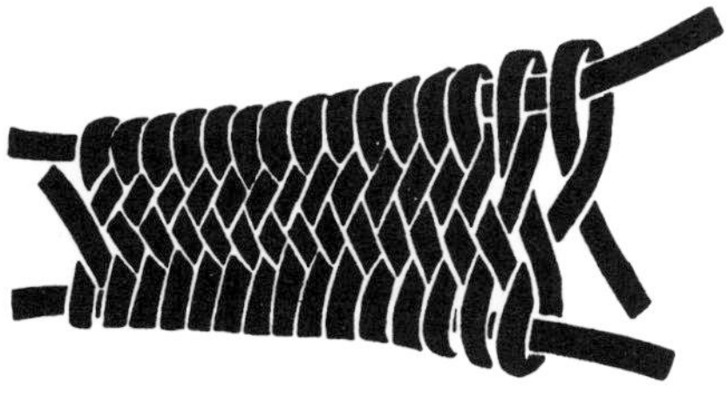

Fig. 65d: Double looped coiling

Other terms used:

Simple looped coiling (Fig. 65a)
Half-hitch coiling (Davidson 1919:285)
Half-hitch coil over a foundation (O'Neale 1949:77)
Simple looping over a foundation element (interlocked stitches) (Emery 1966:53)
Einfach verschlingendes Wulsthalbflechten (Seiler-Baldinger 1991:43)
Einfaches Wulsthalbflechten (Müller 1967:245)
Vannerie spiralée vraie (Leroi-Gourhan 1943:286)
Vannerie spiralée demi-clef (Balfet 1952:271)
Cestería en espiral de armazón libre (Mora de Jaramillo 1974: 342)
Espiral de armadura libre de encaje (Barcelona 1976)
Trançado costurado com ponto de nó (Ribeiro 1988:66)
Omslingen (Keppel 1984:52)

Loop-and-twist coiling (Fig. 65b):
Twisted half-hitch over a coiled foundation (Lothrop 1928:137)
Loop-and-twist on a foundation element (Emery 1966:54)
Zweifach verschlingendes Wulsthalbflechten (Seiler-Baldinger 1991:43)

Double-looped interconnected coiling (Fig. 65c-d):
Mousing knot (Mason 1908:27)
Figure-of-eight wrapping (Collingwood 1968:241)
Mariposa weave (Navajo school 1972:29)
Doppelschlaufig verschlingendes Wulsthalbflechten (Seiler-Baldinger 1991:44)
Höhere Form des Wulsthalbflechtens (Müller 1967:250f.)
Encadenado y enlace (Millán de Palavecino 1960)
Espiral trenzado simple o compuesta (Barcelona 1976)

1.5. Knotted Coiling

As in looped coiling it is possible here also to bind the passive elements together with the help of different kinds of knots (cf. Knotting). Very often suspended knots with double loops are employed. Fixed knots are possible in theory but seldom used.

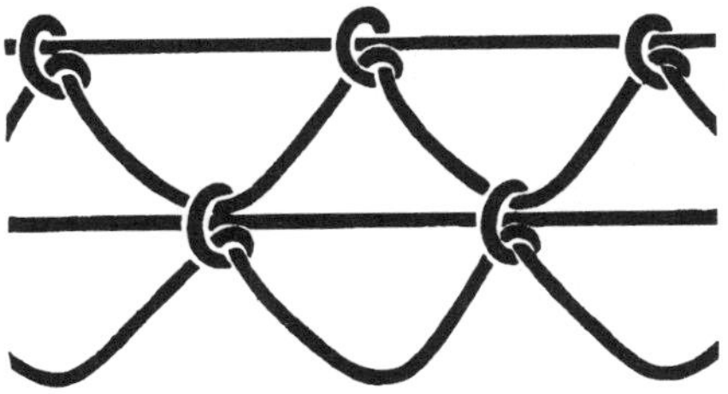

Fig. 66a: Coiling with simple or overhand knot

Fig. 66b: Coiling with double-looped knot

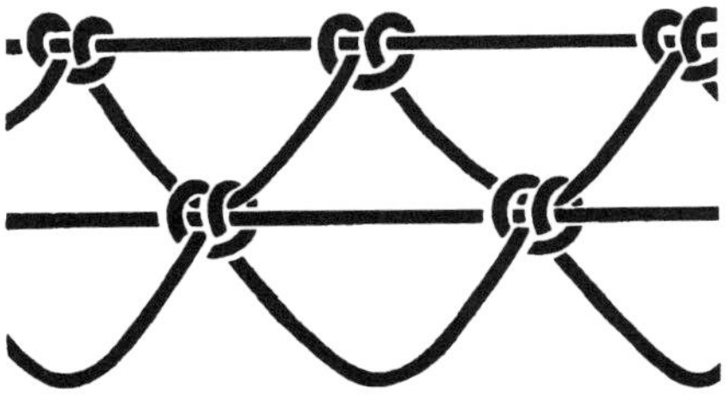

Fig. 66c: Coiling with clove hitches

Other terms used:
Verknotendes Wulsthalbflechten (Seiler-Baldinger 1991:44)

Coiling with overhand knot (Fig. 66a):
Knotted loops on a foundation element, simple knot (Emery 1966:54)
Wulsthalbflechten mit Finger-oder Pfahlbauknoten (Seiler-Baldinger 1991:44)
Espiral anudada (Barcelona 1976)

Coiling with double-looped knot (Fig. 66b):
Wulsthalbflechten mit doppelschlaufigem Knoten (Seiler-Baldinger 1991:44)
Höhere Form des Wulsthalbflechtens (Müller 1967:256)

Coiling with clove hitches (Fig. 66c):
Knotted loops on a foundation element, clove hitch (Emery 1966:54)
Wulsthalbflechten mit halbem asymmetrischem Knoten (Seiler-Baldinger 1991:44)

2. Split Coiling

In these forms, the active thread pierces either the passive system or the active system of the previous row or both. in theory there are as many variations possible as in wrapped coiling although simpler techniques such as split coiling (Fig. 67) and split linked coiling (Fig. 68) predominate in practice.

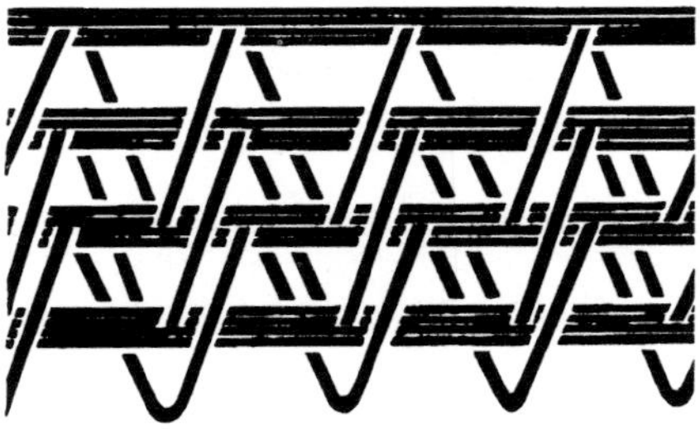

Fig. 67: Wrapped split coiling

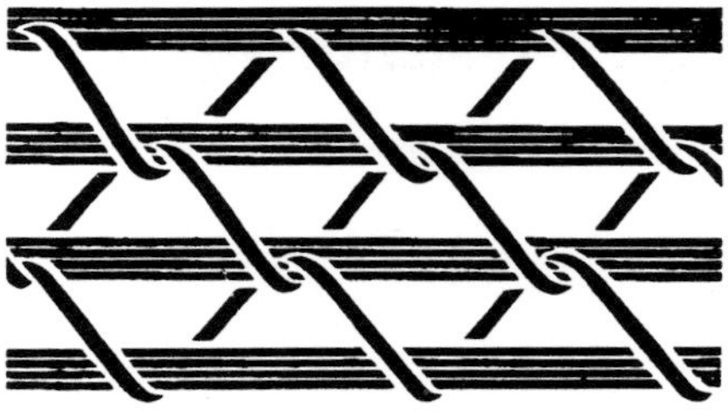

Fig. 68: Linked split coiling

Other terms used:
Wrapped split coiling (Fig. 67):
Uninterlocked coiling technique (Green Gigli et al. 1974:24)
Uninterlocked coiling: split stitch (Elsasser 1978:626)
Regular split stitch (Gallinger 1975:146)
Durchstechendes Wulsthalbflechten (Seiler-Baldinger 1991:44)
Spiralwulstflechterei (Vogt 1937:8)
Vannerie spiralée cousue (Balfet 1952:268)
Cestería en espiral con armazón cogido (Mora de Jaramillo 1974:342)

Split linked coiling (Fig. 68):
Coiled basketry, split stitch (Loud/Harrington 1929:15ff.)
Plain split stitch (Tanner 1968:31)
Durchstechend einhängendes Wulsthalbflechten (Seiler-Baldinger 1991:44)
Schling-oder Spiralwulsttechnik (Staub 1936:26)
Spiralwulstflechterei Art 2 (Vogt 1937:8)
Vannerie spiralée à points fendus (Balfet 1952:269)
Tejido cosido en espiral (Reichel-Dolmatoff 1960:156)
Cestería cosida en espiral (Alfaro Giner 1984:168)

Transitional Forms to Plaiting with Active Systems and Advanced Techniques of Fabric Manufacture

Transitional forms from passive-active to active-active plaiting occur whenever an active element is introduced additionally which actually interlaces with the passive or with the active system. On the other hand, techniques such as weft wrapping or warp twining which employ a tensioned warp or otherwise fixed system belong to the advanced techniques of fabric manufacture (cf. Warp Methods).

As has been constantly reiterated, the two main criteria (technique of manufacture and structure) of the present classification often overlap, especially in this transition group.

Plaiting with Active Systems

In plaiting the fabric is formed by the interlacing of elements of two or more systems. The operations can be performed in one or the other system at will. Their functions are interchangeable (hence the name active-active).

Depending on the number of systems used, plaiting can be in two or more directions and in two or three dimensions. Plaiting in two directions can be divided into: oblique or diagonal plaiting, right-angled plaiting, ply-splitting, and oblique intertwining. Multi-directional plaiting must be differentiated according to the number of elements or directions. To these must be added a number of complex operations for the production of fabrics whose width is relatively small compared with their length (braids, tubular plaiting, etc.) along with methods which combine two-directional and multi-directional plaiting (bobbin lace) and even certain meshwork techniques (macramé).

Plaiting is mostly done without the use of implements, although needles or bobbins are employed for the finer forms. Plaiting is a widespread art and has many variations.

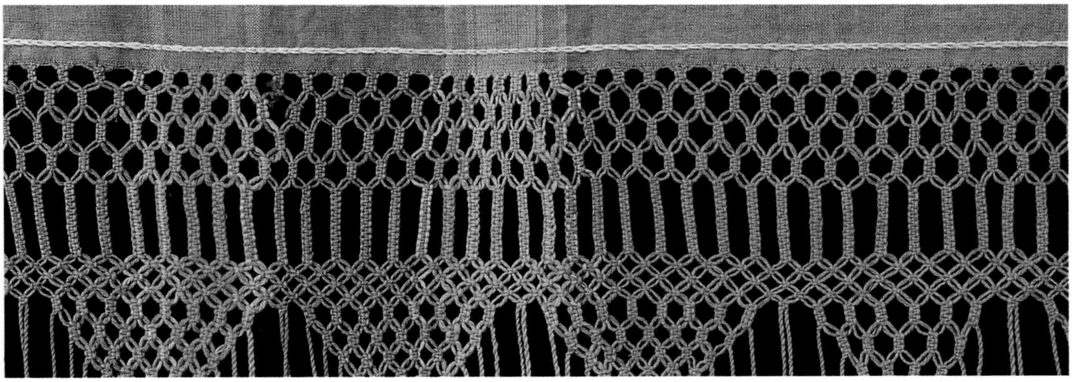

Interknotted fringe of a sarong from Sumbawa, IIc 14575

Plaiting in Two Directions

The structures in two-directional plaiting are analogous to those in weaving (cf. Weaving).

1. Right-angled Plaiting

The two directions of plaiting are parallel or perpendicular to the edges of the fabric (Fig. 69). Here again, the crossings are genuine interlacings as in weaving (see p. 71-102). In most instances of right-angled plaiting, the two systems are interchangeable in their function. However, in one special form, wickerwork (Fig. 70), one system is continuously active and the other more or less passive. Wickerwork is hence closely related to plaiting with an active and a passive system, especially to wrapping, binding and twining. Mechanical aids are rarely used and there are few variations.

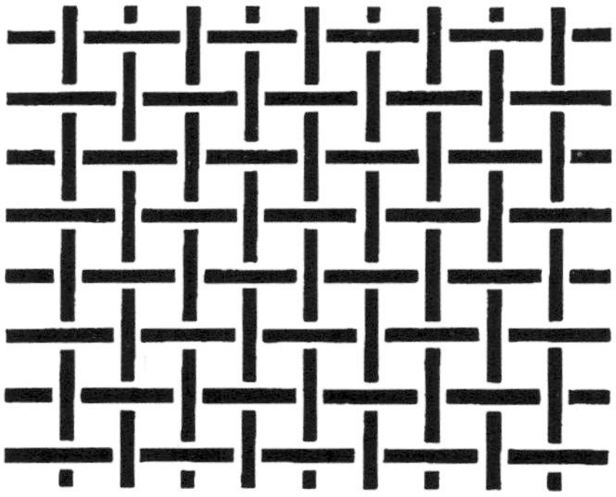

Fig. 69: Right-angled plaiting in plain weave

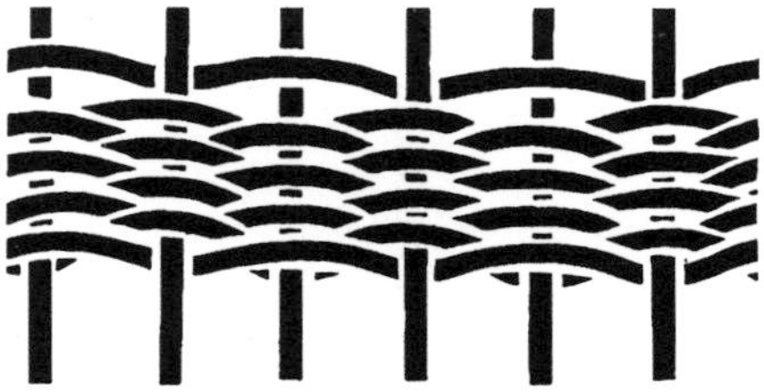

Fig. 70: Wickerwork

Other terms used:
Right-angled plaiting:
Right-angled interlacing (Emery 1966:62)
Randparalleles Flechten (Seiler-Baldinger 1991:46)
Vannerie tissée, type natte à deux nappes perpendiculaires, droite (Balfet 1952:273)
Tissage croisé (Anquetil 1979:15)
Cestería tejida derecha (Mora de Jaramillo 1974:299)
Tejido asargado (Reichel-Dolmatoff 1960:154)
Entrecruzado perpendicular (Saugy 1974:174)
Recht vlechtwerk (Ahlbrinck 1925:640)
Kruisvlechtingen (Lamster 1926: Fig. 1-2)
Recht vlechten (Keppel 1984:61)

Wickerwork:
Wicker weave (Lyford 1943:94)
Wicker basket weave (Underhill 1948:20)
Ribbed and stem type of basket weave (Belen 1952:48)
Randed type (Cardale-Schrimpff 1972:180)
Stakenflechten (Seiler-Baldinger 1991:46)
Stangenflechterei (Gandert 1963:23)
Vannerie tissée type clayonné (Balfet 1952:273)
Montants passifs – type clayonné (Pellaton-Chable 1980:122)
Tejido en cerco (Barcelona 1976)
Cestería derecha en bardal (Mora de Jaramillo 1974:299)
Trançado cruzado arqueado (Ribeiro 1980:35)
Stakenvlechten (Keppel 1984:65)

2. Diagonal or Oblique Plaiting

The two directions of plaiting are at an angle of less than 90 degrees to the edges of the fabric. The crossings are genuine interlacings which are analogous to those of weaving. Although diagonal plaiting is one of the simplest methods of plaiting from the technical point of view, derived forms such as two- and three-dimensional braiding represent highly complex techniques which must therefore be dealt with as a separate group.

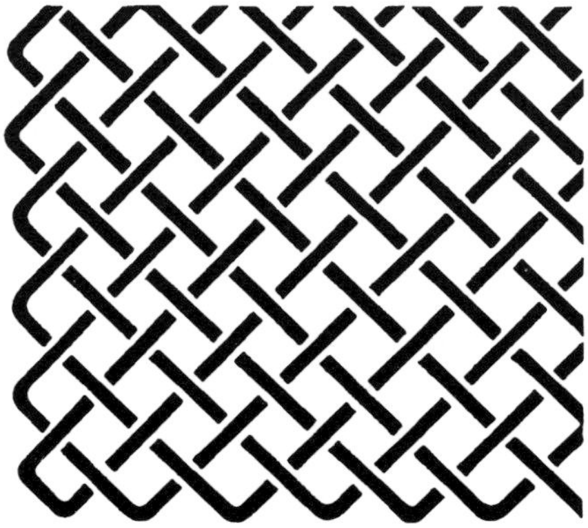

Fig. 71: Diagonal or oblique plaiting in plain weave

Other terms used:
Old Indian weave, finger weaving (Lyford 1943:69f.)
Diagonal braiding (Hald 1950:115)
Braiding (Peck Kent 1957:593)
Oblique interlacing (braiding) (Emery 1966:62)
Diagonalflechten (Seiler-Baldinger 1991:46)
Vannerie diagonale (Leroi-Gourhan 1943:281)
Vannerie tissée, type natte à deux nappes perpendiculaires, diagonale (Balfet 1952:273)
Montants actifs – type natté (Pellaton-Chable 1980:122)
Tissage diagonal (Anquetil 1979:15)
Cestería tejida diagonal simple (Barcelona 1976)
Cestería tejida diagonal (Mora de Jaramillo 1974:297)
Entrecruzado oblicuo (Saugy 1974:174)
Tejido jaquelado (Reichel-Dolmatoff 1960:154)
Trançado entrecruzado em diagonal (Ribeiro 1986:300)
Trançado xadrezado em diagonal (Ribeiro 1980:113)
Trançado diagonal (Melo Taveira 1980:229)
Diagonaal viechten (Keppel 1984:57)
Diagonal vlechtwerk (Loeber 1902:14)
Diagonalfletning (Hald 1975:9)

3. Braiding

The process, which is basically derived from diagonal plaiting (rarely from right-angled plaiting) is used for the production of textiles which are considerably greater in length than in width or diameter. A distinction is to be made between two- and three-dimensional braids of this kind, the methods of manipulating the elements and the structures. The latter correspond to those used in two-directional plaiting and/or twining.

Braiding is used for making narrow fabrics, cords etc. which in turn are sometimes used as "elements" in fabric production. Braids of this kind are particularly elastic and sturdy. Simple braids and tubular braids can be made without any accessories. Dead weights and other devices (e.g. bobbins, frames) are used to keep the threads taut in the manufacture of the more complicated forms, especially for passementeries (trimmings). The elements are often fixed at one end to facilitate working. Instead of using loose threads, an odd or even number of loops can be interworked (loop braiding).

3.1. Two-dimensional Braiding

Two-dimensional braiding is quite simply narrow two-directional plaiting done mainly diagonally. Braiding can be done with an odd (minimum 3) or even (minimum 4) number of elements. These may be fixed at one end (Fig. 72a) and consist of loose elements, or where the number of elements is even, of thread loops (Fig. 73). The simplest two-dimensional plait is the three-strand braid, which can be worked with loose or fixed ends (Fig. 72b). If both ends are fixed, the same interlacings occur at both ends, i.e. we obtain a special form (Fig. 72c) closely related to interlaced sprang (see p. 53) Another special form is obtained when three elements are braided together but, after a brief series of crossings with the other elements in a horizontal direction, are taken in a vertical to oblique direction relative to the plane. The individual movements thus perform a stepwise motion over the whole fabric (Fig. 74).

The commonest basic interlacements are in general plain and twill (see p. 87, pp. 89-92), but it is also possible to link the elements together laterally or to twine them (see Intertwining pp. 41-43).

By colouring and thread configuration a number of interesting and pleasing variants and patternings can be obtained (Fig. 76).

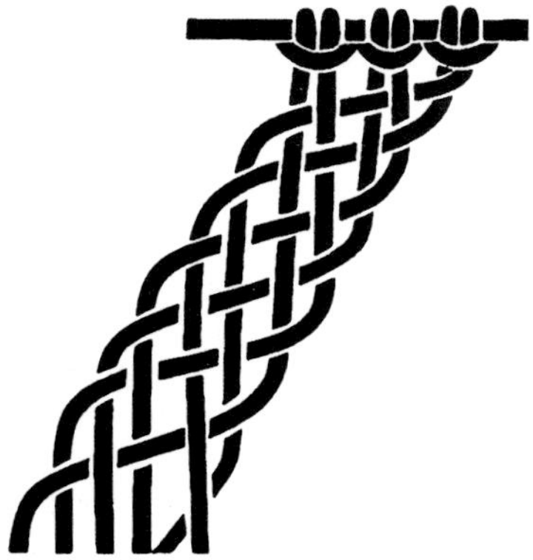

Fig. 72a: Six-strand braid with loose ends

Fig. 72b: Three-strand braid with fixed ends

Fig. 72c: Five-strand braid with fixed ends

Fig. 73: Two-dimensional loop braiding

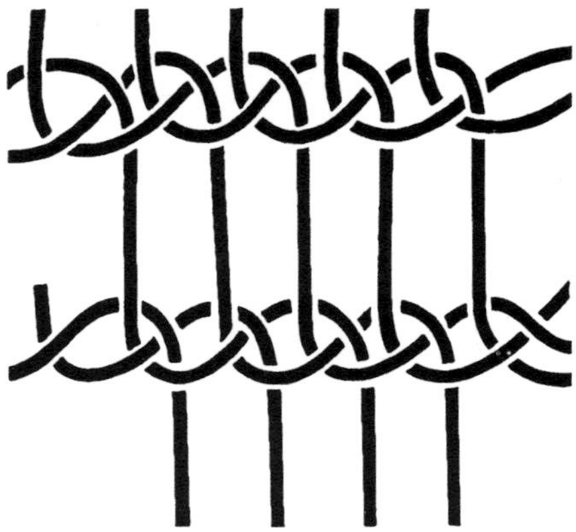

Fig. 74: Two-dimensional braiding (special form)

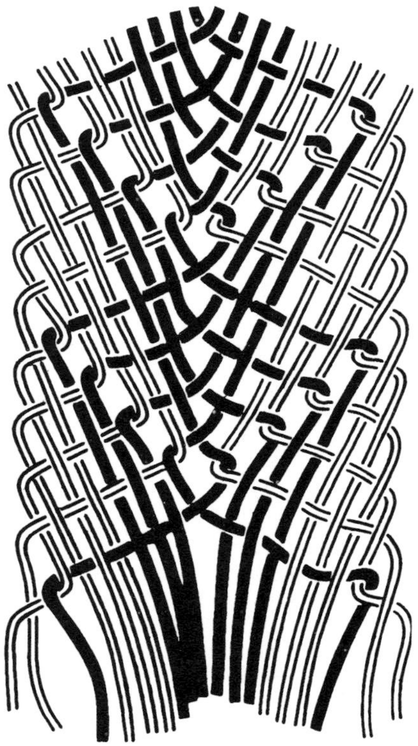

Fig. 75: Two-dimensional braiding with interlinking of individual elements

Fig. 76: Nine-strand braid

Other terms used:

Two-dimensional loop braiding:
Reciprocal plaiting (Cardale-Schrimpff 1984:249)
Zweidimensionales Schlaufenflechten (Seiler-Baldinger 1991:49)
Special form of two-dimensional braiding:
Neolithic braiding (Larsen 1986:82)
Braided (weft-) twining (Emery 1966:203)
Zweidimensionales Zopfflechten (Sonderform) (Seiler-Baldinger 1991:48)

Two-dimensional braiding:
Three strand braid (Mason 1908:14)
Braiding (Miner 1935/36:185)
X-strand braid plaiting (Miner 1935/36:182)
Three-strand plait (O'Neale 1937:196)
Flat braids (flache Geflechte) (Speiser 1983:31, 234)
Flat sennit of ... strands (Crowfoot 1938:71)
Flat braiding (Larsen 1986:80)
Multiple-strand plaiting (O'Neale 1942:162)
Three-ply braid (Buck 1944:301)
Three-strand flat braid (Peck Kent 1954:65)
Whip cording with three etc. strands (Hald 1957:248)
Zweidimensionales Zopfflechten (Seiler-Baldinger 1991:49)
Flechtband aus drei usw. Fäden, vier (usw.)-fädige Verflechtung (Hartung 1963:18)
Tresse à trois brins, tresse à brins multiples (Leroi-Gourhan 1943:271)
Trenzado plano (Millán de Palavecino 1970:22)
Trenza múltiple (Mora de Jaramillo 1974:335)
Trenza de tres hilos (Mora de Jaramillo 1974:294)
Trenzado de 3 a n hebras (Barcelona 1976)
Bandvlechten (Keppel 1984:72)
Piskefletning med ... traade (Hald 1975:27)
Virkede baand (Hald 1975:9)

3.2. Three-dimensional Braiding

In the three-dimensional forms we distinguish between tubular braids and compact braids.

3.2.1. Tubular Braiding

Tubular braids consist of an even number of elements, one half of which is interworked with the other in a plain weave or twill pattern along opposed helical lines. Tubular braids cannot be based on looped threads. Tubular plaits are hollow "inside" but can be made round an inlay (core).

Fig. 77: Tubular braid in twill pattern

Other terms used:
Hollow braid, oblique tubular (Larsen 1986:86)
Schlauchflechten (Seiler-Baldinger 1991:49)

3.2.2. Compact Three-dimensional Braiding

The possible number of variations within this group is almost unlimited. The braids may have a round, oval, triangular, square, hexagonal or octagonal cross section (Fig. 78). The elements are interworked not only on the surface but also in the interior, resulting in very sturdy and decorative braids and cords.
These braids can be made with loose elements and also with loop threads. Braids made with loop threads are closely related to French knitting and crocheting (see pp. 23,25, Fig. 79).

Fig. 78: Square braid of four elements

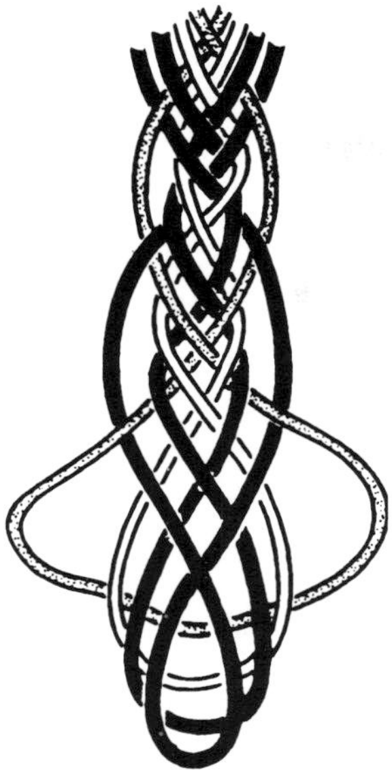

Fig. 79: Three-dimensional loop braiding

Other terms used:
Kompaktes dreidimensionales Kordelflechten (Seiler-Baldinger 1991:49)
With loose elements:
Plattings (Mooi 1977:56)
Solid or three dimensional braids (Speiser 1983:234)
Solid square braid (Larsen 1986:87)
Three-dimensional braiding with elements crossing center (Larsen 1986:88)
With loops:
Loop-plaiting (Cardale-Schrimpff 1984:89)

4. Oblique Intertwining

In contrast to two-directional plaiting in which the elements interlace, they are intertwined. As far as the direction of plaiting is concerned, these methods are allied to diagonal plaiting.
Two main groups – active-passive and active-active intertwining – can be defined by reference to the relation of the sets of elements to one another.

4.1. Active-passive Intertwining

The elements are paired and alternate in their function from active to passive, i.e. the elements a fix the elements b in an S- and/or Z-twisted twine, exchanging roles at the edge of the plait (Fig. 80a) or in the centre (Fig. 80b-c). There are diagonal ribs in the finished fabric. The structure is identical with that of two-strand twining over a passive system and diagonal ply-splitting.

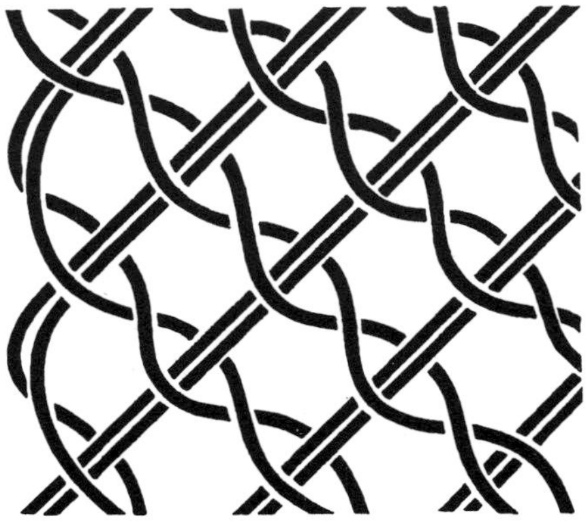

Fig. 80a: Active-passive intertwining, with Z crossing

Fig. 80b: Active-passive intertwining with Z and S crossing

Fig. 80c: Active-passive intertwining with alternate Z and S crossing

Other terms used:

Twined oblique interlacing (Speiser 1983:54)
Oblique twining (Harvey 1976:7)
Single oblique twining (Emery 1966:64)
Aktiv-passives Zwirnflechten (Seiler-Baldinger 1991:50)

4.2. Active-active Intertwining

Both thread groups are equally active, there being the following variant forms: elements a twine round elements b and elements b twine round elements a (Fig. 81a) or a and b are intertwined (Fig. 81b).

Before or after this reciprocal twining, the elements of the groups a and b may be twined once or more round themselves (Fig. 81c). The process can also be combined with braiding (Fig. 81d).

Depending upon the type of variation, the structures are identical with those of diagonal ply-splitting, intertwined sprang and methods akin to bobbin lace (see pp. 44-45, 46-47, 54-55).

Fig. 81a: Active-active intertwining: elements a twine round elements b and vice versa

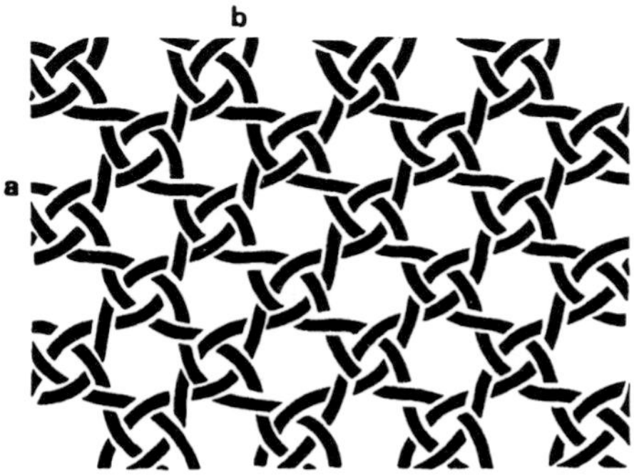

Fig. 81b: Active-active intertwining: elements a and b are intertwined

Fig. 81c: Active-active intertwining with additional twist

Fig. 81d: Active-active intertwining combined with braiding

Other terms used:

Double oblique twining (Emery 1966:65)
Intertwining (Speiser 1983:236)
Aktiv-aktives Zwirnflechten (Seiler-Baldinger 1991:51)
Gegenseitige Zwirnbindung (Speiser 1983:236)

5. Ply-splitting

As the name intimates, this technique is possible only on the basis of plied elements (threads, cords), which is a feature distinguishing it, among other methods, from the splitting of one system (that always remains passive). Needles are used as an aid in splitting. In contrast to oblique intertwining it offers more possibilities of variation.

Other terms used:

Split-ply twining (Harvey 1976)
Zwirnspalten (Seiler-Baldinger 1991:52)

5.1. Interlinked Ply-splitting

Parallel plied elements are "interlinked", i.e. element a splits element b and is then split again by the latter element at the link (Fig. 82a) or vice versa (Fig. 82b). Paired plies can also be used (Fig. 82c).

Fig. 82a: Interlinked ply-splitting: element a splits element b.

Fig. 82b: Interlinked ply-splitting: element b splits element a.

Fig. 82c: Interlinked ply-splitting, with paired plies

Other terms used:
Twined linking (Speiser 1983: 113)
Verhängtes Zwirnspalten (Seiler-Baldinger 1991: 52)

5.2. Right-angled Ply-splitting

In this method the plied elements of one system (passive) are split by those of another system running at right angles (active-passive, Fig. 83a) or there is reciprocal splitting of both systems (active-active, Fig. 83b). In the active-passive process the structures are identical with those of warp twining (see p. 50), tablet and finger weaving (see pp. 72-73).

Fig. 83a: Right-angled ply-splitting, active-passive

Fig. 83b: Right-angled ply-splitting, active-active

Other term used:
Randparalleles Zwirnspalten (Seiler-Baldinger 1992: 53)

5.3. Diagonal Ply-splitting

In this process, which is diagonal in execution, we can make a basic distinction between an alternately active-passive relationship of the thread groups (Fig. 84a) and their reciprocal active penetration (Fig. 84b). With cabled yarns there are other possibilities, depending on where these are split (Fig. 84c).
Attention has already been called to the structural affinity to intertwining and intertwined sprang (see pp. 41-43, 54-55).

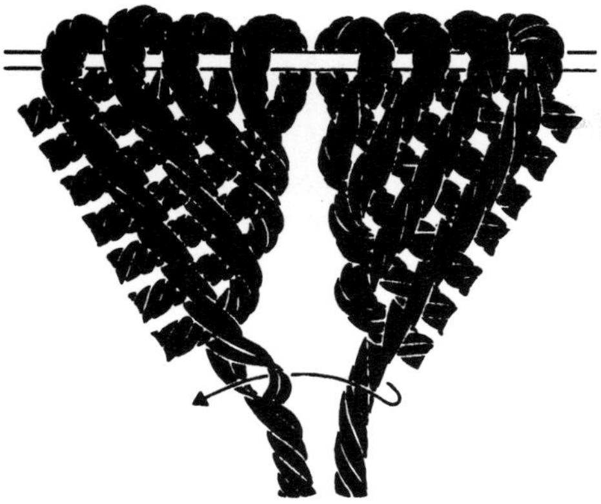

Fig. 84a: Diagonal ply-splitting, alternate active-passive

Fig. 84b: Diagonal ply-splitting, active-active

Fig. 84c: Diagonal ply-splitting, active-active with paired plies

Other terms used:
Oblique interworking by ply-splitting (Speiser 1983:111)
Ply-splitting to produce a single (double) oblique twined fabric (Quick/Stein 1982:32)
Diagonales Zwirnspalten (Seiler-Baldinger 1991:53)

Plaiting in Three and More Directions

For plaiting at least three sets of elements are needed instead of two. If there are more than three systems the elements are sometimes fixed. This method represents a transitional stage leading to more advanced fabric-producing techniques. Depending on the form of interlacement, a distinction can be made between plaitings in which all the elements are interworked equally or plaits with an integrated third, fourth etc. direction, and, in terms of structure, loose or dense multi-directional plaits. Plaiting in three or more directions is a highly specialised final development form of plaiting which allows few variations in the patterns of interlacement.

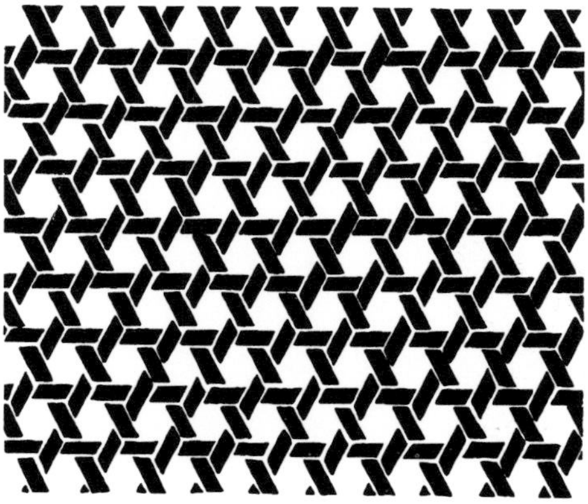

Fig. 85: Plaiting in three directions

Fig. 86: Plaiting in four directions

Other terms used:
Multi-directional plaiting
Lattice-type basket work (O'Neale 1949:76)
Mehrrichtungsflechten (Seiler-Baldinger 1991:54)
Strahlenweberei (Von Kimakowicz-Winnicki 1910:31)
Vannerie tissée à trois nappes et plus (Balfet 1952:273)

Plaiting in three directions (Fig. 85):
Hexagonal plaiting (Miner 1935/36:182)
Interlaced basketry with three sets of elements (Clements Scholz 1975)
Plaiting, three-directional (Dunkelberg 1985:364)
Lattice technique, hexagonal (Cardale-Schrimpff 1972:416)
Dreirichtungsflechten (Seiler-Baldinger 1991:54)
Loses Geflecht aus 3 Flechteinheiten mit hexagonalen Maschen (Detering 1962:66)
Geflecht dreifacher Richtung (Krucker 1940/41:77)
Vannerie tissée type carreau à trois éléments (Balfet 1952:274)
Diagonal compuesta en tres direcciones (Barcelona 1976)
Cestería enrejada (Mora de Jaramillo 1974:338)
Tejido hexagonal (Reichel-Dolmatoff 1960:154)
Trançado hexagonal triangular (Ribeiro 1986b:319)
Spaansche ster (Loeber 1902:16)
Ljlie drierichtingsmethode (Jasper-Pierngadie 1912:51)
Kruisvlechtingen met drie reepen (Lamster 1926:Fig. 5-6)

Plaiting in four directions (Fig. 86)
Octagonal weave (Belen 1952:51)
Caning (Larsen 1986:66)
Vierrichtungsflechten (Seiler-Baldinger 1991:55)
Geflecht mit Leinwandbindung und Diagonalstreifen (Vogt 1937:40)
Diagonal compuesta: rejilla (Barcelona 1976)
Tejido cuadrilateral cruzado (Reichel-Dolmatoff 1960:155)

Combinations of Two-Directional and Multi-Directional Plaiting

In these processes plaiting is done partly in two right-angled and two diagonal directions so as to allow these then to be combined in four-directional plaits, or else two- and three-directional plaits alternate in the same fabric. Elements can be borrowed from other methods such as meshwork techniques. Combinations of this kind require the use of accessories.

1. Interlacing and Intertwining

In the simplest version of this method the threads run diagonally or at right angles in the case of combinations. Interlacing and intertwining are often combined (Fig. 87).
Just as braids were the forerunners of complicated passementerie, oblique intertwining gave rise to bobbin lace with wooden weights, pillows, patterns and pins as aids.

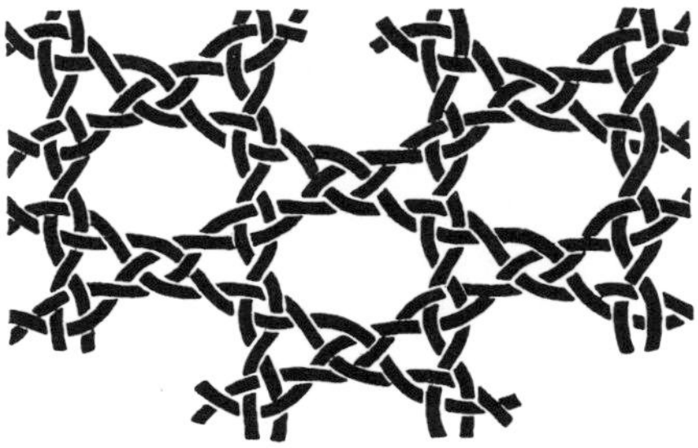

Fig. 87: Bobbin lace by intertwining (fond chant)

Fig. 88 a-d: Bobbin lace by braiding (four-strand braid)

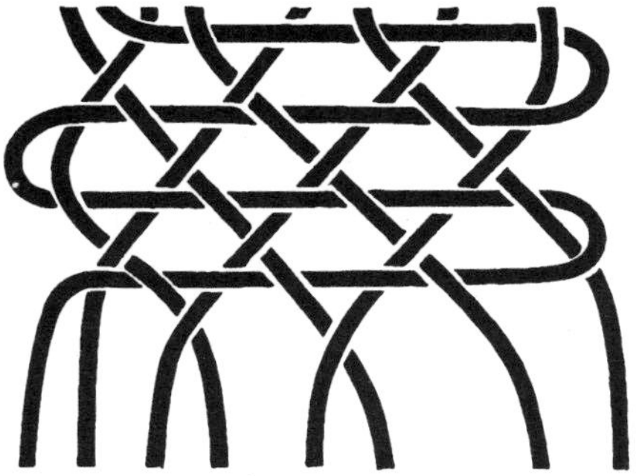

Fig. 89: Bobbin lace: three directional (half stitch)

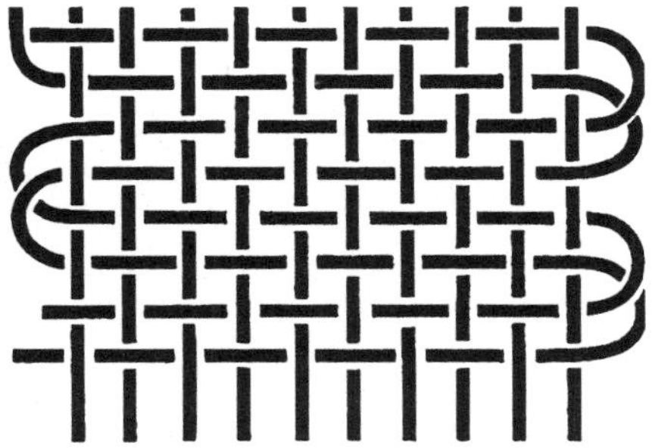

Fig. 90: Bobbin lace with right-angled interlacings (whole stitch)

Other terms used:

Plaiting with twisted yarns (D'Harcourt 1962:76ff.)
Oblique twining (Emery 1966:64)
Klöppeleiartige Verfahren (Seiler-Baldinger 1991:55)
Bolillo (Mora de Jaramillo 1974:293)
Tranzado tipo bolillo (Barcelona 1976)
Finknyppling (Nylén 1969:102)
Slynget snor og dens slaegtninge (Hald 1975:26)

In bobbin lace a four-stranded braid is the equivalent of:
Four strand plait (Start 1948:78)
Flechtenschlag (De Dillmont undated: 654)
Vierteilige Flechte (Müller/Brendler/Spiess 1958:175)
Vävslag (Nylén 1969:297)

A three-directional interlacing (Fig. 89 "halfstitch") is the equivalent of:
Netzschlag (Müller/Brendler/Spiess 1958:175)
Gimpen- oder Halbschlag (Weber 1979:35)

A right-angled interlacing is the equivalent of (Fig. 90):
Whole-stitch clothwork (Freeman 1958:22)
Leinenschlag, toilé (Csernyánszky 1962:7)
Ganzschlag (Schuette 1963:53)

The combination of crossing and twisting (Fig. 87) is the equivalent of:
Löcherschlag (Flemming 1957:367)
Fond chant (Weber 1979:35)
Torchon (Speiser 1983:185)

2. Macramé (interknotting)

The name comes from the Arabic "mucharram", which means lattice or, in the extended sense, "fringe". The technique is closely related to oblique intertwining, the difference being that macramé also involves looping and interknotting. Both methods are often used in combination to make trimmings.

Four or more elements are used in macramé, two of them alternating in forming the ground knot. The clove hitch, the vertical granny knot and the square knot are the three most important macramé knots. The threads not engaged in forming these basic knots can be passed through these in different ways. As in the case of bobbin lace, it is also possible to work in more than two directions.

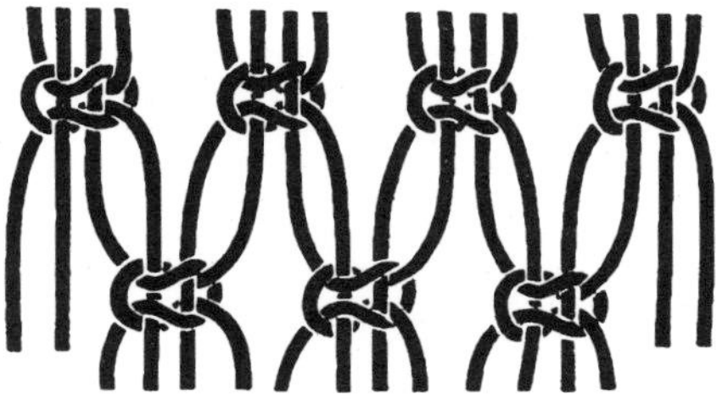

Fig. 91: Macramé with square knot

Other terms used:

Square knotting (Woollard 1953:33f.)
Knüpfarbeit (De Dillmont 1902:403ff.)
Knüpfgewebe, Knüpfgeflecht (Von Kimakowicz-Winnicki 1910:34)

Basic knots, clove hitch:
Halber symmetrischer Knoten (Seiler-Baldinger 1991:56)
Rippenknoten (Zechlin 1966:107)

Basic knots, square knot:
Square or Solomon's knot (O'Neale 1945: Fig. 80b)
Symmetrischer Knoten (Seiler-Baldinger 1991:56)
Flacher Knoten (Thümmel undated:8)
Flacher Doppelknoten (De Dillmont 1902:407)
Flachknoten (Zechlin 1966:107)
Versetzter Kreuzknoten (Lammèr 1975:192)
Dubbelknut (Nylén 1969:280)

References to Plaiting: see pp. 158-160

Advanced Textile Techniques

All advanced techniques of fabric production use a warp, i.e. a tensioned and fixed set of elements. As a rule the warp is passive and the other system, the weft, is active.
The structures are not easily distinguished from those made by plaiting and intertwining or even those of meshwork fabrication. Many of the structures discussed earlier appear here as well, and the various groups can be classified solely on the basis of the method of production.
Technically, weaving is the most advanced method in this group. The other groups represent overall the transition stages to weaving, since all of them use a fixed warp, as in weaving.
It is possible to distinguish between three groups: warp techniques, half-weaving, and weaving.

Woman's sarong of the Belo, Timor, supplementary weft and weft wrapping, IIc 20744

PLATE 7. Sarong from the Philippines, dovetailed tapestry, IIc 20040

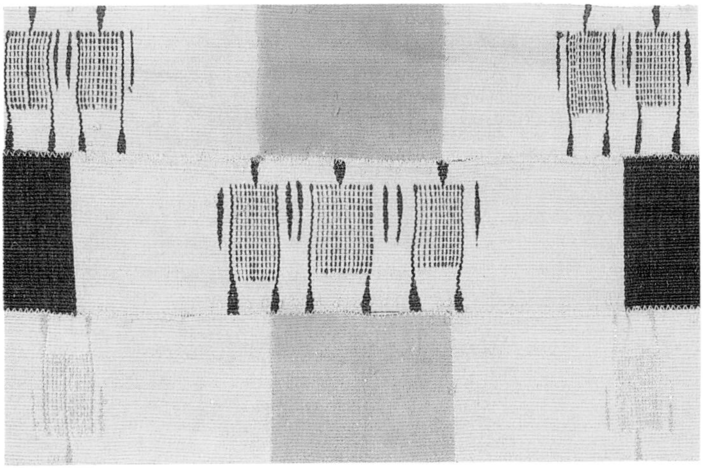

PLATE 8. Weft-faced plain weave, tapestry and supplementary weft. The small bands are sewn together, Konna, Mali, III 21669

PLATE 9. Woman from Tenganan weaving a double ikat cloth on a backstrap loom, Karangasem, Bali

Warp Methods

The warp can be fixed in various ways, e.g. spirally (two-plane) on a cylindrical wooden block; around two stakes driven into the ground, round a frame, or thread by thread with the help of appropriate implements (single-plane). As in weaving, it is possible to work with a double or even a triple warp.

In most of the methods the warp is passive, but "active" in some in the sense that individual warp threads are interlaced, intertwined or twisted round one another. Thus we make a distinction in principle between warp fabrics with an "active" and those with a "passive" warp. The group with an active warp can be subdivided into sprang and warp twining. In the passive warp group further systematic grouping can best be done on the basis of weft insertion methods. This produces the following classification: weft wrapping, weft knotting, weft twining, weft interlacing, tapestry. The technical processes preceding weaving are often combined with it.

Woollen bag, combination of interlinked and intertwined sprang, Egypt, Coptic, 400-700 A.D., III 15485

Fabric Production with an Active Warp (warp interlacing, interlinking and intertwining)

Unlike other methods where the position of the warp threads relative to each other is not altered, this method uses interlacing, interlinking and twining of individual warp threads. The weft yarns may be parallel or may be absent. In the production process it is primarily the warp that is worked. The methods represent special forms of warp fabric manufacture.

Warp Twining

Pairs (or groups) of warp threads fixed at one end are twisted round the weft in the same (Fig. 92a) or alternately different directions (Fig. 92b). Warp twining can be done only with loose warp yarns fixed at one end. If the warp were fixed at both ends it would have to be classified as half-weaving with shed reservation (see p. 70). In both cases the weft is invisible, at least in the case of dense fabrics.

The structure is identical with that of right-angled ply-splitting, finger and tablet weaving and also half-weaving with shed reservation.

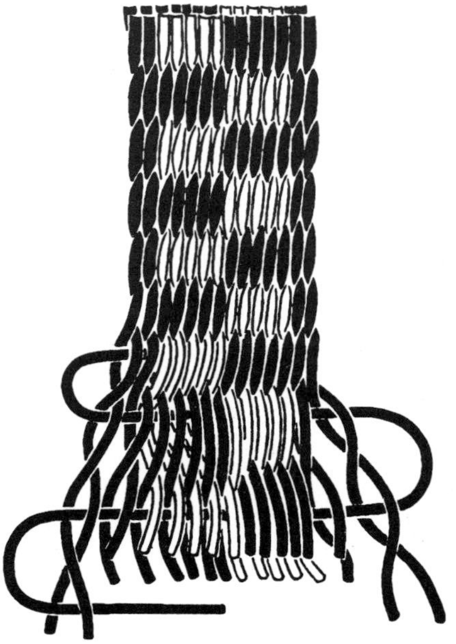

Fig. 92a: Warp twining in Z direction

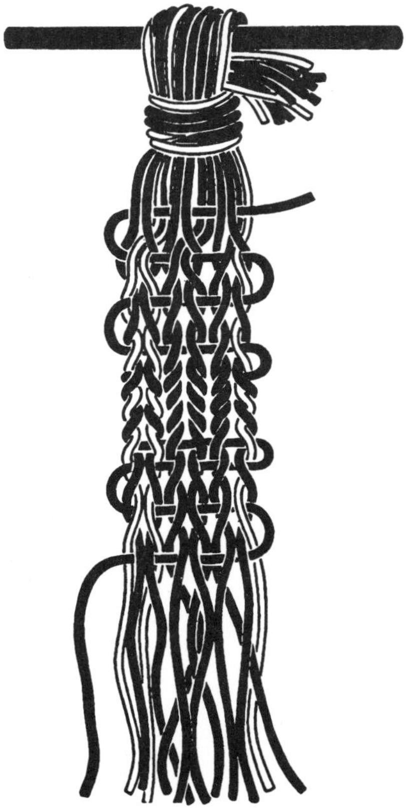

Fig. 92b: Warp twining in S and Z direction (countered)

Other terms used:

Warp twine tie (Kent Peck 1957:580)
Bands with twisted warp yarns (D'Harcourt 1962:62ff.)
Zwirnbinden der Kette (Seiler-Baldinger 1991:59)
Galons à fils de chaîne enroulés (D'Harcourt 1934:67ff.)
Torcido de urdimbre (Nardi 1978:40)
Kettingtwijnen (Brommer 1988:90)

Sprang

The warp is fixed at both ends. Its threads are twisted or interlaced and are sometimes held in position during the working process by bars or sticks. (Fig. 93a-c). In this case the warp is active. Work is started at one end of the warp. The same structures are produced automatically at the other end. These are likewise fixed with bars. The interworkings, which are mirror images of one another, are formed in this manner from the two ends towards the middle and must be fixed there in some way so as to prevent unravelling.

Fig. 93a: Interlinked sprang

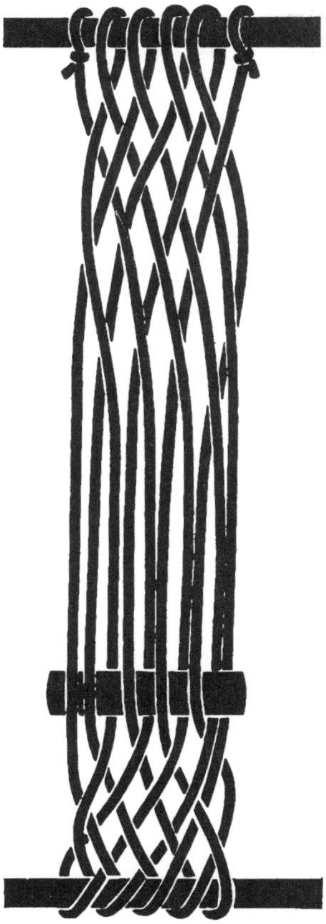

Fig. 93b: Interlaced sprang

The fabrics are highly elastic. They look strikingly similar to fabrics produced by diagonal plaiting, linking, or oblique intertwining. Depending on which yarns are crossed with which, i.e. on the sequence in which the warp threads are picked up and lowered, we obtain various forms of interworking which can be designated in terms of those used for primary fabric-producing techniques. We thus distinguish between interlinked, interlaced and intertwined sprang (Fig. 93a-c). The word sprang is of Swedish origin.

Fig. 93c: Intertwined sprang

Other terms used:

Warp twining (O'Neale 1937:196ff.)
Netting (Lyford 1943:66ff.)
Twine-plaiting (Weitlaner-Johnson 1956:198ff.)
Loom-plaiting (Engel 1963:38)
Sprang or Egyptian plaitwork (Collingwood 1946:6ff.)
Frame plaiting (Cardale-Schrimpff 1972:700)
Ägyptische Flechttechnik (Von Kimakowicz-Winnicki 1910:32)
Geflecht in Sprangtechnik (Schlabow 1958:7)
Tissage torsadé (Chantreaux 1946:65ff.)
Acoplado tipo Tumupasa (Ribeiro 1988:96)
Egyptisch Vlechtwerk (Siervertsz van Reesema undated)
Starobylém pleteni (Smolková 1904)

1. Interlinked Sprang

In interlinked sprang structures like simple linking (Fig. 93a, 94a, 95), multiple linking (Fig. 94b-c) and linking with skipping of rows (Fig. 94d) are possible.
In simple interlinked sprang the thread configuration may be of the 11/11 and also 2/2 variety (see pp. 7-8, Fig. 95a-b). In multiple interlinked sprang the typical diagonal thread pattern (relative to the long edge) is conspicuous whereas it is not so clearly apparent in the simple interlinked variety.
The various types of interlinked sprang can be combined at will and in particular openwork patterns can be produced. Sprang thus offers many more opportunities for patterning than the homonymous meshwork process.

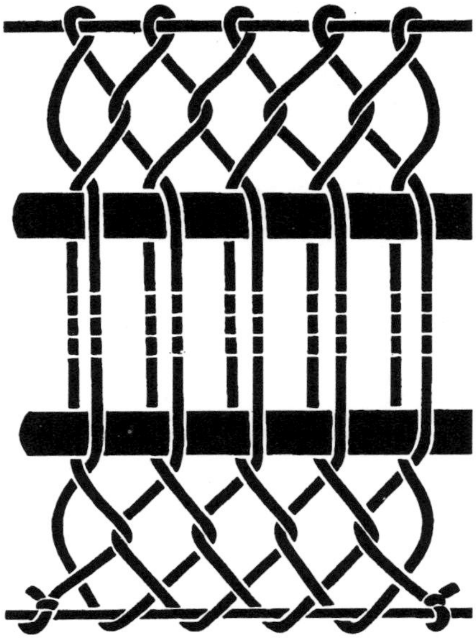

Fig. 94a: Simple interlinked sprang

Fig. 94b:
Double interlinked sprang

Fig. 94c:
Multiple interlinked sprang

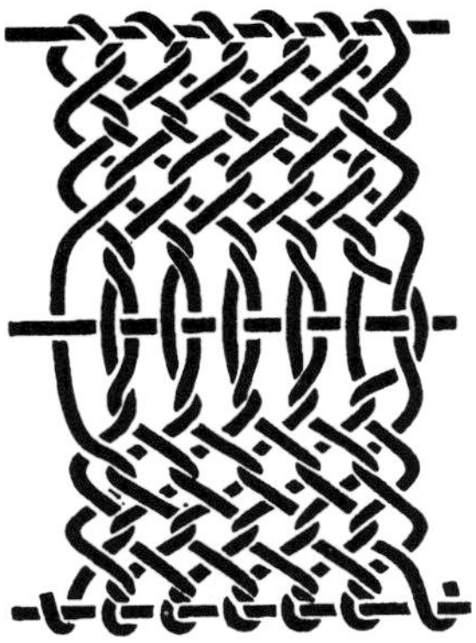

Fig. 94d: Skipped interlinked sprang

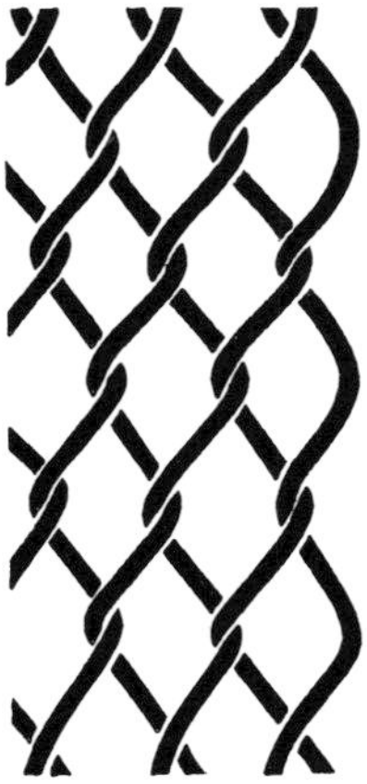

Fig. 95a:
Simple interlinked sprang
2/2

Fig. 95b:
Simple interlinked sprang
1 1/1 1

Other terms used:

Simple and multiple interlinked sprang:
Interlinking with an added twist (Emery 1966:62)
Simple plaiting (D'Harcourt 1962:80ff.)
Half-twist mesh, complete twist mesh (Weitlaner-Johnson 1956: 198ff.)
Einfacher und mehrfacher Einhängesprang (Seiler-Baldinger 1991:61)
Let og vrang (Broholm/Hald 1935:40)

Skipped interlinking:
Lattice sprang (Collingwood 1964:6ff.)
Cestería de saltos (Alfaro Giner 1984:109)
Gennenbrudt sprang: grundslaget, doppelslag (Hald 1975:20)

2. Interlaced Sprang

The simplest form of interlaced sprang is a three-strand braid (Fig. 96a-e) in which thread 1 is crossed over thread 2 and then thread 3 over thread 1 etc. As compared with interlinked sprang, only the sequence in which the thread is raised and lowered is altered.
Interlaced sprang is suitable for the production of dense, elastic fabrics which are comparable in structure to those obtained by diagonal plaiting (Fig. 97a-c) or plain and twill weaving. In the latter case, however, (see pp. 87-88, 101), the twill must be even (see pp. 90-91) and always oblique to the selvedges. Interlaced and interlinked sprang can be combined at will.

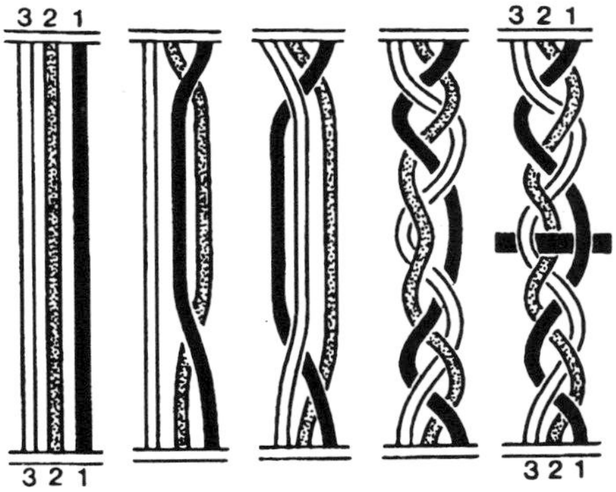

Fig. 96 a-e: Spranged three-strand "braiding": sequence of operations

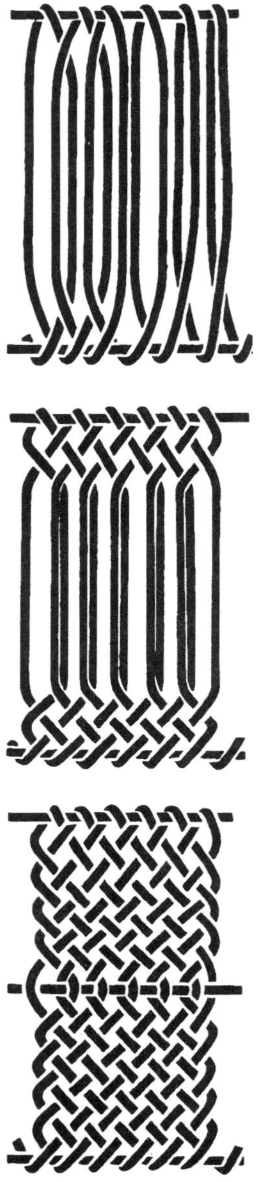

Fig. 97 a-c: Interlaced sprang in plain weave: sequence of operations

Other terms used:

Double plaiting (D'Harcourt 1962: 79ff.)
Simple 1:1 frame plaiting (Cardale-Schrimpff 1972: 615)
Flechtsprang (Seiler-Baldinger 1991: 62)
Sprang entrelazado (Cardale-Schrimpff 1987: 7)

3. Intertwined Sprang

There are two basic forms of intertwined sprang. In one of these (additional) pairs of threads are twined round another thread (e.g. of interlinked sprang), the direction of twist being altered depending on the pattern required (active-passive intertwined sprang, Fig. 98). In the second form all the pairs of threads are actively engaged by being intertwined in a manner depending on the pattern desired (active-active intertwined sprang, Fig. 99). Instead of each thread being intertwined, twists can be added (Fig. 100a). Paired intertwining is also possible (Fig. 100b). Repeating two passes one after the other yields other possibilities of forming patterns (Fig. 101) which, like the preceding variants, are strikingly similar in structure to forms of oblique intertwining, ply-splitting and bobbin lace.

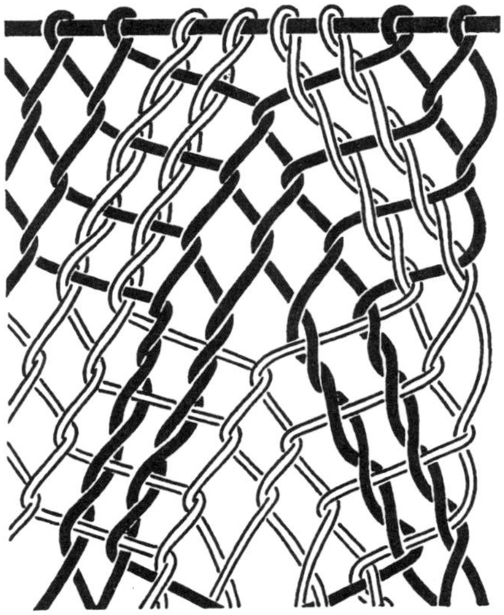

Fig. 98: Active-passive intertwined sprang combined with interlinked sprang

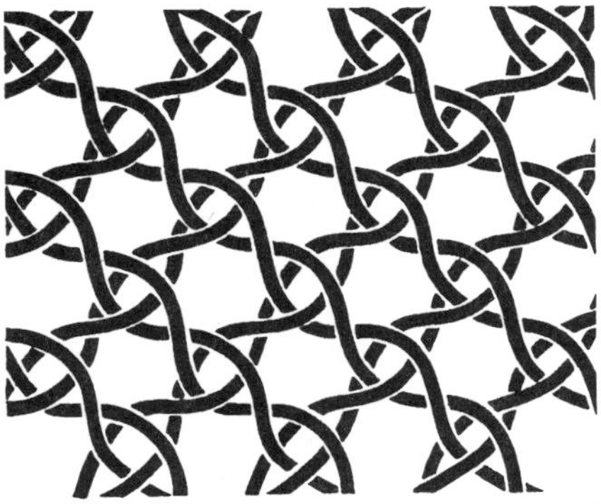

Fig. 99: Active-active intertwined sprang with Z crossing

Fig. 100a: Multiple intertwined sprang

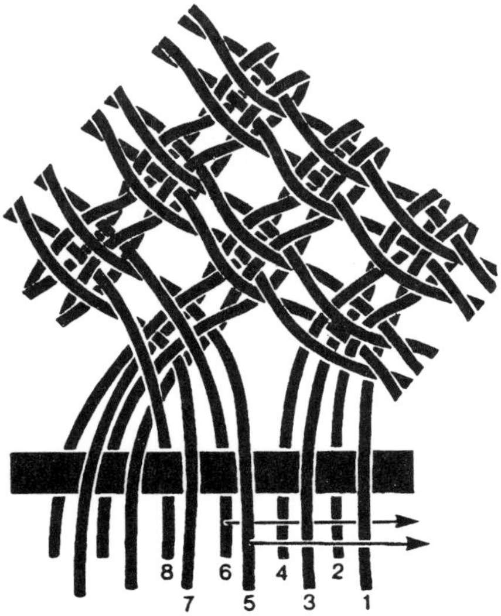

Fig. 100b: Intertwined sprang with two pairs

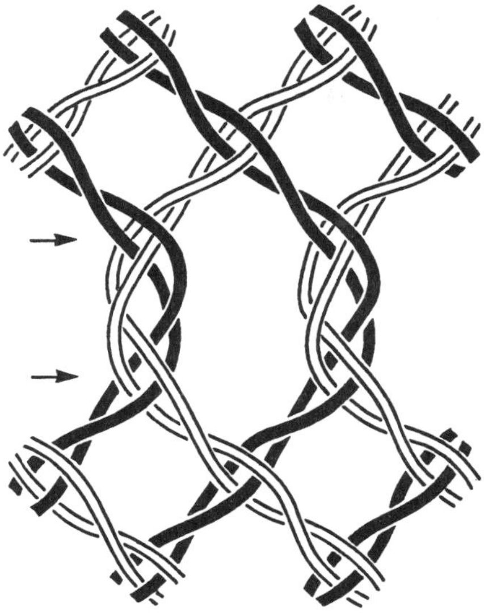

Fig. 101: Intertwined sprang with repetition of a pass

Other terms used:
Oblique intertwining (Rowe 1984:55)
Zwirnbindesprang (Seiler-Baldinger 1991:63)

4. Fixing the Warp in Position

Although sprang depends mainly on the manipulation of the warp threads, some means must be found of fixing them in the centre where the two mirror image halves of the fabric meet. The simplest solution is to insert a yarn or element at that point, in other words to introduce a single weft yarn (Fig. 102a). Another possibility is to fix the warp by forming the warp threads into single (Fig. 102b) or double (Fig. 102c) loops or, as in crossed knitting or encircled looping (Fig. 102d-e), by producing a row of loops with the terminal loop held in position by means of a thread ("minimal weft", see Fig. 102b). With a circular warp there are still other means of minimal fixation.

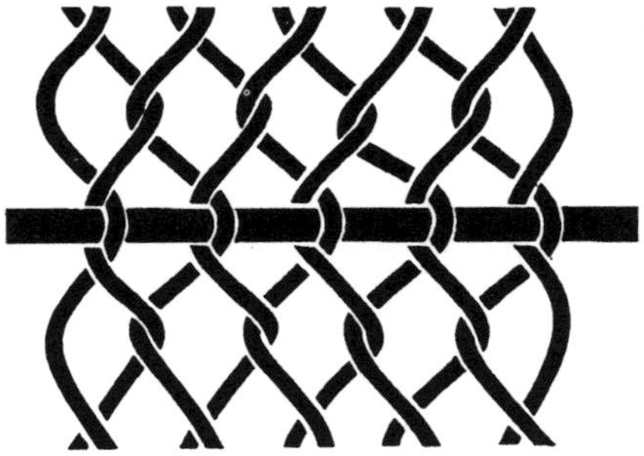

Fig. 102a: Fixing by insertion of a weft yarn

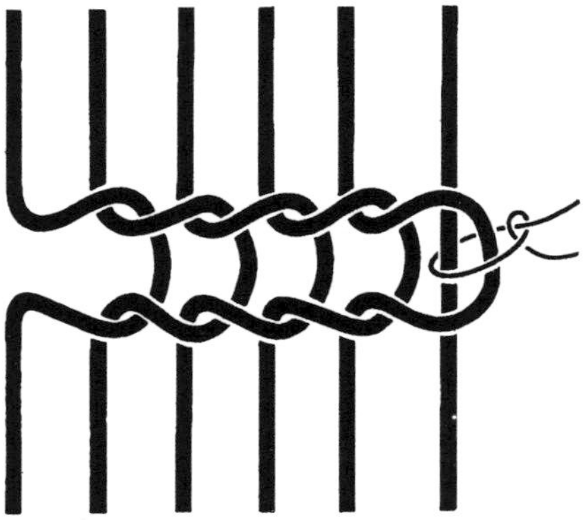

Fig. 102b: Fixing by forming the warp into single loops and a "minimal weft"

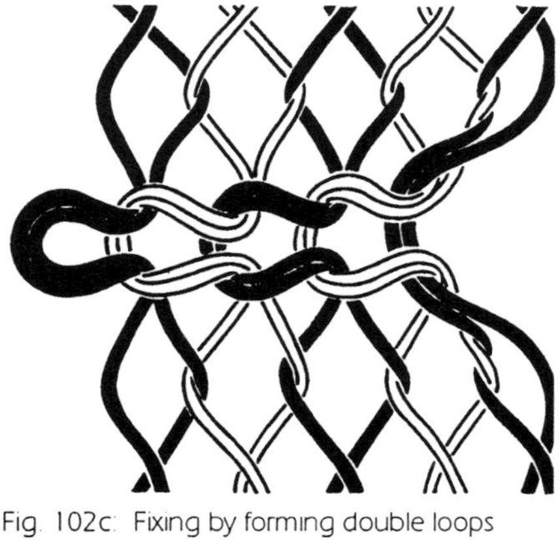

Fig. 102c: Fixing by forming double loops

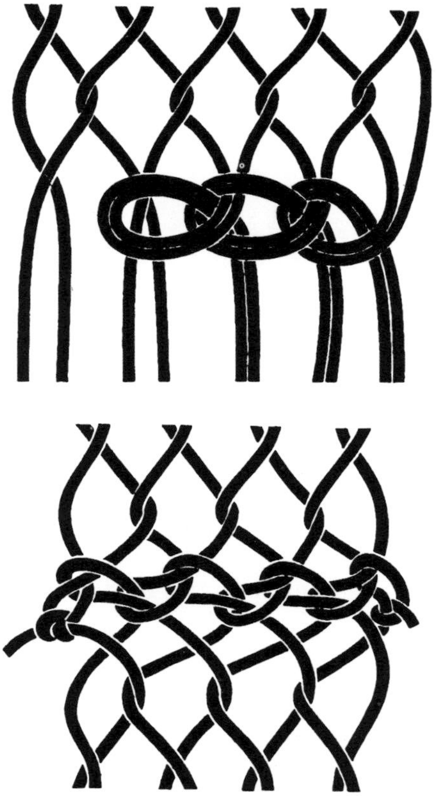

Fig. 102d-e: Fixing by forming encircled loops

Fabric Production with a Passive Warp

The passive warp yarns are secured by one (or more) active wefts. These processes thus have a greater technical affinity with heddle weaving than the methods using an active warp which can be associated rather with special types of weaving (finger and tablet weaving). The crucial point is that the weft must be introduced absolutely by hand on each pass with no automatic shedding.
The forms of interlacing are mainly identical with those of plaiting with an active and a passive system.

Weft Wrapping

The structures are the same as used in wrapping. The only difference consists in the type of manipulation, specifically in the use of a fixed warp. In the literature these methods are sometimes referred to misleadingly as "flat woven fabrics" (in contrast to carpets, i.e., piled fabrics) or sometimes, in more specialised jargon, under the Caucasian name "soumak". In this method the weft is wrapped round the warp threads. This can be done so that the weft runs at right angles, diagonally or even parallel to the warp (Fig. 103a-b), running its whole length or only part thereof (Fig. 109). There are very many types of weft wrapping. They may take the form of wrapping a warp yarn several times instead of once, wrapping several warp yarns at the same time, skipping warp yarns or wrapping alternate warps. Further varieties of design can be achieved by means of the direction of twist of the wefts, which may all be wrapped in the same direction or in opposite directions.
A feature common to them all is a forwards-and-backwards motion of the weft which can be described as similar to the wrapping processes used in plaiting with an active and a passive system (see pp. 26-29).
The most important variant forms are wrapping and looped wrapping of the weft.

Fig. 103a: Diagonal weft wrapping

Fig. 103b: Weft wrapping parallel to the warp

Other terms used:
Wrapped weaving (O'Neale 1937:201)
Wrapped weave, Soumak weave (Hodges 1964:143)
Soumak wrapping (Anderson 1978: Fig. 86)
Wickeln des Eintrages (Seiler-Baldinger 1991:66)
Diagonale und vertikale Wickelbroschierung (Dombrowski/Pfluger-Schindlbeck 1988:23)
Enroulement de la trame (Tanavoli 1985:66)
Snärjväv (CIETA 1970:57)

1. Simple and Multiple Weft Wrapping

The weft can be wrapped round the warp yarns once (Fig. 104a-b) or several times, and either with an S- or a Z-slant (Fig. 105).

If the weft is inserted without turning the workpiece round, the right and reverse sides will be different (Fig. 106a-b).

Depending on the float of the weft on the right and reverse sides, in other words on the number of wrapped warp threads, other variations are possible (Fig. 107a-d). Very pleasing patterns can be obtained by the use of several staggered wefts and combinations of S- and Z-slants (Fig. 108). The wefts may be wrapped round only one part of the warp and then, as in tapestry (see p. 63), carried back to their starting point (Fig. 109).

Notation and theoretical observations:

The characteristic feature of weft wrapping is that, if the thread is carried forward over n warp yarns (fn) the weft must be "returned" (back = b) under 1 to n-1 warp threads. In the case of fn there are thus b under 1 to n-1 warp threads.

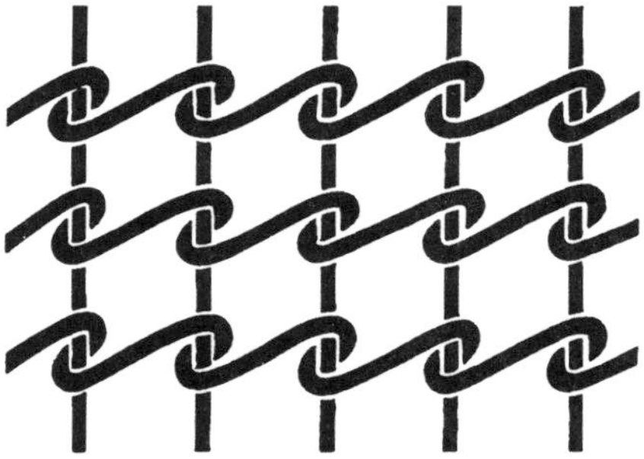

Fig. 104a: Simple weft wrapping f2 b/1: face

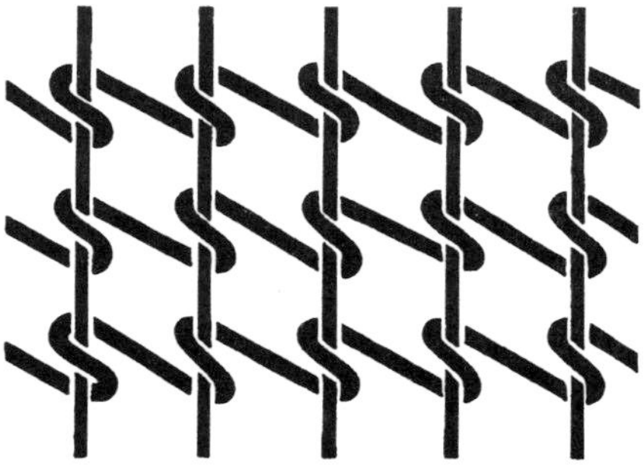

Fig. 104b: Simple weft wrapping f2 b/1: reverse

Fig. 104c: Multiple weft wrapping f2 b/1 f1 b/1

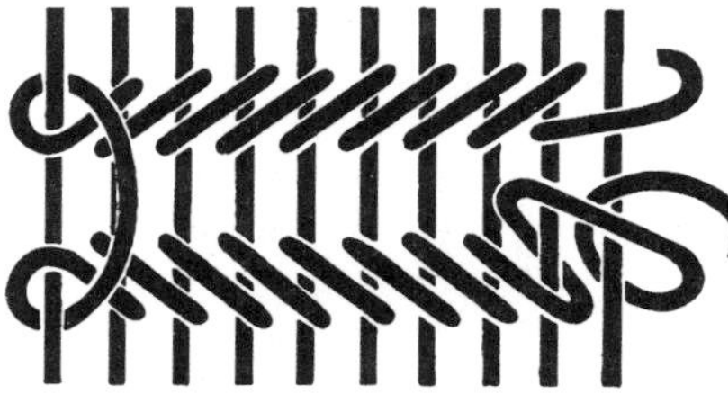

Fig. 105: Countered weft wrapping (S and Z twist)

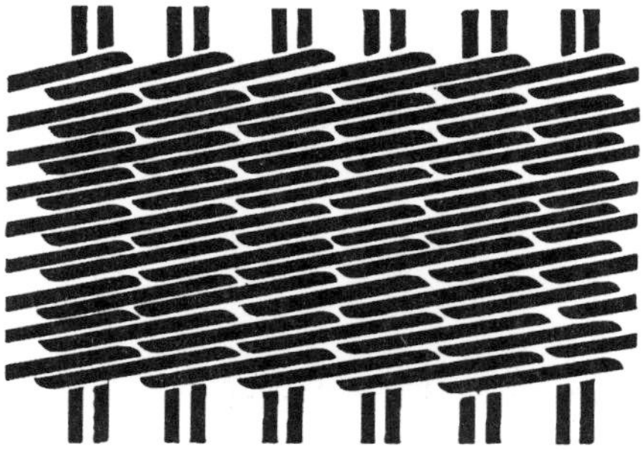

Fig. 106a: Weft wrapping f4/b2: face

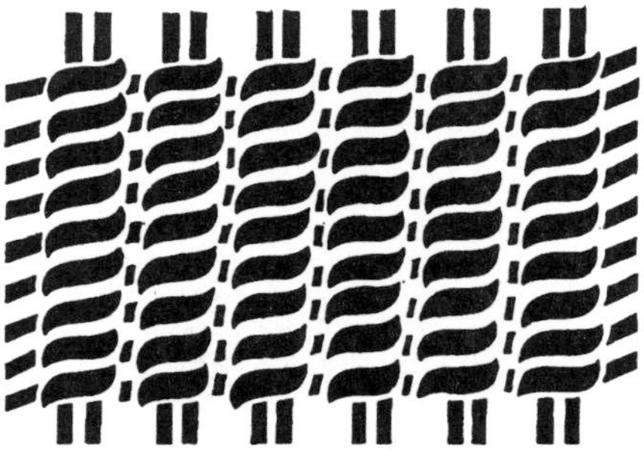

Fig. 106b: Weft wrapping f4/b2: reverse

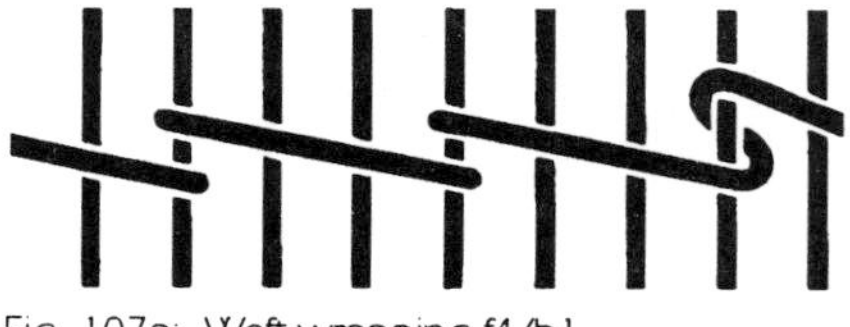

Fig. 107a: Weft wrapping f4/b1

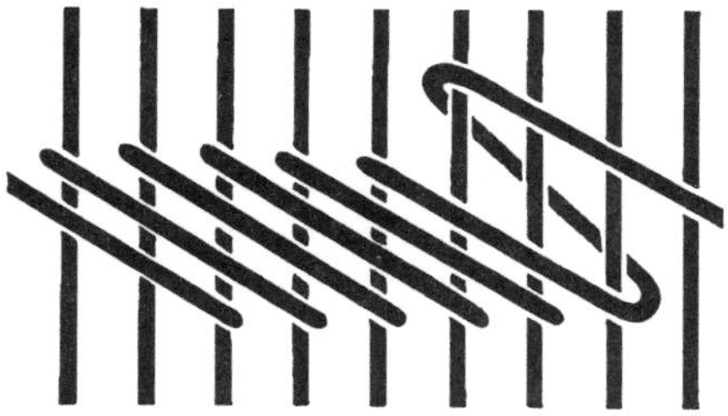

Fig. 107b: Weft wrapping f4/b3

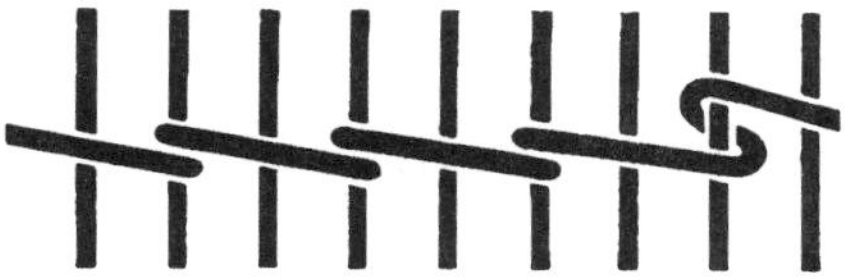

Fig. 107c: Weft wrapping f3/b1

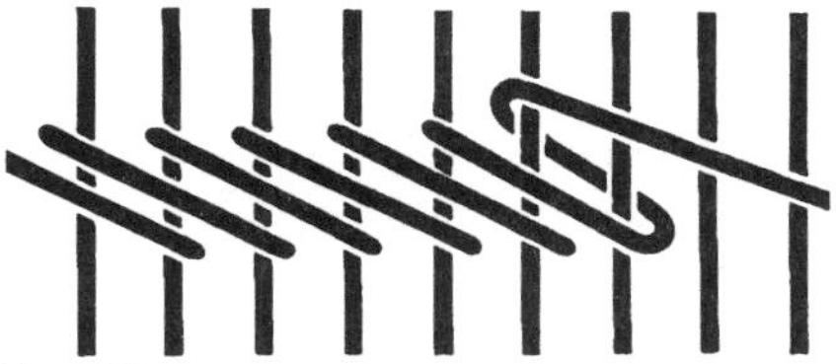

Fig. 107d: Weft wrapping f3/b2

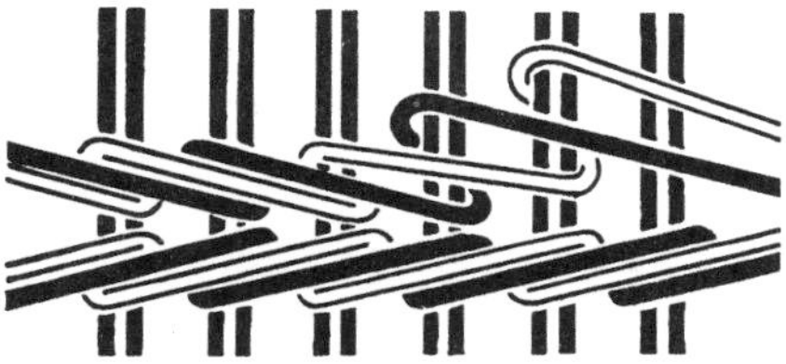

Fig. 108: Countered wrapping of staggered wefts f6/b2 (S and Z twist)

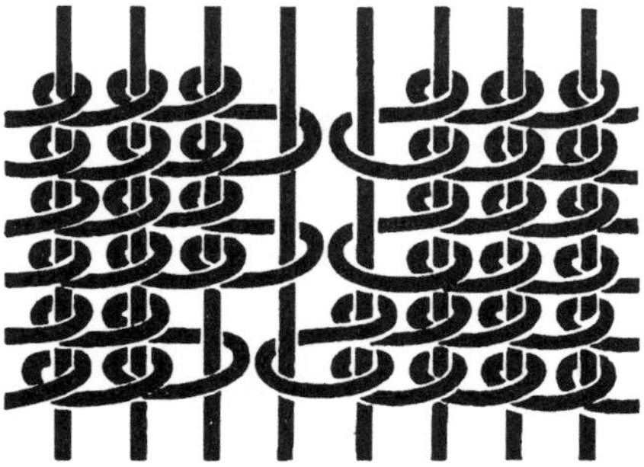

Fig. 109: Discontinuous weft wrapping (as in tapestry)

Other terms used:
Plain weft-wrapping (Emery 1966:215)
Plain and countered weft-wrapping (Tanavoli 1985:81)
Einfaches und mehrfaches Umwickeln des Eintrages (Seiler-Baldinger 1991:67)
Omwikkelen (Brommer et al. 1988:86)

2. Weft Wrapping with Skipping (or interlacing) of Warp Threads

The weft is not wrapped round all the warp threads but only round every third one, i.e. a warp thread is interlaced or skipped between wrappings (Fig. 110a).

If the weft were to be cut after every second warp thread, the result would be the "asymmetrical knot" of carpet weaving (see p. 111).

Only if there is an odd number of skipped (or crossed) warp threads between two wrapped warps can there be any genuine interlacings, always presupposing that the wefts are moved on by one warp thread (Fig. 110b).

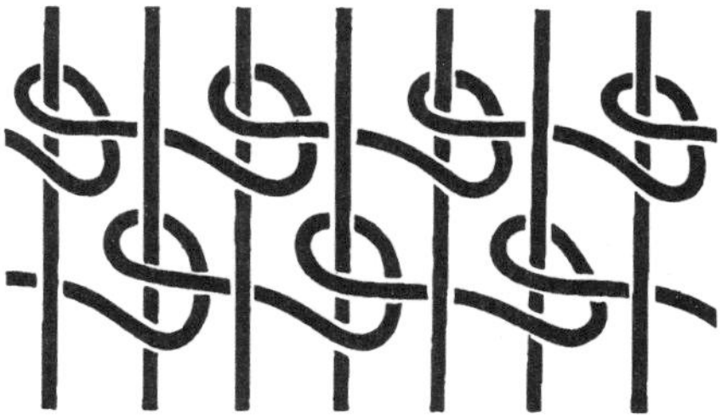

Fig. 110a: Weft wrapping with skipping of one warp thread

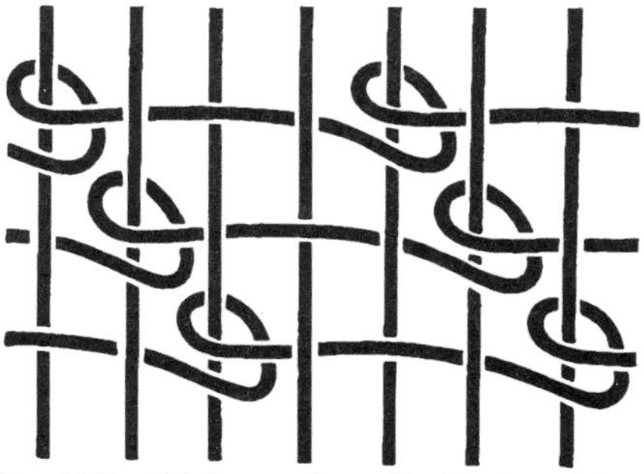

Fig. .110b: Weft wrapping with skipping of three warp threads

Other terms used:
Wickeln des Eintrages mit Überspringen (bzw. Kreuzen) von Kettfäden (Seiler-Baldinger 1991:68)
Steppstichähnliche und Sumakähnliche Reihe (Dombrowski/Pfluger-Schindlbeck 1988:23)

3. Alternating Weft Wrapping

The weft is wrapped round one warp thread and then passed over two (or more) adjacent warp threads, the last of which is wrapped round again. If the warp threads were to be cut after every second warp thread, the result would be the "symmetrical knot" of carpet weaving (see p. 110).

Unlike simple weft wrapping, this method is characterised by the fact that the span must be at least two warp threads.

It can be the same or different at the "bottom" or "top" (Fig. 111a-b).

Notation and theoretical observations:

Depending on the point of view the weft pattern in Fig. 111a can be described as f2/b1, f2/b1 or as f1/b1, f2/b1, f1. The first method of computation is unlike the others in that the symmetrical configuration of the thread (longitudinal glide reflection with transverse mirror image) shows up more clearly.

Fig. 111a: Alternating weft wrapping with equal spans

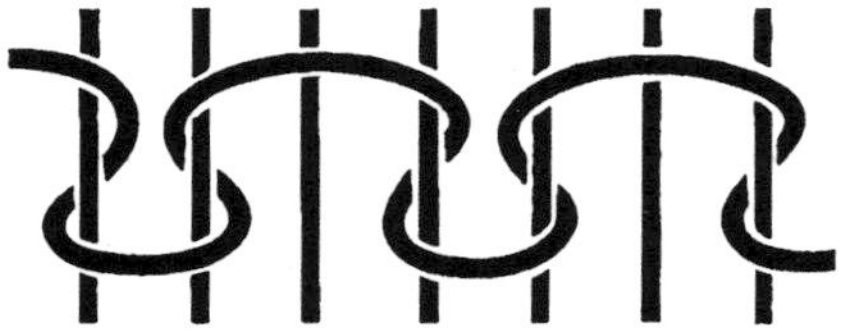

Fig. 111b: Alternating weft wrapping with unequal spans

Other terms used:

Umkehrendes Wickeln des Eintrages (Seiler-Baldinger 1991:69)
Enroulement alterné (Tanavoli 1985: Fig. 118)

4. Looped Weft Wrapping

In contrast to the preceding methods, the weft fixes the warp threads in loops (Fig. 112), which is also expressed in the numerical sequence of the thread pattern (namely, 111 instead of 21 as in simple weft wrapping).

As in the methods of looping in meshwork techniques, similar variations are to be found here, e.g. double-looped weft wrapping. The face and the reverse display a different pattern. Whereas on the face the weft span (float) appears to be parallel and horizontal, there are S- or Z-twisted wrappings of the warp threads on the reverse (Fig. 113a-b). The structures are identical with those of looped wrapping in plaiting with an active and a passive system (see pp. 26-29). There is no need for the weft to be at right angles to the warp in this method either.

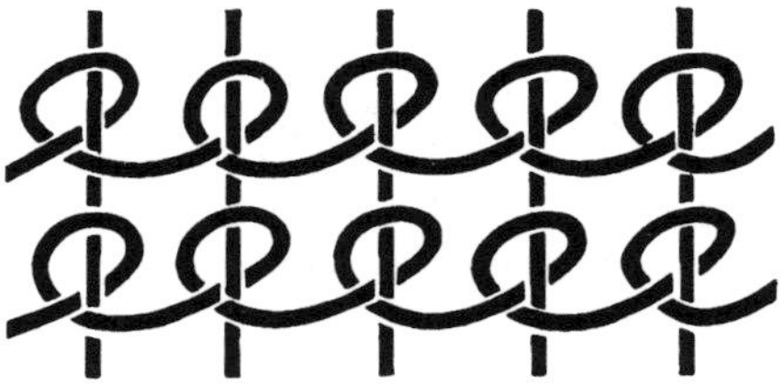

Fig. 112: Looped weft wrapping: thread configuration 1/1/1

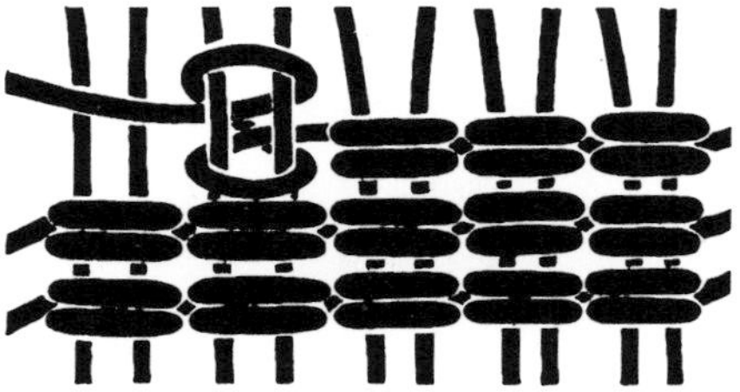

Fig. 113a: Double looped weft wrapping over two warp threads: face

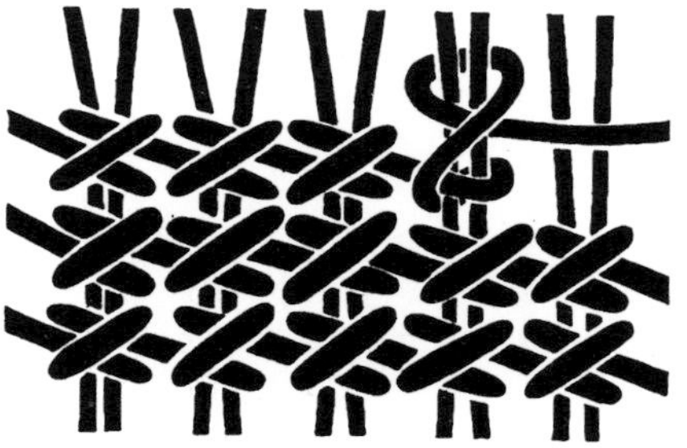

Fig. 113b: Double looped weft wrapping over two warp threads: reverse

Other terms used:

Variation of plain weft-wrapping (Emery 1966:216)
Umschlingendes Wickeln des Eintrages (Seiler-Baldinger 1991: 69)
Geknotetes umschlingendes Wickeln (Tanavoli 1985: Fig. 107)
Trame enroulée avec noeud (Tanavoli 1985: Fig. 86)

Knotted Weft Wrapping:

Knotting the weft is a particularly suitable means of producing gauze-like fabrics. In this process the weft yarns can be clustered together and the wefts are mainly knotted round the warp yarns in suspended knots (Fig. 114a-b).

Fig. 114a: Knotted weft with simple knots

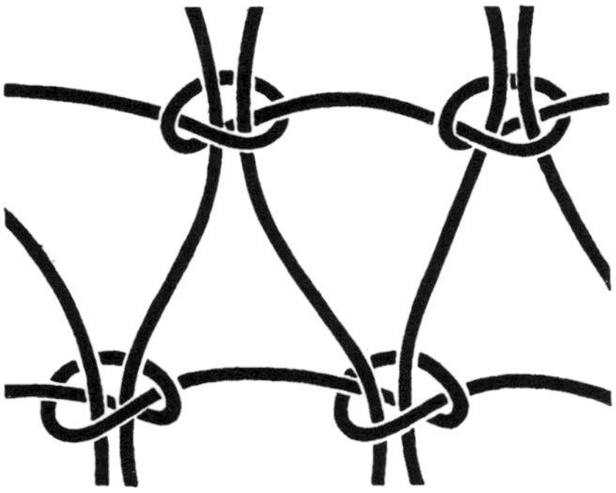

Fig. 114b: Knotted weft with overhand knots and transposed warp

Other terms used:
Simple-knotted weft wrapping (Tanavoli 1985:86)
Knoten des Eintrages (Seiler-Baldinger 1991:70)
Enroulement avec noeud (Tanavoli 1965: Fig. 86)

Weft Twining

The wefts are twined in pairs round one or more warp yarns, i.e. the paired wefts are twisted before and after each warp yarn (or pair of warp yarns) (Fig. 115).
Variations can be obtained by altering the direction of twist of the twined weft threads and their sequence in the fabric as a whole, by varying the number of twined warp threads per twist, by moving the weft obliquely, and by not passing the weft over the full width of the cloth (Fig. 116).
Another possibility is to use more than two wefts together, just as in twining, which produces structures similar to those obtained by this plaiting method.
Additional types of variation can be obtained by, for instance, twisting one (or both) of the weft threads round itself (or themselves) before twisting round the warp thread (Fig. 117), by staggering the paired weft threads (Fig. 118) or by transposing the warp (Fig. 119a-c).

Fig. 115: Weft twining around one warp thread, with Z twist

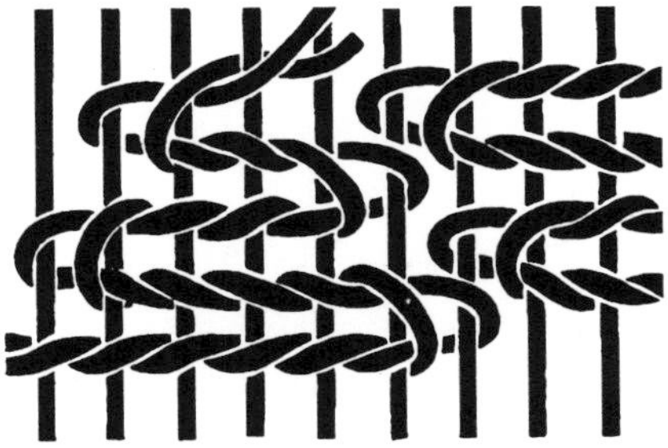

Fig. 116: Countered weft twining with discontinuous wefts

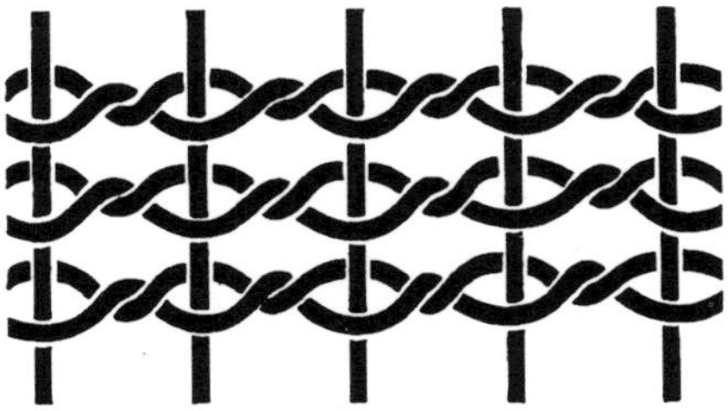

Fig. 117: Weft twining with added twist

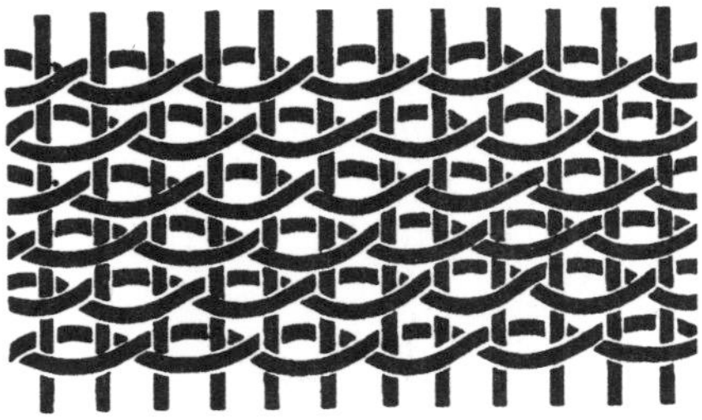

Fig. 118: Weft twining with staggering of weft pairs over two warp threads

Fig. 119a: Staggered weft twining with transposed warp

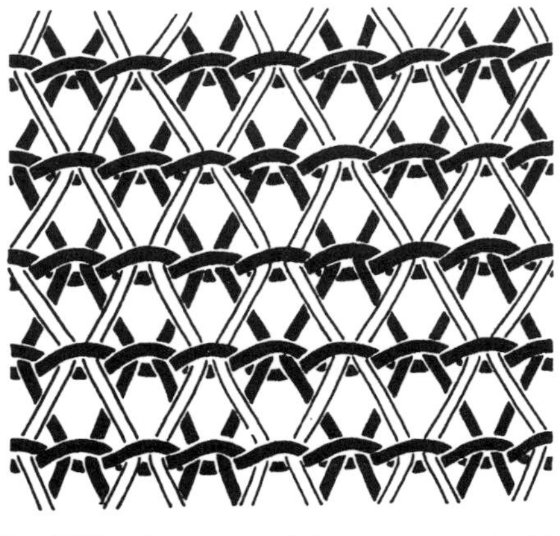

Fig. 119b: Staggered weft twining over a double, transposed warp

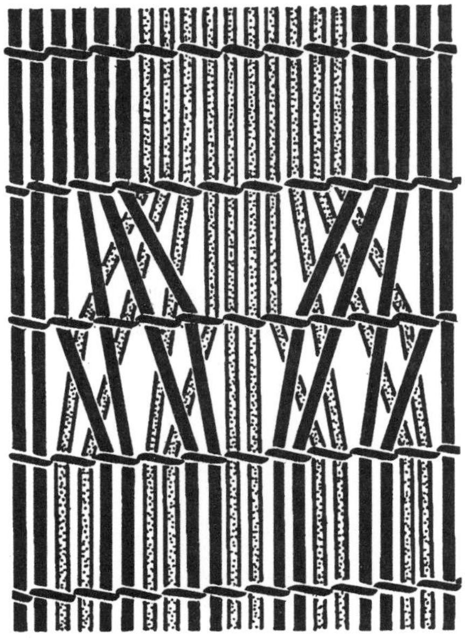

Fig. 119c: Pattern variation: staggered weft twining with transposed warp

Other terms used:

Twined weaving (Underhill 1948)
Weft-twine technique (Kent Peck 1957:477)
Fabrics with twisted weft, twining (D'Harcourt 1962:66)
Twined weave (Hodges 1964:143)
Single or double-pair twining (Pendergast 1987:14)
Taaniko (Pendergast 1987:15)
Double-twining (Cardale-Schrimpff 1972:626ff.)
Weft-faced twining (Hecht 1989:70)
Zwirnbinden des Eintrages (Seiler-Baldinger 1991:70)
Doppelfadengeflecht (Schmidt 1905)
Trames cordées (Tanavoli 1985:78)
Tissus à tramè double entrecroisée (Nooteboom 1945:1ff.)
Torcido de trama (Nardi 1975:79)
Entramado atado o cordado (Alfaro Giner 1984:116)
Ligamento de enlazado (Mirambell/Martínez 1986: Fig. 16)
Técnica de amarra (Ulloa 1985:16)
Técnica de "cadena" (Millán de Palavecino 1960: Lam. 2, Fig. 11-12)
Tejido torcido o encordado (Mora de Jaramillo 1974:336)
Trenzado con hilo doble (Susnik 1986:73)
Torção da trama (Ribeiro 1980:13)
Trançado de fio duple (Schultz 1964:208)
Twijnen (Gerlings 1952:33)
Inslagtwijnen of fitsen (Brommer 1988:90)

Weft Interlacing and Tapestry

With the aid of a needle or bobbin or by hand the weft threads are interlaced with the warp. The structures are identical with those of weaving or the corresponding forms of plaiting parallel to the edges and alternate half-weaving.

As a rule narrow widths of cloth and ribbons are made by weft interlacing (Fig. 120a).

Tapestry can be regarded as a special form of weft interlacing since the wefts do not progress over the full width of the fabric but turn back on themselves (Fig. 120b). Although in practice this is often achieved by automatic shedding, this technique, when seen from a theoretical point of view, should be classified here since, in principle, the individual warp yarns can be picked up by hand.

Tapestry is used mainly for patterning with wefts of different colours, the warp remaining invisible (structure: weft rib, weft-faced plain weave). The technique is also used to produce openwork, in which case the warp can also be deviated (Fig. 121).

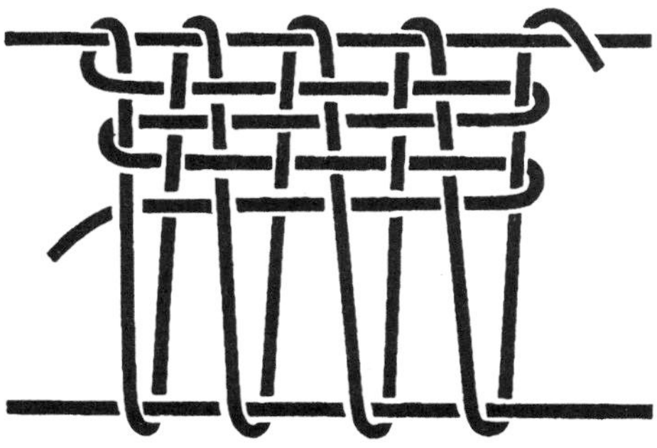

Fig. 120a: Weft interlacing (plain weave)

Fig. 120b: Tapestry (weft-faced plain weave)

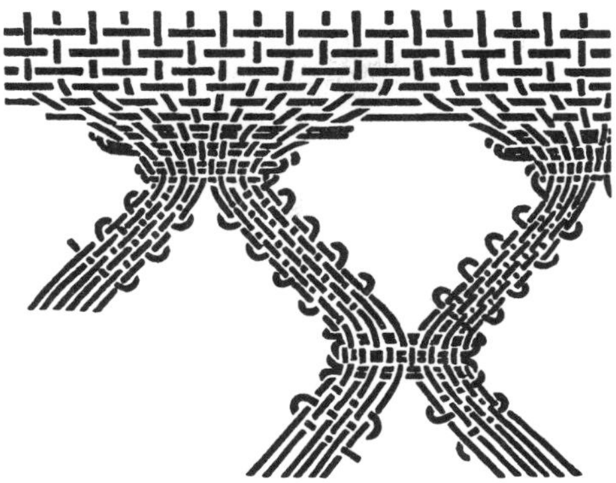

Fig. 121: Openwork tapestry with displaced warp

Other terms used:

Weft interlacing:
Flechten des Eintrages (Seiler-Baldinger 1991:72)

Tapestry:
Wirken (Seiler-Baldinger 1991:72)
Tapisserie, tapestry weaving, arazzo, tapezzeria, tapiz, flamskväv, gobelängvävnad (CIETA 1970:67)
Kuvakudos (Geijer/Hoffmann 1974:22)

Openwork:
Plain weave openwork (Emery 1966:84)
Jour-Wirkerei (Seiler-Baldinger 1991:72)

Where the various weft threads meet one another, slits arise when the wefts are passed back round warp threads. Another possibility is to loop these elements round the same warp thread or to interlink them in various ways and thus avoid the formation of slits. In the following discussion the classification will be based on precisely these points. Other differences arise from the direction of the weft threads in relation to the warp. Apart from thread configurations at right angles to the warp, there can also be, depending on the pattern, markedly deviant directions which often result in the warp threads being displaced.

Other terms used:

Eccentric tapestry wefting (Crawford 1912:120)
Non-horizontal weft (Emery 1966:83)
Oblique and curved wefts, eccentric wefts (Collingwood 1968: 159)

1. Slit Tapestry

Where parts of different colours meet, i.e. where the weft threads turn back on themselves, there will be slits of lesser or greater length which are characteristic in particular of what is known as kelim technique in carpets from the Near East (Fig. 122a-b).

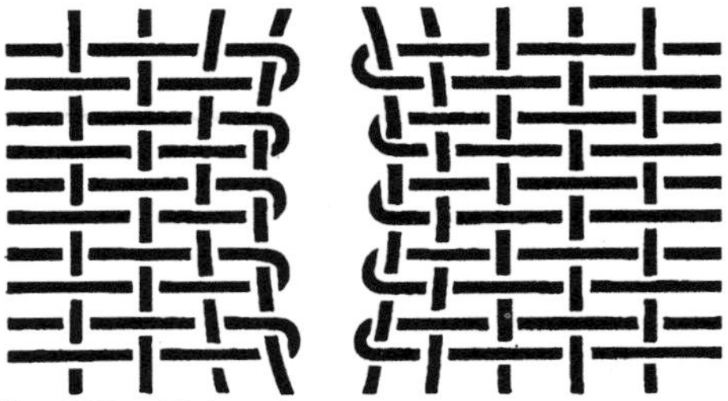

Fig. 122a: Slit tapestry

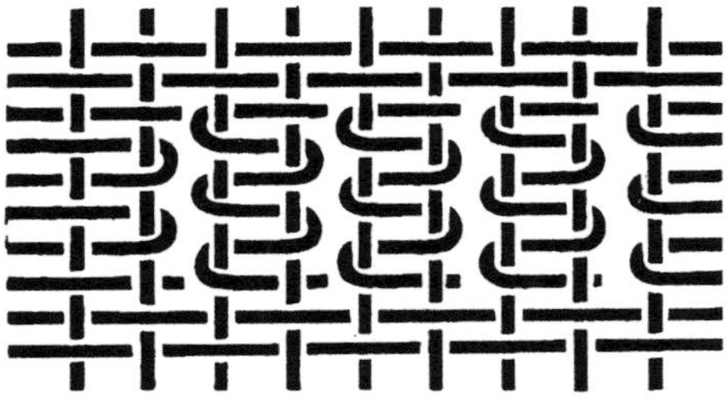

Fig. 122b: Slit tapestry with short slits

Other terms used:

Slit-tapestry weave (Kent Peck 1954:11)
Kelim-tapestry (Lothrop/Mahler 1957:33f.)
Schlitzwirkerei (Seiler-Baldinger 1991:73)
Arrazzo sparato, tapiz a ranura (CIETA 1970:48)
Tapicería con ranuras (Cardale-Schrimpff 1977/78:268)
Tapiz a ojales o ranuras (Vreeland/Muelle 1977:14)
Tapicería ojalada (Ulloa 1985:18)
Flamskvävnad (Nylén 1969:155)

2. Avoidance of Slits

To avoid major slits during tapestry weaving and also to lend emphasis to certain outlines of the pattern, a number of processes have been developed, the most important of which are detailed here.

2.1. Interlocking of Wefts

Adjacent wefts are interlocked before reversal of direction. This can be achieved in a number of ways; for instance by simple interlinking of the weft threads (simple interlocked tapestry, Fig. 123a) or by double interlocking of two weft threads at the points of reversal (double interlocked tapestry, Fig. 123b).

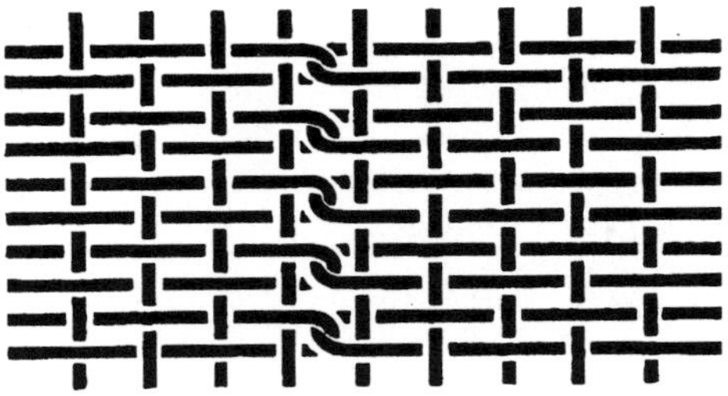

Fig. 123a: Interlocking tapestry

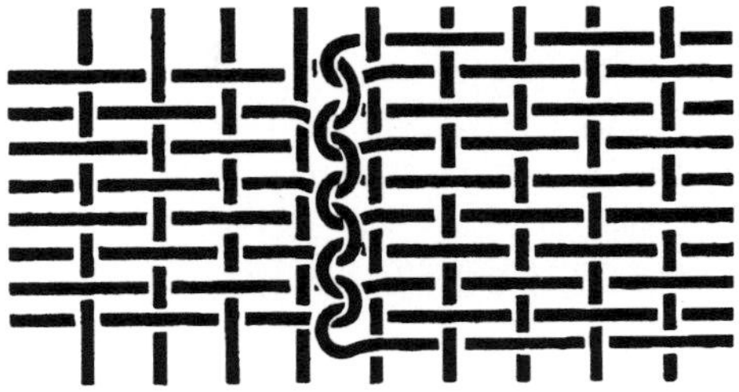

Fig. 123b: Interlocking tapestry

Other terms used:

Interlocking weft (Means 1932:29)
Interlocking tapestry weave (Emery 1966:81)
Interlocking and double interlocking wefts (Tanavoli 1985:71)
Interlocked (single or double) tapestry (Collingwood 1968:175)
Linked wefts (Hecht 1989:56)
Ineinanderhängen der Einträge (Seiler-Baldinger 1991:73)
Kelimtechnik mit verzahnten Schüssen bzw. mit doppelt verhängten Schüssen (Dombrowski/Pfluger-Schindlbeck 1988:17)
Tapisserie à trames entrelacées (Tanavoli 1985:71)
Gobelino enlazado (Lindberg 1964:197)
Tapicería entrelazado (Mirambell/Martínez 1986: Fig. 28)
Enkelslingning, dubbelslingning (Nylén 1969:155)

2.2 Linking the Weft Thread Over a Common Warp (dovetailed tapestry)

The weft threads of two adjacent parts are taken back round a common warp thread.

PLATE 10. Woman's apron, beadwork of the Aparai, Pará, Brazil, Vc 4133

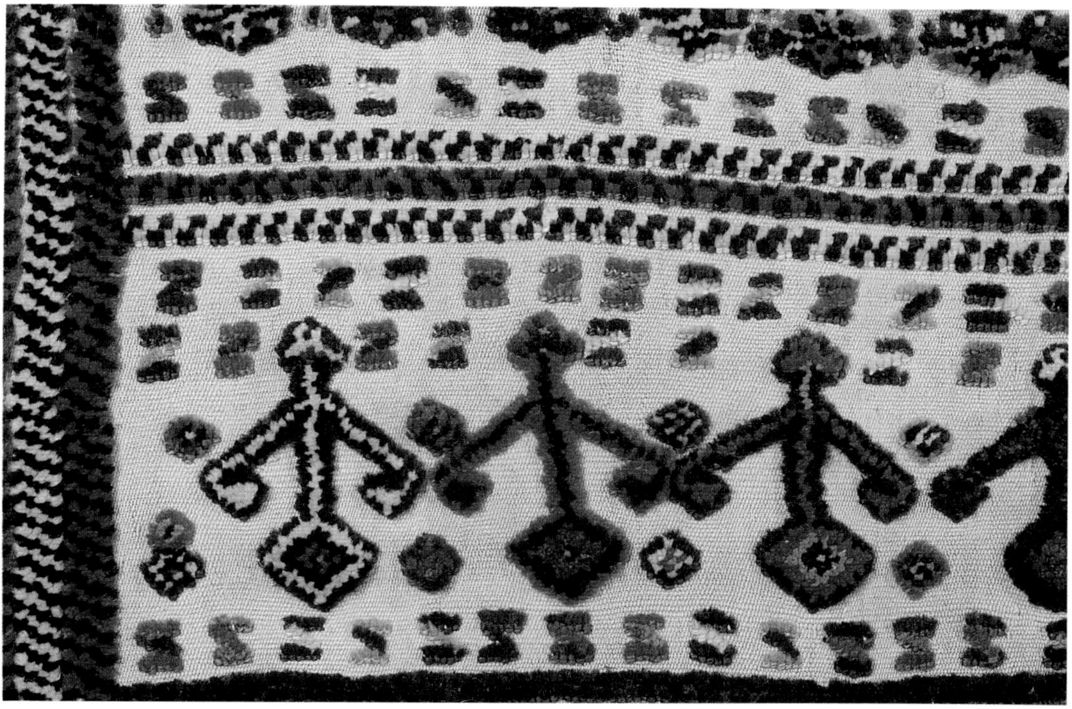

PLATE 11. Horse blanket of the Kashkai, symmetrical knot, Shiraz, Iran, IIe 1924

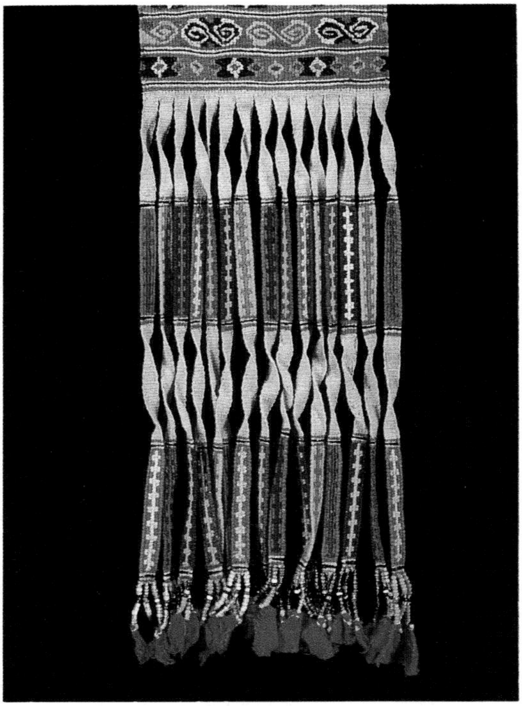

PLATE 12. Warp-faced plain woven and weft-twined fringes of a band, Timor, IIc 5071

PLATE 13. Twisted fringes of a woman's loincloth, Cameroon, III 3910

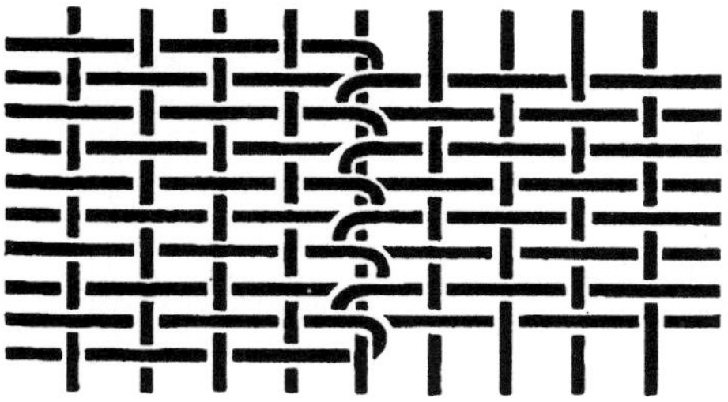

Fig. 124a: Dovetailed tapestry

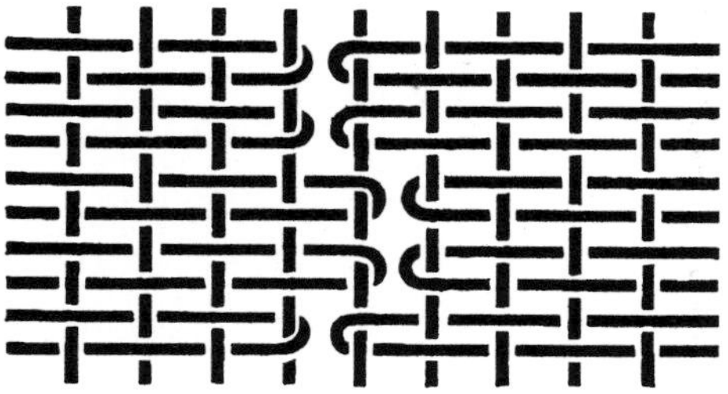

Fig. 124b: Staggered dovetailed tapestry

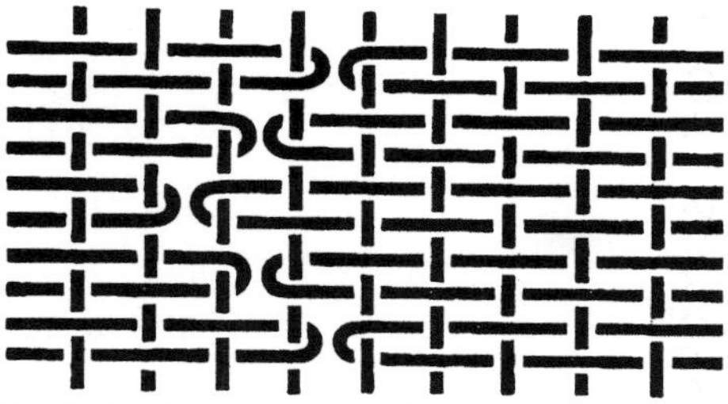

Fig. 124c: Staggered dovetailed tapestry with small slits

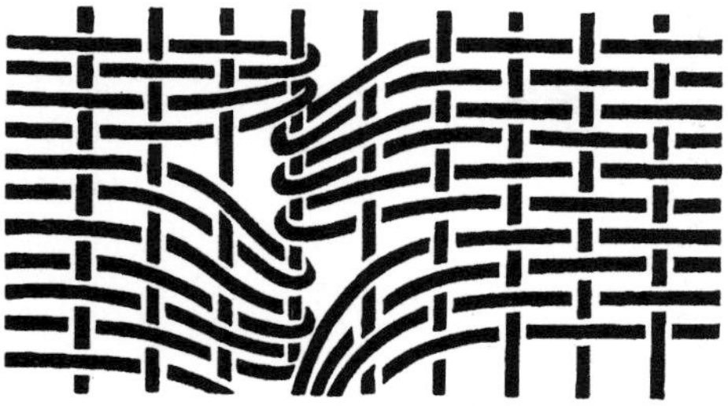

Fig. 124d: Dovetailed tapestry with grouped wefts

Other terms used:
Dovetailed tapestry weave (single dovetailing or toothing) (Emery 1966:80)
Dovetailing weave (Tanavoli 1985:70)
Single dovetailing (Collingwood 1968:80)
Weft interlocking on key warp (Willey/Corbett 1954:90)
Einhängen der Einträge über einen gemeinsamen Kettfaden (verzahnte Wirkerei) (Seiler-Baldinger 1991:74)
Kelimtechnik mit einfach verhängten Schüssen (Dombrowski/Pfluger-Schindlbeck 1988:17)
Tapisserie à trames jointes en dents de scie (Tanavoli 1985:70)
Enlace de cortas tramas (Millán de Palavecino 1970:22)
Tapiz de cola de Milano (Vreeland/Muelle 1977:10)
Tapicería dentada (Mirambell/Martínez 1986: Fig. 29)
Tandad (Geijer/Hoffmann 1974:85)

2.3. Partial Wrapping of a Single Warp Thread

The free end of a warp thread between the back-and-forth pattern of the weft is wrapped round another pick of a different colour in the form of a gimp thread (cf. thread formation). In this way certain motifs are framed and emphasized.

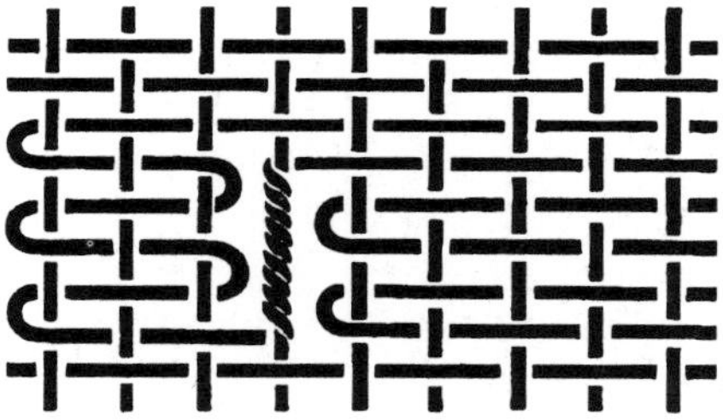

Fig. 125a: Partial wrapping of a single warp thread

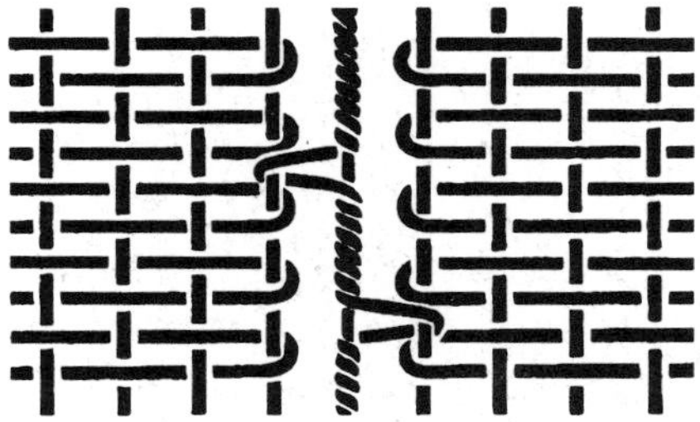

Fig. 125b: Partial wrapping of a warp thread linking with adjacent warp threads

Other terms used:
Stellenweises Umwickeln eines einzigen Kettfadens (Seiler-Baldinger 1991:74)
Gewickelter Konturenschuss (Dombrowski/Pfluger-Schindlbeck 1988:18)
Wirkerei mit Gimpenkontur (CIETA 1970:67)

2.4. Interlocking the Wefts in an Intervening Pick

The back-and-forth wefts of two adjacent portions are interlocked in a warp thread passing over one (rarely over several) warp thread(s).

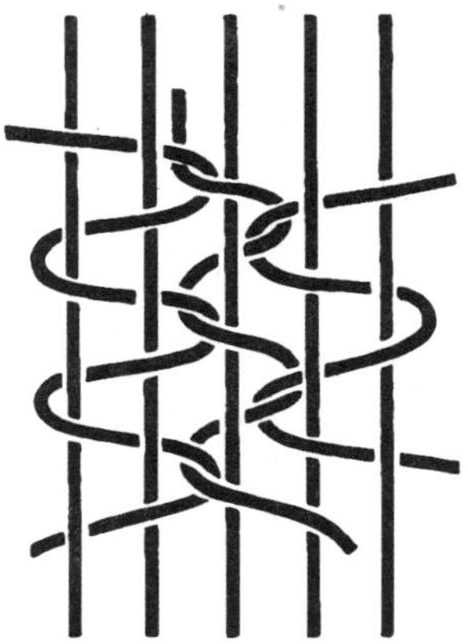

Fig. 126a: Interlocking the wefts in an intervening pick: over one warp thread

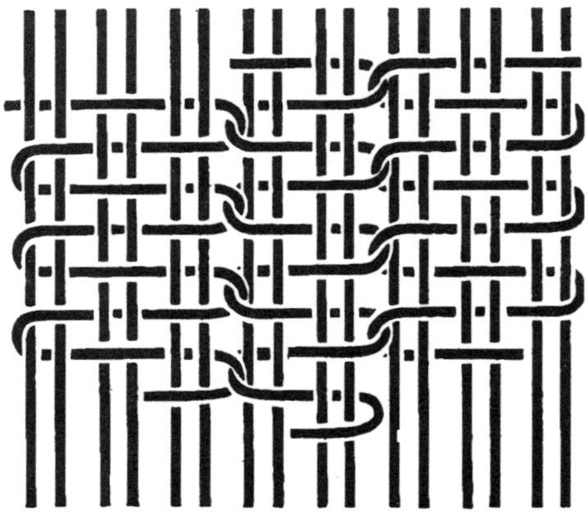

Fig. 126b: Interlocking the wefts in an intervening pick: over several warp threads

Other terms used:
Interlocking weft with limning (Means 1932:29)
Einhängen der Einträge in einem dazwischenliegenden Schussfaden (Seiler-Baldinger 1991:75)

Slits can also be avoided by passing the weft threads back and forth in a staggered pattern (Fig. 124b) or with the aid of contour threads (Fig. 125b).

2.5. Interlocking of Discontinuous Warps and Wefts

This technique is a special form of tapestry since both the warp and the weft are discontinuous.
In this type both the warp and the weft threads pass only over parts of the fabric. At the points of contact between the various portions of warp and weft threads, they are interlocked in a manner similar to tapestry technique. It is also possible to pass the weft thread through the full width of the cloth with only the warp thread being passed back and forth (discontinuous warps).
The technique is particularly well known from Ancient Peru. There is reason to suppose that in those days recourse was had to auxiliary threads which were subsequently removed (on the warp being returned to its starting point) (Rowe 1977:26ff.).

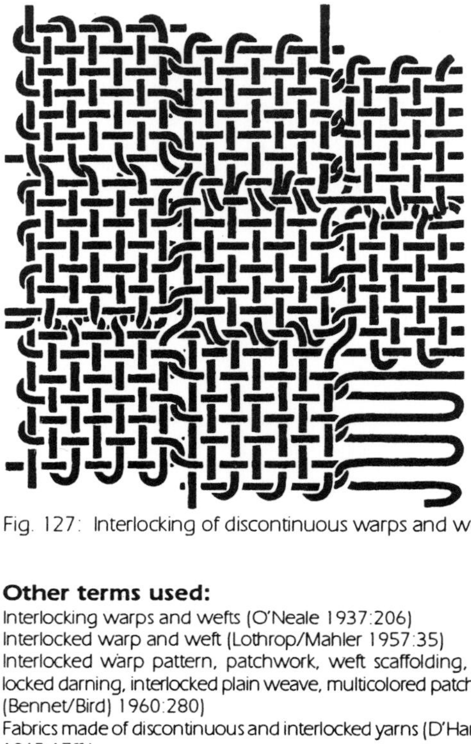

Fig. 127: Interlocking of discontinuous warps and wefts

Other terms used:
Interlocking warps and wefts (O'Neale 1937:206)
Interlocked warp and weft (Lothrop/Mahler 1957:35)
Interlocked warp pattern, patchwork, weft scaffolding, interlocked darning, interlocked plain weave, multicolored patchwork (Bennet/Bird) 1960:280)
Fabrics made of discontinuous and interlocked yarns (D'Harcourt 1962:17ff.)
Patchwork weaving (VanStan 1963/64:166ff.)
Double or Swedish interlocking (King 1968:373)
Plain weave with discontinuous warps and wefts (Rowe 1977:31)
Bildung von Partialstoffen (Seiler-Baldinger 1991:75)
Tejido de urdimbres entrelazadas (Weitlaner-Johnson 1977:70)
Tejidos de urdimbre y trama discontinuas (Vreeland/Muelle 1977:9)
Lapptäckesteknik (Hellervik 1977:32)

Warp Laces

Almost all warp techniques (excepting sprang and those with discontinuous warps) are found combined in what is known as sun and Teneriffe laces (Niedner/Weber undated). Their production involves the use of a round card on which the warp threads are stretched radially. Insertion of the weft is facilitated with a needle. The weft threads are looped or twined, interlaced or tapestry woven. The result is circular pieces of openwork lace which are used mainly as borders and trimmings.

Fig. 128: Warp lace

Other term used:

Kettenstoffspitzen (Seiler-Baldinger 1991:76)

References to Warp Methods: see pp. 160-162.
References to Tapestry: see pp. 162-163.

Half-weaving

In all the techniques of fabric production discussed so far, the interlacing between individual threads or groups of threads is brought about entirely by hand. Nowhere have implements been used which lighten or simplify the repetitive tasks. It is only in half-weaving that the first attempts in this direction occur.
Half-weaving is a process in which the warp is tensioned or fixed at both ends (the warp can be endless or finite) and the fabric is produced by forming one shed automatically for insertion of the weft whereas the countershed must be opened individually by hand. It is immaterial whether the half-automatic shedding is alternating, i.e. takes place every second time, or whether the sheds are reserved continuously until one half of the fabric is made. The most important feature of the weaving process – namely automatic shed formation – (see Weaving) is recognized but only employed for one shed. Hence the designation half-weaving.
From the technical but not the historical point of view half-weaving is to be classified between a) warp processes with a passive warp, in particular weft interlacing and warp twining, and b) true weaving as an independent technique. Shedding can in principle be achieved in two different ways. In the first of these the first shed is invariably formed by what is called the shed rod whereas the other shed is formed by hand. As these two operations alternate, I call this form "half-weaving with alternating automatic shedding" or "alternating half-weaving" for short. In the second way half of the sheds of the future fabric are prepared, i.e. reserved for the weft. I should like to call this "half-weaving with continuous shed reservation".

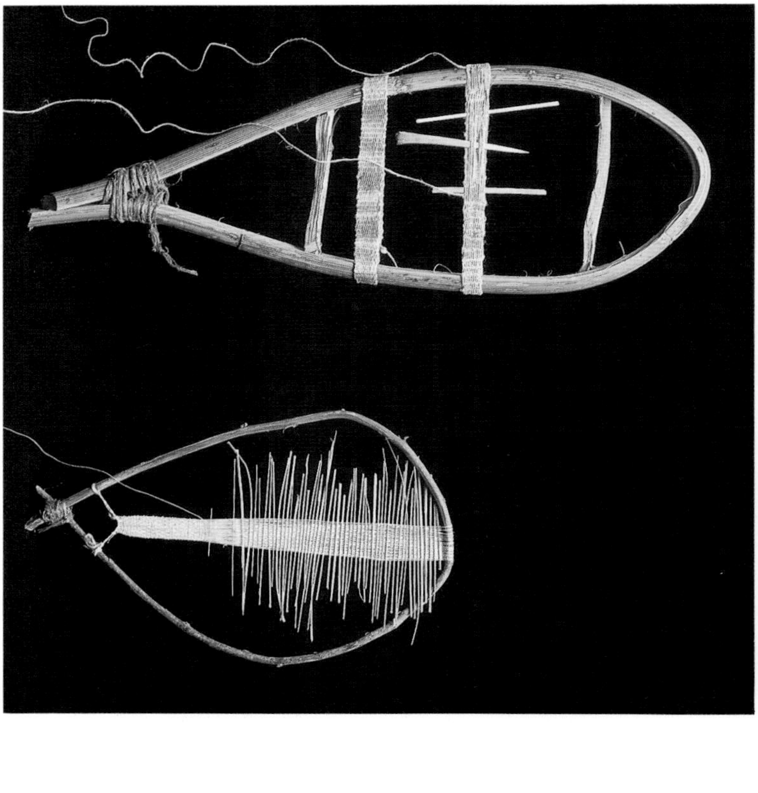

Half-weaving implements:
above: of the Atbalmin of Tumolbil, Telefomin Distr., West Sepik Province, Papua New Guinea, example of half-weaving with alternate shed formation, Vb 29558
below: of the Campa Indians, Dep. Ucayali, Peru, example of reserved half-weaving, IVc 574

Half-weaving with Alternate Shed Formation

A rod (shed rod) is inserted in the tensioned or fixed warp to separate the odd and even numbered threads, thus forming a natural shed (Fig. 129a). The weft can be thrust by hand or with a shuttle through the whole warp, thus bringing about an interlacing of the threads; or, using a plaiting needle, it is possible to open the shed, i.e. to separate the odd and even threads from one another, pull through the weft, and then insert a rod. Thus the implement used to form the first shed, subsequently referred to as a shed rod, can be left permanently in the warp, thrust in the direction of the warp as work proceeds, and every second weft can be inserted in this preformed shed. However, it is not possible to proceed in the same way with the countershed, for two inserted rods would interfere with each other (Fig. 129b). This method can be used only for plain weave (warp-faced, balanced or with multiple warps) and weaves derived from it (see pp. 87-89).

Fig. 129a: Half-weaving with alternate shed formation: formation of the first shed with the shed rod

Other term used:

Alternierendes Halbweben (Seiler-Baldinger 1991:78)

Fig. 129b: Half-weaving with alternate shed formation: formation of the countershed by hand by picking up threads

Fig. 129c: Half-weaving with alternate shed formation: formation of the first shed by moving down the shed rod

Fig. 129d: Half-weaving with alternate shed formation: formation of the countershed by hand

Half-weaving with Continuous Shed Reservation

Instead of forming sheds alternately by hand and shed rod, this method involves preparing or reserving the sheds up to half the size of the future fabric by means of sticks and/or by twisting the warp threads.
For instance, the warp threads are twisted actively with one another, so that, as in warp twining, the twist can be in the same or an opposed direction, and a weft is inserted. As the warp is tensioned there are, as in sprang, mirror-image crossings formed at the opposite end which must be fixed with sticks (Fig. 130) until they are replaced by wefts.
It is also possible to form the first shed with the plaiting needle without twisting the warp threads and at the same time to slip in along with the weft a stick which is subsequently pushed to the other end of the warp so that the corresponding shed is already formed there. The countershed and the other sheds proceed in the same way until the fabric in the centre meets up with the sticks. These are now pulled out from the centre to the end of the warp and replaced in turn by the weft.
This method also allows a "passive" twisting of the warp threads (similar to gauze weaves, see p. 100). In a continuous process two even warp threads are picked up while two odd threads are left, then twice in alternating order one even-numbered thread is picked up while the odd-numbered is left, and then two even-numbered and two odd-numbered and so on.
Interlacing is not achieved actively but through displacement of the two- and one-groups being picked up (Fig. 131). Very pleasing patterns can be obtained by altering the sequence in which the warp threads are picked up.
In contrast to alternate half-weaving, the reserved version has the advantage of allowing complicated structures such as twill and simple gauze weaves as well as those of warp twining to be created. The pattern obtained is always in a mirror-image relationship to the transverse axis of the fabric. This kind of half-weaving can also be combined with weaving.

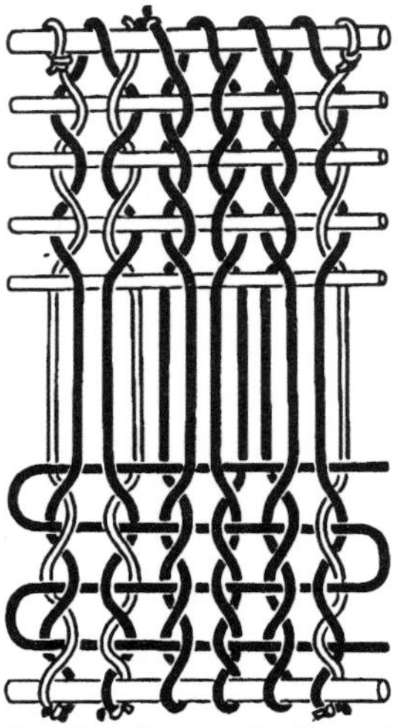

Fig. 130: Reserved half-weaving with twisting of the warp threads

Fig. 131: Reserved half-weaving combining gauze and plain weaves

Other term used:
Reservierendes Halbweben (Seiler-Baldinger 1991:79)

References to Half-weaving: see page 163.

Weaving

Weaving is primarily characterised by the possibility of forming at least two separate sheds in the tensioned warp by mechanical or automatic means; it is thus possible to obtain at least two distinct interlacings of warp which are separated by the weft thread. Secondary features, which are not always present, are the interlacing at right angles of the essentially passive warp and the usually active continuous weft and the use of several warp and weft systems.

Various features already present in the warp fabric process also logically occur in weaving. Thus a one- or two-plane warp can be used, along with several warp and/or weft systems, which is then, of course, reflected in the forms of interlacing (e.g. double warp, supplementary warp or weft, etc.).

We also must distinguish between "active" and "passive" warp. What we have here is a phenomenon analogous to those found in the appropriate warp fabric techniques. As a technical (but not a historical) sequence we might propose:

	Active Warp	Passive Warp
Half-weaving:	reserving	alternating
Weaving:	finger weaving	heddle
	tablet weaving	rigid heddle

The crucial step from half-weaving to weaving is therefore the fully automatic shedding achieved by implements specially designed for the purpose (tablets, heddles and shed rod, rigid heddle).

Accordingly we distinguish by reference to the type of shedding between finger, tablet, rigid heddle and heddle weaving, and by reference to the form of warp, between weaving with a one- or two-plane warp (spiral). Heddle weaving is by far the most capable of development and variation. From the simplest weaving equipment furnished with only the most essential components, the path of development leads via continual innovation to the treadle loom and finally to modern mechanical weaving.

Processes using an active warp, by comparison, offer little scope for development, for automatic shedding tends to interfere with the activity of the warp. It follows, then, that these allow less variation than those with a passive warp.

Other points of difference are the form of interlacing which will be dealt with at the appropriate place (see pp. 87-95).

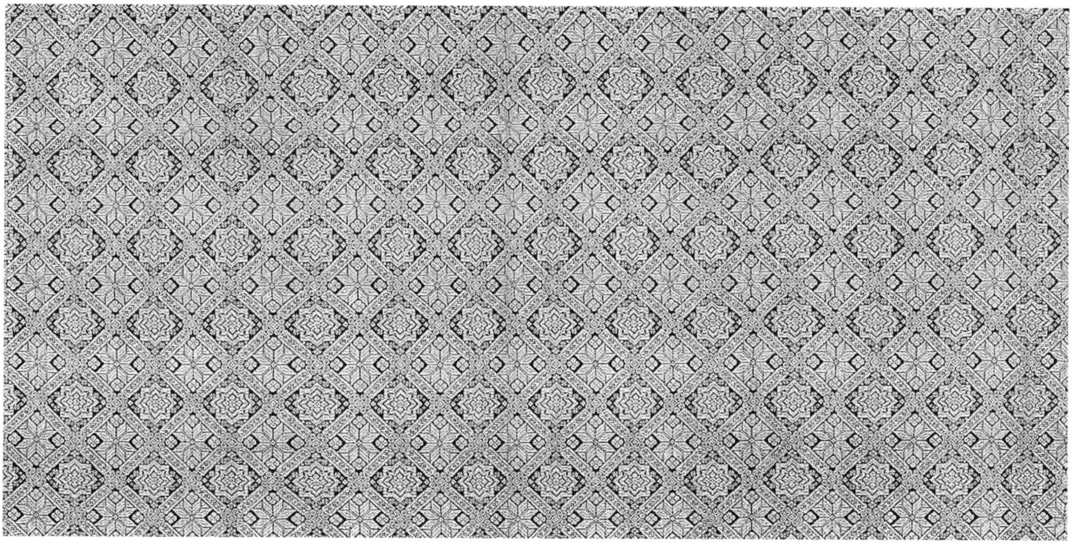

Woven songket silk shawl from Palembang, Sumatra, IIIc 243

Weaving with an "Active" Warp

Weaving with an active warp, which can be derived technically from the allied warp fabric processes (such as warp twining) and from half-weaving with shed reservation, is only suitable for making narrow fabrics. This method is characterised by twining the warps round the usually invisible wefts. We distinguish between finger and tablet weaving according to the type of shed formation.

Finger Weaving

Finger weaving allows the simplest form of automatic shedding, which is achieved without any form of instrument. However, at least two persons are needed. One holds the warp threads while the other introduces the weft. It is an absolute prerequisite that the warp should consist not of individual threads but of loops. A maximum number of ten loops can be used per person, one round each finger. The thread loops are now drawn in sequence from the fingers of the right hand through those of the left, which in turn pass over to the right. Shed and countershed are made by the spreading of hands, the warp threads being twined round the weft (Fig. 132).

The working method must proceed smoothly, the loops of the right hand always being passed through those of the left (or vice versa) and not in an alternating manner otherwise the twining would be undone. If there are two pairs of threads (Fig. 132a-c) there will be two countermoving twines with virtually the same covered pick. Consequently we obtain structures similar to those of warp twining, ply-splitting, tablet weaving and half-weaving with reserved sheds.

There is also a close relationship with loop braiding, except that in finger weaving the number of loops must always be even.

Patterns can be produced in finger weaving by using warp loops of various colours (Fig. 133a), two-coloured warp loops with different colour sequences (Fig. 133b-c) and types of loop manipulation (Fig. 134a-e), and also by the use of a "double" warp (Fig. 135).

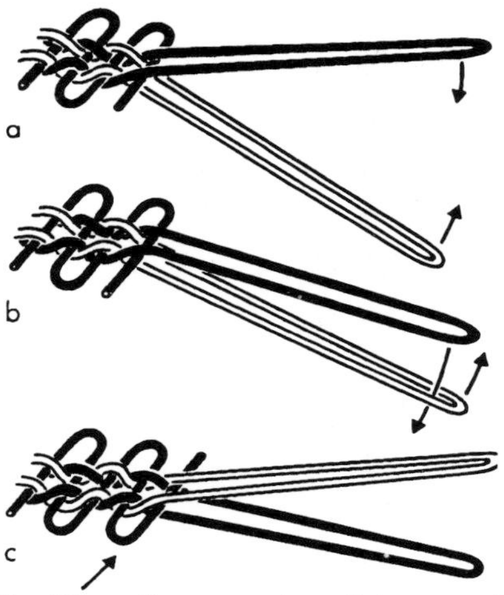

Fig. 132a-c: Finger weaving with two warp loops (two pairs of warp threads): manipulation of loops

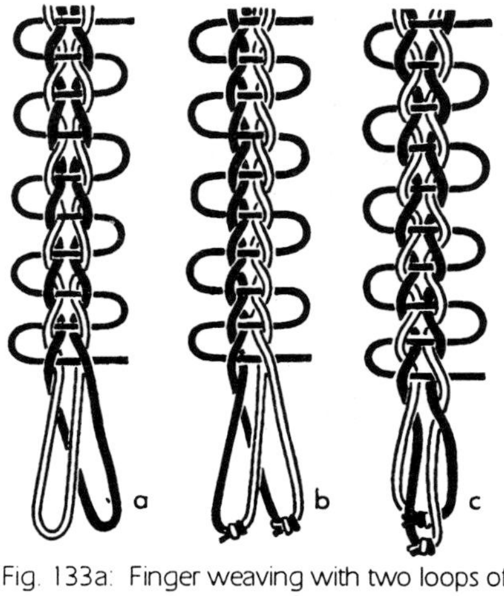

Fig. 133a: Finger weaving with two loops of different colours
Fig. 133b: Finger weaving with two-coloured warp loops (arrangement: black-white, black-white)
Fig. 133c: Finger weaving with two-coloured warp loops (arrangement: white-black, black-white)

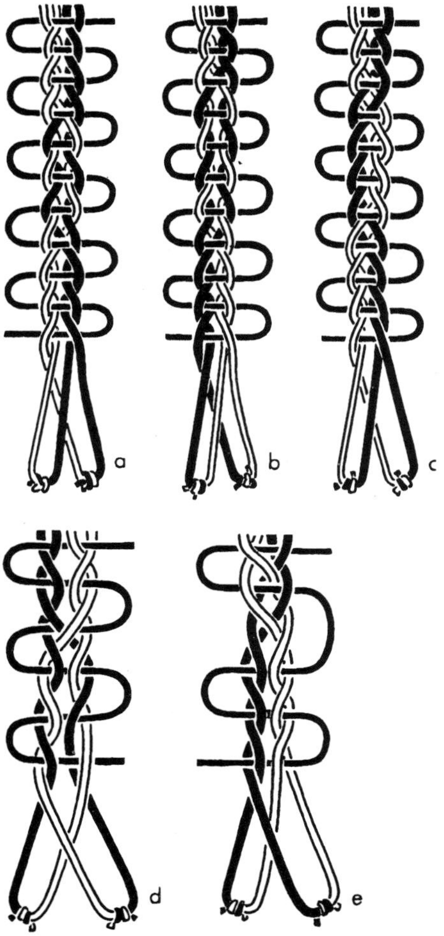

Fig. 134a-e: Finger weaving with two-coloured warp loops with different arrangement and different manipulation

Fig. 135: Finger weaving with double warp loops (double warp)

Other terms used:
Loop-manipulated warp twining (Speiser 1983:119)
Fingerweben (Seiler-Baldinger 1991:81)

Tablet Weaving

Shedding is accomplished with the aid of tablets (cards) of triangular to octagonal shape with holes pierced in the corners near the edge.

There is a warp thread running through each hole. In the tensioned warp the cards are parallel to the warp and their surfaces rest against each other. It is easy to move them all together with one hand to the left or the right (in an S- or Z- direction) and to revolve them through a quarter turn or a whole turn about their own longitudinal or transverse axis (Fig. 136a). The upper and lower pairs of threads of all the cards then form constantly changing groups with changing sheds into which the weft is inserted. The weft remains invisible between the warp threads which spiral round each other.

A twist also occurs at the other end of the warp (Fig.

137). After some time the cards used for shedding must be turned in the opposite direction in order to counteract this twisting along with the shortening or tensioning of the warp that is thus caused. Tablet weaving allows a number of variations, depending on the number of tablets and their perforations, on the direction of twist and on the pairs of threads between which the weft is inserted. It is not necessary to turn all the tablets at the same time but only, say, one without using the others. This, of course, results in a change in the pattern at this place. In principle, therefore, any desired number of tablets can be turned so as to produce a host of patterns (e.g. letters).
Double weaves can also be readily produced by taking advantage of the division of warps into pairs when the tablet is turned up and using two wefts (Fig. 138a-b). Although warp twining and reversal (slackening of the warp tension) are characteristic of tablet weaving (Fig. 139a-b), the process also affords possibilities of using other forms of interlacing; for instance, warp rib with the aid of four-hole tablets with two threads, with a quarter turn forwards alternating with a quarter backwards.
In this way the warp tension is slackened and there is no reversal in the pattern (Fig. 140). Diagonal plain weaves and twills are made possible by arrangement of the warp threads and their distribution on the tablet.

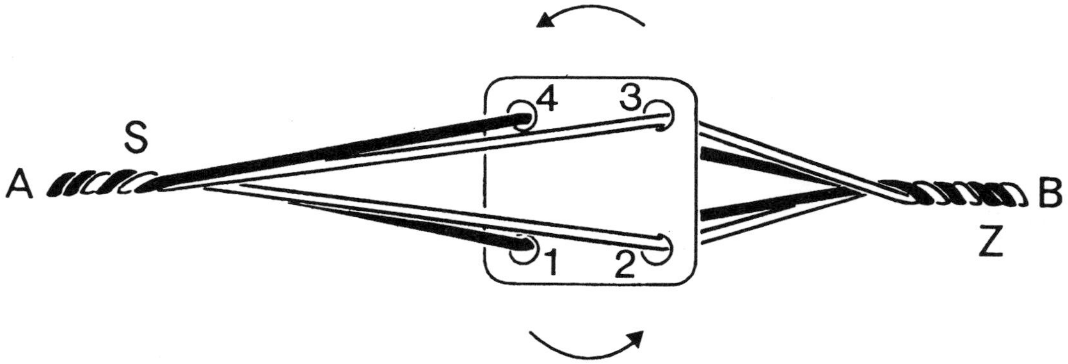

Fig. 136a: Tablet weaving: twining of warp threads according to direction of rotation about longitudinal axis

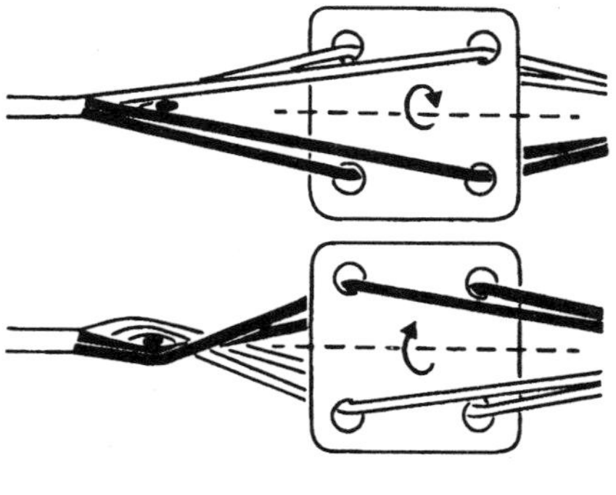

Fig. 136b: Tablet weaving: with rotation about transverse axis

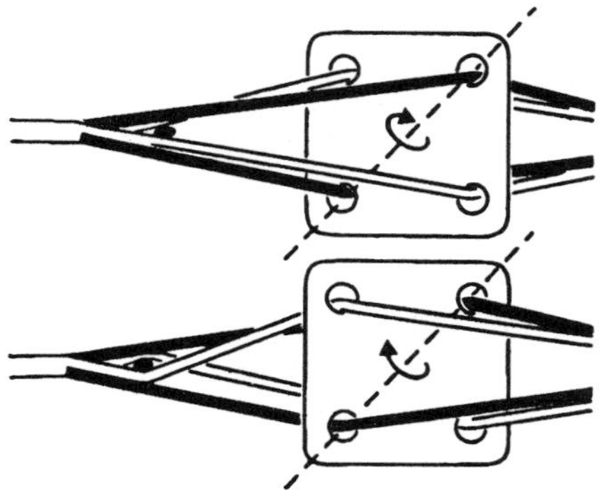

Fig. 136c: Tablet weaving: with rotation about diagonal axis

Fig. 137: Tablet weaving with four 4-holed cards

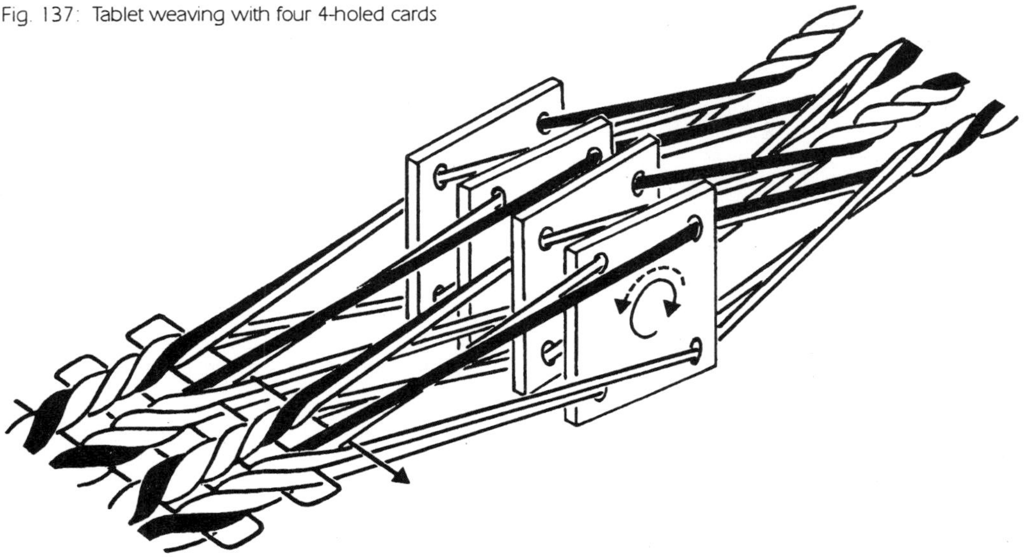

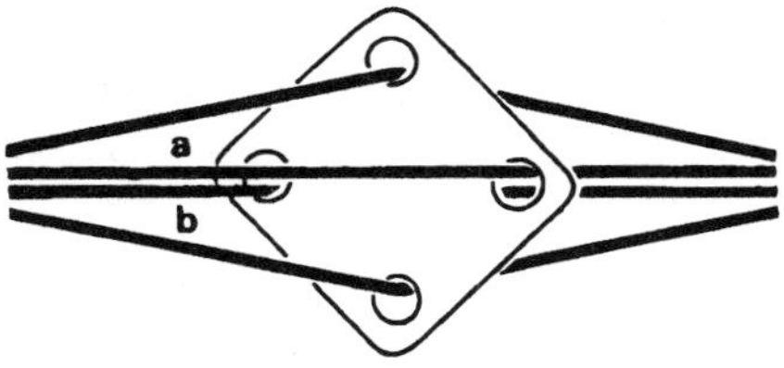

Fig. 138a: Making a quarter turn to produce a double weave (a= upper shed, b= lower shed)

Fig. 138b: Cross section showing double wefts

Fig. 139a: Typical structure of tablet weaving: with inversion of twist direction

Fig. 139b: Structure in finished tablet-woven fabric

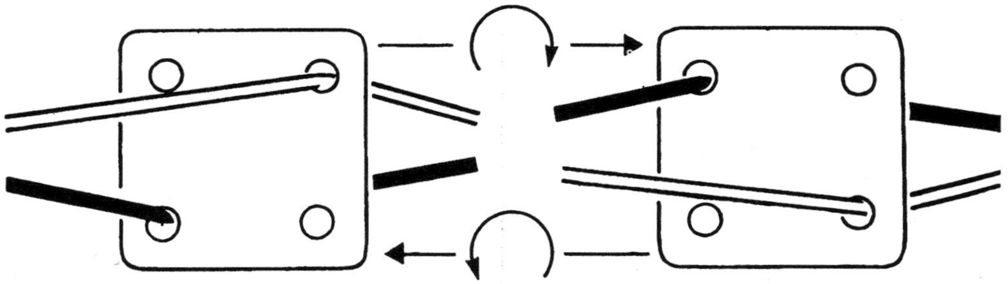

Fig. 140: Tablet manipulation to produce warp rib interlacing

Other terms used:
Card weaving (Burnham 1964:139)
Weaving on tablet (CIETA 1970:7)
Brettchenweben (Seiler-Baldinger 1991:82)
Plättchenweben (Zechlin 1966:132ff.)
Tissage aux cartons ou aux planchettes (Van Gennep 1912:3)
Tissage aux plaques (Hald 1933)
Telar de placas (Alfaro Giner 1984:85)
Brikvaevning (Hald 1950: Fig.81)
Brickvävning, tessitura a cartoni, tecido per cartões, tejido de cartones (Burnham 1980:139)
Kaartweven (Bolland 1970:160)

Weaving with a "Passive" Warp

Woven fabrics with a "passive" warp are characterised by genuine interlacings, i.e. by crossings of warp and weft threads as already encountered in the field of plaiting and warp fabric production. (The only exceptions are gauze weaves, see pp. 99-101.) The adjective "passive" is to be taken in its most general connotation and to be related to the "active" twisting in the preceding processes. In these techniques the warp is passive in that it is "only" raised and lowered.

Weaving with a Rigid Heddle

The shed is formed with the aid of one single device, the rigid heddle. As a rule this consists of a wooden board with a specific number of slits alternating with holes. Through the slits are passed the warp threads forming the group needed for shedding whereas those of the other group pass through the holes. Both ends of the warp can be fixed whereas the frame hangs loose. When the frame is raised, the threads passing through the holes are also lifted whereas those in the slits remain below. In this way the weft for the first shed is created. If the frame is then lowered, all the "hole threads" also move, but this time downwards. The "slit threads", in contrast, are raised, thus producing the second shed for the next weft. It is also possible to work with an immobile frame secured to a board or a bench. In this case the warp thread is held in the hand and alternately raised and lowered for shedding. Weaving with a rigid heddle is only suitable for making narrow fabrics.

Only plain weave structures are possible in weaving with a rigid heddle.

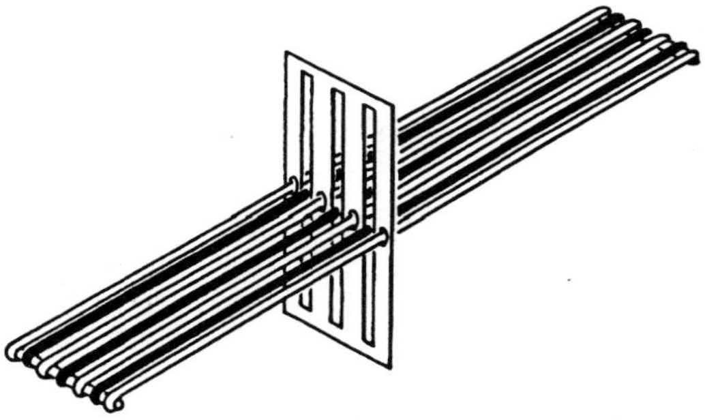

Fig. 141a: Weaving with a rigid heddle: starting position

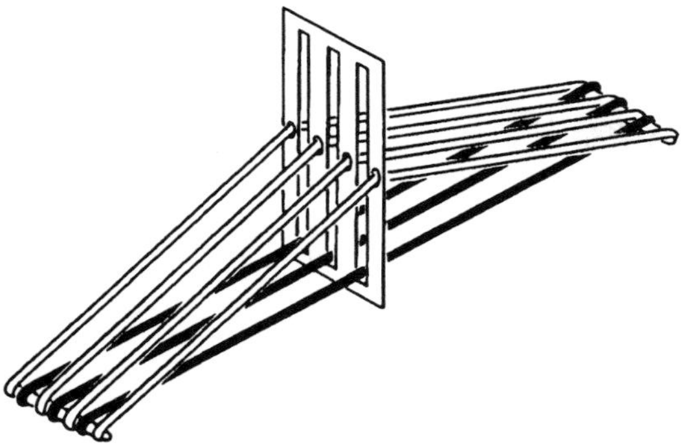

Fig. 141b: Raising the frame: opening the first shed

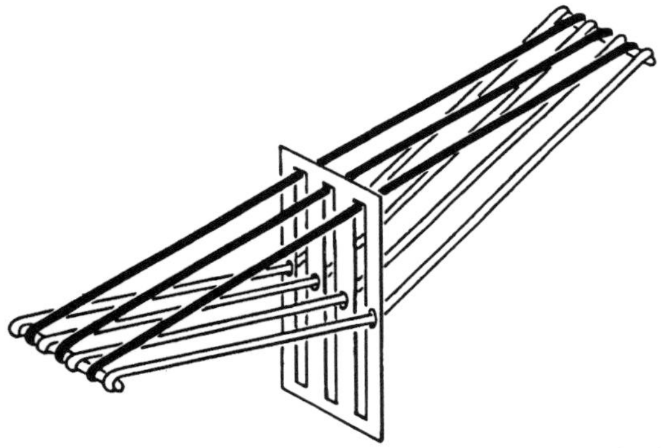

Fig. 141c: Lowering the frame: opening the countershed

Other terms used:

Weaving with a heddle frame (Galinger 1975:158ff.)
Gitterweben (Seiler-Baldinger 1991:85)
Gatterweberei (Nevermann 1938:257ff.)
Kammweberei (Meyer-Heisig 1956:18)
Weben mit dem Kamm (Zechlin 1966:128)
Tissage à la grille, rigid heddle weaving, grata telaio, verja tejedurĺa (CIETA 1970:11)
Telar de rejilla (Alfaro Giner 1984:90)
Tear de grade (Veiga de Oliveira et al. 1978:151)
Lizo rĺgido, bandgrind, bandspjäll (Burnham 1980:112)

Weaving with the Aid of Heddles

In discussing half-weaving with the aid of a shed rod, we referred to the impossibility of using two shed rods for automatic shedding. The rigid heddle affords one means of avoiding this dilemma. Another ingenious method consists in the introduction of heddles. Heddles are loops through which pass the warp threads forming the shed, i.e. the ends of the warp lying under the shed rod are individually threaded through loops which pass through the threads of the upper warp sheet and are fixed to a rod lying transverse to it or to a handle or a loop. With the aid of these heddles or loops and the heddle rod, the warp threads can be crossed a second time, thereby forming the countershed (artificial shed) with a single action, which may be called mechanical or automatic.

When we want to form the second shed, we lift, for instance, all the odd-numbered ends lying below up past all the even-numbered warps and insert the weft. If we release the heddle rod and lower the shed rod that has previously been pushed back, the first (natural) shed is formed again (Fig. 142a-b).

The heddles and the heddle rod must be positioned in front of the shed rod, i.e. between shed rod and working position. The shed rod cannot therefore be used for beating up the new wefts. For this a special flat implement with pointed ends is used (called a sword) which is inserted into the shed and turned on edge to enlarge it for insertion of the weft. The simplest loom of this kind must have the following minimum parts (cf. Fig. 143):

a) Device for fixing the warp: warp beam and breast beam, usually cylindrical timbers, the warp beam generally being fixed to posts, etc. whereas the breast beam lies in front of the weaver. A belt may be attached which can be used to tension or loosen the warp at will;
b) Shed rod;
c) Heddle rod with heddles;
d) Sword;
e) Weft stick for weft insertion with the weft thread wound round it or a shuttle.

All the other components of the simple loom are not strictly necessary for weaving but rather additional features which are used in particular to keep the warp in order (cross sticks).

The following weaving devices, which all function on the basis of heddles for shedding, are incorporated in the loom according to the position of the weft and also the use of secondary implements (especially the comb beater and its subsequent developments). This produces the two main groups of vertical and horizontal looms. The most important variations within these two groups are listed and defined below.

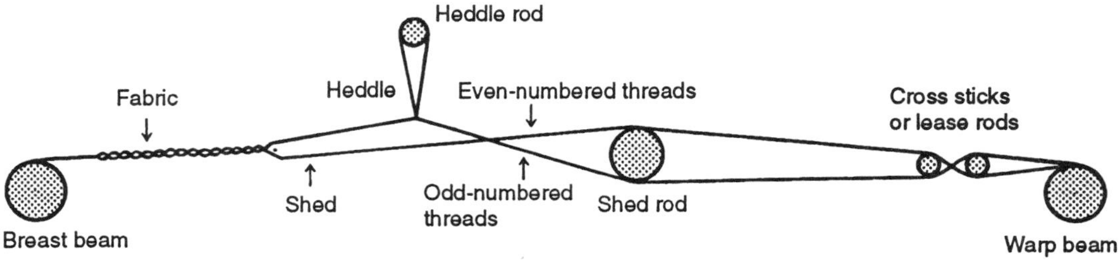

Fig. 142a: Principle of heddle weaving: opening the first shed

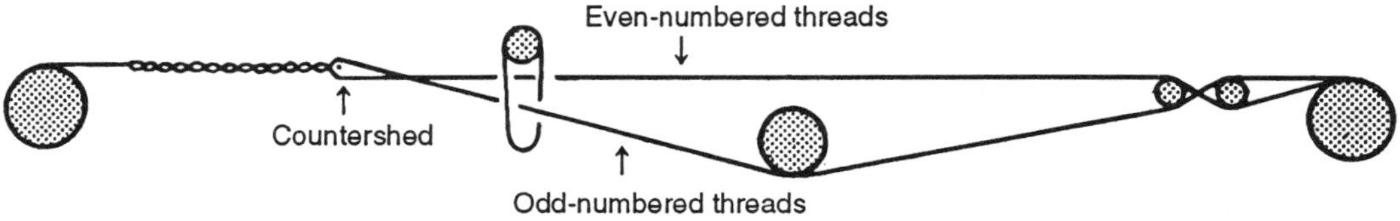

Fig: 142b: Principle of heddle weaving: opening the countershed

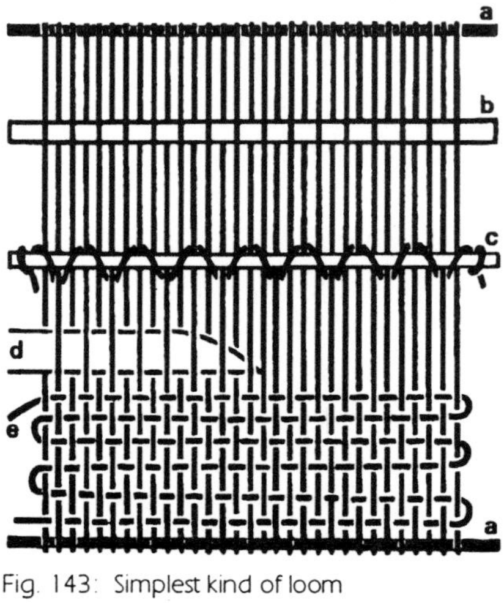

Fig. 143: Simplest kind of loom

Looms

Vertical Looms

In vertical looms the warp is stretched between two beams or tensioned by the fixing of weights to the threads.

1. Warp-weighted Loom

The warp, which is fixed to a transverse beam, is tensioned with stone or clay weights which are usually attached to groups of warp threads or, more rarely, individual warp threads. The warp is always in one plane.

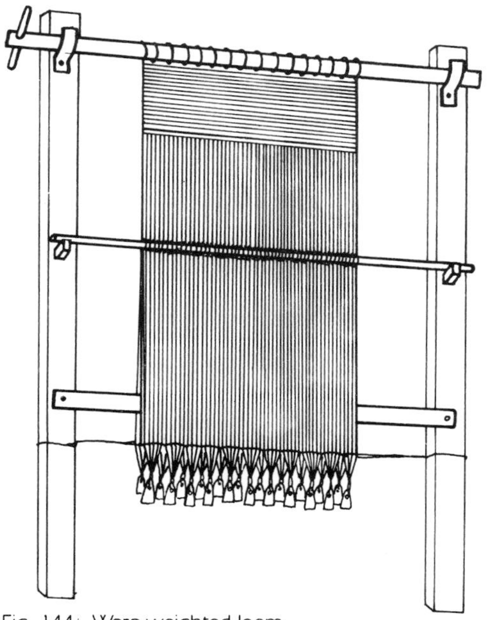

Fig. 144: Warp-weighted loom

Other terms used:

Vertical warp-weighted loom (Hald 1950:205ff.)
Warp-weight loom (Albers 1963:23)
Weight-tensioned loom (Hodges 1965:134ff.)
Gewichtwebgerät (Seiler-Baldinger 1991:88)
Métier à poids (CIETA 1970:20)
Telaio a pesi (Burnham 1980:177)
Telar vertical de pesos (Alfaro Giner 1984:87)
Telar de pesos (Mirambell/Martínez 1986:13)
Tear tensionado a pesos (Ribeiro 1980:14)
Lodret vaegvaevstol (Hald 1950:205ff.)
Oppstadgogn, uppstadgogn (CIETA 1970:20)

2. Two-beam Vertical Loom

In the two-beam vertical loom the warp is stretched between two beams. It can be continuous or single-ended (Fig. 145). This loom is particularly popular for tapestries (see pp. 64-66).

Other terms used:

Vertical loom (Kent Peck 1957:482ff.)
Upright loom (Noss 1966:118ff.)
Vertical frame loom (Collingwood 1968:43ff.)
Gobelinwebgerät (Seiler-Baldinger 1991:88)
Hautelissesstuhl (Von Schorn 1885:77ff.)
Hochwebstuhl (CIETA 1970:24)
Métier vertical (Loir 1935:32)
Métier à haute lisse (CIETA 1970:24)
Telaio verticale (Farno 1968:130)
Telaio ad alti lici (CIETA 1970:24)
Telar vertical (Taullard 1949:71)
Telar de lizos altos (CIETA 1970:24)
Flamskvävstol (CIETA 1970:24)

With continuous warp:
Upright tubular loom (Underhill 1944:45ff.)
Tubular loom with spiral warp (Hald 1950:215)
Vertical loom, tubular warp weave (Kent Peck 1957:482 ff.)
Rundvaev med spiral bende kaede (Hald 1950:215)

Horizontal Looms

Unlike vertical looms, the horizontal type offers more possibilities of variation and development. These are usually heddle looms and their derivatives and are less frequently of the rigid heddle type.

Other terms used:

Horizontal loom (CIETA 1970:16)
Horizontal frame loom (Collingwood 1968:47ff.)
Horizontale Webgeräte (Seiler-Baldinger 1991:88)
Flachwebstuhl (CIETA 1970:16)
Métier horizontal (CIETA 1970:16)
Telaio orizontale (CIETA 1970:16)
Telar horizontal (Barendse/Lobera 1987:12ff.)
Tear horizontal (Ribeiro 1980:28)

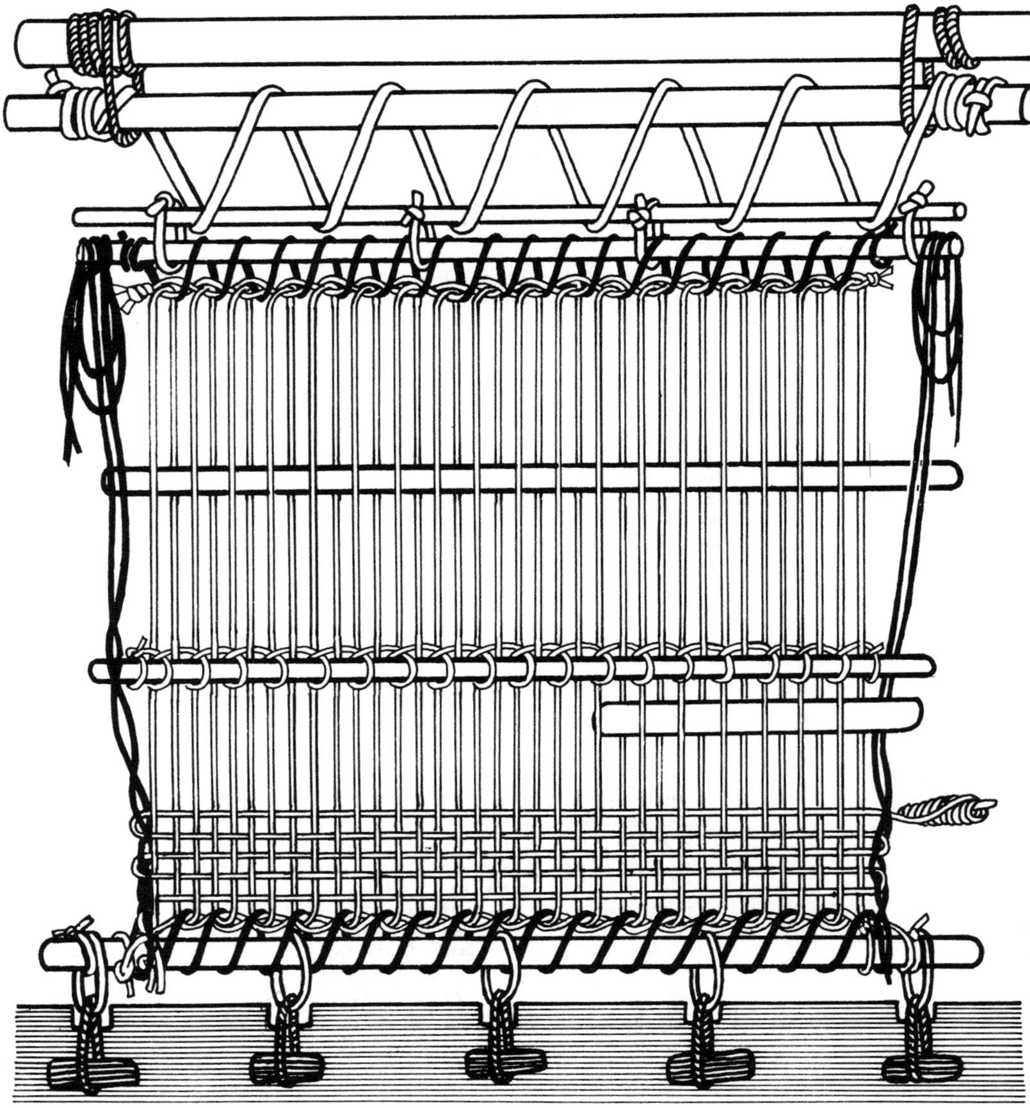

Fig. 145: Two-beam vertical loom

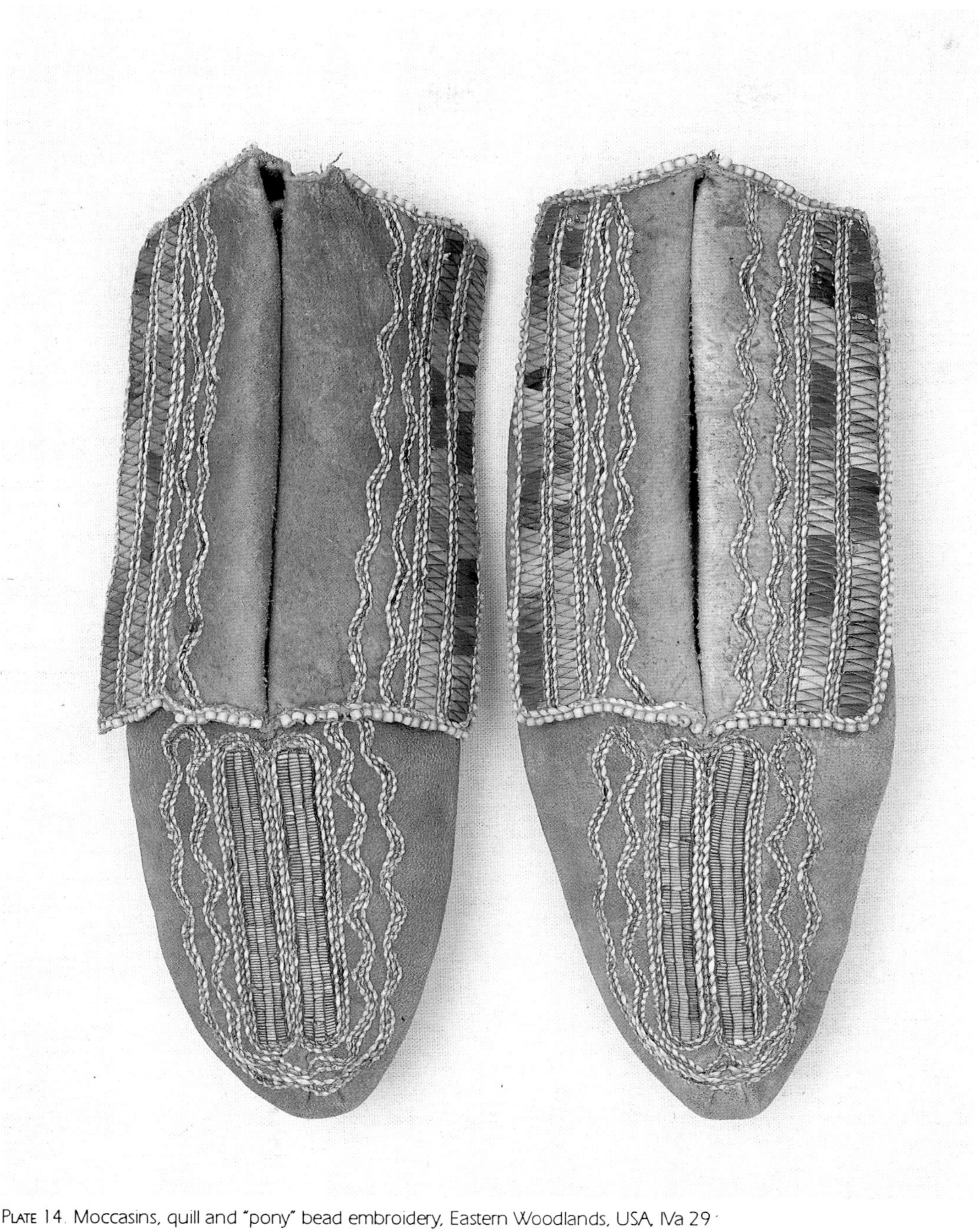

PLATE 14. Moccasins, quill and "pony" bead embroidery, Eastern Woodlands, USA, IVa 29

PLATE 15. Man's shawl, embroidery and appliqué, Sindh, Pakistan, IIa 5488

PLATE 16. Batik loincloth from Cheriben, West Java, IIc 16091

1. Horizontal Ground Loom

The warp beam and breast beam lie on the ground and are fixed with stakes. The warp can be spiral or one plane.

Other terms used:
Staked loom (Schevill 1986:13)
Liegendes horizontales Webgerät (Seiler-Baldinger 1991:90)
Telar horizontal (Chertudi/Nardi 1960:74)

With fixed heddle rod:
Horizontal fixed heddle loom (Ling Roth 1934:40)

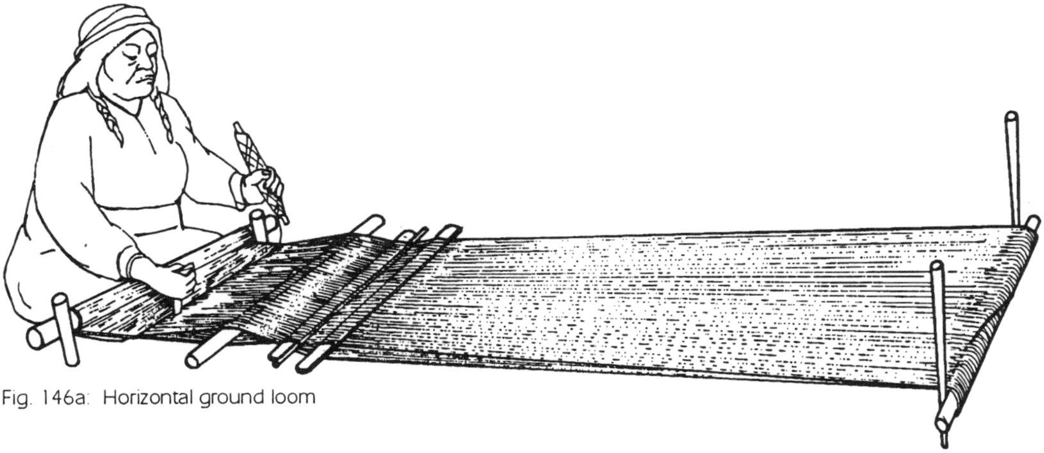

Fig. 146a: Horizontal ground loom

Fig. 146b: Horizontal fixed heddle loom

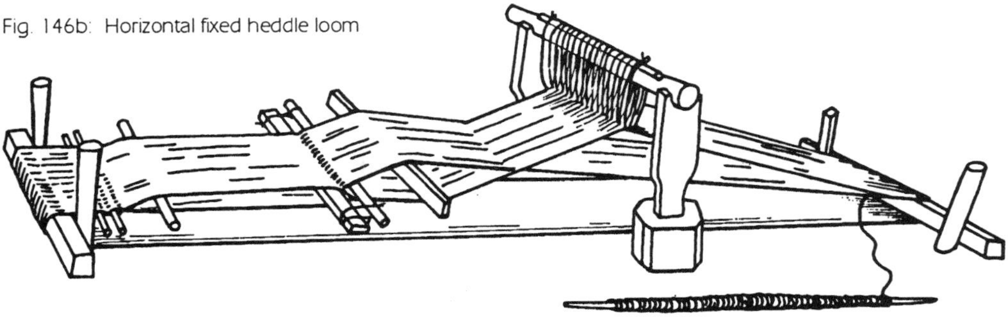

2. Horizontal Backstrap or Body-tensioned Loom

The advantage of this loom is that the tension of the warp can be adjusted at will with the aid of a belt secured to the breast beam. The warp threads can simply be wound round a peg instead of a warp beam. Backstrap looms are found very widely. They are often combined with a rigid heddle or with pattern rods which enable more complicated patterns to be picked up. Needless to say, a number of heddle rods can be fitted to all the looms described, depending on the interlacing and/or patterning required.

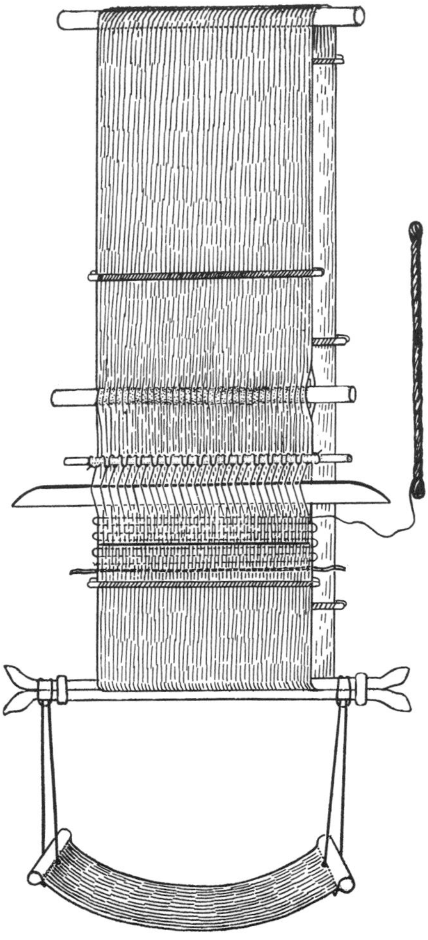

Fig. 147: Backstrap loom

Other terms used:
Waist-loom (Amsden 1932:228ff.)
Backstrap loom, stick(s)-loom (Start 1948:109)
Belt loom (Kent Peck 1957:482ff.)
Hip-strap loom (Osborne de Jongh 1965:50)
Body tensioned loom, métier à ceinture, tear primitivo de cintura, bältesväv (Burnham 1980:10)
Horizontales Webgerät mit Rückengürtel oder Joch (Seiler-Baldinger 1991:90)
Rückenspannungsgerät (Kauffmann 1937:120)
Rückengurtweberei (Jaques 1969:366)
Telar de cintura (Barendse/Lobera 1987:15ff.)
Tear de cintura (Ribeiro 1980:14)
Bältesväv (Geijer/Hoffmann 1974:12)

3. Shaft Looms

In these looms the shedding components take the form of shafts which are called harness. They are actuated by treadles or drawing devices. The comb and sword are often united to form a comb beater and the warp and breast beam equipped for winding and unwinding. Frequently there is a third beam (cloth beam) for taking up the fabric on completion. All parts are incorporated in a fixed framework. Non-continuous warp is virtually the only form used.

Other terms used:
Schaftwebstühle (Seiler-Baldinger 1991:91)
Métier à lisses, métier d'armure (CIETA 1970:47)
Telaio a liccio (CIETA 1970:47)
Telar de lizos (CIETA 1970:47)
Tear de lisos (Burnham 1980:118)
Skaftvävstol (CIETA 1970:47)

3.1. Treadle Looms

The shafts are raised and lowered by foot pedals. If the pedals are in a pit, the loom is called a pit treadle loom (Fig. 148). The warp beam can be omitted from the simple forms of treadle looms. Backstrap types are also known (Fig. 149b), similarly movable heddle frames can also be combined with treadles (Fig. 149a).

Other terms used:
Foot treadle loom (Crawford 1915:62)
Foot-loom (Osborne de Jongh 1965:55)
Foot power loom (Tovey 1965:14ff.)
Trittwebstühle (Seiler-Baldinger 1991:91)
Métier à releveur à pédalier (Montandon 1934)
Telar con pedales (Chertudi/Nardi 1960:57)
Tear de pedais (Ribeiro 1980:19)

Pit loom:
Pit treadle loom (Ling Roth 1934:26)
Grubenwebstuhl (Seiler-Baldinger 1991:91)
Métier à tisser à marches et à fosse (Boser-Sarivaxévanis 1972:222)
Telar de foso (Barendse/Lobera 1987:18)

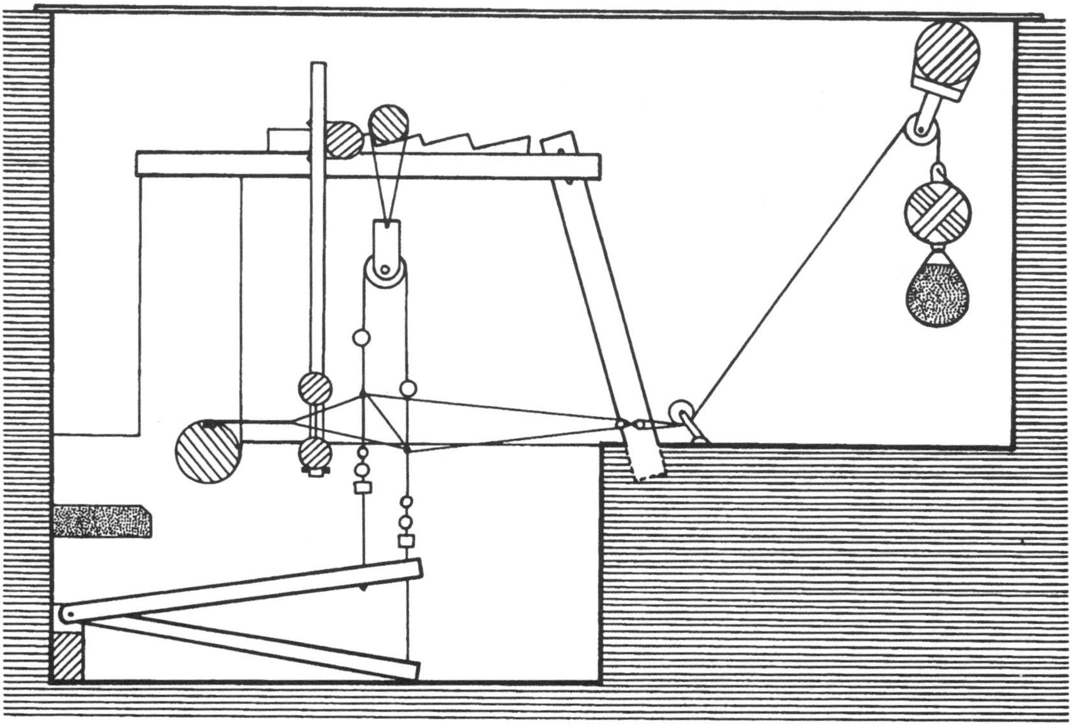

Fig. 148: Pit treadle loom

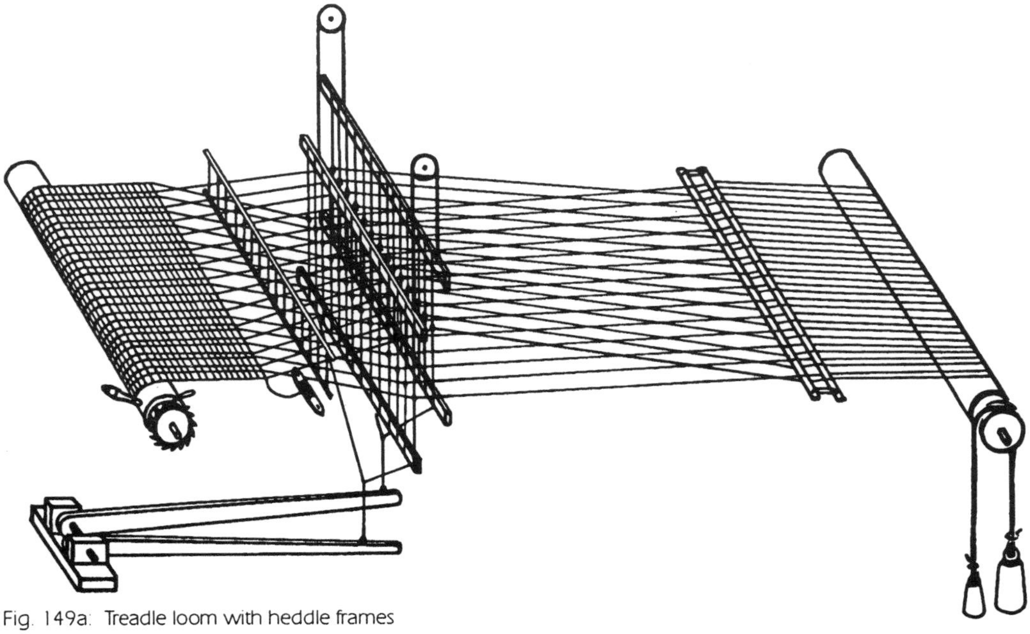

Fig. 149a: Treadle loom with heddle frames

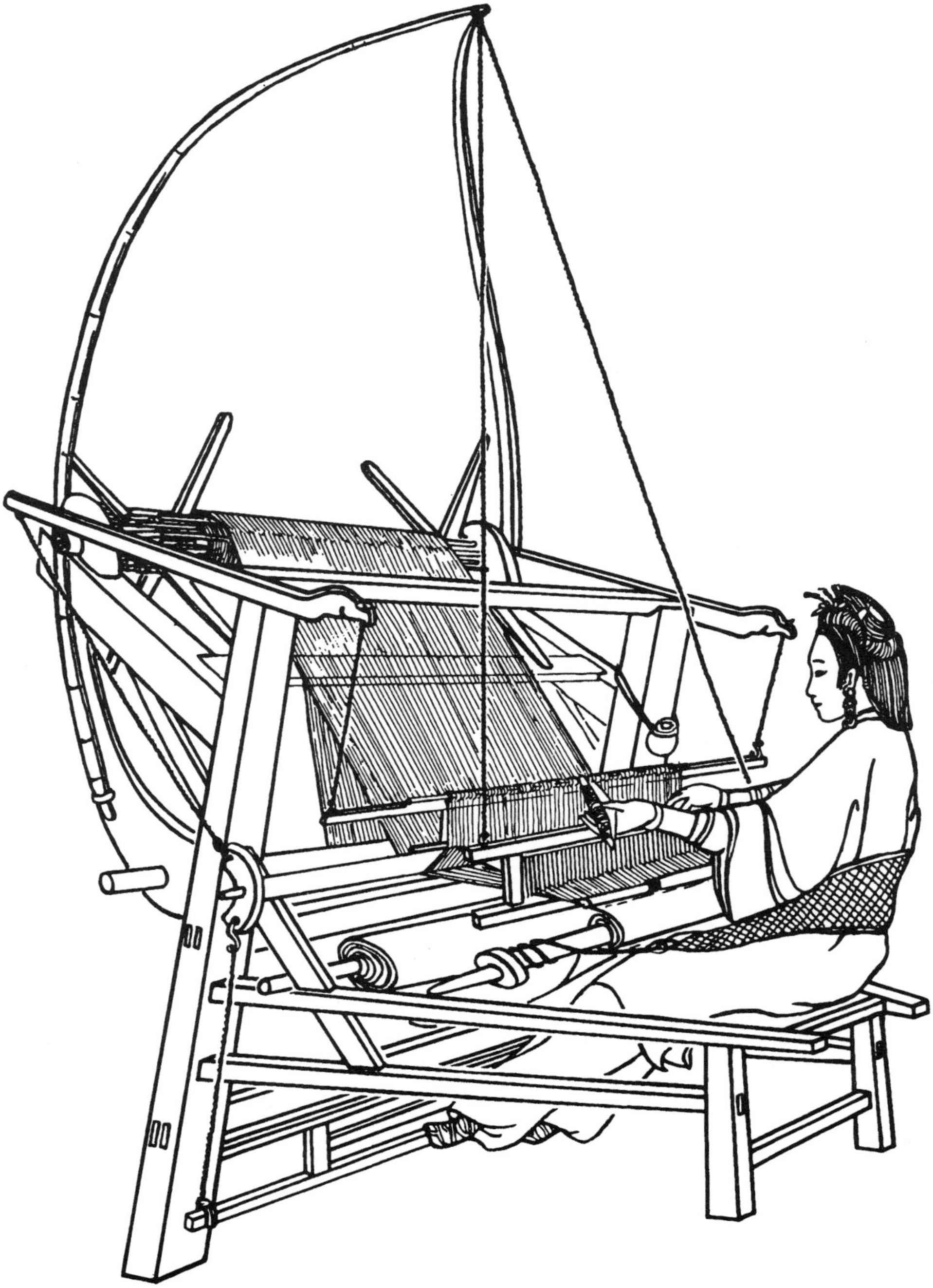

Fig. 149b: Treadle loom with backstrap and "C" arrangement

Fig. 150: Draw loom

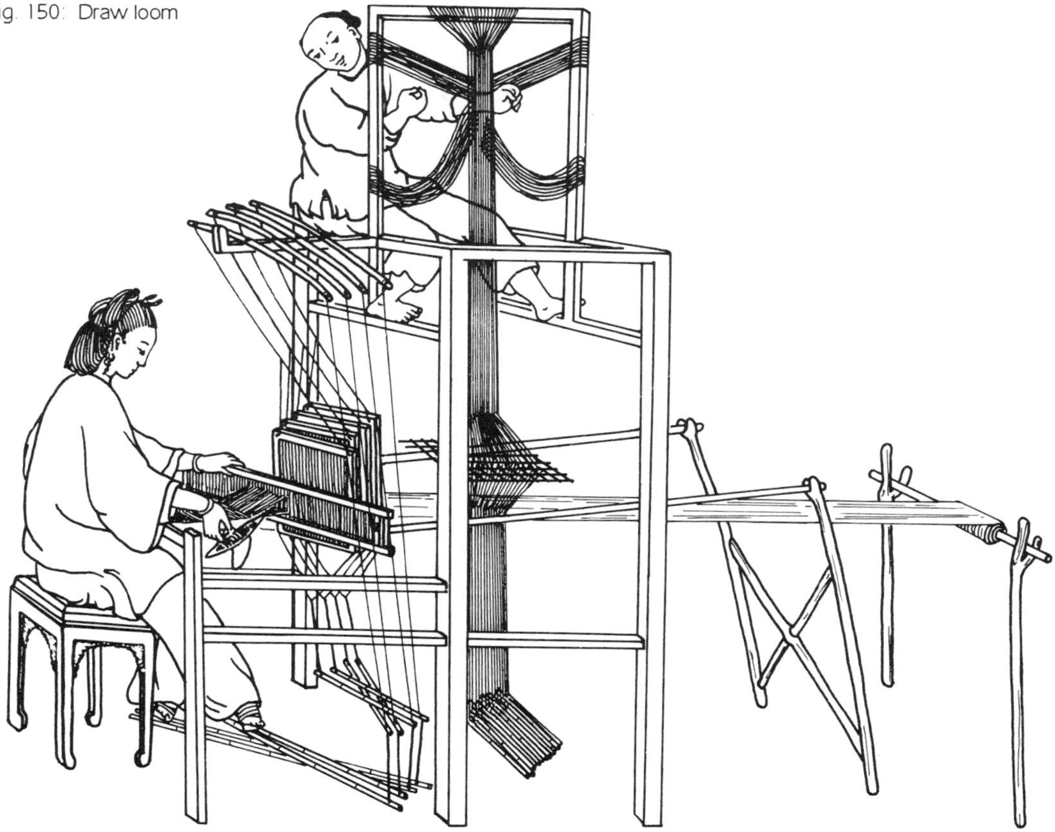

3.2. Draw Looms

Whereas with treadle looms only a limited number of sheds can be formed (although the number is perfectly adequate for basic interlacings), the draw loom allows patterns of any desired complexity to be produced because the heddles bunched together to form cords occupy much less space than shafts actuated by treadles. In the simple loom (Fig. 150) the creation of the desired shed is left to an assistant (drawboy), who has to lift certain groups of appropriately united cords depending on the pattern.

Other terms used:

Zugwebstühle, Zampelstühle (Seiler-Baldinger 1991:94)
Métier à la tire (CIETA 1970:69)
Telaio al tiro (CIETA 1970:69)
Telar de tiro, de lazos (CIETA 1970:69)
Tear de laçadas, tear de cordas (Burnham 1980:48)
Dragvävstol (CIETA 1970:69)

The warp threads of the button draw loom are also lifted by means of individual heddles. These are bunched in draw cords running vertically upwards over pulleys and continue horizontally to a point where they are fixed to the wall. From each of these draw cords a cord runs downwards. Depending on the pattern desired, certain cords are grouped together, passed through a perforated board (button board) and fitted with buttons at the ends (Fig. 151).

Other terms used:

Kegelstühle (Seiler-Baldinger 1991:94)
Métier aux boutons, métier à la petite tire (CIETA 1970:26)
Telaio a bottoni (CIETA 1970:26)
Telaio al piccolo tiro (CIETA 1970:26)
Kägelvävstol (CIETA 1970:26)

Fig. 151: Button draw loom

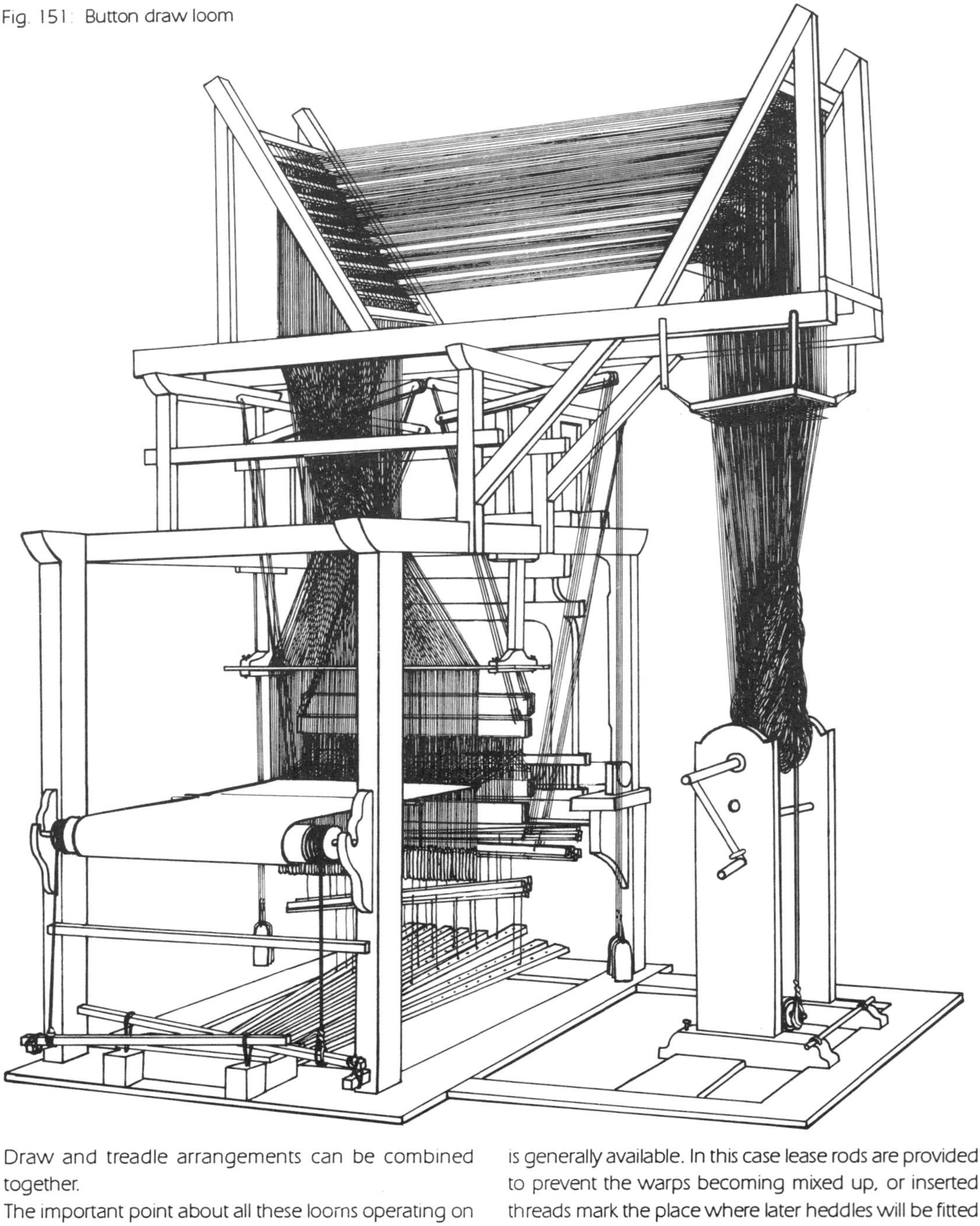

Draw and treadle arrangements can be combined together.

The important point about all these looms operating on the basis of heddles is that it is not the weaving operation as such that is crucial but rather its preparation, i.e. the warping, for which a special device, the warping frame, is generally available. In this case lease rods are provided to prevent the warps becoming mixed up, or inserted threads mark the place where later heddles will be fitted and the lease rod inserted.

Weaving itself then follows automatically.

Weaves or Binding Structures

The way warp and weft interlace is called the binding system. The various forms can be most accurately illustrated as a draw-plan on a point paper, the vertical and horizontal lines representing the warp and weft threads respectively. The points of interlacing between warp and weft threads (e.g. warp threads up, as seen by the viewer) are marked and designated as binding points. The number of intercrossing warp and weft threads required for a complete description of the interlacing pattern is called a repeat or a weave unit. Plain weave, for example, has 2 warps and 2 wefts. It is also described as based on a unit of two ends and two picks because, after the insertion of two weft threads, the binding points are always located in the same places and an identical arrangement of warps and wefts is retained (Fig. 152a-b). Repeat can also be referred to as translation, a term derived from the principles of symmetry (cf. pp. 7-8) as applied to mesh fabrics. Fabric structures are determined by the translation of a point along an axis parallel or perpendicular to the plane in a network pattern.

For a complete description of the characteristics of a weave, the information in the drafts must be supplemented by details of the form and fineness of warp and weft yarns, their number per unit surface (weave density per sq. cm., i.e. thread count) and the form of selvedge.

There is a multitude of different ways of interlacing threads. We distinguish between basic weaves (plain weaves) and their derivatives (float weaves, compound weaves [complementary and supplementary], combined [composite] and gauze weaves).

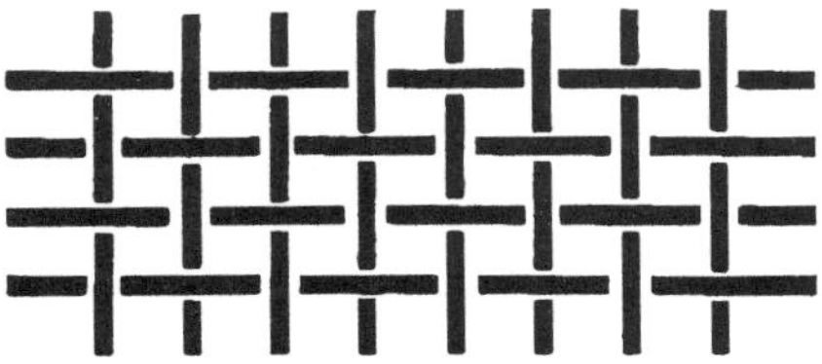

Fig. 152a: Plain weave 1/1

Fig. 152b: Draft of plain weave

Plain Weaves and Derived Float Weaves

Basic weaves can in principle be divided into two types: those in which each warp thread is interlaced with a weft thread, and those in which warp and/or weft threads float or pass over threads before being bound in. This group in turn can be subdivided into weaves with adjacent binding points (twill) and those without (satin). Variants on these basic weaves can be produced by increasing the number of repeats and/or arranging the interlacing points on the lines of the 17 symmetry groups of one-colour, two-dimensional patterns. Details of such plain derived weaves follow immediately upon the description of the basic weaves. Fabrics with discontinuous warps and wefts are classified with the warp fabrics on theoretical grounds (see Tapestry pp. 63-66, Plain weave with discontinuous warp and/or weft (p. 66).

1. Plain Weaves

Plain weave is the simplest form of interlacing warp and weft. It is based on a unit of two ends and two picks, its repeat extending over two warp and two weft threads (Fig. 152), i.e. its warp and weft are combined in such a way (1/1) that both warp and weft threads are equally spaced. Both sides of the fabric are identical in structure.

Other terms used:

Plain or tabby single warp and weft (Start 1948:23)
Balanced plain weave (Emery 1966:78)
Tabby or plain weave, taffeta weave, cloth weave (Hodges 1965: 140)
Leinwandbindung (Seiler-Baldinger 1991:96)
Taft-, Tuch-, Kattunbindung (Bühler-Oppenheim 1948:180)
Armure toile (Leroi-Gourhan 1943:294)
Taffetas, toile (CIETA 1970:34)
Taffeta, tela (CIETA 1970:34)

Taffetas, plana, tela (CIETA 1970:34)
Entramado liso (Alfaro Giner 1984:103)
Tejido liso (Cardale-Schrimpff 1977/78:269)
Tuskaftbindning, lärftsbindning (CIETA 1970:34)
Laerred (Bender-Jørgensen 1986:14)
Taskaftsbindning, lerretsbindning (Geijer/Hoffmann 1974:88)

Plain weaves with large distances between individual ends and picks are known as Stramin in German.

1.1. Extended Plain Weaves (plain weave with paired warps and wefts)

Basket weaves, as they are also called, are obtained by combining two or more threads of warp, weft or both in a plain weave; thus the crossing is between systems of threads instead of individual threads. If the group contains the same number of threads in warp and weft, the weave is called natté in French (Fig. 153). Extended plain weaves can also be done with thread groups of varying thickness (mixed basket weaves), yielding numerous opportunities for patterning (Fig. 154a-b).

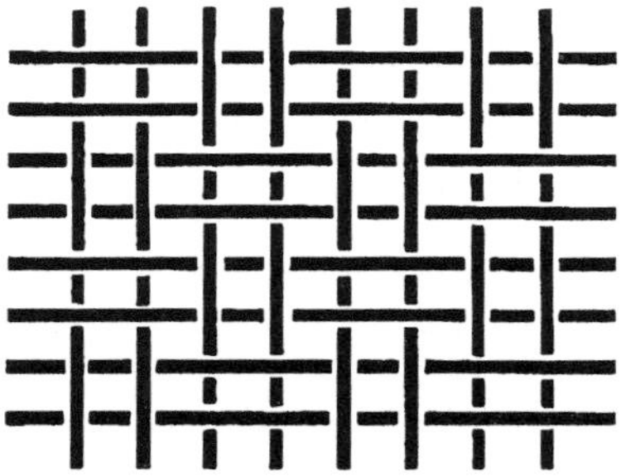

Fig. 153: Plain weave with paired warps and wefts 2/2

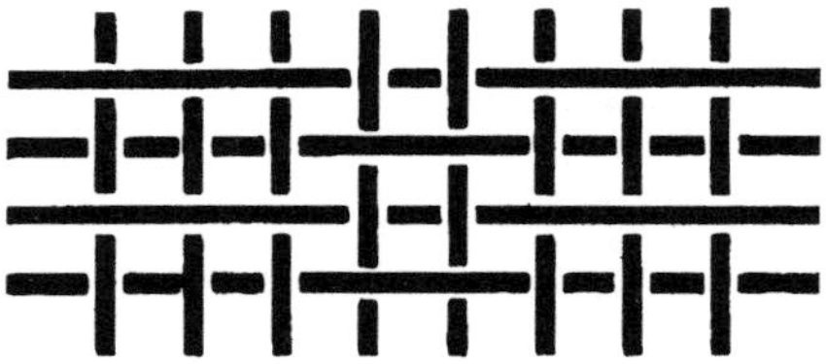

Fig. 154a: Basket weave 3/2

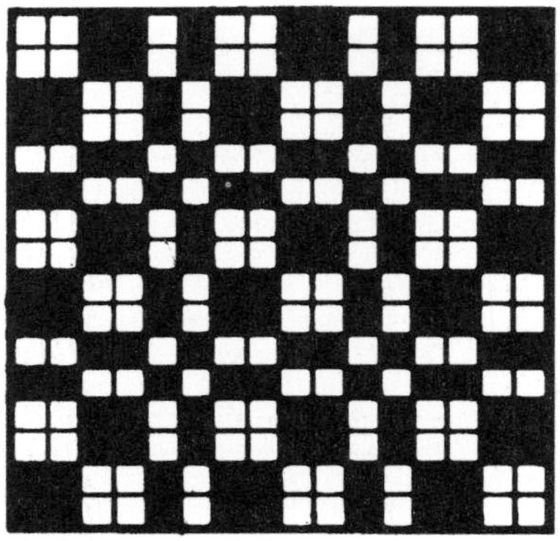

Fig. 154b: Mixed basket weave 2/2/1/1

Other terms used:

Extended tabby, Panamabindungen (Burnham 1980:53)
Würfelbindungen (Seiler-Baldinger 1991:97)

1/2:
Plain weave with paired warps (wefts) (Emery 1966:77)
Half-basket weave (Kent Peck 1957:490ff.)
Louisine cannelé (Burnham 1980:53)

2/2:
Plain twin weave, twin or paired warp and weft (Start 1948:23)
Canvas weave, basket weave, ordinary hopsack or matt weave (Hodges 1965:140)
Plain weave with paired warps and wefts (Emery 1966:77)
Panama (Bender J/orgensen 1986:14)
Natté (Burnham 1980:53)

3/3:
Panama weave (Hodges 1965:140)
Plain weave with tripled warps and wefts (3/3 basket or 3/3 matt weave) (Emery 1966:77)
Ligamento de esterilla (Mirambell/Martínez 1986: Fig. 15)

1.2. Weft- or Warp-faced Plain (rib) Weaves

Rib weave is an important special form of plain weave. The method of interlacing and repeat are the same as in the plain weave; the warp and weft threads may also be combined in groups. But the main feature of rib weave is that only one system of threads is visible in the fabric. As such we have warp-faced fabrics and weft-faced fabrics. Rib weaves display patterns of fine ribs at right angles to the direction of the visible threads.

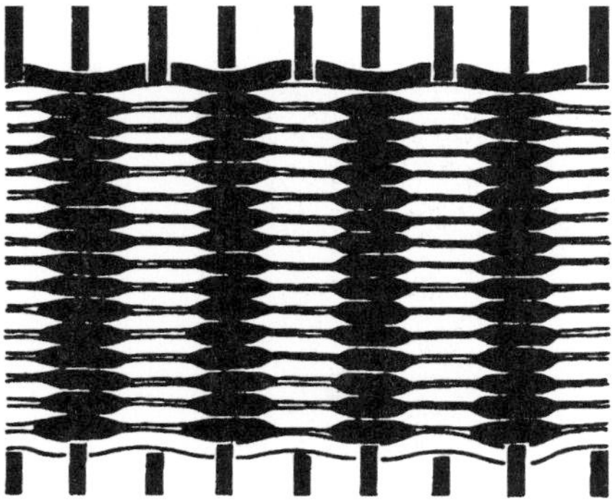

Fig. 155: Weft-faced rib weave

Other terms used:
Repp or poplin (Start 1948:23)
Plain weave rep (D'Harcourt 1962:19f.)
Rep, repp or ribbed tabby weave (Hodges 1965:143ff.)
Reps (Seiler-Baldinger 1991:97)
Côtelé, tessuto a coste, gorgorão, canutillo, ripsartaed (Burnham 1980:111)

Warp-faced weave:
Plain weave warp-face (Kent Peck 1957:535)
Warp-faced tabby with weftwise rib (Burnham 1980:111)
Kettenreps (Seiler-Baldinger 1991:98)

Weft-faced weave:
Weft-faced tabby with warpwise rib (Burnham 1980:111)
Schussreps (Seiler-Baldinger 1991:98)
Tejido simple de cara de urdimbre (Weitlaner-Johnson 1977:61)

1.3. Plain Weave Openwork

Openwork effects are mainly special forms of plain weave (although this can be produced in tapestry weaving as well). In the simple cases, the warp is arranged in groups separated from one another and interlaced by wefts. In the most complicated variations, the warp may be displaced; a continuous weft yarn is used for weaving and for wrapping. The resulting fabric is a combination of weaving and weft wrapping.

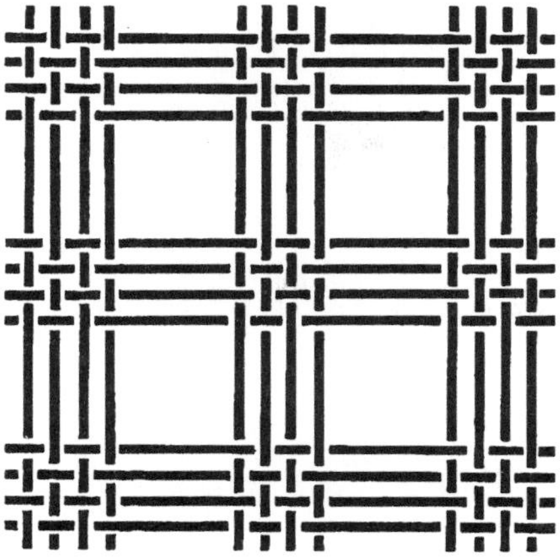

Fig. 156: Plain weave openwork

Other terms used:
Mock leno (Burnham 1980:90)
Jour-Gewebe (Seiler-Baldinger 1991:98)
Scheindrehergewebe, fausse gaze, tessuto a imitazione di gaza, imitacão de gaze, semi-gasa, myggtjäll (Burnham 1980:90)

2. Float Weaves

Float weaves are obtained when, for example, warps and wefts are skipped at certain points for decorative purposes. Both warp and weft threads may float. Depending on arrangement, the interlacings are of a compound (complementary) or combined nature (see pp. 94-100).

If floating threads are arranged in a diagonal pattern over the whole fabric, the result is a twill weave.

2.1. Twill Weaves

The main feature of the twill weave is a looser binding of the two yarn systems. Each weft thread passes over/under at least two warp threads and only under/over one warp thread (three-end twill, Fig. 157). Moreover, the points of interlacing in each successive pick are shifted to the right or left by one warp thread. In other forms of twill the weft passes over/under at least two warp threads regularly, but there is again a lateral displacement of the binding point from pick to pick (Fig. 158). The lateral shift in the binding point causes a diagonal rib to appear in the fabric. The smallest possible repeat for a twill weave is 3 ends and 3 picks. It cannot be increased at will for practical reasons. In the case of an uneven twill, the two sides of the fabric differ in appearance and structure.

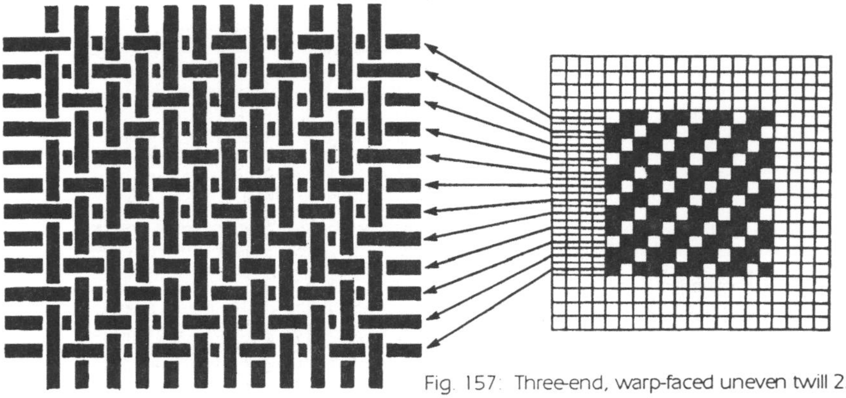

Fig. 157: Three-end, warp-faced uneven twill 2/1 or 1/2

We speak therefore of a warp-faced or weft-faced twill, the diagonal rib being laid in and S- or Z-direction.
Numerous variations of the twill weave can be derived from the basic three-end weave by increasing the number of crossings (by equal or different amounts in the warp and weft direction) and varying the arrangement of the binding points.
We refer, for instance, to a single-diagonal twill if each repeat contains only one diagonal rib (Fig. 157, 159) or to a composite twill if each repeat contains two or more diagonal ribs (Fig. 160). Twill can have identical (even twill, Fig. 158) or differing faces (uneven twill, Fig. 157, 159), according to the ratios of interlacing in warp and weft (i.e. 2/2 even, 1/2 uneven). These in turn can be one- or two-sided.(Fig. 164). If the numerical ratio of the repeat is balanced, we speak of even twills (Fig. 158).
Herringbone twills differ from the variations mentioned so far in that the direction of their diagonal ribs reverses to form an acute angle. This may take place in either the warp or the weft direction (Fig. 161), and the repeat in the two directions may be different (e.g. 4 and 6 ends respectively as in this case) or the same so as to produce lozenges or diamonds (Fig. 162).
Other variants of broken twills result if after a number of warp and weft threads the diagonal rib is interrupted, shifted and simultaneously reversed (Fig. 163).
Notation and theoretical observations:
Twill weaves are described by stating over/under how many warp threads the weft runs, in which connection the addition of the relevant numbers determines the number of ends in the repeat. Fig. 157 accordingly represents a 2/1 warp twill (the reverse side would be a 1/2 weft twill), Fig. 159 a 3/1 warp twill, Fig. 158 a 2/2 even-sided twill. In twills with identical faces the numbers are equal or symmetrically arranged, e.g. ${}^{2}_{1}{}^{1}_{1}{}^{1}_{2}$ (Fig. 164). Twills can readily be recognised by their number combinations.
The repeat must always result in an even number of numbers (but must not be composed only of 1, which gives a plain weave). An even number of complementary numbers in a repeat results in twill weaves, and, furthermore, this applies to all symmetrical number sequences. The number of possible twill weaves in a given repeat partitioned into an even number of summands is accordingly 2^{n-2}.

Fig. 158a: Four-end even twill 2/2

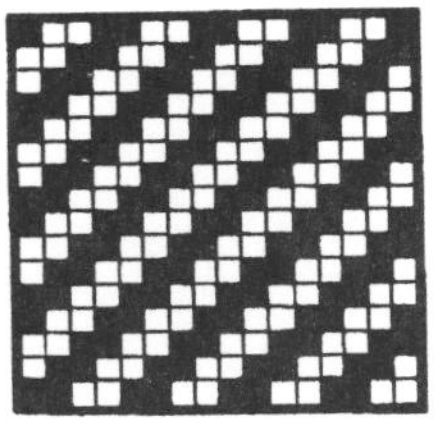

Fig. 158b: Draft of a four-end even twill

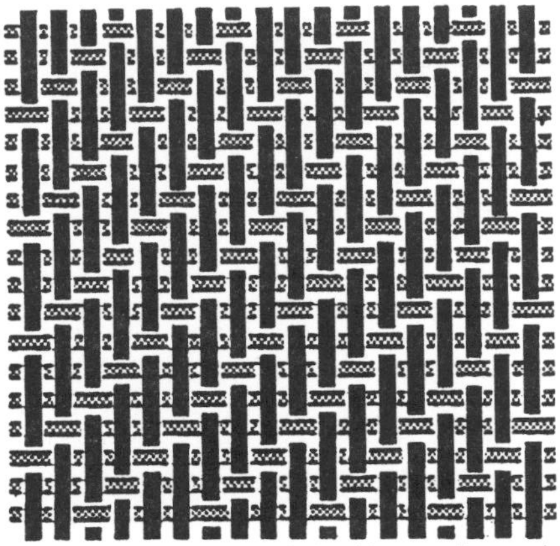

Fig. 159: Four-end twill 3/1 with one diagonal rib

Fig. 160: Six-end composite twill 1/1/1/3 with two diagonal ribs

Fig. 161a: 3/1 weft chevron twill

Fig. 161b: Herringbone twill

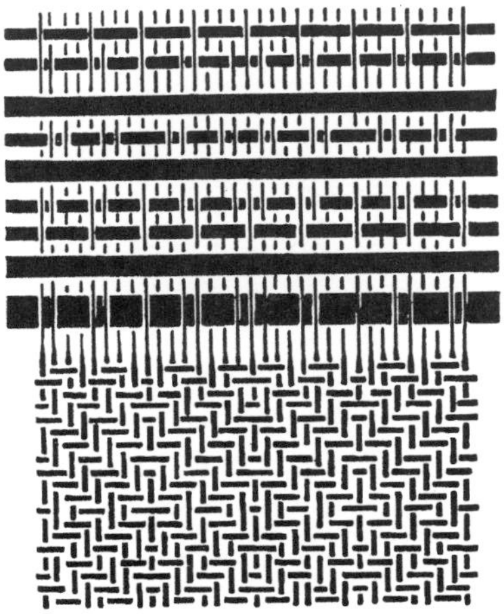

Fig. 162: Diamond twill with heddle and pattern rods

Fig. 163: Draft of a broken twill in the warp and the weft

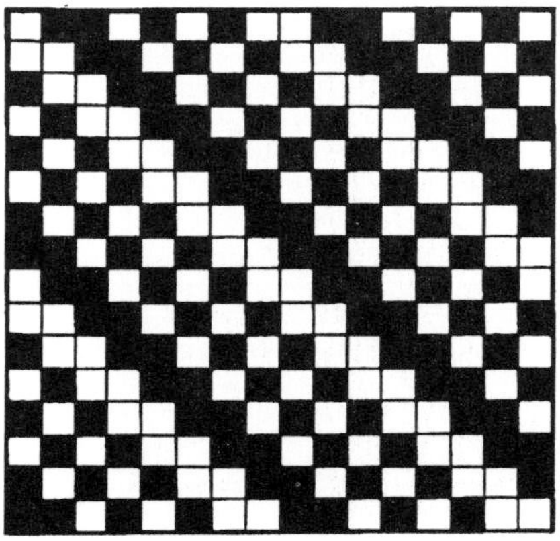

$$\frac{2\ \ 1\ \ 1}{1\ \ 1\ \ 2}$$

Fig. 164: Draft of an even multiple-diagonal rib twill

Other terms used:

Twill:
Twill weaves (Kent Peck 1957:535ff.)
Köperbindungen (Seiler-Baldinger 1991:98)
Armure croisée (Leroi-Gourhan 1943:294)
Sergé (CIETA 1970:29)
Sarga (CIETA 1970:29)
Spina, diagonale (CIETA 1970:29)
Entramado cruzado o en sarga (Alfaro Giner 1984:104)
Kiperbindinger (Hald 1950:145ff.)
Kypert (CIETA 1970:29)

Uneven twill:
1/2 Prunella (Hodges 1965:140ff.)
Zweiseitiger Köper (Seiler-Baldinger 1991:101)

Even twill:
Gleichseitiger Köper (Seiler-Baldinger 1991:101)
Sarga de caras iguales (Barendse/Lobera 1987:53)

Warp- and weft-faced twills:
Ketten- und Schussköper (Seiler-Baldinger 1991:101)
Sarga de urdimbre/trama (Barendse/Lobera 1987:53)

Composite twill:
Mehrgratköper (Seiler-Baldinger 1991:101)
Sergé composé, spina composta, sarja composta, sarga compuesta, graderat kypert (Burnham 1980:29)

Herringbone twill:
Chevron twill (Burnham 1980:155)
Spitzköper (Seiler-Baldinger 1991:101)
Sarga de espiga (Barendse/Lobera 1987:54)

Diamond twill:
Lozenge twill (Burnham 1980:156)
Rautenköper (Seiler-Baldinger 1991:101)

Broken twill:
Gebrochener Köper (Seiler-Baldinger 1991:101)
Sarga cruzada (Barendse/Lobera 1987:54)
Sarga interrumpida (Barendse/Lobera 1987:56)

2.2. Satin Weaves

The binding points in the satin weave are separated even further apart than in the twill weave. Moreover, they are set over two or more ends on successive picks, so that they never "touch" each other. The smallest possible repeat is on 5 ends (Fig. 165a).

Between each crossing point each end passes over or under four or more adjacent picks. The crossing of warp and weft is never at adjacent threads (in contrast to plain and twill weaves). In this case too the repeat cannot be increased at will because this will lead to an excessive reduction in thread interlacing. The binding points are shifted to the left or right from pick to pick by at least two ends. The size of the shift is stated by the so-called interruption or decochement. Similarly, the "move" indicates the number of picks by which a binding point is advanced between adjacent warps. As in the case of twill, a distinction is made between warp and weft satin. With regard to the distribution of the binding points, satins are classified as regular or irregular.

Satins with an even distribution of the binding points, which furthermore are usually covered by the floating threads, have a smooth, glossy surface.

Notation and theoretical observations:

Satins are generally described by their interruption (i) and move (m) numbers. One speaks, for instance, of a five-end satin with an interruption of two and a move of three or vice versa (Fig. 165a). Furthermore, the notation of satin weaves in the warp or weft direction is always 1 under/over repeat number-1, because only one thread at a time is bound. The interruption and move numbers cannot be varied at will, but are subject to certain conditions.

The interruption and move numbers must both be relatively prime to the repeat number. They must be not less than 2 and not more than the repeat number -2. For a given repeat (e.g. R = 9), one thus seeks an interruption (i) between 2 and R-2 which is relatively prime to R. When this has been found (in our case i = 2, 4, 5 or 7) the move (m) has to satisfy the additional condition that im-1 is divisible by the repeat (in our case 5, 7, 2 or 4). Thus i times m-1 must be a multiple of the repeat (in our case m = 4 or 5). Satin weaves with regularly distributed binding points are not possible for every repeat. It is impossible, for instance, to construct a regular 6-end satin since there are no numbers relatively prime to 6 between 2 and 4 and thus adjacent binding points occur between successive repeats (Fig. 166a).
Such adjacent binding points can be avoided by irregularly arranging the binding points (Fig. 166b). This is also possible in repeats that allow a regular weave such as 8-end satin (Fig. 167a-b). In such cases the different move and interruption numbers must be stated. Satin weaves of this type are known as irregular or broken satins (Fig. 167c).

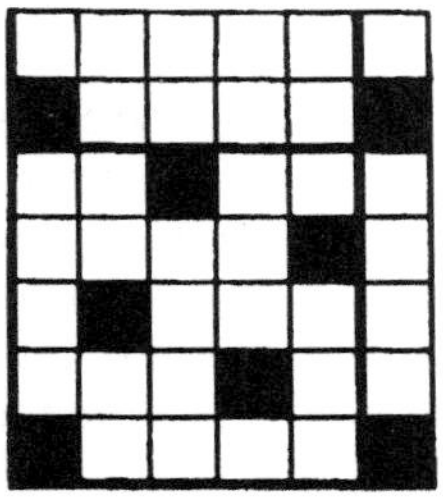

Fig. 165a: 5-end satin weave

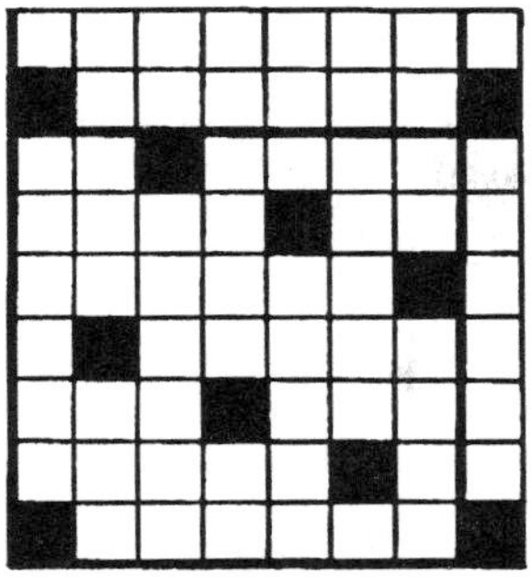

Fig. 165b: 7-end satin weave

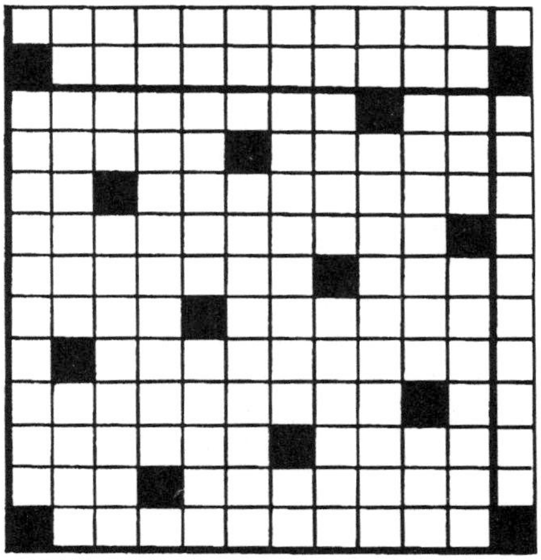

Fig. 165c: 11-end satin weave

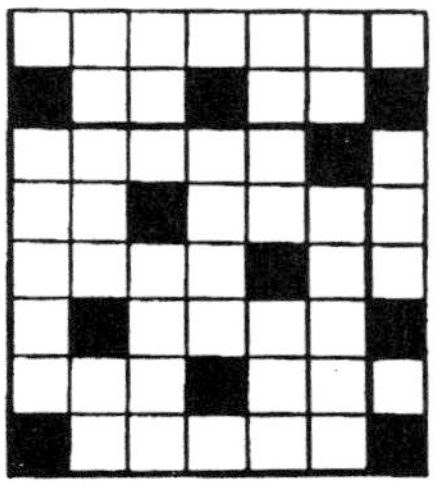

Fig. 166a: 6-end regular satin weave with two adjacent binding points

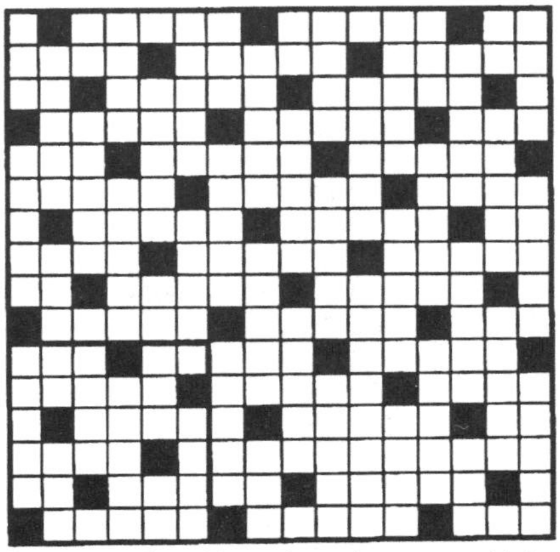

Fig. 166b: 6-end irregular satin weave with irregular interruption and move

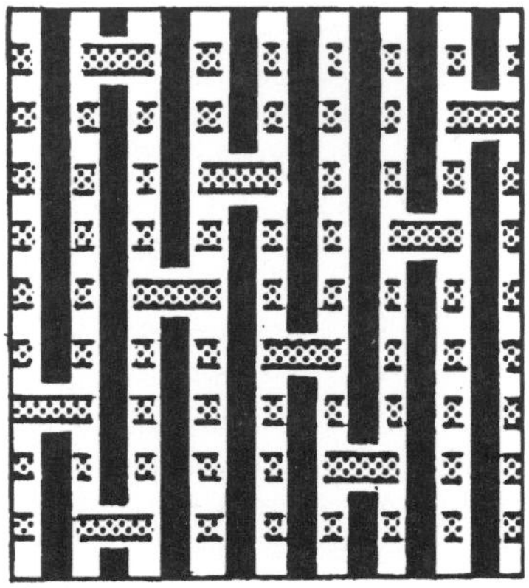

Fig. 167c: 8-end irregular satin weave with variable moves and interruptions

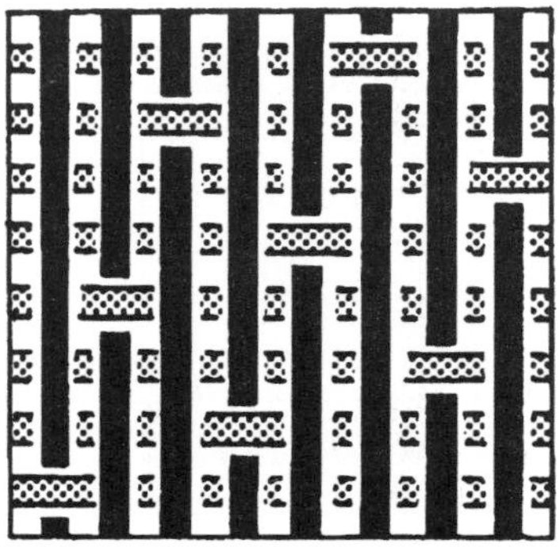

·Fig. 167a: 8-end regular satin weave with move = interruption = 3

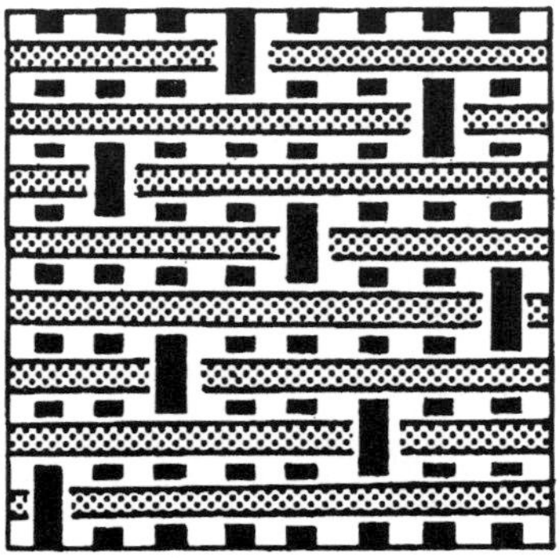

Fig. 167b: Regular satin weave with move = interruption = 5

Other terms used:

Satin (CIETA 1970:2)
Satins (Hodges 1965:141)
Atlas- oder Satinbindungen (Seiler-Baldinger 1991:101)
Raso (CIETA 1970:2)
Raso o satén (Barendse/Lobera 1987:57)
Satin, atlasbindning (CIETA 1970:2)

Regular and irregular satins:
Regelmässiger oder unregelmässiger Atlas (Seiler-Baldinger 1991:103)

Compound Weaves

Compound weaves can be produced in a very wide variety of patterns and can be very complex. In principle they can be divided into those which combine a number of different weave principles and their derivatives within a repeat and within at least one thread system (warp, weft or both), and those which are made up of a basic structure and supplementary yarn systems (in the warp and weft direction). We thus distinguish between complementary and supplementary weaves.

Other terms used:

Zusammengesetzte Bindungen (Seiler-Baldinger 1991:103)
Abgeleitete Bindungen (Bühler 1948:188)
Ligamentos mixtos (Barendse/Lobera 1987:65)

1. Complementary Weaves

All warp and weft threads play a part in the formation of the fabric, i.e. two (or more) groups of warp or weft threads, often in different colours, are used together and in equal parts for the formation of the fabric. Thus in each system the warp and weft systems behave with respect to each other in a complementary fashion. According to the form of weave, the warp may be more prominent on one side of the fabric and the weft more prominent on the other side (complementary weft or warp weave, Fig. 168a). The faces of the fabric are either the same or different, depending upon whether all threads on one side are floated or if the complementary threads include balanced proportions of floats and interlaces on both sides (reciprocal complementary weave, Fig. 168b-c). The relevant structures are plain and twill weaves (Fig. 169), in which differently coloured threads can alternate to form a pattern, i.e. the threads of one colour behave in a complementary and reciprocal manner towards the other.

In this connection it is possible in the weave for the warp threads to alternate with each other 3/1 and 1/3 while the corresponding weft threads alternate 1/1 and 2/2 (Fig. 168a) so that the warp and weft show different alternations, or for the warp and weft to have the same alternation in both systems, e.g. 3/1 and 1/1 (Fig. 168b) or for the warp and weft to have the same reversal, e.g. 3/1 and 1/3 (Fig. 168c).

All groups can be combined with each other in order to form a pattern. The transitions between them, derived twill weaves and the floating of the warp and/or weft to form patterns of basic weaves, are fluid and often make exact technical classification difficult. In order exactly to describe complementary weaves, it is always necessary to state the ratio of warp and weft within a repeat in figures for each thread.

Fig. 168a: Complementary weave: alternating 3/1 and 1/3 in the warp and 1/1 and 2/2 in the weft

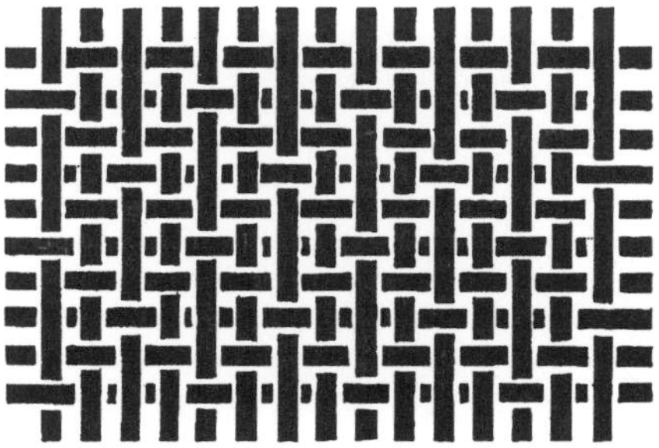

Fig. 168b: Complementary weave: alternating 1/1 and 1/3 in both warp and weft

Fig. 168c: Complementary weave: alternating 3/1 and 1/3 in both warp and weft

Other terms used:

Complementary weft- or warp-faced weaves (Fig. 169):
Double (two)-faced weave with complementary sets of wefts (warps) (Emery 1966:144, 150ff.)
Warp (weft)-faced compound weave (Burnham 1980:177, 180)
Two colour complementary weaves with variable interlacing (Tanavoli 1985:77)
Komplementäre abgeleitete Köper (Seiler-Baldinger 1991:104)
Leinwand-, Köper-, Kett-, (Schuss-), Kompositbindung (Burnham 1980:173,180)

Tejido flotante complementario de urdimbre (Rolandi/Pupareli 1983:5)

Complementary regularly alternating weaves:
Alternating float weave, plain-weave derived (Emery 1966:114ff.)
Complementary double faced floats in alternate alignment (Emery 1966:150)
Complementary-warp (weft) weave with (x)-span float in alternating alignment (Rowe 1977:77ff.)
Reciprocal-warp weave with (x-span) floats aligned in alternate pairs (Rowe 1984:84)
Komplementäre regelmässig alternierende Bindungen (Seiler-Baldinger 1991:104)
Urdimbre complementaria compuesta (Gisbert 1984:27)

2. Supplementary Weaves

In contrast to the methods discussed up to now, these techniques employ supplementary decorative threads in the warp and/or weft which do not essentially form part of the ground weave. The sole purpose of interlacing the decorative threads is to fix decorative floats on the often single-coloured ground fabric. Such patterned fabrics are similar in appearance to embroidery. In many simple methods using supplementary decorative threads the shed for ground fabric is formed mechanically and that for the pattern manually (using needles, lease rods etc.). As a rule the two sides of the fabric differ.

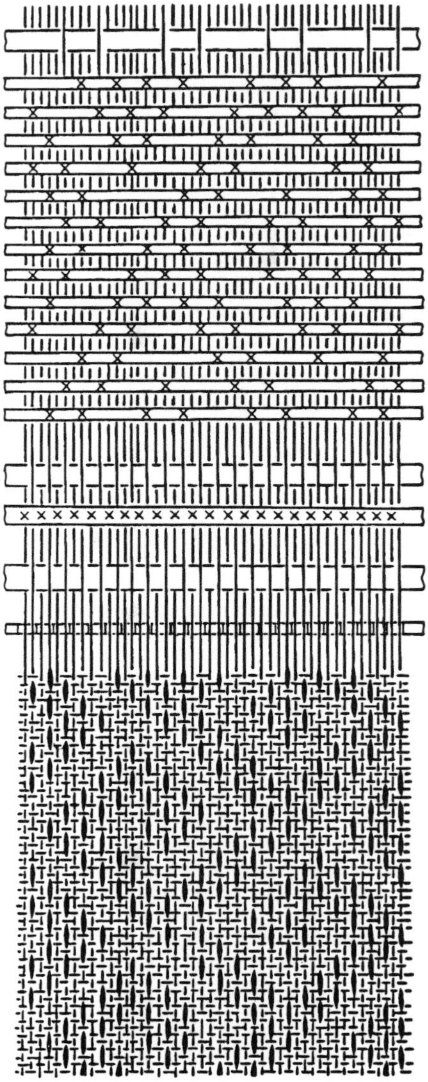

Fig. 169: Complementary derived twill weave: warp alternating 1/1 and 1/1/1/1/3/1/3/1/3 etc., weft 1/1

Other terms used:

Compound weaves with supplementary sets (Emery 1966:140)
Supplementäre Bindungen (Seiler-Baldinger 1991:105)

PLATE 17. Ceremonial loincloth from Mamara, batik and plangi, Galumpang, Celebes, IIc 14946

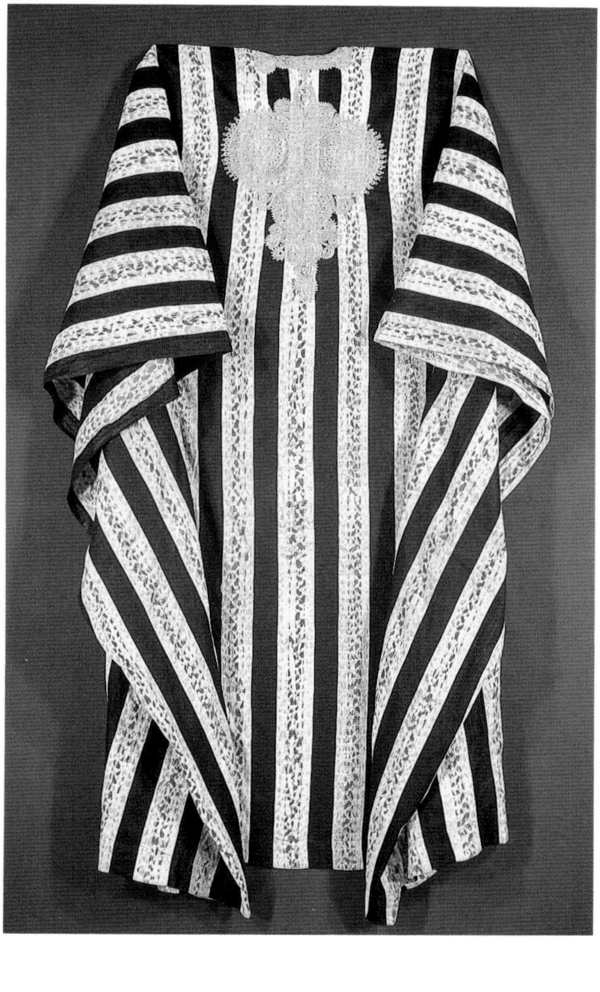

PLATE 18. Wolof man's robe, resist-dyed and embroidered, Gandiol, Senegal, III 20345

PLATE 19. Stencil resist dyed linen from China, IId 6736

2.1. Supplementary Warp Weaves

The fabrics and the corresponding techniques are related to certain complementary warp techniques (Fig. 169), particularly where the pattern or figure warp threads run parallel with those of the ground warp and markedly transitional forms can be ascertained (Fig. 170a-c). Extra warp techniques can be used with a plain, basket or twill ground weave (Fig. 171). The extra warp need not run over the whole warp length, and its direction can also differ from that of the ground warp.

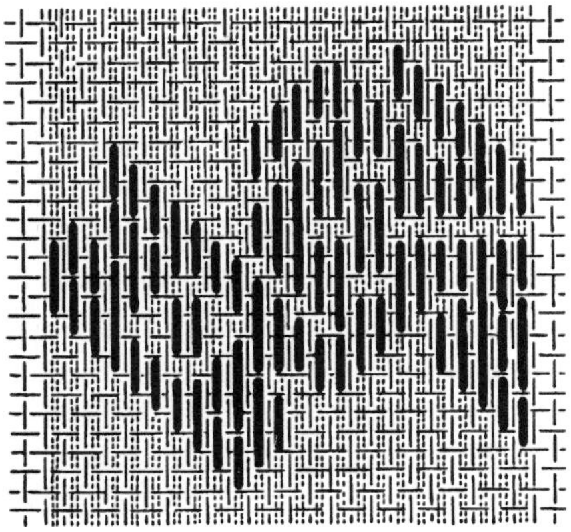

Fig. 170a: Supplementary warp weave on plain weave

Fig. 170b
One supplementary warp

Fig. 170c
Two supplementary warps

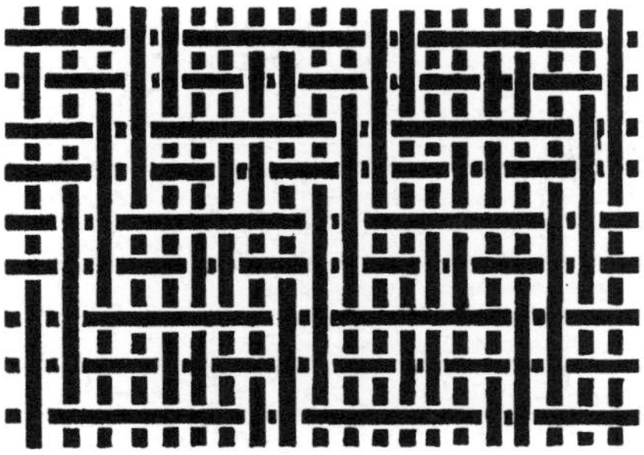

Fig. 171: Supplementary weave in 6/2 twill on 2/2 twill ground weave

Other terms used:

Supplementary decorative warp brocade (D'Harcourt 1962:38ff.)
Extra-warp patterning (Emery 1966:140f.)
Supplementary warp floats (Rowe 1977:34ff.)
Zierkettentechniken (Seiler-Baldinger 1991:105)

Flottierbindung (Burnham 1980:174)
Dibujo de urdimbre adicional (Vreeland/Muelle 1977:10)
Ytvarpsbindningar (Burnham 1980:174)

2.2. Supplementary Weft Weaves

Additional ornamental threads are much more commonly used in the weft than in the warp. The principle is exactly the same as in extra warp. One set of weft threads forms the ground fabric. In between these weft threads the supplementary or figure wefts are introduced which have a purely decorative function and which partially cover the ground threads. Any form of interlacing can be chosen for the figure threads. The figure weft can be parallel or oblique to the ground weft. Further, it may be restricted to certain portions (brocade weave), swivel in the fabric or run from edge to edge (weft-patterned technique). In brocade weaving (Fig. 172) the extra weft extends only across the width of the pattern. Within the pattern the threads usually lie closely together and are cut at the end of the pattern or float at the back till the next pattern. Depending on the method of incorporating the extra threads, brocade fabrics may have the same appearance on both sides or the patterning effect may be confined to one side. In pattern weft weaves (Fig. 173) the figure weft passes from one selvedge of the fabric to the other and usually floats at the back. The figure weft is generally a continuous thread, as is the ground weft.
Extra wefts with a twill weave can be combined with a ground fabric in plain weave just as well as with a twill ground fabric.

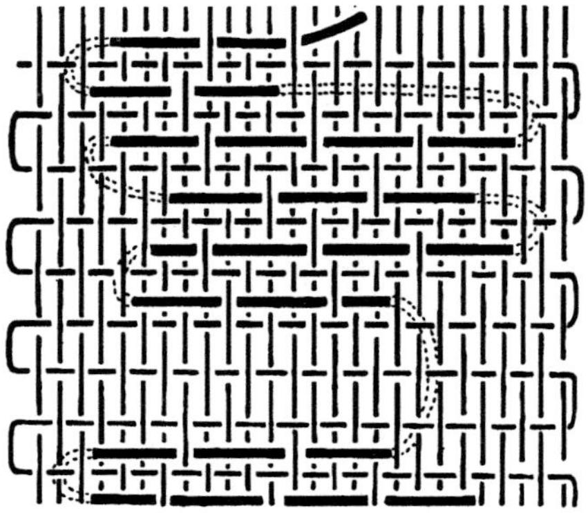

Fig. 172: Brocading

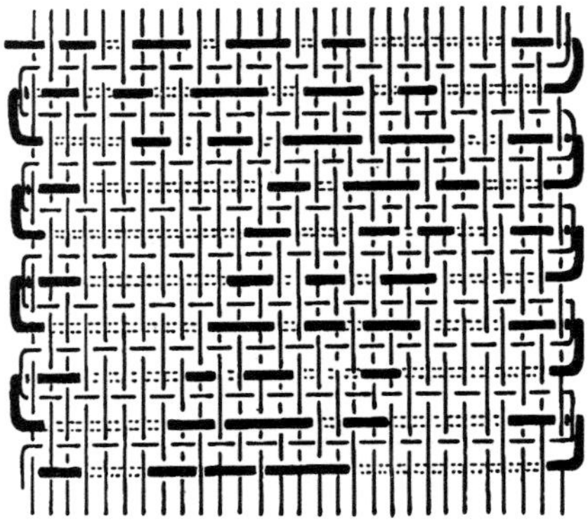

Fig. 173: Weft-patterned weave

Other terms used:

Supplementary decorative weft brocade (D'Harcourt 1962:38ff.)
Extra-weft patterning (Emery 1966:140ff.)
Brocade: weft-float pattern weave (Kent Peck 1957:510ff.)
Ziereintrag- oder Zierschusstechniken (Seiler-Baldinger 1991:106)
Façonnés (Müller/Brendler/Spiess 1958:98)

Brocade weaving:
Double face (or single) pattern motive, onlay brocading, inlay laid in weaving (O'Neale 1945:313, 315)
Extra-weft floats discontinuous (Emery 1966:141ff.)
Brocade, broccare, brocher, spolinado, brochado, broschera (Burnham 1980:14)
Discontinuous supplementary wefts inlaid (Rowe 1977:34)
Broschieren (Seiler-Baldinger 1991:107)
Brokadvävning (Hellervik 1977)

Weft-patterned weaves:
Weft float-patterned two-faced fabric (Emery 1966:154)
Lancieren (Seiler-Baldinger 1991:107)
Weven med een extra inslagdraad (Bolland 1975:19)
Lancé, schussgemustert, lanciato, trama lassada, efecto de perdido por trama, lanserad (Burnham 1980:184)

2.3. Double Weaves (weaves with double or multiple warps and/or wefts)

In this technique the interlacing is as if it were intended to produce two fabrics one over the other by means of four sets of elements, the wefts being interchanged at the edges so that they are transferred from the upper to the lower layer of the fabric and vice versa. Both the warp and the weft can also be interchanged at will (Fig. 174). This results in the formation of common points of interlacing spread over the length and width of the fabric. Double cloths produced in this way have the same patterns on both sides, but with the colours interchanged (Fig. 175a-c).
Double-weave fabrics may be in plain or twill, or may exhibit complementary binding systems. Fabrics with a

triple or multiple warp or weft system can also be woven by the same principle as double weaves.

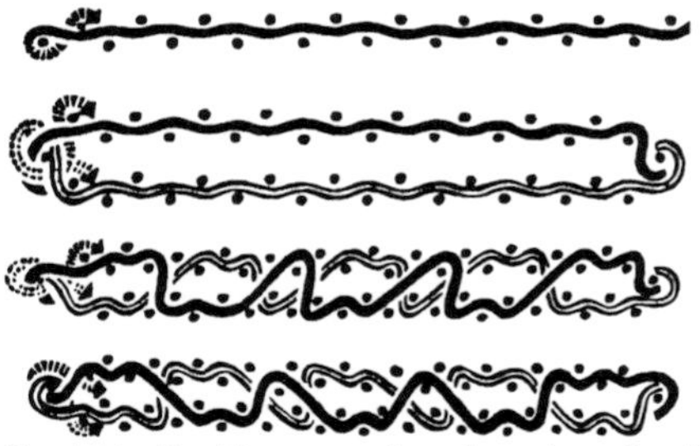

Fig. 174: Double weave, interchanging of wefts

Fig. 175a: Double weave, interchanging of warps

Fig. 175b: Double weave, interchanging of warp and weft, plan view

Fig. 175c: Double weave, interchanging of warp and weft, cross section

Other terms used:
Double cloth, tubular weaving (D'Harcourt 1962:44ff.)
Double-faced weave (CIETA 1970:11)
Doppelgewebe (Seiler-Baldinger 1991:107)
Double étoffe (CIETA 1970:11)
Armatura doppia-faccia (CIETA 1970:11)
Tubico, tecido duplo, doble tela, dubbelväv (Burnham 1980:39)
Ligamento de tela a dos caras (CIETA 1970:11)
Tejidos dobles (Vreeland/Muelle 1977:10)
Dubbelsidiga bindningar (CIETA 1970:11)
Dubbelweefsel (Brommer 1988:79)
Dobbelväv, doppeltvev (Geijer/Hoffmann 1974:18)

Gauze Weaves

Gauze weave differs from all other interlacing methods in weaving in that the warp is activated. Pairs or even larger groups of warp threads are alternately crossed over or twisted around each other, and fixed in this position by the weft thread. In the simplest case, with a pair of warp threads as the basic unit (simple gauze weave,

Fig. 176a-c), one warp thread (the fixed end), passes below the weft; the other warp thread (the doup end) is positioned to the left of the fixed end on one pick and to the right of the fixed end on the following pick. (Fig. 176c). Thus the fixed end and the doup end throughout remain respectively below and above the weft threads. If the weft threads were to be removed, all the warp threads would reassume their original parallel position, without any twist.

Gauze weaves fix the weft better than other weaves. They are hence widely used in open constructions (real gauze) and in fabrics with openwork patterning when the weft threads could otherwise be easily displaced. Mechanical shedding devices can be employed for twisting the warp threads with one another. In this case, however, the heddles are attached to the doup ends running above the shed rod and not to the ends below the shed rod; moreover, the doup ends are not lifted straight but first passed under the adjoining thread on the left or right (Fig. 176a). As a result, a half turn is formed between two warp threads which is removed when the next shed is formed. Heddles can be arranged to twist together groups of two or more warp threads.

More complex forms in which more than two warp threads are alternately twisted cannot be produced automatically on simple weaving devices, so that the relevant processes are akin to weft wrapping.

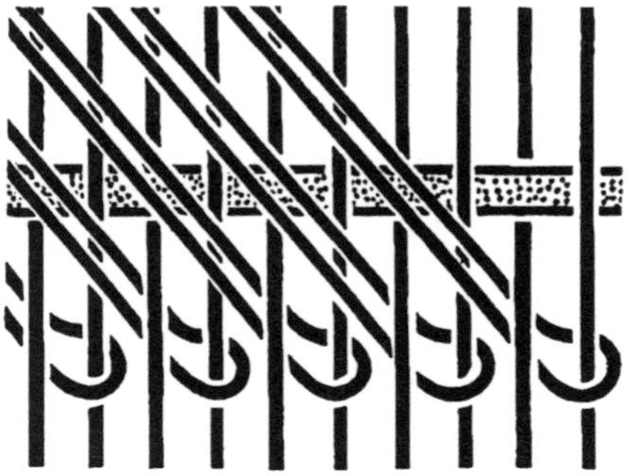

Fig. 176a: Simple gauze weave: position of shed rod and heddles

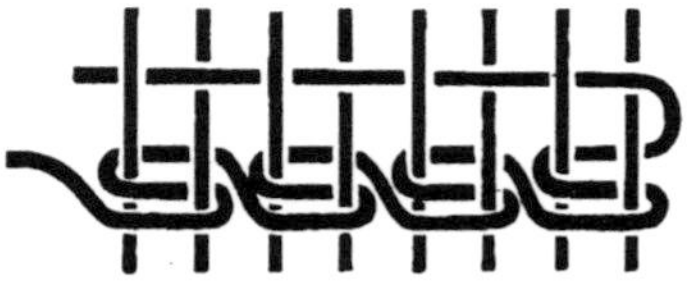

Fig. 176b: Simple gauze weave: weft insertion

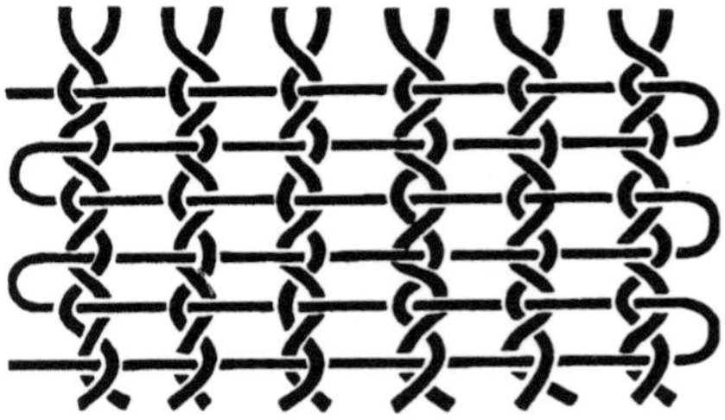

Fig. 176c: Simple gauze weave

Other terms used:

Lace weave (Cordry 1941:121)
Gauze technique (O'Neale 1942:157)Leno, gauze weaving or cross weaving (Frey 1955:4ff.)
Gauze weave techniques(Kent Peck 1957:509ff.)
Gauze or leno weave (Albers 1963: Pl.25)
Gauze or leno (Hodges 1965:141)
Gauze or crossed-warp weaves (Emery 1966:180ff.)
Dreherbindungen (Seiler-Baldinger 1991:108)
Gaze (CIETA 1970:11)
Gaza a giro (CIETA 1970:11)
Twining de urdimbre (Chertudi/Nardi 1961:123)
Gasa de vuelta (Burnham 1980:62)
Gasbindning (CIETA 1970:11)
Gasväv (Hellervik 1977:36)

1. Simple Gauze Weaves

The warp threads are crossed only in pairs along the entire length of the fabric and these pairs do not cross the adjacent threads. The pairs may be twisted through a full instead of only a half turn before the direction is changed again (Fig. 177). The structures obtained are similar to those produced by half-weaving with continuous shed reservation (see p. 70).

Fig. 177: Simple and full-turn gauze

Other terms used:
Simple gauze (O'Neale 1945:74)
Two-yarn gauze (D'Harcourt 1962:50ff.)
Simple gauze weaves, plain gauze weave 1/1 (Emery 1966:181)
Simple and full turn gauze (Rowe 1977:99ff.)
Einfache Dreherbindung (Seiler-Baldinger 1991:109)
Gaze à deux fils (D'Harcourt 1934:54ff.)
Gasa de vuelta completa (Gil 1974:60)
Gasa simple (Mirambell/Martínez 1986: Fig. 25)
Slingbindning, gazebindning, slyngvev (Geijer/Hoffmann 1974: 26)

2. Complex Gauze Weaves

In the simplest cases, here too only two warp threads are twisted together at a time; however, each warp thread is twisted alternately with the neighbouring thread on the left and right. As a result, the threads are always combined in groups of three in the warp direction so as to produce a net-like diamond pattern (Fig. 178a).
Complex variations and mixed forms combine two- and three-thread twisting. Other pattern possibilities include periodic omission of crossings, twisting of thread groups, crossing of non-adjacent threads etc.(Fig. 178b).

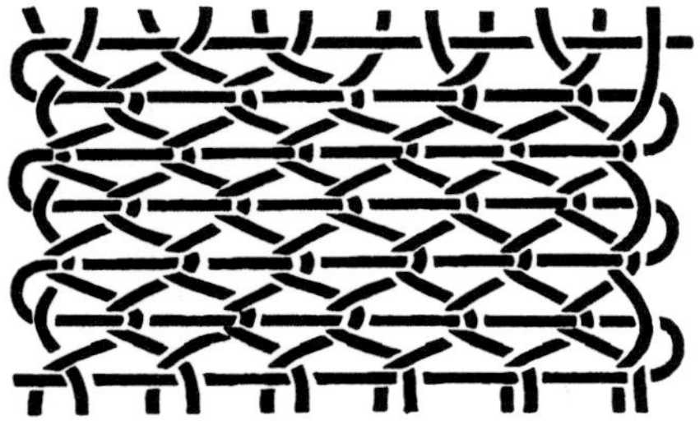

Fig. 178a: Complex gauze weave

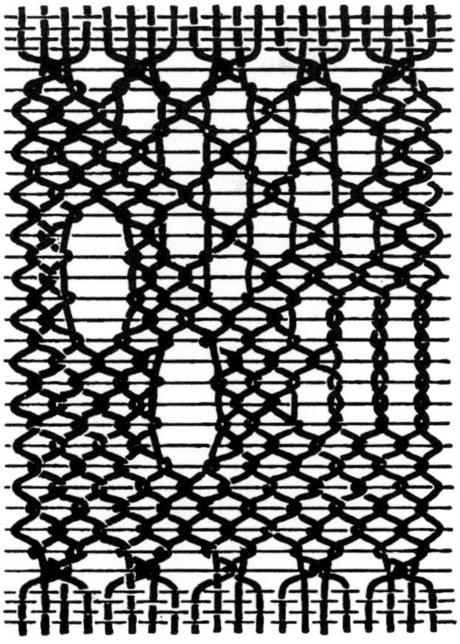

Fig. 178b: Complex gauze weave

Other terms used:
Fancy gauze, Peruvian gauze (O'Neale 1945:74)
Alternating gauze weave, complex gauze weave, complex alternating gauze weave, uneven gauze crosses (Emery 1966: 183ff.)
Komplizierte Dreherbindungen (Seiler-Baldinger 1991:109)
Gazes à trois fils, gazes irrégulières (D'Harcourt 1934:55ff.)
Gasa combinada (Gil 1974:60)

Combined Weaves

Combined weaves offer a wide scope for patterning since any two or more basic and derived weaves can be jointly employed. Weft wrapping and weft twining can also be freely combined with the above-mentioned weaves, such mixtures being very frequently seen (e.g.) in the Near East (Fig. 179a).
In the most complex variants, a dislocation of the warp can be achieved by simultaneously weaving and wrapping with the same continuous weft thread (Fig. 179b).
In order to describe combined weaves, all components and their arrangement in the textile must be stated.

Fig. 179a: Combination of weaving and warp fabric techniques (multiple, diagonal weft wrapping)

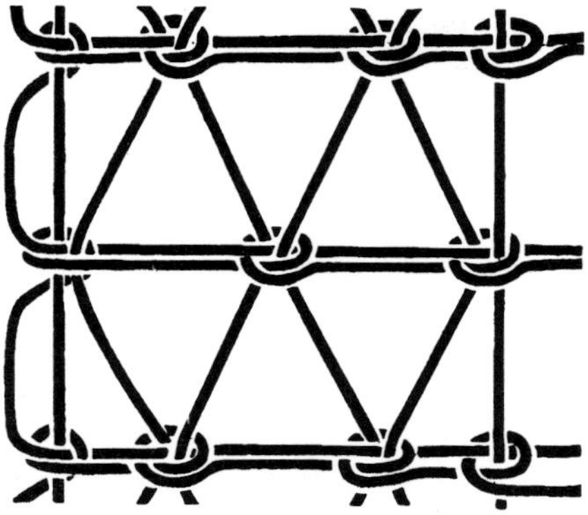

Fig. 179b: Weaving with dislocated warp, combined with looped weft wrapping

Other terms used:

Composite structures (Rowe 1977:109ff.)
Kombinierte Bindungen (Seiler-Baldinger 1991:110)
Zusammengesetzte Bindungen (Hauptmann 1952:29ff.)
Tejido de tramas envolventes (Mirambell/Martínez 1986:17)

References to Weaving: see pp. 163-166.

The Techniques of Fabric Ornamentation

A broad distinction can be made between methods in which the fabric is embellished during and after its manufacture, and the transitional group of border trimmings.

Raphia velvet of the Kuba, Zaïre, III 25487

Ornamentation by Additional Elements During Fabric Production

This group includes methods in which the fabric is embellished during its actual formation but the elements involved in ornamentation do not play a fundamental or essential part in its formation. In typical techniques of this kind, the fabric is embellished with the aid of additional elements during the process of manufacture. On the basis of the nature of these elements (soft, pliable or stiff) and their resultant mode of attachment (binding or stringing) the relevant ornamentation methods can be classified into techniques for the formation of pile fabrics and beadwork techniques.

The classification of techniques into these groups becomes increasingly difficult as the basic fabric-forming technique grows more complex. The transitions between pure fabric formation and ornamentation are very often fluid (e.g. weaving with additional ornamental warp and weft threads) and a clear-cut classification is often impossible.

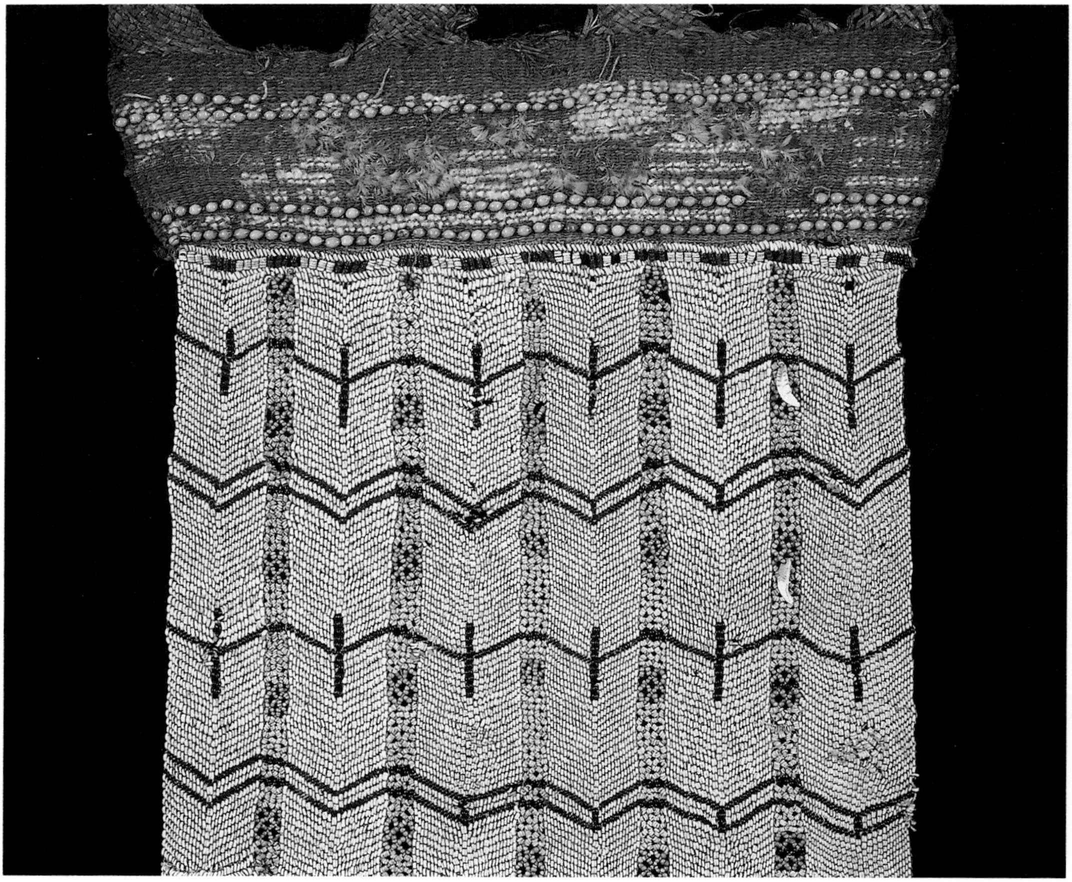

Woman's dancing costume from Pitiliu Island, bead-weave, Admiralty Islands, Melanesia, Vb 9800

Formation of Pile or Tuft Fabrics

In principle, pile or tuft fabrics can be produced on the basis of any fabric-forming technique by the incorporation of pile-forming elements, which can consist of widely differing materials (tufts, threads, feathers etc.). The present discussion is confined to methods in which piles are formed during and not before (e.g. by twisting or plying piles into a thread) or after the manufacture of the fabric (e.g. by additional knotting or attaching pieces of thread to the finished fabric).
Logically, the techniques are again classified according to the basic textile technique, thus: pile formation

- in meshwork
- in plaited systems
- in warp fabrics
- in half-woven fabrics
- in woven fabrics.

Here it should be borne in mind that in a similar way to beadwork (see pp. 114-121), with certain stiff materials (particularly large feathers) the fabric is held together not by the binding of the basic elements but by the binding of the "pile". This particularly applies in the case of meshwork.

Pile Formation in Meshwork

Pile Formation by Looping

In contrast to the linking methods (see pp. 7-8), the looping techniques are relatively well suited for the formation of pile fabrics. In the case of simple looping the pile-forming element can, for instance, be fixed in an additional loop (Fig. 180a) or by several rows of loops which, however, need not be linked (Fig. 180b). Simple interconnected looping is also a suitable technique for tying-in pile (Fig. 180c).

Fig. 180a: Pile formation by simple looping

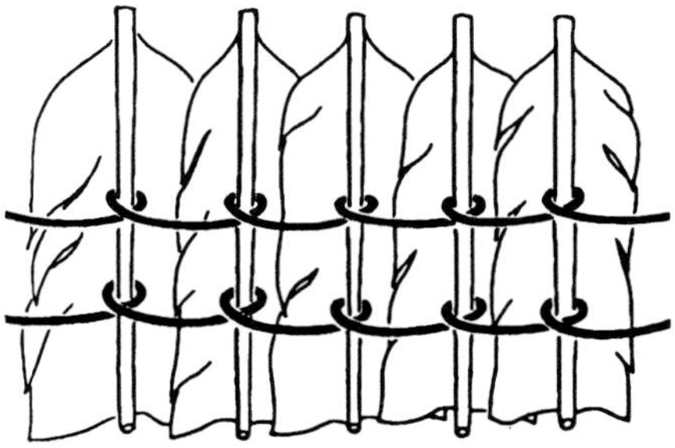

Fig. 180b: Pile formation by simple looping

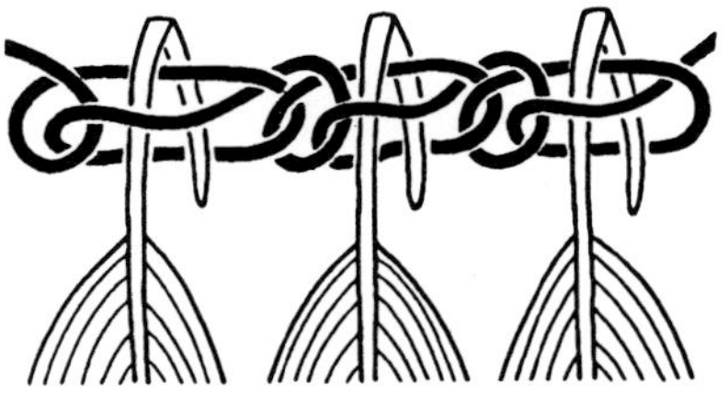

Fig. 180c: Pile formation by interconnected looping

Pile Formation by Knotting

Knotting, since it is a technically more appropriate technique, is far more commonly used as a method of pile formation. This method exhibits the greatest scope for variation among the primary fabric-forming techniques.

1. Pile Formation by Simple Knotting

Simple or overhand knots are generally used to fix coarser decorative elements (feather quills, leaves etc.). Fixing may be by several rows of knots (Fig. 181a-b) or by the loop of a single knot (Fig. 182a-b).

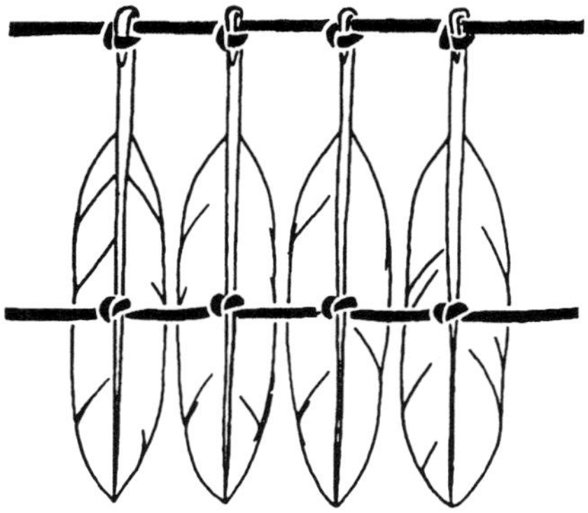

Fig. 181a: Pile formation by simple knotting, multiple rows, not connected

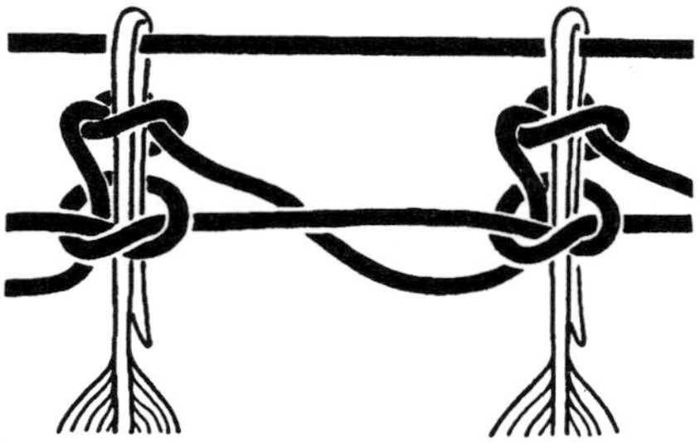

Fig. 181b: Pile formation by simple knotting, multiple rows, connected

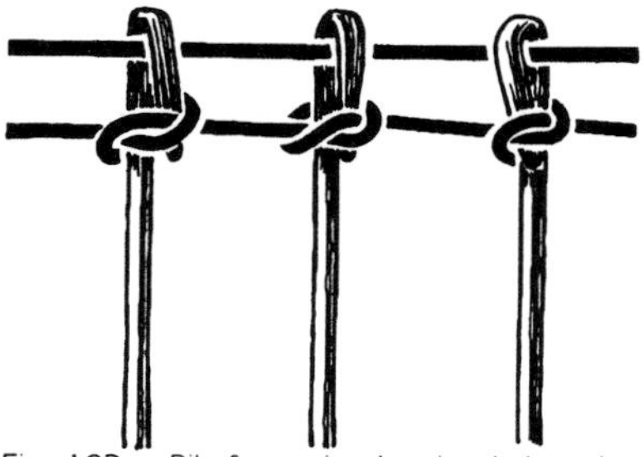

Fig. 182a: Pile formation by simple knotting, single row

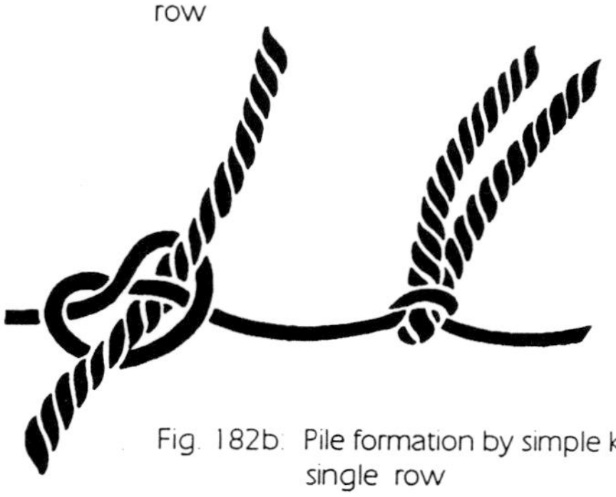

Fig. 182b: Pile formation by simple knotting, single row

Other terms used:

Florbildung mit Fingerknoten (Seiler-Baldinger 1991:113)
Fieira de penas sobre cordel-base, nó verdadeiro (Ribeiro 1986:193)

2. Pile Formation by Cow Hitch

The cow hitch is relatively rarely used in its original form to fix tuft-forming elements (Fig. 183a); wherever it is used, the knots are arranged at right angles and not parallel to the row of meshes (Fig. 183b).

In more complex variations an additional looping at the base of the knot can be used to fix the tuft-forming element more firmly (Fig. 184).

Other term used:

Florbildung mit halbem symmetrischem Knoten (Seiler-Baldinger 1991:114)

3. Pile Formation by Square Knotting

The square knot in its basic form is the one most frequently used in tuft formation. The tuft can at the same time be tied parallel to the knotting thread (Fig. 185a) or merely threaded through the knot (Fig. 185b).

Fig. 183a: Pile formation by cow hitch: horizontal

Fig. 183b: Pile formation by cow hitch: vertical

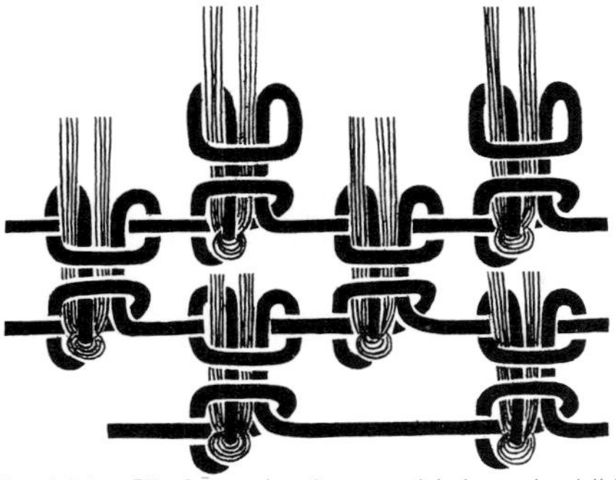

Fig. 184: Pile formation by cow hitch and additional loop

Fig. 185a: Pile formation by square knotting

Fig. 185b: Pile formation by square knotting

Other terms used:
Pile knot (Crawford 1912:157)
Florbildung mit symmetrischem Knoten (Seiler-Baldinger 1991: 114)
Falscher Samt (D'Harcourt 1960:29)
Simili velours (Izikowitz 1933:11)

4. Pile formation by Peruke Stitches

The form of knot known as a peruke stitch provides an even better fixation. It is a further development of the square knot in which the thread forms an additional two-loop flat knot at the base (Fig. 186). In more artistic variants the pile is fixed in complex loops running in opposite directions (Fig. 187a-b).

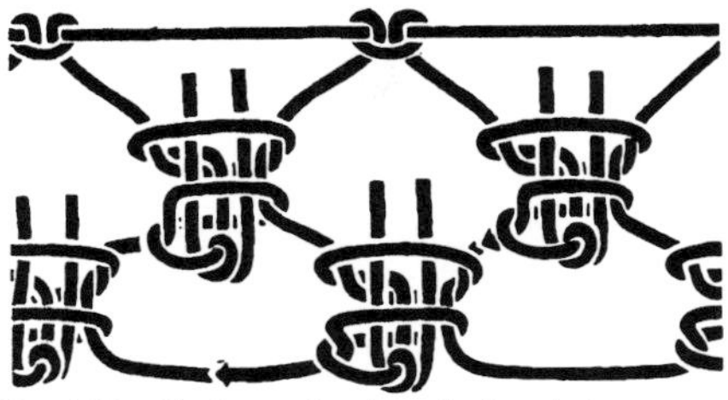

Fig. 186: Pile formation by pêruke stitches

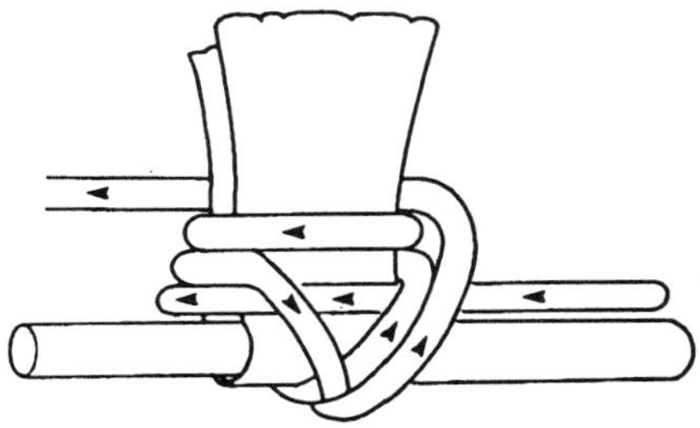

Fig. 187a: Pile formation by variant of peruke stitch

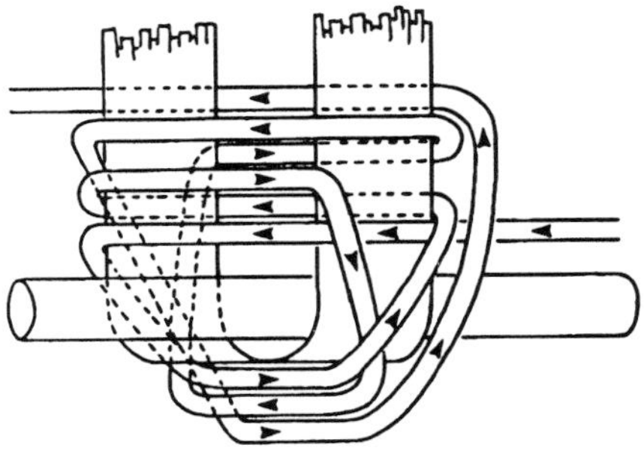

Fig. 187b: Variant of peruke stitch: thread configuration

Other term used:
Florbildung mit Perückenknoten (Seiler-Baldinger 1991:115)

5. Pile Formation by Fishnet Knot

The fishnet knot is also eminently suited for fixing pile elements (Fig. 188a); in the case of stiff, firm elements an additional thread may be employed.

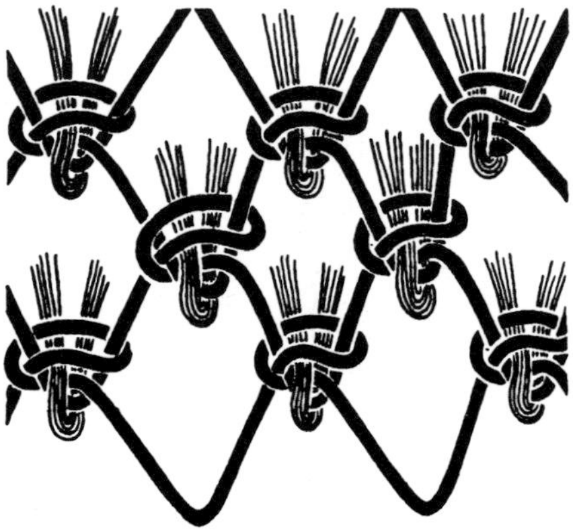

Fig. 188a: Pile formation by fishnet knot

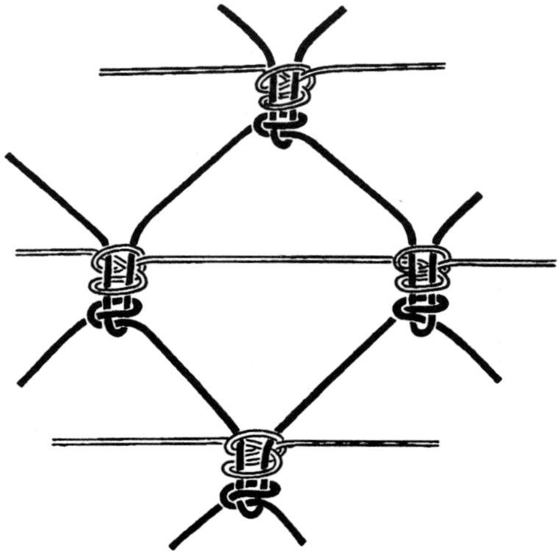

Fig. 188b: Pile formation by fishnet knot and cow hitch

Other term used:
Florbildung mit Filetknoten (Seiler-Baldinger 1991:115)

Pile Formation on Element Systems

Pile Formation in Association with Plaiting

In contrast to plaiting with two active systems, plaiting with an active and a passive system is preferred for pile formation.

1. Pile Formation by Looped Wrapping

The active thread system fixes in each loop both the passive system and the pile-forming elements (Fig.189).

Fig. 189: Pile formation by looped wrapping

Other terms used:
Pile knot (Crawford 1912:158ff.)
Florbildung durch Umwickeln (Seiler-Baldinger 1991:116)

2. Pile Formation by Twining

There are various possibilities of forming a pile by twining. The pile-forming elements can be fixed parallel to the active or passive system with one or more rows of single or double twining (Fig. 190a-c).

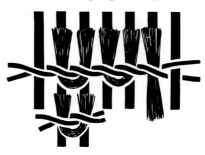

Fig. 190a: Pile formation by twining: fixing of one pile element per twist

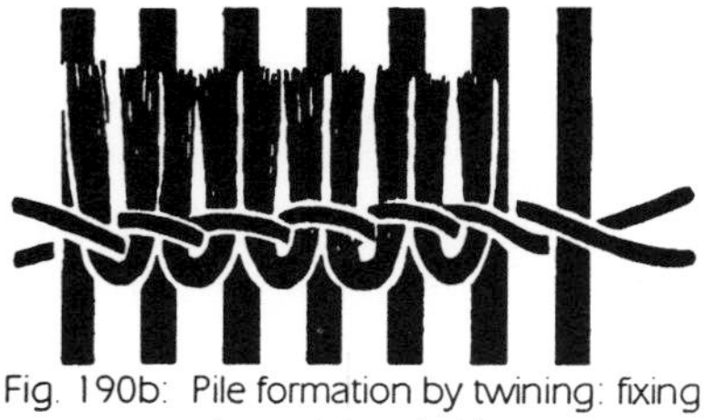

Fig. 190b: Pile formation by twining: fixing of two pile elements per twist

Fig. 190c: Pile formation by twining: looped pile element

Other terms used:

False fringe (Emmons 1907:341)
Florbildung durch Zwirnbinden (Seiler-Baldinger 1991:116)
Vliessgeflechte mit Zwirnbindung (Vogt 1937:20ff.)

3. Pile Formation by Coiling

Wrapped coiling and its variants are also suitable for fixing pile elements. There are a number of possibilities depending on the material (Fig. 191a-b).

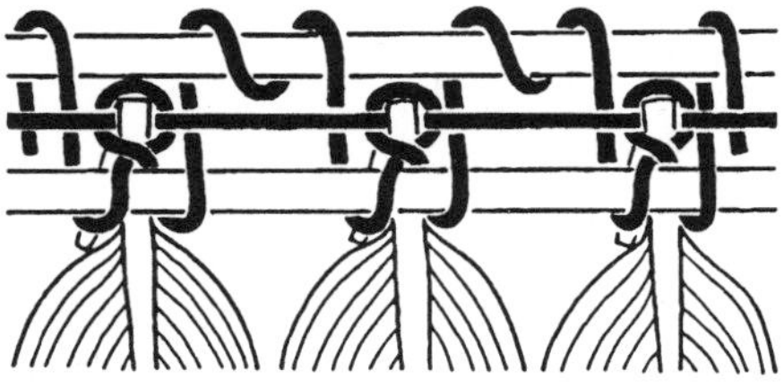

Fig. 191a: Pile formation by wrapped coiling

Fig. 191b: Pile formation by variation of wrapped coiling

Other term used:

Florbildung durch Wulsthalbflechten (Seiler-Baldinger 1991:117)

4. Pile Formation by Two- and Multi-directional Plaiting

Plaiting with two or more active systems enables additional ornamental elements to be fixed in place in a number of different ways along lines running parallel with one of the systems (Fig. 192a-c).

Fig. 192a: Pile formation on diagonal plaiting

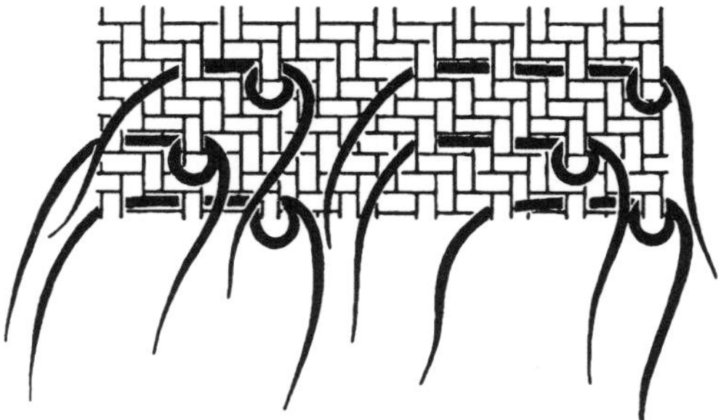

Fig. 192b: Pile formation on right-angle plaiting

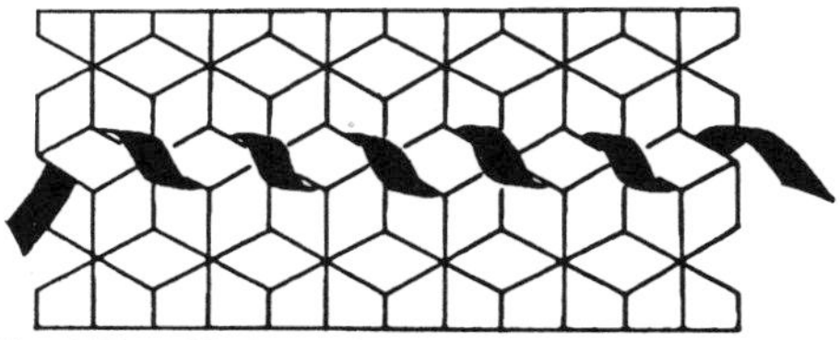

Fig. 192c: Pile formation on multi-directional plaiting

Other term used:
Florbildung durch Zwei- und Mehrrichtungsflechten (Seiler-Baldinger 1991:117)

Pile Formation on a Warp Fabric Basis

Among the active warp techniques, warp twining is the one that best lends itself to pile formation (Fig. 193). In the passive warp techniques (weft wrapping and weft twining) the same applies as for the looped wrapping techniques. However, the most important forms of pile and tuft formation are based on tapestry, to which they are closely related.

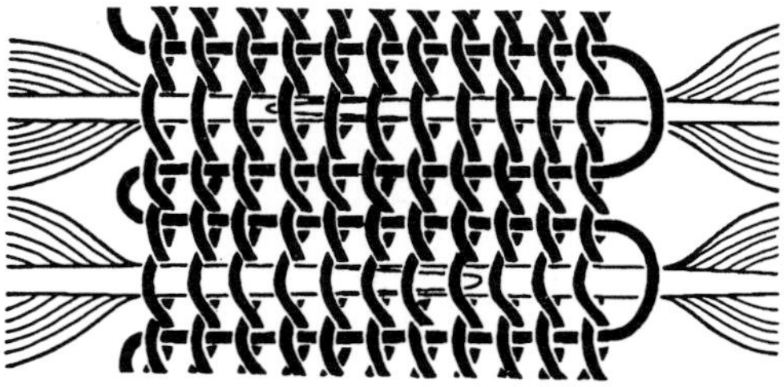

Fig. 193: Pile formation by warp twining

1. Knotted Pile Technique (carpet knotting)

In the simplest forms of these techniques, short lengths of weft are knotted or looped into the warp. In order to obtain a coherent fabric, the successive weft threads should be linked to at least one common warp thread. Techniques of this kind are rarely used.
Carpet knotting is one of the more complex techniques. From the technical point of view it is a combination of interlacing ground weft and short lengths of tuft-forming weft. The first set of weft threads gives coherence to the fabric and the second set provides thickness and ornamentation. If automatic shed-forming devices are used for the insertion of the ground weft, carpet knotting can be considered as a special form of weaving. On the other hand the knotting of the shorter weft threads, with or without the help of a hooked needle, is always done manually.
The work is usually done on a vertical loom and, more rarely, on a horizontal loom.

Other terms used:
Looped-pile fabric (D'Harcourt 1962:27ff.)
Knotted pile (Emery 1966:148ff.)
Florbildung in Verbindung mit Wirken (Teppichknüpferei) (Seiler-Baldinger 1991:118)
Etoffes à trame nouée, point noué (Leroi-Gourhan 1943:298)
Technique de tapis noué (CIETA 1970:30)
Tappeti annodati (CIETA 1970:30)
Tejidos con pelo (Chertudi/Nardi 1961:137ff.)
Alfombra anudada, flossa (CIETA 1970:30)
Knuten flossa (Burnham 1980:78)

The different methods of knotting are distinguished essentially according to the way in which the short weft lengths are knotted or looped in, and also according to whether the warp threads are arranged in one or two planes and the number of ground weft threads between rows of knots.

1.1. Carpet Knotting with Symmetrical Knots

The pile thread is looped round two warp threads in the manner of the cow hitch. The pile-forming threads thus emerge between alternate pairs of warp threads. The symmetrical knot holds more firmly than the asymmetrical knot.

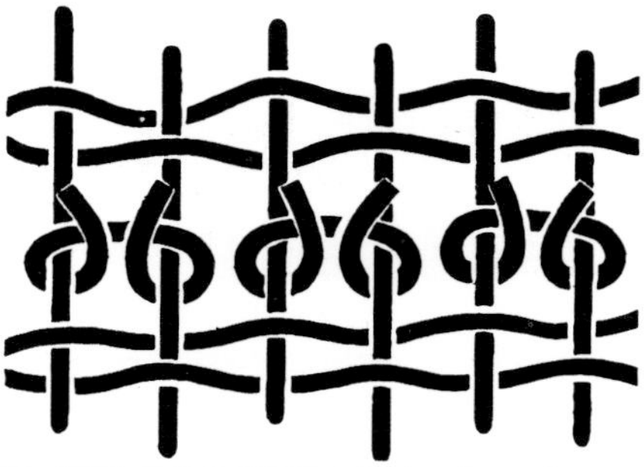

Fig. 194a: Symmetrical knot: view from above

Fig. 194b: Symmetrical knot: section, with warp threads in various positions

Other terms used:
Closed knot (Burnham 1980:29)
Turkish rug knot (Albers 1963: Pl. 26)
Ghiordes (Smyrna or Turkish) knot (Emery 1966:221ff.)
Teppichknüpfen mit symmetrischem Knoten (Seiler-Baldinger 1991:118)
Smyrnaknoten (Hartung 1963:34)

Smyrna-, Rya- oder Ghiördesknoten (Zechlin 1966:140ff.)
Gördes- oder Turkknoten (Hubel 1967/68:7)
Noeud symétrique (Tanavoli 1985:89)
Nudo de Ghiordes, nudo de Smirna (Chertudi/Nardi 1961: 137ff.)
Nudo turco o cerrado (Mirambell/Martínez 1986:31)

1.2. Carpet Knotting with Asymmetrical Knots

The pile thread passes under one warp thread and loops round the next one. Since the knot is asymmetrical, each warp thread is followed by a protruding pile end. The effect is similar to that of cutting a weft wrapping thread after every two warp threads (cf. p. 59).

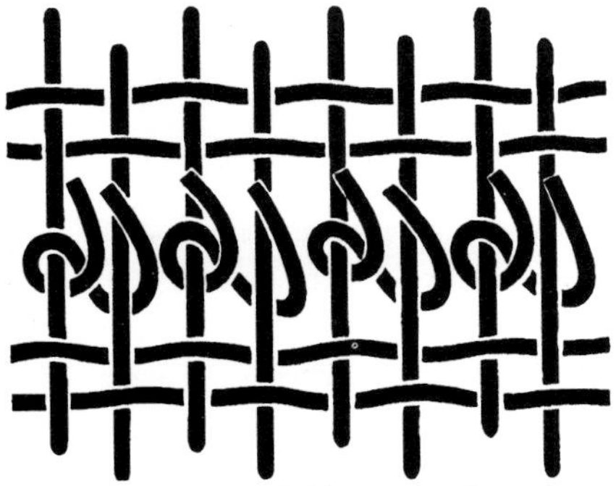

Fig. 195a: Asymmetrical knot: view from above

Fig. 195b: Asymmetrical knot: section, with warp threads in various positions

Other terms used:

Open knot (Burnham 1980:79)
Senna knot (Hunter 1953)
Lahore rug knot (Innes 1959:40)
Persian rug knot (Albers 1963: Pl.26)
Sehna (or Persian) knot (Emery 1966:222)
Teppichknüpfen mit asymmetrischem Knoten (Seiler-Baldinger 1991:119)
Senne-Knüpfung (Neugebauer/Orendi 1923:76ff.)
Sinäh- oder persischer Knoten (Hubel 1967/68:7)
Sennehknoten (halber oder persischer Knoten) (Nabholz 1980: 23)
Persischer oder türkischer Knoten (Hongsermeier 1987:80)
Noeud persian (CIETA 1970:42)
Noeud asymétrique (Tanavoli 1985:90)
Nodo persiano (CIETA 1970:42)
Nudo perso (CIETA 1970:42)
Nudo perso o abierto (Mirambell/Martínez 1986:31)

1.3. Carpet Knotting with Asymmetrical Knots Around Two Warp Threads

In contrast to the customary asymmetrical knot, the pile thread passes beneath two warp threads before being looped twice round the following two warp threads (Fig. 196a). As a result, two pile threads appear one above the other after each pair of warp threads (Fig. 196b).

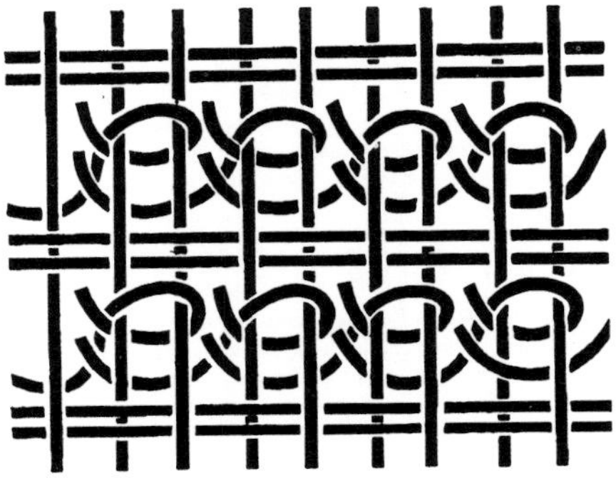

Fig. 196a: Asymmetrical knots around two warp threads: view from above

Fig. 196b: Asymmetrical knots around two warp threads: section

Other terms used:

Teppichknüpfen mit asymmetrischem Knoten um zwei Kettfäden (Seiler-Baldinger 1991:119)
Tibetischer Knoten (Hongsermeier 1987:80)

1.4. Carpet Knotting with a Single Warp Knot

The knot is formed around each warp thread so that there are two pile weft ends between each warp thread.

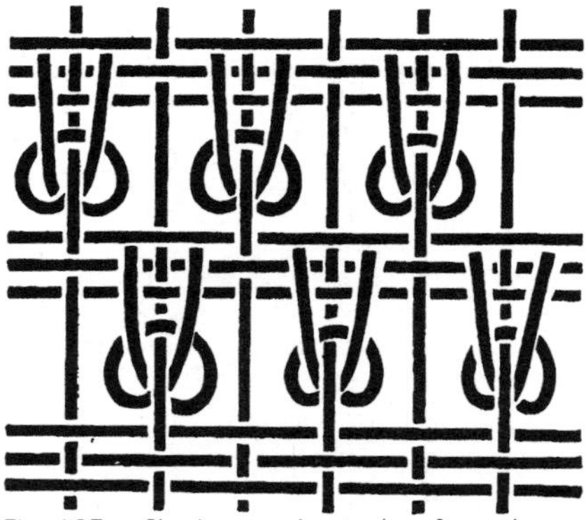

Fig. 197a: Single warp knot: view from above

Fig. 197b: Single warp knot: section

Other terms used:

Spanish knot (Burnham 1980:79)
Spanish single knot (Hunter 1953)
Single-warp (or Spanish) knot (Emery 1966:222ff.)
Teppichknüpfen mit gekreuztem Knoten (Seiler-Baldinger 1991: 120)
Ghiordes-Knoten über einen Kettfaden (Bühler-Oppenheim 1948:78c)
Nudo español (Mirambell/Martínez 1986:31)

Pile Formation in Weaving

1. Weft Pile Weaving

In the simplest form the weft threads, for instance in a plain weave, are not interlaced tightly (see Fabric Production), but allowed to remain loose, between the warp threads, in the form of protruding tufts (Fig. 198a-b) or loops. Such loops can be formed intermittently; they can also be left uncut or be cut subsequently.

In the more complex variants, the pile is formed during weaving by additional ornamental threads between the basic weft threads.

We thus have a combination of supplementary weft threads and loops (Fig. 199).

In this case too, the pile may be cut or uncut. In contrast to the group in which pile is formed from warp threads, widely differing forms are found here. In some methods the figure weft forms genuine interlacings with the warp (slip loop type). The ornamental weft thread may be continuous or in relatively short, individual pieces, generally in different colours, which are woven in as in the case of brocading (Fig. 199a-b). In the second case the weft thread retraces its path after pile formation, thus looping round a group of warp threads, and then again proceeds in the original direction as in looped weft wrapping (Fig. 200).

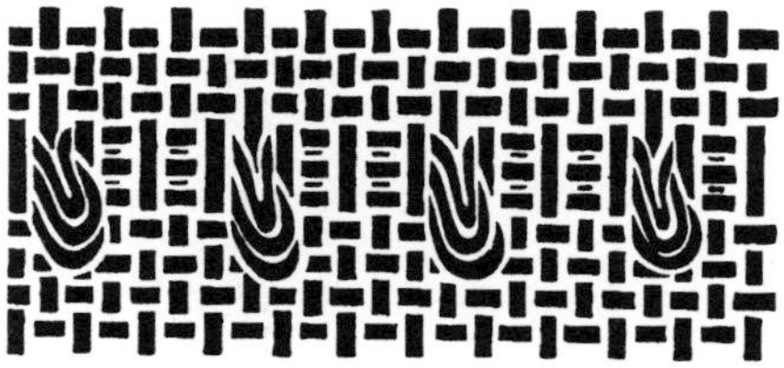

Fig. 198a: Weft pile formation: view from above

Fig 198b: Weft pile formation: section

Fig. 199a: Slip loop type fabric: section

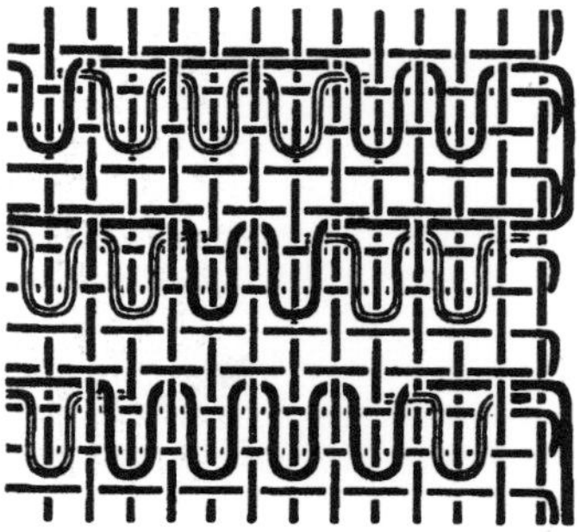

Fig. 199b: Complex loop fabric: view from above

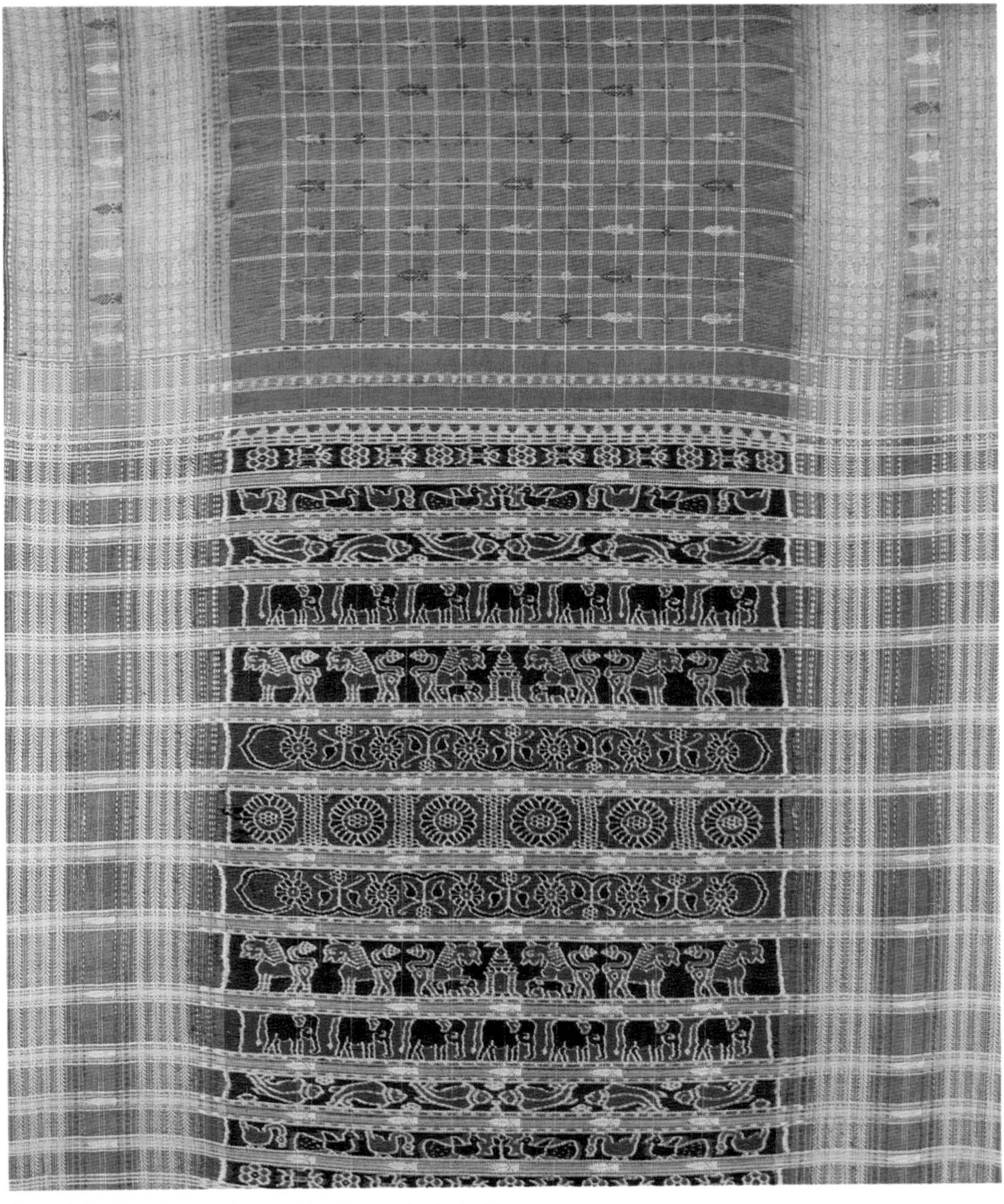

PLATE 20. Sari from Phulbani, weft ikat, Orissa, India, IIa 6414

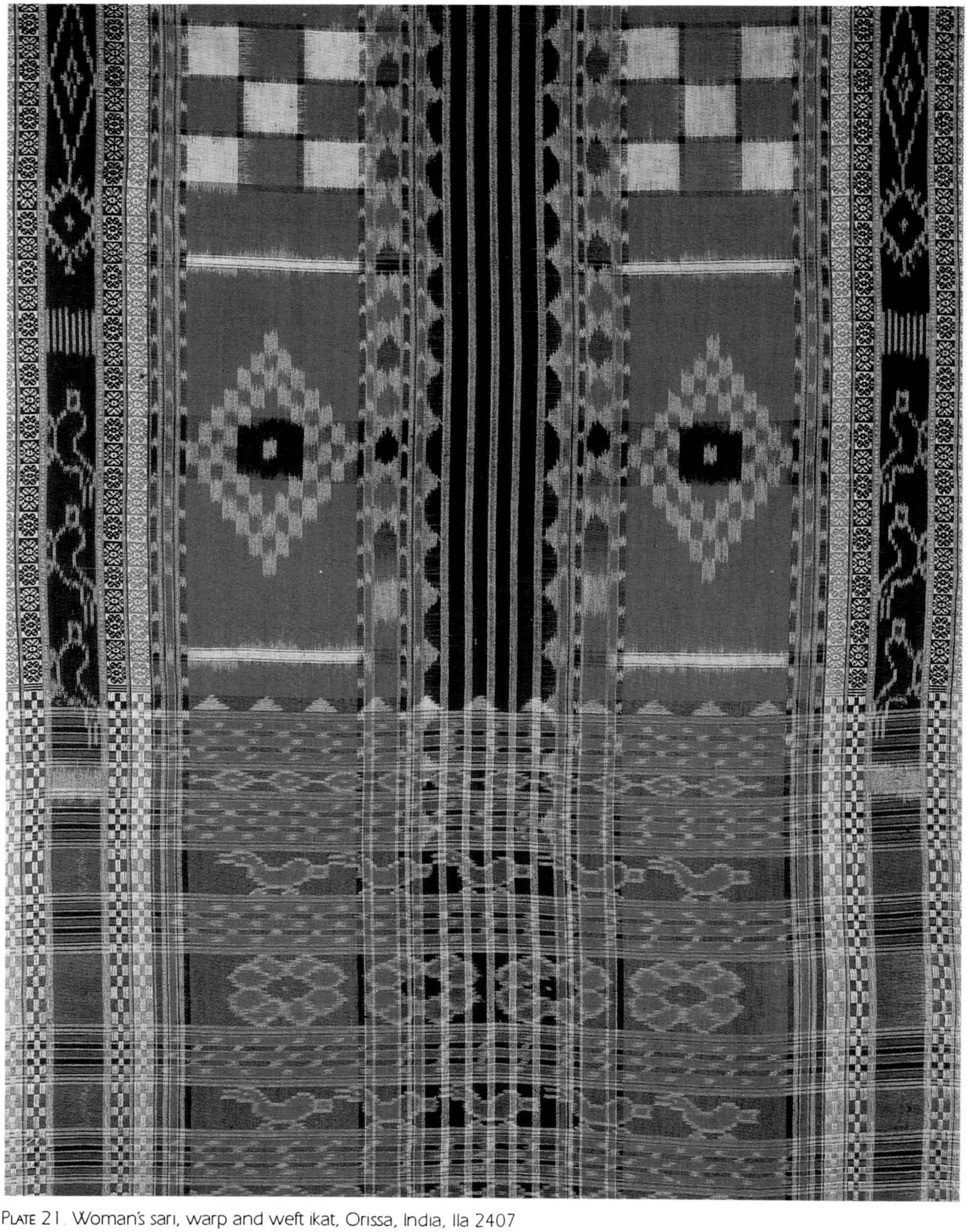

PLATE 21. Woman's sari, warp and weft ikat, Orissa, India, IIa 2407

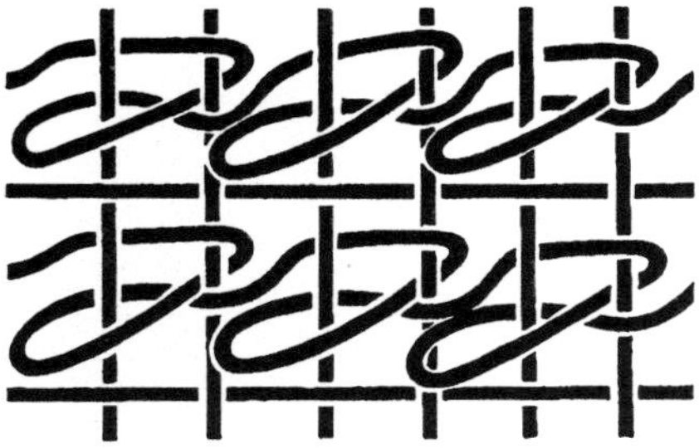

Fig. 200: Reversing weft threads in loop fabric

Other terms used:
Weft loop (Bellinger 1955: Fig. 1-2)
Florbildung im Eintrag (Seiler-Baldinger 1991:120)
Schussamt (Müller/Brendler/Spiess 1958:100ff.)
Lussenweefsel (Brommer 1988:80)
Velours par trame, velvet, veludilho, terciopelo por trama, inslag-sammet, velluto por trama (Burnham 1980:186)

Uncut:
Terry weave (Hodges 1965:144)
Weft-loop weave (Burnham 1980:182)
Noppengewebe, Schlingengewebe (Seiler-Baldinger 1991:120)
Noppväv, nuppevev (Geijer/Hoffmann 1974:9)
Bouclé par la trame, arriciato per trama, anelado por trama, tecido repuxado, anillado por trama, boutonné (Burnham 1980: 182)

Cut:
Velvet weave (Hodges 1965:144)
Loop weave (Rosenberg et al. 1980:12)
Woven pile, laid in or extra weft-loop pile (Emery 1966:148ff.)
Weft looping (Collingwood 1968:211ff.)
Weft pile weave, velveteen (CIETA 1970:51)
Schlingenschuss (Henneberg 1932:10)
Schussamt (Burnham 1980:186)
Velours par trame (CIETA 1970:51)
Velluto per trama (CIETA 1970:51)
Terciopelo por trama (CIETA 1970:51)
Veludilho (Burnham 1980:186)
Inslagsammet (CIETA 1970:51)
Knutar i senantik flossa (Sylwan 1934:216)

2. Warp Pile Weaving (velvet)

Instead of in the weft, the pile is formed in the warp. In addition to the ground warp, more complex fabrics have a pile warp of appropriate fineness. The pile warp threads are passed in the loom over needles or transverse rods in such a way that they form protruding loops between the ground warp threads and the weft (uncut velvet, Fig. 201a). These may be subsequently cut (cut velvet, Fig. 201b). Among the best-known forms in this group are the true velvets. These, however, are no longer produced in the manner described above but like a double-weave fabric with the pile warp alternating between the face and back fabrics and being cut subsequent to weaving (double velvet Fig. 201c).

Fig. 201a: Uncut velvet

Fig. 201b: Cut velvet

Fig. 201c: Double velvet

Other terms used:
Warp-pile weave (CIETA 1970:29)
Warp-pile fabrics, velvet, plush, terry (Emery 1966:149)
Florbildung in der Kette (echter Samt) (Seiler-Baldinger 1991:121)
Velours, veludo, sammet (Burnham 1980:163)
Velluto per catena (CIETA 1970:29)
Terciopelo por urdimbre (CIETA 1970:29)

3. Pile Formation by Tablet Weaving

Pile can also be formed in tablet weaving (Fig. 202a) by working with pile warp pairs in which one pile warp forms the pile on one side and the other pile warp forms the pile on the reverse face (Fig. 202b).

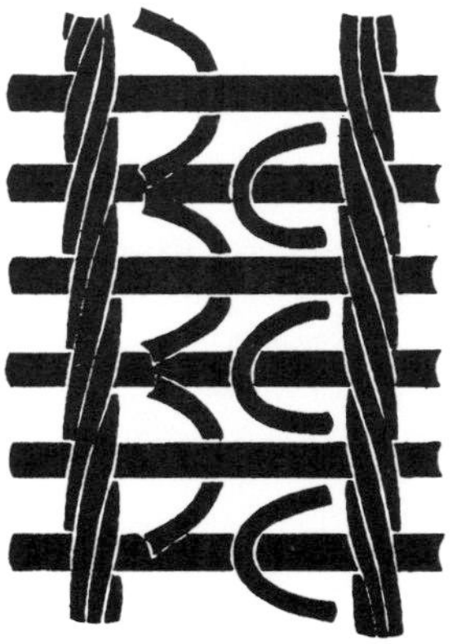

Fig. 202a: Pile formation in tablet weaving: view from above

Fig. 202b: Pile formation in tablet weaving: section

Other term used:
Florbildung in Verbindung mit Brettchenweben (Seiler-Baldinger 1991:121)

References to Pile Formation: see pp. 166-167.

Beadwork

In principle beadwork is similar to pile formation. Beads, being rigid, can be strung together on the working threads. However, completely new variations are possible in which the interworking is paradoxically not between the threads of the ground fabric but by the beads themselves. The decorative elements can be shells (whole or parts), beads of glass, clay, metal or rubber; seeds, fruits; metal discs or tubes; cylindrical pieces of metal or wood etc.

Beaded fabrics can be fundamentally formed in two different ways: either by interworking the ground elements, in which case the beads have a purely ornamental function, or by fixing through the beads (so that the fabric would not hold together without them). The two methods can readily be combined.

Beadwork by Interworking the Ground Elements

Beadwork by Meshing

All meshwork techniques can be used for beadwork.

1. Linked Beadwork

Only simple linking is suitable for this purpose. The simplest method differs from ordinary linking only in that the beads are strung along the thread (Fig. 203a). In another variation the links are covered by a bead and thereby also better fixed (Fig. 203b).
In a related form, the ascending and descending limbs of a mesh pass through the same bead (Fig. 203c). This method can be varied by linking with skipping of rows (Fig. 203d).

Fig. 203a: Simple linking with strung beads

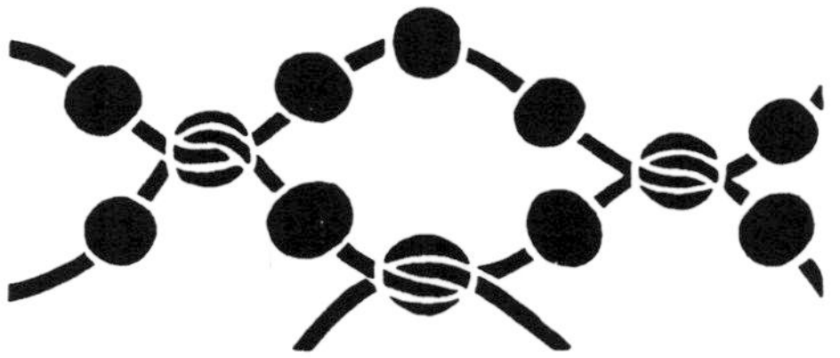

Fig. 203b: Beadwork by simple linking (bead fixes links)

Fig. 203c: Beadwork by simple linking

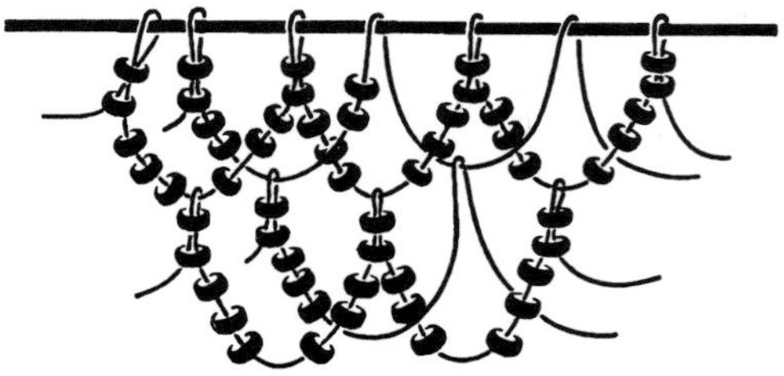

Fig. 203d: Beadwork by linking with skipping of rows

Other terms used:
Perlenstoffbildung durch Einhängen (Seiler-Baldinger 1991:122)
Bausteinverbindung (Lemaire 1960:216)

2. Looped Beadwork

The techniques of simple (Fig. 204) and simple interconnected looping (Fig. 205 a-d) are very popular. The beads are usually placed on the mesh loops.

Fig. 204: Beadwork by simple looping

Fig. 205a: Beadwork by interconnected looping

Fig. 205b: Beadwork by interconnected looping

Fig. 205c: Beadwork by interconnected looping

Fig. 205d: Beadwork by interconnected looping

Other terms used:
Perlenstoffbildung durch Verschlingen (Seiler-Baldinger 1991:123)
Simple interconnected looping:
Method in assembling shells in a crochet-like stitch (Orchard 1929:23ff.)
Perlenstoffbildung durch verhängtes Verschlingen (Seiler-Baldinger 1991:123)

3. Knotted Beadwork

Knotting is not in general very suitable for the production of beadwork, with the exception of transitional forms between suspended and fixed knots. Knotted beadwork is therefore made only in a single row (Fig. 206).

Fig. 206: Beadwork by knotting

Other term used:
Perlenstoffbildung durch Verknoten (Seiler-Baldinger 1991:123)

4. Crocheted and Knitted Beadwork

The thread on which the beads are strung is crocheted or knitted in the usual manner (Fig. 207) with the beads being placed in the loops.

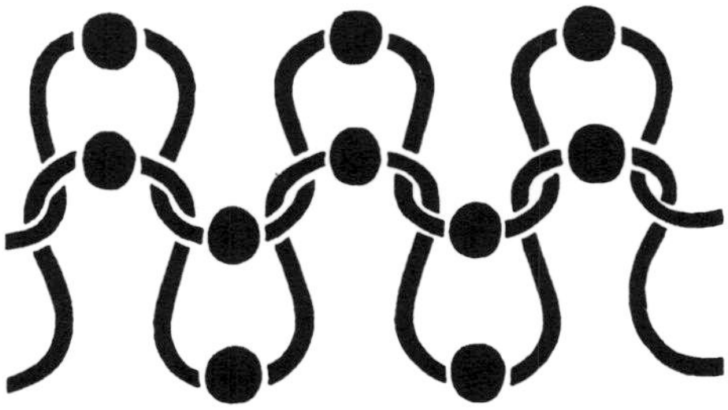

Fig. 207: Beadwork by knitting

Other terms used:
Knitting and crocheting with beads (Edwards 1966:157ff.)
Perlenstoffbildung durch Häkeln und Stricken (Seiler-Baldinger 1991:123)
Häkeln und Stricken mit Perlen (Lammèr 1975:307)

Plaited Beadwork

Of the various techniques using an active and a passive system, wrapping (Fig. 208), binding and coiling (Fig. 209) are the ones preferred for beadwork. These include, for instance, wrapped coiling (Fig. 210), simple linked coiling (Fig. 211a), cross-linked coiling (Fig. 211b) and looped coiling (Fig 212a-b).

Plaiting with two active systems is also valued as a means of producing beadwork, in particular diagonal plaiting (Fig. 213), three-strand braiding (Fig. 214), macramé or other variations. A technique is frequently used in which the beads are strung on paired threads which then "split" the other threads moving at right or oblique angles. (Fig. 215a-b).

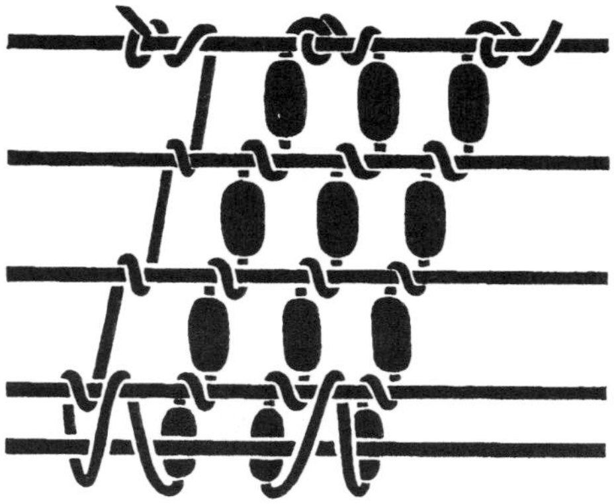

Fig. 208: Beadwork by wrapping

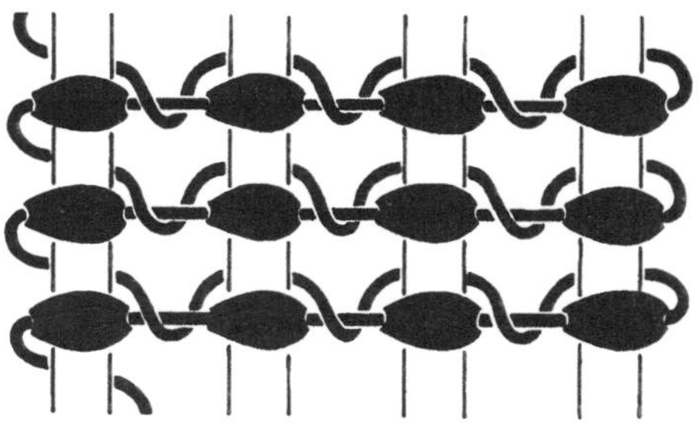

Fig. 209: Beadwork by wrapped binding

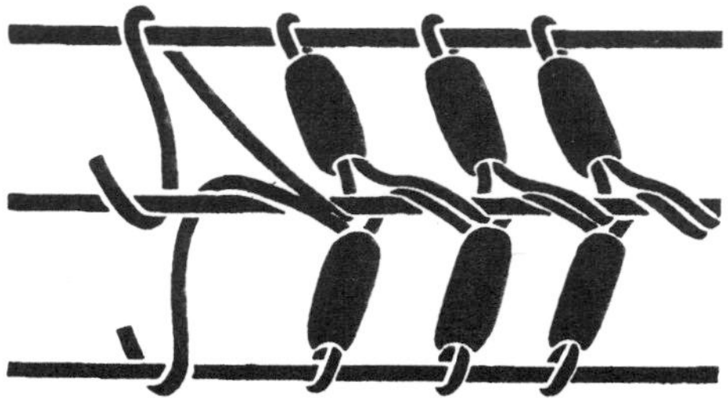

Fig. 210: Beadwork by wrapped coiling

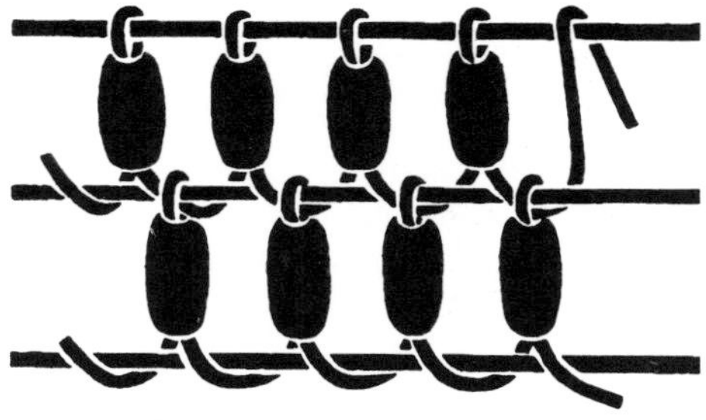

Fig. 211a: Beadwork by simple linked coiling

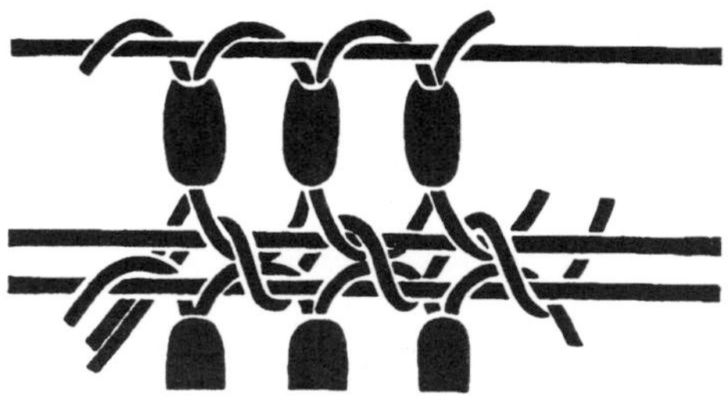

Fig. 211b: Beadwork by cross-linked coiling

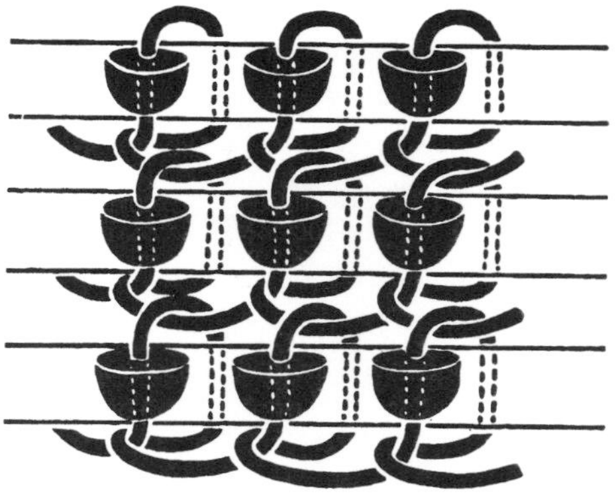

Fig. 212a: Beadwork by simple looped coiling

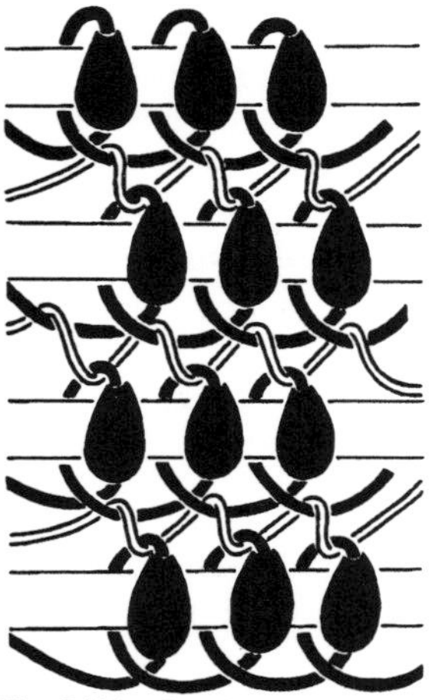

Fig. 212b: Beadwork by looped coiling over a linked thread

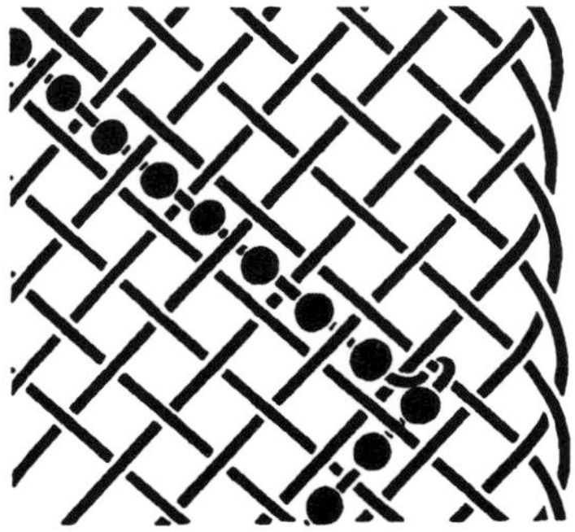

Fig. 213: Beadwork by diagonal plaiting

Fig. 214: Beadwork by braiding

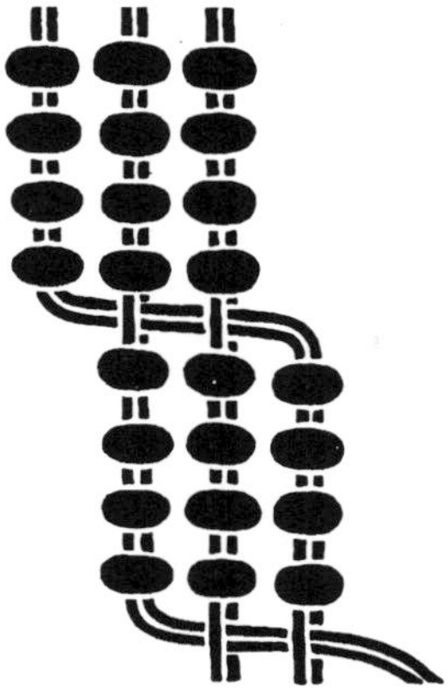

Fig. 215a: Beadwork with a set of paired elements

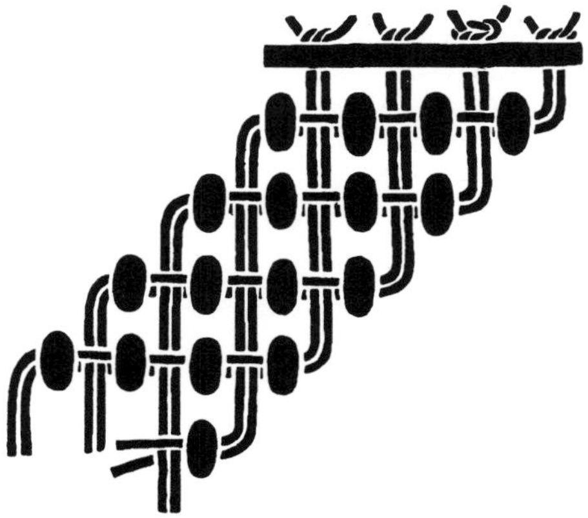

Fig. 215b: Beadwork with a set of paired elements

Other terms used:

Perlenstoffbildung durch Flechten (Seiler-Baldinger 1991:123)

Wrapping:
Perlenstoffbildung durch Wickeln (Seiler-Baldinger 1991:124)

Coiling:
Coiled weave with beads interwoven (Orchard 1929: Pl. XXI)
Perlenstoffbildung durch Wulsthalbflechten (Seiler-Baldinger 1991:124f)
Befestigung der Perlen auf gleichlaufenden oder spiraligen Bändern (Lemaire 1960:218)

Binding:
Perlenstoffbildung durch Binden (Seiler-Baldinger 1991:124)

With a set of paired elements:
Bias weave (Orchard 1929:112ff.)
Perlenstoffbildung durch klöppeleiartige Verfahren (Seiler-Baldinger 1991:125)

Beadwork with Warp Techniques

Warp techniques are the most popular in beadwork manufacture, in particular the techniques of weft interlacing and warp or weft twining.
Simple plaiting frames are used for fixing the warp and needles for inserting the weft.

1. Beadwork by Weft Interlacing

In beadwork of this type, the weft may go through the whole width of the fabric, or it may also reverse. The beads are fixed either by a single weft thread or a pair of weft threads. When a pair of weft threads is used for fixation, one of them passes above all warp threads and the other, below, and the two threads are interchanged at the selvedges (Fig. 216a).
The same effect can be obtained with one continuous weft thread by passing it twice through the same row of beads (Fig. 216b).

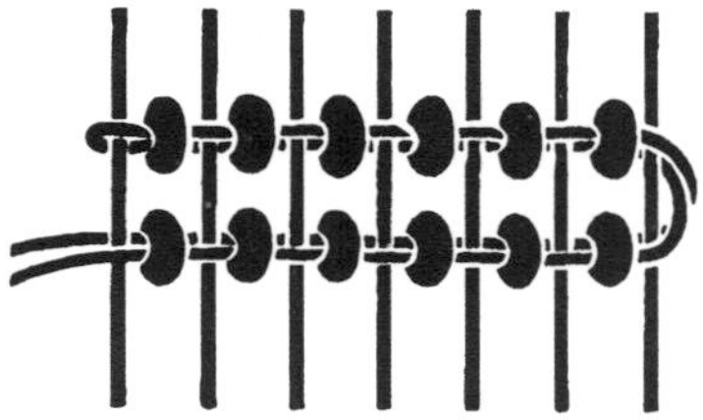

Fig. 216a: Beadwork by interlacing a pair of weft threads

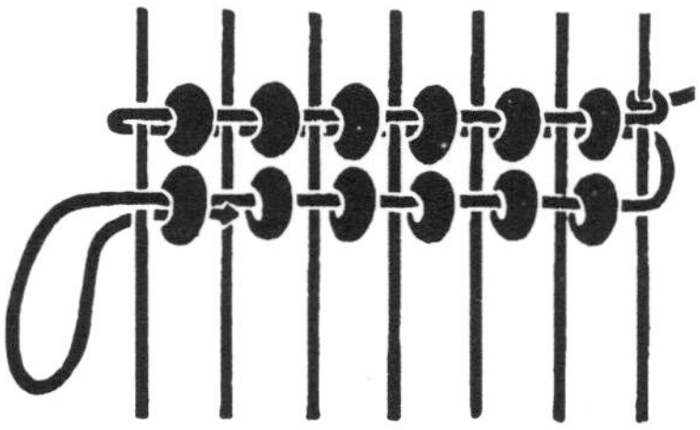

Fig. 216b: Beadwork by interlacing a continuous weft thread

Other terms used:
Square weave (Orchard 1929:92ff.)
Bead weaving, single or double weft (Lyford 1940:64ff.)
Simple beadweaving technique (beadweaving on a bow loom) (Edwards 1966:179ff.)
Perlenstoffbildung durch Flechten des Eintrages (Seiler-Baldinger 1991:126)

2. Warp or Weft Twined Beadwork

In the case of warp twining the beads are strung on the weft thread in such a way that one bead is located between two pairs of twisted warp threads (Fig. 217).
In weft twining, the beads are arranged on the twining weft thread and held in place by the warp (Fig. 218).

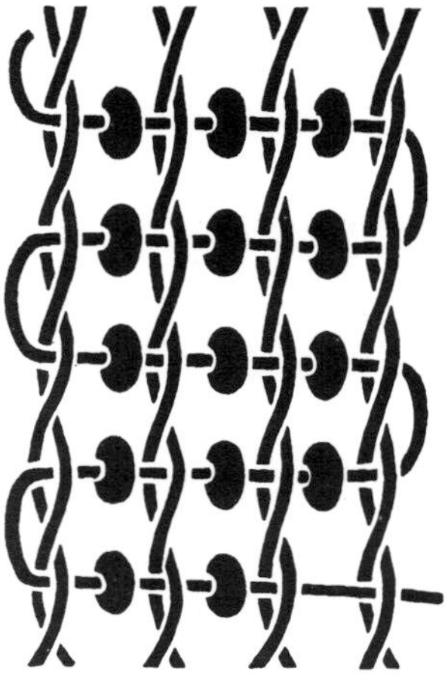

Fig. 217: Beadwork by warp twining

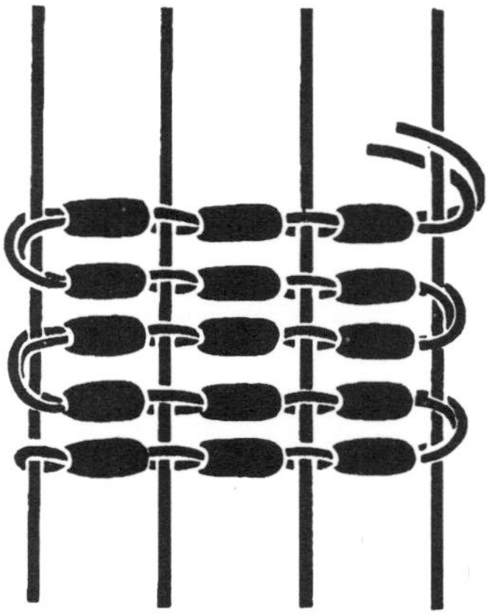

Fig. 218: Beadwork by weft twining

Other terms used:
Technique of double-thread weave (Orchard 1929:104,109)
Perlenstoffbildung durch Zwirnbinden der Kette oder des Eintrages (Seiler-Baldinger 1991:126)

Woven Beadwork

The use of weaving to produce beadwork is extremely limited. Mainly narrow beaded ribbons are made by means of rigid-heddle weaving (Fig. 219a), every second warp thread usually being followed by a bead (Fig. 219b).

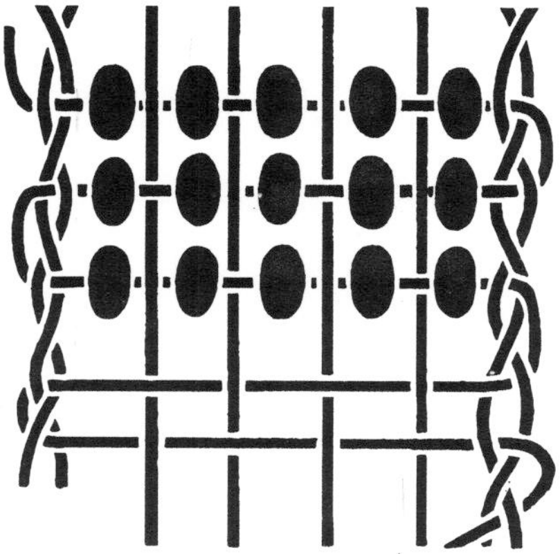

Fig. 219a: Beadwork by weaving

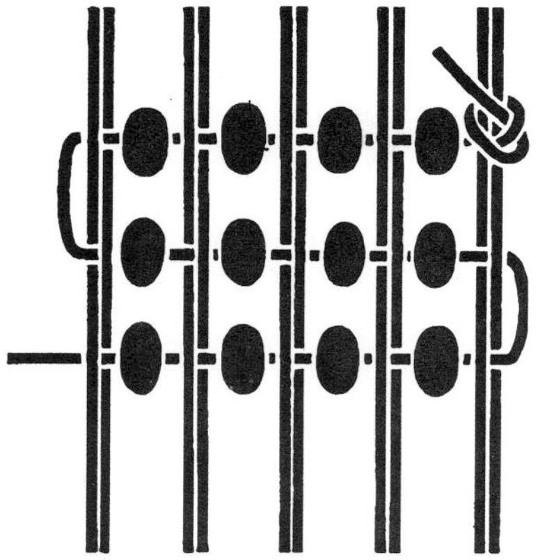

Fig. 219b: Beadwork by weaving

Other terms used:
Bead weaving (Burnham 1981:30)
Perlenstoffbildung durch Weben (Seiler-Baldinger 1991:127)
Perlenweberei (Lammèr 1975:308)

Beadwork by Interconnecting of Beads

This group differs from the beadwork techniques dealt with so far in that a coherent fabric is produced not by the interworking of the basic elements but by an interconnection through the ornamental elements themselves. These techniques employ a single continuous thread (only of limited length) or sets of elements.

Beadwork with a Continuous Thread

The path followed by the thread is similar to that in meshwork with a continuous thread of limited length. Linking takes place only at the bead and not at the mesh of the preceding row (simple linking into the bead of the preceding row, horizontal or vertical, Fig. 220a-b). Similarly, the thread may be looped through two beads (Fig. 221).

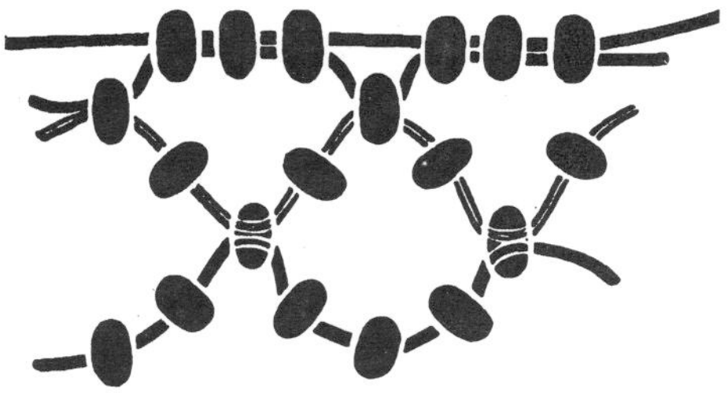

Fig. 220a: Horizontal linking through beads

Fig. 220b: Vertical linking through beads

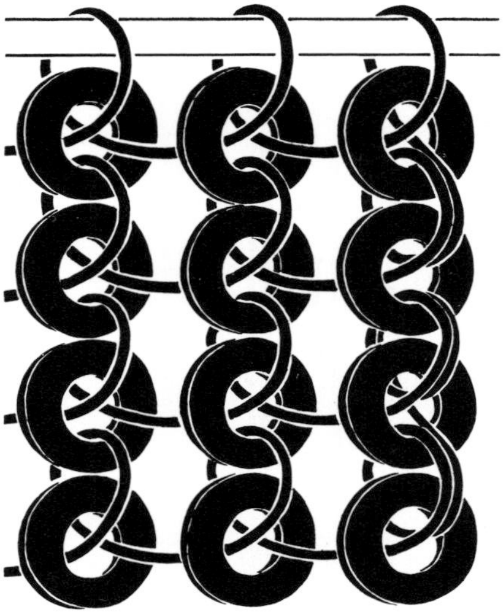

Fig. 221: Looping through beads

Other terms used:
Net-like weave (Orchard 1929:124)
Weaving with needle and thread (Edwards 1966:187ff.)
Openwork variety (Cardale-Schrimpff 1972:96)
Perlenstoffbildung durch Einhängen oder Verschlingen in die Perlen (Seiler-Baldinger 1991:127)
Netzverbindung (Lemaire 1960:216ff.)
Perlenfädeln (Lammèr 1975:304)

Beadwork with Sets of Elements

Instead of single threads, a set of elements is used. However, there is no crossing of threads in the sense of true interlacings, but at the most a superposing of threads which are fixed by the beads at the crossing points.
We can distinguish between plaiting-like and warp-fabric-like techniques. Thus the addition of the suffix "like" always denotes that binding is effected by the bead.

1. Beadwork with Plaiting-like Techniques

These techniques resemble the ones used in plaiting, especially macramé and braiding.
In the simplest case, paired threads are employed which without interlacing periodically pass through a common bead. Structurally these fabrics differ little from those produced by simple linking to the bead in the preceding row. In more complex variations the threads pass over each other at right angles or diagonally without forming any true interlacings. This is achieved by the threads passing through a common bead (Fig. 222a-b).

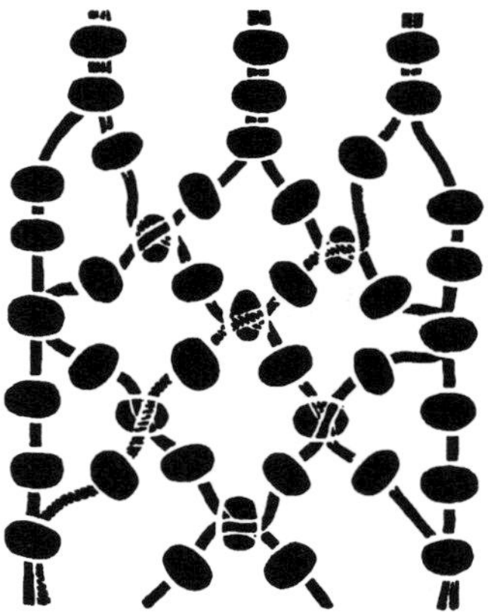

Fig. 222a: Beadwork with plaiting-like technique: diagonal

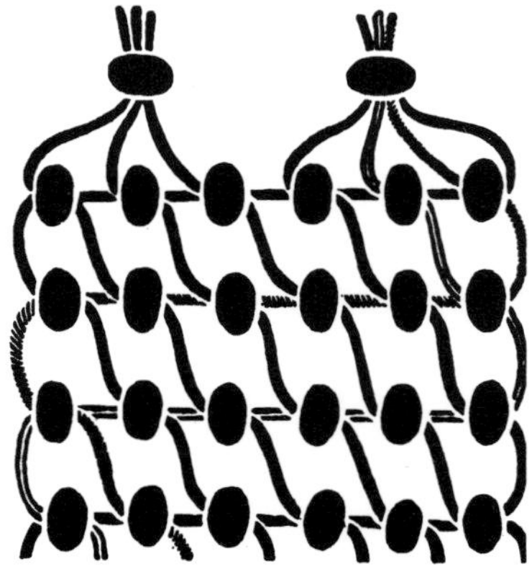

Fig. 222b: Beadwork with plaiting-like technique

Other terms used:
Close-mesh variety (Cardale-Schrimpff 1972:96)
Flechtereiartige Perlenstoffbildung (Seiler-Baldinger 1991:128)
Netzverbindung (Lemaire 1960:230ff.)

2. Beadwork with Warp-fabric-like Techniques

A tensioned warp is used whose threads may be either active or passive. Here again there are no genuine interworkings in the sense of interlacings or twinings. The fabric is held together only by the ornamental elements (Fig. 223a-b).

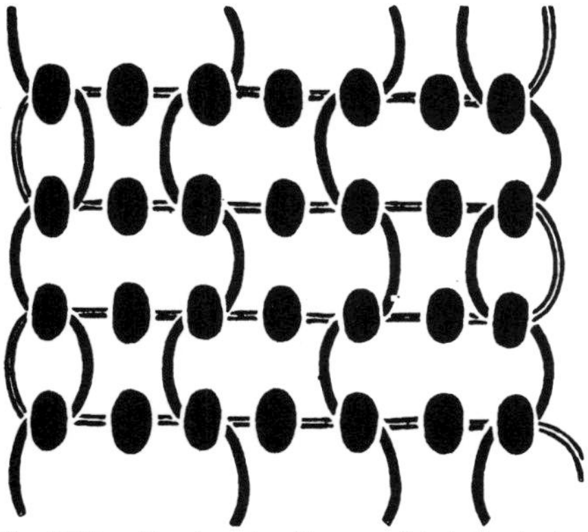

Fig. 223a: Beadwork with warp-fabric-like technique

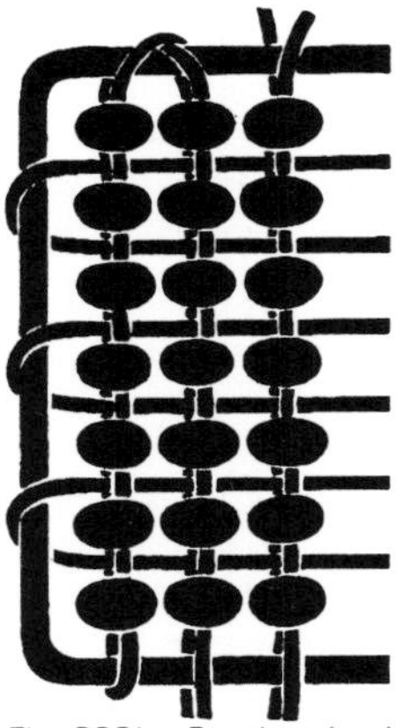

Fig. 223b: Beadwork with warp-fabric-like technique

Other terms used:

Skip weave (Orchard 1929:112)
Kettenstoffartige Perlenstoffbildung (Seiler-Baldinger 1991:129)

References to Beadwork Techniques: see pp. 168-169.

Making of Borders and Fringes

The methods included in this group are employed immediately after the production of the fabric and are often identical with fabric-producing techniques. Their purpose, however, is not solely decorative.
Borders perform a double function: they fix and strengthen the edges of the fabric and provide ornamentation. Borders are often formed as a part of the production of the fabric itself, but can also be added to the fabric after its manufacture.
A purely external distinction can be made between borders with and without fringes. Strictly speaking, these groups contain all the techniques discussed so far as well as variations that have not yet been mentioned. Only by going once more through the whole classification would it be possible to do some kind of justice to the enormous diversity of border techniques. In the following section, for each group a number of selected, typical forms, in particular new techniques and variations on known methods, are presented as examples. The simplest forms such as seaming, i.e. folding over and sewing the edge of a fabric, are not discussed.

Warp-faced plain woven and weft-twined fringes of a dancing apron from Timor, IIc 5064

Borders Without Fringes

It is a striking fact that particularly with primary fabric-producing techniques, border formation often uses variations of the process used to make the fabric. In this case the close relationship between fabric production and borders is clearly apparent. With more advanced techniques of fabric production, border formation deviates more from the basic technique and a broader variety of techniques are used.

Borders in Meshwork Techniques

Most meshwork techniques, with the exception of linking, are well suited for making borders. They are most frequently used for borders on meshwork fabrics themselves, and occur rarely on woven textiles (with the exception of crocheting and knitting) and not at all on plaited fabrics.

Looped Borders

The most popular looping border techniques are ones which impart a certain thickness and stability. These include above all the many variations of interconnected (Fig. 224a-b) and twisted interconnected looping (Fig. 225), as well as cord looping (Fig. 226) and simple looping on a foundation (Fig. 227, also see pp. 11-12).

Fig. 225: Borderwork by interconnected linked hourglass looping with equal spacing

Fig. 224a: Border formed by interconnected looping in the second turn

Fig. 224b: Border formed by interconnected looping in the second turn

Fig. 226: Borderwork by cord looping

Fig. 227: Looping on a foundation as border

Other terms used:

Looped and braided borderwork (Mason 1908:9)
Needleknitted cords, tabbed and fringed (O'Neale/Kroeber 1937:216)
False braid top selvedge (Green Gigli et al. 1974:84,109)
Verschlungene Randabschlüsse (Seiler-Baldinger 1991:131)

Knotted Borders

Borderwork in this category generally uses special forms of knots employed for fabric production. Different knots – the overhand knot and the two-loop flat knot, for instance – are often combined and interconnected to create completely new forms of knots (Fig. 228a-b). The outermost row of the border is formed by overhand knots. The thread in the next row passes downwards through the first loop of the overhand knot and forms a two-loop flat knot. It then passes through the second loop of the same overhand knot and then through the first loop of the next overhand knot and so on (Fig. 228b).

Fig. 228a: Border with simple knots

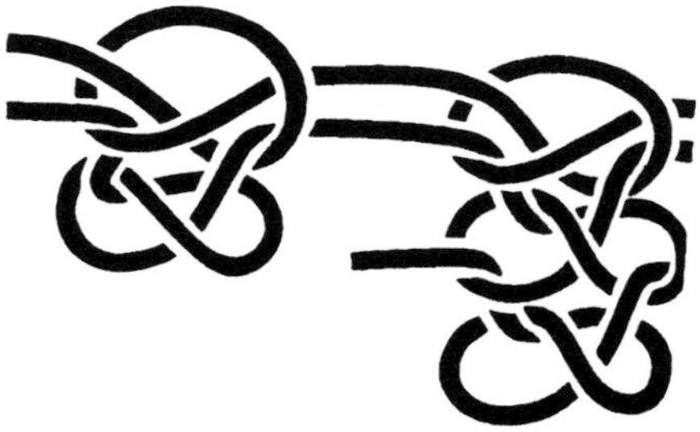

Fig. 228b: Combined borderwork of simple knots and two-loop flat knots

Other terms used:

Geknotete Randabschlüsse (Seiler-Baldinger 1991:132)
Arrêt par nouage (Balfet 1952:278)

Crocheted and Knitted Borders

Crocheted and knitted borders are very popular. They can be combined with any fabric-producing technique, and have a more purely ornamental character than any of the methods mentioned so far.

Simple variations employ plain or chain crocheting and the more complex forms have lace-like structures. Ordinary knitting stitches are not commonly used; knitted cordages are preferred for stable borders (Fig. 229a-b).

Fig. 229a: Simple "French"-knitted border

Fig. 229b: "French"-knitted border with skipping of meshes

Other term used:

Gehäkelte und gestrickte Randabschlüsse (Seiler-Baldinger 1991: 132)

Plaited Borders

Because of its wide scope for variation and combination, plaiting is one of the most commonly used border-making techniques. Although, as one would expect, it is encountered primarily in plaited fabrics, it also is often used with woven and warp fabrics.

Active-Passive Plaited Borders

This kind of borderwork is encountered almost exclusively on plaited fabrics. There are numerous variations and special forms, only a few of which can be mentioned here. Popular forms include wrapped borderwork, bound, twined and coiled borderwork.

1. Wrapped Borders

Among the various forms of wrapped borderwork, crosswise double-looped wrapping is particularly suited for producing stable edges (Fig. 230a-b).

Fig. 230a: Double-loop cross-wrapped border

Fig. 230b: Double-loop cross-wrapped border

Other terms used:
Figure-of-8 borderwork (Mason 1908:9, Fig. 2)
Gewickelte Randabschlusse (Seiler-Baldinger 1991:133)

2. Bound Borderwork

Binding techniques are also widely employed, i.e. a variation of knotted binding with clove hitches, effected with two alternately used threads (Fig. 231).

Fig. 231: Bound border

Other terms used:
Borderwork concealing rough ends with hoops and knotwork (Mason 1908:10, Fig. 4).
Gebundene Randabschlüsse (Seiler-Baldinger 1991:133)

2.1. Twined Borders

Twining and braiding are among the commonest and most popular forms of borderwork in plaited fabrics (Fig. 232).

Fig. 232: Twined borderwork

Other terms used:
Braid finish (Buck 1957:148, Fig. 38,8)
Crossed paired bend (Green Gigli et al. 1974:82)
Zwirngebundene Randabschlüsse (Seiler-Baldinger 1991:133)
Randabschluss der Zuschlag (Zechlin 1966:200)
Bord renversé cordé (Leroi-Gourhan 1943:290)

3. Coiled Borders

As the simplest and most effective technique, wrapped coiling is a widely used and popular form of borderwork (Fig. 233a-b).

Fig. 233a: Borderwork by wrapped coiling

Fig. 233b: Borderwork by wrapped coiling

Other terms used:
Wrapped loop finish (Buck 1957:148)
Bord renversé lié (Leroi-Gourhan 1943:290)
Arrêt en queue de spirale à brins roulés (Balfet 1952:278)

Other frequently used methods are looped coiling (Fig. 234a) and double-loop coiling, simple or crosswise (Fig. 234b).

Fig. 234a: Borderwork by looped coiling

Fig. 234b: Borderwork by cross double-looped coiling

Other terms used:
Wulsthalbgeflochtene Randabschlüsse (Seiler-Baldinger 1991: 133)
Arrêt en queue de spirale en 8 (Balfet 1952:278)
Acabamento anelar (Ribeiro 1988:72)

Active-Active Plaited Borders

Amongst the techniques of plaiting, three-strand braiding is particularly well suited for borderwork. Decorative borders are produced using macramé and bobbin lace techniques.

1. Diagonally Plaited Borders

These techniques are relatively rare and use a comparatively small number of elements so that they can be more correctly classified as multiple-strand braiding (Fig. 235).

Fig. 235: Diagonally plaited border

Other term used:
Diagonalgeflochtene Randabschlüsse (Seiler-Baldinger 1991: 134)

2. Perpendicularly Plaited Borders

This type of borderwork is almost entirely restricted to plaited fabrics, especially wickerwork. In the simplest form, one system (here passive) is bent and fixed by the other (active) system in a plain weave interlacing (Fig. 236a).

Fig. 236a. Perpendicularly plaited border

Other terms used:
Randparallel geflochtene Randabschlüsse (Seiler-Baldinger 1991: 134)
Ösen-Abschluss (Zechlin 1966:200a)
Bord renversé tissé (Leroi-Gourhan 1943:290)

In another variation, the passive elements are bent over at an acute angle and interlace with one another (but not quite at right angles) in a plain weave (Fig. 236b).

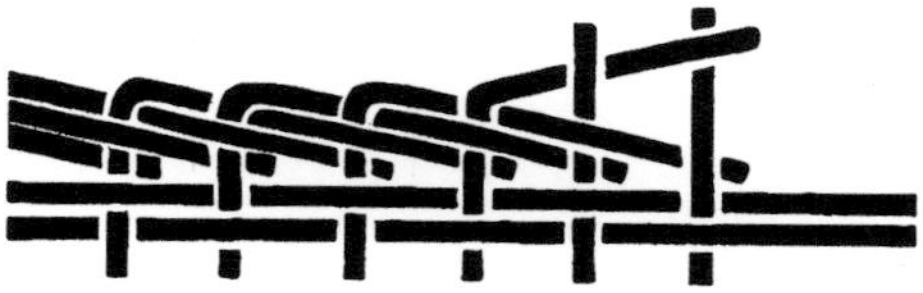

Fig. 236b: Perpendicularly plaited border

Other term used:
Übersteck-Randabschluss (Zechlin 1966:200c)

In another form each stake is arched over and its end pushed in beside the next stake but one (Fig. 236c).

Fig. 236c: Perpendicularly plaited border

Other terms used:
Simple turn-in border (Mason 1908:10, Fig. 5)
Bogen-Randabschluss (Zechlin 1966:200b)

A plaited border on a woven fabric is more complicated. Threads are laid on both sides, parallel to the fabric edges and braided with the aid of a thread which passes spirally and also through the fabric. A tubular border covering the fabric edges is thus formed (Fig. 237).

Fig. 237: Tubular plaited border

Other term used:
Schlauchgeflochtener Randabschluss (Seiler-Baldinger 1991:135)

3. Braided Borders

Very stable and attractive borders can be formed by braiding with three or more elements (Fig. 238a-b).

Fig. 238a: Braided border

Fig. 238b: Braided border

Other terms used:
Braid finish (Buck 1957:148)
Plaited border (Hodges 1964:147, Fig. 9)
Gezopfte Randabschlüsse (Seiler-Baldinger 1991:135)
Einfacher Zöpfchenschluss, Randabschluss der Zopf (Zechlin 1966:200f.;d,e)
Bord renversé tressé (Leroi-Gourhan 1943:290)

Making of Borders in More Advanced Fabric-producing, Decorative and Combined Techniques

More advanced fabric-producing techniques are used for making borders only in warp and woven fabrics.

Weft-wrapped Borders

In warp fabrics and woven textiles, wrapping the weft is quite frequently used as a means of reinforcing the edge (Fig. 239 a-b).

Other terms used:
Parallel wrapping (Tanavoli 1985:97)
Randabschluss durch Wickeln des Eintrages (Seiler-Baldinger 1991:135)
Seitenverstärkung durch einfache Umwicklung oder durch Umwicklung in Achterschlingen mit zusätzlichem Faden (Nabholz 1980:26)

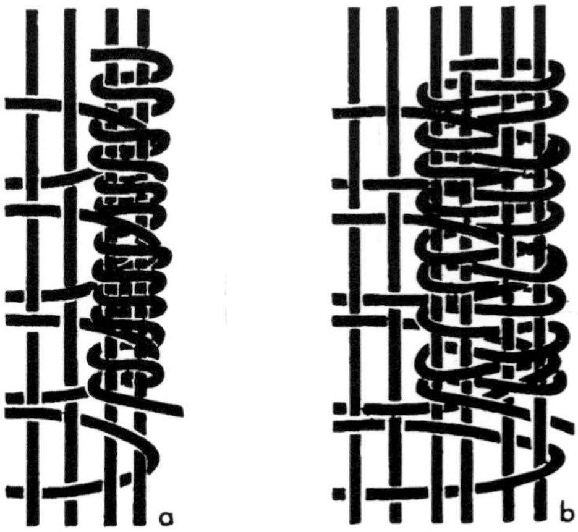

Fig. 239a-b: Weft-wrapped border

Weft- or Warp-twined Borders

Weft (Fig. 240a) or warp twining (Fig. 240b) is the most commonly used of all warp fabric techniques for bordering.

Fig. 240a: Weft-twined border

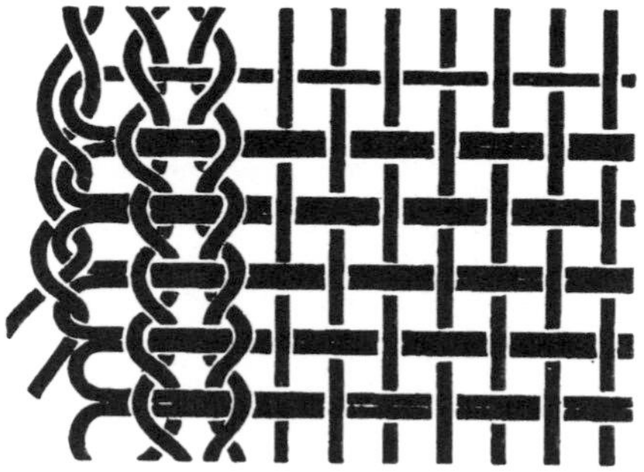

Fig. 240b: Warp-twined border

Other terms used:
Twine-stitches (Kent Peck 1957:575)
Twine edge (Collingwood 1968:503)
Zwirngebundene Randabschlüsse im Eintrag oder in der Kette (Seiler-Baldinger 1991:136)
Fils toronnés autour des fils de chaîne (Boser-Sarivaxévanis 1972: 53)

Woven Borders

Apart from narrow woven tapes which are attached to the fabric after its manufacture, woven borders (not selvedges) are quite rare. An ornamental thickening can, for instance, be produced at the edge. At the ends of the fabric the weft threads are inserted separately through the upper and lower warp threads as if in a separate fabric, so that a tubular structure is obtained (Fig. 241). Tablet- and finger-woven borders, however, are very common.

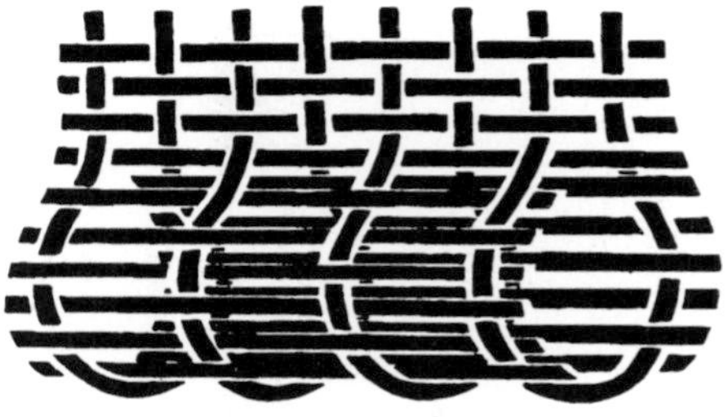

Fig. 241: Woven border

Other terms used:
Thickened edge made by the weaving of terminal loops of warp yarns (D'Harcourt 1962:135)
Tubular selvedge (Cardale-Schrimpff 1972:242)
Gewobene Randabschlüsse (Seiler-Baldinger 1991:136)

Stitched and Embroidered Borders

Stitched and embroidered borders form a large and widely varied group of their own. Since most of the employed methods are truly ornamental techniques (cf. embroidery, Fig. 242c), only a very simple form is mentioned here, namely borderwork by overcasting or whipping (Fig. 242a-b).

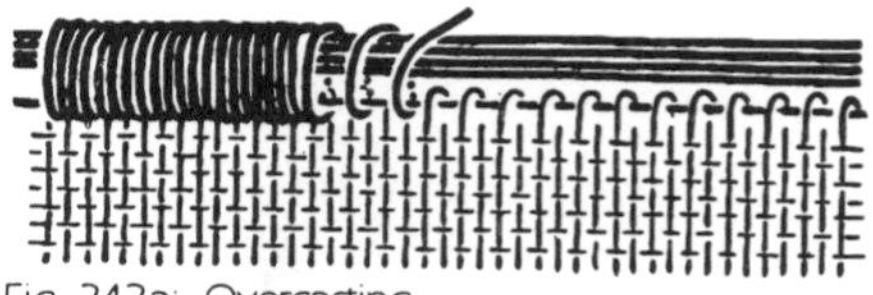

Fig. 242a: Overcasting

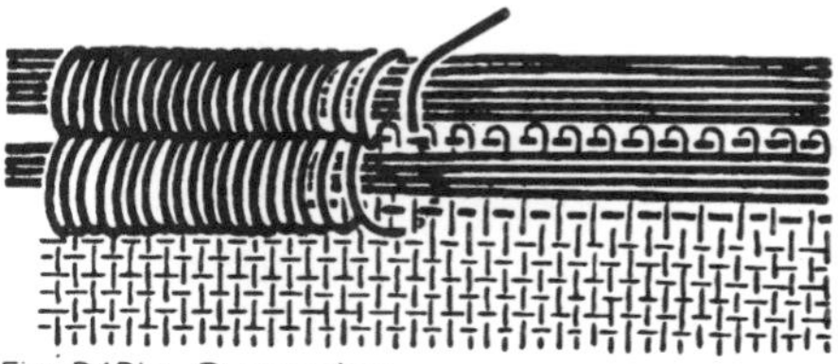

Fig. 242b: Overcasting

Fig. 242c: Embroidered border

Other term used:
Genähte und gestickte Randabschlüsse (Seiler-Baldinger 1991: 136)

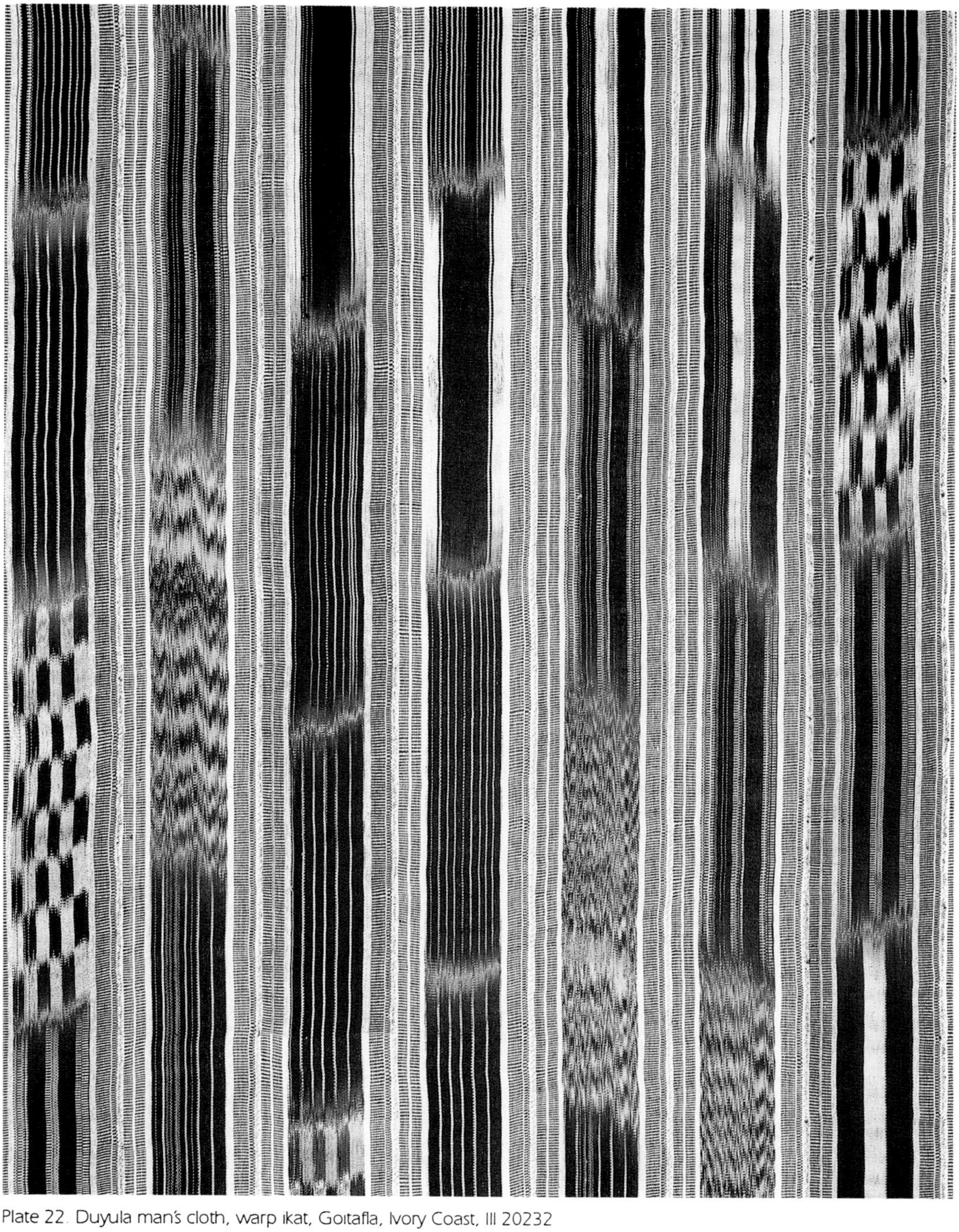

Plate 22. Duyula man's cloth, warp ikat, Goitafla, Ivory Coast, III 20232

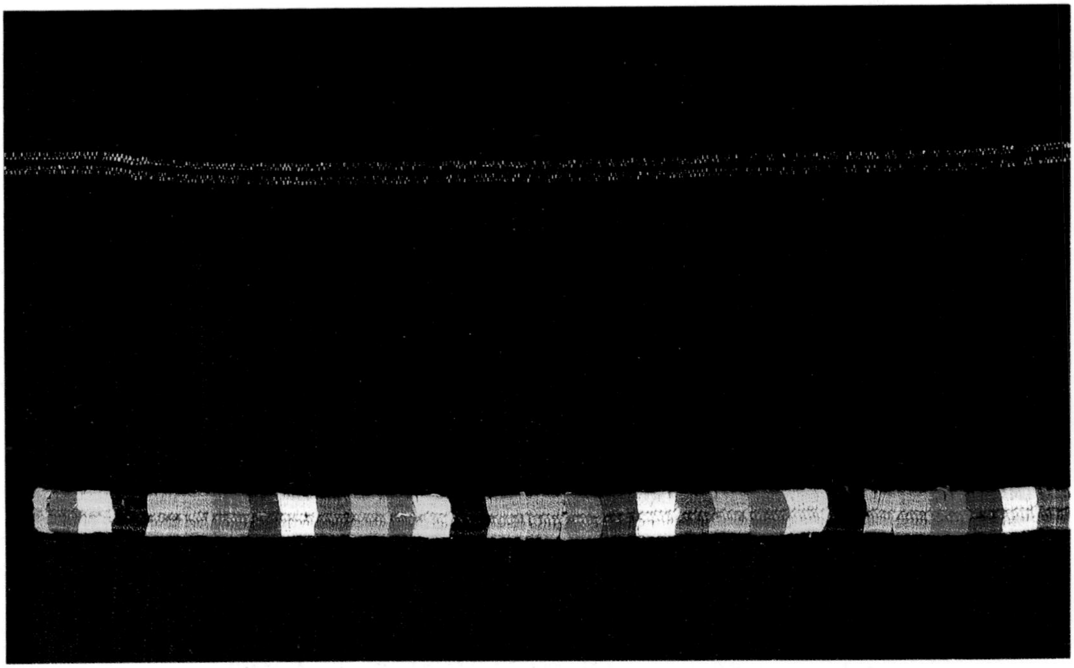

Plate 23. Embroidered seam of a Maya woman's skirt, Nahuala, Guatemala, collection A. Seiler-Baldinger

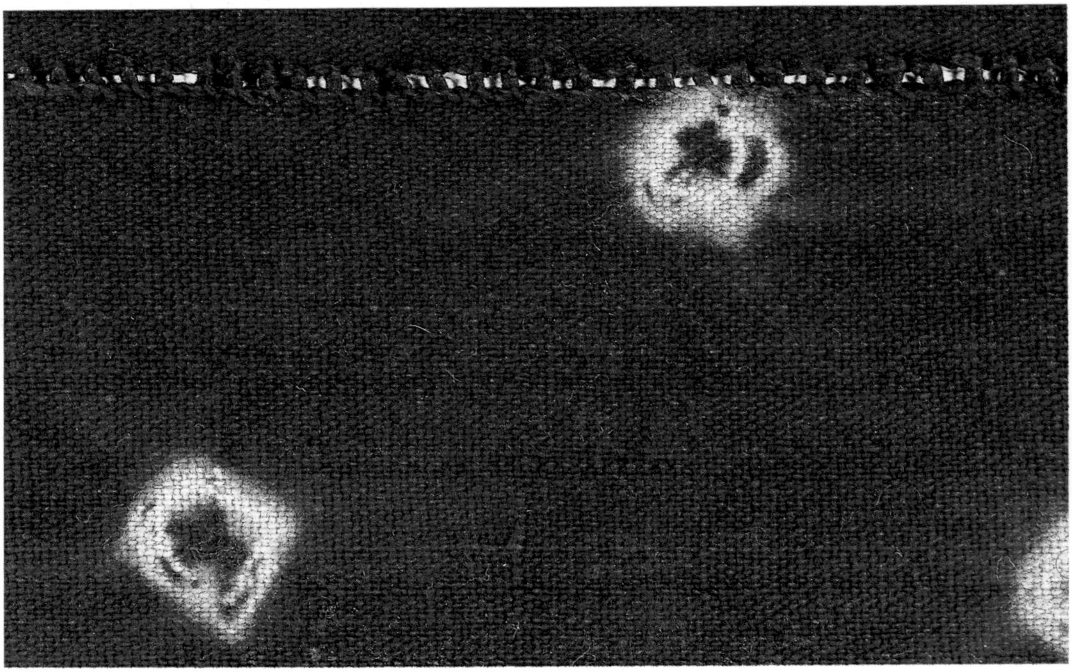

Plate 24. Decorative seam on a tie-dyed textile of the Dogon, Pinyar, Mali, III 25954

Combined Borderwork

The above-mentioned techniques can naturally be combined with each other to produce a virtually unlimited range of new variations.
Only two examples must suffice as an illustration:

1. Twisted and Plied Borders

This simple borderwork is seen quite often, particularly on woven fabrics. A number of warp or weft threads, usually in the form of a bundle, are continuously twisted together and twined or simply linked into a thread running at right angles to them (Fig. 243b-c).

Fig. 243a: Twisted and twined borderwork

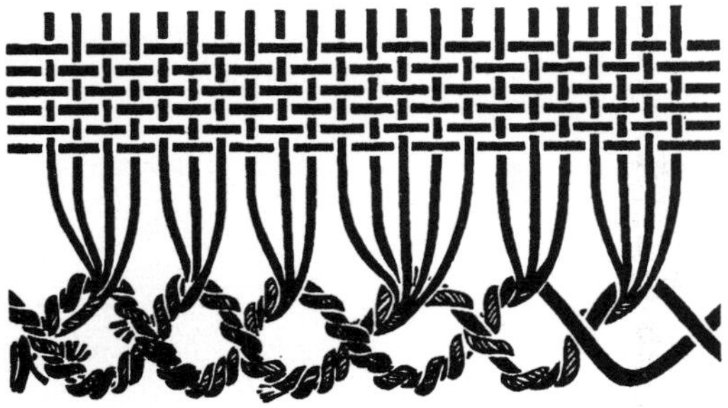

Fig. 243b: Twisted and twined borderwork

Fig. 243c: Twisted and twined borderwork

Other terms used:

Twining selvedge strings between warp or weft threads (Kent Peck 1957:577)
Gedrillte und verzwirnte Randabschlüsse (Seiler-Baldinger 1991: 137)
Fils de chaîne roulés en cordon courant dans le sens de la trame et adhérent étroitement au bord du tissu (Boser-Sarivaxévanis 1972:59)
Refuerzo de enlazado simple (Weitlaner-Johnson 1977:37)

2. Twisted and Braided Borders

A combination of different plaiting techniques is a very popular method of border formation (Fig. 244). In one possible variation, warp threads assembled into groups can be diagonally braided into a band and the ends emerging from this band twisted into two cords which are again plied together (Fig. 245).

Fig. 244: Combined border: diagonal plaiting and braiding

Fig. 245: Combined border: braiding and twining

Other terms used:

Kombiniert geflochtene und verzwirnte Randabschlüsse (Seiler-Baldinger 1991:137)
Madeira-Rand (Zechlin 1966:202)

Fringed Borders

Fringes and tassels can be formed either by protruding elements of the fabric itself or they can be subsequently added by insertion into the edge of the fabric or by sewing-on. The possibilities of fringe formation are at least as numerous and varied as those of ordinary borderwork.

Simple Fringes by Twisting, Knotting and Linking

In the simplest form of fringes on plaited or woven fabrics threads of one and/or the other system are left to protrude beyond the edges and subsequently twisted together in pairs or groups (Fig. 246).

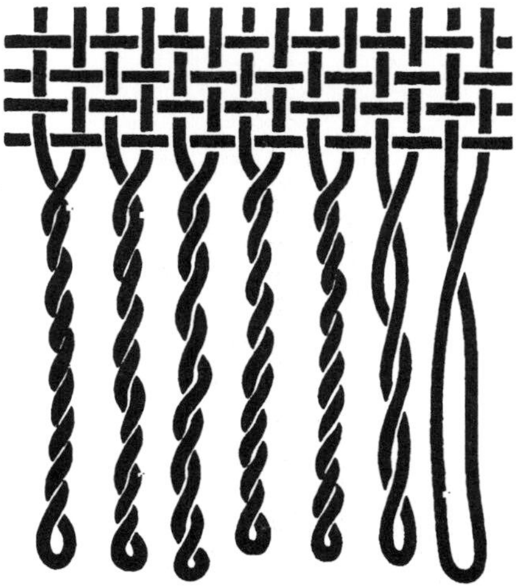

Fig. 246: Fringe formation by twisting of warp threads

Twisted, Plied and Knotted Fringes

Warp and weft threads at the edges can also be twisted with themselves or with a separate thread introduced for this purpose, and the cords thus formed knotted together at the corners where they stand out as fringes or tassels (Fig. 247).

Fig. 247: Fringe formation by twisting of warp and weft threads

Other terms used:
Corner tassels (Kent Peck 1957:477)
Fransenbildung durch Drillen und Zwirnen (Seiler-Baldinger 1991:138)
Fils de chaîne torsadés, fringe of twisted warp (Tanavoli 1985: 101)

The knotting of groups of warp threads (Fig. 248) is another popular way of forming fringes.

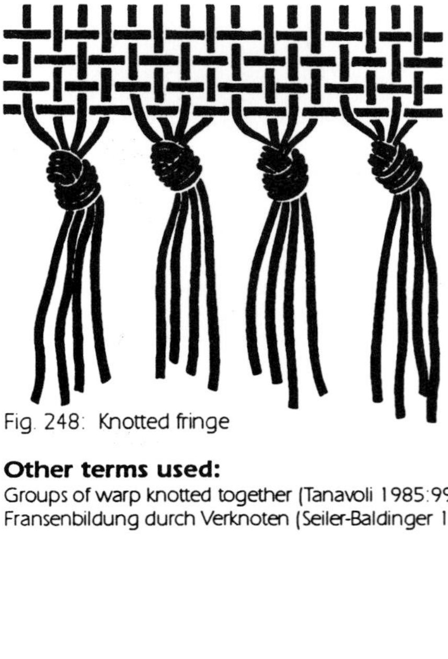

Fig. 248: Knotted fringe

Other terms used:
Groups of warp knotted together (Tanavoli 1985:99)
Fransenbildung durch Verknoten (Seiler-Baldinger 1991:138)

Fringe Formation by Linking or Knotting in a Running Thread

A running thread is loosely looped into the edges of the fabric (Fig. 249a-c). The loops thus formed twist together, usually in pairs. The fringe thread can also be knotted in (Fig. 249d).

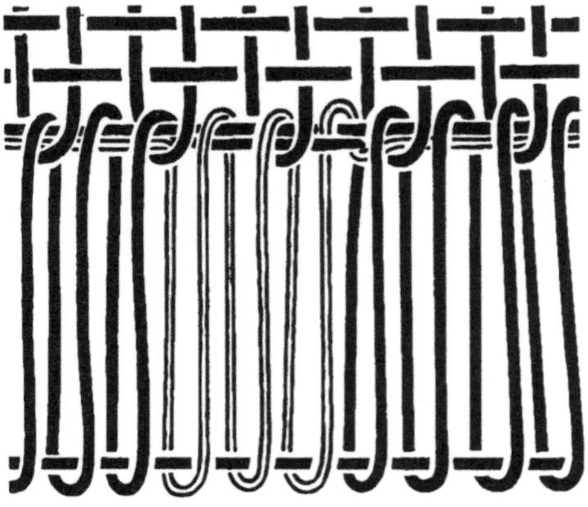

Fig. 249a: Fringe formation by linking in a running thread

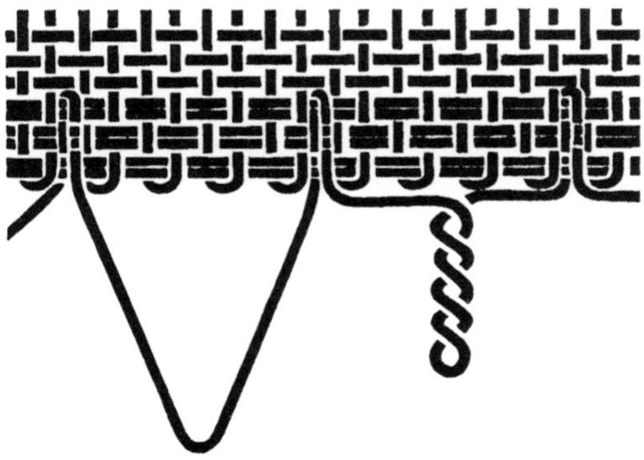

Fig. 249b: Fringe formation by linking in a running thread

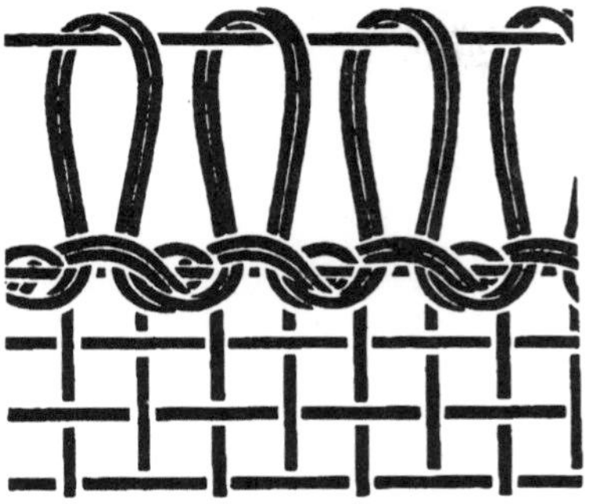

Fig. 249c: Fringe formation by looping in a running thread

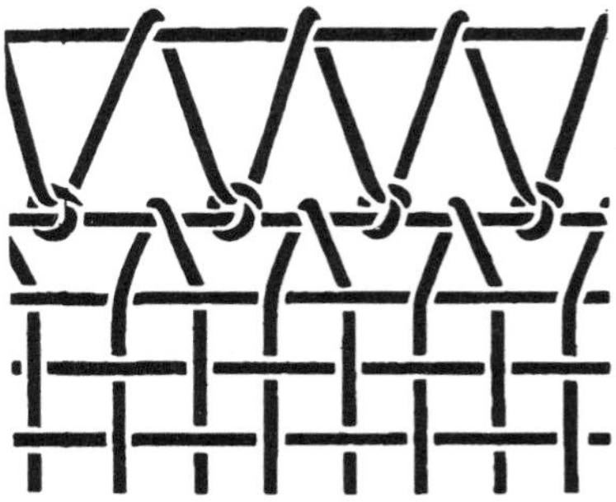

Fig. 249d: Fringe formation by knotting in a running thread

Other terms used:

Overcast fringe (Bird/Bellinger 1954:101)
Fransenbildung durch Einhängen oder Einknoten eines fortlaufenden Fadens (Seiler-Baldinger 1991:139)

In a somewhat more complex variation, the running thread is passed through the fringe loops at regular intervals and holds them together in groups (Fig. 250).

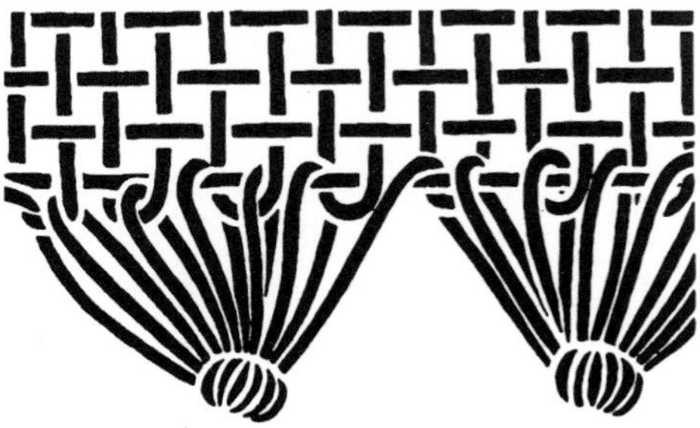

Fig. 250: Bundled fringe

Other terms used:

Bundled fringe (Bird/Bellinger 1954:101)
Gebündelte Fransenbildung (Seiler-Baldinger 1991:139)

Fringe Formation by Fabric-producing Techniques

Meshwork techniques have only a limited suitability for producing fringes: linking and knitting are hardly ever used. Variations of looping are more frequently employed.
Fringes can also be formed by plaiting. In active-passive plaiting the fringes constitute the passive system, which is fixed by wrapping and twining. In plaiting with active systems, the fringe-forming elements themselves are active.

Looped Fringes

Attractive borders are produced by simple (Fig. 251a-b) and twisted looping (Fig. 252) and complex special forms of double looping (Fig. 253a-b).

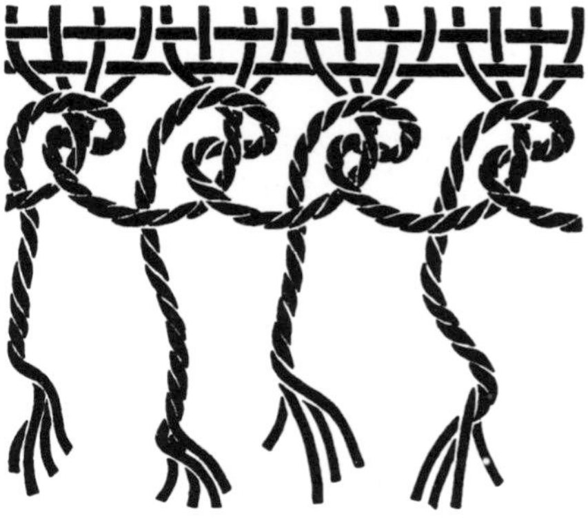

Fig. 252: Fringe formation by twisted looping

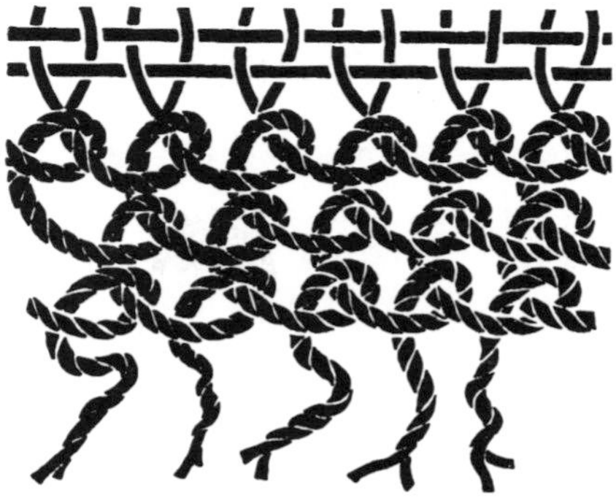

Fig. 251a: Fringe formation by simple looping

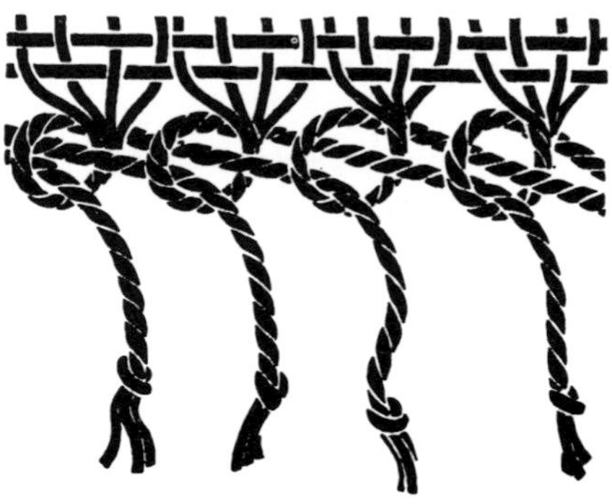

Fig. 251b: Fringe formation by simple looping

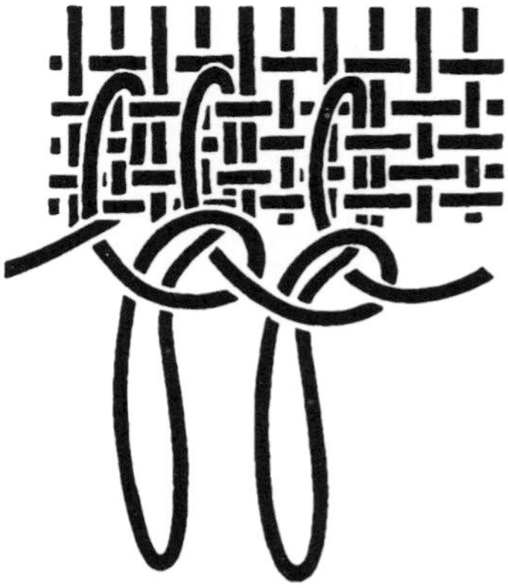

Fig. 253a: Double-looped fringe

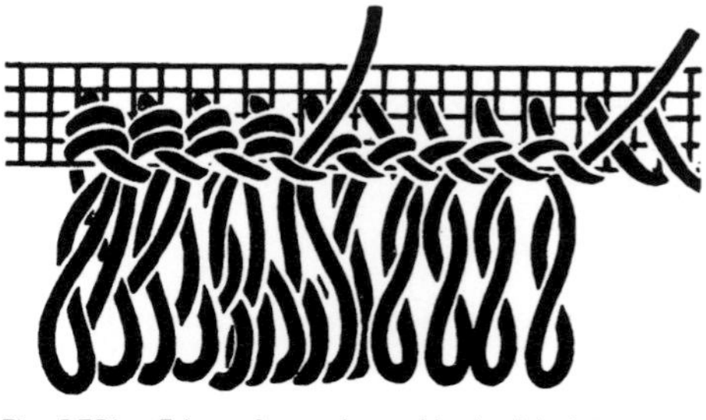

Fig. 253b: Fringe formation with double loops

Other terms used:
Buttonhole loop fringe (Bird/Bellinger 1954:101)
Einfach, zweifach oder doppelschlaufig verschlungene Fransenbildung (Seiler-Baldinger 1991:140)

Interconnected looping can also be used for making fringes by simply allowing the mesh loops to hang down loosely (Fig. 254a) or by means of a complex double-looped technique (Fig. 254b).

Fig. 254a: Fringe formation by interconnected looping

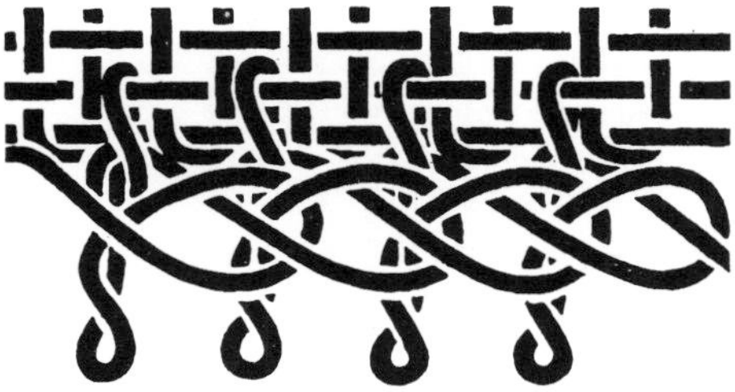

Fig. 254b: Fringe formation by interconnected looping

Other term used:
Verhängt verschlungene Fransenbildung (Seiler-Baldinger 1991: 141)

Crocheted Fringes

In a similar way to that of interconnected looping, fringes can be produced by simple crochet stitches with a loosely formed loop (plain crocheting).

Fig. 255: Crocheted fringe

Other term used:
Gehäkelte Fransenbildung (Seiler-Baldinger 1991: 141)

Fringe Formation by Active-passive Plaiting

Wrapping (Fig. 256a-b) and knotted wrapping techniques (Fig. 257a-b) are frequently used to form bundled warp fringes. The active thread can also be linked or looped into the edge of the fabric (Fig. 256a).

Fig. 256a: Wrapped fringe

Fig. 256b: Fringe fixed by looped wrapping

Fig. 257a: Fringe fixed by knotted wrapping

Fig. 257b: Fringe formed by knotted wrapping with twining

Other terms used:

Gewickelte und geknotete Franse (Seiler-Baldinger 1991:141)
Fil continu noué autour des fils de chaîne terminaux pris par groupes (Boser-Sarivaxévanis 1972:52)

Fringes are also fixed by wrapped binding (Fig. 258) and twining (Fig. 259).

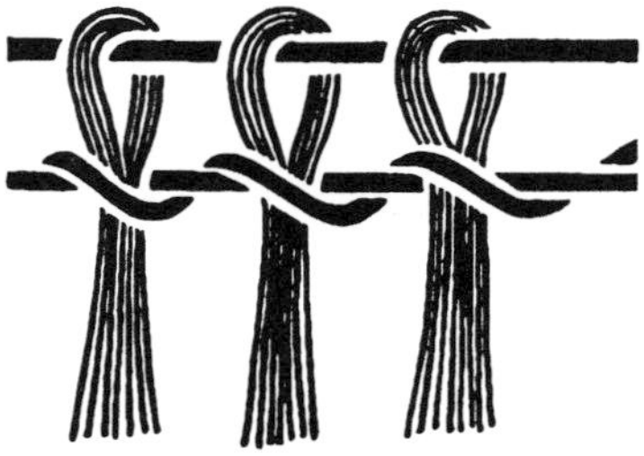

Fig. 258: Fringe fixed by wrapped binding

Fig. 259: Fringe formed by twining

Other term used:

Gebundene und zwirngebundene Franse (Seiler-Baldinger 1991:142)

Braided Fringes

Warp fringes with braided warp thread ends are particularly popular in woven fabrics. The braiding may be either parallel to the fabric edge with hanging threads (Fig. 260a-b) or the fringes may be simply braided (Fig. 261). Fringed borders produced by oblique intertwining and macramé techniques are also common (Fig. 262).

Fig. 260a: Fringe formed by braiding parallel to fabric edge

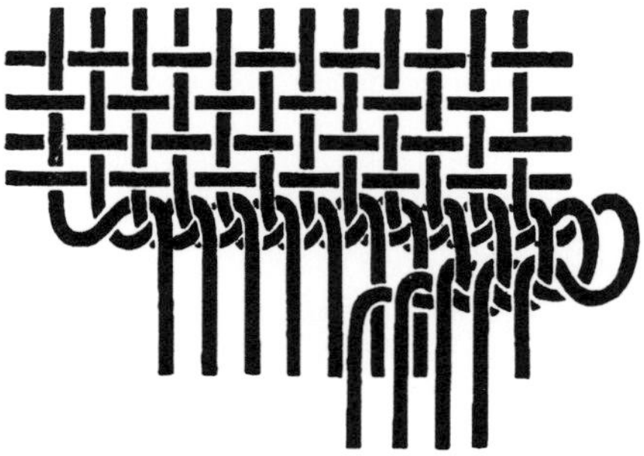

Fig.260b: Fringe formed by braiding parallel to fabric edge

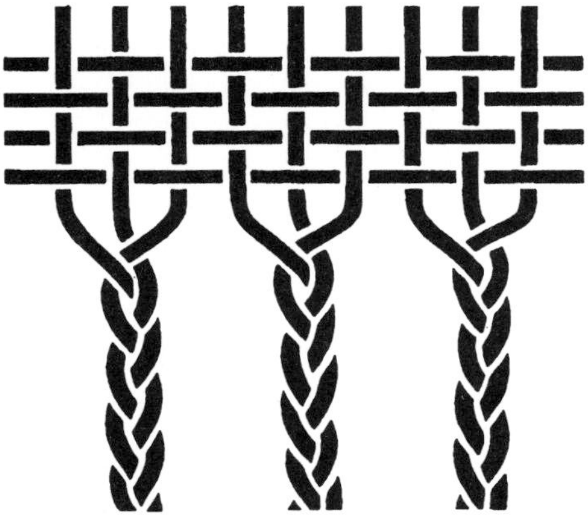

Fig.261: Braided warp fringe

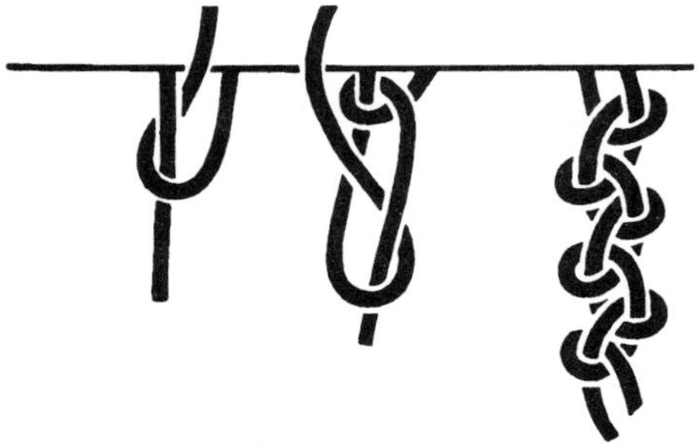

Fig.262: Macramé fringe

Other terms used:
Finishing warp ends with alternative hitches (Collingwood 1968: 496)
Knotted fringe (O'Neale 1945: Fig. 49)
Warps interlooped in a chain-like manner (Tanavoli 1985: Fig. 150)
Gezopfte Fransen (Seiler-Baldinger 1991:142)
Knüpffransen (De Dillmont, undated:418ff.)
Fils de chaîne noués en filet (Boser-Sarivaxévanis 1972:58)
Fils de chaîne tressés en natte plate, groups of warp braided (Tanavoli 1985:100)

Fringe Formation by More Advanced Fabric-producing Techniques

Fringe formation in the warp fabric technique is the same in principle as in plaiting by wrapping and twining, whereas fringes in weaving techniques are produced, for instance, by reversing the weft over only a few warp threads (Fig. 263).

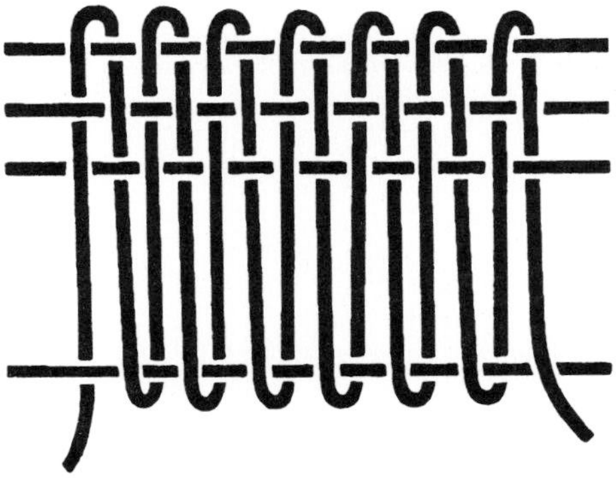

Fig.263: Woven fringe

Other terms used:
Woven fringe (Bird/Bellinger 1954:101)
Gewobene Franse (Seiler-Baldinger 1991:143)

Fringes can also be substituted or supplemented by sewing to the fabric tassels, feathers, bundles of fibres etc., and the edges ornamented by stitching on beads, etc.

References to Borders and Fringes: see pp. 168-169.

Ornamentation After Production of the Fabric

Instead of being ornamented during their production, fabrics can also be decorated after they are finished. The techniques can be divided into two main groups according to the substances used: Ornamentation with solid and liquid materials. These two groups can be further subdivided.

Woman's sarong, glass beads and shells, of the Iban Dayak, West Kalimantan, Indonesia, IIc 14904

Ornamentation with Solid Materials

The ornamentation of fabrics with solid materials offers a wealth of decoration possibilities. These differ a) in the technique of ornamentation and b) in the character of the employed material.

Application Techniques

One of the oldest techniques of ornamentation is to attach to the fabric pieces of other fabrics, feathers, threads, shells, hairs, beads, bristles, quills, pieces of wood and bark, leather etc. The methods used are relatively simple from the technical point of view. The ornamental elements can be fixed to the fabric in the desired arrangement by sewing or gluing. The employed sewing stitches often have a decorative character and are akin to embroidery. The techniques are generally classified according to the type of accessory and the fixing method. The most important methods are briefly discussed below.

Sewing on of Accessory Fabric Pieces

Fabric pieces cut into different shapes are sewn on to the base fabric (Fig. 264).

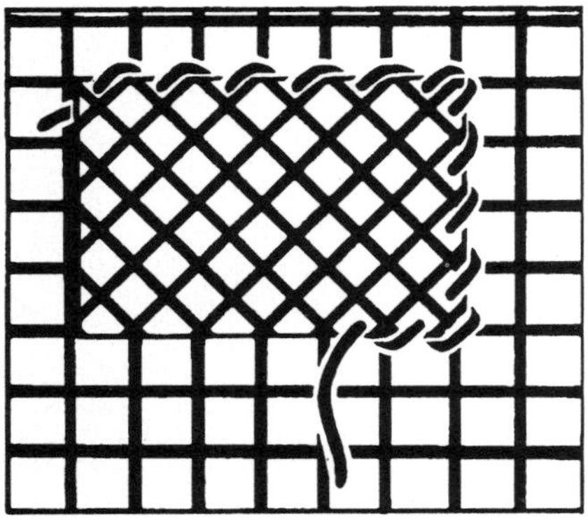

Fig. 264:. Sewing on accessory fabric pieces

Other terms used:
Appliqué (Emery 1966:251)
Ribbonwork (Lyford 1943:131)
Applied work (Cox 1959c:5)
Aufnähen von Stoffstücken (Seiler-Baldinger 1991:145)
Flickenstepperei, Patchwork (Lammèr 1975:269)
Aufnäh- und Fleckelarbeiten (Meyer-Heisig 1956:59ff.)
Aplicado (Vreeland/Muelle 1977:9)

Sewing Together Pieces of Fabric (quilting)

Two or more superimposed pieces of fabric are sewn together with running stitches in such a way that fine patterns are created by the stitches themselves as well as by the relief effect thus produced. The relief effects can be accentuated by padding the individual fabric pieces (Fig. 265).

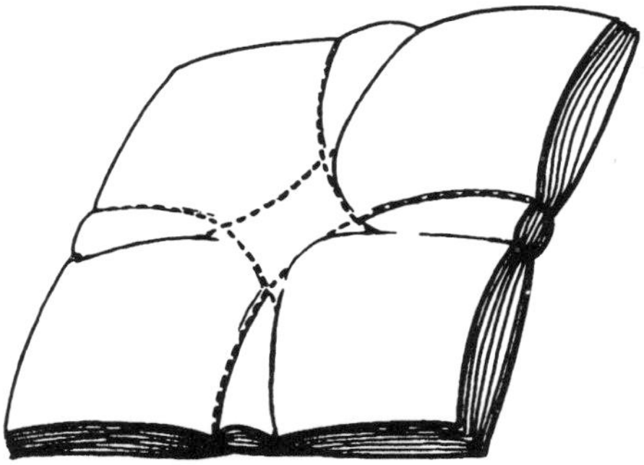

Fig. 265: Quilting

Other terms used:
Quilting (Fitzrandolph 1954:7ff.)
Quilt making (Wulff 1966:227ff.)
Zusammennähen von Stofflagen (Steppen) (Seiler-Baldinger 1991:145)
Appliqué quilt (Bishop/Coblentz 1975:71)

Sewing Together and Cutting Out Layers of Fabric

In this technique, the sewing together of layers of fabric is combined with the sewing on of pieces of fabric and the cutting out of specific parts of the fabric layers thus formed (Fig. 266 a-d). This technique is known primarily from the Mola work of the Kuna Indians (Panama/ Colombia), but is also seen elsewhere.

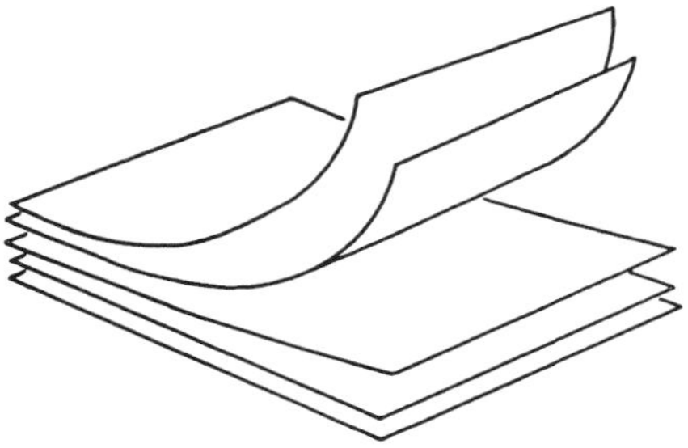

Fig. 266a: Cutout appliqué technique: placing the layers of fabric upon each other

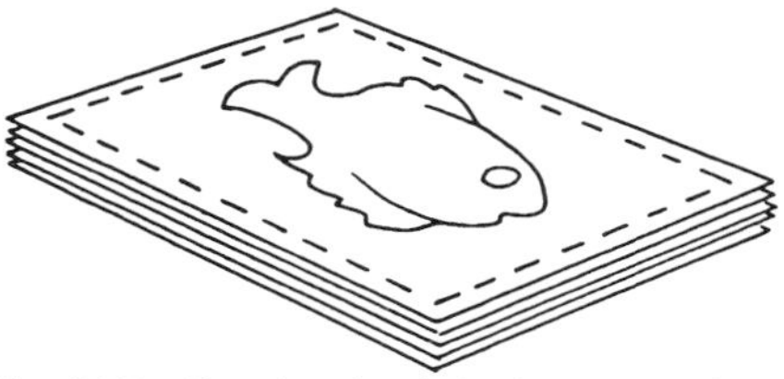

Fig. 266b: Drawing the desired pattern and sewing together the layers

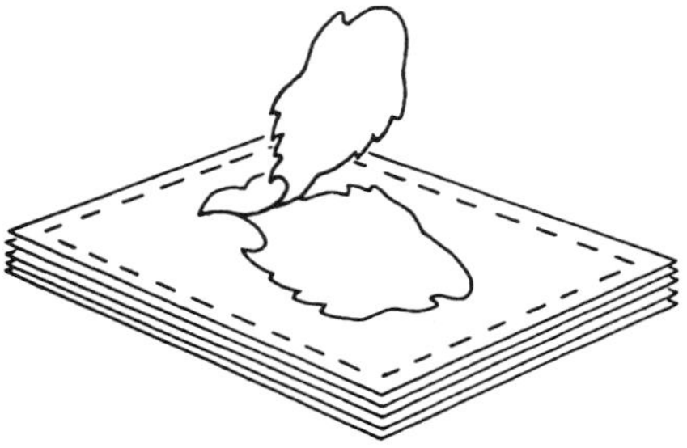

Fig. 266c: Cutting out the pattern

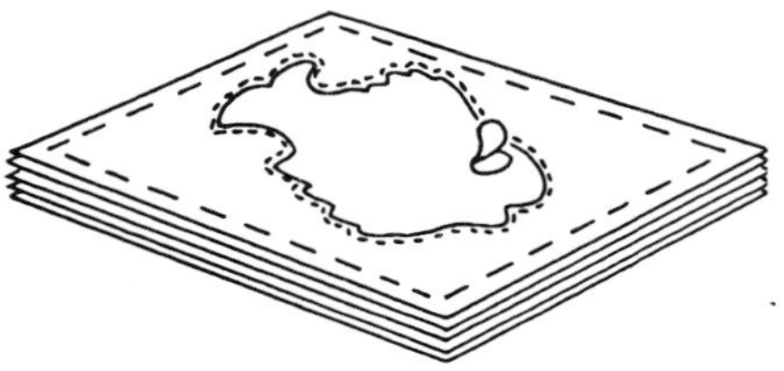

Fig. 266d: Sewing round the edges and cutting out a further layer of fabric, etc.

Other terms used:
Set in (inlay) (Emery 1966:252)
Zusammennähen und Ausschneiden von Stofflagen (Seiler-Baldinger 1991:146)

Sewing on of Beads, Hair, Strings, Quills, Bristles etc.

In these methods the stitches have no decorative function but serve only for the fixing of the accessory. Only the accessory is seen on the fabric surface, and often the stitches are visible only on the reverse side.

1. Bead Embroidery

The beads can be fixed to the fabric in two ways. In the more simple form, the beads are strung on a thread which is periodically passed through the fabric (Fig. 267a). The other method is to fix the bead thread to the base with additional stitches (Fig. 267b).

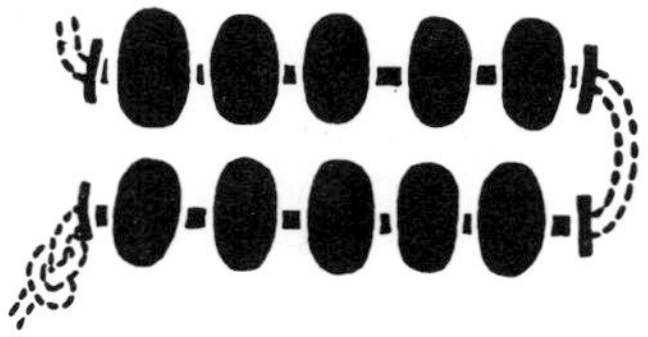

Fig. 267a: Bead embroidery

Fig. 267b: Bead embroidery

Other terms used:
Beadwork, sewing technique (Orchard 1929:128ff.)
Beadwork technique (Lyford 1940:60ff.)
Lazy stitch (Orchard 1929:129)
Overlaid or spot stitch (Orchard 1929:129)
Spot or couched stitch (Lyford 1943:125)
Perlenstickerei (Seiler-Baldinger 1991:146)

2. Quill Embroidery

This method is closely related to bead embroidery. The main difference is that a thread, or often two parallel threads, are first fixed on the base fabric with simple stitches (e.g. spotstitch, backstitch or loopstitch, Fig. 268a-c), after which the moistened quills or bristles are wrapped or bent round the floating parts of the threads (Fig. 269a-b).

Fig. 268a: Quill embroidery with two parallel threads

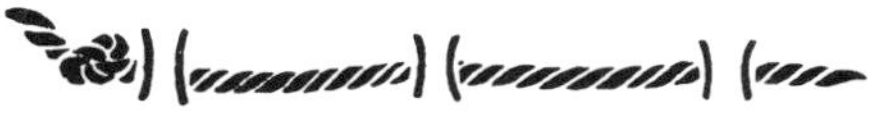

Fig. 268b: Quill embroidery: fixing thread from reverse side: running stitch

Fig. 268c: Quill embroidery: fixing thread from reverse side: loop stitch

Fig. 269a: Quill embroidery around a single thread

Fig. 269b: Quill embroidery around two parallel threads

Other terms used:
Quill sewing (Lyford 1940:48ff.)
Quillwork techniques (Ewers 1945:30ff.)
Federkiel- oder Borstenstickerei (Seiler-Baldinger 1991:147)
Travail aux piquants (Best/McClelland 1977)

3. Hair Embroidery

In the simplest method, tufts of hair are placed on the fabric and fixed by means of stitches running at right angles to the tufts. As the work progresses, successive new tufts of hair are attached. These may also be twisted. Instead of hair, threads and cords may be fixed in the same way (Fig. 270a).

Fig. 270a: Hair embroidery

Other terms used:
Hair embroidery, simple oversewn line (Turner 1955:31, Fig. 3, 5)
Haarstickerei (Seiler-Baldinger 1991:147)

In another variation, the same method is used as in quill embroidery (Fig. 270b). Similar methods are used for fixing thin metal spirals on the fabric.

Fig. 270b: Hair embroidery

Other terms used:
Hairs wound over straight stitching (Turner 1955:32, Fig. 6)
Metallstickerei (Meyer-Heisig 1956:56ff.)

Embroidery and Related Methods

The embroidery-like methods differ from the application techniques in that the embroidery thread itself has a decorative function without being used to fix additional elements.

Embroidery

The term embroidery is used for ornamental methods in which fabrics are decorated with a thread which is also used to fix itself to the base. Many embroidery techniques have close similarities with sewing, as can be seen in particular in decorative stitches in which embroidery has the function not only of ornamentation but of joining pieces of fabric as well. The relation to appliqué has already been mentioned.
Embroidery exists in many forms, which are classified according to the stitches. In many cases the stitches show the same looping and interlacing forms as those used in fabric production techniques – with the difference, of course, that embroidery is done on a finished fabric and with the use of needles (e.g. the structure of the looping stitch is related to looping).
Since an excellent and comprehensive classification of stitch forms appeared in 1968 (Boser/Müller, reprinted 1984), it is not necessary to discuss the various forms again. Only a few transitional and special forms will be mentioned here.

Decorative Seams

Embroidery in this case has the function not only of ornamentation but also of joining pieces of fabric. Two-dimensional stitches formed by crossing or looping (e.g. cross stitch or looping stitch, Fig. 271) are generally preferred.

Fig. 271: Decorative loop stitch

Smocking

The fabric is uniformly pleated by means of threads running through it (Fig. 272a) and the individual pleats are fixed as desired by means of suitable stitches. The charm of the pattern lies both in the embroidery and in the contrast between the smooth and pleated areas (Fig 272b-c).

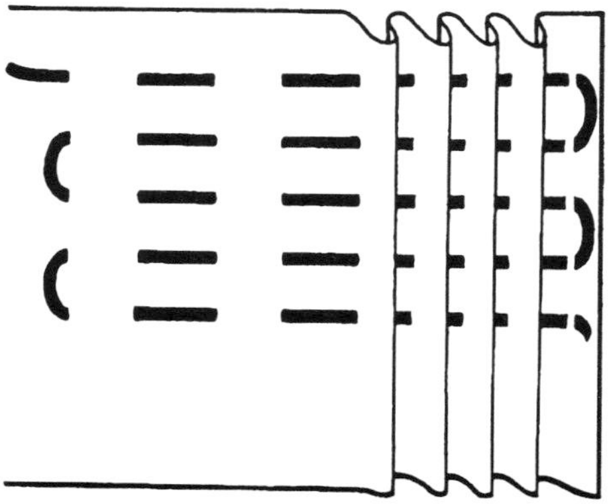

Fig. 272a: Smocking: sewing and pleating the fabric

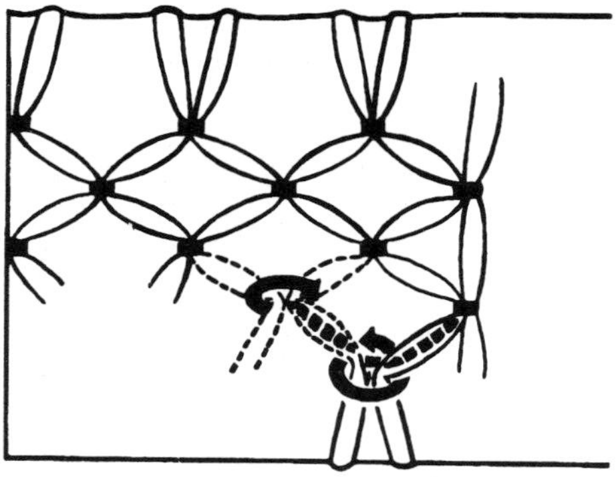

Fig. 272b: Fixing the pleats by various types of stitches

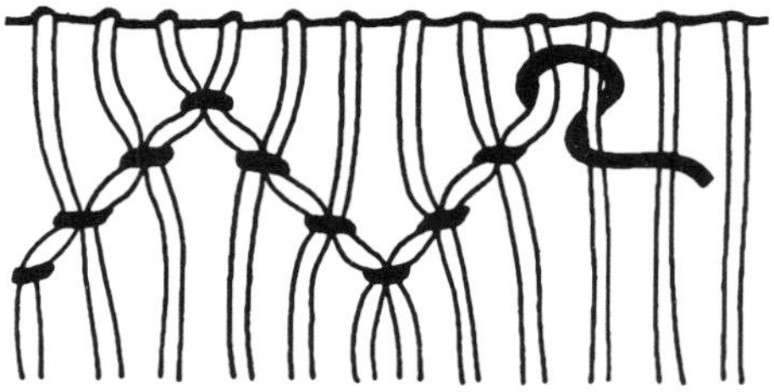

Fig. 272c: Fixing the pleats by various types of stitches

Embroidery-like Decoration of Net Fabrics

These methods can be classified as embroidery in as much as they involve the fixing of decorative threads on the fabric. However, since the base fabric is very open (net-like), the decorative threads must be either looped or knotted to keep them firm. (Fig. 273).

This method is closely related to weft wrapping techniques.

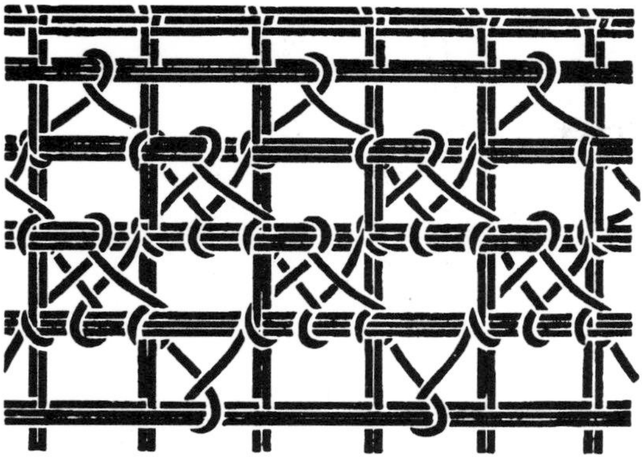

Fig. 273: Embroidery-like decoration of net fabrics

Other terms used:

Embroidery on fabric with square open spaces and on network (D'Harcourt 1962:129ff.)
Stickereiartige Verzierung von Netzgründen (Seiler-Baldinger 1991:149)
Filetstickerei, Guipure, Lacis (Von Schorn 1885:164)
Netzstickerei, Guipure, Tüllspitzen (De Dillmont, undated: 470ff., 576ff.)
Netznadelarbeiten (Meyer-Heisig 1956:54ff.)
Filetspitze (Müller/Brendler/Spiess 1958:180)
Zugstickerei, Tüllstickerei (Zechlin 1966:75, 77ff.)
Broderie sur filet (Hardouin, undated:19ff.)
Tejido reticular anudado y enlazado (Fung Pineda 1978:325)

Openwork

The methods used in this group differ from those already discussed in that the decorative effects are obtained primarily by removing parts of the fabric. The opening of the base fabric (in most cases this is a woven fabric) can be effected either by pulling out individual threads or groups of threads (drawn work) or by cutting out parts of the fabric (cut work). In the open spaces thus created the threads are now "embroidered" in groups by techniques such as binding, interlacing or looping to form patterns. In cut work the open portions are bordered by stitches. In drawn work, the threads removed may be from only the warp or from the weft (weft or warp openwork) or from both (weft-warp openwork). The simplest form of openwork is the hemstitch (Fig. 274). Similar decorative effects can be obtained if parts of the fabric are left open at the time of fabric production itself, so that the threads of one system are free. They are then decorated as described. This type of openwork is so closely related to plain-weave openwork, and the transitions are often so gradual, that it is difficult to draw a boundary between the methods (Fig. 275).

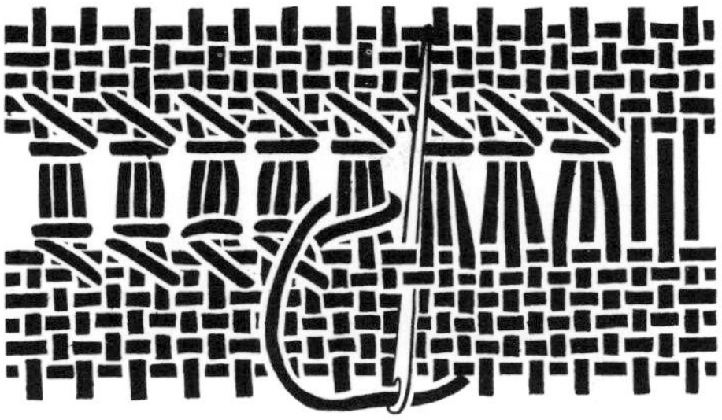

Fig. 274: Hemstitch

Fig. 275: Openwork

Other terms used:

Openwork embroidery (Emery 1966:247)
Weft-warp openwork (Weitlaner-Johnson 1976:64)
Durchbrucharbeiten (Seiler-Baldinger 1991:149)

Drawn work:
Substractive embroidery (Dendel 1974:26)
Withdraw element work (Coleman/Sonday 1977:35)
Gezogener Durchbruch (Seiler-Baldinger 1991:150)
Ausziehspitze, point tiré, punto tirato (Von Schorn 1885:264ff.)

Warp or weft openwork:
Einfacher Durchbruch (Seiler-Baldinger 1991:150)
Punto tirato (De Dillmont, undated: 515ff.)

Warp-weft openwork:
Doppeldurchbruch (Seiler-Baldinger 1991:150)
Point coupé (Preising 1987:94)
Punto tagliato (De Dillmont, undated: 515ff.)

Cut work:
Cut fabric work (Coleman/Sonday 1977:35)
Geschnittener Durchbruch (Seiler-Baldinger 1991:150)
Ausschnittstickerei (Niedner 1924:10)
Point coupé (Von Schorn 1885:164ff.)
Broderie Richelieu, Broderie Colbert, Broderie anglaise etc. (Hardouin, undated:8ff.)

References to Ornamentation with Solid Material: see pp.169-170.

Ornamentation with Liquid Materials

Materials in liquid (or powder) form can be used to pattern fabrics either directly or indirectly. Whereas direct patterning employs technically simple methods, the processes used for indirect forms of ornamentation can be highly complex.

Direct Ornamentation

The direct patterning methods were originally carried out with pigment colouring materials, i.e. with colouring matter which does not have the same affinity for the fabric as in true dyeing.

Transitional Forms: Application of Dry Colouring Substances

Instead of solid material, colouring substances can be used for the ornamentation of fabrics. Only in the very simplest techniques, however, are such substances – e.g. soot, chalk, red chalk – applied in their dry form. Strictly speaking, these techniques are application processes using very finely divided solid material. The same also applies to the use of mineral pigments mixed with liquids.

Painting with Liquid Colours

Painting is undoubtedly one of the earliest methods of surface ornamentation. Although it allows a very large degree of individual freedom, it is more suited for woven than for plaited fabrics.

Block Printing

Direct printing of coloured patterns represents an advance over painting since the blocks used in printing allow a motif to be applied quickly and an unlimited number of times.

Immersion Methods

Multi-coloured fabrics can be obtained by dipping portions of the cloth in a dye bath. This method has the advantage of imparting a more intensive coloration to both sides of the fabric, but cannot be used to produce complex patterns. Natural dyestuffs can be used for the bath in order to obtain fast dyeings. These may be either direct dyes (oxidation dyes) or mordant dyes which become fixed only on suitably prepared fabric (e.g. madder).

Indirect Ornamentation

Indirect ornamentation with liquid material includes all resist dyeing methods. The simplest example of a resist effect is that of a surface exposed to sunlight on which an object has intentionally or unintentionally been left. The object has a blocking-off or resist effect (sun tan).
As a rule, resist methods are used for the ornamentation of fabrics after their production, although one special process (ikat) is used for yarn.
From the viewpoint of the broad classification of ornamentation techniques, this process should be assigned to the methods of ornamentation during fabric production. Within the overall system of classification, however, ikat so clearly belongs to the resist processes that it would make little sense to separate it from these.

Covering Certain Parts of the Fabric Prior to Dyeing (resist dyeing)

In resist dyeing, a coloured ornamentation of fabrics or yarns is achieved by covering certain portions of the material prior to dyeing. Patterning is thus obtained not by the direct application of colour but indirectly. In the simplest examples of these techniques, the resultant patterns appear uncoloured on a coloured ground. Multi-coloured decorations can be obtained by previously dyeing the entire fabric, by the repeated application of resists, or by their removal in a series of stages in association with successive dyeings.

The resist techniques for fabrics can be classified into the following groups: folding, stitching, tie dyeing, use of stencils, application of pastes or liquids, and mordant and negative resist methods. Corresponding forms for yarn are named ikat (see pp. 147-148).

1. Fold Resist Dyeing

When the fabric is folded into an appropriate form and pressed together, some parts are protected from the dye, which is unable to penetrate into the interior of the pressed material. Thus, in this case, parts of the fabric itself act as resists (Fig. 276 a-c).

A folded fabric can be better held together by pressing (Fig. 277 a-c).

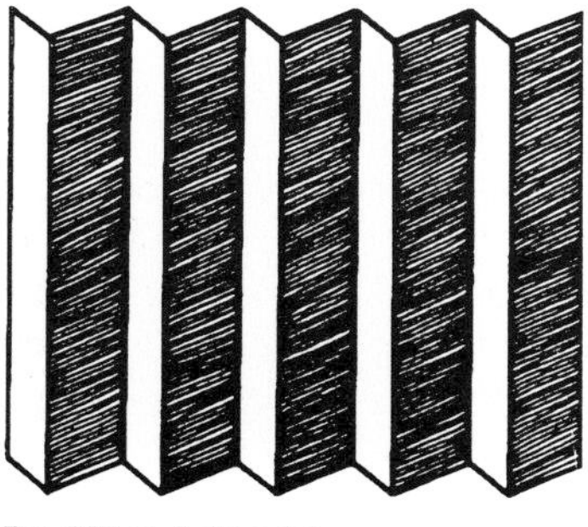

Fig. 276a: Fold resist

Fig. 276b: Fold resist

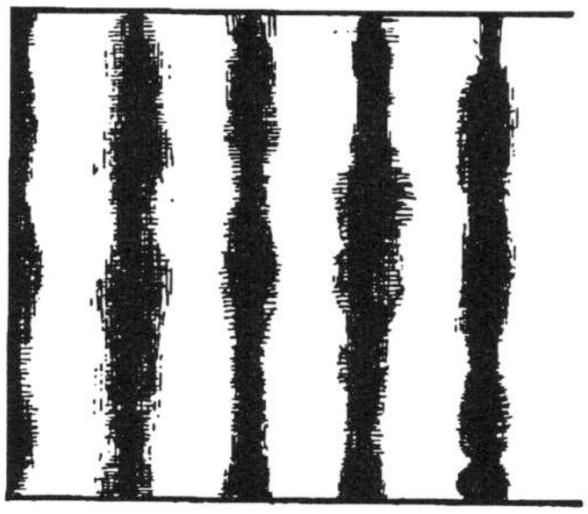

Fig. 276c: Resist pattern by folding

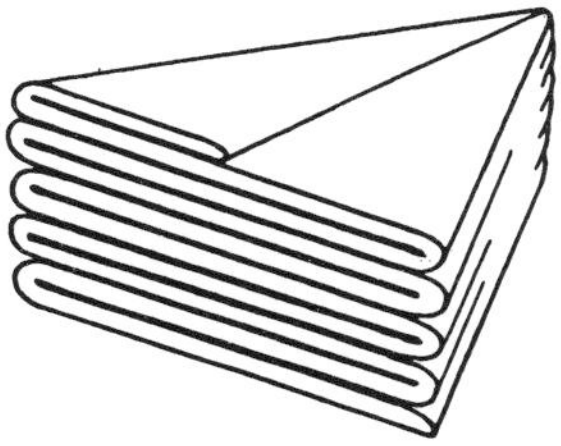

Fig. 277a: Fold resist

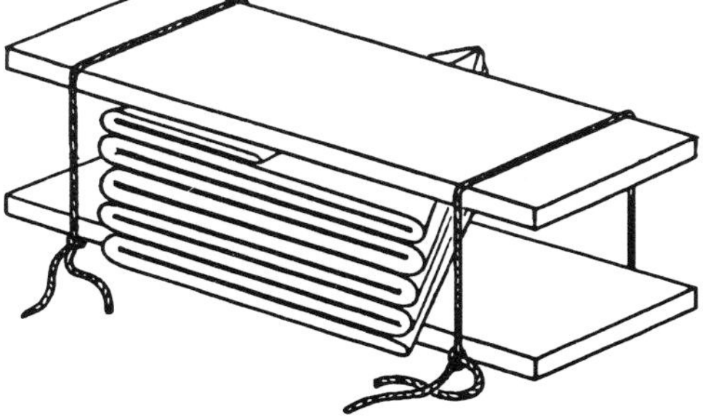

Fig. 277b: Folding and pressing resist

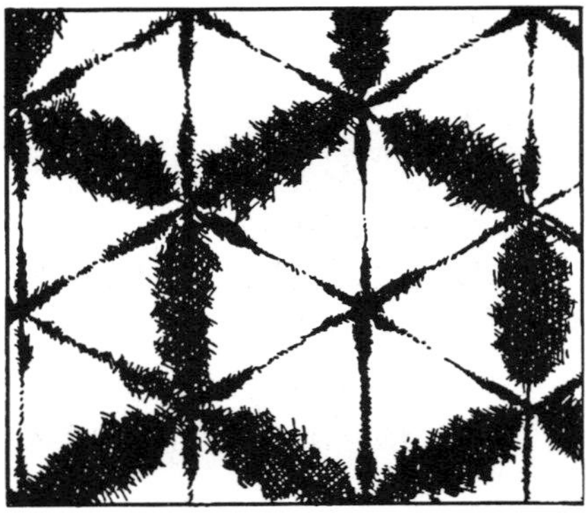

Fig. 277c: Resist pattern by folding and pressing

Other terms used:
Tie-and-dye: folding (Maile 1963:52ff.)
Board clamping (Wada et al. 1983:118)
Reservierung durch Falten (Seiler-Baldinger 1991:152)

2. Stitch Resist Dyeing (tritik)

In the most typical form of this group, running stitches are made in the fabric, the fabric is pushed together on the threads and the ends of the threads are knotted. In another variation the fabric is pinched together in single or double folds which are sewn with thread using running or overcasting stitches, after which the fabric is also drawn together on the threads (Fig.278). Another possibility is to stitch together a number of layers of the fabric at the edges. In order to obtain a coloured sewn pattern on a white ground, which is more difficult than the converse, it is necessary to reserve the fabric which has been prepared by sewing, by (e.g.) winding it on a cylindrical core (Fig. 279a-b). A resist effect is achieved by tightly winding the fabric on the roller. In the dye bath the colour penetrates only into the stitches so as to produce a coloured pattern on a white ground (Fig. 279c). Folding and stitching methods are often combined in order to obtain complex patterns.

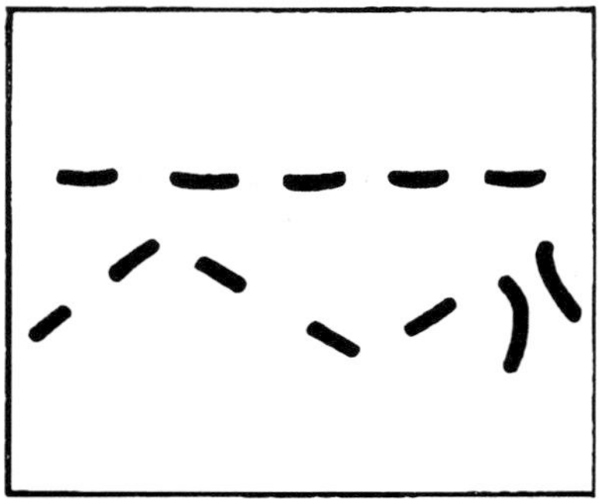

Fig. 278a: Resist stitches in place

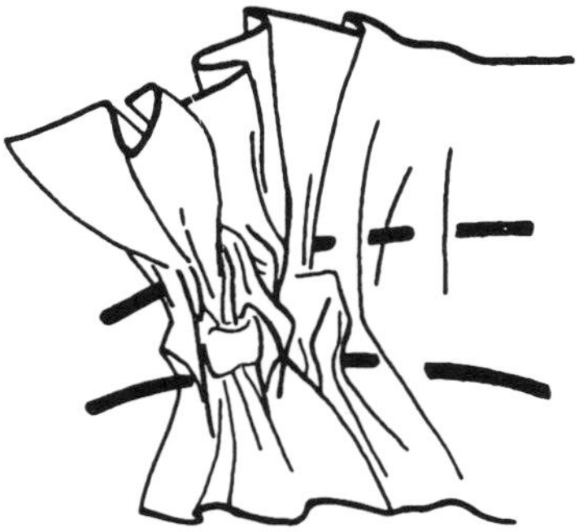

Fig. 278b: Drawing together the fabric on the thread

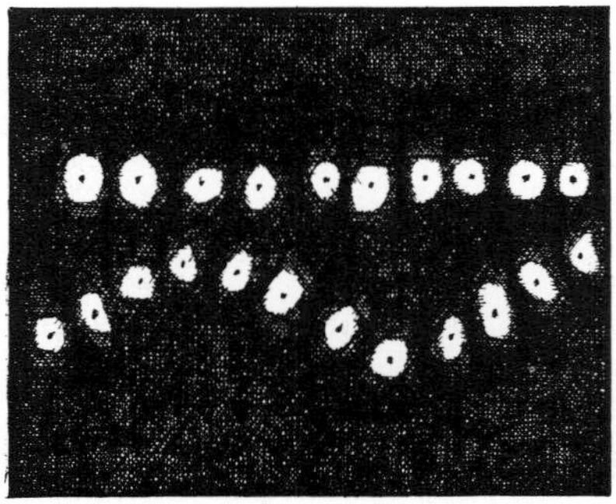

Fig. 278c: Tritik on coloured ground

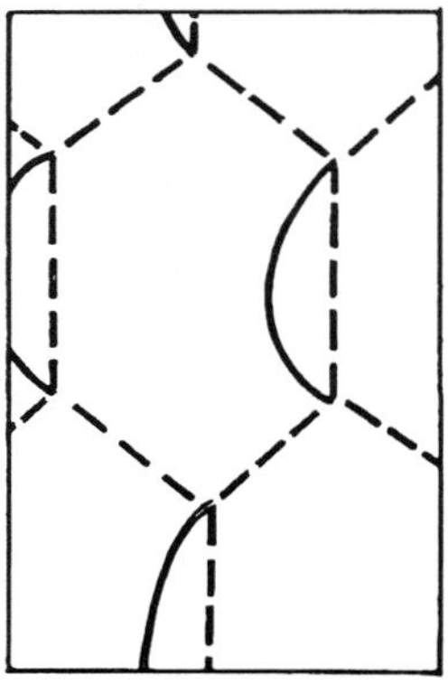

Fig. 279a: Resist stitches in place

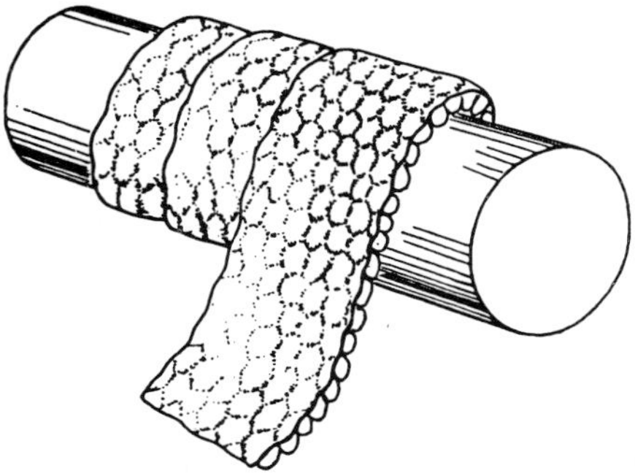

Fig. 279b: Rolling onto a core

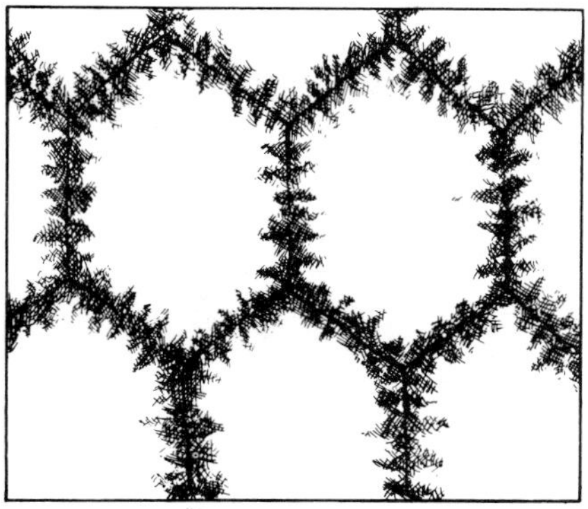

Fig. 279c: Tritik on white ground

Other terms used:
Rope tying ou réserves cordées (Boser-Sarivaxévanis 1969:157)
Tie-and-dye: twisting and coiling, binding (Maile 1963:19ff.)
Stitching (Wada/Kellog/Barton 1983:73)
Reservierung durch Nähen (Tritik) (Seiler-Baldinger 1991:153)

3. Tie Dyeing

The fabric or skein yarn is rolled or folded and tied in different places with strings, threads or ribbons. Fabrics woven from yarns dyed in this fashion are known as ikat (see pp. 147-148).

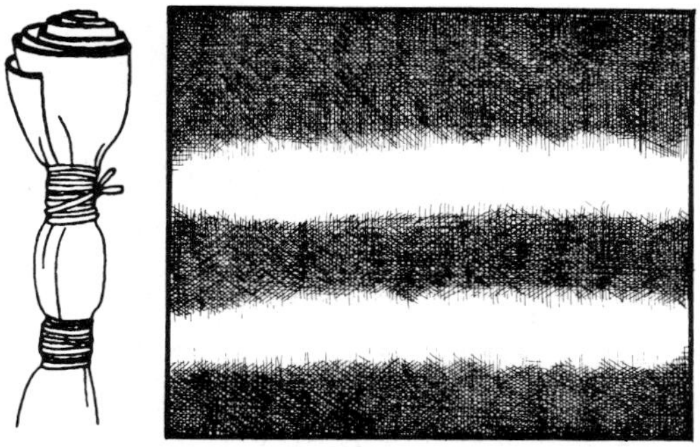

Fig. 280: Coil resist

Other terms used:
Rope tying ou réserves cordées (Boser-Sarivaxévanis 1969:157)
Tie-and-dye: twisting and coiling, binding (Maile 1963:19ff.)
Reservierung durch Umwickeln (Seiler-Baldinger 1991:154)
Oprollen en afbinden (Claerhout 1975:2)

3.1. Plangi

This is a special form of tie dyeing. Parts of the fabric are pulled into a knob-like or conical form and wholly or partially tied with threads (Fig. 281). These and in some cases additional flat material (pieces of leaf and bast) are used as a resist. With this method it is possible to cover very large areas. Techniques of the plangi type are often combined with stitch resisting. In order to save time, a number of layers of cloth are often tied at the same time so that the same patterns are repeated in the finished fabric.

Other terms used:
Tie-and-dye: binding (Maile 1963:38ff.)
Reservierung durch Abbinden (Plangi) (Seiler-Baldinger 1991:154)
Knüpf-Batik (Zechlin 1966:161)
Indian: bandhani, bandhni (Bühler 1952:5)
Chungri, chundri, chunri (Nabholz 1969a:7)
Japanese: maki shibori (Bühler 1952:5)
Dofjesuitsparingen (Claerhout 1975:8)

4. Stencil Resist Dyeing

In this process, stencils made of various materials impervious to the dye (leaves, wood, paper, string) are cut out in accordance with the desired pattern and fixed on the fabric. In the simplest form, portions of the material are protected from the dye by knotting (Fig. 282a-b). With this method as with the folding technique it is possible to obtain only simple stripes or dots. The colour can be applied with a brush or in a dye bath. In the latter case, stencils of matching form must be applied to both sides of the fabric in order to protect it completely (pressing or clamping, Fig. 283).

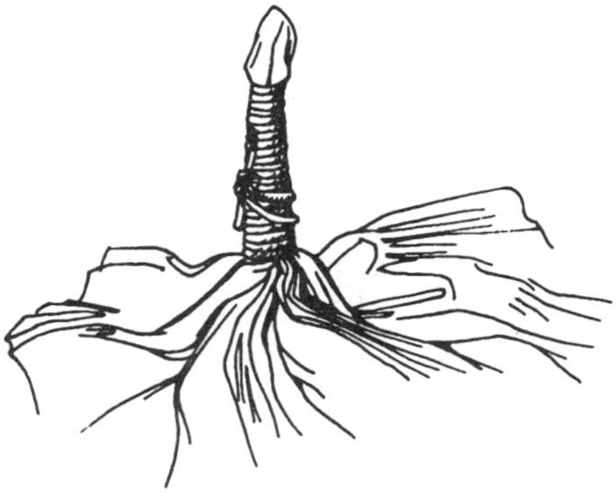

Fig. 281a: Tie dye (plangi)

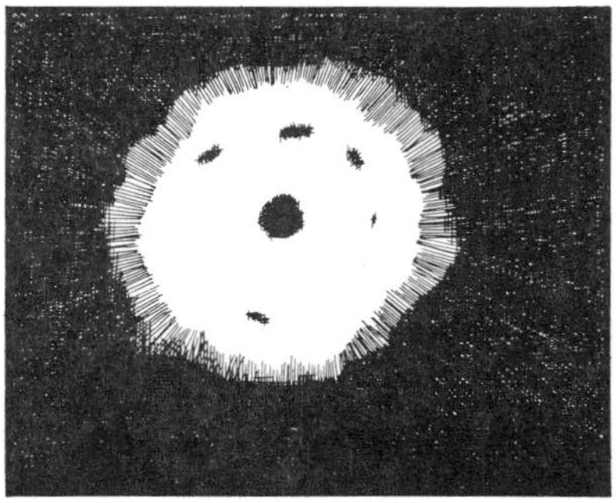

Fig. 281b: Tie dye (plangi)

Fig. 282a: Stencil resist by knotting

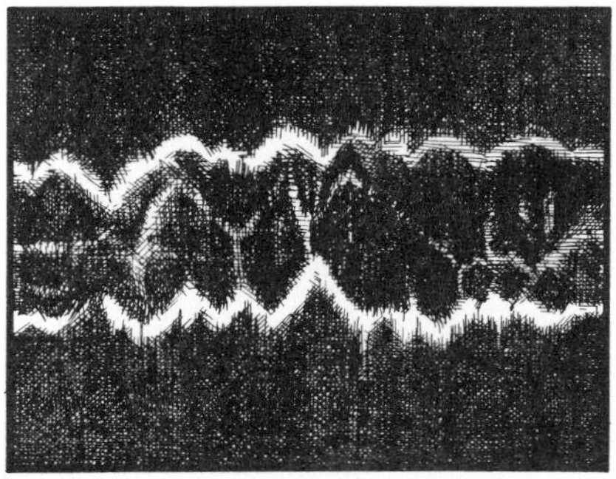

Fig. 282b: Stencil resist by knotting

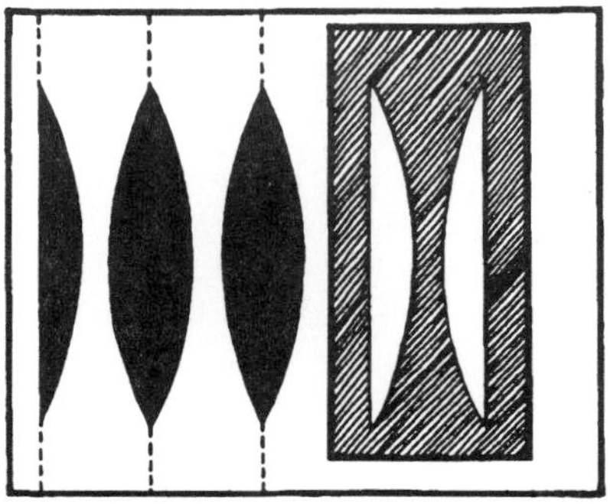

Fig. 283: Stencil resist with stencil

Other terms used:

Tie-and-dye: knotting (Maile 1963:21ff.)
Folding and clamping (Wada et al. 1983:116)
Reservierung durch Schablonieren (Seiler-Baldinger 1991:155)
Schabloonuitsparing (Claerhout 1975:12)

5. Paste or Liquid Resist Dyeing (batik)

The portions of the fabric which are not to be coloured are painted, brushed or printed before dyeing with pastes of gum, mud, resin or liquid wax, the dried resist material being removed after dyeing by washing or boiling (Fig. 284a-c). The resists can be applied by hand, with brushes, nozzles or jugs, or with the aid of stencils and blocks.

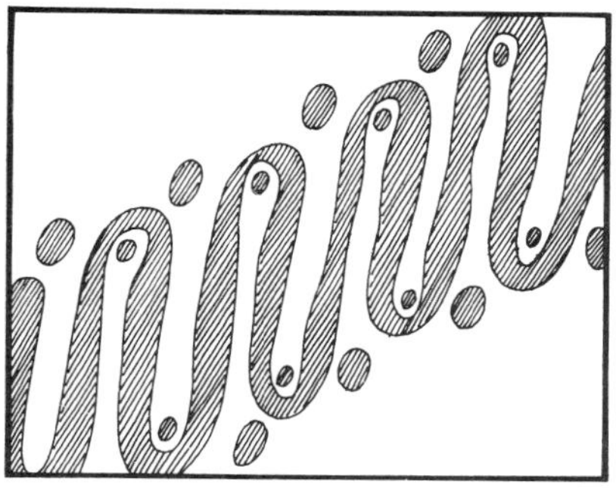

Fig. 284a: Batik: resist applied

Fig. 284b: Batik: dyeing

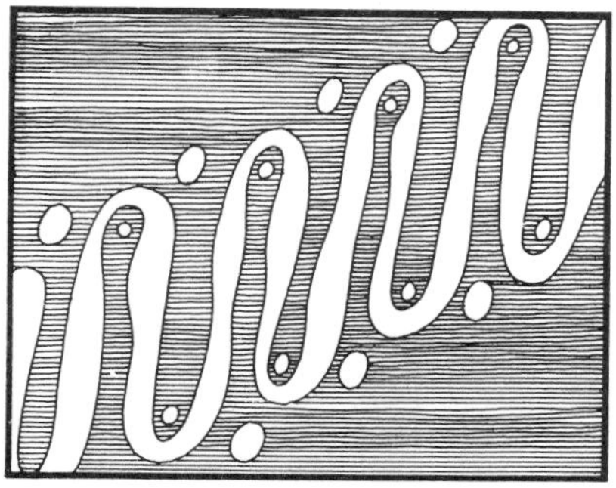

Fig. 284c: Batik: resist removed

6. Mordant and Negative Resist Dyeing

These methods differ from the batik-type methods in that in mordant and negative resist techniques the fabric serves as the resist and the parts to be patterned must be treated accordingly.

6.1. Mordant Resist Dyeing

In this method, specific parts of the fabric are prepared (e.g. with alum) in such a way that the dye becomes fixed only to these and not to the untreated parts. The untreated portions thus act as resists. The patterns are painted on or printed with mordant dyes.

Other term used:

Beizenreserven (Seiler-Baldinger 1991:156)

6.2. Negative Resist Dyeing

Certain parts of the fabric consist of material which does not pick up the dye (e.g. cotton). These portions act as resists while other parts (e.g. of wool) readily take up the dye.

Other terms used:

Negativreservierung (Seiler-Baldinger 1991:156)
Uitsparen met een vloeibaar aangebrachte ... substantie (Claerhout 1975:12)

Resist Dyeing of Yarn Before Weaving (ikat)

Since patterning is effected not only on the finished fabric but on the yarn meant for weaving and is closely linked with the weaving process, ikat techniques represent a special form of resist dyeing. Different designations – warp, weft or double ikat – are used depending on whether the warp or weft threads or both are patterned (Fig. 285a-d).

Before dyeing, skeins of yarn are reserved by knotting, partial wrapping, pressing by means of plates or other methods. Imitation ikats are produced by a direct application of colour on the yarn with (e.g.) brushes, or sticks, or by yarn printing.

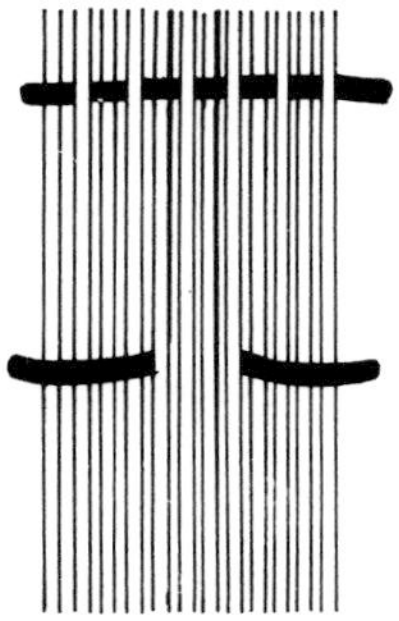

Fig. 285a:
Warp ikat: distribution of warp threads

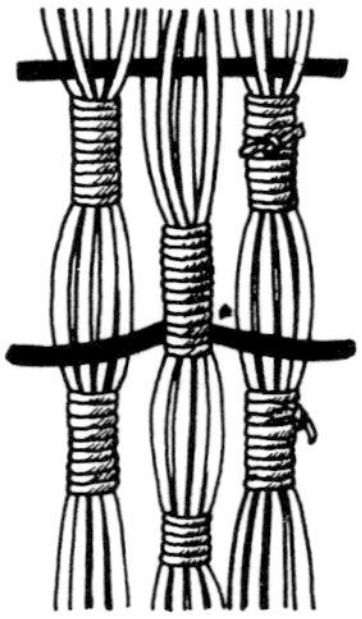

Fig. 285b:
Warp ikat: tying the bundled warp threads

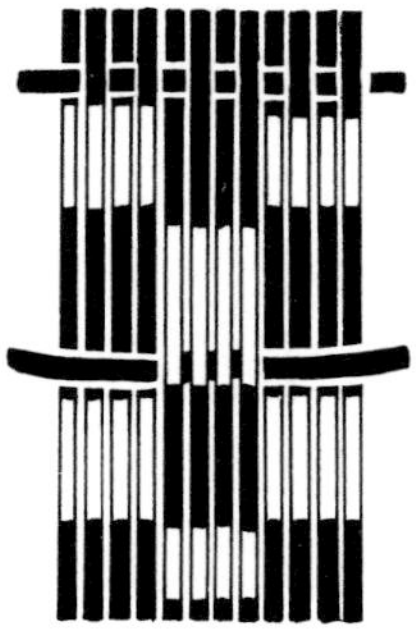

Fig. 285c:
Warp ikat: yarn after resist dyeing

Fig. 285d:
Warp ikat: woven yarn

Other terms used:
Ikat or Jaspé dyeing (Start 1948:49ff.)
Klem- en afbinduitsparingen op weefgarens (Claerhout 1975:14)

Warp ikat:
Kettenikat (Seiler-Baldinger 1991:157)
Ikat châine (CIETA 1970:28)
Catena ikat (CIETA 1970:28)
Urdimbre ikat (CIETA 1970:28)
Ikat de urdimbre (Chertudi/Nardi 1961:139)
Varpikat (CIETA 1970:28)

Weft ikat:
Schussikat (Seiler-Baldinger 1991:157)
Ikat trame (CIETA 1970:50)
Ikat trama (CIETA 1970:50)
Ikat de trama (Chertudi/Nardi 1961:140)
Inslagikat (CIETA 1970:50)

Double ikat:
Doppelikat (Seiler-Baldinger 1991:157)
Doppio ikat (CIETA 1970:11)
Doble ikat (Chertudi/Nardi 1961:140)

Warp printing:
Chiner, chinieren (Loeber 1908:273)
Japanese: Kasuri

References to Ornamentation with Liquid Material: see pp. 170-172.

The Techniques of Fabric Processing (joining of fabrics)

The term "fabric processing" embraces the cutting (fabric division) and sewing together (fabric combination) of fabrics for specific purposes such as the making of clothes. The division of fabrics is of minor importance in cultures with a simple technology since these almost always use fabrics in the form in which they are made, as loin cloths, saris, ponchos, etc. Moreover, the techniques of textile cutting go far beyond the scope of a textile classification, and therefore will not be discussed here.

Since the techniques of fabric combination often are closely related to those of fabric ornamentation (embroidery), it seems appropriate to consider them briefly here. Fabrics can be combined either by fabric-forming processes or by typical fabric-joining processes. On the other hand the beating of layers of fabric placed one upon the other, as is commonly used for bark cloth and felts, or the joining of fabrics by means of adhesives, are techniques with little relevance to textiles within the sense of the present classification.

Woven blanket of the Mabo-Peul, brocade and tapestry with embroidered seam, Youvaru, Mali, III 20468

Joining Fabrics by Manufacturing Techniques

For meshwork, plaited fabrics and warp fabrics, techniques exist in which protruding threads of the fabric itself are used to join parts together. Very many of the techniques used for fabric manufacture can also be used for fabric combination, so that within this group the same classification applies. Other points to be considered are whether or not the same technique is used for the production of a fabric and for joining its parts together, and in what way fabrics made by different methods are combined. Then it must also be considered whether special threads are used to combine pieces of fabric or if parts of the fabrics themselves are employed.

Fabric-combining Techniques

True fabric-combining techniques are generally new working methods which cannot be regarded as variations of fabric-producing processes. They employ a special material, in most cases an additional thread, and not parts of the fabrics to be combined.

Fastening

The technically most simple method of combining pieces of fabric is to fasten them together with thorns, wooden pins, needles etc. It is of so little importance for the textiles conforming to our definition that to mention it is sufficient.

Knotting

The edges of fabric pieces are joined together by passing short lengths of yarn through them at regular intervals and knotting the two ends of the yarn. Even if the knotting points are relatively close together, the join remains relatively loose.

Sewing

In sewing, pieces of cloth are joined together with a continuous thread which passes through the superposed or adjoining pieces in the desired stitch form so as to form a seam (Fig. 286a-f). Although certain types of stitch can also be used to join together very loose fabrics, sewing methods are largely restricted to dense, tightly interlaced textiles, especially warp and woven fabrics. This method generally requires mechanical aids (awls, needles, bodkins) for passing the thread, and devices for protecting the fingers and the ball of the thumb.

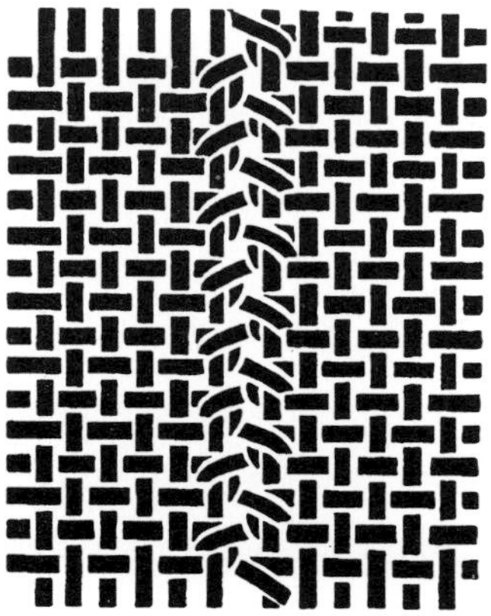

Fig. 286a: Sewn fabric

Fig. 286b: Fabric joined by running stitches: view from above

Fig. 286c: Fabric joined by running stitches: section

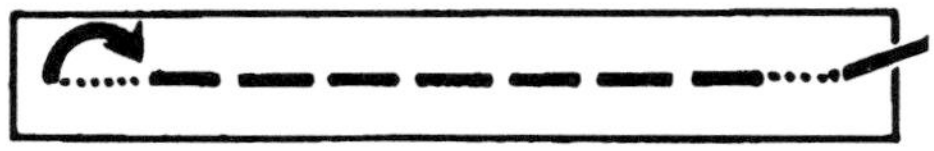

Fig. 286d: Fabric joined by back-stitches: view from above

Fig. 286e: Fabric joined by back-stitches: section

Other terms used:
Seaming (Emery 1966:233)
Nähen (Seiler-Baldinger 1991:160)

Embroidery

Embroidery techniques for fabric combination are somewhat akin to sewing; the main difference lies in their predominantly decorative character, for which reason the relevant techniques are classified under the heading of fabric decoration (cf. Decorative Stitches).

Dovetailing

Dovetailing is suitable only for meshwork fabrics or fabrics in which threads of one system reverse in loops at the fabric edges, i.e. warp fabrics or woven textiles. The two parts are juxtaposed in such a way that the loops at the edges face each other, and a common thread is then drawn through the loops (Fig. 287).

Fig. 286f: Fabric joined by overcasting stitch

Clasping

Fabric combination by clasping is a refinement of dovetailing. The thread is replaced by stiff materials such as hooks, buttons, pieces of wood etc. which are fixed to the edge of one piece of fabric and drawn through the loops of the other piece. The loops can also be replaced by openings and slits (Fig.288a-c).

References to fabric processing: see page 172.

Fig. 287: Dovetailing

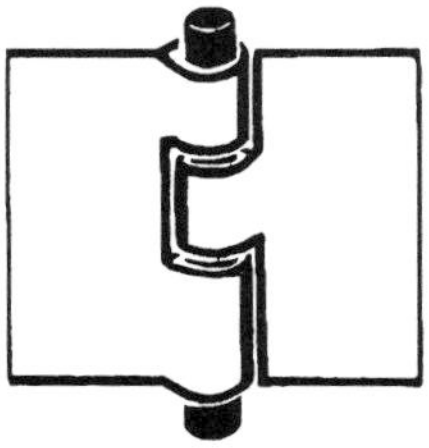

Fig. 288a:
Clasping with hinge

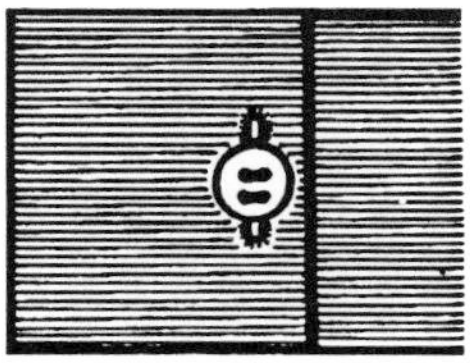

Fig. 288b:
Button closure

Fig. 288c: Loop closure

Appendix

Structures and Possible Ways of Production and Identification

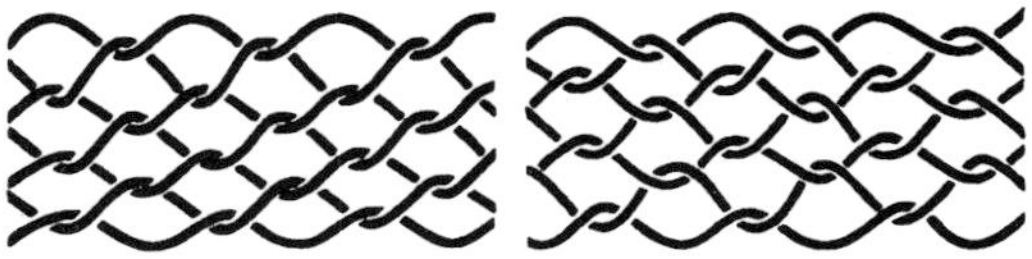

1. Simple linking (thread configuration 2/2, 11/11).
2. Interlinked sprang clearly identifiable when parts of the fabric are mirror images of each other or a minimal weft is present, or if this technique is combined with the skipping of rows, intertwining, interlacing etc. so as to form patterns or openwork.

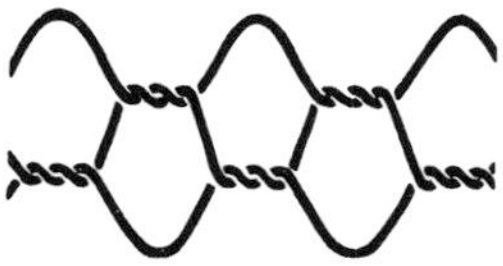

1. Twisted linking.
2. Interlinked sprang, if combined with simple linking for pattern and openwork formation or if a minimal weft is present.

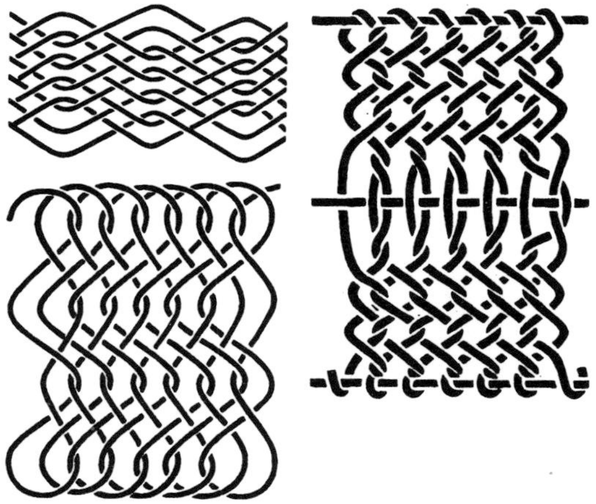

1. Linking with skipping of rows: if worked horizontally over more than 20 links.
2. Interconnected linked hourglass looping: if worked vertically over less than 20 links.
3. Interlinked sprang, if not more than two rows are skipped, if combined with simple interlinked sprang, and/or if a minimal weft is present.

1. Interconnected looping.
2. Crocheting, simple crochet stitch: only if worked in single row; thread configuration must be made up of the number 1 plus the number of turns minus 1.

1. Encircled looping, if no runs form when fabric is damaged.
2. Crossed knitting, if runs form.
3. Transition to embroidery, if base is present.

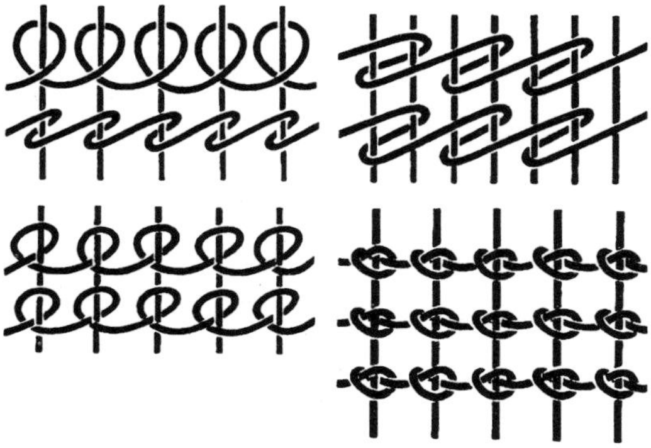

1. Plaiting with an active and a passive system: wrapping.
2. Warp techniques with a passive warp: weft wrapping. The differences can be ascertained, if at all, through the material. If the difference (stiffness of the passive element) between the two systems is large, plaiting is the more probable technique.

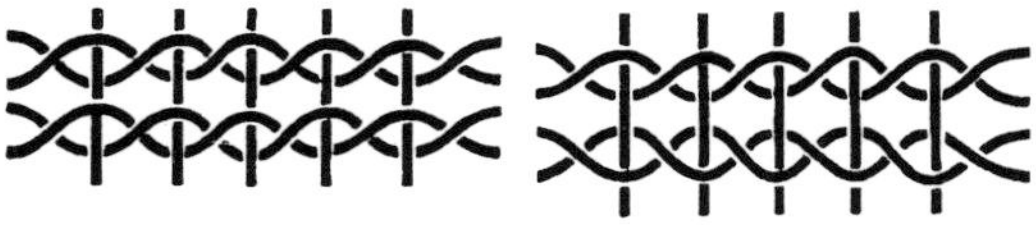

1. Twining over a passive system: the differences between plaiting and warp fabric techniques (weft twining) are determined by the material.
2. Active-passive intertwining.
3. Right-angled ply-splitting (active-passive).
4. Weft twining.

1. Linked or looped coiling: when sets of elements are used.
2. Linking (or looping etc.) over a foundation, if using a single continuous element. This also applies to all other coiling techniques which are not pierced (not dealt with here).

1. Two-directional plaiting (parallel or diagonal to edges) in plain or twill weave.
2. Two-dimensional braiding in plain or twill weave.
3. Three-dimensional tubular braiding in plain or twill weave. The techniques are distinguished on the basis of the number of elements (many = two-directional plaiting; few = braiding, tubular braiding).
4. Bobbin lace: whole-stitch clothwork; generally combined with other forms of oblique intertwining, very fine material.
5. Interlaced sprang: diagonal thread direction, axially symmetrical fabric parts, minimal weft.
6. Weft interlacing and tapestry (the latter if wefts turn back on themselves).
7. Half-weaving with alternate shed formation.
8. Weaving: plain or twill weave.

Note: Weft interlacing, half-weaving and weaving cannot be distinguished in the finished product.

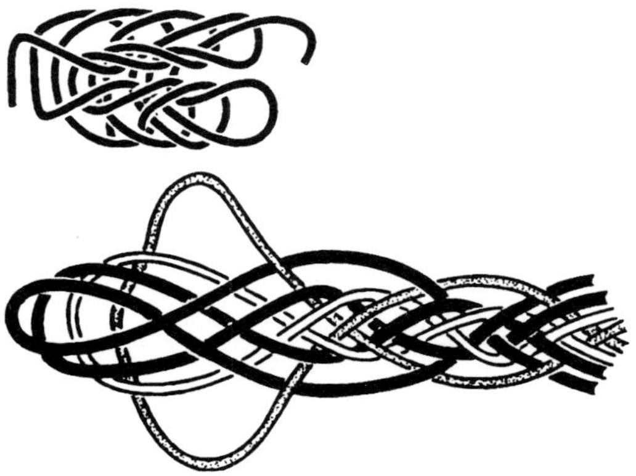

1. Compact three-dimensional looped braiding.
2. French knitting and crocheting. In the analysis, attention must be paid to the ends: loose ends indicate braiding, loops indicate mesh fabric or looped braiding.

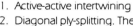

1. Active-active intertwining
2. Diagonal ply-splitting. The differences are manifested in the character of the elements (i.e. plied yarn).
3. Intertwined sprang, if fabric exhibits axial symmetry or weft insert.
4. Bobbin lace: finer material than 1. and 2.

1. Right-angled ply-splitting: passive-active (plied yarn).
2. Warp twining: warp ends loose at one end, fixed at other end.
3. Half-weaving with continuous shed reservation: fabric parts axially symmetrical.
4. Tablet weaving: reversal points in twist direction of threads, dense structure, narrow fabrics.
5. Finger weaving: if warp consists of an even number of loops, narrow fabrics.

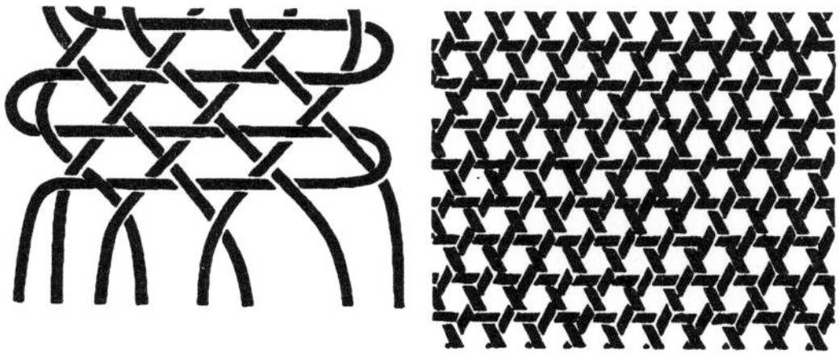

1. Plaiting in three directions.
2. Bobbin lace: the differences are material-dependent.

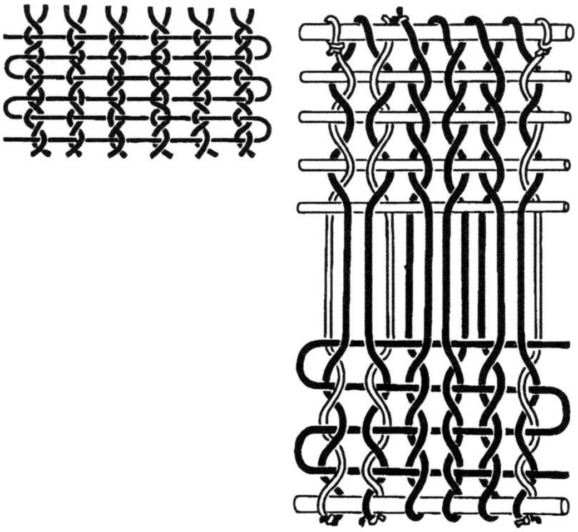

1. Half-weaving with continuous shed reservation if fabric displays axially symmetrical parts. Often seen in combination with twill weave.
2. Gauze weaves.

References

Techniques of Element Production

Classification:

Baines (1977), Bühler (1972), Burnham (1980), Cahlander (1980), Connor (1983), Crowfoot (1954), Dixon (1957), Emery (1952, 1966), Frödin & Nordenskiöld (1918), Hinderling (1959, 1960), Leroi-Gourhan (1943), Osborne (1954), Schnegelsberg (1971), Seiler-Baldinger (1971, 1979, 1991), Tanavoli (1985)

Analysis:

Anonym (1957), Baines (1977), Bel & Ricard (1913), Bender-Jorgensen (1986), Bluhm (1952), Braulik (1900), Brauns & Löffler (1986), Brommer et al. (1988), Burnham (1980, 1981, 1986), Cahlander (1980), Campbell & Pongnoi (1978), Caspar (1975), Connor (1983), Cordry & Cordry (1973), Crawford (1915-16), Crowfoot (1931, 1954), Dombrowski & Pfluger-Schindlbeck (1988), Durand-Forest (1966), D'Harcourt (1962), Farke (1986), Feltham (1989), Fox (1978), Furger & Hartmann (1983), Gaitzsch (1986), Geijer (1979), Gordon (1980), Hald (1980), Hecht (1989), Henshall (1950), Hissink & Hahn (1989), Hodges (1965), Hundt (1969, 1980), Hyslop & Bird (1985), Justin (1980), Kaufmann (1986), Kent Peck (1957), Keppel (1984), King (1965), Koch-Grünberg (1923), Konieczny (1979), Lamb (1984), Lewis & Lewis (1984), Linder (1967), Lorenz (1980), Lorenzo (1933), Lothrop & Mahler (1957, 1957), MacKenzie (1986), Mc Neish et al. (1967), Menzel (1973), Millán de Palavecino (1960), Mirambell & Martínez (1986), Nachtigall (1955), Nevermann (1938), Nordenskiöld (1924), Osborne (1965), O'Neale (1946), Pownall (1976), Prümers (1990), Reswick (1985), Riester (1971), Roth (1910), Sanoja Obediente (1979), Sayer (1988), Schaedler (1987), Schlabow (1976), Segal et al. (1973), Seiler-Baldinger (1971, 1981), Sharma (1968), Sillitoe (1988), Stanková (1989), Sylwan (1941), Tanavoli (1985), Taullard (1949), Textilmuseum Krefeld (1978), Ullemeyer & Tidow (1973), Underhill (1948), Van Stan (1958), Veiga de Oliveira & Galhano (1978), Walton (1989), Weitlaner-Johnson (1976), West (1980), Willey & Corbett (1954), Wilson (1979), Wulff (1966)

Ethnography:

Adams (1969), Adovasio & Maslowski (1980), Ahmed (1967), Ali (1900), Amborn (1990), Analsad (1951), Anderson (1978), Archambault (1988), Aretz (1979), Baer (1972), Bailey (1947), Beals (1969), Bel & Ricard (1913), Bird (1960, 1968), Bolinder (1925), Brauns & Löffler (1986), Brigham (1908), Bühler (1972), Campbell (1836), Campbell & Pongnoi (1978), Cardale de Schrimpff (1972), Cardenas et al. (1988), Carreira (1968), Caspar (1975), Chevallier (1964), Connor (1983), Cordry & Cordry (1973), Cresson & Jeannin (1943), Crowfoot (1931), Dalman (1964), Dauer (1978), Delawarde (1967), Deuss (1981), Devassy (1964), Dombrowski & Pfluger-Schindlbeck (1988), Drucker et al. (1969), Duby & Blom (1969), Dürr (1978), Dunlop (1966), Durand-Forest (1966), Easmon (1924), Etienne-Nugue (1982, 1982, 1984), Feltham (1989), Fischer & Mahapatra (1980), Fischer & Shah (1970, 1970), Forelli & Harries (1977), Fowler (1989), Fox (1978), Foy (1909), Franquemont (1986), Frödin & Nordenskiöld (1918), Gardi (1976), Germann (1963), Gifford (1931-33), Goodell (1968), Gräbner (1909), Haas (1970), Haberland (1963), Harvey & Kelly (1969), Hecht (1989), Hennemann (1975), Hissink & Hahn (1989), Hooper (1915), Justin (1980), Kauffmann (1963, 1967), Kaufmann (1986), Keppel (1984), Kissel (1916), Koch (1961, 1965, 1965, 1969), Koch-Grünberg (1923), Konieczny (1979), Korsching (1980), Kron-Steinhardt (1989), Kussmaul & Snoy (1964), Labin (1979), Lakwete (1977), Lamb (1984), Lamb & Lamb (1981), Landreau & Yoke (1983), Lane (1952), Leach (1951), Lenser (1964), Lewis & Lewis (1984), Littlefield (1976), Luz & Schlenker (1967), Luz (1961), Mac Leish (1940), MacKenzie (1986), Manndorff & Scholz (1967, 1967), Manrique (1969), Menzel (1973), Métraux (1928), Moos, von (1983), Nachtigall (1955), Nambiar (1966), Nevermann (1938), Nordenskiöld (1924), Nordquist & Aradeon (1975), Ortiz (1979), Osborne, de Jongh (1935), Ottaviano de (1974), Ottovar & Munch-Petersen (1980), O'Neale (1946), Pangemanan (1919), Picton & Mack (1979), Pleyte (1912), Pownall (1976), Reswick (1981, 1985), Ribeiro (1982, 1983, 1985, 1988), Riester (1971, 1972), Roessel (1983), Rolandi & Pupareli, de (1985), Ross (1988), Rossie & Claus (1983), Roth (1910), Roy (1982), Sanoja-Obediente (1961), Sayer (1985, 1988), Scarce (1988/89), Schaedler (1987), Schlenker (1973, 1974, 1975), Scholz (1967, 1974, 1974), Schultz (1962), Schuster (1962), Schuster & Schuster (1981), Schweeger-Hefel (1973/74), Seiler-Baldinger (1971, 1973, 1981), Sharma (1968), Sharma (1964), Shiroishi Miyagi Prefecture (1946), Siegenthaler (1989), Signi (1988), Sillitoe (1988), Susnik (1986), Tanavoli (1985), Taullard (1949), Tietze (1941), Trivedi (1967), Underhill (1948), Vreeland (1986), Weber (1977), Weiner & Schneider (1989), Weir (1970, 1976), Weitlaner-Johnson (1976), Weitlaner-Johnson & Mac Dougall (1966), West (1980), Westfall (1981), Wilbert (1974), Wilson (1979), Wulff (1966), Yde (1965), Zerries (1976, 1976)

Folk Art:

Aguirre (o.J.), Anonym (1957, 1985), Aretz (1972), Baines (1977), Bodmer (1940), Boeve (1974), Bretz (1977), Burnham (1981, 1986), Cardenas et al. (1988), Debétaz (1965), Eaton (1937), Gordon (1980), Gubser (1965), Hentschel (1949), Holm (1978), Kimakowicz-Winnicki (1910), Linder (1967), Lorenz (1980), Lorenzo (1933), Lühning (1963, 1963, 1963, 1971, 1980, 1981), Marková (1967), Pocius (1979), Rural Industries Bureau (1930), Sanoja Obediente (1979), Schwarz (1945), Shivo (1978), Simon (1965), Stanková (1989), Svobodová & Kûava (1975), Thompson (1964), Ungricht (1917), Vallinheimo (1956), Veiga de Oliveira & Galhano (1978), Wanner (1979), Weiner & Schneider (1989), Wilson (1979)

Archaeology:

Adovasio & Maslowski (1980), Alfaro Giner (1984), Amsden (1932), Azzola & Azzola (1986), Batigné & Bellinger (1965), Bellinger (1959), Bender-Jorgensen (1986), Bender-Jorgensen & Tidow (1981), Bennett & Bird (1960), Bird (1979), Bird & Mahler (1952), Bluhm (1952), Bluhm & Grange (1952), Bollinger (1983), Braulik (1900), Brommer et al. (1988), Clements-Scholtz (1975), Crawford (1946), Crowfoot (1931), Durand-Forest (1966), D'Harcourt (1962, 1974), Feltham (1989), Furger & Hartmann (1983), Gaitzsch (1986), Hald (1980), Hecht (1989), Henshall (1950), Hoffmann & Burnham (1973), Hooper (1915), Hundt (1969, 1980), Hyslop & Bird (1985), Kent Peck (1957), King (1965), La Baume (1968), Lothrop & Mahler (1957, 1957), Mayer Thurman & Williams (1979_), Mc Neish et al. (1967), Millán de Palavecino (1960), Mirambell & Martínez (1986), Olsen Bruhns (1989), Ortiz (1979), O'Neil (1974), Patterson (1956), Petrucci (1982), Prümers (1983, 1990), Rast (1990, 1991),

Rosenberg & Haidler (1980), Ryder (1962, 1964), Schlabow (1976), Schoch (1985), Segal et al. (1973), Seiler-Baldinger (1971), Singer et al. (1954-57), Snethlage (1930), Stokar (1938), Swanson & Bryon (1954), Sylwan (1941), Taullard (1949), Thurmann & Williams (1979), Ullemeyer & Tidow (1973), Van Stan (1958), Walton (1989), Weiner & Schneider (1989), Weitlaner-Johnson (1976), Whitford (1943), Wilbert (1974), Wild (1976), Willey & Corbett (1954), Wilson (1979)

Collections:

Aguirre (o.J.), Anderson (1978), Bird (1965), Brommer et al. (1988), Crawford (1946), Dürr (1978), Petrucci (1982), Riester (1971), Schlabow (1976), Signi (1988), Thompson (1964)

Working Instructions:

Burgess (1981), Cahlander (1980), Crawford Post (1961), La Plantz (1982), Markus (1974), Pownall (1976)

Films:

Baer (1972), Boeve (1974), Dauer (1978), Dunlop (1966), Germann (1963), Hennemann (1975), Kauffmann (1963, 1967), Koch (1961, 1965, 1965, 1969), Kussmaul & Snoy (1964), Lenser (1964), Lorenz (1980), Lühning (1963, 1963, 1963, 1971, 1980, 1981), Luz & Schlenker (1967), Luz (1961), Manndorff & Scholz (1967, 1967), Schlenker (1973, 1974, 1975), Scholz (1967, 1974, 1974), Schultz (1962), Schuster (1962), Schuster & Schuster (1981), Schweeger-Hefel (1973/74), Seiler-Baldinger (1973), Simon (1965), Svobodová & Kûava (1975), Zerries (1976, 1976)

General, Historical:

Ahmed (1967), Anonym (o.J.), Batigné & Bellinger (1965), Bohnsack (1981), Bussagli (1980), Cavallo (1977), Chesley (1949), Franquemont (1986), Hahn (1924), Hausner (1963), Horwitz (1934), Karmasch (1858), Kelsey & Osborne, de Jongh (1939), Lévi-Strauss (1987), Little (1931), Lombard (1978), Müller & Brendler (1958), Naupert (1938), Patterson (1957), Stirling (1938), Warburg & Friis (1975), Wehmeyer (1949)

Production of Mesh Fabrics

Classifications:

Brügger (1947), Bühler & Bühler-Oppenheim (1948), Bühler-Oppenheim (1947), Cahlander (1980), Collingwood (1974), Connor (1983), Davidson (1933, 1935), Dickey (1964), Emery (1955, 1966), Hinderling (1959), Larsen (1986), Lehmann (o.J.), Leroi-Gourhan (1943), Müller (1967), Neuwirth (1979), Nordland (1961), Oppenheim (1942), Reidemeister (1932), Ribeiro (1986, 1986), Seiler-Baldinger (1968, 1971, 1977, 1979, 1981, 1991), Singer Wieder (1935), Vogt (1935)

Analysis:

Albers (1965), Amano & Tsunoyama (1979), Amsden (1934), Anton (1984), Bahr (1983), Bel & Ricard (1913), Belen (1952), Bianchi et al. (1982), Biebuyck (1984), Bird & Bellinger (1954), Birrel (1959), Bluhm (1952), Brandt, von (1957, 1962), Brigham (1974), Brügger (1947), Buck (1944, 1957), Cahlander (1980), Califano (1982), Campbell & Pongnoi (1978), Caspar (1975), Caulfeild & Saward (1882), Collingwood (1974, 1987, 1988), Connor (1983), Cordry & Cordry (1973), Day (1967), Deuss (1981), Donner & Schnebel (1913), Dudovikova (1986), Dussan de Reichel (1960), D'Harcourt (1930, 1934, 1960, 1962), Eisleb (1975), Engel (1963, 1966), Feick (1917), Feldman (1986), Feltham (1989), Flury von Bültzingslöwen (1955, 1955), Fox (1978), Fuhrman (1941), Gaitzsch (1986), Gibson & Mc Gurk (1977), Graumont (1945), Graumont & Hensel (1942), Graumont & Wenstrom (1948), Grieder (1986), Grieder et al. (1988), Grünberg (1967), Hald (1950, 1975, 1980), Hundt (1980), Hyslop & Bird (1985), Iklé (1963), Kaufmann (1980, 1986), Kent Peck (1957, 1983), Keppel (1984), Kidder & Guernsey (1921), King (1965), Kissel (1916), Koch-Grünberg (1923), Kroeber & Wallace (1954), La Baume (1955), Lamb (1984), Lamster (1926), Larsen (1986), Lehmann (1908), Lothrop (1928), Mac Laren (1955), MacKenzie (1986), Mc Neish et al. (1967), Millán de Palavecino (1960), Miner (1936), Mooi (1974), Müller (1967), Museo Chileno (1989), Nachtigall (1955), Nordenskiöld (1919, 1920), Nordland (1961), Nylén (1969), Oezbel (1976), Oppenheim (1942), O'Neale (1942, 1945, 1986), O'Neale & Kroeber (1930), Prümers (1989, 1990), Ribeiro (1986), Riddell (1978), Riester (1971), Roth (1910, 1918, 1929), Rutt (1987), Sayer (1988), Schlabow (1976), Schuster (1989), Schuster (1976), Segal et al. (1973), Seiler-Baldinger (1971, 1981, 1987, 1991), Siewertsz van Reseema (1926), Signorini (1979), Sillitoe (1988), Speiser (1983), Taullard (1949), Tsunoyama (1980), Villegas & Rivera (1982), Vogt (1935, 1937), Walton (1989), West (1980), Wiedemann (1975), Willey & Corbett (1954), Wilson (1979), Zechlin (1966)

Ethnography:

Adovasio & Maslowski (1980), Albers (1965), Amsden (1934), Anderson (1978), Aretz (1977, 1979), Baer (1972), Bahr (1983), Ball (1924), Bel & Ricard (1913), Bianchi et al. (1982), Biebuyck (1984), Bolinder (1925), Borgatti (1983), Boulay (1990), Brigham (1908), Brügger (1947), Buck (1944, 1957), Bühler-Oppenheim (1945), Burch (1984), Califano (1982), Câmara Cascudo, da (1959), Campbell & Pongnoi (1978), Cannizzo (1969), Cardale de Schrimpff (1972, 1977), Caspar (1975), Chaumeil (1987), Collingwood (1987, 1988), Connor (1983), Cordry & Cordry (1941, 1973), Crawford (1981), Davidson (1933, 1935), Dendel (1974), Deuss (1981), Dickey (1964), Drucker et al. (1969), Duby & Blom (1969), Dussan de Reichel (1960), D'Harcourt (1930), Ekpo (1978), Emery & Fiske (1977), Espejel & Català Roca (1978), Feick (1917), Fejos (1943), Feltham (1989), Femenias (1988), Fischer & Shah (1970, 1970), Foster (1969), Fowler & Matley (1979), Fox (1978), Frame (1983, 1989), Gayton (1948), Gibson & Mc Gurk (1977), Gifford (1931-33), Gowd (1965), Gräbner (1909, 1913), Grünberg (1967), Guhr & Neumann (1982), Guiart (1945), Haas (1970), Haberland (1963), Hammel & Haase (1962), Hauser-Schäublin (1989), Heermann (1989), Heizer (1987), Henking (1955), Hinderling (1965), Houwald, von (1990), Izikowitz (1932), Kaufmann (1980, 1986), Kelly & Fowler (1986), Kemp (1984), Keppel (1984), Kissel (1916), Koch (1969), Koch-Grünberg (1923), Kooijman (1959), Lamb (1984), Lamster (1926), Lane (1952), Lantis (1984), Lehmann (1907, 1908), Leib & Romano (1984), Lips (1947), Littlefield (1976), Lothrop (1928), MacKenzie (1986), Malkin (1974), Müller (1967), Nachtigall (1955), Nordenskiöld (1919, 1920), Oezbel (1967, 1976), Ortiz (1979, 1983), Ottenberg & Knudsen (1985), Ovalle Fernandez (1982), O'Neale (1945, 1986), Radin (1906), Reichel-Dolmatoff (1946), Ribeiro (1980, 1985, 1986, 1986, 1988), Riddell (1978), Riester (1971, 1972), Rogers (1967), Rogers & Smith (1981), Roth (1910, 1918, 1929), Rutt (1987), Rydén (1935), Saraf (1987), Saugy de Kliauga (1984), Sayer (1985, 1988), Schevill (1986), Schultz (1963), Schuster (1989), Schuster (1976), Seiler-Baldinger (1968, 1971, 1974, 1977, 1981, 1987), Sieber (1987),

Signorini (1979), Sillitoe (1988), Singer Wieder (1935), Stokes (1906), Susnik (1986), Taullard (1949), Van Gennep (1909), Venegas (1956), Villegas & Rivera (1982), Von Bayern (1908), Vreeland (1974), Vrydagh (1977), Waite (1987), Wallace (1978), Washburn & Crowe (1988), Weisswange (1966), Weitlaner-Johnson (1977), Weitlaner-Johnson & Mac Dougall (1966), West (1980), Wiedemann (1975, 1979), Wilson (1979), Wirz (1934), Yde (1965), Zerries & Schuster (1974)

Folk Art:

Albers (1965), Apostolaki (1956), Aretz (1972, 1977), Ashley (1977, 1986), Collin (1917), Csernyánsky (1962), Dahl (1987), Dudovikova (1986), Eaton (1937), Haberlandt (1912), Hald (1945), Heikinmäki (1970), Kurrick (1932), Müller (1948), Nixdorff (1977), Nordland (1961), Nylén (1969), Pearson's (1984), Pocius (1979), Rutt (1987), Schinnerer (1897), Schneider (1975), Strömberg & Arbman (1934), Upitis (1981), Václavík (1956), Václavik & Orel (o.J.), Wilson (1979)

Archaeology:

Adovasio & Maslowski (1980), Albers (1965), Alfaro Giner (1984), Amano & Tsunoyama (1979), Anton (1984), Bellinger (1954), Bird (1952), Bird & Bellinger (1954), Bird & Mahler (1952), Bird et al. (1981), Bluhm (1952), Bluhm & Grange (1952), Bollinger (1983), Broholm & Hald (1948), Bültzingslöwen, von & Lehmann (1951), Cardale de Schrimpff (1978, 1987), Clements-Scholtz (1975), Collingwood (1974), Conklin (1975), Cortes Moreno (1987), Dickey (1964), D'Harcourt (1934, 1952, 1962, 1974), Eisleb (1975), Engel (1960, 1963, 1966), Feldman (1986), Feltham (1989), Frame (1990), Fuhrman (1941), Gaitzsch (1986), Grieder (1986), Grieder et al. (1988), Hald (1950, 1980), Harner (1979), Holmes (1884, 1896), Hundt (1980), Hyslop & Bird (1985), Izikowitz (1932), Jaques (1968), Kent Peck (1957, 1983), Kidder & Guernsey (1919, 1921), King (1962, 1965, 1979), Kroeber (1944), Kroeber & Wallace (1954), Lautz (1982), Lehmann & Bültzingslöwen, von (1954), Levillier (1928), Lindberg (1964), Lynch (1980), Martin et. al. (1954), Mc Neish et al. (1967), Millán de Palavecino (1960), Museo Chileno (1989), Ortiz (1979), O'Neale (1934, 1942), O'Neale & Bacon (1949), O'Neale & Kroeber (1930), Petrucci (1982), Prümers (1983, 1989, 1990), Rast (1990, 1991), Rau (1884), Reindel (1987), Rolandi (1971, 1985), Rutt (1987), Schinnerer (1891), Schlabow (1976, 1983), Schoch (1985), Segal et al. (1973), Seiler-Baldinger (1971), Siewertsz van Reseema (1926), Silva Celis (1978), Singer (1947), Singer Wieder (1936), Spahni (1967), Steffensen (1975, 1978, 1978), Steward (1937), Taullard (1949), Taylor (1966), Tidow (1982), Ulloa (1985), Van Stan (1964), Vogt (1937), Vreeland (1974), Walton (1989), Washburn & Crowe (1988), Wassén (1972), Whitford (1943), Willey & Corbett (1954), Wilson (1979)

Collections:

Amano & Tsunoyama (1979), Anderson (1978), Bird (1965), Borgatti (1983), Boulay (1990), Eisleb (1975), Femenias (1988), Fowler & Matley (1979), Frame (1990), Grünberg (1967), Guhr & Neumann (1982), Gyula (1984), Hauser-Schäublin (1989), Heermann (1989), Iklé (1935), Iklé & Vogt (1935), Jaques (1968), Museo Chileno (1989), Nixdorff (1977), Petrucci (1982), Riester (1971), Schlabow (1976), Schmedding (1978), Schneider (1975), Seiler-Baldinger (1987), Tsunoyama (1980), Waite (1987)

Working Instructions:

Belash (1936), Belen (1952), Burgess (1981), Cahlander (1980), Caulfeild & Saward (1882), Chamberlain & Crookelt (1974), Collingwood (1974), De Leon (1978), Dendel (1974), Dillmont, de (o.J.), Donner & Schnebel (1913), Floses (1960), Hald (1975), Hartung (1963), Hochfelden (o.J.), Lammèr (1975), Liebert (1916), Mooi (1974), Phillips (1971), Schachenmayr (1934), Speiser (1983), Steffensen (1975, 1978, 1978), Steven (1950), Strömberg & Arbman (1934), Thomas (1972, 1972), Tiesler (1980), Upitis (1981), Weldon's Encyclopaedia (o.J.), Zechlin (1966)

Films:

Baer (1972), Kaufmann (1980), Koch (1969), Schultz (1963), Weisswange (1966)

General, Historical:

Ferchion (1971), Glassmann (1935), Kiewe (1967), Oezbel (1981), Oka (1982), Rogers (1967), Schuette (1963), Seiler-Baldinger (1986), Singer Wieder (1937), Stirling (1938), Thomas (1926, 1936), Wehmeyer (1949)

Plaiting

Classification:

Balfet (1952, 1957, 1986), Brügger (1947), Bühler & Bühler-Oppenheim (1948), Bühler-Oppenheim (1947), Burnham (1980), Cahlander (1980), Collingwood (1968), Connor (1983), Crowfoot (1954), Davidson (1933), Emery (1955, 1966), Harvey (1976), Larsen (1986), Leroi-Gourhan (1943), Mason (1902), Müller (1967), Museo Etnografico (1976), Oppenheim (1942), Quick & Stein (1982), Ribeiro (1985, 1986, 1986), Seiler-Baldinger (1979, 1991)

Analysis:

Adovasio (1977), Ahlbrinck (1925), Albers (1965), American Indian Basketry Magazine (1979), Amsden (1934), Anonym (1957), Arbeit (1990), Bahr (1983), Balfet (1986), Barkow (1983), Bel & Ricard (1913), Belen (1952), Bianchi et al. (1982), Biebuyck (1984), Bird & Bellinger (1954), Bluhm (1952), Brauns & Löffler (1986), Brigham (1974), Brommer et al. (1988), Broudy (1979), Brügger (1947), Buck (1944, 1957), Bühler et al. (1972), Burnham (1980), Cahlander (1980), Cahlander & Cason (1976), Califano (1982), Campbell & Pongnoi (1978), Caspar (1975), Caulfeild & Saward (1882), Collings (1987), Collingwood (1987, 1988), Colyer Ross (1989), Connor (1983), Cordry & Cordry (1973), Corey (1987), Cornet (1982), Corrie Newman (1985), Crowfoot (1954), Detering (1962), Disselhoff (1981), Donner & Schnebel (1913), Douglas (1935), D'Harcourt (1934, 1940, 1960, 1962), Eisleb (1975), Elsasser (1978), Engel (1963), Etienne-Nugue (1985), Farke (1986), Feldman & Rubinstein (1986), Fenelon-Costa & Malhano (1986), Fernandez Distel (1983), Flemming (1923), Fox (1978), Freyvogel (1959), Furger & Hartmann (1983), Gaitzsch (1986), Gass & Lozado (1985), Geijer (1979), Grant (1954), Green Gigli et al. (1974), Grieder et al. (1988), Grünberg (1967), Guss (1989), Häberlin (1907), Haeberlin & Teit (1928), Hald (1950, 1962, 1975), Harvey (1976, 1986), Heissig & Müller (1989), Henshall (1950), Hissink & Hahn (1984, 1989), Hodges (1965), Hugger (1967), Hundt (1969, 1980), Jager-Gerlings (1952), Jasper & Pirngadie (1912-16), Jones (1983), Kaudern (1935), Kelly (1932), Kent Peck (1954, 1957, 1983), Keppel (1984), Kidder & Guernsey (1921), King (1965), Kissel (1916), Koch-Grünberg (1923), Kogan (1985), Kok (1979), Kuhn (1980), Lamster (1926), Lane (1981), Lane (1986), Larsen (1986), Lehmann (1912), Leigh-Theisen (1988), Leontidi

(1986), Lewis & Lewis (1984), Lismer (1941), Lothrop (1928), Lothrop & Mahler (1957), Mantuba-Ngoma (o.J.), Marková (1962), Martin (1986), Mason (1890, 1901, 1901, 1904, 1907, 1908), Mc Clellan & Denniston (1981), Mc Lendon & Holland (1979), Mc Neish et al. (1967), Meyers & & Co. (o.J.), Miner (1936), Mooi (1974), Müller (1967), Nabholz-Kartaschoff (1986), Nachtigall (1955), Newman (1974, 1977), Nixdorff (1977), Nordenskiöld (1919, 1920, 1924), Oppenheim (1942), O'Neale (1942, 1945, 1946, 1986), O'Neale & Kroeber (1937), Paulis (1923), Pendergast (1982, 1987), Pestalozzianum (1990), Petersen (1963), Pownall (1976), Prümers (1989, 1990), Quick & Stein (1982), Ranjan & Yier (1986), Rendall & Tuohy (1974), Ribeiro (1980, 1985, 1986), Riddell (1978), Riester (1971), Rodel (1949), Roquette-Pinto (1954), Roth (1910, 1918, 1929), Rydén (1955), Sahashi (1988), Schaar & Delz (1983), Schier (1951), Schlabow (1976), Schmidt (1905), Schneider (1988), Schuster (1976), Seiler-Baldinger (1987), Sillitoe (1988), Speiser (1983), Sylwan (1941), Tanner (1968), Tiesler (1980), Turnbaugh & Turnbaugh (1986), Underhill (1945, 1948), Valonen (1952), Villegas & Rivera (1982), Vogt (1937), Walton (1989), Widmer (o.J.), Wiedemann (1975), Wilbert (1975), Will (1978), Willey & Corbett (1954), Zechlin (1966), Zerries (1980), Zorn (1980)

Ethnography:

Adams (1989), Adovasio & Maslowski (1980), Ahlbrinck (1925), Albers (1965), All India Handicrafts Board(o.J.), Alvarez de Williams (1983), American Indian Basketry Magazine (1979), Amsden (1934), Anderson (1978), Anonym (1964, 1990), Arbeit (1990), Aretz (1977), Ashabranner & Ashabranner (1981), Ave & King (1986), Baer (1960, 1973, 1977), Bahr (1983), Balbino Camposeco (1983), Balfet (1986), Barrett (1905, 1908), Bates (1982), Bel & Ricard (1913), Berin (1978), Bianchi et al. (1982), Biebuyck (1984), Blackwood (1950), Bliss (1982), Bolinder (1925), Boulay (1990), Branford (1984), Brasser (1975), Brauns & Löffler (1986), Brigham (1906, 1908), Brügger (1947), Buck (1944, 1950, 1957), Burnham (1977), Cahlander & Cason (1976), Califano (1982), Campbell & Pongnoi (1978), Cannizzo (1969), Cardale de Schrimpff (1972, 1977), Caspar (1975), Cervellino (1979), Chattopadhyaya (1976), Chaumeil (1987), Cocco (1972), Collings (1987), Collingwood (1987, 1988), Connor (1983), Cordry & Cordry (1973), Corey (1987), Cornet (1982), Corrie Newman (1985), Crawford (1981), Danneil (1901), Das (1979), Davidson (1933), Delawarde (1967), Dendel (1974), Desrosiers (1982), Detering (1962), Devassy (1964), Dhamija (1966, 1970), Douglas (1935, 1937, 1940), Douglas & D'Harcourt (1941), Drucker et al. (1969), Dürr (1978), Dunsmore (1985), Dusenbury (1983), D'Azevedo (1986), D'Harcourt (1940, 1948), Ellis & Walpole (1959), Ellis (1980), Elsasser (1978), Emmons (1903), Engelbrecht (1986), Espejel & Català Roca (1978), Etienne-Nugue (1982, 1982, 1984, 1985), Farrand (1975), Fejos (1943), Feldman & Rubinstein (1986), Fenelon-Costa & Malhano (1986), Fernandez Distel (1983), Fischer & Mahapatra (1980), Forde (1931), Foss (1978), Fowler (1989), Fowler & Dawson (1986), Fowler & Matley (1979), Fox (1978), Frame (1989), Freyvogel (1959), Gass & Lozado (1985), Geary (1987), Gettys (1984), Gifford (1931-33), Gluck & Gluck (1974), Goddard (1931, 1934), Goggin (1949), Gowd (1965), Gräbner (1909, 1913), Green Gigli et al. (1974), Grosset (1978), Grünberg (1967), Guhr & Neumann (1982), Guss (1989), Haas (1970), Haberland (1963), Haberland (1979), Haeberlin & Teit (1928), Hald (1962), Hames (1976), Hartmann (1966, 1971, 1972), Harvey & Kelly (1969), Hauser-Schäublin (1989), Heathcote (1976), Heermann (1989), Heissig & Müller (1989), Heizer (1987), Henking (1957), Henley & Mattei-Muller (1978), Henninger (1971), Herle (1990), Herzog (1985), Higuera (1987), Hissink & Hahn (1984, 1989), Hobi (1982), Hodge (1982), Holm & Reid (1975), Holter (1983), Houlihan et al. (1987), Houwald, von (1990), Idiens (1990), Jager-Gerlings (1952), James (1903), Jensen (1971), Jones (1983), Jones (o.J.), Kasten (1990), Kaudern (1935), Keller (1988), Kelly (1930, 1932), Kelly & Fowler (1986), Kenagy et al. (1987), Kensinger (1975), Keppel (1984), Kissel (1916), Klausen (1957), Koch (1961, 1969, 1969), Koch & König (1956), Koch-Grünberg (1909, 1923), Kogan (1985), Kooijman (1959), Kremser & Westhart (1986), Kroeber (1905), Krucker (1941), Kuhn (1980), Kussmaul & Snoy (1980), La Pierre (1984), Lambrecht (1981), Lamster (1926), Lane (1981), Lane (1986), Lantis (1984, 1984), Lehmann (1907, 1912), Leigh & Kerajinan (1989), Leigh-Theisen (1988), Levinsohn (1979, 1980, 1983), Lewis & Lewis (1984), Linden-Museum (1989), Lippuner (1981), Lips (1947), Lismer (1941), Loebèr (1902, 1909, 1914, 1916), Lothrop (1928), Lumholtz (1904), Luz & Schlenker (1974), Lyford (1943), Malkin (1975, 1975, 1975, 1976), Manrique (1969), Mantuba-Ngoma (o.J.), Mapelli Mozzi & Castello Yturbide (1987), Martin (1986), Mason (1912), Mason (1890, 1900, 1904, 1908), Mathews (1983), Matsumoto (1984), Matthews (1894), Mauldin (1977), Mc Clellan & Denniston (1981), Mc Lendon (1981), Mc Lendon & Holland (1979), Melo Taveira (1980), Métraux (1928), Miles & Bovis (1977), Moore (1989), Morrison (1982), Mowat (1989), Müller (1967), Mukharji (1888), Munan (1989), Nabholz-Kartaschoff (1986), Nachtigall (1955), Navajo School of Indian Basketry (1949), Nettinga Arnheim (1977), Nevermann (1960), Newman (1974, 1977), Newton (1981), Nieuwenhuis (1913), Nordenskiöld (1919, 1920, 1924), Ortiz (1979, 1983), Ottovar & Munch-Petersen (1980), Ovalle Fernandez (1982), O'Neale (1932, 1945, 1946, 1986), Palm (1958), Paul (1944), Pelletier (1982), Pendergast (1982, 1987), Pérez de Micou (1984), Petersen (1963), Porter (1988), Pownall (1976), Quick & Stein (1982), Ranjan & Yier (1986), Ray (1984), Reichel-Dolmatoff (1960, 1985), Rendall & Tuohy (1974), Ribeiro (1978, 1980, 1980, 1982, 1982, 1984, 1985, 1985, 1986, 1986, 1986, 1988, 1988, 1989), Richman (1980), Riddell (1978), Riester (1971, 1972), Roberts (1929), Roessel (1983), Rogers & Leacock (1981), Rogers & Smith (1981), Rohrer (1928), Ronge (1982), Roquette-Pinto (1954), Rossbach (1973), Rossie & Claus (1983), Roth (1910, 1918, 1929), Sahashi (1988), Sanoja-Obediente (1960, 1961), Saraf (1987), Sayer (1985), Schindler (1990), Schlesier (1967), Schmidt (1905), Schneebaum (1985), Schneider (1988), Scholz (1967, 1968, 1968), Schultz (1963-65, 1965), Schultz (1981), Schulze-Thulin (1989), Schuster (1962, 1976), Schuster & Schuster (1980, 1981), Schweeger-Hefel (1973/74, 1973/74), Sedlak (1987), Seiler-Baldinger (1987), Sibeth (1990), Sieber (1972, 1981), Signi (1988), Sillitoe (1988), Smith (1978), Solyom & Solyom (1984), Speiser (1925), Speiser (1972, 1985), Spencer (1984), Staub (1936), Streiff (1967), Susnik (1986), Suttles (1990), Swartz (1958), Tada (1986), Tanner (1968, 1982, 1983), Taylor & Moore (1948), Taylor (1984), Torres (1980), Trigger (1978), Trivedi (1961), Trupp (1980), Tschopik (1940), Turnbaugh & Turnbaugh (1986), Underhill (1941, 1941, 1945, 1948), Uplegger (1969), Valentin (1970), Vanstone (1984), Vasco Uribe (1987), Verma (1961), Verswijver (1983), Villegas & Rivera (1982), Wagner (1949), Waite (1987), Wallace (1978), Wardle (1912), Washburn & Crowe (1988), Weber (1986), Weiner & Schneider (1989), Weir (1989), Wells (1982), Weltfish (1930, 1930), Westphal-Hellbusch (1980), Whiteford (1988), Wiedemann (1975), Wilbert (1975), Willoughby (1905), Woolley (1929, 1932), Wright (1977), Yamamoto (1986), Yde (1965), Yoffe (1978), Zaldivar (1982), Zerries (1974, 1980), Zerries & Schuster (1974), Zigmond (1986), Zorn (1980)

Folk Art:

Abadia Morales (1983), Aguirre (o.J.), Albers (1965), Anonym (1928, 1957, 1985, 1985), Aretz (1972, 1977), Ashley (1977, 1986), Bianconi (1965), Burnham (1977), Csernyánsky (1962), Dahl (1987), Eaton (1937), Eddy (1989), Efthymiou-Chatzilakou (1980), Flemming (1923), Frantisek (1960), Freeman (1958), Gabric (1962), Gandert (1963), Gusic (1955), Haberlandt (1912), Häberlin (1907), Herzog (1985), Horvàth & Werder (1978), Hugger (1967), Kuhar (1970), Kurrick (1932), Leontidi (1986), Linden-Museum (1989), Lippuner (1981), Marková (1962), Martin (1984), Meyers & & Co. (o.J.), Meyer- Heisig (1956), Müller (1948), Munksgaard (1980), Musée d'Art (1984), Nixdorff (1977, 1977), Nordiska Museet (1984), Palotay (o.J.), Paulis (1923), Pelanzy & Català (1978), Pellaton-Chable (1987), Petrasch (1970), Reichelt (1956), Rodel (1949), Rosengarten (1986), Rossbach (1973), Schier (1951), Schier & Simon (1975), Schneider (1975), Seeberger (1987), Sonderausstellung des Steirischen Bauernmuseums (1976), Suter (1978), Teleki (1975), Tucci (1963), Václavík (1956), Valonen (1952), Weber (1979), Weiner & Schneider (1989), Will (1978), Wright (1977)

Archaeology:

Adovasio (1977, 1980, 1986), Adovasio & Maslowski (1980), Albers (1965), Alfaro Giner (1984), Bedaux & Bolland (1989), Bird & Bellinger (1954), Bird et al. (1981), Bluhm (1952), Brommer et al. (1988), Brown (1981), Cardale de Schrimpff (1978, 1987), Cardale de Schrimpff & Falchetti de Sáenz (1980), Clements-Scholtz (1975), Csalog (1965), Dawson (1979), Dellinger (1936), Disselhoff (1967, 1981), D'Azevedo (1986), D'Harcourt (1934, 1948, 1948, 1962, 1974), Egloff (1984), Eisleb (1975), Engel (1960, 1963), Feldtkeller & Schlichtherle (1987), Forbes (1956), Furger & Hartmann (1983), Gaitzsch (1986), Geijer (1938), Grant (1954), Grieder et al. (1988), Hald (1950), Harner (1979), Harvey (1975), Henshall (1950), Holmes (1889), Hundt (1969, 1980), Kent Peck (1954, 1957, 1983), Kidder & Guernsey (1919, 1921), King (1965, 1979), Kroeber (1937, 1944), Lambert & Ambler (1961), Lapiner (1976), Laurencich-Minelli & Ciruzzi (1981), Lavalle, de & Lang (1980), Lothrop & Mahler (1957), Loud & Harrington (1929), Lucas (1948), Lynch (1980), Martin et. al. (1954), Massey & Osborne (1961), Mc Neish et al. (1967), Meyer (1987), Millán de Palavecino (1957, 1966), Mohr & Sample (1955), Morris (1975), Ortiz (1979), O'Neale (1942), O'Neale & Bacon (1949), Perini (1990), Pestalozzianum (1990), Petrucci (1982), Plazas de Nieto (1987), Prümers (1989, 1990), Rast (1990, 1991), Rolandi (1981, 1985), Rydén (1955), Schaar & Delz (1983), Schlabow (1976), Schulze-Thulin (1989), Seipel (1989), Singer et al. (1954-57), Spahni (1967), Steward (1937), Sylwan (1941), Taylor (1966), Turnbaugh & Turnbaugh (1986), Ulloa (1985), Van Stan (1959), Vogt (1937), Walton (1989), Washburn & Crowe (1988), Wassén (1972), Weiner & Schneider (1989), Weitlaner-Johnson (1971), Weltfish (1930, 1932), Whitford (1943), Willey & Corbett (1954)

Collections:

Aguirre (o.J.), American Indian Basketry Magazine (1979), Anderson (1978), Anonym (1964), Boulay (1990), Branford (1984), Brommer et al. (1988), Bühler et al. (1972), Corey (1987), Dürr (1978), Eisleb (1975), Fowler & Matley (1979), Genoud (1981), Grünberg (1967), Guhr & Neumann (1982), Gusic (1955), Hartmann (1952), Hauser-Schäublin (1989), Heathcote (1976), Heermann (1989), Hobi (1982), Iklé (1935), Iklé & Vogt (1935), Kahlenberg (1976), Kundegraber (1976), Laurencich-Minelli & Ciruzzi (1981), Lavalle, de & Lang (1980), Linden-Museum (1989), Mapelli Mozzi & Castello Yturbide (1987), Meyer (1987), Museum für Völkerkunde Basel (1970), Nixdorff (1977), Okada (1958), Petrucci (1982), Rabineau (1975), Riester (1971), Schlabow (1976), Schneider (1975), Schulze-Thulin (1989), Seiler-Baldinger (1987), Signi (1988), Start (1948), Sonderausstellung des Steirischen Bauernmuseums (1976), Streiff (1967), Tenri Sankokan Museum (1981), Verswijver (1983), Waite (1987), Weber (1986), Zerries (1980)

Working Instructions:

American Indian Basketry Magazine (1979), Anonym (1964), Anquetil (1979), Arbeit (1990), Atwater (1976), Barker (1973), Barkow (1983), Barnes & Blake (1976), Belash (1936), Belen (1952), Blanchard (1937), Brotherton (1977), Burgess (1981), Cahlander (1980), Cahlander & Cason (1976), Caulfeild & Saward (1882), Chamberlain & Crookelt (1974), Churcher & Gloor (1986), Corrie Newman (1985), De Leon (1978), Dendel (1974), Dillmont, de (o.J., 1902, 1910), Donner & Schnebel (1913), Finckh-Haelsing (o.J.), Floses (1960), Gallinger-Tod & Benson (1975), Georgens & Von Gayette Georgens (o.J.), Glashauser & Westfall (1976), Hald (1975), Hartung (1963), Heinze (1969), Huber & Stöcklin (1977), Kunz (1980), La Plantz (1982), Lammèr (1975), Martin (1986), Mas (1978), Mooi (1974), Navajo School of Indian Basketry (1949), Osornio Lopez (1938), Pestalozzianum (1990), Pownall (1976), Speiser (1983), Thümmel (o.J.), Tiesler (1980), Voshage (1910), Widmer (o.J.), Will (1978), Wright (1977), Zechlin (1966), Zorn (1980), Zschorsch & Wallach (1923)

Films:

Baer (1973, 1977), Hugger (1967), Koch (1969, 1969), Kussmaul & Snoy (1980), Luz & Schlenker (1974), Malkin (1975, 1975, 1975, 1976), Schier & Simon (1975), Schlesier (1967), Scholz (1967, 1968, 1968), Schultz (1963-65, 1965), Schultz (1981), Schuster (1962), Schuster & Schuster (1980, 1981), Schweeger-Hefel (1973/74), Suter (1978), Trupp (1980), Zerries (1974)

General, Historical:

Chattopadhyaya (1976), Douglas & D'Harcourt (1941), Kelsey & Osborne, de Jongh (1939), Kok (1979), Laufer (1925), Lübke (1969), Müller & Brendler (1958), Nevermann (1960), Oka (1982), Okada (1958), Schneebaum (1985), Schuette (1963), Seiler-Baldinger (1986), Underhill (1941, 1941), Wirz (1955)

Warp Methods

Classification:

Bühler (1938), Bühler & Bühler-Oppenheim (1948), Burnham (1980), Cahlander (1980), Collingwood (1964, 1968, 1974), Crowfoot (1954), Emery (1966), Larsen (1986), Leroi-Gourhan (1943), Oppenheim (1942), Ribeiro (1986), Seiler-Baldinger (1979, 1991), Tanavoli (1985), Vogt (1935)

Analysis:

Acar (1975), Acar (1983), Albers (1965), Amano & Tsunoyama (1979), Anton (1984), Azadi & Andrews (1985), Bergman (1975), Bird (1979), Bird & Bellinger (1954), Bird & Skinner-Dimitrijevic (1974), Birrel (1959), Bolland (1989), Broholm & Hald (1935), Broudy (1979), Burnham (1980), Cahlander (1980), Caspar (1975), Castle (1977), Caulfeild & Saward (1882), Collingwood (1974), Crawford (1915-16), Crowfoot (1985), Crowfoot (1977),

Crowfoot (1954), Disselhoff (1981), Dombrowski (1976), Dombrowski & Pfluger-Schindlbeck (1988), D'Harcourt (1934, 1960, 1962), Eiland (1979), Emmons & Boas (1907), Engel (1963), Farke (1986), Feldman (1986), Feltham (1989), Fernandez Distel (1983), Frame (1981, 1986), Fraser-Lu (1988), Gervers (1977), Gittinger (1971, 1989), Grieder (1986), Grieder et al. (1988), Haebler (1919), Hald (1950), Hecht (1989), Hissink & Hahn (1984, 1989), Hodges (1965), Hyslop & Bird (1985), Kent Peck (1954, 1957), King (1965), Koch-Grünberg (1923), Konieczny (1979), La Baume (1955), Landreau & Pickering (1969), Larsen (1986), Lothrop & Mahler (1957), Mc Neish et al. (1967), Mead (1968), Millán de Palavecino (1960), Mirambell & Martínez (1986), Nabholz-Kartaschoff (1979), Nabholz-Kartaschoff & Näf (1980), Nevermann (1932, 1938), Nooteboom (1948), Nordenskiöld (1919, 1920, 1924), Oppenheim (1942), O'Neale (1942, 1945), O'Neale & Kroeber (1937), Pendergast (1987), Pestalozzianum (1990), Pownall (1976), Prümers (1989), Reath & Sachs (1937), Reswick (1985), Ribeiro (1986, 1986), Riester (1971), Rodee (1987), Roquette-Pinto (1954), Roth (1910, 1918), Rowe (1984), Rutt (1987), Sayer (1988), Schaar & Delz (1983), Schlabow (1976), Schmidt (1905), Schuster (1976), Siewertsz van Reesema (o.J.), Sillitoe (1988), Skinner (1986), Smith (1975), Speiser (1974, 1983), Stoltz Gilfoy (1987), Sylwan (1941), Tanavoli (1985), Tanner (1968), Tattersall (1927), Taullard (1949), Topham (1981), Treiber-Netoliczka (1970), Tsunoyama (1980), Ullemeyer & Tidow (1973), Underhill (1948), Villegas & Rivera (1982), Vogt (1935, 1937), Weitlaner-Johnson (1950, 1976), Wertime (1979), Willey & Corbett (1954), Willoughby (1910), Wilson (1979), Ziemba & Abdulkadir (1979)

Ethnography:

Acar (1983), Adovasio & Maslowski (1980), Albers (1965), Amar & Littleton (1981), Anderson (1978), Aretz (1977), Azadi & Andrews (1985), Baer (1960), Barrow (1962), Bidder (1964), Bighorse & Bennett (1978), Bird (1979), Bolland (1989), Brandford (1977), Buck (1911, 1924), Câmara Cascudo, da (1959), Cardale de Schrimpff (1972, 1977), Caspar (1975), Chantreaux (1946), Cocco (1972), Crowfoot (1943), Danneil (1901), Deuss (1981), Dombrowski (1976), Dombrowski & Pfluger-Schindlbeck (1988), Duby & Blom (1969), Feltham (1989), Fernandez Distel (1983), Fischer & Shah (1970, 1970), Forelli & Harries (1977), Fraser-Lu (1988), Gayton (1948), Gervers (1977), Gittinger (1971, 1975, 1989), Grosset (1978), Grossmann (1955), Haberland (1979), Haebler (1919), Hartmann (1972), Hecht (1989), Heizer (1987), Henking (1957), Herzog (1985), Hissink & Hahn (1984, 1989), Holm & Reid (1975), Indianapolis Museum of Art (1976), James (1971, 1974), Kaeppler (1978), Kahlenberg & Berlant (1976), Kaufmann (1989), Kenagy et al. (1987), Kent Peck (1940, 1961), Kidder (1935), King (1977), Kissel (1928), Koch-Grünberg (1923), Konieczny (1979), Kooijman (1959), Landreau (1973, 1978), Landreau & Pickering (1969), Landreau & Yoke (1983), Lindblom (1928), Lyford (1943), Mead (1945), Mead (1968, 1969), Miller (1988), Moschner (1955), Nabholz-Kartaschoff (1979), Nestor (1987), Nevermann (1938), Newton (1974), Nooteboom (1948), Nordenskiöld (1919, 1920, 1924), Ottaviano de (1974), O'Neale (1945), Pendergast (1987), Pownall (1976), Reichel-Dolmatoff (1946), Reinhard (1974), Reswick (1985), Ribeiro (1978, 1980, 1983, 1985, 1986, 1986, 1989), Riester (1971, 1972), Rodee (1987), Rogers (1983), Roquette-Pinto (1954), Roth (1910, 1918), Rowe (1977), Rutt (1987), Samuel (1982), Sanoja-Obediente (1961), Sayer (1985, 1988), Schmidt (1905), Scholz (1967), Schultz (1963, 1964), Schulze-Thulin (1989), Schuster (1962, 1962, 1976), Signi (1988), Sillitoe (1988), Smith (1975), Stoltz Gilfoy (1987), Susnik (1986), Suttles (1990), Tanavoli (1985), Tanner (1968), Taullard (1949), Topham (1981), Underhill (1948), Villegas & Rivera (1982), Vreeland (1974), Washburn & Crowe (1988), Weitlaner-Johnson (1950, 1956, 1976, 1977), Wertime (1979), Wheat (1977), Wiedemann (1979), Willoughby (1910), Wilson (1979), Zerries & Schuster (1974), Ziemba & Abdulkadir (1979)

Folk Art:

Albers (1965), Aretz (1972, 1977), Collin (1924), Dahrenberg (1936), Gabric (1962), Gervers (1977), Herzog (1985), Meyer-Heisig (1956), Millán de Palavecino (1952), Nixdorff (1977), Palotay & Ferenc (1934), Plá (1990), Preysing (1987), Rutt (1987), Schneider (1975), Sheltman (1922), Smolková (1904), Tkalcic (1929), Treiber-Netoliczka (1970), Vuia (1914), Wilson (1979)

Archaeology:

Adovasio & Maslowski (1980), Albers (1965), Alfaro Giner (1984), Amano & Tsunoyama (1979), Amsden (1932), Anton (1984), Beckwith (1959), Bedaux & Bolland (1989), Bennett & Bird (1960), Bergman (1975), Bird (1952), Bird & Bellinger (1954), Bird & Mahler (1952), Bird & Skinner-Dimitrijevic (1974), Bollinger (1983), Bourguet, du (1964), Broholm & Hald (1935,. 1940, 1948), Cardale de Schrimpff (1977, 1987), Collin (1924), Collingwood (1974), Conklin (1971, 1975), Crowfoot (1985), Crowfoot (1977), Dahrenberg (1936), Dellinger (1936), Disselhoff (1967, 1981), Dwyer (1979), D'Harcourt (1934, 1962, 1974), Egger (1964), Eisleb (1964), Eisleb & Strelow (1965), Engel (1960, 1963), Feldman (1986), Feldtkeller & Schlichtherle (1987), Feltham (1989), Frame (1981, 1982, 1986), Garaventa (1979), Gazda et al. (1980), Geijer (1938), Gervers (1977), Grieder (1986), Grieder et al. (1988), Hald (1950), Hecht (1989), Heizer & Weitlaner-Johnson (1953), Hellervik (1977), Hoffmann & Burnham (1973), Hoffmann & Traetteberg (1959), Holmes (1889), Horn (1968), Hyslop & Bird (1985), Jenkins & Williams (1987), Kent Peck (1954, 1957), Kidder & Guernsey (1919), King (1965, 1968, 1969, 1983), King & Gardner (1981), Laurencich-Minelli & Ciruzzi (1981), Lehmann & Bültzingslöwen, von (1954), Lindberg (1964), Lothrop & Mahler (1957), Lynch (1980), Mc Neish et al. (1967), Means (1932), Millán de Palavecino (1960), Mirambell & Martínez (1986), Moseley & Barrett (1969), Nevermann (1932), O'Neale (1942), Pestalozzianum (1990), Peter (1976), Pfister (1934), Pittard (1946), Prümers (1983, 1989), Rast (1990, 1991), Rosenberg & Haidler (1980), Rowe (1972, 1977, 1979, 1984), Rutt (1987), Schaar & Delz (1983), Schinnerer (1891), Schlabow (1958, 1976, 1983), Schoch (1985), Schulze-Thulin (1989), Siewertsz van Reesema (o.J., 1920), Skinner (1986), Stone (1987), Sylwan (1941), Taullard (1949), Thurmann & Williams (1979), Tsunoyama (1966), Ullemeyer & Tidow (1973), Ulloa (1985), Van Stan (1964), Vogt (1937), Vreeland (1974, 1977), Washburn & Crowe (1988), Weitlaner-Johnson (1950, 1967, 1976), Wey (1990), Whitford (1943), Willey & Corbett (1954), Wilson (1979), Wyss (1990)

Collections:

Amano & Tsunoyama (1979), Amar & Littleton (1981), Anderson (1978), Barten (1976), Boralevi & Faccioli (1986), Bourguet, du (1964), Egger (1964), Enderlein (1986), Landreau (1978), Landreau & Pickering (1969), Laurencich-Minelli & Ciruzzi (1981), Nixdorff (1977), Peter (1976), Preysing (1987), Ramos & Blasco (1976), Reath & Sachs (1937), Riester (1971), Schlabow (1976),

Schneider (1975), Schürmann (o.J.), Schulze-Thulin (1989), Signi (1988), Stoltz Gilfoy (1987), Straka & Mackie (1978), Tattersall (1927), Tsunoyama (1966, 1980)

Working Instructions:
Atwater (1976), Bighorse & Bennett (1978), Cahlander (1980), Caulfeild & Saward (1882), Collingwood (1974), Dillmont, de (o.J.), Gerhardt-Wentzky (1984), Gerhardt-Wenzky (o.J.), Grostol (1932), Hartung (1963), Johnson (1949), Mead (1968), Niedner & Weber (1915), Nilsson (1928), Pestalozzianum (1990), Pownall (1976), Reijnders-Baas (1988), Smith (1975), Speiser (1974, 1983)

Films:
Scholz (1967), Schultz (1963), Schuster (1962, 1962)

General, Historical:
Aga-Dglu (1941), Beattie (1971), Biggs (1983), Black (1985), Black & Loveless (1977), Boralevi & Faccioli (1986), Boyd (1974), Eiland (1979), Flint (1974), Gans-Ruedin (1971), Gazda et al. (1980), Horn (1968), Muthmann (1977), Schürmann (o.J.), Seiler-Baldinger (1986), Straka & Mackie (1978), Sylwan (1928), Victoria and Albert Museum (1931)

Tapestry

Classification:
Burnham (1980), Emery (1966), Seiler-Baldinger (1979, 1991)

Analysis:
Acar (1975), Acar (1983), Amano & Tsunoyama (1979), Amsden (1934), Baerlocher (1978, 1978), Bauspack (1983), Birrel (1959), Brommer et al. (1988), Burnham (1980), Collingwood (1987, 1988), Cootner (1981), Disselhoff (1981), Dombrowski & Pfluger-Schindlbeck (1988), Egloff (1976), Feltham (1989), Fisher & Bowen (1979), Fox (1978), Geijer (1979), Gervers (1977), Jager-Gerlings (1952), Justin (1980), Kahlenberg & Berlant (1976), King (1965), Kroeber & Wallace (1954), Kümpers (1961), Landreau & Pickering (1969), Lothrop & Mahler (1957), Means (1925), Mellaart & Hirsch (1989), Mirambell & Martínez (1986), Museo Chileno (1989), Nabholz-Kartaschoff & Näf (1980), Nevermann (1932), Nylén (1969), O'Neale & Kroeber (1930, 1937), Petsopoulos (1980), Prümers (1990), Ramos & Blasco (1977), Rapp & Stucky (1990), Reswick (1985), Schaar & Delz (1983), Segal et al. (1973), Taullard (1949), Van Stan (1958, 1967), Willey & Corbett (1954), Ziemba & Abdulkadir (1979)

Ethnography:
Acar (1983), Amar & Littleton (1981), Amsden (1934), Andrews (o.J.), Balbino Camposeco (1983), Blomberg (1988), Brandford (1977), Cohen (1982), Collingwood (1987, 1988), Dockstader (1978, 1987), Dombrowski & Pfluger-Schindlbeck (1988), Douglas & D'Harcourt (1941), Dutton (1961), Eggebrecht (1979), Feltham (1989), Fisher & Bowen (1979), Fox (1978), Frauenknecht & Frantz (1975), Frost (1977), Getzwiller (1984), Gisbert & Arze (1987), Gluck & Gluck (1974), Goetz (1952), Haegenbart (1982), Herrli (1985), Housego (1978), Jager-Gerlings (1952), James (1971, 1974), James (1988), Justin (1980), Kahlenberg & Berlant (1972), Kenagy et al. (1987), Kent Peck (1961, 1985), Kiewe (1952), King (1977), Klingmüller & Münch (1989), Kümpers (1961), Landreau (1973, 1978), Landreau & Pickering (1969), Matsumoto (1984), Mellaart & Hirsch (1989), Montell (1925), Myers (1989), Osborne, de Jongh (1964), Payne Hatcher (1967), Pendelton (1974), Petsopoulos (1980), Philip Stoller (1977), Reichard (1936, 1974), Reinhard (1974), Renne (1986), Reswick (1981, 1985), Riboud (1989), Rodee (1977, 1981), Roessel (1983), Schevill (1986), Schulze-Thulin (1989), Segal Brandford (1977), Taullard (1949), Washburn & Crowe (1988), Wegner (1974), Weir (1976), Wells (1969), Wheat (1984), Whitaker (1986), Wiet (1935), Wissa (1972), Zick-Nissen (1968), Ziemba & Abdulkadir (1979)

Folk Art:
Egloff (1976), Geijer (1972), Hicks (1976), Klingmüller & Münch (1989), Millán de Palavecino (1957), Montell (1925), Nylén (1969), Petrasch (1970), Petrescu (1967), Vergara Wilson (1988)

Archaeology:
Amano & Tsunoyama (1979), Baerlocher (1978, 1978), Bajinski & Tidhar (1980), Beckwith (1959), Bellinger (1952, 1954, 1962), Bird (1964), Bird et al. (1981), Bourguet, du (1964), Brommer et al. (1988), Cortes Moreno (1987), Coulin-Weibel (1952), Disselhoff (1967, 1981), D'Harcourt (1936), Egger (1964), Einstein (1922), Eisleb (1964), Feltham (1989), Flemming (1957), Forbes (1956), Frame (1990), Garaventa (1981), Gazda et al. (1980), Gervers (1977), Jaekel-Greifswald (1911-12), Jaques (1963), Kendrick (1922, 1924), King (1965), Krafft (1956), Kroeber & Wallace (1954), Lapiner (1976), Lavalle, de & Lang (1980), Lothrop & Mahler (1957), Maurer (1951), Means (1925, 1927, 1930), Mellaart & Hirsch (1989), Millán de Palavecino (1941), Mirambell & Martínez (1986), Murra (1962), Museo Chileno (1989), Nauerth (1978), Nevermann (1932), Oakland (1986), O'Neale (1933), O'Neale & Kroeber (1930), Peter (1976), Pleyte (1900), Prümers (1990), Ramos & Blasco (1977), Renner (1974, 1985), Renner-Volbach (1988), Riboud (1989), Rowe (1972, 1978, 1979), Rowe (1979), Sawyer (1963, 1966), Schaar & Delz (1983), Schmidt (1910, 1911), Schulze-Thulin (1989), Segal et al. (1973), Shurinova (1967), Stone (1987), Taullard (1949), Turner (1971), Van Stan (1958, 1961, 1964, 1964, 1967), Wace (1944, 1954), Washburn & Crowe (1988), Wassén (1972), Willey & Corbett (1954), Zaloscer (1962)

Collections:
Amano & Tsunoyama (1979), Amar & Littleton (1981), Andrews (o.J.), Blomberg (1988), Boralevi & Faccioli (1986), Bourguet, du (1964), Brommer et al. (1988), Cerny (1975), Cootner (1981), Coulin-Weibel (1952), Egger (1964), Enderlein (1986), Flemming (1957), Frame (1990), Gruber (1990), Haegenbart (1982), Harmsen (1977), Herrli (1985), Jaques (1963), Kahlenberg & Berlant (1976), Kendrick (1924), Kiewe (1952), Landreau (1978), Landreau & Pickering (1969), Lavalle, de & Lang (1980), Means (1927), Museo Chileno (1989), Nauerth (1978), Peter (1976), Renne (1986), Renner (1974, 1985), Renner-Volbach (1988), Rodee (1977), Schulze-Thulin (1989), Van Stan (1967), Wace (1944), Zick-Nissen (1968)

Working Instructions:
Pendelton (1974), Reichard (1974)

Film:
Egloff (1976)

General, Historical:
Aga-Dglu (1941), Black (1985), Black & Loveless (1979), Boralevi

& Faccioli (1986), Douglas & D'Harcourt (1941), Forman & Wasseff (1968), Frauenknecht & Frantz (1975), Gans-Ruedin (1971), Gazda et al. (1980), Gombos (1980), Hubel (1972), Jarry (1976), Kadow (1973), Muthmann (1977), Pianzola & Coffinet (1971), Sylwan (1928), Victoria and Albert Museum (1931)

Half-weaving

Classification:

Bühler & Bühler-Oppenheim (1948), Bühler-Oppenheim (1947), Oppenheim (1942), Seiler-Baldinger (1979, 1991), Seiler-Baldinger & Ohnemus (1986)

Analysis:

Brommer et al. (1988), Collingwood (1987, 1988), Kent Peck (1957, 1983), Lamb (1984), Nordenskiöld (1924), Oppenheim (1942), Schaar & Delz (1983)

Ethnography:

Cardale de Schrimpff (1972), Collingwood (1987, 1988), Desrosiers (1980), Dürr (1978, 1989), Lamb (1984), Ling Roth (1920), Nordenskiöld (1924), Ohnemus (1989), Schmidt (1907), Seiler-Baldinger & Ohnemus (1986), Simon (1989)

Archaeology:

Brommer et al. (1988), Kent Peck (1957, 1983), Schaar & Delz (1983)

Collections:

Brommer et al. (1988), Dürr (1978)

Film:

Ohnemus (1989), Simon (1989)

Weaving

Classification:

Bühler (1938, 1943, 1972), Bühler & Bühler-Oppenheim (1948), Bühler-Oppenheim (1947), Burnham (1980), Collingwood (1968), Crowfoot (1954), Emery (1966), Larsen (1986), Leroi-Gourhan (1943), Ling Roth (1934), Oppenheim (1942), Praeger (1986), Ribeiro (1986, 1986), Rowe (1984), Schams (o.J.), Schnegelsberg (1971), Seiler-Baldinger (1979, 1991), Tanavoli (1985), Vial (1986)

Analysis:

Albers (1952, 1965), Amano & Tsunoyama (1979), Amsden (1934), Anonym (1957), Anquetil (1977), Anton (1984), Aronson (1989), Baerlocher (1978), Barendse & Lobera (1987), Bel & Ricard (1913), Bellinger & Kühnel (1952), Bender-Jorgensen (1986), Bergman (1975), Bianchi et al. (1982), Bird & Bellinger (1954), Birrel (1959), Bluhm (1952), Bolland (1970, 1975, 1977, 1979), Boser-Sarivaxévanis (1972, 1972, 1975, 1980), Braulik (1900), Brauns & Löffler (1986), Brigham (1974), Broholm & Hald (1935), Brommer et al. (1988), Broudy (1979), Buck (1944), Bühler (1943), Bühler & Ramseyer-Gygi (1975), Bühler et al. (1972), Burnham (1977, 1980, 1981, 1986), Cahlander & Baizerman (1985), Cahlander & Cason (1976), Cahlander et al. (1978), Campbell & Pongnoi (1978), Castle (1977), Caulfeild & Saward (1882), Cheesman (1988), Chertudi & Nardi (1960, 1961), Christensen (1979), Claerhout & Bolland (1975), Collingwood (1982, 1987, 1988), Conklin (1979), Cootner (1981), Cordry & Cordry (1973), Cornet (1982), Crawford (1915-16), Crowfoot (1985), Crowfoot (1977), Crowfoot (1939, 1948/49, 1954), Desrosiers (1986), Deuss (1981), Disselhoff (1981), Dombrowski (1976), Dombrowski & Pfluger-Schindlbeck (1988), Donat (1899), Durand-Forest (1966), D'Harcourt (1934, 1960), Egloff (1976), Eisleb (1975), Ephraim (1904), Etienne-Nugue (1985), Farke (1986), Feldman & Rubinstein (1986), Feltham (1989), Fisher & Bowen (1979), Flemming (1923), Fox (1978), Franquemont (1983), Fraser-Lu (1988), Frey (1955), Furger & Hartmann (1983), Gallinger-Tod & Couch del Deo (1976), Geijer (1979, 1982), Gervers (1977), Gittinger (1971, 1989), Gordon (1980), Gräbner (1922), Grieder (1986), Grünberg (1967), Hagino & Stothert (1983), Hald (1950, 1980), Hansen (1990), Hecht (1989), Heissig & Müller (1989), Henshall (1950), Hentschel (1937), Hissink & Hahn (1984, 1989), Hodges (1965), Hoffmann (1964), Hundt (1969, 1980), Hyslop & Bird (1985), Innes (1959), Jager-Gerlings (1952), Jaques & Wencker (1967), Jasper & Pirngadie (1912-16), Jelmini & Clerc-Junier (1986), Johl (1924), Jongh, de (1985), Justin (1980), Kahlenberg & Berlant (1976), Kalter (1983), Kauffmann (1937), Kent Peck (1941, 1954, 1957), King (1965, 1979), Klein (1961), Knottenbelt (1983), Konieczny (1979), Koob (1979), Krishna (1966), Kroeber & Wallace (1954), Kümpers (1961), La Baume (1955), Laczko (1979), Lamb (1975, 1984), Lamb & Lamb (1975), Landreau & Pickering (1969), Larsen (1986), Lehmann-Filhes (1901), Lewis & Lewis (1984), Linder (1967), Lipton (1989), Loir (1935), Lorenz (1980), Lorenzo (1933), Lothrop (1928), Lothrop & Mahler (1957, 1957), Mannová (1972), Mason (1901), Mc Neish et al. (1967), Means (1925), Meisch (1986), Menzel (1973), Meurant & Tunis (1989), Millán de Palavecino (1960), Mirambell & Martínez (1986), Museo Chileno (1989), Nabholz-Kartaschoff (1979), Nachtigall (1955), Nevermann (1938), Newman (1974, 1977), Niessen (1989), Noppe & Castillon, du (1988), Nordenskiöld (1920), Nylén (1969), Oppenheim (1942), Osborne (1965), O'Neale (1942, 1945, 1946), O'Neale & Clark (1948), O'Neale & Kroeber (1930, 1937), Pancake & Baizerman (1981), Pestalozzianum (1990), Ponting & Chapman (1980), Prümers (1989, 1990), Ramos & Blasco (1977), Reath & Sachs (1937), Reswick (1985), Ribeiro (1986, 1986), Riboud & Vial (1970), Riesenberg & Gayton (1952), Riester (1971), Rodee (1987), Roth (1918), Rowe (1975, 1984, 1984), Roy (1979), Rutt (1987), Sanoja Obediente (1979), Sayer (1988), Schaar & Delz (1983), Schaedler (1987), Schlabow (1957, 1976), Segal et al. (1973), Seiler-Baldinger (1987), Selvanayagam (1990), Sharma (1968), Signorini (1979), Simpson & Weir (1932), Snow & Snow (1973), Sonday (1979), Sonday & Kajitani (1971), Standigel (1975), Stanková (1989), Stanley (1983), Stoltz Gilfoy (1987), Stout (1976), Sylwan (1941), Tanavoli (1985), Taullard (1949), Textilmuseum Krefeld (1978), Topham (1981), Tsunoyama (1980), Tunis & Meurant (1989), Ullemeyer & Tidow (1973), Underhill (1945, 1948), Van Stan (1967), Veiga de Oliveira & Galhano (1978), Veltman & Fischer (1912), Vial (1976, 1980, 1986, 1986), Villegas & Rivera (1982), Vogt (1937), Vollmer (1977), Voskresensky & Tikhonov (1936), Walton (1989), Weitlaner-Johnson (1976, 1979), Wertime (1979), Willey & Corbett (1954), Wilson (1979), Wulff (1966), Zechlin (1966), Zumbühl (1988)

Ethnography:

Adams (1984), Adams (1969, 1971, 1977, 1978, 1989), Adelson & Tracht (1983), Adovasio & Maslowski (1980), Agthe (1975), Ahmed (1967), Albers (1965), Ali (1900), Alman (1960), Amborn

(1990), Amsden (1934), Anand (1974), Anderson (1978), Ankermann (1922), Anonym (1944, 1956, 1965), Archambault (1988), Aretz (1977), Aronson (1982, 1986, 1989), Baer & Seiler-Baldinger (1989), Bailey (1947), Ball (1924), Baranowicz, de & Bernheimer (1957), Barker (1985), Barnes (1987, 1989), Bayley Willis (1987), Beals (1969), Becker-Donner (1968), Bedford (1974), Bel & Ricard (1913), Bellinger (1961), Ben-Amos (1978), Berin (1978), Bhavani (1968), Bhushan (1985), Bianchi et al. (1982), Billeter (o.J., o.J.), Bird (1960, 1979), Bird & Skinner-Dimitrijevic (1964), Bjerregaard (1977, 1979), Blinks (1960, 1979), Blomberg (1988), Bolinder (1925), Bolland (1956, 1970, 1971, 1975, 1977, 1979), Bombay Government (o.J.), Borgatti (1983), Boser-Sarivaxévanis (1972, 1972, 1972, 1975, 1980), Boyd (1964), Boyer (1983), Brauns & Löffler (1986), Braunsberger de Solari (1983), Breguet & Martin (1983), Bubolz-Eicher (o.J.), Buck (1944), Bühler (1943, 1947, 1972), Bühler & Ramseyer-Gygi (1975), Burnham (1962, 1965), Cahlander & Cason (1976), Cahlander et al. (1978), Câmara Cascudo, da (1959), Campbell (1836), Campbell & Pongnoi (1978), Cannizzo (1969), Cardale de Schrimpff (1972, 1977), Cardenas et al. (1988), Cardoso et al. (1988), Carreira (1968), Casagrande (1977), Cervellino (1979), Chantreaux (1941, 1945), Chao (1977), Chattopadhyaya (1963, 1976), Chattopadhyaya (1923), Cheesman (1982, 1988), Chertudi & Nardi (1960, 1961), Chishti & Sanyal (1989), Chor Lin (1987), Christensen (1979), Cisneros (1981), Claerhout & Bolland (1975), Clarke (1938), Claude (1928), Cohen (1957), Cole & Ross (1977), Collingwood (1987, 1988), Combe (1947, 1948), Cook de Leonard et al. (1966), Cordry & Cordry (1940, 1941, 1973), Cornet (1982), Crawford (1916), Cresson & Jeannin (1943), Crowfoot (1943, 1945, 1956), Cuéllar (1977), Dalman (1964), Dalrymple (1984), Damm (1960), Danneil (1901), Deimel (1982), Delgado (1963), Deuss (1981), Devassy (1964), Dhamija (1970, 1985), Dhamija & Jain (1989), Dietrich (1979), Dijk van (1980), Dockstader (1978, 1987), Does, de (o.J.), Dombrowski (1976), Dombrowski & Pfluger-Schindlbeck (1988), Dongerkery (o.J.), Dornheim (1948), Drewal & Pemberton (1989), Dürr (1978), Dunsmore (1983, 1985), Dupaigne (1974), Duponchel (1987), Duque Gomez (1945), Durand-Forest (1966), Durban Art Gallery (1977), Dutton (1961), D'Harcourt (1948, 1970), Easmon (1924), Elmberg (1968), Emery & Fiske (1977, 1979), Engelbrecht (1986), Espejel & Català Roca (1978), Etienne-Nugue (1982, 1982, 1984, 1985), Fauconnier (1980), Feldman & Rubinstein (1986), Feltham (1989), Femenias (1988), Fenton & Stuart-Fox (1976), Fischer (1965), Fischer & Shah (1970, 1970), Fischer et al. (1979), Fisher & Bowen (1979), Forelli & Harries (1977), Foster (1969), Fox (1978), Frame (1983, 1989), Franquemont (1986), Franquemont (1983), Fraser-Lu (1988), Freshley (1979), Galestin et al. (1956), Gardi (1976, 1985), Gardi & Seydou (1989), Gardi (1958), Geirnaert (1989), Gerhards (1987), Gervers (1977), Ghose (1948), Gil del Pozo (1974), Gilfoy (1979), Girault (1969), Gisbert (o.J.), Gisbert & Arze (1987), Gittinger (1971, 1972, 1974, 1979, 1989, 1989), Gluck & Gluck (1974), Goddard (1931), Goetz (1952), Goitein (1955), Goody (1982), Gräbner (1909), Grünberg (1967), Guelton (1989), Guhr & Neumann (1982), Haas (1970), Haberland (1963), Haddon & Start (1982), Hagino & Stothert (1983), Hahn-Hissink (1971), Hailey (1904), Hamilton (1979), Hansen (1960), Hartkamp-Jonxis (1989), Hartkopf (1971), Harvey & Kelly (1969), Hauser-Schäublin & Nabholz-Kartaschoff (1991, 1991), Heathcote (1976), Hecht (1989), Heissig & Müller (1989), Henriksen (1978), Heringa (1989), Hissink & Hahn (1984, 1989), Hitchcock (1985), Hodge (1982), Högl (1980), Holmgren & Spertus (1980), Hooper (1915), Houlihan et al. (1987), Huang & Wenzhao (1982), Imperato (1979), Indianapolis Museum of Art (1976), Irwin (1973, 1978), Jacobs (1983), Jager-Gerlings (1952), James (1971, 1974), James (1988), Jayakar (1962, 1967, 1978), Jingshan (1982), Joplin (1977), Joseph (1978), Justin (1980), Kahlenberg & Berlant (1972), Kalter (1983), Kann (1982), Karsten (1972), Kartiwa (1980, 1982, 1986), Kauffmann (1937, 1963, 1967), Kensinger (1975), Kent Peck (1940, 1941, 1977, 1985, 1989), Khan Majlis (1977, 1984, 1985), Kidder (1935), King (1988), King (1974, 1979), Kissel (1910), Klein (1974, 1979), Klein (1961), Klingmüller & Münch (1989), Knottenbelt (1983), Koch (1973), Koch-Grünberg (1909), Konieczny (1979), Korsching (1980), Kosswig (1967), Kreischer (1907), Krishna (1966), Kron-Steinhardt (1989), Kümpers (1961), Kuhn (1977), Kussmaul & Moos, von (1981), Labin (1979), Laczko (1979), Lakwete (1977), Lamb (1975, 1984), Lamb & Lamb (1975, 1981), Landreau (1978), Landreau & Pickering (1969), Landreau & Yoke (1983), Langewis (1956), Langewis & Wagner (1964), Laquist (1947), Lehmann (1945), Leigh & Kerajinan (1989), Lévi-Strauss (1984), Lewis & Lewis (1984), Lin (1987), Lindahl & Knorr (1975), Lindblom (1928), Ling Roth (1920, 1934), Lipton (1989), Loebèr (1903), Loir (1935), Lorm, de (1938), Lothrop (1928), Lyman (1962), Mac Leish (1940), Mack (1987, 1989), Manderloot (1971), Manndorff & Scholz (1967, 1968), Manrique (1969), Mapelli Mozzi & Castello Yturbide (1987), March (1983), Marschall (1989), Mason (1910), Matthews (1891-92), Maxwell (1990), Mayer Stinchecum (1984), Mc Creary (1975), Mc Kelvy Bird & Mendizábal Losak (1986), Mc Reynolds (1982), Medlin (1983, 1986), Mege Rosso (1990), Meisch (1981), Meisch (1986), Menzel (1973), Merritt (1989), Metha (1970), Métraux (1928), Meurant (1986), Meurant & Tunis (1989), Miller (1979), Miller (1988), Mom Dusdi (1975), Montandon (1934), Montell (1925), Moos, von (1983), Morris (1980), Morton (1981), Moshkova (1970), Mukharji (1888), Munan (1989), Muraoka & Okamura (1973), Murray (1938), Myers (1989), Nabholz-Kartaschoff (1979), Nachtigall (1955, 1963, 1966, 1969), Nambiar (1961, 1964, 1966), Nestor (1987), Nettleship (1970), Nevermann (1938), Newman (1974, 1977), Niessen (1989), Niggemeyer (1952, 1955, 1966), Nooteboom (1958), Nooy-Palm (1980), Noppe & Castillon, du (1988), Nordenskiöld (1920), Nordquist & Aradeon (1975), Olagniers-Riottot (1972), Olschak (1966), Ortiz (1979, 1983), Osborne, de Jongh (1935, 1964, 1965), Ottovar & Munch-Petersen (1980), Ovalle Fernandez (1982), O'Neale (1945, 1946), Palm (1958), Pancake & Baizerman (1981), Pangemanan (1919), Pauly & Corrie (1975), Payne Hatcher (1967), Pelras (1962, 1972), Perani (1979, 1989), Philip Stoller (1977), Picton & Mack (1979), Pleyte (1912), Ploier (1988), Plumer (1971), Polakoff (1982), Ponting & Chapman (1980), Powell (1985), Poynor (1980), Prangwatthanakun & Cheesman (1987), Ramseyer (1987), Rangnekar (1966), Rau (1970), Ravicz & Romney (1969), Ravines (1978), Ray (1989), Redwood (1974), Reichard (1936, 1974), Renne (1986), Reswick (1981, 1985), Ribeiro (1978, 1980, 1980, 1985, 1986, 1986, 1986, 1988), Riboud (1989), Riedinger & Riedinger (1980), Riefstahl (1923), Riesenberg & Gayton (1952), Riester (1971), Rodee (1987), Rodee (1977, 1981), Rodgers (1985), Rodgers-Siregar (1980), Roessel (1983), Rolandi & Pupareli, de (1985), Ronge (1982), Rossie & Claus (1983), Roth (1918), Rouffaer (1902), Rowe (1975, 1977, 1977, 1978, 1981), Roy (1982), Roy (1979), Rutt (1987), Ryesky (1977, 1977), Salomon (1977), Saraf (1987), Saugy (1973), Sayer (1985, 1988), Sayles (1955), Scarce (1988/89), Schaedler (1987), Schermann (1913), Schevill (1986), Schindler (1990), Schmidt-Thome & Tsering (1975), Schneider (1987), Scholz (1967, 1968, 1974, 1974, 1977), Schulze-Thulin (1989), Sedlak (1987), Seiler-Baldinger (1987), Selvanayagam (1990), Sharma (1968), Sharma (1964), Shepherd (1973), Shiroishi Miyagi Prefecture (1946), Sibeth (1990), Sieber (1972,

1987), Siegenthaler (1989), Signorini (1979), Silverman-Proust (1986, 1988, 1989), Siskin (1977), Snoddy-Cuellar (1977), Solyom & Solyom (1979, 1984), Sperlich & Sperlich (1980), Spier (1924), Spring (1989), Stanley (1983), Start (1917), Steinman (1937), Stoeckel (1921-23), Stoltz Gilfoy (1987), Stout (1976), Strupp-Green (1971), Supakar (1985), Susnik (1986), Suwati (1982), Tanavoli (1985), Tanner (1975), Taullard (1949), Therik (1989), Thompson (1983), Tietze (1941), Topham (1981), Torres (1980), Trivedi (1967), Tunis & Meurant (1989), Turnbull (1982), Underhill (o.J., 1945, 1948), University of Singapore Art Museum (1964), Van Gennep (1912, 1914), Vargas (1985), Veltman & Fischer (1912), Verma (1965), Vial (1980, 1985, 1986), Victoria and Albert Museum (1928), Villegas & Rivera (1982), Völger & Weck (1987), Vogelsanger (1980), Vollmer (1977), Vreeland (1979), Wacziarg & Nath (1987), Warming & Gaworski (1981), Washburn & Crowe (1988), Wass & Murnane (1978), Wassermann & Hill (1981), Wassing-Visser (1982), Watkins (1939), Watson-Franke (1974), Weber (1935), Weber (1977), Weigand, de & Weigand, de (1977), Weiner & Schneider (1989), Weir (1970, 1976), Weisswange (1975), Weitlaner-Johnson (1976, 1977, 1979), Wells (1969), Wertime (1979), Westfall (1981), Wheat (1977, 1984), Whitaker (1986), Whiting (1977), Wiedemann (1979), Wiet (1935), Wilson (1979), Wulff (1966), Yorke & Allen (1980), Zebrowski (1989), Zorn (1979), Zumbühl (1988)

Folk Art:

Abadia Morales (1983), Aguirre (o.J.), Albers (1965), Anawalt (1979), Andersen (1980), Anonym (1893, 1957, 1985), Anquetil (1977), Apostolaki (1956), Aretz (1972, 1977), Barendse & Lobera (1987), Barletta (1985), Berbenni (1984), Bodmer (1940), Bouza & Calzada (1977), Bretz (1977), Brunner-Littmann & Hahn (1988), Burnham (1981, 1986), Cardenas et al. (1988), Collin (1924), Cyrus (1956), Dahl (1987), Eaton (1937), Eddy (1989), Egloff (1976), Endrei (1985), Engelstad (1958), Eyk, van (1977), Fink (1979), Flemming (1923), Gehret & Keyser (1976), Geijer (1964, 1972, 1982), Gervers (1977), Gimbatas (1966), Gordon (1980), Grabowicz (1977), Grabowicz & Wolinetz (1981), Gustafson (1980), Haberlandt (1912), Hald (1932), Heikinmäki (1970), Henschen (1943, 1951), Hicks (1976), Hörlèn (1948, 1950), Hoffmann (1958, 1964, 1965, 1979, 1979), Juhasz (1990), Kaukonen (1961), Kerkhoff-Hader (1989), Kimakowicz-Winnicki (1910), King (1988), Klingmüller & Münch (1989), Kurrick (1932), Lechner (1958), Linder (1967), Lönnqvist (1972), Lorenz (1980), Lorenzo (1933), Mannová (1972), Marková (1967), Mayer (1969), Meyer-Heisig (1956), Millán de Palavecino (1957, 1961), Montell (1925), Müller-Christensen (1975), Müller-Peter (1983), Nixdorff (1977), Nordiska Museet (1984), Noss (1966), Nylén (1969), O_tric (1981), Pelanzy & Català (1978), Petrasch (1970), Pocius (1979), Rauter (1969), Reichelt (1956), Rural Industries Bureau (1930), Rutt (1987), Sanoja Obediente (1979), Scarin et al. (1989), Schneider (1975), Shepherd (1943), Shivo (1978), Simpson & Weir (1932), Spirito (1964), Stanková (1975, 1989), Stapeley (1924), Stojanovic (1962), Sturtevant (1977), Svobodová (1975, 1975), Swiezy (1958), Taszycka (1972), Tidow (1978), Tkalcic (1929), Torella Nuibò (1949), Tucci (1963), Ungricht (1917), Václavík (1956), Václavik & Orel (o.J.), Valansot (1986), Veiga de Oliveira & Galhano (1978), Vergara Wilson (1988), Volkart (1907, 1915, 1916), Weiner & Schneider (1989), Wencker (1968), Wilson (1979)

Archaeology:

Adovasio (1975), Adovasio & Maslowski (1980), Albers (1952, 1965), Alfaro Giner (1984), Amano & Tsunoyama (1979), Amsden (1932), Anonym (1944), Anton (1984), Baerlocher (1978), Bajinski & Tidhar (1980), Becker (1981), Bedaux & Bolland (1980, 1981), Bellinger (1952, 1954, 1959, 1959, 1962), Bellinger & Kühnel (1952), Bender-Jorgensen (1986), Bender-Jorgensen & Tidow (1981), Bennett (1935, 1954), Berberian (1941), Bergman (1975), Billeter (o.J.), Bird (1983), Bird & Bellinger (1954), Bird & Skinner-Dimitrijevic (1964), Bird et al. (1981), Bluhm (1952), Bollinger (1983), Braulik (1900), Bray (1987), Broholm & Hald (1935, 1940, 1948), Brommer et al. (1988), Bruce (1986), Cachot (1949), Cammann (1964), Cardale de Schrimpff (1977, 1978, 1987, 1988), Cardale de Schrimpff & Falchetti de Sáenz (1980), Carvajal (1938), Chaves (1984), Cherblanc (1935), Collin (1924), Conklin (1978, 1978, 1979), Cortes Moreno (1987), Coulin-Weibel (1952), Crawford (1916, 1946), Crowfoot (1985), Crowfoot (1977), Crowfoot (1939, 1943, 1947, 1948/49), Crowfoot & Davies (1941), Dawson (1979), Dimand (1930), Disselhoff (1967, 1981), Durand-Forest (1966), Dwyer (1979), D'Harcourt (1934, 1948), Egger (1964), Eisleb (1975), Eisleb & Strelow (1965), Emery & King (1971), Faxon (1932), Feltham (1989), Flemming (1957), Forbes (1956), Frame (1990), Freshley (1979), Furger & Hartmann (1983), Garaventa (1979), Gardner (1982), Gazda et al. (1980), Geijer (1964, 1967), Geijer & Franzen (1956), Gervers (1977), Grieder (1986), Grossman (1958), Guliev (1961), Hägg (1984), Hald (1933, 1950, 1963, 1980), Harner (1979), Hecht (1989), Hellervik (1977), Henneberg, von (1932), Henshall (1950), Hentschel (1937), Hissink (1965), Hoffmann & Burnham (1973), Hoffmann & Traetteberg (1959), Hooper (1915), Hsian (1963), Hundt (1960, 1963, 1969, 1970, 1970, 1974, 1980), Hyslop & Bird (1985), Ingstad (1982), Jaques (1968), Jerusalimskaia (1967), Johl (1917, 1924), Joyce (1921, 1922), Kent Peck (1954, 1957), King (1956, 1962, 1965, 1974, 1974, 1979), Kjellberg (1982), Krafft (1956), Krause (1921), Kroeber (1937, 1944), Kroeber & Wallace (1954), Lapiner (1976), Laurencich-Minelli & Ciruzzi (1981), Lavalle, de & Lang (1980), Lehmann (1920), Lindström (1981), Ling Roth (1951), Lothrop & Mahler (1957, 1957), Lucas (1948), Lynch (1980), Magnus (1982), Mailey & Hathaway (1958), Marcos (1979), Mastache (1971), Mc Neish et al. (1967), Means (1925, 1927), Meyer (1987), Millán de Palavecino (1941, 1960, 1966), Mirambell & Martínez (1986), Müller-Christensen (1972, 1977), Munksgaard (1982), Murra (1962), Museo Chileno (1989), Olsen Bruhns (1989), Ortiz (1979), Osborne (1950), O'Neale (1930, 1937, 1942, 1943, 1943, 1947), O'Neale & Bacon (1949), O'Neale & Clark (1948), O'Neale & Kroeber (1930), Patterson (1956), Paul (1979, 1980, 1986), Pedersen (1982), Pestalozzianum (1990), Peter-Müller (1978), Petrucci (1982), Pfister (1934, 1937, 1937-40, 1938, 1946, 1950, 1951), Pfister & Bellinger (1945), Portillo (1976), Prümers (1983, 1989, 1990), Ramos & Blasco (1977), Raymond & Bayona (1982), Reindel (1987), Renner (1985), Renner-Volbach (1988), Restrepo (1972), Riboud (1973, 1975, 1975, 1977, 1989), Riboud & Vial (1968), Rolandi (1979), Rowe (1977, 1979, 1979, 1984), Rowe & Bird (1981), Rutt (1987), Sawyer (1966), Schaar & Delz (1983), Schinnerer (1891), Schlabow (1951, 1958, 1961, 1965, 1972, 1976, 1983), Schmidt (1910, 1911), Schoch (1985), Schottelius (1946), Schulze-Thulin (1989), Segal et al. (1973), Seipel (1989), Shepherd (1974), Silva Celis (1978), Singer et al. (1954-57), Skinner (1974), Smart & Gluckman (1989), Spahni (1967), Spuhler (1978), Standigel (1975), Stettiner (1911), Stokar (1938), Strupp-Green (1971), Sylwan (1941, 1949), Taullard (1949), Thurmann & Williams (1979), Tidow (1982, 1982, 1983), Timmerman (1982), Tsunoyama (1966), Ullemeyer & Tidow (1973), Ulloa (1985), Van Gennep & Jéquier (1916), Van Stan (1965, 1967, 1967, 1970, 1979), Vial (1976), Völger & Weck

(1987), Vogt (1937, 1952, 1958, 1964), Vollmer (1977, 1979), Voskresensky & Tikhonov (1936), Wace (1944), Wallace (1967, 1975, 1979), Walton (1989), Wardle (1944), Washburn & Crowe (1988), Wassén (1972), Weiner & Schneider (1989), Weitlaner-Johnson (1971, 1976, 1977), Wild (1976), Willey & Corbett (1954), Wilson (1979), Zebrowski (1989), Zerries (1968), Zimmermann (1981, 1982, 1984), Zimmern (1949)

Collections:

Adams (1984), Adelson & Tracht (1983), Agthe (1975), Aguirre (o.J.), Altman & Lopez (1975), Amano & Tsunoyama (1979), Anderson (1978), Barten (1976), Bartholomew (1985), Billeter (o.J.), Bird (1965), Blomberg (1988), Blomberg de Avila (1980), Borgatti (1983), Bridgewater (1986), Brommer et al. (1988), Bühler et al. (1972), Castello Yturbide & Martinez del Rio, de (1979), Cootner (1981), Coulin-Weibel (1944, 1952), Crawford (1946), Davidson & Christa (1973), Dietrich (1979), Dürr (1978), Durban Art Gallery (1977), Egger (1964), Eisleb (1975), Enderlein (1986), Errera (1907), Femenias (1988), Flemming (1957), Frame (1990), Gimbatas (1966), Gisbert (o.J.), Grabowicz (1977), Grabowicz & Wolinetz (1981), Gruber (1990), Grünberg (1967), Guhr & Neumann (1982), Hahn-Hissink (1971), Hald (1967), Harmsen (1977), Heathcote (1976), Innes (1959), Jaques (1968), Jaques & Wencker (1967), Kahlenberg & Berlant (1976), Lamb & Lamb (1975), Landreau (1978), Landreau & Pickering (1969), Laurencich-Minelli & Ciruzzi (1981), Lavalle, de & Lang (1980), Lemberg (1973), Lin (1987), Lindahl & Knorr (1975), Lipton (1989), Mackie & Rowe (1976), Mapelli Mozzi & Castello Yturbide (1987), Mayer (1969), Mayer Stinchecum (1984), Means (1927), Mege Rosso (1990), Meyer (1987), Mikosch (1985), Museo Chileno (1989), Nabholz-Kartaschoff (1986), Niggemeyer (1966), Nixdorff (1977), Nooteboom (1958), O_tric (1981), Pauly & Corrie (1975), Peebles (1982), Pence Britton (1938), Petrucci (1982), Ploier (1988), Powell (1985), Rabineau (1975), Ramos & Blasco (1976), Reath & Sachs (1937), Renne (1986), Renner (1985), Renner-Volbach (1988), Riboud & Vial (1970), Riester (1971), Rodee (1977), Rouffaer (1901, 1902), Rowe (1948), Schlabow (1976), Schmedding (1978), Schmidt (1975), Schneider (1975), Schulz (1988), Schulze-Thulin (1989), Seiler-Baldinger (1987), Singh (1979), Singh & Mathey (1985), Smith (1925, 1931), Spuhler (1978), Start (1948), Stoltz Gilfoy (1987), Taszycka (1972), Tenri Sankokan Museum (1981), Torella Nuibò (1949), Tsunoyama (1966, 1980), Turnbull (1982), Van Stan (1967), Vial (1980), Victoria and Albert Museum (1928), Völger & Weck (1987), Volbach (1932), Wace (1944), Wencker (1968), Yorke & Allen (1980), Zerries (1968), Zimmern (1949)

Working Instructions:

Ankermann (1922), Anonym (1964), Atwater (1976), Baizerman & Searle (1980), Barendse & Lobera (1987), Barker (1973), Bjerregaard (1979), Bolland (1977), Buff (1985), Burgess (1981), Cahlander & Baizerman (1985), Cahlander & Cason (1976), Caulfeild & Saward (1882), Clifford (1947), Collingwood (1982), Crawford Post (1961), Debétaz-Grünig (1977), Gallinger-Tod & Benson (1975), Gallinger-Tod & Couch del Deo (1976), Gil del Pozo (1974), Hansen (1990), Hentschel (1937), Hörlèn (1948, 1950), Holzklau (1977), Johnson (1942, 1949), Joliet van der Berg (1975), Lammèr (1975), Machschefes (1983), Markus (1974), Morton (1981), Pestalozzianum (1990), Redwood (1974), Reichard (1974), Riedinger & Riedinger (1980), Simpson & Weir (1932), Snow & Snow (1973), Specht & Rawlings (1973), Thorpe (1952), Tovey (1965), Zechlin (1966), Zolles (1942), Zumbühl (1981)

Films:

Berbenni (1984), Egloff (1976), Kauffmann (1963, 1967), Koch (1973), Kussmaul & Moos, von (1981), Lorenz (1980), Manndorff & Scholz (1967, 1968), Nachtigall (1963, 1969), Rauter (1969), Scholz (1967, 1968, 1974, 1974, 1977), Svobodová (1975, 1975), Weisswange (1975)

General, Historical:

Aga-Dglu (1941), Ahmed (1967), Altman (o.J.), Bartholomew (1985), Bernès (1974), Bernès & Jacob (1974), Black (1985), Black & Loveless (1977), Bohnsack (1981), Bombay Government (o.J.), Boyd (1974), Braun, Pater (1907), Bushell (1924), Chattopadhyaya (1976), Chesley (1949), Cook de Leonard et al. (1966), Denny (1972), Fischer (1979), Flint (1974), Forcart-Respinger (1942), Forman & Wasseff (1968), Franquemont (1986), Gayet (1900), Gazda et al. (1980), Gehret & Keyser (1976), Geijer & Lamm (1944), Glazier (1923), Goody (1982), Graw, de & Kuhn (1981), Grothe (1883), Gruber (1984), Guicherd (1952), Hahn (1924), Hahn (1971), Huang & Wenzhao (1982), Irwin (1973), Kadow (1973), Kelsey & Osborne, de Jongh (1939), Kreischer (1907), Kuhn (1977), Lévi-Strauss (1987), Lewis (1953), Little (1931), Lombard (1978), Mc Kelvy Bird & Mendizábal Losak (1986), Meisch (1986), Mikosch (1985), Müller & Brendler (1958), Müller-Christensen (1973), Olson (1929), Opt'land (1969), Otavsky (1987), Patterson (1957), Paul (1986), Pfister (1946, 1948, 1950), Rau (1970), Rickenbach (1944), Rossbach (1980), Rowe (1985), Schaefer (1937), Schermann & Schermann (1922), Schlabow (1961), Schneider (1987), Seiler-Baldinger (1986), Shenai (1974), Singh (1981), Stirling (1938), Taber & Anderson (1975), Timmermann (1986), Underhill (o.J.), Usher (1959), Volbach (1932), Von Schorn (1885), Wehmeyer (1949), Weitlaner-Johnson (1976), Wirz (1955), Wroth (1977), Zorn (1986)

Pile or Tuft Fabrics

Classification:

Bühler & Bühler-Oppenheim (1948), Burnham (1980), Cahlander (1980), Collingwood (1968), Emery (1966), Leroi-Gourhan (1943), Ribeiro (1957, 1986), Rowe (1984), Schnegelsberg (1971), Schoepf (1971), Seiler-Baldinger (1974, 1979, 1991), Tanavoli (1985)

Analysis:

Albers (1965), Amano & Tsunoyama (1979), Anton (1984), Bender-Jorgensen (1986), Bergman (1975), Bianchi et al. (1982), Biebuyck (1984), Birrel (1959), Brommer et al. (1988), Buck (1944, 1957), Burnham (1980, 1986), Burnham (1959), Cahlander (1980), Califano (1982), Chertudi & Nardi (1961), Collingwood (1987, 1988), Cootner (1981), Corey (1987), Crawford (1915-16), Crowfoot (1985), Crowfoot (1948/49), Detering (1962), Disselhoff (1981), Due (1980), D'Harcourt (1934, 1960, 1962), Eiland (1979), Emmons & Boas (1907), Engel (1963), Farke (1986), Fawcett (1979), Feick (1917), Feltham (1989), Gallinger-Tod & Couch del Deo (1976), Geijer (1979), Gräbner (1922), Grünberg (1967), Gupta (1966), Hodges (1965), Hongsermeier (1987), Hunter (1953), Innes (1959), Izikowitz (1933), Justin (1980), Kalter (1983), Kent Peck (1971), King (1965), Klein (1961), Koch-Grünberg (1923), La Baume (1955), Lamb (1984), Laurencich-Minelli & Bagli (1984), Lipton (1989), Lothrop & Mahler (1957), Mead (1908), Mead (1968), Mellaart & Hirsch (1989), Meurant & Tunis (1989), Millán de Palavecino (1960), Mirambell & Martínez (1986), Museo

Chileno (1989), Nabholz-Kartaschoff & Näf (1980), Nicola & Dorta (1986), Nordenskiöld (1924), Nylén (1969), O'Neale (1945), Pendergast (1987), Petersen (1980), Pownall (1976), Rapp & Stucky (1990), Rendall & Tuohy (1974), Reswick (1985), Riddell (1978), Rodee (1987), Rowe (1984), Schaedler (1987), Schoepf (1985), Segal et al. (1973), Seiler-Baldinger (1974, 1987), Sillitoe (1988), Stritz (1971), Sylwan (1934), Tanavoli (1985, 1985), Tattersall (1927), Taullard (1949), Textilmuseum Krefeld (1978), Tsunoyama (1980), Tunis & Meurant (1989), Turnbaugh & Turnbaugh (1986), Vial (1986), Vogt (1937), Wattal (1965), Wulff (1966), Zechlin (1966), Zerries (1980)

Ethnography:

Albers (1965), Andrews (o.J.), Anonym (o.J.), Arthur (1926), Azadi (1970), Ball (1924), Baranowicz, de & Bernheimer (1957), Berthoud (1964), Bhushan (1985), Bianchi et al. (1982), Biebuyck (1984), Billeter (o.J.), Bolinder (1925), Brigham (1899), Buck (1944, 1957), Califano (1982), Cannizzo (1969), Chattopadhyaya (1963, 1965, 1969), Chertudi & Nardi (1961), Collingwood (1987, 1988), Corey (1987), Costa Fénelon & Monteiro (1968), Denwood (1974), Detering (1962), Dhamija (1965, 1970), Due (1980), Fawcett (1979), Feick (1917), Feltham (1989), Ferraro-Dorta (1981, 1986), Fontaine (1982), Forelli & Harries (1977), Fowler & Matley (1979), Gewerbemuseum Basel (1974), Gil del Pozo (1974), Gluck & Gluck (1974), Gräbner (1909), Grünberg (1967), Guhr & Neumann (1982), Gupta (1966), Hartmann (1971), Heizer (1987), Henking (1955), Holt (1985), Hongsermeier (1987), Housego (1978), Hussak von Velthem (1975), Izikowitz (1932), Justin (1980), Kaeppler (1978), Kaeppler et al. (1978), Kalter (1983), Kaufmann (1989), Kensinger (1975), Kent Peck (1971), Klein (1961), Koch (1969), Koch-Grünberg (1923), Lamb (1984), Lamb & Lamb (1981), Landreau (1978), Lindahl & Knorr (1975), Linden-Museum (1989), Lipton (1978, 1989), Mackie & Thomson (1980), Mead (1908), Mead (1945), Mead (1968), Mege Rosso (1990), Mellaart & Hirsch (1989), Métraux (1928), Meurant & Tunis (1989), Michell (1986), Milhofer (1979), Moschner (1955), Moshkova (1970), Myers (1984), Nabholz-Kartaschoff (1972), Nambiar (1965), Navajo School of Indian Basketry (1949), Nicola & Dorta (1986), Nordenskiöld (1924), Opie (1986), O'Neale (1945), Pendergast (1987), Petersen (1980), Ploier (1988), Pownall (1976), Price (1979), Quadiri (o.J.), Rendall & Tuohy (1974), Reswick (1981, 1985), Ribeiro (1957, 1988, 1989), Ribeiro (1957), Riboud (1989), Riddell (1978), Rodee (1987), Rogers & Smith (1981), Ronge (1982), Rose (1978), Rossbach (1973), Schaedler (1987), Schindler (1990), Schoepf (1971, 1985), Schulze-Thulin (1989), Seiler-Baldinger (1974, 1987), Sekhar (1964), Sharma (1964), Sieber (1972), Signi (1988), Sillitoe (1988), Spring (1989), Streiff (1967), Stritz (1971), Susnik (1986), Tanavoli (1974, 1978, 1985, 1985), Taullard (1949), Tunis & Meurant (1989), Turnbaugh & Turnbaugh (1986), Valentin (1970), Verswijver (1983, 1987), Vial (1986), Wacziarg & Nath (1987), Watt (1903), Wattal (1965), Wegner (1964), Wegner (1974), Whiting (1925), Wulff (1966), Yde (1965), Zerries (1980)

Folk Art:

Akkent & Franger (1987), Albers (1965), Anjou (1934), Anonym (1985), Bouza & Calzada (1977), Burnham (1986), Collin (1924), Geijer (1972), Henschen (1951), Juhasz (1990), Kissling (1982), Linden-Museum (1989), Mantscharowa (1960), Marková (1964), Mayer (1969), Meyer-Heisig (1956), Nylén (1969), O_tric (1981), Pelanzy & Català (1978), Petrasch (1970), Pocius (1979), Pylkkanen (1974), Rossbach (1973), Shivo (1978), Sylwan (1934), Tkalcic (1929)

Archaeology:

Albers (1965), Amano & Tsunoyama (1979), Anton (1984), Bender-Jorgensen (1986), Bender-Jorgensen & Tidow (1981), Bergman (1975), Billeter (o.J.), Bird et al. (1981), Brommer et al. (1988), Cherblanc (1937), Collin (1924), Cortes Moreno (1987), Crowfoot (1985), Crowfoot (1948/49), Denis (1875), Disselhoff (1981), D'Harcourt (1933, 1934, 1962, 1974), Engel (1963), Feldtkeller & Schlichtherle (1987), Feltham (1989), Frame (1990), Hellervik (1977), Izikowitz (1932, 1933), Jaekel-Greifswald (1911-12), King (1965, 1968, 1969), Lapiner (1976), Laurencich-Minelli & Bagli (1984), Laurencich-Minelli & Ciruzzi (1981), Lavalle, de & Lang (1980), Lindberg (1964), Lindström (1981), Lothrop & Mahler (1957), Massey & Osborne (1961), Mellaart & Hirsch (1989), Millán de Palavecino (1960), Mirambell & Martínez (1986), Museo Chileno (1989), Rast (1990, 1991), Riboud (1989), Rolandi (1971), Rosenberg & Haidler (1980), Rowe (1986), Schulze-Thulin (1989), Segal et al. (1973), Smart & Gluckman (1989), Spuhler (1978), Taullard (1949), Turnbaugh & Turnbaugh (1986), Ulloa (1985), Van Stan (1959), Vogt (1937), Zerries (1968), Zimmern (1949)

Collections:

Amano & Tsunoyama (1979), Andrews (o.J.), Billeter (o.J.), Bolour (1981), Brommer et al. (1988), Brüggemann & Böhmen (1980), Cootner (1981), Corey (1987), D'Hennezel (1924), Ellis (1975), Enderlein (1986), Ettinghausen & Dimand (1974), Fowler & Matley (1979), Frame (1990), Grünberg (1967), Guhr & Neumann (1982), Hubel (1967), Innes (1959), Landreau (1978), Laurencich-Minelli & Bagli (1984), Laurencich-Minelli & Ciruzzi (1981), Lavalle, de & Lang (1980), Lindahl & Knorr (1975), Linden-Museum (1989), Lipton (1989), Mackie (1969), Mackie & Rowe (1976), Mayer (1969), Mc Mullan & Sylvester (1972), Mege Rosso (1990), Mostafa (1953), Museo Chileno (1989), Oytric (1981), Ploier (1988), Provence (1946), Rabineau (1975, 1980), Reed (1966), Schoepf (1985), Schürmann (o.J.), Schulze-Thulin (1989), Seiler-Baldinger (1987), Signi (1988), Singh (1979), Spuhler (1978), Straka & Mackie (1978), Streiff (1967), Tanavoli (1974, 1978, 1985), Tattersall (1927), Tsunoyama (1980), Verswijver (1983), Watt (1903), Zerries (1968, 1980), Zimmern (1949)

Working Instructions:

Cahlander (1980), Gallinger-Tod & Couch del Deo (1976), Gil del Pozo (1974), Hartung (1963), Lammèr (1975), Mead (1968), Navajo School of Indian Basketry (1949), Pownall (1976), Zechlin (1966)

Films:

Kissling (1982), Koch (1969), Nabholz-Kartaschoff (1972)

General, Historical:

Aga-Dglu (1941), Anawalt (1981), Biggs (1983), Black (1985), Black & Loveless (1979), Bosc du (1948), Bushell (1924), Chattopadhyaya (1965, 1969), Denny (1973), Eiland (1979), Ellis (1969), Ettinghausen & Dimand (1974), Gans-Ruedin (1971), Grote-Hasenbalg (1922), Hubel (1972), Lettenmair (1962), Lipton (1978), Lombard (1978), Mc Mullan & Sylvester (1972), Milhofer (1979), Mostafa (1953), Müller & Brendler (1958), Myers (1984), Neugebauer & Orendi (1923), Revault (1973), Ricard (1926), Rose (1978), Rowe (1986), Schlosser (1960), Schürmann (o.J.), Straka & Mackie (1978), Victoria and Albert Museum (1931), Wegner (1980)

Beadwork

Classification:
Burnham (1980), Lemaire (1960), Orchard (1929), Rowe (1984), Seiler-Baldinger (1979, 1991)

Analysis:
Anquetil (1977), Bianchi et al. (1982), Biebuyck (1984), Birrel (1959), Burnham (1980, 1981), Collingwood (1987, 1988), Dubin (1987), Heissig & Müller (1989), Koch-Grünberg (1923), Lyford (1940), Newman (1977), Riesenberg & Gayton (1952), Roth (1918, 1929), Rowe (1984), Schuster (1976), Sillitoe (1988), Turnbaugh & Turnbaugh (1986)

Ethnography:
Alvarez de Williams (1983), Beier (1981), Berin (1978), Bianchi et al. (1982), Biebuyck (1984), Burnham (1977), Cannizzo (1969), Cardale de Schrimpff (1972), Collingwood (1987, 1988), Deimel (1982), Drewal & Pemberton (1989), Dubin (1987), Ellis (1980), Forno (1966), Guhr & Neumann (1982), Haug (1988), Heermann (1989), Heissig & Müller (1989), Heizer (1987), Henking (1957), Houwald, von (1990), Klingmüller & Münch (1989), Koch-Grünberg (1923), Lambrecht & Lambrecht (1977), Lemaire (1953), Linden-Museum (1989), Loeb (1983), Loebèr (1913), Lyford (1940), Mathews (1983), Maxwell (1980), Maxwell (1990), Morrison (1982), Munan (1989), Munan-Oettli (1987), Nanavati & Vora (1966), Newman (1977), Ohnemus (1989), Orchard (1929), Pemberton (1980), Picton & Mack (1979), Pokornowsky (1979), Ribeiro (1988), Richman (1980), Riesenberg & Gayton (1952), Rossbach (1973), Roth (1918, 1929), Salzer (1961), Schulze-Thulin (1989), Schuster (1976), Scoville (1922), Sedlak (1987), Sibeth (1990), Sieber (1972), Signi (1988), Sillitoe (1988), Simon (1989), Smith (1983), Susnik (1986), Torres (1980), Trigger (1978), Turnbaugh & Turnbaugh (1986), Verswijver (1983), Washburn & Crowe (1988), Wassing-Visser (1982), Wells (1982), Westfall (1981), Wildschut & Ewers (1985), Wissler (1919)

Folk Art:
Anquetil (1977), Burnham (1977, 1981), Dubin (1987), Haberlandt (1912), Klingmüller & Münch (1989), Linden-Museum (1989), Rossbach (1973)

Archaeology:
Dubin (1987), Lavalle, de & Lang (1980), Loud & Harrington (1929), Schulze-Thulin (1989), Seipel (1989), Turnbaugh & Turnbaugh (1986), Washburn & Crowe (1988)

Collections:
Gogol (1985), Guhr & Neumann (1982), Heermann (1989), Lavalle, de & Lang (1980), Lemaire (1953), Linden-Museum (1989), Pemberton (1980), Schulze-Thulin (1989), Signi (1988), Verswijver (1983)

Working Insrtuctions:
Anquetil (1979), Heinze (1969), Lammèr (1975), Scholz-Peter (1975)

Films:
Ohnemus (1989), Simon (1989)

General, Historical:
Edwards (1966), Pazaurek (1911)

Borders

Classification:
Balfet (1952), Bühler & Bühler-Oppenheim (1948), Burnham (1980), Collingwood (1968), Leroi-Gourhan (1943), Müller (1967), Oppenheim (1942), Ribeiro (1985, 1986), Seiler-Baldinger (1971, 1979, 1991), Tanavoli (1985)

Analysis:
Bender-Jorgensen (1986), Bergman (1975), Bianchi et al. (1982), Bird & Bellinger (1954), Bird & Skinner-Dimitrijevic (1974), Bolland (1989), Boser-Sarivaxévanis (1972), Braulik (1900), Brigham (1974), Brommer et al. (1988), Buck (1944, 1957), Burnham (1980), Collingwood (1987, 1988), Detering (1962), Dombrowski (1976), D'Harcourt (1934, 1960), Emmons & Boas (1907), Gass & Lozado (1985), Geijer (1979), Gittinger (1989), Green Gigli et al. (1974), Grünberg (1967), Haeberlin & Teit (1928), Hald (1950, 1980), Harvey (1986), Hodges (1965), Hundt (1980), Hyslop & Bird (1985), Kelly (1932), Kent Peck (1957, 1983), Keppel (1984), King (1965), Konieczny (1979), Kroeber & Wallace (1954), La Baume (1955), Leigh-Theisen (1988), Leontidi (1986), Lismer (1941), Mason (1908), Mc Neish et al. (1967), Mead (1908), Mead (1968), Müller (1967), Museo Chileno (1989), Nabholz-Kartaschoff & Näf (1980), Oppenheim (1942), O'Neale & Kroeber (1937), Pendergast (1987), Petersen (1963), Pilar de (1968), Prümers (1989, 1990), Ramos & Blasco (1977), Ranjan & Yier (1986), Rendall & Tuohy (1974), Ribeiro (1980, 1985), Roth (1918), Rowe (1984), Schlabow (1976), Schuster (1989), Sillitoe (1988), Snow & Snow (1973), Sylwan (1941), Tanavoli (1985), Tanner (1968), Tattersall (1927), Turnbaugh & Turnbaugh (1986), Underhill (1945, 1948), Van Stan (1967), Walton (1989), West (1980), Wiedemann (1975), Willey & Corbett (1954), Zechlin (1966)

Ethnography:
Baizerman & Searle (1978), Bianchi et al. (1982), Bolland (1989), Boser-Sarivaxévanis (1972, 1972), Buck (1944, 1957), Cardale de Schrimpff (1972), Collingwood (1987, 1988), Detering (1962), Dombrowski (1976), Gass & Lozado (1985), Gittinger (1989), Green Gigli et al. (1974), Grünberg (1967), Haeberlin & Teit (1928), Kelly (1932), Keppel (1984), Konieczny (1979), Krucker (1941), Leigh-Theisen (1988), Lismer (1941), Mason (1908), Mead (1908), Mead (1968), Müller (1967), Nettinga Arnheim (1977), Paul (1944), Pendergast (1987), Petersen (1963), Pilar de (1968), Ranjan & Yier (1986), Rendall & Tuohy (1974), Ribeiro (1980, 1980, 1985, 1988), Roth (1918), Sanoja-Obediente (1960), Sayer (1985), Schuster (1989), Seiler-Baldinger (1971), Sillitoe (1988), Susnik (1986), Tanavoli (1985), Tanner (1968), Turnbaugh & Turnbaugh (1986), Underhill (1945, 1948), Wardle (1912), West (1980), Wiedemann (1975)

Folk Art:
Leontidi (1986), Lühning (1971), Pilar de (1968), Start (1939)

Archaeology:
Alfaro Giner (1984), Bender-Jorgensen (1986), Bender-Jorgensen & Tidow (1981), Bergman (1975), Bird & Bellinger (1954), Bird & Skinner-Dimitrijevic (1974), Braulik (1900), Brommer et al. (1988), Clements-Scholtz (1975), D'Harcourt (1934), Hägg (1984), Hald (1950, 1980), Hellervik (1977), Henneberg, von (1932), Hoffmann & Burnham (1973), Hoffmann & Traetteberg

(1959), Hundt (1980), Hyslop & Bird (1985), Kent Peck (1957, 1983), King (1957, 1965), Kjellberg (1982), Kroeber & Wallace (1954), Loud & Harrington (1929), Mc Neish et al. (1967), Museo Chileno (1989), Prümers (1983, 1989, 1990), Ramos & Blasco (1977), Rast (1991), Rowe (1984), Schlabow (1976), Seiler-Baldinger (1971), Sylwan (1941), Turnbaugh & Turnbaugh (1986), Van Stan (1958, 1967), Wallace (1979), Walton (1989), Weitlaner-Johnson (1967), Willey & Corbett (1954)

Collections:

Boralevi & Faccioli (1986), Brommer et al. (1988), Castello Yturbide & Martinez del Rio, de (1979), Grünberg (1967), Museo Chileno (1989), Schlabow (1976), Start (1939), Tattersall (1927), Van Stan (1967)

Working Insrtuctions:

Anquetil (1979), Baizerman & Searle (1978), Dillmont, de (o.J., 1902), Finckh-Haelsing (o.J.), Gallinger-Tod & Benson (1975), Kunz (1980), Mead (1968), Snow & Snow (1973), Zechlin (1966)

Film:

Lühning (1971)

General, Historical:

Boralevi & Faccioli (1986)

Ornamentation with Solid Materials

Classification:

Boser-Sarivaxévanis & Müller (1968), Bühler & Bühler-Oppenheim (1948), Burnham (1980), Coleman & Sonday (1974), Emery (1966), Oppenheim (1942), Orchard (1929), Seiler-Baldinger (1979, 1991)

Analysis:

Abbass (1986), Adi-Rubin (1983), All India Handicrafts Board (o.J.), Amano & Tsunoyama (1979), Anonym (1957), Anton (1984), Asch (1981), Basilov & Naumova (1989), Bel & Ricard (1913), Biebuyck (1984), Bird & Bellinger (1954), Birrel (1959), Black & Loveless (1981), Boser-Sarivaxévanis (1972), Boser-Sarivaxévanis & Müller (1968), Brommer et al. (1988), Bühler et al. (1972), Burnham (1980, 1986), Campbell & Pongnoi (1978), Caulfeild & Saward (1882), Chung (1979), Collingwood (1987, 1988), Colyer Ross (1989), Cornet (1982), Cousin (1972), Crawford (1915-16), Crowfoot (1985), Day & Buckle (1907), Disselhoff (1981), Dombrowski (1976), Dudovikova (1986), D'Harcourt (1934, 1960), Eisleb (1975), Feltham (1989), Fisher & Bowen (1979), Flemming (1923), Fraser-Lu (1988), Geijer (1982), Gervers (1977), Gittinger (1971, 1989), Goodman (1976), Gordon (1980), Gostelow (1977), Hald (1950), Hecht (1989), Heissig & Müller (1989), Hemert, van (1967), Iklé (1930), Jaques & Wencker (1967), Kalter (1983), Kent Peck (1983), King (1965), Kümpers (1961), Landreau & Pickering (1969), Lang-Meyer & Nabholz-Kartaschoff (1987), Lewis & Lewis (1984), Lorenzo (1933), Lyford (1940), Mannová (1972), Markrich (1976), Mattern-Pabel (1981), Mead (1968), Mersich (1982), Museo Chileno (1989), M'hari (1975), Nabholz-Kartaschoff (1979), Newman (1974), Noppe & Castillon, du (1988), Nylén (1969), Oppenheim (1942), O'Neale (1942, 1945), O'Neale & Kroeber (1937), Paine (1989), Pandit (1976), Prümers (1989, 1990), Puls (1988), Ramos & Blasco (1977), Rol (1980), Rowe (1984), Sayer (1988), Schaedler (1987), Segal et al. (1973), Sharma (1968), Taullard (1949), Tsunoyama (1980), Tunis & Meurant (1989), Turner (1955), Van Stan (1967), Wanner (1983), Weitlaner-Johnson (1976), Yoshimoto (1988), Zechlin (1966)

Ethnography:

Abbasi (o.J.), Abbass (1986), Adams (1984), Adams (1974, 1978, 1980, 1989), Adler (1980), Agthe (1975), All India Handicrafts Board(o.J.), Anand (1974), Anderson (1978), Andrews (1976), Anonym (1990), Aryan (1984), Asch (1981), Ashton & Wace (1929), Baker & Lunt, M. (1977), Basilov & Naumova (1989), Bayley Willis (1987), Beer (1970), Bel & Ricard (1913), Berin (1978), Best (1977), Bhagwat & Jayakar (1972), Bhattacharyya (1968), Bhavani (1968), Bhushan (1985), Biebuyck (1984), Billeter (o.J.), Biro & Fondation Dapper (1988), Bliss (1982), Borgatti (1983), Boser-Sarivaxévanis (1972), Boyer (1983), Brandenbourg (1987), Bubolz-Eicher & Erekosima (1982), Bühler (1951), Burman (1970), Cadoux (1990), Campbell & Pongnoi (1978), Chattopadhyaya (1963, 1964, 1976, 1977), Chongkol (1982), Chung (1979), Cohen (1990), Cohen (1977), Cole & Ross (1977), Collingwood (1987, 1988), Cornet (1982), Cousin (1972, 1986), Dalrymple (1984), Deimel (1982), Dendel (1974), Deuss (1981), Devi (1982), Dhamija (1964, 1966, 1970, 1970), Dhamija & Jain (1989), Dixit (1965), Djajasoebrata & Adams (1965), Dombrowski (1976), Dongerkery (1951), Douglas (1941), Douglas & D'Harcourt (1941), Drewal & Pemberton (1989), Drucker et al. (1969), Durban Art Gallery (1977), Elmberg (1968), Elson (1979), Erekosima & Bubolz-Eicher (1981), Etienne-Nugue (1982, 1982, 1984), Ewers (1945), Feltham (1989), Fischer (1989), Fischer & Shah (1970), Fischer et al. (1979), Fisher & Bowen (1979), Forsythe (1982, 1987), Fowler & Matley (1979), Fraser-Lu (1982, 1988), Frater (1975), Geary (1987), Geirnaert (1989), Gervers (1977), Gewerbemuseum Basel (1974), Gill (1977), Gittinger (1971, 1989), Gluck & Gluck (1974), Goodman (1976), Guelton (1989), Guhr & Neumann (1982), Gwinner, von (1987), Haas et. al. (1987), Haberland (1979), Hartmann (1980), Hartmann (1985, 1986), Heathcote (1973, 1974, 1975, 1976, 1979), Hecht (1989), Heissig & Müller (1989), Herzog (1985), Hitkari (1980, 1985, 1989), Holm & Reid (1975), Icke-Schwalbe (1989), Irwin & Jayakar (1956), Jaitly (1985), Janata & Jawad (1983), Joseph (1978), Kalter (1983), Kasten (1990), Khan Majlis (1984), Kiewe (1952), Klingmüller & Münch (1989), Korea-Britain Centennial Committee (o.J.), Kroeber (1905), Kron-Steinhardt (1989), Kümpers (1961), Lamb (1980), Lamb & Lamb (1981), Landreau (1978), Landreau & Pickering (1969), Lang-Meyer & Nabholz-Kartaschoff (1987), Lantz (1938), Leigh & Kerajinan (1989), Lewis & Lewis (1984), Lindahl & Knorr (1975), Lumholtz (1904), Lyford (1940, 1943), Ma & Zhan (1981), Mack (1989), Majmudar (1968), Mapelli Mozzi & Castello Yturbide (1987), Matsumoto (1984), Maxwell (1980), Maxwell (1990), Mayer Stinchecum (1984), Mead (1968), Metha (1970), Meurant (1986), Michell (1986), Miller (1988), Mirza (o.J.), Moes & Tay Pike (1985), Mohanty (1980), Mollet (1976), Mom Dusdi (1975), Mueller (1973), Nabholz-Kartaschoff (1979, 1987), Nachtigall (1966), Nana (1975), Nanavati & Vora (1966), Newman (1974), Noppe & Castillon, du (1988), Nordquist & Aradeon (1975), Omar (1987), Orchard (1929), Ortiz (1979), Ovalle Fernandez (1982), O'Neale (1945), Paine (1989), Pandit (1976), Parker & Neal (1977, 1977), Perani (1979), Pfister (1936), Picton & Mack (1979), Puls (1988), Rajab (1984, 1987), Riboud (1989), Rose (1985), Roy (1982), Roze (1989), Salvador (1976), Saraf (1987), Sayer (1985, 1988), Schaedler (1987), Schevill (1986), Schneider (1987), Schulze-

Thulin (1989), Scott (1981), Sedlak (1987), Segawa (1985), Sekhar (1964), Sharma (1968), Sheares (1987), Sibeth (1990), Siderenko (1981), Sieber (1972), Solyom & Solyom (1984), Spring (1989), Stanislaw (1987), Susnik (1986), Taullard (1949), Torres (1980), Tunis & Meurant (1989), Turnbull (1982), Turner (1955), University of Singapore Art Museum (1964), Victoria and Albert Museum (1931), Völger & Weck (1987), Vollmer (1981), Vollmer & Gilfoy (1981), Wacziarg & Nath (1987), Wallace (1978), Wang (1986), Washburn & Crowe (1988), Wass & Murnane (1978), Wassén (1964), Wassén (1962), Wastraprema (1976), Watt (1903), Wegner (1983), Wegner (1974), Weiner & Schneider (1989), Weir (1970, 1989), Weitlaner-Johnson (1976), Westfall (1981), Westfall & Desai (1987, 1987), Westphal-Hellbusch (1965), White (1982), Wilbush (1976), Yoshimoto (1988), Zebrowski (1989)

Folk Art:

Anonym (1957, 1985), Apostolaki (1956), Azizbekova (1971, 1972), Balke (1976), Brunner-Littmann & Hahn (1988), Burnham (1986), Colby (1958), Cooper & Buferd (1978), Dahlin (o.J.), Dillmont, de (o.J.), Dudovikova (1986), Dunare (1985), Eaton (1937), Emery (1949), Fél (1976), Ferenc & Palotay (1940), Flemming (1923), Geijer (1982), Gervers (1977), Gockerell (1980), Gordon (1980), Grabowicz (1977, 1980), Grabowicz & Wolinetz (1981), Gudjonsson (1977), Gusic (1955), Gwinner, von (1987), Haberlandt (1912), Hänsel (1983), Hamilton & Hamilton (1976), Harvey (1983), Hemert, van (1967), Herzog (1985), Johnstone (1961), Juhasz (1990), Kiewe (1954), King (1977), Klingmüller & Münch (1989), Lorenzo (1933), Lundbäck & Ingers (1952), Magalhaes Calvet de (o.J.), Mannová (1972), Matterna (1982), Mattern-Pabel (1981), Mayer (1969), Mersich (1982), Meyer- Heisig (1956), Mozes (1975), Nelson (1977), Nelson & Houck (1984), Nistoroaia (1975), Nixdorff (1977), Nordiska Museet (1984), Nylén (1969), Palotay & Szabó (1940), Patterson & Gellermann (1979), Pelanzy & Català (1978), Pocius (1979), Pottinger (1983), Powers (1987), Preysing (1987), Rapp (1976), Reichelt (1956), Robinson (1987), Safford & Bishops (1980), Scarin et al. (1989), Schneider (1975), Sebba (1979), Shivo (1978), Sonday (1982), Stanková (1985), Stapeley (1924), Start (1939), Trilling (1983), Trudel (1954), Václavík (1956), Václavik & Orel (o.J.), Wahlman (1986), Walker (1985), Wanner (1979), Weiner & Schneider (1989), Young (1974), Zoras (1966)

Archaeology:

Amano & Tsunoyama (1979), Anton (1984), Batigné & Bellinger (1965), Bennett (1954), Billeter (o.J.), Bird (1961), Bird & Bellinger (1954), Bird et al. (1981), Bollinger (1983), Broholm & Hald (1948), Brommer et al. (1988), Clabburn (1977), Crawford (1946), Crowfoot (1985), Crowfoot & Davies (1941), Disselhoff (1981), Dwyer (1979), D'Harcourt (1934, 1948, 1954), Eisleb (1975), Feltham (1989), Fung-Pineda (1978), Gervers (1977), Hald (1950), Hecht (1989), Hellervik (1977), Iklé (1930), Jaques (1968), Kent Peck (1983), King (1965), Lamm (1938), Lapiner (1976), Laurencich-Minelli & Ciruzzi (1981), Lautz (1982), Lavalle, de & Lang (1980), Mailey (1978), Means (1927), Merlange (1928), Museo Chileno (1989), Ortiz (1979), O'Neale (1934, 1942, 1943), O'Neale & Whitaker (1947), Paul (1979, 1980, 1986), Pfister (1934), Prümers (1989, 1990), Ramos & Blasco (1977), Riboud (1989), Rowe (1984), Sawyer (1960), Schulze-Thulin (1989), Segal et al. (1973), Stafford (1941), Taullard (1949), Van Stan (1961, 1967, 1967), Völger & Weck (1987), Wallace (1960), Wardle (1939), Washburn & Crowe (1988), Wassén (1972), Weiner & Schneider (1989), Weitlaner-Johnson (1976), Zebrowski (1989), Zerries (1968), Zimmern (1949)

Collections:

Adams (1984), Adams (1964), Agthe (1975), Amano & Tsunoyama (1979), Anderson (1978), Ashton & Wace (1929), Azizbekova (1971, 1972), Beer (1970), Bhattacharyya (1968), Billeter (o.J.), Bird (1965), Bishop & Coblentz (1975), Black & Loveless (1981), Borgatti (1983), Brommer et al. (1988), Bühler et al. (1972), Crawford (1946), Devi (1982), Djajasoebrata & Adams (1965), Durban Art Gallery (1977), Eisleb (1975), Elson (1979), Fowler & Matley (1979), Grabowicz (1977, 1980), Grabowicz & Wolinetz (1981), Gruber (1990), Guhr & Neumann (1982), Gusic (1955), Haas et. al. (1987), Hartmann (1980), Heathcote (1976), Hwa (1987), Icke-Schwalbe (1989), Irwin & Jayakar (1956), Jaques (1968), Jaques & Wencker (1967), Johnson (1985), Jones (1973), Kiewe (1952), Landreau (1978), Landreau & Pickering (1969), Laurencich-Minelli & Ciruzzi (1981), Lavalle, de & Lang (1980), Lindahl & Knorr (1975), Mapelli Mozzi & Castello Yturbide (1987), Mayer (1969), Mayer Stinchecum (1984), Means (1927), Merlange (1928), Moes & Tay Pike (1985), Moss (1984), Museo Chileno (1989), Museum für Völkerkunde Basel (1970), Nabholz-Kartaschoff (1986), Nixdorff (1977), Okada (1958), Peebles (1982), Pottinger (1983), Preysing (1987), Ramos & Blasco (1976), Rapp (1976), Schneider (1975), Schulz (1988), Schulze-Thulin (1989), Sheares (1987), Singh (1979), Singh & Mathey (1985), Start (1939), Tsunoyama (1980), Turnbull (1982), Van Stan (1967), Victoria and Albert Museum (1931), Völger & Weck (1987), Vollmer & Gilfoy (1981), Wanner (1983), Watt (1903), Yoshimoto (1988), Zerries (1968), Zimmern (1949)

Working Instructions:

Adi-Rubin (1983), Baker (1975, 1975), Cammann (1973), Caulfeild & Saward (1882), Colby (1958), Dawson (1985), Day & Buckle (1907), Dendel (1974), Dillmont, de (o.J., o.J., o.J., 1902), Fitzrandolph (1954), Georgens & Von Gayette Georgens (o.J.), Gostelow (1977), Grafton (1975), Gross (1981), Hänsel (1983), Hardouin (o.J.), Harvey (1983), James (1978, 1981), Jessen (1972), Kahmann (1985), Lammèr (1975), Lundbäck & Ingers (1952), Mallin (o.J.), Malon (o.J.), Markrich (1976), Mead (1968), Nel (1980), Nelson & Houck (1984), Niedner (1921, 1924), Pottinger (1983), Rol (1980), Schäpper (1984), Tiesler (1977), Timmins (1968), Walker (1985), Wark (1984), Weldon's Encyclopaedia (o.J.), Westfall & Desai (1987), Zechlin (1966)

General, Historical:

Adler (1980), Anthony (o.J.), Aryan (o.J.), Barista (1981), Basilov & Naumova (1989), Batigné & Bellinger (1965), Bernès (1974), Boyd (1974), Bunting (1980), Burrows (1921), Bushell (1924), Chattopadhyaya (1964, 1976), Clabburn (1984), Coomaraswamy (1964), Douglas & D'Harcourt (1941), Edwards (1966), Gombos (1980), Hwa (1987), Kiewe (1954), Lancet-Müller (1967), Little (1931), Müller & Brendler (1958), Okada (1958), Paul (1986), Powers (1987), Schneider (1987), Seiler-Baldinger (1986), Sigerus (1922), Simeon (1979), Sonday (1982), Steinmann (1939), Targonska (1985), Von Schorn (1885), Webster (1948), White (1982), Wroth (1977), Zaman (1981)

Ornamentation with Liquid Materials

Classification:

Bühler (1943, 1953, 1972), Bühler & Bühler-Oppenheim (1948), Burnham (1980), Seiler-Baldinger (1979, 1991), Wada (1983)

Analysis:

Ackermann-Ando (1978), Albers (1965), All India Handicrafts Board (o.J.), Amano & Tsunoyama (1979), Anton (1984), Barnes (1989), Basilov & Naumova (1989), Birrel (1959), Boser-Sarivaxévanis (1969, 1972, 1972, 1975, 1980), Bühler (1939, 1941, 1943, 1953, 1963, 1969), Bühler & Fischer (1979), Bühler & Ramseyer-Gygi (1975), Bühler et al. (1972), Burnham (1980), Campbell & Pongnoi (1978), Cheesman (1988), Chertudi & Nardi (1961), Claerhout (1975), Claerhout & Bolland (1975), Claerhout (1964), Cordry & Cordry (1973), Crawford (1915-16), Crill (1989), De Bone (1976), Desai (1988), Djambatan (1985), Donner & Schnebel (1913), D'Harcourt (1962), Elliot-Mc Cabe (1984), Etienne-Nugue (1985), Feltham (1989), Fisher & Bowen (1979), Flanagan (1957), Fraser-Lu (1988), Gervers (1977), Gittinger (1971, 1989), Golden de Bone (1976), Haake (1984), Hecht (1989), Heuermann (1972), Iklé (1941), Iklé (1928), Ito (1981), Jager-Gerlings (1952), Jasper & Pirngadie (1912-16), Kalter (1983), Kent Peck (1957, 1971, 1983), King (1965), Klein (1961), Kümpers (1961), Laczko (1979), Lamster (1930), Larsen et al. (1976), Lewis & Lewis (1984), Loebèr (1908), Maile (1963), Mohanty & Krishna (1974), Mohanty & Mohanty (1983), Moser (1974), Murphy & Crill (1989), Museo Chileno (1989), Nabholz-Kartaschoff (1979), Nevermann (1938), Newman (1974, 1977), Polakoff (1980), Ponting & Chapman (1980), Prümers (1990), Ritch & Wada (1975), Rogers (1986), Rouffaer (1902), Sayer (1988), Schaedler (1987), Schevill (1986), Segal et al. (1973), Selvanayagam (1990), Sheares (1975), Spée (1977), Stanfiled & Barbour (1971), Stanková (1989), Steinmann (1947, 1953), Taullard (1949), Theisen (1982), Tomita (1982), Tsunoyama (1980), Van Gelder (1980), Van Stan (1967), Veltman & Fischer (1912), Wada (1983), Wilson (1979), Zechlin (1966)

Ethnography:

Abdurachman (1982), Adam (1935), Adams (1969, 1971, 1974, 1977, 1989), Agthe (1975), Albers (1965), All India Handicrafts Board(o.J.), Anderson (1978), Anonym (1956, 1970, 1975, 1978, 1978, 1980), Archambault (1988), Arseven (1953), Bachinger (1979), Baker (1921), Barbour (1970), Barbour & Simmonds (1971), Barkley (1980), Barnes (1989, 1989), Barton et al. (1980), Basilov & Naumova (1989), Becker-Donner (1968), Bergman (1954), Berg, van den (1984), Bezemer (1920), Bhavani (1968), Bhushan (1985), Billeter (o.J.), Blackwood (1950), Blakemore (1979, 1982), Bohackova (1975), Boser-Sarivaxévanis (1969, 1972, 1972, 1975, 1980), Boyd (1964), Brandon (1986), Breguet & Martin (1983), Bruignac, de et al. (1982), Bühler (1939, 1943, 1946, 1951, 1959, 1963, 1977), Bühler & Boser-Sarivaxévanis (1969), Bühler & Fischer (1974, 1979), Bühler & Ramseyer-Gygi (1975), Burman (1970), Buser-Abt (1977), Campbell (1836), Campbell & Pongnoi (1978), Cannizzo (1983), Cardale de Schrimpff (1972), Chandra (1938), Chattopadhyaya (1963), Cheesman (1988), Chertudi & Nardi (1961), Chevallier (1962), Chishti & Sanyal (1989), Chongkol (1982), Claerhout (1975), Claerhout & Bolland (1975), Cohen (1990), Cordry & Cordry (1973), Cousin (1975, 1976), Couvreur & Goslings (o.J.), Crill (1989), Crystal (1979), Daniel (1938), Delahaye (1983), Dendel (1974), Desai (1988), Deuss (1981), Devi (1982), Dhamija (1970, 1985), Dhamija & Jain (1989), Djajasoebrata & Adams (1965), Djambatan (1985), Djoemena (1986, 1990), Djumena (1990), Does, de (o.J.), Drewal & Pemberton (1989), Dürr (1978), Dunham (1980), Dupaigne (1968, 1974, 1983), Duponchel (1987), Dusenbury (1978, 1985), Elliot- Mc Cabe (1984), Ellis (1980), Enserinck (o.J.), Erikson (1984), Etienne-Nugue (1982, 1984, 1985), Feltham (1989), Fenton & Stuart-Fox (1976), Fischer (1972), Fischer & Jain (1982), Fischer & Pathy (1982), Fischer & Shah (1970, 1970), Fischer et al. (1979), Fisher & Bowen (1979), Fraser-Lu (1986, 1988), Fukuni (1973), Futagami & Plötz (1983), Gardi (1957, 1958), Geirnaert (1989), Geirnaert & Heringa (1989), Geirnaert-Martin (1981), Gewerbemuseum Basel (1974), Gittinger (1971, 1976, 1976, 1979, 1979, 1980, 1982, 1989, 1989), Gluck & Gluck (1974), Godon (1944), Golden de Bone (1976), Guelton (1989), Gulati (1951), Haake (1984), Haas (1966), Hacker (1982), Hadaway (1911), Haddon & Start (1982), Hall & Irwin (1971), Hambruch (1929), Hardjonagoro (1980), Harris (1986), Hartkamp-Jonxis (1989), Hartland-Rowe (1985), Haselberger (1965), Hauser-Schäublin & Nabholz-Kartaschoff (1991, 1991), Haussmann (1847), Hecht (1989), Heringa (1989), Hitchcock (1985), Hodge (1982), Holz (1980), Hurwitz (1962), Icke-Schwalbe (1989), Iklé (1931, 1941), Ito (1981), Jager-Gerlings (1952), Janata (1978), Jannes (1973), Jayakar (o.J., 1947), Jeanneret (1965), Jenny (1919), Jingshan (1982), Joseph (1978), Joseph (1986), Juel (1984), Jusuf et al. (1984), Kahlenberg (1977, 1980), Kalter (1983), Kartiwa (1963, 1982), Kent Peck (1971), Khan Majlis (1984, 1985), Kidder (1935), King (1988), Kitley (1981), Klein (1961), Klopfer (1988), Kooijman (1974), Kreischer (1907), Kron-Steinhardt (1989), Kümpers (1961), Labin (1979), Laczko (1979), Lamb (1980), Lamb & Lamb (1981), Lamster (1930), Landolt-Tüller (1976/77), Langewis (1960, 1963), Langewis & Wagner (1964), Leib & Romano (1984), Lestrange, de (1950), Levinsohn (1980), Lewis & Lewis (1984), Lindahl & Knorr (1975), Linden-Museum (1989), Loebèr (1902, 1903, 1914, 1926), Lorm, de (1938), Mack (1989), Majmudar (1968), Matsumoto (1984), Maxwell (1990), Maxwell (1980, 1984), Mc Kinnon (1989), Mege Rosso (1990), Metha (1970), Moes & Tay Pike (1985), Mohanty & Krishna (1974), Mohanty & Mohanty (1983), Mollet (1976), Moser (1974), Moss (1979), Mukharji (1888), Munan (1989), Muraoka & Okamura (1973), Murphy & Crill (1989), Mylius (1979), Nabholz-Kartaschoff (1970, 1979, 1980, 1982, 1989, 1989, 1989), Nabholz-Kartaschoff & Krehl-Eschler (1980), Nevermann (1938), Newman (1974, 1977), Nieuwenhuis (1913), Niggemeyer (1965), Nooteboom (1958), Nordquist & Aradeon (1975), Oei (1982, 1985), Okamura & Muraoka (1973), Ong (1970), Palmieri & Ferentinos (1979), Paravicini (1924), Peacock (1977), Pfister (1936, 1939), Picton & Mack (1979), Pleyte (1912), Polakoff (1980, 1982), Ponting & Chapman (1980), Prangwatthanakun & Cheesman (1987), Raadt-Apel (1981), Rajab (1987), Ramseyer (1980, 1984, 1987), Ramseyer & Ramseyer-Gygi (1979), Riboud (1989), Ricard (1925), Ritch & Wada (1975), Robinson (1969), Robyn (1989), Rodgers (1985), Rolandi & Pupareli, de (1985), Ronge (1982), Rose (1985), Rouffaer (1914), Rowe (1977), Saraf (1987), Saugy (1973), Sayer (1985, 1988), Schaedler (1987), Schermann (1910), Schevill (1986, 1986), Schindler (1990), Schneider (1987), Scholz (1974, 1974), Schuster (1948), Schuster & Schuster (1980), Schwartz (1977), Schwartz (1962), Selvanayagam (1990), Senthna (1985), Sheares (1975, 1987), Sibeth (1990), Sieber (1972), Sievers, von (1911), Skyring & Bogle (1982), Soekawati, (1941), Solyom & Solyom (1979, 1984), Solyom & Solyom (1973, 1980, 1980), Sorber (1983), Spée (1977), Speiser (1985), Spring (1989), Stanfiled & Barbour (1971), Steinmann (o.J., 1941, 1947, 1949, 1953), Sugimura & Suzuki (1973), Sumadio (1976), Supakar (1985), Swallow (1987), Taullard (1949), Theisen (1982), Therik (1989), Tietze (1941), Tirta (1974), Tirtaamidjaja & Anderson (1966), Tomoyuki (1966), Trivedi (1969), Tsevan (1956), Turnbull (1982), University of Singapore Art Museum (1964), Van Gelder (1979, 1980), Varadarajan (1978, 1982, 1983), Veldhuisen- Djajasoebrata (1972, 1984), Veldhuisen-Djajasoebrata (1980, 1988), Veltman

& Fischer (1912), Viatte & Pinault (1987), Völger & Weck (1987), Vogelsanger (1980), Vollmer & Gilfoy (1981), Vromen (1970, 1970), Vuldy (1987), Wacziarg & Nath (1987), Wagner (1949), Warming & Gaworski (1981), Washburn & Crowe (1988), Wass & Murnane (1978), Wassing-Visser (1982), Watt (1903), Weber (1977), Wegner (1974), Weir (1989), Westfall (1981), Westfall & Desai (1987), Wilson (1979), Wirz (1932), Yamanobe (1966), Yanagi & Ota (1932), Yogi (1980), Yoshida (1980), Yoshioka & Yoshimoto (1980), Zebrowski (1989), Zeller (1907, 1926)

Folk Art:
Albers (1965), Anonym (1949, 1954), Bachmann & Reitz (1962), Boser-Sarivaxévanis (1972), Brailaschwili (1964, 1964), Brett (1949), Dahlin (o.J.), Domonkos (1981), Henschen (1942), King (1988), Linden-Museum (1989), Mantscharowa (1960), Meyer-Heisig (1956), Müllers (1977), Nabholz-Kartaschoff (1968, 1969), Orel & Stanková (1960), Phillips (1932), Reichelt (1956), Scheller (1941), Schmalenbach (1950), Schneider (1975), Stanková (1989), Trnka (1959), Vahter (1951), Vergara Wilson (1988), Vydra (1954), Wallace (1972), Wiasmitinow (1963), Wilson (1979)

Archaeology:
Albers (1965), Amano & Tsunoyama (1979), Anton (1984), Bedaux & Bolland (1980), Billeter (o.J.), Bird (1952), Bird et al. (1981), Bollinger (1983), Cardale de Schrimpff (1986), Carter (o.J.), Clabburn (1987), Crawford (1946), Crowfoot (1947), Dawson (1979), D'Harcourt (1962, 1974), Eisleb & Strelow (1964, 1965), Feltham (1989), Gardner (1982), Gervers (1977), Haberland (1964), Hägg (1984), Hecht (1989), Jaques (1968), Katara (1972), Kent Peck (1957, 1983), King (1958, 1965), Kobel-Streiff (1972), Kroeber (1944), Lapiner (1976), Laurencich-Minelli & Ciruzzi (1981), Lavalle, de & Lang (1980), Lindberg (1964), Linné (1953), Mastache (1973), Museo Chileno (1989), Pfister (1938), Prümers (1983, 1990), Reichlen (1965), Riboud (1989), Rowe (1977), Sawyer (1979), Segal et al. (1973), Snethlage (1931), Stephani & Tolmachoff (1942), Taullard (1949), Tsunoyama (1966), Valette (1913), Van Stan (1955, 1957, 1961, 1963, 1967), Völger & Weck (1987), Washburn & Crowe (1988), Weitlaner-Johnson (1970, 1971), Wilson (1979), Zebrowski (1989)

Collections:
Adams (1972), Agthe (1975), Amano & Tsunoyama (1979), Anderson (1978), Anonym (1962), Bachinger (1979), Bezault (1954), Billeter (o.J.), Brett (1949), Bühler (1953, 1969), Bühler & Boser-Sarivaxévanis (1969), Bühler et al. (1972), Castello Yturbide & Martinez del Rio, de (1979), Chandra (1938), Claerhout (1964), Crawford (1946), Devi (1982), Djajasoebrata & Adams (1965), Djoemena (1990), Dürr (1978), Gittinger (1976), Hall & Irwin (1971), Hartland-Rowe (1985), Hartmann (1952), Heine-Geldern, von (1949), Hurwitz (1962), Icke-Schwalbe (1989), Jaques (1968), Jaquet (1975), Jusuf et al. (1984), Klimburg & Pinto (1986), Laurencich-Minelli & Ciruzzi (1981), Lavalle, de & Lang (1980), Lindahl & Knorr (1975), Linden-Museum (1989), Louber (1937), Mangkdilaga & Hutapea (1980), Mege Rosso (1990), Moes & Tay Pike (1985), Museo Chileno (1989), Museum für Völkerkunde Basel (1970), Nabholz-Kartaschoff (1970, 1986), Okada (1958), Peacock (1977), Peebles (1982), Pence Britton (1938), Rogers (1986), Rouffaer (1901), Schneider (1975), Schulz (1988), Sheares (1987), Singh (1979), Singh & Mathey (1985), Smith (1924, 1924), Solyom & Solyom (1973, 1979), Start (1948), Steinmann (1925), Sumadio (1976), Tenri Sankokan Museum (1981), Tsunoyama (1966, 1980), Turnbull (1982), Van Stan (1967), Völger & Weck (1987), Vollmer & Gilfoy (1981), Watt (1903), Zeller (1907)

Working Instructions:
Battenfield (1978), Dendel (1974), Donner & Schnebel (1913), Haake (1984), Heinze (1969), Houston (1975), Lammèr (1975), Lechuga (1979), Maile (1963), Mijer (1928), Nakamo (1982), Proud (1965), Rachman (o.J.), Rangkuty (o.J.), Reichert (1984), Spée (1977), Tidball (1957), Ursin & Kilchenmann (1979), Van Gelder (1980), Vesper (1922), Zechlin (1966)

Films:
Mylius (1979), Ramseyer & Ramseyer-Gygi (1979), Scholz (1974, 1974), Schuster & Schuster (1980)

General, Historical:
Altman (o.J.), Basilov & Naumova (1989), Beauvais-Raseau (1770), Boyd (1974), Brinckmann (1892), Bunting (1980), Grothe (1912), Hambruch (1929), Holz (1980), Jaques (1950), Jean-Richard (1968), Jenny (1919), Kreischer (1907), Lancet-Müller (1967), Lewis (1924), Metha (1951, 1961), Moss (1979), Noma (1977), Okada (1958), Osumi (1963), Pfister (1939), Raaschou (1967), Réal (1923, 1977), Rowe (1985), Schneider (1987), Schuster (1965), Schwartz (1962, 1967), Seiler-Baldinger (1986), Steinmann (o.J., 1958), Storey (1974), Strickler-Streiff (1925), Swallow (1987), Talwar & Krishna (1979), Timmermann (1984), Vuldy (1987)

Fabric Processing

Classification:
Emery (1966), Seiler-Baldinger (1979, 1991)

Analysis:
Cousin (1972), Deuss (1981), Hald (1980), Kent Peck (1957, 1983), La Baume (1955), Lothrop & Mahler (1957), Mattern-Pabel (1981), O'Neale (1942), Schlabow (1976), Snow & Snow (1973), Ullemeyer & Tidow (1973), West (1980), Zechlin (1966)

Ethnography:
Cousin (1972), Deuss (1981), Dürr (1978), Kremser & Westhart (1986), Sedlak (1987), West (1980)

Folk Art:
Johnson (1985), Mattern-Pabel (1981), Müller (1957), Nixdorff (1977), Reichelt (1956)

Archaeology:
Bender-Jorgensen & Tidow (1981), Bird & Mahler (1952), Cherblanc (1937), Hägg (1984), Hald (1980), Hellervik (1977), Hundt (1960), Kent Peck (1957, 1983), King (1956), Lothrop & Mahler (1957), O'Neale (1942), Pedersen (1982), Renner-Volbach (1988), Schlabow (1976), Ullemeyer & Tidow (1973), Weitlaner-Johnson (1977)

Collections:
Dürr (1978), Nixdorff (1977), Renner-Volbach (1988), Schlabow (1976)

Working Instructions:
Dillmont, de (1902), Snow & Snow (1973), Zechlin (1966)

General, Historical:
Fontaine (1986)

Bibliography

Abadia Morales, G.: Compendio General de Folklore Colombiano. Bogotá 1983 [Folk Art; Plaiting; Weaving]

Abbasi, S.: "Embroidery", Traditional Arts of Hyderabad, o.O. o.J.: 37-39 [Ethnography; Ornamentation with Solid Material(s)]

Abbass, D.K.: "American Indian Ribbonwork", Lore 36 (2), Milwaukee 1986: 8-15 [Analysis; Ethnography; Ornamentation with Solid Material(s)]

Abdulkadir, A.: see also Ziemba, W.T.

Abdurachman, P.R.: "The batik tradition", Abdurachman, P.R. (ed.) Cerbon. Jakarta 1982: 129-157 [Ethnography; Ornamentation with Liquid Material(s)]

Acar, B.K: Kilim ve düz dokuma yaygilar. Istanbul 1975 [Analysis; Warp Fabric; Tapestry]

Acar, B.K.: Kilim, Cicim, Zili, Sumak: Türkische Flachgewebe. Istanbul 1983 [Analysis; Ethnography; Warp Fabric; Tapestry]]

Ackermann-Ando, H.: Die Shibori-Textilmustertechnik von Arimatsu, Japan. Basel 1978 [Analysis; Ornamentation with Liquid Material(s)]

Adam, T.: "The Art of Batik in Java", The Needle and Bobbin Club 18, New York 1935: 3-17 [Ethnography; Ornamentation with Liquid Material(s)]

Adams, B.: Traditional Buthanese Textiles. Bangkok 1984 [Ethnography; Collections; Weaving; Ornamentation with Solid Material(s)]

Adams, L.G.: Textile Arts: From the 16th to the Early 19th Century. New York 1964 [Collections; Ornamentation with Solid Material(s)]

Adams, M.: System and Meaning in East Sumba Textile Design: A Study in traditional Indonesian Art. Cultural Report Series N°16, New Haven 1969 [Ethnography; Threads; Weaving; Ornamentation with Liquid Material(s)]

Adams, M.: "Designs in Sumba Textiles, Local Meanings and Foreign Influences", Textile Museum Journal 3 (2), Washington 1971: 28-37 [Ethnography; Weaving; Ornamentation with Liquid Material(s)]

Adams, M.: "Classic and Eccentric Elements in East Sumba Textiles", Bulletin of the Needle and Bobbin Club 55 (1+2), New York 1972 [Collections; Ornamentation with Liquid Material(s)]

Adams, M.: "Dress and Design in Highland Southeast Asia:: The Hmong (Miao) and Yao", Textile Museum Journal Vol.4 N°1, Washington 1974: 51-66 [Ethnography; Ornamentation with Solid Material(s); Ornamentation with Liquid Material(s)]

Adams, M.: "Style in Southeast Asian Materials Processing", Lechtman, H. & Merill, R. S. (ed.) Material Culture 1975, St. Paul 1977: 21-52 [Ethnography; Weaving; Ornamentation with Liquid Material(s)]

Adams, M.: "Kuba Embroidered Cloth", African Arts Vol.12 N°1, Los Angeles 1978: 24-39 [Ethnography; Weaving; Ornamentation with Solid Material(s)]

Adams, M.: "Fon Appliqued Cloths", African Arts Vol.13 N°2, Los Angeles 1980: 28-41 [Ethnography; Ornamentation with Solid Material(s)]

Adams, M.: "Beyond symmetry in middle African design", African Arts Vol.23 N°1, Los Angeles 1989: 34-43 [Ethnography; Plaiting; Weaving; Ornamentation with Solid Material(s); Ornamentation with Liquid Material(s)]

Adams, M.: see also Djajasoebrata, V.A.

Adelson, L. & Tracht, A.: Aymara Weavings. Ceremonial Textiles of Colonial and Nineteenth Century Bolivia. Washington 1983 [Ethnography; Collections; Weaving]

Adi-Rubin, M.: Israeli Yemenite Embroidery. Cone-Heiden 1983 [Analysis; Working Instruction; Ornamentation with Solid Material(s)]

Adler, A.: Textilkunst der Cuna im Grenzgebiet von Kolumbien und Panama. Koblenz 1980 [Ethnography; General, Historical; Ornamentation with Solid Material(s)]

Adovasio, J.M.: "Prehistoric Great Basin Textiles", I.Emery Roundtable on Museum Textiles 1974, Washington 1975: 141-149 [Archaeology; Weaving]

Adovasio, J.M.: Basketry Technology, a Guide to Identification and Analysis. Chicago 1977 [Analysis; Archaeology; Plaiting]

Adovasio, J.M.: "Prehistoric Basketry of Western North America and Mexico", Browman, D. (ed.) Early Native America. New York 1980: 341-362 [Archaeology; Plaiting]

Adovasio, J.M.: "Prehistoric Basketry", Handbook of North American Indians 11, Washington 1986: 194-205 [Archaeology; Plaiting]

Adovasio, J.M. & Maslowski, R.F.: "Cordage, Basketry and Textiles", Lynch, Th.F. (ed.) Guittarero Cave – Early Man in the Andes. London 1980: 253-289 [Ethnography; Archaeology; Threads; Mesh Fabric; Plaiting; Warp Fabric; Weaving]

Aga-Dglu, M.: Safawid Rugs and Textiles. New York 1941 [General, Historical; Warp Fabric; Weaving; Pile Fabric; Tapestry]

Agthe, J.: Kunsthandwerk in Afrika im Wandel. Roter Faden zur Ausstellung 2, Frankfurt 1975 [Ethnography; Collections;Weaving; Ornamentation with Solid Material(s); Ornamentation with Liquid Material(s)]

Aguirre, J.: Eusko-Bilkin – Degi: Museo Vasco (Etnográfico). Museo Municipal de S.Sebastián 3 & 5, San Sebastián n.d. [Folk Art; Collections; Threads; Plaiting; Weaving]

Ahlbrinck, W.: "Over de vlechtmethoden gebruikelijk bij de Kalina", Anthropos 20, Freiburg 1925: 638-652 [Analysis; Ethnography; Plaiting]

Ahmed, M.: A monograph on village Manhira. Census of India, Village Survey 12 (6), 1961, New Delhi 1967 [Ethnography; General, Historical; Threads; Weaving]

Akkent, M. & Franger, G.: Das Kopftuch: Ein Stückchen Stoff in Geschichte und Gegenwart. Frankfurt 1987 [Folk Art; Pile Fabric]

Albers, A.: A Structural Process in Weaving. New Haven 1952 [Analysis; Archaeology; Weaving]

Albers, A.: On Weaving. Middletown 1965 [Analysis; Ethnography; Folk Art; Archaeology; Mesh Fabric; Plaiting; Warp Fabric; Weaving; Pile Fabric; Ornamentation with Liquid Material(s)]

Alfaro Giner, C.: Tejido y cestería en la peninsula Ibérica. Bibl. Praehist. Hispana 21, Madrid 1984 [Archaeology; Threads; Mesh Fabric; Plaiting; Warp Fabric; Weaving; Borders]

Ali, Y.: A monograph on silk fabrics produced in the North-Western provinces and Oudh. Allahabad 1900 [Ethnography; Threads; Weaving]

All India Handicrafts Board: Cane grass and bamboo crafts of India. New Delhi n.d. [Ethnography; Plaiting]

All India Handicrafts Board: Indian printed textiles. New Delhi]
Analysis; Ethnography; Ornamentation with Solid Material(s); Ornamentation with Liquid Material(s)]

Allen, M.: see also Yorke, R.

Alman, J.H.: "Bajau Weaving", Sarawak Museum Journal 9 (15-26), Kuching,Sarawak 1960: 603-618 [Ethnography; Weaving]

Altman, B. & Lopez, R.: Guatemala: Quetzal and Cross. Los Angeles 1975 [Collections; Weaving]
Altman, P.H.: The Loom, the needle and dye pot. n.p., n.d. [General, Historical; Weaving; Ornamentation with Liquid Material(s)]
Alvarez de Williams, A.: "Cocopa", Handbook of North Am. Indians 10, Washington 1983: 99-112 [Ethnography; Plaiting; Beadwork]
Amano, Y.& Tsunoyama, Y. (ed.): Textiles of the Andes: Catalog of Amano Collection Lima. San Francisco 1979 [Analysis; Archaeology; Collections; Mesh Fabric; Warp Fabric; Weaving; Pile Fabric; Ornamentation with Solid Material(s); Ornamentation with Liquid Material(s); Tapestry]
Amar, A.B. & Littleton, C.: Traditional Algerian flat-weavings. Cullowhee 1981 [Ethnography; Collections; Warp Fabric; Tapestry]
Ambler, R.: see also Lambert, M.F.
Amborn, H.: Differenzierung und Integration. Notos Band 1, München 1990 [Ethnography; Threads; Weaving]
American Indian Basketry Magazine:, Portland from 1979 on]
Analysis; Ethnography; Collections; Working Instruction; Plaiting]
American Society for testing Materials: Standard Methods of Identification of Fibres in Textiles. Philadelphia 1949 [General, Historical]
Amsden, C.: "The Loom and its Prototypes", American Anthropologist Vol.34 N°2, Menasha 1932: 216-235 [Archaeology; Threads; Warp Fabric; Weaving]
Amsden, C.: Navajo Weaving:its Technique and History. Santa Ana 1934 [Analysis; Ethnography; Mesh Fabric; Plaiting; Weaving; Tapestry]
Analsad, D.M.: Cotton Hand Spinning. Madras 1951 [Ethnography; Threads]
Anand, M.R.: "The Art of living in the Punjab village", Marg 28 (1), Bombay 1974 [Ethnography; Weaving; Ornamentation with Solid Material(s)]
Anawalt, P. R.: "The Ramifications of Treadle Loom Introduction in 16th Century Mexico", I.Emery Roundtable on Museum Textiles 1977, Washington 1979: 170-187 [Folk Art; Weaving]
Anawalt, P.R.: Indian clothing before Cortés: Mesoamerican costumes from the Codices. Norman 1981 [General, Historical; Pile Fabric]
Andersen, E.: "Solution of the mystery", Folk 21-22, 1979-80, Kobenhagen 1980 [Folk Art; Weaving]
Anderson, B.R.O.: see also Tirtaamidjaja, N.
Anderson, M.: Guatemalan Textiles Today. New York 1978 [Ethnography; Collections; Threads; Mesh Fabric; Plaiting; Warp Fabric; Weaving; Ornamentation with Solid Material(s); Ornamentation with Liquid Material(s)]
Anderson, M.: see also Taber, B.
Andrews, M.: Türkmen Needlework: Dressmaking and Embroidery among the Türkmen of Iran. Central Asian Research Centre, London 1976 [Ethnography; Ornamentation with Solid Material(s)]
Andrews, P.: The Turcoman of Iran. Kendal n.d. [Ethnography; Collections; Pile Fabric; Tapestry]
Andrews, P.A.: see also Azadi, S.
Anjou, S.: "Ryer i det Nordenfjelske Norge", Röhsska Konstslöjdenusects, Arstryck 1934 [Folk Art; Pile Fabric]
Ankermann, B.: "Gemusterte Raphiagewebe vom unteren Niger", Baessler–Archiv 6, Berlin 1922: 204-206 [Ethnography; Working Instruction; Weaving]
Anonym: Guimaraes Gualterianos: Abbildungen spinnender Frauen. Journal de Noticias, n.p., n.d. [General, Historical; Threads]
Anonym: Orient-Teppiche: eine erste Einführung. Binningen n.d. [Ethnography; Pile Fabric]
Anonym: Arts and crafts in Indonesia. Djakarta n.d. [Ethnography]
Anonym: Der antike Webstuhl. Mitteil. K. u. K. öster. Mus. für Kunst und Industrie N°8, Wien 1893 [Folk Art; Weaving]
Anonym: Das Spitzenschulwesen: Das Schulwesen der Spitzenklöppelei in der Tschechoslowakei. Prag 1928 [Folk Art; Plaiting]
Anonym: Two thousand years of silk weaving. New York 1944 [Ethnography; Archaeology; Weaving]
Anonym: European printed textiles. London 1949 [Folk Art; Ornamentation with Liquid Material(s)]
Anonym: Présentation de la Collection Louis Becker: Mouchoirs et Tissus imprimés du XVIIIe et XIXe siècle. Mulhouse 1954 [Folk Art; Ornamentation with Liquid Material(s)]
Anonym: Indonésie. Les Arts et les Dieux. Sumatra, Java, Bali, Timor , Borneo, Célébes, Iles du Sud-Ouest. Neuchâtel 1956 [Ethnography; Weaving; Ornamentation with Liquid Material(s)]
Anonym: Slovensky l'udovy textil. Tkaniny, vysivky cipky, kroje. Osveta 1957 [Analysis; Folk Art; Threads; Plaiting; Weaving; Ornamentation with Solid Material(s)]
Anonym: Craft designs. Delhi 1961 [Ethnography; General, Historical]
Anonym: Exposition de toiles peintes anciennes des Indes. Mulhouse 1962 [Collections; Ornamentation with Liquid Material(s)]
Anonym: Catalogue of exhibition of Shoso-in treasures. Nara 1964 [Working Instruction; Plaiting; Weaving]
Anonym: Chumash Indian Art. The Art Gallery University of California 18, n.p. 1964 [Ethnography; Collections; Plaiting]
Anonym: Handwoven Textiles. Bombay 1965 [Ethnography; Weaving]
Anonym: The art of tie-dyeing. Standard Bangkok Magazine 30 (8), Bangkok 1970 [Ethnography; Ornamentation with Liquid Material(s)]
Anonym: Ein Museum für Textiles: Sammlung Iklé im Industrie- und Gewerbe Museum St.Gallen. St. Gallen 1972 [Collections]
Anonym: Cultural relics unearthed in Sinkiang. Bejing 1975 [Archaeology; General, Historical]
Anonym: Ikats from central Asia. New York 1975 [Ethnography; Ornamentation with Liquid Material(s)]
Anonym: Hommage to Kalam-kari. Marg 31.4, Bombay 1978 [Ethnography; Ornamentation with Liquid Material(s)]
Anonym: Ikat: Indonesian Textile Traditions. Glasgow 1978 [Ethnography; Ornamentation with Liquid Material(s)]
Anonym: Kanoko aus Kyoto. Kyoto 1980 [Ethnography; Ornamentation with Liquid Material(s)]
Anonym: Volkskunst. München 1985 [Folk Art; Threads; Plaiting]
Anonym: Weben und Knüpfen. Ausstellung des bildnerischen Volksschaffens in der DDR. Leipzig 1985 [Folk Art; Plaiting; Weaving; Pile Fabric; Ornamentation with Solid Material(s)]
Anonym: Nias: Tribal Treasures. Delft 1990 [Ethnography; Plaiting; Ornamentation with Solid Material(s)]
Anquetil, J.: Le Tissage. Paris 1977 [Analysis; Folk Art; Weaving; Beadwork]
Anquetil, J.: La Vannerie. Paris 1979 [Working Instruction; Plaiting; Beadwork; Borders]
Anthony, I.E.: "Quilting and Patchwork in Wales", Bulletin of the Natural Museum Wales, Portsmouth n.d. [General, Historical; Ornamentation with Solid Material(s)]
Anton, F.: Altindianische Textilkunst aus Peru. Leipzig 1984 [Analysis; Archaeology; Mesh Fabric; Warp Fabric; Weaving; Pile Fabric; Ornamentation with Solid Material(s); Ornamentation

with Liquid Material(s)]
Aoki, M.: see also Sekido, M.
Apostolaki, A.: Kentimata Mallina. Benaki Mus. Athen 1956 [Folk Art; Mesh Fabric; Weaving; Ornamentation with Solid Material(s)]
Aradeon, S.B.: see also Nordquist, B.K.
Arbeit, W.: Baskets in Polynesia. Honolulu 1990 [Analysis; Ethnography; Working Instruction; Plaiting]
Arbman, H.: see also Strömberg, E.
Archambault, M.: Tissus royaux, tissus villageois de Thailande. Mulhouse 1988 [Ethnography; Threads; Weaving; Ornamentation with Liquid Material(s)]
Aretz, I.: Manual de Folklore Venezolano. Carácas 1972 [Folk Art; Threads; Mesh Fabric; Plaiting; Warp Fabric; Weaving]
Aretz, I.: El traje del Venezolano. Carácas 1977 [Ethnography; Folk Art; Mesh Fabric; Plaiting; Warp Fabric; Weaving]
Aretz, I.: La artesanía folklórica de Venezuela. Carácas 1979 [Ethnography; Threads; Mesh Fabric]
Aronson, L.: "Popo Weaving: The Dynamics of Trade in Southeastern Nigeria", African Arts Vol.15 N°3, Los Angeles 1982: 43-47 [Ethnography; Weaving]
Aronson, L.: Akwete weaving: a study of change in response to the palmoil trade in the nineteenth century. Ann Arbor 1986 [Ethnography; Weaving]
Aronson, L.: "Akwete Weaving: Tradition and Change", Basler Beiträge zur Ethnologie Band 30, Basel 1989: 35-64 [Analysis; Ethnography; Weaving]
Arseven, C.E.: Le yazama. Les arts décoratifs Turcs. Istanbul 1953 [Ethnography; Ornamentation with Liquid Material(s)]
Arthur, L.: Der echte Teppich. Wien 1926 [Ethnography; Pile Fabric]
Aryan, K.C.: Rural art of the Western Himalaya. New Delhi 1985 [Ethnography]
Aryan, S.: Himachal Embroidery. New Delhi n.d. [General, Historical; Ornamentation with Solid Material(s)]
Aryan, S.: "Pahari Embroidery", Arts of Asia Vol.14 N°5, Hong Kong 1984: 81-91 [Ethnography; Ornamentation with Solid Material(s)]
Arze, S.: see also Gisbert, T.
Asch, M.I.: "Slavey", Handbook of North Am. Indians 6, Washington 1981: 338-349 [Analysis; Ethnography; Ornamentation with Solid Material(s)]
Ashabranner, B. & Ashabranner, M.: "The Basket Art of Northern Luzon", Arts of Asia Vol.11 N°5, Hong Kong 1981: 120-126 [Ethnography; Plaiting]
Ashabranner, M.: see also Ashabranner, B.
Ashley, C.W.: The Ashley Book of Knots. London 1977 [Folk Art; Mesh Fabric; Plaiting]
Ashley, C.W.: Das Ashley Buch der Knoten. Hamburg 1986 [Folk Art; Mesh Fabric; Plaiting]
Ashton, L. & Wace, A.J.B.: Brief Guide to the Persian Embroideries. Victoria and Albert Museum, London 1929 [Ethnography; Collections; Ornamentation with Solid Material(s)]
Atwater, M.M.: Byways in hand-weaving. New York 1976 [Working Instruction; Plaiting; Warp Fabric; Weaving]
Ave, J.B. & King, V.T.: Borneo: People of the Weeping Forest. Leiden 1986 [Ethnography; Plaiting]
Azadi, S.: Turkmenische Teppiche. Hamburg 1970 [Ethnography; Pile Fabric]
Azadi, S. & Andrews, P.A.: Mafrash. Berlin 1985 [Analysis; Ethnography; Warp Fabric]
Azizbekova, P.A.: Aserbeidschanische Stickereien. Moskau 1971 [Folk Art; Collections; Ornamentation with Solid Material(s)]
Azizbekova, P.A.: Aserbeidschanische Nationaltracht. Moskau 1972 [Folk Art; Collections; Ornamentation with Solid Material(s)]
Azzola, F.K.: see also Azzola, J.
Azzola, J. & Azzola, F.K.: "Die Tuchschere im Bergischen Museum auf Schloss Burg an der Wupper", Das Kleindenkmal N°1, 11, Burg a.d. Wupper 1985 [Folk Art]
Azzola, J. & Azzola, F.K.: "Spinnrocken und Handspindel, zwei steinerne Denkmale von 1447", Schwäbische Heimat N°1, 36, Stuttgart 1986 [Archaeology; Threads]

Bachinger, R.: Pua: Zeremonialtücher der Iban aus Borneo. Frankfurt 1979 [Ethnography; Collections; Ornamentation with Liquid Material(s)]
Bachmann, M. & Reitz, G.: Der Blaudruck. Leipzig 1962 [Folk Art; Ornamentation with Liquid Material(s)]
Bacon, E.: see also O'Neale, L.M.
Baer, G.: Beiträge zur Kenntnis des Xingu-Quellgebietes. Basel, München 1960 [Ethnography; Plaiting; Warp Fabric]
Baer, G.: Matsigenka(Ostperu, Montaña), Schnurdrehen und Netzknüpfen. Encyclopaedia Cinematographica E 1718, Göttingen 1972 [Ethnography; Films; Threads; Mesh Fabric]
Baer, G.: Matsigenka(Ostperu, Montaña), Herstellen eines Deckelkorbes. Encyclopaedia Cinematographica E 1719, Göttingen 1973 [Ethnography; Films; Plaiting]
Baer, G.: Píro (Ostperu, Montaña) Herstellen einer Matte. Encyclopaedia Cinematographica 7 (29), E 1716, Göttingen 1977: 3-10 [Ethnography; Films; Plaiting]
Baer, G. & Seiler-Baldinger, A.: "Cushmas der Matsingenka, Ost-Peru", Basler Beiträge zur Ethnologie Band 30, Basel 1989: 421-431 [Ethnography; Weaving]
Baerlocher, M.: Veränderungen in der Arbeitsweise der Aegyptisch-Koptischen Wirkereien. Dissertation. Basel 1978 [Analysis; Archaeology; Tapestry]
Baerlocher, M.: Vorbereitungsschritte zu Wirkereien, Fadenverläufe als Ausdruck der Stoffbildungsmöglichkeiten. Anhang zur Dissertation. Basel 1978 [Analysis; Archaeology; Weaving; Tapestry]
Bagli, M.: see also Laurencich-Minelli, L.
Bahr, D.M.: "Pima and Papago Social Organization", Handbook of North American Indians 10, Washington 1983: 178-192 [Analysis; Ethnography; Mesh Fabric; Plaiting]
Bailey, T.E.: The manual industries of Peru. New York 1947 [Ethnography; Threads; Weaving]
Baines, P.: Spinning wheels: Spinners and spinning. London 1977 [Classification; Analysis; Folk Art; Threads]
Baizerman, S. & Searle, K.: Finishes in the Ethnic Tradition. St. Paul 1978 [Ethnography; Working Instruction; Borders]
Baizerman, S. & Searle, K.: Latin American brocades: Explorations in supplementary weft techniques. St. Paul 1980 [Working Instruction; Weaving]
Baizerman, S.: see also Cahlander, A.
Baizerman, S.: see also Pancake, C.M.
Bajinski, A. & Tidhar, A.: Textiles from Egypt: 4th – 13th Century. Tel Aviv 1980 [Archaeology; Weaving; Tapestry]
Baker, G.P.: Calico Painting and Printing in the East Indies in the 17th. and 18th. centuries. London 1921 [Ethnography; Ornamentation with Liquid Material(s)]
Baker, M. & Lunt, M.: Blue and white: The cotton embroideries of rural China. New York 1977 [Ethnography; Ornamentation with Solid Material(s)]
Baker, M.L.: The abc's of Canvas embroidery. Sturbridge 1975 [Working Instruction; Ornamentation with Solid Material(s)]
Baker, M.L.: The xyz's of Canvas embroidery. Sturbridge 1975 [Working Instruction; Ornamentation with Solid Material(s)]
Balbino Camposeco, M.J.: La Cestería de la Aldea Cerro Alto,

San Juan Sacatepéquez. Guatemala 1983 [Ethnography; Plaiting; Tapestry]
Balfet, H.: "La vannerie: Essai de classification", L'Anthropologie 56, Paris 1952: 259-280 [Classification; Plaiting; Borders]
Balfet, H.: Basketry: A Proposed Classification. Univ. Calif. Arch. Survey Rep. 37, Pap. Cal. Arch. 47, Berkeley 1957: 1-21 [Classification; Plaiting]
Balfet, H.: "Essai de classification de la vannerie", Schweiz. Arbeitslehrerinnen Zeitung 9, N°69, Biel 1986: 7 [Classification; Analysis; Ethnography; Plaiting]
Balfet, H. & Desrosiers, S.: "Où en sont les classifications textiles", Techniques et Culture 10, Paris 1987: 207-212 [Classification]
Balke, L.: Serbische Stickereien. Bautzen 1976 [Folk Art; Ornamentation with Solid Material(s)]
Ball, S.C: Clothing. Mus. Handbook 2, B.P. Bishop Mus. Special Publ. 9, Honolulu 1924 [Ethnography; Mesh Fabric; Weaving; Pile Fabric]
Baranowicz, de, I. & Bernheimer, L.& Soustiel, J.: Udstilling af orientalske textiler tilhorende I. de Baranowicz. Kobenhaven 1957 [Ethnography; Weaving; Pile Fabric]
Barbour, J.: "Nigerian Adire Cloths", Baessler-Archiv NF 18(2), Berlin 1970: 363-426 [Ethnography; Ornamentation with Liquid Material(s)]
Barbour, J.& Simmonds, D. (ed.): Adire Cloth in Nigeria. Ibadan 1971 [Ethnography; Ornamentation with Liquid Material(s)]
Barbour, J.: see also Stanfiled, N.
Barendse, R. & Lobera, A.: Manual de Artesanía Textil. Barcelona 1987 [Analysis; Folk Art; Working Instruction; Weaving]
Barista, O.: "Broderies turques du XIXe siècle: Les serviettes de bain", Objets et Mondes 21, Paris 1981 [General, Historical; Ornamentation with Solid Material(s)]
Barker, D.K.: "Bhutanese Handwoven Textiles", Arts of Asia Vol.15 N°4, Hong Kong 1985: 103-111 [Ethnography; Weaving]
Barker, J.: Decorative Braiding and Weaving. Newton Centre, Massachussets 1973 [Working Instruction; Plaiting; Weaving]
Barkley, S.: Adire: Indigo Cloth of Nigeria. Toronto 1980 [Ethnography; Ornamentation with Liquid Material(s)]
Barkow, I.: Klöppelspitzen in Idriatechnik. Hannover 1983 [Analysis; Working Instruction; Plaiting]
Barletta, R.: Appunti e immagini su cartapula, terracotta, teintura e telaio. n.p. 1985 [Folk Art; Weaving]
Barnes, C. & Blake, D.P.: Creative macramé projects. New York 1976 [Working Instruction; Plaiting]
Barnes, R.: "Weaving and non-weaving among the Lamaholot", Indonesian Circle 42, London 1987 [Ethnography; Weaving]
Barnes, R.: The Ikat Textiles of Lamalera: A Study of an Eastern Indonesian Weaving Tradition. Leiden 1989 [Analysis; Ethnography; Ornamentation with Liquid Material(s)]
Barnes, R.: "The Bridewealth Cloth of Lamalera, Lembata", Gittinger, M. (ed.) To Speak with Cloth. Los Angeles 1989 [Ethnography; Weaving; Ornamentation with Liquid Material(s)]
Barrett, L.K.: see also Moseley, M.
Barrett, S.A.: "Basket Designs of the Pomo Indians", American Anthropologist 7, Menasha 1905 [Ethnography; Plaiting]
Barrett, S.A.: "Pomo Indian Basketry", UCLA Publ. Amer. Arch. and Ethnology 7, 1907-10, Berkeley 1908: 134-266 [Ethnography; Plaiting]
Barrow, T.: "Die Taniko-Weberei der Maori auf Neuseeland", Palette 9, Basel 1962 [Ethnography; Warp Fabric]
Barten, S.: Navajo blankets. Zürich 1976 [Collections; Warp Fabric; Weaving]
Bartholomew, M.: Thunder dragon textiles from Bhutan: The Bartholomew collection. Tokyo 1985 [Collections; General, Historical; Weaving]
Barton, J. et al.: Itchiku Kubota: Kimono in the Tqujigahana Tradition: Exhibition Catalogue. Fullerton Art Gallery, Fullerton, Ca. 1980 [Ethnography; Ornamentation with Liquid Material(s)]
Basilov, V.N.& Naumova, O.B. (ed.): Yurts, rugs, felts. Nomads of Eurasia. Los Angeles 1989: 97-110 [Analysis; Ethnography; General, Historical; Ornamentation with Solid Material(s); Ornamentation with Liquid Material(s)]
Bates, C.D.: Coiled basketry of the Sierra Miwok. San Diego 1982 [Ethnography; Plaiting]
Batigné, R. & Bellinger, L.: "The significance and technical analysis of ancient textiles as historical documents", Proceedings of American Philos. Soc. 97, Philadelphia 1965: 670-680 [Archaeology; General, Historical; Threads; Ornamentation with Solid Material(s)]
Battenfield, J.: Ikat technique. New York 1978 [Working Instruction; Ornamentation with Liquid Material(s)]
Bauspack, P.: Kelim: antike orientalische Flachgewebe. München 1983 [Analysis; Tapestry]
Bayley Willis, E.: "The Textile Arts of India's North-East Borderlands", Arts of Asia Vol.17 N°1, Hong Kong 1987: 93-115 [Ethnography; Weaving; Ornamentation with Solid Material(s)]
Bayona, B.: see also Raymond, P.
Beals, R.: "The Tarascans", Handbook of Middle Am. Indians 8, Austin 1969: 725-773 [Ethnography; Threads; Weaving]
Beattie, M.H.: "Some weft-float brocaded rugs of the Bergama Ezine Region", Textile Museum Journal 3.2, Washington 1971: 20-27 [General, Historical; Warp Fabric]
Beauvais-Raseau: Die Kunst des Indigobereitens. Paris 1770 [General, Historical; Ornamentation with Liquid Material(s)]
Becker, J.: "Silk-weaving techniques of Han-China: The monochrome patterned weaves", CIETA, Lyon 1981 [Archaeology; Weaving]
Becker-Donner, E.: "Die Bedeutung der Weberei in Dorfgemeinschaften Guatemalas", Verhand. des Internat. Amerik. Kongress Band 2, München 1968 [Ethnography; Weaving; Ornamentation with Liquid Material(s)]
Beckwith, J.: "Koptische Textilien", Ciba Rundschau Band 13, N°145, Basel 1959: 2-27 [Archaeology; Warp Fabric; Tapestry]
Bedaux, R.M.A. & Bolland, R.: "Tellem, reconnaissance archéologique d'une culture de l'ouest africaine au moyen-âge: les textiles", Journal des Africanistes 50, Paris 1980 [Archaeology; Weaving; Ornamentation with Liquid Material(s)]
Bedaux, R.M.A. & Bolland, R.: "Medieval textiles from the Tellem Caves in Central Mali, West Afrika", Textile Museum Journal 19-20, 1980-81, Washington 1981: 65-74 [Archaeology; Weaving]
Bedaux, R.M.A. & Bolland, R.: "Vêtements féminins médiévaux du Mali: les cache-sexes de fibre des Tellem", Basler Beiträge zur Ethnologie Band 30, Basel 1989: 15-34 [Archaeology; Plaiting; Warp Fabric]
Bedford, M.C.: Pit loom weaving: Blampur and Fatepur, Swat, West Pakistan. California Uni. 1974 [Ethnography; Weaving]
Beer, A.B.: Trade Goods: A study of Indian Chintz. Washington 1970 [Ethnography; Collections; Ornamentation with Solid Material(s)]
Beier, U.: Yoruba beaded crowns: Sacred regalias of the Olokuku of Okuku. London 1981 [Ethnography; Beadwork]
Bel, A. & Ricard, P.: Le travail de la laine à Tlemcen: Les industries indigènes de l'Algérie. Jourdan 1913 [Analysis; Ethnography; Threads; Mesh Fabric; Plaiting; Weaving; Ornamentation with Solid Material(s)]
Belash, C.A.: Braiding and Knotting Techniques and Projects. Repr. 1974, New York 1936 [Working Instruction; Mesh Fabric; Plaiting]

Belen, H.F.: Philippine Creative Handicrafts. Manila 1952 [Analysis; Working Instruction; Mesh Fabric; Plaiting]
Bellinger, L.: "Textile Analysiss. Early techniques in Egypt and the Near East. Part 3", Workshop Notes, Textile Museum Paper 6, Washington 1952 [Archaeology; Weaving; Tapestry]
Bellinger, L.: "Patterned stockings: possibly Indian, found in Egypt, and textile analysis: early techniques in Egypt and Near East", Workshop Notes, Textile Museum N°2-3, 10, Washington 1954 [Archaeology; Mesh Fabric; Weaving; Tapestry]
Bellinger, L.: "Craft Habits: 1", Workshop Notes, Textile Museum 19, Washington 1959 [Archaeology; Weaving]
Bellinger, L.: "Craft Habits 2: Spinning and fibres in warp yarns", Workshop Notes, Textile Museum 20, Washington 1959 [Archaeology; Threads; Weaving]
Bellinger, L.: "Repeats in Silk Weaving in the Near East", Workshop Notes, Textile Museum 24, Washington 1961 [Ethnography; Weaving]
Bellinger, L.: "Textiles from Gordion", Bull. Needle and Bobbin Club Vol.46 N°1 & 2, New York 1962 [Archaeology; Weaving; Tapestry]
Bellinger, L. & Kühnel, E.: Catalogue of Dated Tiraz Fabrics. The Textile Museum, Washington 1952 [Analysis; Archaeology; Weaving]
Bellinger, L.: see also Batigné, R.
Bellinger, L.: see also Bird, J.B.
Bellinger, L.: see also Pfister, R.
Bender-Jorgensen, L.: Forhistoriske textiler i Skandinavien. Nordiske Fortidsminder Serie B, Band 9, Kopenhagen 1986 [Analysis; Archaeology; Threads; Weaving; Pile Fabric; Borders]
Bender-Jorgensen, L. & Tidow, K.: Textilsymposium Neumünster: Archäologische Textilfunde. Neumünster 1981 [Archaeology; Threads; Weaving; Pile Fabric; Borders; Fabric Processing]
Bennett, N.: see also Bighorse, T.
Bennett, W.C.: "Weaving in the Land of the Incas", Natural History 35 (1), New York 1935: 63-72 [Archaeology; Weaving]
Bennett, W.C.: Ancient Arts of the Andes. New York 1954 [Archaeology; Weaving; Ornamentation with Solid Material(s)]
Bennett, W.C. & Bird, J.B.: Andean Culture History. Handbook Series. American Mus. of Natural History 15, New York 1960 [Archaeology; Threads; Warp Fabric]
Benson, H.O.: see also Gallinger-Tod, O.
Ben-Amos, P.: "Owina N'ido: Royal Weavers of Benin", African Arts Vol.11 N°4, Los Angeles 1978: 49-53 [Ethnography; Weaving]
Berbenni, A.: "Mitteleuropa, Lombardei: Weaving von Flickenteppichen auf dem Trittwebstuhl", Encyclopaedia Cinematographica 14 (3), Göttingen 1984: 3-15 [Folk Art; Films; Weaving]
Berberian, E.E.: "Enterratorios de Adultos en Urnas en el Area Valliserrana del Noroeste Argentino", Instituto de Antropología 29, 1969, Córdoba 1941: 1-71 [Archaeology; Weaving]
Bergman, I.: Late Nubian Textiles. The Scandinavian Joint Expedition to Sudanese Nubia, Vol. 8, Stockholm 1975 [Analysis; Archaeology; Warp Fabric; Weaving; Pile Fabric; Borders]
Bergman, R.A.M.: Kleur of doek: Hoe exotische weefsels worden gekleurd. Amsterdam 1954 [Ethnography; Ornamentation with Liquid Material(s)]
Berg, van den, R.: "Het grafische borduurwerk van de Akhavrouwen uit het dorp Pa Mee", Handwerken zonder grenzen 1, Utrecht 1984 [Ethnography; Ornamentation with Liquid Material(s)]
Berin, K. (ed.): Art of the Huichol Indians. New York 1978 [Ethnography; Plaiting; Weaving; Beadwork; Ornamentation with Solid Material(s)]
Berlant, A.: see also Kahlenberg, M.H.
Bernès, J.P.: Arts et objets du Maroc: Costumes, broderies, brocats. Paris 1974 [General, Historical; Weaving; Ornamentation with Solid Material(s)]
Bernès, J.P. & Jacob, A.: Arts et objets du Maroc: Meubles, zellidjs, tapis. Paris 1974 [General, Historical; Weaving]
Bernheimer, L.: see also Baranowicz, de, I.
Berry, G.M. & Hersh, P.A.: Properties of some Archaeological Textiles. Zagreb 1974 [Archaeology]
Berthoud, G.: "Considérations sur la culture matérielle des Kuba", Bulletin Annuel: Musée et Inst. d'Ethnography N°7, Genève 1964: 49-60 [Ethnography; Pile Fabric]
Best, A.: Traveaux en piquants de porc-épic exécutés par les autochtones au Canada. Toronto 1977 [Ethnography; Ornamentation with Solid Material(s)]
Beutlich, T.: The Technique of Woven Tapestry. London 1982 [Tapestry]
Bezault, P.: La collection Louis Becker 1ère partie: Les Indiennes 17e, 18e, 19e siècles. Bull. de la Soc. Ind. de Mulhouse N°3-16, Mulhouse 1954 [Collections; Ornamentation with Liquid Material(s)]
Bezemer, T.J.: Indonesisches Kunstgewerbe. Den Haag 1920 [Ethnography; Ornamentation with Liquid Material(s)]
Bhagwat, D. & Jayakar, P.: "Stickerei in Indien: Dichtung und Wahrheit", Ciba Rundschau N°3, Basel 1972 [Ethnography; Ornamentation with Solid Material(s)]
Bhattacharyya, A.K.: Chamba Rumal. Indian Museum Monograph N°2, Calcutta 1968 [Ethnography; Collections; Ornamentation with Solid Material(s)]
Bhavani, E.: Decorative designs and craftmanship of India: With over 10.000 designs and motifs from crafts of India. Bombay 1968 [Ethnography; Weaving; Ornamentation with Solid Material(s); Ornamentation with Liquid Material(s)]
Bhushan, J.B.: The Costumes and Textiles of India. Bombay 1985 [Ethnography; Weaving; Pile Fabric; Ornamentation with Solid Material(s); Ornamentation with Liquid Material(s)]
Bianchi, C. et al.: Artesanías y técnicas shuar. Mundo Shuar 4, Quito 1982 [Analysis; Ethnography; Mesh Fabric; Plaiting; Weaving; Pile Fabric; Beadwork; Borders]
Bianconi, G.: Artigianati scomparsi. L'industria della paglia in Onsernone. Locarno 1965 [Folk Art; Plaiting]
Bidder, H.: Teppiche aus Ost-Turkestan. Tübingen 1964 [Ethnography; Warp Fabric]
Biebuyck, D.P.: The power of headdresses: A cross-cultural study of forms and functions. Brüssel 1984 [Analysis; Ethnography; Mesh Fabric; Plaiting; Pile Fabric; Beadwork; Ornamentation with Solid Material(s)]
Biggs, R.D.: Discoveries from Kurdish looms. Illinois 1983 [General, Historical; Warp Fabric; Pile Fabric]
Bighorse, T. & Bennett, N.: "Weaving, the Navajo Way", Interweave Vol. 4, 1978: 12-19 [Ethnography; Working Instruction; Warp Fabric]
Billeter, E. (ed.): Textilparadies Indien. n.p., n.d. [Ethnography; Weaving]
Billeter, E. (ed.): Aussereuropäische Textilien. Kunstgewerbemuseum, Zürich n.d. [Ethnography; Archaeology; Collections; Weaving; Pile Fabric; Ornamentation with Solid Material(s); Ornamentation with Liquid Material(s)]
Billeter, E. (ed.): Europäische Textilien. Kunstgewerbemuseum. Sammlungskatalog, Zürich n.d. [Folk Art; Collections]
Bird, J.B.: "A Pre-Spanish Peruvian Ikat", American Fabrics N°20, 1951-52, New York 1952: 73-77 [Archaeology; Ornamentation with Liquid Material(s)]
Bird, J.B.: "Before heddles were invented", Handweaver and Craftsman Vol.3 N°3, New York 1952 [Archaeology; Mesh Fabric; Warp Fabric]

Bird, J.B.: "Suggestions for the recording of data on spinning and weaving and the collecting of Material", Kroeber Anthropol. Series 20-23, 1959-60, Berkeley 1960: 1-9 [Ethnography; Threads; Weaving]

Bird, J.B.: "Textile designing and samplers in Peru", Essays in Pre-Columbian Art. Cambridge 1961: 299-316 [Archaeology; Ornamentation with Solid Material(s)]

Bird, J.B.: "Shaped Tapestry Bags from the Nazca – Ica Area of Peru", Textile Museum Journal 1 (3), Washington 1964: 2-7 [Archaeology; Tapestry]

Bird, J.B.: Ancient Peruvian textiles from the Collection of the Textile Museum Washington. New York 1965 [Collections; Threads; Mesh Fabric; Weaving; Ornamentation with Solid Material(s)]

Bird, J.B.: "Handspun Yarn Production Rates in the Cuzco Region of Peru", Textile Museum Journal 2 (3), Washington 1968: 9-16 [Ethnography; Threads]

Bird, J.B.: "Heta weaving", Museum of Natural History: Anthropol. Papers Vol.55 Part 6, New York 1979: 425-434 [Analysis; Ethnography; Warp Fabric]

Bird, J.B.: "Fibres and Spinning Procedures in the Andean Area", The J.B.Bird Pre-Columbian Tex. Conf. 1973, Washington 1979: 13-17 [Archaeology; Threads]

Bird, J.B.: "New World Fabric Production and the Distribution of the Backstrap Loom", I.Emery Roundtable on Mus. Textiles 1977, Washington 1979: 115-126 [Ethnography; Weaving]

Bird, J.B.: "A Matched Pair of Archaeological Looms from Peru", Rogers, N. & Stanley, M. (ed.) In Celebration of the Curious Mind. Loveland 1983: 1-8 [Archaeology; Weaving]

Bird, J.B. & Bellinger, L.: Paracas Fabrics and Nazca Needlework. Washington 1954 [Analysis; Archaeology; Mesh Fabric; Plaiting; Warp Fabric; Weaving; Borders; Ornamentation with Solid Material(s)]

Bird, J.B. & Mahler, J.: "America's Oldest Cotton Fabrics: A Report on Textiles Made in Peru", American Fabrics N°20 1951-52, New York 1952: 73-79 [Archaeology; Threads; Mesh Fabric; Warp Fabric; Fabric Processing]

Bird, J.B. & Skinner-Dimitrijevic, M.: "The Care and Conservation of Ethnological and Archaeological Backstrap Looms", Curator Vol.12 N°2, Washington 1964: 99-120 [Ethnography; Archaeology; Weaving]

Bird, J.B. & Skinner-Dimitrijevic, M.: "The technical features of a Middle Horizon tapestry shirt from Peru", Textile Museum Journal 4 (1), Washington 1974: 5-13 [Analysis; Archaeology; Warp Fabric; Borders]

Bird, J.B. et al.: Museums of the Andes. Tokyo / New York 1981 [Archaeology; Mesh Fabric; Plaiting; Weaving; Pile Fabric; Ornamentation with Solid Material(s); Ornamentation with Liquid Material(s); Tapestry]

Bird, J.B.: see also Bennett, W.C.

Bird, J.B.: see also Hyslop, J.S.

Bird, J.B.: see also Rowe, A.P.

Biro, A.& Fondation Dapper, (ed.): Au royaume du signe. Paris 1988 [Ethnography; Ornamentation with Solid Material(s)]

Birrel, V.: The Textile Art. New York 1959 [Analysis; Mesh Fabric; Warp Fabric; Weaving; Pile Fabric; Beadwork; Ornamentation with Solid Material(s); Ornamentation with Liquid Material(s); Tapestry]

Bishop, R. & Coblentz, P.: New discoveries in American quilts. New York 1975 [Collections; Ornamentation with Solid Material(s)]

Bishops, R.: see also Safford, L.

Bjerregaard, L.: "Recent Changes of Pattern in Guatemalan Backstrap Weaving", I.Emery Roundtable on Mus. Textiles 1976, Washington 1977: 133-142 [Ethnography; Weaving]

Bjerregaard, L.: Techniques of Guatemalan Weaving. New York 1979 [Ethnography; Working Instruction; Weaving]

Black, D. (ed.): World Rugs and Carpets. London 1985 [General, Historical; Warp Fabric; Weaving; Pile Fabric; Tapestry]

Black, D. & Loveless, C.: The undiscovered kilim. London 1977 [General, Historical; Warp Fabric; Weaving]

Black, D. & Loveless, C.: Woven Gardens. London 1979 [General, Historical; Pile Fabric; Tapestry]

Black, D. & Loveless, C.: Embroidered Flowers from Thrace to Tartary. London 1981 [Analysis; Collections; Ornamentation with Solid Material(s)]

Blackwood, B.: The Technology of a Modern Stone Age People in New Guinea. Occ. Papers on Technology, Pitt Rivers Museum 3, Oxford 1950 [Ethnography; Plaiting]

Blackwood, B.M.: "Reserve Dyeing in New Guinea", Man Vol. 50, London 1950: 52-55 [Ethnography; Ornamentation with Liquid Material(s)]

Blake, D.P.: see also Barnes, C.

Blakemore, F.: Japanese design through textile patterns. New York 1979 [Ethnography; Ornamentation with Liquid Material(s)]

Blakemore, F.: "Kataami: the Japanese Stencil", Orientations Vol.13 N°1, Hong Kong 1982: 60-65 [Ethnography; Ornamentation with Liquid Material(s)]

Blanchard, M.M.: The Basketry Book. New York 1937 [Working Instruction; Plaiting]

Blasco, M.C.: see also Ramos, L.J.

Blinks, A.: "An unusual pattern-loom from Bangkok", Bull. Needle and Bobbin Club 44, New York 1960: 15-21 [Ethnography; Weaving]

Blinks, A.: "An Unusual Shedding Device from Thailand", I.Emery Roundtable on Mus. Textiles 1977, Washington 1979: 76-77 [Ethnography; Weaving]

Bliss, F.: "Das Kunsthandwerk der Oase Siwa (Ägypten)", Baessler-Archiv NF 30, Berlin 1982: 1-68 [Ethnography; Plaiting; Ornamentation with Solid Material(s)]

Blom, F.: see also Duby, G.

Blomberg, N.J.: Navajo Textiles: The William Randolph Hearst Collection. Tucson 1988 [Ethnography; Collections; Weaving; Tapestry]

Blomberg de Avila, A.: Catalog for an exhibition of Mexican textiles from the Middle Am. Research Inst. at the Dep. of Art, Newcomb Coll. New Orleans 1980 [Collections; Weaving]

Bluhm, E.: "Clothing and Textiles", Martin, P. et al. (ed.) Mogollan Cultural Continuity and Change, Fieldiana Anthrop. 40, Chicago 1952: 231-330 [Analysis; Archaeology; Threads; Mesh Fabric; Plaiting; Weaving]

Bluhm, E. & Grange, R.: "Cordage, Knots and Cordage Artifacts", Martin P. et al. (ed.) Mogollan Cultural Continuity and Change. Fieldiana Anthrop. 40, Chicago 1952: 205-230 [Archaeology; Threads; Mesh Fabric]

Boas, F.: see also Emmons, G.T.

Bodmer, A.: "Spinnen und Weaving im französischen und deutschen Wallis", Romanica Helvetica 459, N°15-17, Zürich 1940 [Folk Art; Threads; Weaving]

Böhmen, H.: see also Brüggemann, W.

Boeve, E.: "Westeuropa, Overijssel: Spinnen von Wolle mit dem Spinnrad in Staphorst", Encyclopaedia Cinematographica 4 (3), Göttingen 1974: 242-252 [Folk Art; Films; Threads]

Bogle, M.: see also Skyring, F.

Bohackova, L.: "Katazome – die japanische Schablonenmusterung der Stoffe", Abhandlungen, Staatl. Mus. Dresden 34, Dresden 1975: 417-428 [Ethnography; Ornamentation with Liquid Material(s)]

Bohnsack, A.: Spinnen und Weben. Hamburg 1981 [General,

Historical; Threads; Weaving]
Bolinder, G.: Die Indianer der tropischen Schneegebirge. Stuttgart 1925 [Ethnography; Threads; Mesh Fabric; Plaiting; Weaving; Pile Fabric]
Bolland, R.: "Weaving a Sumba woman's skirt", Galestin, Th.P. et al. (ed.) Lamak and Malat in Bali and a Sumba Loom. Amsterdam 1956: 49-56 [Ethnography; Weaving]
Bolland, R.: "Three Looms for Tablet Weaving", Tropical Man 3, Amsterdam 1970: 160-189 [Analysis; Ethnography; Weaving]
Bolland, R.: "A comparison between the looms used in Bali and Lombok for weaving sacred cloths", Tropical Man 4, Amsterdam 1971: 171-182 [Ethnography; Weaving]
Bolland, R.: "Het Roller-Ophalergetouw en enkele van zijn variaties", Enkele niet-westerse textieltechnieken, Amsterdam 1975: 17-42 [Analysis; Ethnography; Weaving]
Bolland, R.: "Weaving the pinatkan, a warp-patterned kain bentenan from North Celebes", Gervers, V. (ed.) Studies in Textile History. Toronto 1977: 1-17 [Analysis; Ethnography; Working Instruction; Weaving]
Bolland, R.: "Demonstration of Three Looms", I. Emery Roundtable on Mus. Textiles 1977, Washington 1979: 69-75 [Analysis; Ethnography; Weaving]
Bolland, R.: "Batak bags in weft twining", Gittinger, M. (ed.) To Speak with Cloth. Los Angeles 1989: 213-223 [Analysis; Ethnography; Warp Fabric; Borders]
Bolland, R.: see also Bedaux, R.M.A.
Bolland, R.: see also Claerhout, A.
Bollinger, A.: So kleideten sich die Inka. Institut Lateinamerikaforschung Band 2, St. Gallen 1983 [Archaeology; Threads; Mesh Fabric; Warp Fabric; Weaving; Ornamentation with Solid Material(s); Ornamentation with Liquid Material(s)]
Bolour, Y.: "Knotted Persian Saddle-Covers", Hali 3 (4), London 1981 [Collections; Pile Fabric]
Bombay Government Cottage Industries: Handwoven Textiles: Bombay Government Cottage and small scale Industries. Bombay n.d. [Ethnography; General, Historical; Weaving]
Boralevi, A. & Faccioli, R.: Sumakh: tappati tessuti del Caucaso: Flat-woven carpets of the Caucasus. Firenze 1986 [Collections; General, Historical; Warp Fabric; Borders; Tapestry]
Borgatti, J.: Cloth as metapher: Nigerian Textiles from the Museum of Cultural History. Los Angeles 1983 [Ethnography; Collections; Mesh Fabric; Weaving; Ornamentation with Solid Material(s)]
Bosc du, J.P.: "Contribution à l'étude des tapisseries d'époque Song", Artibus Asiae Vol.11 N°1-2, Ascona 1948: 73-89 [General, Historical; Pile Fabric]
Boser-Sarivaxévanis, R.: "Aperçus sur la teinture à l'indigo en Afrique Occidentale", Verh. der Naturforschenden Gesellschaft 80 (1), 1968, Basel 1969: 152-208 [Analysis; Ethnography; Ornamentation with Liquid Material(s)]
Boser-Sarivaxévanis, R.: "Anciennes techniques textiles artisanales de la Thrace et la Macédonie", Verh. der Naturforschenden Gesellschaft 82 (2) 1971, Basel 1972: 230-241 [Folk Art; Ornamentation with Liquid Material(s)]
Boser-Sarivaxévanis, R.: "Les tissus de l'Afrique Occidentale à dessin réservé par froissage", Ethnologische Zeitschrift Zürich 1, Zürich 1972: 53-60 [Ethnography; Weaving; Borders; Ornamentation with Solid Material(s); Ornamentation with Liquid Material(s)]
Boser-Sarivaxévanis, R.: Les tissus de l'Afrique occidentale. Basler Beiträge zur Ethnologie 13, Basel 1972 [Analysis; Ethnography; Weaving; Borders; Ornamentation with Liquid Material(s)]
Boser-Sarivaxévanis, R.: Textilhandwerk in Westafrika. Basel 1972 [Analysis; Weaving; Ornamentation with Solid Material(s); Ornamentation with Liquid Material(s)]
Boser-Sarivaxévanis, R.: "Weaving", Schweiz. Arbeitslehrerinnen Zeitung 1, Biel 1972 [Ethnography; Weaving]
Boser-Sarivaxévanis, R.: "Recherche sur l'histoire des textiles traditionnels tissés et teints de l'Afrique occidentale", Verhandl. der Naturforschenden Gesellschaft 86, Basel 1975: 301-341 [Analysis; Ethnography; Weaving; Ornamentation with Liquid Material(s)]
Boser-Sarivaxévanis, R.: West African Textiles and Garments. Minneapolis 1980 [Analysis; Ethnography; Weaving; Ornamentation with Liquid Material(s)]
Boser-Sarivaxévanis, R. & Müller, I.: Stickerei: Systematik der Stichformen. Basel 1968 [Classification; Analysis; Ornamentation with Solid Material(s)]
Boser-Sarivaxévanis, R.: see also Bühler, A.
Boulay, R. (ed.): De jade et de nacre.Réunion des musées nationaux, Paris 1990 [Ethnography; Collections; Mesh Fabric; Plaiting]
Bourguet, du, P.: Catalogue des étoffes coptes I. Paris 1964 [Archaeology; Collections; Warp Fabric; Tapestry]
Bouza, Y.L. & Calzada, M.S.: "Aproximación al arte popular en Galicia", Sesena, N. (ed.) Cuardernos del Seminario 22, 23, Sargadelos 1977 [Folk Art; Weaving; Pile Fabric]
Bovis, P.: see also Miles, C.
Bowen, D.D.: see also Fisher, N.
Boyd, E.: "Rio Grande Blankets Containing Hand Spun Cotton Yarn", El Palacio, Winter, Santa Fe 1964: 22-27 [Ethnography; Weaving; Ornamentation with Liquid Material(s)]
Boyd, E.: Popular arts of Spanish New Mexico. New Mexico 1974 [General, Historical; Warp Fabric; Weaving; Ornamentation with Solid Material(s); Ornamentation with Liquid Material(s)]
Boyer, R.M.: "Yoruba Cloths with Regal Names", African Arts Vol.16 N°2, Los Angeles 1983: 42-45 [Ethnography; Weaving; Ornamentation with Solid Material(s)]
Brailaschwili, N.P.: Bedruckte Stoffe. Tiflis 1964 [Folk Art; Ornamentation with Liquid Material(s)]
Brailaschwili, N.P.: "Blaue Tischtücher", VIIe Cong. Int. de Science Ethn. Tiflis 1964 [Folk Art; Ornamentation with Liquid Material(s)]
Brandenbourg, M.: Seminole Patchwork. Batsford 1987 [Ethnography; Ornamentation with Solid Material(s)]
Brandford, J.S.: "The old Saltillo Sarape", I. Emery Roundtable on Museum Textiles 1976, Washington 1977: 271-292 [Ethnography; Warp Fabric; Tapestry]
Brandon, R.M.: Country Textiles of Japan: The Art of Tsutsugaki. New York 1986 [Ethnography; Ornamentation with Liquid Material(s)]
Brandt, von, A.: Fischnetzknoten: aus der Geschichte der Fischnetzherstellung. Schriften der Bundesforschungs-Anstalt, Berlin 1957 [Analysis; Mesh Fabric]
Brandt, von, A.: Netzstricken mit Hakennadeln. Schriften der Bundesforschungs-Anstalt, Berlin 1962 [Analysis; Mesh Fabric]
Branford, J.S.: From the Tree Where the Bark Grows. Chicago 1984 [Ethnography; Collections; Plaiting]
Brasser, T.J.: A basketful of Indian culture change. Mercury Series 22, Ottawa 1975 [Ethnography; Plaiting]
Braulik, A.: Altägyptische Gewebe. Stuttgart 1900 [Analysis; Archaeology; Threads; Weaving; Borders]
Brauns, C.D. & Löffler, L.G.: Mru: Bergbewohner im Grenzgebiet von Bangladesh. Basel 1986 [Analysis; Ethnography; Threads; Plaiting; Weaving]
Braunsberger de Solari, C.: "Una Manta de Taquile: Interpretación de sus Signos", Boletín de Lima N°29, Lima 1983: 57-73 [Ethnography; Weaving]

Braun, Pater, J.: Die liturgische Gewandung in Occident und Orient. n.p. 1907 [General, Historical; Weaving]
Bray, W.: The Gold of El Dorado. London 1987 [Archaeology; Weaving]
Breguet, G. & Martin, J.: Art textile traditionnel d'Indonésie. Los Angeles 1983 [Ethnography; Weaving; Ornamentation with Liquid Material(s)]
Brendler, E.: see also Müller, E.
Brett, G.: European printed Textiles. Victoria and Albert Museum, London 1949 [Folk Art; Collections, Ornamentation with Liquid Material(s)]
Bretz, G.: Die mundartliche Fachsprache der Spinnerei und Weberei in Hetau, Siebenbürgen. Marburg 1977 [Folk Art; Threads; Weaving]
Bridgewater, A.& G.: Guide to Weaving. London 1986 [Collections; Weaving]
Brigham, W.T.: Additional Notes on Hawaiian Feather Work. Mem. Bernice Bishop Mus. 1 (5), Honolulu 1899 [Ethnography; Pile Fabric]
Brigham, W.T.: Mat and Basket Weaving of the Ancient Hawaiians. Mem. Bernice Bishop Mus. 2 (1), Honolulu 1906 [Ethnography; Plaiting]
Brigham, W.T.: The Ancient Hawaiian House. Mem. o. t. B.P.Bishop Mus. Vol.2 N°3, Honolulu 1908 [Ethnography; Threads; Mesh Fabric; Plaiting]
Brigham, W.T.: Mat and basket weaving of the Ancient Hawaiians: Reprint. New York 1974 [Analysis; Mesh Fabric; Plaiting; Weaving; Borders]
Brinckmann, J.: Ein Beitrag zur Kenntnis des japanischen Kunstgewerbes. Aarau 1892 [General, Historical; Ornamentation with Liquid Material(s)]
Britton, N.P.: A study of some early Islamic textiles in the Museum of Fine Arts Boston. Boston 1938 [Archaeology; General, Historical]
Broholm, H.C. & Hald, M.: "To Sprangede Textilarbeijder i Danske Oldfund", Saertryk af Aarbger for nordisk olkyndighed og historie 35, Copenhagen 1935: 29-46 [Analysis; Archaeology; Warp Fabric; Weaving]
Broholm, H.C. & Hald, M.: Costumes of the Bronze Age in Denmark. Copenhagen 1940 [Archaeology; Warp Fabric; Weaving]
Broholm, H.C. & Hald, M.: Bronze Age Fashion. Copenhagen 1948 [Archaeology; Mesh Fabric; Warp Fabric; Weaving; Ornamentation with Solid Material(s)]
Brommer, B. et al.: 3000 jaar weven in de Andes. Gemeente Museum Helmond, Helmond 1988 [Analysis; Archaeology; Collections; Threads; Plaiting; Half-weaving; Weaving; Pile Fabric; Borders; Ornamentation with Solid Material(s); Tapestry]
Brotherton, G.: Rush and Leafcraft. Boston 1977 [Working Instruction; Plaiting]
Broudy, E.: The Book of Looms. New York 1979 [Analysis; Plaiting; Warp Fabric; Weaving]
Brown, J.A.: "The Potential of Systematic Collections for Archaeological Research", Annales of the New York Academy of Science Vol. 376, New York 1981: 65-75 [Archaeology; Plaiting]
Bruce, S.L.: "Textile Miniatures from Pacatnamu, Peru", Rowe, A.P. (ed.) J.B. Bird Conf. on Andean Textiles 1984, Washington 1986: 183-204 [Archaeology; Weaving]
Brüggemann, W. & Böhmen, H.: Teppiche der Bauern und Nomaden in Anatolien. Hannover 1980 [Collections; Pile Fabric]
Brügger, M.: Die primären textilen Techniken der Neu-Hebriden und Banks- Insulaner. Basel 1947 [Classification; Analysis; Ethnography; Mesh Fabric; Plaiting]
Bruignac, de, V. et al. (ed.): Teinture, Expression de la Tradition en Afrique Noire. Mulhouse 1982 [Ethnography; Ornamentation with Liquid Material(s)]
Brunner-Littmann, B. & Hahn, R.: Motiv und Ornament: Textilien aus der Sammlung des Rätischen Museums Chur. Schriftenreihe des Rätischen Museums N°34, Chur 1988 [Folk Art; Weaving; Ornamentation with Solid Material(s)]
Bryan, N.G. & Young, S.: Navajo Native Dyes and their Preparation and Use. Indian Handicrafts N°2, Los Angeles 1940 [Ethnography]
Bryon, A.: see also Swanson, E.
Bubolz-Eicher, J.: Nigerian Handcrafted Textiles. University of Ife Press, Ile-Ife n.d. [Ethnography; Weaving]
Bubolz-Eicher, J.: African Dress. Michigan 1969 [Ethnography]
Bubolz-Eicher, J. & Erekosima, T.V.: Pelet bite: Kalabari cut-thread cloth. St.Paul 1982 [Ethnography; Ornamentation with Solid Material(s)]
Bubolz-Eicher, J.: see also Erekosima, T.V.
Buck, P.H: "On the Maori art of weaving cloaks, capes and kilts", Dominion Museum Bull. 3, 1911: 69-90 [Ethnography; Warp Fabric]
Buck, P.H: "The evolution of Maori clothing", Journ. of the Polynesian Soc. Wellington 33, 1924/25/26, Wellington 1924: 24 ff. [Ethnography; Warp Fabric]
Buck, P.H.: Arts and Crafts of the Cook Islands. B.P.Bishop Mus. Bull. 179, Honolulu 1944 [Analysis; Ethnography; Mesh Fabric; Plaiting; Weaving; Pile Fabric; Borders]
Buck, P.H.: Material Culture of the Kapingamarangi. Honolulu 1950 [Ethnography; Plaiting]
Buck, P.H.: Arts and Crafts of Hawai. B.P. Bishop Mus. Special Publ. 45, Honolulu 1957 [Analysis; Ethnography; Mesh Fabric; Plaiting; Pile Fabric; Borders]
Buckle, M.: see also Day, L.F.
Bühler, A.: "Die Entwicklung des Webens bei den Naturvölkern", Ciba Rundschau 25, Basel 1938: 912-922 [Classification; Warp Fabric; Weaving]
Bühler, A.: "Die Herstellung von Ikattüchern auf der Insel Rote", Verh. der Naturforschenden Gesellschaft Band L, Basel 1939 [Analysis; Ethnography; Ornamentation with Liquid Material(s)]
Bühler, A.: "Ikatten", Ciba Rundschau 51 N°8, Basel 1941 [Analysis; Ornamentation with Liquid Material(s)]
Bühler, A.: Materialien zur Kenntnis der Ikattechnik. Int. Archiv für Ethnographie 43 Suppl. Band, Leiden 1943 [Classification; Analysis; Ethnography; Weaving; Ornamentation with Liquid Material(s)]
Bühler, A.: "Die Reservemusterungen: Versuch einer zusammenfassenden Betrachtung ihrer Technik, Entstehung und Herkunft", Acta Tropica 3, Basel 1946: 242-271, 322-366 [Ethnography; Ornamentation with Liquid Material(s)]
Bühler, A.: Indonesische Gewebe. Gewerbemuseum Basel, Basel 1947 [Ethnography; Weaving]
Bühler, A.: "Sumba-Expedition des Museums für Völkerkunde und des Naturhistorischen Museums in Basel", Verh. der Naturforschenden Gesell. Basel Band 62, Basel 1951 [Ethnography; Ornamentation with Solid Material(s); Ornamentation with Liquid Material(s)]
Bühler, A.: "Plangi", Ciba Rundschau 111, Basel 1953: 4062-4083 [Classification; Ornamentation with Liquid Material(s)]
Bühler, A.: Primitive Stoffmusterung. Führer durch das Museum für Völkerkunde Basel, Basel 1953 [Analysis; Collections; Ornamentation with Liquid Material(s)]
Bühler, A.: "Patola Influences in Southeast Asia", Journal of Indian Textiles IV 55, N°129, 1959: 4-47 [Ethnography; Ornamentation with Liquid Material(s)]

Bühler, A.: "Shibori und Kasuri", Folk 5, Kopenhagen 1963: 45-64 [Analysis; Ethnography; Ornamentation with Liquid Material(s)]
Bühler, A.: Plangi. Führer durch das Museum für Völkerkunde Basel 58, Basel 1969 [Analysis; Collections; Ornamentation with Liquid Material(s)]
Bühler, A.: Vokabular der Textiltechniken. Centre Int. d'Etude Textiles Anciens, Lyon 1971 [Bühler, A.: Ikat, Plangi, Batik. Basel 1972 [Classification; Threads; Weaving; Ornamentation with Liquid Material(s)]
Bühler, A.: "Hanfverarbeitung und Batik bei den Meau in Nordthailand", Ethnologische Zeitschrift Zürich 1, Zürich 1972:61-82 [Ethnography; Threads; Weaving, Ornamentation with Liquid Material(s)]
Bühler, A.: Clamp Resist Dyeing of Fabrics. Ahmedabad 1977 [Ethnography; Ornamentation with Liquid Material(s)]
Bühler, A. & Boser-Sarivaxévanis, R.: Exposition de tissus japonais. Mulhouse 1969 [Ethnography; Collections; Ornamentation with Liquid Material(s)]
Bühler, A. & Bühler-Oppenheim, K.: Die Textiliensammlung Fritz Iklé-Huber. Denkschrift d. Naturforschenden Gesell. 78, Zürich 1948 [Classification; Mesh Fabric; Plaiting; Warp Fabric; Half-weaving; Weaving; Pile Fabric; Borders; Ornamentation with Solid Material(s); Ornamentation with Liquid Material(s)]
Bühler, A. & Fischer, E.: Musterung von Stoffen mit Hilfe von Pressschablonen. Basler Beiträge zur Ethnologie 16, Basel 1974 [Ethnography; Ornamentation with Liquid Material(s)]
Bühler, A. & Fischer, E.: The Patola of Gujarat: Double Ikat in India. Basel 1979 [Analysis; Ethnography; Ornamentation with Liquid Material(s)]
Bühler, A. & Ramseyer-Gygi, U.& N.: Patola und geringsing: Zeremonialtücher aus Indien und Indonesien. Basel 1975 [Analysis; Ethnography; Weaving; Ornamentation with Liquid Material(s)]
Bühler, A. et al.: "Die Textilsammlung im Museum für Völkerkunde Basel", Schweiz. Arbeitslehrerinnen Zeitung 1, Biel 1972: 2-22 [Analysis; Collections; Plaiting; Weaving; Ornamentation with Solid Material(s); Ornamentation with Liquid Material(s)]
Bühler-Oppenheim, K.: Primäre textile Techniken. Ciba Rundschau 73, Basel 1947 [Classification; Mesh Fabric; Plaiting; Half-weaving; Weaving]
Bühler-Oppenheim, K.: "Textiltechnologischer Beitrag: Die Technik der Ziertasche aus Kaup", Annali Lateranensi Vol. 9, Rom 1945: 298-302 [Ethnography; Mesh Fabric]
Bühler-Oppenheim, K.: see also Bühler, A.
Bültzingslöwen, von, R. & Lehmann, E.: Nichtgewebte Textilien vor 1400. Bisingen 1951 [Archaeology; Mesh Fabric]
Bültzingslöwen, von, R.: see also Lehmann, E.
Buferd, N. B.: see also Cooper, P.
Buff, R.: Bindungslehre – ein Webmusterbuch. Bern 1985 [Working Instruction; Weaving]
Bunting, E-J.W.: Sindhi tombs and textiles: The persistence of pattern. Maxwell Mus. Anthro. Publ. Albuquerque 1980 [General, Historical; Ornamentation with Solid Material(s); Ornamentation with Liquid Material(s)]
Burch, E.S.: "Kotzebue Sound Eskimo", Handbook of North Am. Indians 5, Washington 1984: 301-319 [Ethnography; Mesh Fabric]
Burgess, J.T.: Die praktische Knotenfibel. München 1981 [Working Instruction; Threads; Mesh Fabric; Plaiting; Weaving]
Burman, B.K.R.: Textile dyeing and hand-painting in Madhya Pradesh. Census of India, Monograph Series Vol.1 Part 7 N°3,61, New Delhi 1970 [Ethnography; Ornamentation with Solid Material(s); Ornamentation with Liquid Material(s)]
Burnham, D.K.: "Constructions used by Jacquard coverlet weavers in Ontario", Gervers, V. (ed.) Studies in Textile History. Toronto 1977: 34-40 [Analysis; Weaving]
Burnham, D.K.: "Braided "Arrow" Sashes of Quebec", I.Emery Roundtable on Mus. Textiles 1976, Washington 1977: 356-365 [Ethnography; Folk Art; Plaiting; Beadwork]
Burnham, D.K.: Warp and Weft, a Textile Terminology. Toronto 1980 [Classification; Analysis; Threads; Plaiting; Warp Fabric; Weaving; Pile Fabric; Beadwork; Borders; Ornamentation with Solid Material(s); Ornamentation with Liquid Material(s); Tapestry]
Burnham, D.K.: The comfortable Arts: Traditional spinning and weaving in Canada. Ottawa 1981 [Analysis; Folk Art; Threads; Weaving; Beadwork]
Burnham, D.K.: Unlike the lilies: Doukhobor textile traditions in Canada. Royal Ontario Museum, Toronto 1986 [Analysis; Folk Art; Threads; Weaving; Pile Fabric; Ornamentation with Solid Material(s)]
Burnham, H.B.: Chinese Velvets. Occ. Papers Art and Archaeology 2, Toronto 1959 [Analysis; Pile Fabric]
Burnham, H.B.: "Four Looms", Annual Royal Ontario Museum, Toronto 1962: 77-128 [Ethnography; Weaving]
Burnham, H.B.: Japanese Country Textiles. Toronto 1965 [Ethnography; Weaving]
Burnham, H.B.: Canadian Textiles: 1750-1900. Toronto 1965 [Folk Art; Collections]
Burnham, H.B.: see also Hoffmann, M.
Burrows, L.B.: Note on Indian Chikan Works. Calcutta 1921 [General, Historical; Ornamentation with Solid Material(s)]
Buser-Abt, V.: Exporttextilien aus Gujarat. Basel 1977 [Ethnography; Ornamentation with Liquid Material(s)]
Bushell, S.W.: Chinese Art. Victoria and Albert Museum, London 1924 [General, Historical; Weaving; Pile Fabric; Ornamentation with Solid Material(s)]
Bussagli, M.: Cotton and silk making in Manchu China. New York 1980 [General, Historical; Threads]

Cachot, R.C.: Paracas: Cultural Elements. Lima 1949 [Archaeology; Weaving]
Cadoux, A.M.: "Asian Domestic Embroideries", Arts of Asia Vol.20 N°3, Hong Kong 1990: 138-145 [Ethnography; Ornamentation with Solid Material(s)]
Cahlander, A.: Sling braiding of the Andes. Weaver's Journal Monograph IV, Boulder 1980 [Classification; Analysis; Working Instruction; Threads; Mesh Fabric; Plaiting; Warp Fabric; Pile Fabric]
Cahlander, A. & Baizerman, S.: Double-woven treasures from old Peru. St.Paul 1985 [Analysis; Working Instruction; Weaving]
Cahlander, A. & Cason, M.: The Art of Bolivian Highland Weaving. New York 1976 [Analysis; Ethnography; Working Instruction; Plaiting; Weaving]
Cahlander, A. et al.: Bolivian tubular edging and crossed warp techniques. Weaver's Journal Monograph 1, Boulder 1978 [Analysis; Ethnography; Weaving]
Califano, M.: Etnografía de los Mashco. Buenos Aires 1982 [Analysis; Ethnography; Mesh Fabric; Plaiting; Pile Fabric]
Calzada, M.S.: see also Bouza, Y.L.
Câmara Cascudo, da, L.: Rede de dormir. Rio de Janeiro 1959 [Ethnography; Mesh Fabric; Warp Fabric; Weaving]
Cammann, N.F.: Embroidery: Designs from American Indian Art. London 1973 [Working Instruction; Ornamentation with Solid Material(s)]
Cammann, S.: "Chinese Influence in Colonial Peruvian Tapestries", Textile Museum Journal Vol.1 N°3, Washington 1964 [Ar-

chaeology; Weaving]
Campbell, A.: "Notes on the state of the arts of cotton, spinning, printing and dyeing in Nepal", Journ. of the Asiatic Soc. of Bengal 5, 1836: 219-227 [Ethnography; Threads; Weaving; Ornamentation with Liquid Material(s)]
Campbell, M. & Pongnoi, N.: From the hands of the hills. Hong Kong 1978 [Analysis; Ethnography; Threads; Mesh Fabric; Plaiting; Weaving; Ornamentation with Solid Material(s); Ornamentation with Liquid Material(s)]
Cannizzo, J.: Into the Heart of Africa. Toronto 1969 [Ethnography; Mesh Fabric; Plaiting; Weaving; Pile Fabric; Beadwork]
Cannizzo, J.: "Gara Cloth by Senesse Tarawallie", African Arts Vol.16 N°4, Los Angeles 1983: 60-64 [Ethnography; Ornamentation with Liquid Material(s)]
Cardale de Schrimpff, M.: Techniques of hand-weaving and allied arts in Colombia. St. Hughs 1972 [Ethnography; Threads; Mesh Fabric; Plaiting; Warp Fabric; Half-weaving; Weaving; Beadwork; Borders; Ornamentation with Liquid Material(s)]
Cardale de Schrimpff, M.: "Textiles arqueológicos de Nariño", Revista Colombiana de Antropología Vol. 21, 1977-78, Bogotá 1977: 245-282 [Archaeology; Warp Fabric, Weaving]
Cardale de Schrimpff, M.: "Weaving and other Indigenous Textile Techniques in Colombia", I. Emery Roundtable on Mus. Textiles 1976, Washington 1977: 44-60 [Ethnography; Mesh Fabric; Plaiting; Warp Fabric; Weaving]
Cardale de Schrimpff, M.: "Informe preliminar sobre una mochila Muisca hallada en la región de Pisba", Bol. Museo del Oro 1, Bogotá 1978: 18-21 [Archaeology; Mesh Fabric; Plaiting; Weaving]
Cardale de Schrimpff, M.: "Painted Textiles from Caves in the Eastern Cordillera, Colombia", The J.B.Bird Precolumbian Textile Conf. 1984, Washington 1986: 205-217 [Archaeology; Ornamentation with Liquid Material(s)]
Cardale de Schrimpff, M.: "Informe preliminar sobre el hallazgo de textiles y otros elementos perecederos, conservados en cuevas en Purnia", Boletín de Arqueología N°3, Año 2, Bogotá 1987: 3-23 [Archaeology; Mesh Fabric; Plaiting; Warp Fabric; Weaving]
Cardale de Schrimpff, M.: "Nota sobre un fragmento de tela hallado en la hoya del Quindio", Museo del Oro, Boletín N°20, Bogotá 1988: 13-15 [Archaeology; Weaving]
Cardale de Schrimpff, M.: "Textiles arqueológicos del Bajo Río San Jorge", Museo del Oro, Boletín N°20, Bogotá 1988: 88-95 [Analysis; Archaeology]
Cardale de Schrimpff, M. & Falchetti de Sáenz, A.M: "Objetos prehispánicos de madera procedentes del altiplano nariñense, Colombia", Bol. Museo del Oro 3, Bogotá 1980: 1-15 [Archaeology; Plaiting; Weaving]
Cardenas, H. et al.: Artesanía Textil Andina. Lima 1988 [Ethnography; Folk Art; Threads; Weaving]
Cardoso, L. et al.: Alguns aspectos da tecelagem Manjaca. Bissau 1988 [Ethnography; Weaving]
Carreira, A.: Panaria. Lisboa 1968 [Ethnography; Threads; Weaving]
Carter, T.F.: The invention of printing in China and its spread westward. n.p., n.d. [Archaeology; Ornamentation with Liquid Material(s)]
Carvajal, M.: "Cerámica y restos indígenas de Santander", Estudio 7, 83-84, Santander 1938 [Archaeology; Weaving]
Casagrande, J.B.: "Looms of Otavalo", Natural History 86 (8), New York 1977: 48-59 [Ethnography; Weaving]
Cason, M.: see also Cahlander, A.
Caspar, F.: Die Tupari: ein Indianerstamm in Westbrasilien. Berlin 1975 [Analysis; Ethnography; Threads; Mesh Fabric; Plaiting; Warp Fabric]
Castany Saladrigas, F.: Análisis de tejidos. Barcelona 1944 [Weaving]
Castany Saladrigas, F.: Diccionario de tejidos. Barcelona 1949 [Weaving]
Castello, C.M.: see also Yturbide, M.T.
Castello Yturbide, T. & Martinez del Rio, de, R.: El rebozo. Artes de Mexico 142, Repr. Mexico 1979 [Collections; Weaving; Borders; Ornamentation with Liquid Material(s)]
Castello Yturbide, T.: see also Mapelli Mozzi, C.
Castillon, du, M.F.: see also Noppe, C.
Castle, N.: "A peruvian crossed-warp weave", Textile Museum Journal 4 (4), Washington 1977: 61-70 [Analysis; Warp Fabric; Weaving]
Català, R.: see also Pelanzy, A.
Català Roca, F.: see also Espejel, C.
Caulfeild, S.T.A. & Saward, B.C.: Dictionary of Needlework. London 1882 [Analysis; Working Instruction; Mesh Fabric; Plaiting; Warp Fabric; Weaving; Ornamentation with Solid Material(s)]
Cavallo, A.S: A festival of fibres. Masterworks of textile art from the collection of the Honolulu Academy of Arts. Honolulu 1977 [General, Historical; Threads]
Cerny, C.: Navajo pictorial weaving. New Mexico 1975 [Collections; Tapestry]
Cervellino, M.: "Colorantes vegetales chilenos y textiles Mapuches", Actas d. 7 Cong. de Arqueología de Chile 1979, Santiago 1979: 193-215 [Ethnography; Plaiting; Weaving]
Chamberlain, M. & Crookelt, C.: Beyond Weaving. New York 1974 [Working Instruction; Mesh Fabric; Plaiting]
Chandra, M.: A Handbook to the Indian Art Collection. Prince of Wales Museum of Western India, Bombay 1938 [Ethnography; Collections; Ornamentation with Liquid Material(s)]
Chantreaux, G.: Le tissage sur métier de haute lisse à Ait-Hichem et dans le Haut-Sébaou. Rev. Africaine N°85, Alger 1941 [Ethnography; Weaving]
Chantreaux, G.: "Les tissages décorés chez les Beni-Mguild", Hésperis Tome 32, Paris 1945: 19-33 [Ethnography; Weaving]
Chantreaux, G.: "Notes sur un procédé de tissage torsadé", Héspéris Tome 33, Paris 1946: 65-81 [Ethnography; Warp Fabric]
Chao, K.: The Development of Cotton Textile Production in China. Harvard East As. Monogr. 74, Cambridge 1977 [Ethnography; Weaving]
Chapman, S.D.: see also Ponting, K.G.
Chattopadhyaya, K.: Indian Handicrafts. New Delhi 1963 [Ethnography; Weaving; Pile Fabric; Ornamentation with Solid Material(s); Ornamentation with Liquid Material(s)]
Chattopadhyaya, K.: "Origins and Development of Embroidery in our Land", Marg Vol. 17, Bombay 1964: 5-10 [Ethnography; General, Historical; Ornamentation with Solid Material(s)]
Chattopadhyaya, K.: "The origin of pile carpets and their development in India", Marg Vol.18. N°4, Bombay 1965 [Ethnography; General, Historical; Pile Fabric]
Chattopadhyaya, K.: Carpets and Floor Coverings of India. Bombay 1969 [Ethnography; General, Historical; Pile Fabric]
Chattopadhyaya, K.: The glory of Indian handicrafts. New Delhi 1976 [Ethnography; General, Historical; Plaiting; Weaving; Ornamentation with Solid Material(s)]
Chattopadhyaya, K.: Indian embroidery. New Delhi 1977 [Ethnography; Ornamentation with Solid Material(s)]
Chattopadhyaya, K.P.: "An essay on the history of the Newar culture", Journ. and Proc. Asiatic Soc. of Bengal 19 (10), 1923: 465-560 [Ethnography; Weaving]

Chaumeil, J.P.: Nihamwo: Los Yagua del Nor-Oriente Peruano. Lima 1987 [Ethnography; Mesh Fabric; Plaiting]
Chaves, A.: "Trama y urdimbre en la historia del tejido muisca", Lampana 94, Vol.12, 1984 [Archaeology; Weaving]
Cheesman, P.: "The Antique Weavings of the Lao Neua", Arts of Asia Vol.12 N°4, Hong Kong 1982: 120-125 [Ethnography; Weaving]
Cheesman, P.: Lao textiles: ancient symbols – living art. Bangkok 1988 [Analysis; Ethnography; Weaving; Ornamentation with Liquid Material(s)]
Cheesman, P.: see also Prangwatthanakun, S.
Cherblanc, E.: "Mémoire sur l'invention du tissu", Histoire Générale du Tissu Vol 1, Paris 1935 [Archaeology; Weaving]
Cherblanc, E.: Etude critique d'après les textes, les monuments figurés et les survivances supposées du tissu. Histoire Générale du Tissu Vol 2, Paris 1937 [Archaeology; Pile Fabric; Fabric Processing]
Chertudi, S. & Nardi, R.L.J.: "El tejido en Santiago del Estero", Cuadernos del Inst. Nac. Inv. Folkl. 1, Buenos Aires 1960: 53-82 [Analysis; Ethnography; Weaving]
Chertudi, S. & Nardi, R.L.J.: "Tejidos Araucanos en la Argentina", Cuadernos del Inst. Nac. Inv. Folkl. 2, Buenos Aires 1961: 97-182 [Analysis; Ethnography; Weaving; Pile Fabric; Ornamentation with Liquid Material(s)]
Chesley, B.: Man is a weaver. New York 1949 [General, Historical; Threads; Weaving]
Chevallier, D.: "Les tissus ikatés d'Alep et de Damas", Revue Syria 39, Paris 1962: 300-324 [Ethnography; Ornamentation with Liquid Material(s)]
Chevallier, D.: "Techniques et societé en Syrie", Bull. d'Etudes Orient. Inst. Fr. Tome 18, 63-64, Damas 1964: 85-93 [Ethnography; Threads]
Chishti, R.K. & Sanyal, A.: Saris of India: Madhya Pradesh. New Delhi 1989 [Ethnography; Weaving; Ornamentation with Liquid Material(s)]
Chongkol, C.: "Textiles and Costumes in Thailand", Arts of Asia Vol.12 N°6, Hong Kong 1982: 121-131 [Ethnography; Ornamentation with Solid Material(s); Ornamentation with Liquid Material(s)]
Chor Lin, L.: Ancestral Ships: Lampung Culture. Nat. Mus. Singapore 1987 [Ethnography; Weaving]
Christa, C.: see also Davidson, M.
Christensen, B.: "Otomi Looms and Quechquemitls from San Pablito, State of Puebla and from Santa Ana Huetlalpan, State of Hidalgo, Mexico", I.Emery Roundtable on Mus. Textiles 1977, Washington 1979: 160-169 [Analysis; Ethnography; Weaving]
Chung, Y.Y.: The Art of oriental embroidery. New York 1979 [Analysis; Ethnography; Ornamentation with Solid Material(s)]
Churcher, E. & Gloor, V.: "Peruanisches Schnurflechten", Schweiz. Arbeitslehrerinnen Zeitung 9, N°69, Biel 1986: 10-14 [Working Instruction; Plaiting]
Ciruzzi, S.: see also Laurencich-Minelli, L.
Cisneros, H.J.: Inventario de diseños en tejidos indígenas de la provincia de Imbabura. Otavalo 1981 [Ethnography; Weaving]
Clabburn, P.: Samplers. Aylesbury 1977 [Archaeology; Ornamentation with Solid Material(s)]
Clabburn, P.: Masterpieces of embroidery. Oxford 1984 [General, Historical; Ornamentation with Solid Material(s)]
Clabburn, P.: Shawls in imitation of the Indian. Aylesbury 1987 [Archaeology; Ornamentation with Liquid Material(s)]
Claerhout, A.: "Uitsparingstechnieken voor Weefselversiering", Enkele niet-westerse textieltechnieken. Amsterdam 1975: 1-16 [Analysis; Ethnography; Ornamentation with Liquid Material(s)]
Claerhout, A.& Bolland, R. (ed.): Enkele niet-westerse textieltechnieken. Amsterdam 1975 [Analysis; Ethnography; Weaving; Ornamentation with Liquid Material(s)]
Claerhout, A.G.: Exposition Textiles Exotiques. Nivelles 1964 [Analysis; Collections; Ornamentation with Liquid Material(s)]
Clark, B.: see also O'Neale, L.M.
Clarke, J.D.: "Ilorin weaving", Nigeria N°14, London 1938: 121-124 [Ethnography; Weaving]
Claude, J.H.: "Los tejidos araucanos", Revista Chilena 12, N°104-104, Santiago 1928 [Ethnography; Weaving]
Claus, G.J.M.: see also Rossie, J.P.
Clements-Scholtz, S.: Prehistoric Plies: A Structural and Comparative Analysis of Cordage, Netting, Basketry and Fabric from Ozark Bluff Shelters. Arkansas Arch. Survey Research Series N°9, Fayetteville 1975 [Archaeology; Threads; Mesh Fabric; Plaiting; Borders]
Clerc-Junier, C.: see also Jelmini, J.P.
Clifford, L.I.: Card Weaving. Illinois 1947 [Working Instruction; Weaving]
Coblentz, P.: see also Bishop, R.
Cocco, P.L.: Iyëwei-teri: Quince años entre los yanomamos. Carácas 1972 [Ethnography; Plaiting; Warp Fabric]
Coffinet, J.: see also Pianzola, M.
Cohen, E.: "Hmong (Meo) Commercialized Refugee Art: From Ornament to Picture", Eban, D. (ed.) Art as Means of Communication in Pre-Literate Societies. Jerusalem 1990: 51-96 [Ethnography; Ornamentation with Solid Material(s); Ornamentation with Liquid Material(s)]
Cohen, J.: An investigation of contemporary weaving of the Peruvian Indians. MA Thesis, Yale Univ. 1957 [Ethnography; Weaving]
Cohen, R.: Contemporary art of Canada: The western Subarctic. Royal Ontario Museum, Toronto 1977 [Ethnography; Ornamentation with Solid Material(s)]
Cohen, S.: The unappreciated Dhurrie. London 1982 [Ethnography; Tapestry]
Colby, A.: Patchwork. London 1958 [Folk Art; Working Instruction; Ornamentation with Solid Material(s)]
Cole, H.M. & Ross, D.H.: The Arts of Ghana. Los Angeles 1977 [Ethnography; Weaving; Ornamentation with Solid Material(s)]
Coleman, E.A. & Sonday, M.: "Practical Definitions for the three Openwork Techniques", Textile Museum Journal Vol.4 N°4, Washington 1974: 35-40 [Classification; Ornamentation with Solid Material(s)]
Collin, M.: "Sydda vantar", Fataburen Häft 2, Styresman 1917 [Folk Art; Mesh Fabric]
Collin, M.: Skånsk Konstvävnad. Lund 1924 [Folk Art; Archaeology; Warp Fabric; Weaving; Pile Fabric]
Collings, J.L.: "Basketry from Foundation Past", Collings, J.L. (ed.) Harmony by Hand. San Francisco 1987: 23-47 [Analysis; Ethnography; Plaiting]
Collingwood, P.: "Sprang", Handweaver and Craftsman 15, New York 1964 [Classification; Warp Fabric]
Collingwood, P.: The Techniques of Rug-Weaving. London 1968 [Classification; Plaiting; Warp Fabric; Weaving; Pile Fabric; Borders]
Collingwood, P.: Rugs and wall-hangings by Peter Collingwood. Victoria and Albert Museum, London 1969 [Warp Fabric; Pile Fabric]
Collingwood, P.: The Techniques of Sprang. London 1974 [Classification; Analysis; Archaeology; Working Instruction; Mesh Fabric; Warp Fabric]
Collingwood, P.: The Techniques of Tablet-Weaving. London

1982 [Analysis; Working Instruction; Weaving]
Collingwood, P.: Textile and weaving structures. London 1987 [Analysis; Ethnography; Mesh Fabric; Plaiting; Half-weaving; Weaving; Pile Fabric; Beadwork; Borders; Ornamentation with Solid Material(s); Tapestry]
Collingwood, P.: Textile Strukturen. Bern 1988 [Analysis; Ethnography; Mesh Fabric; Plaiting; HalfWeaving; Weaving; Pile Fabric; Beadwork; Borders; Ornamentation with Solid Material(s); Tapestry]
Colyer Ross, H.: L'art du costume de l'Arabie. Montreux 1989 [Analysis; Plaiting; Ornamentation with Solid Material(s)]
Combe, E.: Une institution de l'état musulman. Revue des conférences françaises en Orient Jb. 2 N°2, Kairo 1947 [Ethnography; Weaving]
Combe, E.: Introduction à l'étude des tissus musulmans. Revue des conférences françaises en Orient Jb. 12 N°5, Kairo 1948 [Ethnography; Weaving]
Conklin, W.J.: "Chavin textiles and the origin of Peruvian weaving", Textile Museum Journal 3 (2), Washington 1971: 13-19 [Archaeology; Warp Fabric]
Conklin, W.J.: "Pampa Gramalote Textiles", I.Emery Roundtable on Mus. Textiles 1974, Washington 1975: 77-92 [Archaeology; Mesh Fabric; Warp Fabric]
Conklin, W.J.: "Precolumbian South American textiles", I.Emery Roundtable on Mus. Textiles 1974, Washington 1975: 17-33 [Archaeology]
Conklin, W.J.: "Estructura de los tejidos moche", Ravines (ed.) Tecnología Andina. Lima 1978: 299-335 [Archaeology; Weaving]
Conklin, W.J.: "The revolutionary weaving inventions of the Early Horizon", Nawpa Pacha 16, Berkeley 1978: 1-12 [Archaeology; Weaving]
Conklin, W.J.: "Moche Textile Structures", Bird, J. (ed.) The J.B.Bird Precolumbian Textile Conf. 1973, Washington 1979: 155-164 [Analysis; Archaeology; Weaving]
Conn, R.: "Influences of technique upon textile design: Some Examples from the Great Lakes Region", I.Emery Roundtable on Mus. Textiles 1976, Washington 1977: 519-528 [Plaiting; Warp Fabric; Beadwork; Ornamentation with Solid Material(s)]
Connor, J.: "A descriptive classification of Maori fabrics", Journal of the Polyn. Soc. 92, Wellington 1983: 189-213 [Classification; Analysis; Ethnography; Threads; Mesh Fabric; Plaiting]
Cook de Leonard, C. et al.: Indumentaria mexicana. Artes de Mexico 13 (77/78), Mexico 1966 [Ethnography; General, Historical; Weaving]
Coomaraswamy, A.K.: The Arts and Crafts of India and Ceylon. New York 1964 [General, Historical; Ornamentation with Solid Material(s)]
Cooper, P. & Buferd, N. B.: The quilters: Women and domestic Art. New York 1978 [Folk Art; Ornamentation with Solid Material(s)]
Cootner, C.: Flat-woven textiles. Washington 1981 [Analysis; Collections; Weaving; Pile Fabric; Tapestry]
Corbett, J.M.: see also Willey, G.
Cordry, D.B. & Cordry, D.M.: Costumes and Textiles of the Aztec Indians of the Cuetzalán Region, Puebla, Mexico. Southwest Museum Papers N°14, Los Angeles 1940 [Ethnography; Weaving]
Cordry, D.B. & Cordry, D.M.: Costumes and Weaving of the Zoque Indians of Chiapas, Mexico. Southwest Museum Papers 15, Los Angeles 1941 [Ethnography; Mesh Fabric; Weaving]
Cordry, D.B. & Cordry, D.M.: Mexican Indian Costumes. London 1973 [Analysis; Ethnography; Threads; Mesh Fabric; Plaiting; Weaving; Ornamentation with Liquid Material(s)]
Cordry, D.M.: see also Cordry, D.B.
Corey, P.L.: Faces, Voices & Dreams. Alaska 1987 [Analysis; Ethnography; Collections; Plaiting; Pile Fabric]
Cornet, J.: Art Royal Kuba. Milano 1982 [Analysis; Ethnography; Plaiting; Weaving; Ornamentation with Solid Material(s)]
Corrie, R.W.: see also Pauly, S.B.
Corrie Newman, S.: Indian Basket Weaving. Flagstaff 1985 [Analysis; Ethnography; Working Instruction; Plaiting]
Cortes Moreno, E.: "Industria Textil Precolombina Colombiana", Museo del Oro N°18, Bogotá 1987 [Archaeology; Mesh Fabric; Weaving; Pile Fabric; Tapestry]
Costa Fénelon, M.H. & Monteiro, D.: "Dois estilos plumarios: Barroco e Classico", Revista Museu Paulista N.S. Vol. 18, S_o Paulo 1968: 121-143 [Ethnography; Pile Fabric]
Couch del Deo, J.: see also Gallinger-Tod, O.
Coulin-Weibel, A.: The Elsberg collection of Peruvian Textiles. Bull. Detroit Inst. Arts 19 (4), Detroit 1940 [Archaeology; Collections]
Coulin-Weibel, A.: 2000 years of Silk-Weaving. New York 1944 [Collections; Weaving]
Coulin-Weibel, A.: 2000 years of Tapestry Weaving: A loan exhibition. Baltimore 1952 [Archaeology; Collections; Weaving; Tapestry]
Cousin, F.: "Blouses brodées du Kutch", Objets et Mondes 12, Paris 1972: 287-311 [Analysis; Ethnography; Ornamentation with Solid Material(s); Fabric Processing]
Cousin, F.: "Teinture à réserves ligaturées et décor de voiles dans le Kutch", Objets et Mondes Vol.15 N°1, Paris 1975 [Ethnography; Ornamentation with Liquid Material(s)]
Cousin, F.: "Lumière et ombre, bleu et rouge: Les azark du Sind", Objets et Mondes 16, Paris 1976: 65-78 [Ethnography; Ornamentation with Liquid Material(s)]
Cousin, F.: Tissus imprimés du Rajasthan. Paris 1986 [Ethnography; Ornamentation with Solid Material(s)]
Couvreur, A.J.L. & Goslings, B.M.: De timorgroep en de Zuid-Western Eilanden: Weven en ikatten. Gids in het Volkenkundig Mus. N°10, Amsterdam n.d. [Ethnography; Ornamentation with Liquid Material(s)]
Cox, T.: Notes on Applied Work and Patchwork. London 1953 [Ornamentation with Solid Material(s)]
Crawford, A.L: Aida: Life and Ceremony of the Gogodala. Nat. Cultural Council of Papua New Guinea, Bathurst 1981 [Ethnography; Mesh Fabric; Plaiting]
Crawford, M.D.C.: "Peruvian Textiles", Anthro. Pap. Am. Mus. Nat. Hist. 12, 1912, New York 1915-16: 53-191 [Analysis; Threads; Warp Fabric; Weaving; Pile Fabric; Ornamentation with Solid Material(s); Ornamentation with Liquid Material(s)]
Crawford, M.D.C.: "The Loom in the New World", American Mus. Nat. History Journal 16 (6), New York 1916: 381-387 [Ethnography; Archaeology; Weaving]
Crawford, M.D.C.: 5000 years of Fibres and Fabrics. Brooklin 1946 [Archaeology; Collections; Threads; Weaving; Ornamentation with Solid Material(s); Ornamentation with Liquid Material(s)]
Crawford Post, G.: "Setting up a Tape Loom", Handweaver and Craftsman 12, New York 1961 [Working Instruction; Threads; Weaving]
Cresson, & Jeannin, R.: "La toile Méo", Bull. et Travaux Inst. Indoch. Zs.1. 6. Hanoi 1943: 435-447 [Ethnography; Threads; Weaving]
Crill, R.: Indian Ikat Textiles. n.p. 1989 [Analysis; Ethnography; Ornamentation with Liquid Material(s)]
Crill, R.: see also Murphy, V.
Crockett, C.: Cardweaving. New York 1973 [Weaving]
Crockett, C.: "Cardweaving", I.Emery Roundtable on Mus. Textiles 1977, Washington 1978 [Weaving]

Crookelt, C.: see also Chamberlain, M.

Crowe, D.W.: see also Washburn, D.K.

Crowfoot, E.: "The Textiles", Bruce-Mitford R. (ed.) The Sutton Hoo Ship Burial Band 3, London 1985 [Analysis; Archaeology; Warp Fabric; Weaving; Pile Fabric; Ornamentation with Solid Material(s)]

Crowfoot, E.G.: "The Clothing of a Fourteenth-Century Nubian Bishop", Gervers, V. (ed.) Studies in Textile History. Toronto 1977: 43-51 [Analysis; Archaeology; Warp Fabric; Weaving]

Crowfoot, G.M.: "Methods of Hand Spinning in Egypt and the Sudan", Bankfield Museum Notes 12, Halifax 1931 [Analysis; Ethnography; Archaeology; Threads]

Crowfoot, G.M.: "The tablet-woven braids from the vestments of St. Cuthbert at Durham", The Antiquaries Journal Vol.19 N°1, Oxford 1939: 57-80 [Analysis; Archaeology; Weaving]

Crowfoot, G.M.: "The vertical loom in Palestine and Syria", Palestine Exploration Fund 1941-43, London 1943: 141-150 [Archaeology; Weaving]

Crowfoot, G.M.: "Handicrafts in Palestine: Primitive Weaving. Plaiting and finger weaving", Palestine Exploration Quarterly Oct. London 1943: 75-89 [Ethnography; Warp Fabric; Weaving]

Crowfoot, G.M.: "The tent beautiful: A study of pattern weaving in Transjordan", Palestine Exploration Quarterly Apr. London 1945: 34-47 [Ethnography; Weaving]

Crowfoot, G.M.: "Two Textiles from the National Museum, Edinburgh", Proc. Soc. Antiquaries of Scotland Vol. 82 7th, Edinburgh 1947 [Archaeology; Weaving; Ornamentation with Liquid Material(s)]

Crowfoot, G.M.: "Textiles from a Viking Grave at Kildonan", Proc. Soc. Antiquaries of Scotland Vol. 83, Edinburgh 1948/49: 24-28 [Analysis; Archaeology; Weaving; Pile Fabric]

Crowfoot, G.M.: "Textiles, Basketry and Mats", Singer, C. & Holmyard E.J. (ed.) A History of Technology Band 1, Oxford 1954: 413-447 [Classification; Analysis; Threads; Plaiting; Warp Fabric; Weaving]

Crowfoot, G.M.: "The Sudanese Camel Girth", Kush 4, Khartoum 1956: 34-38 [Ethnography; Weaving]

Crowfoot, G.M. & Davies, N.: "The Tunic of Tut'Ankhamun", The Journ. Egyptian Archaeol. Vol. 27, Oxford 1941: 113-130 [Archaeology; Weaving; Ornamentation with Solid Material(s)]

Crowfoot, G.M. & Ling Roth, H.: Hand spinning and wool combing. Bedford 1974 [Threads]

Crystal, E.: "Mountain Ikats and Coastal Silk: Traditional Textiles in South Sulawesi", Fischer, I. (ed.) Threads of Tradition. Berkeley 1979: 53-62 [Ethnography; Ornamentation with Liquid Material(s)]

Csalog, J.: "Die Lehren des neusten Geflechtabdruckes von Kökenyodonb", Mora Ferenc Muzeum 1, 1964-65, Zzeged 1965: 43-45 [Archaeology; Plaiting]

Csernyánsky, M.: Ungarische Spitzenkunst. Budapest 1962 [Folk Art; Mesh Fabric; Plaiting]

Cuéllar, E.S.: "San Augustin Tlacotepec and Mixteca Alta Beltweaving Village", I.Emery Roundtable on Mus. Textiles 1976, Washington 1977: 310-322 [Ethnography; Weaving]

Cyrus, U.: Manual of Swedish Handweaving. Boston 1956 [Folk Art; Weaving]

Dahl, H.: Högsäng och klädbod: ur svenskbygdermas textilhistoria. Folklivsstudier N°18, Helsingfors 1987 [Folk Art; Mesh Fabric; Plaiting; Weaving]

Dahlin, I.: Blekingedräklen. n.p., n.d. [Folk Art; Ornamentation with Solid Material(s); Ornamentation with Liquid Material(s)]

Dahrenberg, T.: ""Sprang" – eine dreitausendjährige Handarbeit", Frauenkultur Heft 9, Leipzig 1936: 6-11 [Folk Art; Archaeology; Warp Fabric]

Dalgaard, H.F.: "Danish needlework", Folk 21-22, 1979-80, Kobenhagen 1980 [Archaeology]

Dalman, G.H.: Arbeit und Sitte in Palästina. Hildesheim 1964 [Ethnography; Threads; Weaving]

Dalrymple, R.E.: "Gold Embroidered Ceremonial Sarongs from South Sumatra", Arts of Asia Vol.14 N°1, Hong Kong 1984: 90-99 [Ethnography; Weaving; Ornamentation with Solid Material(s)]

Damm, H.: "Ein Schiffstuch aus Süd-Sumatra", Jahrbuch Museum für Völkerkunde N°17, 1958, Leipzig 1960: 67-75 [Ethnography; Weaving]

Daniel, F.: "Yoruba Pattern Dyeing", Nigeria N°14, Lagos 1938: 125-129 [Ethnography; Ornamentation with Liquid Material(s)]

Danneil, C.: "Der Übergang vom Flechten zum Weben, nebst einem weiteren Beitrag zur Kenntniss der Weberei in Melanesien", Int. Archiv für Ethnographie 14, Leiden 1901: 227-238 [Ethnography; Plaiting; Warp Fabric; Weaving]

Das, A.K.: Tribal Art and Craft. Delhi 1979 [Ethnography; Plaiting]

Dauer, A.M.: Fulbe: Spinnen eines Baumwollfadens. Encyclopaedia Cinematographica Ser. 8, N°8, Göttingen 1978 [Ethnography; Films; Threads]

Davidson, D.S.: "Australian Netting and Basketry Techniques", Journal of the Polyn. Soc. 42, Wellington 1933: 257-299 [Classification; Ethnography; Mesh Fabric; Plaiting]

Davidson, D.S.: "Knotless netting in America and Oceania", American Anthropologist 37, Menasha 1935: 117-134 [Classification; Ethnography; Mesh Fabric]

Davidson, M. & Christa, C.: Coverlets. Chicago 1973 [Collections; Weaving]

Davies, N.: see also Crowfoot, G.M.

Dawson, B.: The technique of metal thread embroidery: Repr. from an extended version. First published 1968. London 1985 [Working Instruction; Ornamentation with Solid Material(s)]

Dawson, L.E.: "Painted mummy masks of Ica, Peru", The J.B. Bird Precolumbian Textile Conf. 1973, Washington 1979: 83-104 [Archaeology; Plaiting; Weaving; Ornamentation with Liquid Material(s)]

Dawson, L.E.: see also Fowler, C.S.

Day, C.L.: Quipus and Witches Knots. Los Angeles 1967 [Analysis; Mesh Fabric]

Day, L.F. & Buckle, M.: Art in Needlework: A Book about Embroidery. London 1907 [Analysis; Working Instruction; Ornamentation with Solid Material(s)]

D'Azevedo, W.L. (ed.): Great Basin.Handbook of North Am. Indians 11, Washington 1986 [Ethnography; Archaeology; Plaiting]

De Bone, M.G.: "Patola and its techniques", Textile Museum Journal 4 (3), Washington 1976: 49-62 [Analysis; Ornamentation with Liquid Material(s)]

De Leon, S.: The Basketry Book. New York 1978 [Working Instruction; Mesh Fabric; Plaiting]

Debétaz, V.: Von den Spinnerinnen im Eringertal und ihrem Betreuer. Heimatwerk 1, Zürich 1965: 2-17 [Folk Art; Threads]

Debétaz-Grünig, E.: Apprenons à tisser. Fribourg 1977 [Working Instruction; Weaving]

Deimel, C.: "Kleidung und Kultgegenstände der Huichol (Wirarika)", Mitteilungen Museum für Völkerkunde 12 NF, Hamburg 1982: 55-108 [Ethnography; Weaving; Beadwork; Ornamentation with Solid Material(s)]

Delahaye, G.: "Les tissus teints à l'indigo de l'Afrique Occidentale", La Navette 23, Cordes 1983: 22-29 [Ethnography; Ornamentation with Liquid Material(s)]

Delawarde, J.B.: "Les Galibi de la Mana et d'Iracoubo (Guayane Française)", Journ. Soc. Américan. 56 (1), Paris 1967 [Ethnography; Threads; Plaiting]
Delgado, H.: Aboriginal Guatemalan Handweaving and Costume. Thesis Indiana Univ. Ann Arbor 1963 [Ethnography; Weaving]
Delgado-Pang, H.: "Overview and Introduction to Central American Ethnographic Textiles", I.Emery Roundtable on Mus. Textiles 1976, Washington 1977: 84-105 [Ethnography]
Delgado-Pang, H.: "Similarities between certain early Spanish, contemporary Spanish Folk, and Mesoamerican Indian Textile Design Motifs", I.Emery Roundtable on Mus. Textiles 1976, Washington 1977: 386-404 [Folk Art]
Dellinger, S.C.: "Baby Cradles of the Ozark Bluff Dwellers", American Antiquity 1, 1935-36, Salt Lake City 1936: 197-214 [Archaeology; Plaiting; Warp Fabric]
Delz, S.: see also Schaar, E.
Dendel, E.W.: African fabric crafts: Sources of African designs and technique. New York 1974 [Ethnography; Working Instruction; Mesh Fabric; Plaiting; Ornamentation with Solid Material(s); Ornamentation with Liquid Material(s)]
Denis, F.: Arte plumaria – Les plumes dans les Arts au Mexique, au Pérou, au Brésil, etc. Paris 1875 [Archaeology; Pile Fabric]
Denniston, G.: see also Mc Clellan, C.
Denny, W.B.: "Ottoman Turkish textiles", Textile Museum Journal 3 (3), Washington 1972: 55-66 [General, Historical; Weaving]
Denny, W.B.: "Anatolian rugs", Textile Museum Journal 3 (4), Washington 1973: 7-26 [General, Historical; Pile Fabric]
Denwood, P.: The Tibetan Carpet. Warminster 1974 [Ethnography; Pile Fabric]
Desai, C.: Ikat Textiles of India. Tokyo 1988 [Analysis; Ethnography; Ornamentation with Liquid Material(s)]
Desai, D.: see also Westfall, C.D. [Desrosiers, S.: "Un "métier à tisser aux baguettes" du Pérou", Bull. CIETA 1 & 2, Lyon 1980: 36-40 [Ethnography; Half-weaving]
Desrosiers, S.: Le tissu comme être vivant. Paris 1982 [Weaving]
Desrosiers, S.: "Beschreibung einer tibetischen Schleuder", Müller, C.C. (ed.) Der Weg zum Dach der Welt. München 1982: 176-177 [Ethnography; Plaiting]
Desrosiers, S.: "An Interpretation of Technical Weaving Data Found in an Early 17th-Century Chronicle", Rowe, A.P. (ed.) J.B. Bird Conf. on Andean Textiles 1984, Washington 1986: 219-242 [Analysis; Weaving]
Desrosiers, S.: see also Balfet, H.
Detering, D.: "Flechtwerke und Flechttechniken der Kaschuyana-Indianer Nordost Brasilien", Baessler-Archiv NF 10, Berlin 1962: 63-103 [Analysis; Ethnography; Plaiting; Pile Fabric; Borders]
Deuss, K.: Indian Costumes from Guatemala. Twickenham 1981 [Ethnography; Threads; Warp Fabric; Ornamentation with Solid Material(s); Ornamentation with Liquid Material(s)]
Deuss, K.: Fest der Farben: Trachten und Textilien aus dem Hochland Guatemalas. Köln 1981 [Analysis; Ethnography; Mesh Fabric; Weaving; Fabric Processing]
Deutsches Textilforum: Arbeitsgruppe für Textilien. Hannover from 1982 on [Working Instruction; General, Historical]
Devassy, M.K.: Selected Crafts of Kerala. New Delhi 1964 [Ethnography; Threads; Plaiting; Weaving]
Devi, P. (ed.): The master weavers. Bombay 1982 [Ethnography; Collections; Ornamentation with Solid Material(s); Ornamentation with Liquid Material(s)]
Dhamija, J.: "The Survey of Embroidery Traditions", Marg Vol. 17 N°2, Bombay 1964 [Ethnography; Ornamentation with Solid Material(s)]
Dhamija, J.: "Survey of pile carpet industry in India", Marg 18, Bombay 1965 [Ethnography; Pile Fabric]
Dhamija, J.: Survey of crafts of Bihar. Bombay 1966 [Ethnography; Plaiting]
Dhamija, J.: "Survey of Crafts", Marg Vol. 20, Bombay 1966 [Ethnography; Ornamentation with Solid Material(s)]
Dhamija, J.: Indian folk arts and crafts. New Delhi 1970 [Ethnography; Weaving; Pile Fabric; Ornamentation with Solid Material(s); Ornamentation with Liquid Material(s)]
Dhamija, J.: "Arts and Crafts of Himachal Pradesh", Marg 23 (2), Bombay 1970 [Ethnography; Plaiting; Ornamentation with Solid Material(s)]
Dhamija, J.: Crafts of Gujarat: Living traditions of India. New York 1985 [Ethnography; Weaving; Ornamentation with Liquid Material(s)]
Dhamija, J. & Jain, J.: Handwoven Fabrics of India. Ahmedabad 1989 [Ethnography; Weaving; Ornamentation with Solid Material(s); Ornamentation with Liquid Material(s)]
D'Harcourt, R.: "Technique du point de tricot à Nazca", Jour. Soc. Américanistes 22, Paris 1930: 207-209 [Analysis; Ethnography; Mesh Fabric]
D'Harcourt, R.: "Un bonnet péruvien en similivelours", Bull. de Mus. d'Ethno. de Trocadero N°5, Paris 1933: 3-7 [Archaeology; Pile Fabric]
D'Harcourt, R.: Les textiles anciens du Pérou et leurs techniques. Paris 1934 [Analysis; Archaeology; Mesh Fabric; Plaiting; Warp Fabric; Weaving; Pile Fabric; Borders; Ornamentation with Solid Material(s)]
D'Harcourt, R.: "Techniques des tissus Péruviens à fils de chaîne et de trame discontinus", Journ. de la Soc. des Américanistes N.S. 28, Paris 1936: 323-325 [Archaeology; Tapestry]
D'Harcourt, R.: "Le Tressage des Frondes au Pérou et en Bolivie et les Textiles chez les Uro-Cipaya", Jour. Soc. Américanistes Tome 32, Paris 1940: 103-132 [Analysis; Ethnography; Plaiting]
D'Harcourt, R.: Arts de l'Amérique. Paris 1948 [Ethnography; Archaeology; Plaiting; Weaving]
D'Harcourt, R.: "Un tapis brodé de Paracas, Pérou", Journ. de la Soc. des Américanistes N.S. 37, Paris 1948: 241-257 [Archaeology; Ornamentation with Solid Material(s)]
D'Harcourt, R.: "Techniques du tressage des sandales chez les tribus indiennes de la côte du Pérou", Actes du XXVIIe Congrès International des Américan. Paris 1948: 615-619 [Archaeology; Plaiting]
D'Harcourt, R.: "Un réseau à bouclettes décoratives de Nazca: Note technologique", Journ. de la Soc. des Américanistes N.S. 41, Paris 1952: 39-41 [Archaeology; Mesh Fabric]
D'Harcourt, R.: "Une broderie sur filet de Nazca, Pérou", Soc. Suisse des Améric. Bulletin N°8, Genève 1954: 1-2 [Archaeology; Ornamentation with Solid Material(s)]
D'Harcourt, R.: "Peruanische Textiltechnik", Ciba Rundschau 148, Basel 1960: 2-39 [Analysis; Mesh Fabric; Plaiting; Warp Fabric; Weaving; Pile Fabric; Borders; Ornamentation with Solid Material(s)]
D'Harcourt, R.: Textiles of ancient Peru and their techniques. Paris 1962 [Analysis; Archaeology; Threads; Mesh Fabric; Plaiting; Warp Fabric; Pile Fabric; Ornamentation with Liquid Material(s)]
D'Harcourt, R.: "Notes technologiques sur les tissus indiens modernes de Bolivie", Jour. Soc. Américanistes 59, Paris 1970: 171-175 [Ethnography; Weaving]
D'Harcourt, R.: Textiles of Ancient Peru and their techniques. Denny, G.K. & Osborne, C.M. (ed.) Univ. Wash. Press, Seattle 1974 [Archaeology; Threads; Mesh Fabric; Plaiting; Warp Fabric; Pile Fabric; Ornamentation with Liquid Material(s)]
D'Harcourt, R.: see also Douglas, F.H.
D'Hennezel, H.: Catalogue des principales pièces exposées.

Musée Historique des Tissus, Lyon 1924 [Collections; Pile Fabric]
Dickey, S.F.: A Historical Review of Knotless Netting in South America. Berkeley 1964 [Classification; Ethnography; Archaeology; Mesh Fabric]
Dietrich, M.G.: Guatemalan Costume: The Heard Museum Collection. Phoenix 1979 [Ethnography, Collections; Weaving]
Dijk van, T.: Ship Cloths of the Lampung, South Sumatra. Amsterdam 1980 [Ethnography; Weaving]
Dillmont, de, T.: Encyclopédie des ouvrages de dames. Mulhouse n.d. [Working Instruction; Plaiting; Borders; Ornamentation with Solid Material(s)]
Dillmont, de, T.: Die Durchbruchsarbeit. Mülhausen n.d. [Working Instruction; Warp Fabric]
Dillmont, de, T.: Die Bändchenspitze: Point Lace. Mülhausen n.d. [Working Instruction; Mesh Fabric]
Dillmont, de, T.: Motifs de broderie copte. Dornach n.d. [Working Instruction; Ornamentation with Solid Material(s)]
Dillmont, de, T.: Hardanger Arbeiten. Mülhausen n.d. [Folk Art; Working Instruction; Ornamentation with Solid Material(s)]
Dillmont, de, T.: Enzyklopädie der weiblichen Handarbeiten. Dornach 1902 [Working Instruction; Plaiting; Borders; Ornamentation with Solid Material(s); Fabric Processing]
Dillmont, de, T.: Die Klöppelspitzen. Mülhausen 1910 [Working Instruction; Plaiting]
Dimand, M.S.: A Handbook of Muhammadan Art. New York 1974 [General, Historical]
Dimand, M.S.: see also Ettinghausen, R.
Dimand, M.S.: Altislamische Gewebe. n.p. 1930 [Archaeology; Weaving]
Disselhoff, H.D.: Daily Life in Ancient Peru. New York 1967 [Archaeology; Plaiting; Warp Fabric; Weaving; Tapestry]
Disselhoff, H.D.: Leben im alten Peru. München 1981 [Analysis; Archaeology; Plaiting; Warp Fabric; Weaving; Pile Fabric; Ornamentation with Solid Material(s); Tapestry]
Dixit, D.K.: Zari embroidery and batwa making of Bhopal. Census of India 1961 Vol.8,Part 7a,61, Jabalpur 1965 [Ethnography; Ornamentation with Solid Material(s)]
Dixon, K.A.: "Systematic Cordage Structure Analysis", American Anthropologist 59, Menasha 1957: 134-136 [Classification; Threads]
Djajasoebrata, V.A. & Adams, M.: Life and Death on Sumba. Rotterdam 1965 [Ethnography; Collections; Ornamentation with Solid Material(s); Ornamentation with Liquid Material(s)]
Djambatan, P.: Hamzuri: Classical Batik. Jakarta 1985 [Analysis; Ethnography; Ornamentation with Liquid Material(s)]
Djoemena, N.S.: Ungkapan sehelai: Batik: its mystery and meaning. Jakarta 1986 [Ethnography; Ornamentation with Liquid Material(s)]
Djoemena, N.S.: Pameran Lintasan Budaya Dalam Batik Koleksi. Jakarta 1990 [Ethnography; Collections; Ornamentation with Liquid Material(s)]
Djumena, N.S.: Batik and its Kind. Jakarta 1990 [Ethnography; Ornamentation with Liquid Material(s)]
Dockstader, F.J.: Weaving Arts of the North American Indian. London 1978 [Ethnography; Weaving; Tapestry]
Dockstader, F.J.: The Song of the Loom: New Traditions in Navajo Weaving. New York 1987 [Ethnography; Weaving; Tapestry]
Dodds, D.R.: Südpersische Stammeserzeugnisse. New York 1983 [Ethnography]
Dörner, G.: Volkskunst in Mexico: Ausstellung des städtischen Museums für Völkerkunde. Frankfurt 1964 [Ethnography; Collections]
Does, de, A.M.K.: Toestand der Nijverheid in de afdeeling Banjaruegara. n.p., n.d. [Ethnography; Weaving; Ornamentation with Liquid Material(s)]
Dombrowski, G.: "Über eine besondere Form textiler Randverzierung in Turkestan", Baessler-Archiv NF 24, Berlin 1976: 365-387 [Analysis; Ethnography; Warp Fabric; Weaving; Borders; Ornamentation with Solid Material(s)]
Dombrowski, G. & Pfluger-Schindlbeck, I.: Flachgewebe aus Anatolien. Staatl. Museen Preussischer Kulturbesitz N°58 & 59, Berlin 1988 [Analysis; Ethnography; Threads; Warp Fabric; Weaving; Tapestry]
Domonkos, O.: Blaudruckhandwerk in Ungarn. Budapest 1981 [Folk Art; Ornamentation with Liquid Material(s)]
Donat, F.: Methodik der Bindungslehre und Decomposition. Wien 1899 [Analysis; Weaving]
Dongerkery, K.S.: The Indian Sari. New Delhi n.d. [Ethnography; Weaving]
Dongerkery, K.S.: The Romance of Indian Embroidery. Bombay 1951 [Ethnography; Ornamentation with Solid Material(s)]
Donner, M. & Schnebel, C.: Handarbeiten wie zu Grossmutters Zeiten: Faksimiledruck von: Ich kann handarbeiten. Berlin 1913 [Analysis; Working Instruction; Mesh Fabric; Plaiting; Ornamentation with Liquid Material(s)]
Dornheim, A.: "Posición ergológica de los Telares Cordobeses en la América del Sur", Revista del Inst. Nac. Trad. 1, Buenos Aires 1948 [Ethnography; Weaving]
Dorta, S.F.: see also Nicola, N.
Douglas, F.H.: Basketry Construction Technics. Denver Art Mus. Dept. of Indian Art, Leaflet 67, Denver 1935 [Analysis; Ethnography; Plaiting]
Douglas, F.H.: The Main Division of California Indian Basketry. Denver Art Mus. Dept. of Indian Art, Leaflet 83-84, Denver 1937 [Ethnography; Plaiting]
Douglas, F.H.: Southwest Twined, Wicker and Plaited Basketry. Denver Art Mus. Dept. of Indian Art, Leaflets 99-100, Denver 1940 [Ethnography; Plaiting]
Douglas, F.H.: Porcupine Quillwork. Denver Art Mus. Dept. of Indian Art, Leaflet 103, Denver 1941 [Ethnography; Ornamentation with Solid Material(s)]
Douglas, F.H. & D'Harcourt, R.: Indian Art of the United States. New York 1941 [Ethnography; General, Historical; Plaiting; Ornamentation with Solid Material(s); Tapestry]
Drewal, H.J. & Pemberton, J.: Yoruba: Nine Centuries of African Art and Thought. New York 1989 [Ethnography; Weaving; Beadwork; Ornamentation with Solid Material(s); Ornamentation with Liquid Material(s)]
Drinbao, S.: Babi: tekuilt mengergakan tenunan ikat. S.Augustin 1980 [Ethnography; Ornamentation with Liquid Material(s)]
Drucker, S. et al.: "The Cuitlatec", Handbook of Middle Am. Indians 7, Austin 1969: 565-576 [Ethnography; Threads; Mesh Fabric; Plaiting; Ornamentation with Solid Material(s)]
Dubin, L.S.: The History of Beads. New York 1987 [Analysis; Ethnography; Folk Art; Archaeology; Beadwork]
Duby, G. & Blom, F.: "The Lacandon", Handbook of Middle Am. Indians 7, Austin 1969: 276-297 [Ethnography; Threads; Mesh Fabric; Warp Fabric]
Dudovikova, M.: Moravska lidova vysivka. Brno 1986 [Analysis; Folk Art; Mesh Fabric; Ornamentation with Solid Material(s)]
Due, B.: "A shaman's cloak?", Folk 21-22, 1979-80, Kobenhagen 1980 [Analysis; Ethnography; Pile Fabric]
Dürr, A.: Die Weberei in der zentralen peruanischen Montaña. Basel 1978 [Ethnography; Collections; Threads; Plaiting; Halfweaving; Weaving; Ornamentation with Liquid Material(s); Fabric Processing]
Dürr, A.: "Halbweben in der peruanischen Montaña", Basler Beiträge zur Ethnologie Band 30, Basel 1989: 431-442 [Eth-

nography; Half-weaving]
Dunare, N.: Rumänische Stickereien. Bukarest 1985 [Folk Art; Ornamentation with Solid Material(s)]
Dunham, S.A.: Womens work in village industries on Java. Jakarta 1980 [Ethnography; Ornamentation with Liquid Material(s)]
Dunlop, J.: People of the Australian Western Desert: Spinning Hair String. Encyclopaedia Cinematographica N°9, Göttingen 1966 [Ethnography; Films; Threads]
Dunsmore, S.: Weaving in Nepal: Dhaka-Topi Cloth. London 1983 [Ethnography; Weaving]
Dunsmore, S.: The Nettle in Nepal: A Cottage Industry. London 1985 [Ethnography; Plaiting; Weaving]
Dupaigne, B.: "Aperçus sur quelques techniques afghanes", Objets et Mondes 8 (1), Paris 1968: 41-84 [Ethnography; Ornamentation with Liquid Material(s)]
Dupaigne, B.: "Un artisan d'Afghanistan: sa vie, ses problèmes, ses espoirs", Objets et Mondes 14 Fasc. 3, Paris 1974: 143-170 [Ethnography; Weaving; Ornamentation with Liquid Material(s)]
Dupaigne, B.: "Les ikats d'Usbekistan et d'Afghanistan", Textilhandwerk in Afghanistan. Liestal 1983: 77-92 [Ethnography; Ornamentation with Liquid Material(s)]
Duponchel, P.: Le Tissage du Coton à San, République du Mali. Paris 1987 [Ethnography; Weaving; Ornamentation with Liquid Material(s)]
Duque Gomez, L.: Tejidos y Bordados. Bogotá 1945 [Ethnography; Weaving]
Durand-Forest, J.: "Survivances de quelques techniques précolombiennes dans le Méxique moderne", Jour. Soc. Américanistes 55 (2), Paris 1966: 525-561 [Analysis; Ethnography; Archaeology; Threads; Weaving]
Durban Art Gallery: Exhibition of Traditional Indian Costumes of Guatemala: Exhibition Catalogue. Durban 1977 [Ethnography; Collections; Weaving; Ornamentation with Solid Material(s)]
Dusenbury, M.: "Kasuri: a japanese textile", Textile Museum Journal 17, Washington 1978 [Ethnography; Ornamentation with Liquid Material(s)]
Dusenbury, M.: "Braiding in Japan", Rogers, N. (ed.) In celebration of the curious mind. Loveland 1983: 81-102 [Ethnography; Plaiting]
Dusenbury, M.: Textiles of old Japan: Bast-fibre textiles and old Kasuris. San Francisco 1985 [Ethnography; Ornamentation with Liquid Material(s)]
Dussan de Reichel, A.: "La mochila de fique: Aspectos tecnológicos, socio-económicos y etnográficos", Rev. Col. de Folclor Band 11 (4), Bogotá 1960: 137-148 [Analysis; Ethnography; Mesh Fabric]
Dutton, B.: Navaho Weaving Today. 3. Edition, Santa Fe 1961 [Ethnography; Weaving; Tapestry]
Dwyer, E.B.: "Early Horizon Tapestry from South Coastal Peru", The J.B.Bird Precolumbian Textile Conf. 1973, Washington 1979: 61-82 [Archaeology; Warp Fabric; Ornamentation with Solid Material(s)]
Dwyer, J.P.: "The Chronology and Iconography of Paracas Style Textiles", The J.B.Bird Precolumbian Textile Conf. 1973, Washington 1979: 105-128 [Archaeology; Weaving]

Easmon, M.C.F.: Sierra Leone Country Cloths. British Empire Exhibition, London 1924 [Ethnography; Threads; Weaving]
Eaton, A.M.: Handicrafts of the Southern Highlands. New York 1937 [Folk Art; Threads; Mesh Fabric; Plaiting; Weaving; Ornamentation with Solid Material(s)]
Eddy, M.: Crafts and Traditions of the Canary Islands. Shire Ethnography N°17, Dyfed 1989 [Folk Art; Plaiting; Weaving]
Edwards, J.: Bead Embroidery. London 1966 [General, Historical; Beadwork; Ornamentation with Solid Material(s)]
Efthymiou-Chatzilakou, M.: "I Kalathoplektiki tou Argous: Basket-weaving in Argos", Ethnografica 2, 1979-80, Athen 1980: 57-82 [Folk Art; Plaiting]
Eggebrecht, A.: Das Land am Nil: Bildteppiche aus Harrania. Hildesheim 1979 [Ethnography; Tapestry]
Egger, G.: Frühchristliche und koptische Kunst. Wien 1964 [Archaeology; Collections; Warp Fabric; Weaving; Tapestry]
Egloff, M.: "Le panier du cueilleur", Jagen und Sammeln. Jahrbuch Hist. Museum 63-64, 1983-84, Bern 1984 [Archaeology; Plaiting]
Egloff, W.: Weben und Wirken im Lötschental. Schweiz. Gesell. für Volkskunde, Abt. Films, Basel 1976 [Analysis; Folk Art; Films; Weaving; Tapestry]
Eiland, M.L.: Chinese and Exotic Rugs. London 1979 [Analysis; General, Historical; Warp Fabric; Pile Fabric]
Einstein, C.: "Peruanische Bildgewebe der Sammlung Gaus", Westheim, P. (ed.) Das Kunstblatt 6 (4), Potsdam 1922: 172-175 [Archaeology; Tapestry]
Eisleb, D.: "Altperuanische Kelimgewebe aus Pachacamac", Baessler-Archiv NF 12, Berlin 1964: 257-270 [Archaeology; Warp Fabric; Tapestry]
Eisleb, D.: Altperuanische Kulturen, I. Veröffentl. Museum Völkerkunde NF 31. 1974, Berlin 1975 [Analysis; Archaeology; Collections; Mesh Fabric; Plaiting; Weaving; Ornamentation with Solid Material(s)]
Eisleb, D. & Strelow, R.: "Altperuanische Ikat-Gewebe aus den Sammlungen des Berliner Museums für Völkerkunde", Baessler-Archiv NF 12, Berlin 1964: 179-191 [Archaeology; Ornamentation with Liquid Material(s)]
Eisleb, D. & Strelow, R.: "Altperuanische unechte Partialgewebe mit Plangimusterung", Baessler-Archiv NF 13, Berlin 1965: 293-308 [Archaeology; Warp Fabric; Weaving; Ornamentation with Liquid Material(s)]
Ekpo, I.A.: "Ekpe Costume of the Cross River", African Arts Vol.12 N°1, Los Angeles 1978: 72-75 [Ethnography; Mesh Fabric]
Elliot-Mc Cabe, I.: Batik: Fabled cloth of Java. New York 1984 [Analysis; Ethnography; Ornamentation with Liquid Material(s)]
Ellis, C.G.: "The Ottoman prayer rugs", Textile Museum Journal 2 (4), Washington 1969 [General, Historical; Pile Fabric]
Ellis, C.G.: Early caucasian rugs. Textile Museum Washington, Washington 1975 [Collections; Pile Fabric]
Ellis, F. & Walpole, U.: "Posible Pueblo, Navajo and Jicarilla Basketry Relationships", El Palacio 66 (6), Santa Fe 1959: 181-198 [Ethnography; Plaiting]
Ellis, G.R.: "The Art of the Toradja", Arts of Asia Vol.10 N°5, Hong Kong 1980: 94-107 [Ethnography; Plaiting; Beadwork; Ornamentation with Liquid Material(s)]
Elmberg, J.E.: Balance and circulation. Aspects of tradition and change among the Mejprat of Irian Barat. Ethnogr. Mus. Monograph Series 12, Stockholm 1968 [Ethnography; Weaving; Ornamentation with Solid Material(s)]
Elsasser, A.B.: "Basketry", Handbook of North Am. Indians 8, Washington 1978: 626-641 [Analysis; Ethnography; Plaiting]
Elson, V.: Dowries from Kutch. Mus. Cultural History UCLA, Los Angeles 1979 [Ethnography; Collections; Ornamentation with Solid Material(s)]
Emery, I.: "Wool Embroideries of New Mexico: Some Notes on the Stitch Employed", El Palacio 56 (11), Santa Fe 1949: 339-352 [Folk Art; Ornamentation with Solid Material(s)]
Emery, I.: "Naming the Direction of the Twist in Yarn and Cordage", El Palacio 59 (8), Santa Fe 1952: 251-262 [Class-

ification; Threads]

Emery, I.: Note on some of the basic requirements for a terminology of ancient and primitive fabrics. Workshop Notes 11, Washington 1955 [Classification; Mesh Fabric; Plaiting]

Emery, I.: The Primary Structures of Fabrics. New York 1966 [Classification; Threads; Mesh Fabric; Plaiting; Warp Fabric; Weaving; Pile Fabric; Ornamentation with Solid Material(s); Tapestry; Fabric Processing]

Emery, I.& Fiske, P. (ed.): Ethnographic Textiles of the Western Hemisphere.I.Emery Roundtable on Mus. Textiles 1976, Washington 1977 [Ethnography; Mesh Fabric; Weaving]

Emery, I.& Fiske, P. (ed.): Looms and their Products.I.Emery Roundtable on Mus. Textiles 1977, Washington 1979 [Ethnography; Weaving]

Emery, I. & King, M.E.: Vicús Textile Fragments: Vicús eine neu entdeckte altperuanische Kultur. Disselhoff, H.D (ed.) Monumenta Americana Vol. 7, Berlin 1971: 52-53 [Archaeology; Weaving]

Emmons, G.T.: "The Basketry of the Tlingit", Am. Mus. Nat. History Memoirs 3 (2), New York 1903: 229-277 [Ethnography; Plaiting]

Emmons, G.T. & Boas, F.: The Chilkat Blanket. Mem. Americ. Mus. of Nat. Hist 3-4, New York 1907: 329-400 [Analysis; Warp Fabric; Pile Fabric; Borders]

Enderlein, V.: Orientalische Kelims. Berlin 1986 [Collections; Warp Fabric; Weaving; Pile Fabric; Tapestry]

Endrei, W.: Le métier à tisser aux baguettes; Influences orientales dans les costumes polonais et hongrois. Paris 1985 [Folk Art; Weaving]

Engel, F.: "Un Groupe Humain datant de 5000 ans à Paracas, Pérou", Jour. Soc. Américanistes Tome 49, Paris 1960: 1-35 [Archaeology; Mesh Fabric; Plaiting; Warp Fabric]

Engel, F.: A Preceramic Settlement on the Central Coast of Peru, Asia 1. Trans. of the American Philosoph. Soc. Philadelphia 1963 [Analysis; Archaeology; Mesh Fabric; Plaiting; Warp Fabric; Pile Fabric]

Engel, F.: "Le complexe précéramique d'el Paraiso (Pérou)", Jour. Soc. Américanistes 55 (1), Paris 1966: 43-96 [Analysis; Archaeology; Mesh Fabric]

Engelbrecht, B.: Handwerk im Leben der Purhépecha in Mexico. Ethnol. Schriften Zürich 3, Zürich 1986 [Ethnography; Plaiting; Weaving]

Engelstad, H.: Dobbeltvev i Norge. Oslo 1958 [Folk Art; Weaving]

Engelstad, H.: "The big fishes from Pachacamac: Peru", Folk 21-22, 1979-1980, Kobenhagen 1980 [Archaeology]

Engelstad, H.: "Mythology, religion and textile art on the central coast of Old Peru", Folk 26, Kobenhagen 1984: 191-213 [Archaeology; General, Historical]

Enserinck, P.: Van Batikken en Ikatten. Haarlemsche Kunstboekjes 7, Haarlem n.d. [Ethnography; Ornamentation with Liquid Material(s)]

Ephraim, H.: Über die Entwicklung der Webtechnik und ihre Verwendung ausserhalb Europas. Mittl. Städt. Mus. f. Völkerk. 8 N°9, Leipzig 1904 [Analysis; Weaving]

Erekosima, T.V. & Bubolz-Eicher, J.: "Kalabari Cut-Thread and Pulled-Thread Cloth", African Arts 14 (2), Los Angeles 1981: 48-51 [Ethnography; Ornamentation with Solid Material(s)]

Erekosima, T.V.: see also Bubolz-Eicher, J.

Erikson, J.: Mata ni Pachedi: A book on the temple cloth of the mother goddess. Ahmedabad 1984 [Ethnography; Ornamentation with Liquid Material(s)]

Errera, I.: Catalogue d'étoffes anciennes et modernes. Musée Royal des Arts Decoratives, Bruxelles 1907 [Collections; Weaving]

Espejel, C. & Català Roca, F.: Mexican Folk Crafts. Barcelona 1978 [Ethnography; Mesh Fabric; Plaiting; Weaving]

Etienne-Nugue, J.: Artisanats et arts de vivre au Cameroun. n.p. 1982 [Ethnography; Threads; Plaiting; Weaving; Ornamentation with Solid Material(s)]

Etienne-Nugue, J.: Artisanats traditionnels Haute Volta. Dakar 1982 [Ethnography; Threads; Plaiting; Weaving; Ornamentation with Solid Material(s); Ornamentation with Liquid Material(s)]

Etienne-Nugue, J.: Artisanats traditionnels en Afrique Noire: Bénin. Dakar 1984 [Ethnography; Threads; Plaiting; Weaving; Ornamentation with Solid Material(s); Ornamentation with Liquid Material(s)]

Etienne-Nugue, J.: Artisanats traditionnels: Côte d'Ivoire. Dakar 1985 [Analysis; Ethnography; Plaiting; Weaving; Ornamentation with Liquid Material(s)]

Ettinghausen, R. & Dimand, M.S.: Prayer Rugs. Washington Textile Museum, Washington 1974 [Collections; General, Historical; Pile Fabric]

Ewers, J.C.: Blackfeet Crafts. Los Angeles 1945 [Ethnography; Ornamentation with Solid Material(s)]

Ewers, J.C.: see also Wildschut, W.

Eyk, van, R.: My woven diary. Goirle 1977 [Folk Art; Weaving]

Faccioli, R.: see also Boralevi, A.

Falchetti de Sáenz, A.M: see also Cardale de Schrimpff, M.

Farke, H.: Archäologische Fasern, Geflechte, Gewebe: Restaurierung und Museumstechnik. Mus. für Ur- und Frühgeschichte 17, Weimar 1986 [Analysis; Threads; Plaiting; Warp Fabric; Weaving; Pile Fabric]

Farrand, L.: Basketry Designs of the Salish Indians: Reprint of the 1900 edition. New York 1975 [Ethnography; Plaiting]

Fauconnier, F.: Ship cloth from southern Sumatra: Schiffstücher aus Süd-Sumatra. Köln 1980 [Ethnography; Weaving]

Fawcett, M.D.: "The Featherworker: The Karajá of Brazil", Roosevelt, A.C. (ed.) The Ancestors. New York 1979: 24-43 [Analysis; Ethnography; Pile Fabric]

Faxon, H.: "A model of an ancient Greek loom", Bull. of the Met. Mus. of Art Vol.27 N°3, New York 1932: 70-71 [Archaeology; Weaving]

Feick, K.: Die Caraguatábast-Knüpfereien der Chamacoco und Tumanahá: Ein Beitrag zur Ethnography des Chaco Boreal. Giessen 1917 [Analysis; Ethnography; Mesh Fabric; Pile Fabric]

Fejos, P.: Ethnography of the Yagua. Viking Fund Publ. Anthrop. 1, New York 1943 [Ethnography; Mesh Fabric; Plaiting]

Fél, E.: Leinenstickereien der ungarischen Bauern. Budapest 1976 [Folk Art; Ornamentation with Solid Material(s)]

Feldman, J. & Rubinstein, D.H.: The art of Micronesia. Univ. of Hawaii Art Gallery, Honolulu 1986 [Analysis; Ethnography; Plaiting; Weaving]

Feldman, R.A.: "Early Textiles from the Supe Valley, Peru", Rowe, A.P. (ed.) J.B. Bird Conf. on Andean Textiles 1984, Washington 1986: 31-46 [Analysis; Archaeology; Mesh Fabric; Warp Fabric]

Feldtkeller, A. & Schlichtherle, H.: "Jungsteinzeitliche Kleidungsstücke aus Ufersiedlungen des Bodensees", Archäologische Nachrichten aus Baden 38 & 39, Freiburg 1987: 74-83 [Archaeology; Plaiting; Warp Fabric; Pile Fabric]

Feltham, J.: Peruvian Textiles. Shire Ethnography N°16, Aylesbury 1989 [Analysis; Ethnography; Archaeology; Threads; Mesh Fabric; Warp Fabric; Weaving; Pile Fabric; Ornamentation with Solid Material(s); Ornamentation with Liquid Material(s); Tapestry]

Femenias, B.: Two Faces of South Asian Art: Textiles and Paintings. University of Wisconsin, Madison 1984 [Ethnography; Collections]
Femenias, B.: Andean Aesthetics: Textiles of Peru and Bolivia. Wisconsin 1988 [Ethnography; Collections; Mesh Fabric; Weaving]
Fenelon-Costa, M.H. & Malhano, H.B.: "Habitacão Indigena Brasileira", Suma Etnologica Brasileira 2, Petropolis 1986: 27-92 [Analysis; Ethnography; Plaiting]
Fenton, R. & Stuart-Fox, D.: "Woven Textiles of Indonesia", Craft Australia, Spring, 1976: 14-17 [Ethnography; Weaving; Ornamentation with Liquid Material(s)]
Ferchion, S.: Techniques et Sociétés: Exemple de la fabrication des chéchias en Tunisie. Thèse Univ. Paris, Paris 1971 [General, Historical; Mesh Fabric]
Ferdière, A.: Le Travail du Textile en Région Centre de l'Age du Fer au Haut Moyen-Age. Revue Archéologique du Centre de France 23, 1984: 204-275 [Archaeology]
Ferenc, K. & Palotay, G.: Himzömesterség: A magyarországi népé Hunzések ö Uésbecknikaja. Budapest 1940 [Folk Art; Ornamentation with Solid Material(s)]
Ferenc, K.: see also Palotay, G.
Ferentinos, F.: see also Palmieri, M.
Fernandez Distel, A.A.: La Cultura Material de los Ayoreo del Chaco Boreal. Scripta Ethnologica Supplement N°3, Buenos Aires 1983 [Analysis; Ethnography; Plaiting; Warp Fabric]
Ferraro-Dorta, S.: Parľko: Etnografia de um artefato plumário. Col.Mus.Paulista Etnologia 4, São Paulo 1981 [Ethnography; Pile Fabric]
Ferraro-Dorta, S.: "Plumária Bororo", Suma Etnologica Brasileira 3, Petrópolis 1986 [Ethnography; Pile Fabric]
Finckh-Haelsing, M.: Korbflechten mit buntem Peddingrohr für Kinder. Ravensburg n.d. [Working Instruction; Plaiting; Borders]
Fink, P.: Vom Passementerhandwerk zur Bandindustrie. Basel 1979 [Folk Art; Weaving]
Fischer, B.: "Applikationen einer Schuhmachersfrau in Gujarat", Schmitt-Moser, E. et al. (ed.) Indische Frauenkunst. Bayreuth 1989: 20-25 [Ethnography; Ornamentation with Solid Material(s)]
Fischer, E.: "Aufzeichnungen über einen Weber der Bandi", Baessler-Archiv NF 13, Berlin 1965: 83-103 [Ethnography; Weaving]
Fischer, E.: "Das Tempeltuch der Muttergöttin aus Gujarat", Archiv für Völkerkunde 26, Wien 1972: 15-27 [Ethnography; Ornamentation with Liquid Material(s)]
Fischer, E. & Jain, J.: Tempeltücher für die Muttergöttinen in Indien. Zürich 1982 [Ethnography, Ornamentation with Liquid Material(s)]
Fischer, E. & Mahapatra, S.: Orissa: Kunst und Kultur in Nordostindien. Zürich 1980 [Ethnography, Threads; Plaiting]
Fischer, E. & Pathy, D.: "Gita Govinda inscribed Ikat-Textiles from Orissa", Journ. of the Orissa Research Soc. Vol.1 N°2, 1968, Bhubaneswa 1982: 7-15 [Ethnography; Ornamentation with Liquid Material(s)]
Fischer, E. & Shah, H.: Simple weft-ikat from South Gujarat, India; The production of loincloths for the Chadhri tribe in Mandir. Ahmedabad 1970 [Ethnography, Threads; Mesh Fabric; Warp Fabric; Weaving; Ornamentation with Liquid Material(s)]
Fischer, E. & Shah, H.: Rural craftsmen and their work. Equipment and techniques in the Mer village of Ratadi, Saurashtra, India. Ahmedabad 1970 [Ethnography; Threads; Mesh Fabric; Warp Fabric; Weaving; Ornamentation with Solid Material(s)]
Fischer, E. & Shah, H.: "Schlichter Eintragsikat aus Süd-Gujarat (Indien)", Tribus N°19, Stuttgart 1970: 47-69 [Ethnography; Ornamentation with Liquid Material(s)]
Fischer, E.: see also Bühler, A.
Fischer, H.W.: see also Veltman, T.J.
Fischer, J.: "The value of Tradition: An Essay on Indonesian Textiles", Fischer, J. (ed.) Threads of Tradition. Berkeley 1979: 9-14 [General, Historical; Weaving]
Fischer, J. et al. (ed.): Threads of Tradition: Textiles of Indonesia and Sarawak. Berkely 1979 [Ethnography; Weaving; Ornamentation with Solid Material(s); Ornamentation with Liquid Material(s)]
Fisher, N. & Bowen, D.D.: Spanish Textile Tradition of New Mexico and Colorado. Santa Fe 1979 [Analysis; Ethnography; Weaving; Ornamentation with Solid Material(s); Ornamentation with Liquid Material(s); Tapestry]
Fisk, L.L.: see also Strupp-Green, J.
Fiske, P.: "Imported and domestic textiles in 18th century America", I.Emery Roundtable on Mus. Textiles 1975, Washington 1976 [Folk Art; General, Historical]
Fiske, P.: see also Emery, I.
Fitzrandolph, M.: Traditional Quilting. London 1954 [Working Instruction; Ornamentation with Solid Material(s)]
Flanagan, J.F.: "Figured Fabrics", Singer, C. & Holmyard, E.J. (ed.) A History of Technology Band 3, Oxford 1957: 187-206 [Analysis; Ornamentation with Liquid Material(s)]
Flemming, E.: Textile Künste: Weberei, Stickerei, Spitze. Berlin 1923 [Analysis; Folk Art; Plaiting; Weaving; Ornamentation with Solid Material(s)]
Flemming, E.: Das Textilwerk. Tübingen 1957 [Archaeology; Collections; Weaving; Tapestry]
Flint, B.: Formes et symboles dans les arts maghrebins: Tome 2: Tapis, Tissage. Tanger 1974 [General, Historical; Warp Fabric; Weaving]
Floses, L.A.: El Guanasquero: Trenzados Criollos. Buenos Aires 1960 [Working Instruction; Mesh Fabric; Plaiting]
Flury von Bültzingslöwen, R.: "Einhängen", Heydenreich, C.H. & Gall, E. (ed.) Reallexikon zur dt. Kunstgeschichte. Stuttgart 1955 [Analysis, Mesh Fabric]
Flury von Bültzingslöwen, R.: "Endlicher und endloser Faden", Heydenreich, C.H. & Gall, E. (ed.) Reallexikon zur dt. Kunstgeschichte. Stuttgart 1955 [Analysis; Mesh Fabric]
Fondation Dapper: see also Biro, A.
Fontaine, A.: Zur Geschichte der Nähtechnik und der Nähmaschine: Erfindung d. Nähmaschine u. ihre tech. Entwicklung im 19.Jh. Dortmunder Reihe: didak. Mat. Textilunt. Dortmund 1986 [General, Historical; Fabric Processing]
Fontaine, P.: "Notes sur l' évolution qualitative des tapis dans la région d'Arâk (Iran central)", Objets et Mondes Vol. 22, N°1, Paris 1982: 19-24 [Ethnography; Pile Fabric]
Forbes, R.J. (ed.): Studies in Ancient Technology. 4, Leiden 1956 [Archaeology; Plaiting; Weaving; Tapestry]
Forcart-Respinger, E.: Basel und das Seidenband. Basel 1942 [General, Historical; Weaving]
Forde, D.: "Ethnography of the Yuma Indians", Univ. Calif. Publ. in Am. Archaeol. and Ethnol. 28 (4), Berkeley 1931: 57-83 [Ethnography; Plaiting]
Forelli, S. & Harries, J.: "Traditional Berberweaving in Central Marocco", Textile Museum Journal 4 (4), Washington 1977: 41-60 [Ethnography; Threads; Warp Fabric; Weaving; Pile Fabric]
Forman, M. & Wasseff, W.W.: Blumen der Wüste: Aegyptische Kinder Weaving Bildteppiche. Hanau 1968 [General, Historical; Weaving; Tapestry]
Forno, M.: "La raccolta di ornamenti ceremoniali Ghivaro", Annali Lateranensi 30, Rom 1966: 230-255 [Ethnography; Beadwork]

Forno, M.: "La racolta di indumenti Ghivaro", Ann. d. Pont. Mus. Miss. Etnol. Lat. 32, Rom 1968: 127-164 [Ethnography]
Forsythe, M.G.: "Modern Mien Needlework", Arts of Asia Vol.12 N°4, Hong Kong 1982: 83-93 [Ethnography; Ornamentation with Solid Material(s)]
Forsythe, M.G.: "From a Missionary's Closet", Arts of Asia Vol.17 N°1, Hong Kong 1987: 76-86 [Ethnography; Ornamentation with Solid Material(s)]
Foss, S.M.: "Urhobo Mats in Praise of Daughters", African Arts Vol.12 N°1, Los Angeles 1978: 60-62 [Ethnography; Plaiting]
Foster, G.M.: "The Mixe, Zoque, Popoluca", Handbook of Middle Am. Indians 7, Austin 1969: 448-477 [Ethnography; Mesh Fabric; Weaving]
Fowler, C.S. (ed.): Willard Park's Ethnographic Notes on the Northern Paiute of Western Nevada Anthropol. Pap. Uni. Utah 114 Vol.1, Salt Lake City 1989 [Ethnography; Threads; Plaiting]
Fowler, C.S. & Dawson, L.E.: "Ethnographic Basketry", Handbook of North American Indians 11, Washington 1986: 705-737 [Ethnography; Plaiting]
Fowler, C.S.: see also Kelly, I.T.
Fowler, D. & Matley, J.F.: Material culture of the Numa. Smithsonian Contr. to Anthrop. 26, Washington 1979 [Ethnography; Collections; Mesh Fabric; Plaiting; Pile Fabric; Ornamentation with Solid Material(s)]
Fox, N.: Pueblo Weaving and Textile Arts. Museum of New Mexico Press Guidebook N°3, Santa Fe 1978 [Analysis, Ethnography; Threads; Mesh Fabric; Plaiting; Weaving; Tapestry]
Foy, W.: "Australische Spindel", Ethnologica 1, Leipzig 1909: 226-230 [Ethnography; Threads]
Frame, M.: "Nasca Sprang Tassels: Structure, Technique, and Order", Textile Museum Journal, Washington 1981: 67-82 [Analysis; Archaeology; Warp Fabric]
Frame, M.: Ancient Peruvian Sprang Fabrics. Master's thesis, Vancouver 1982 [Archaeology; Warp Fabric]
Frame, M.: "Faugustino's Family: Knitters, Weavers and Spinners on the Island of Taquile, Peru", Rogers, N. et al. (ed.) In Celebration of the Curious Mind. Loveland 1983: 21-34 [Ethnography; Mesh Fabric; Weaving]
Frame, M.: "The Visual Images of Fabric Structures in Ancient Peruvian Art", Rowe, A.P. (ed.) J.B. Bird Conf. on Andean Textiles 1984, Washington 1986: 47-80 [Analysis; Archaeology; Warp Fabric]
Frame, M.: A Family Affair: Making Cloth in Taquile, Peru. Mus. Notes U.R.C. Mus. of Anthropology 26, Vancouver 1989 [Ethnography; Mesh Fabric; Plaiting; Weaving]
Frame, M.: Andean Four-Cornered Hats. Metrop. Mus. of Art, New York 1990 [Archaeology; Collections; Mesh Fabric; Weaving; Pile Fabric; Tapestry]
Franger, G.: see also Akkent, M.
Franquemont, C.R.: "Chinchero Pallays: An Ethnic Code", Rowe, A.P. (ed.) J.B. Bird Conf. on Andean Textiles 1984, Washington 1986: 331-338 [Ethnography; General, Historical; Weaving]
Franquemont, E.M.: "Reserved shed pebble weave in Peru", Rogers, N. (ed.) In Celebration of the Curious Mind. Loveland 1983: 43-53 [Analysis; Ethnography; Weaving]
Franquemont, E.M.: "Cloth Production Rates in Chinchero, Peru", Rowe, A.P. (ed.) J.B. Bird Conf. on Andean Textiles 1984, Washington 1986: 309-330 [Ethnography; General, Historical; Threads]
Frantisek, K.: Ein Beitrag zur Frage der Herkunft der Klöppelspitze in der Slowakei. Ethnographica, Brünn 1960 [Folk Art; Plaiting]
Frantz, K.: see also Frauenknecht, B.
Franzen, A.M.: see also Geijer, A.
Fraser-Lu, S.: "Kalagas: Burmese Wall Hangings and Related Embroideries", Arts of Asia Vol.12 N°4, Hong Kong 1982: 73-82 [Ethnography; Ornamentation with Solid Material(s)]
Fraser-Lu, S.: Indonesian Batik: Processes, patterns and places. New York 1986 [Ethnography; Ornamentation with Liquid Material(s)]
Fraser-Lu, S.: Handwoven textiles of South-East Asia. Singapore 1988 [Analysis; Ethnography; Warp Fabric; Weaving; Ornamentation with Solid Material(s); Ornamentation with Liquid Material(s)]
Frater, J.: "The meaning of folk art in Rabari life", Textile Museum Journal 4 (2), Washington 1975 [Ethnography; Ornamentation with Solid Material(s)]
Frauenknecht, B. & Frantz, K.: Anatolische Gebetskelims. Nürnberg 1975 [Ethnography; General, Historical; Tapestry]
Freeman, C.: The Pillow Lace in the East Midlands. Letchworth 1958 [Folk Art; Plaiting]
Freshley, K.T.: "Archaeological and Ethnographic Looms: A Bibliography", I.Emery Roundtable on Mus. Textiles 1977, Washington 1979: 269-314 [Ethnography; Archaeology; Weaving]
Frey, B.: "What is Leno?", Handweaver and Craftsman 6, New York 1955: 4-9 [Analysis; Weaving]
Freyvogel, T.: "Eine Sammlung geflochtener Matten aus dem Ulanga Distrikt Tanganyika", Acta Tropica Vol.16 N°4, Basel 1959: 289-301 [Analysis; Ethnography; Plaiting]
Friis, L.: see also Warburg, L.
Frödin, O. & Nordenskiöld, E.: Über Zwirnen und Spinnen bei den Indianern Südamerikas. Göteborgs Kungl. Vet. Vitt. Samm. 4, Göteborg 1918 [Classification; Ethnography; Threads]
Frost, G.: "Little known textiles of Guatemala: An Arbitrary Selection", I.Emery Roundtable on Mus. Textiles 1976, Washington 1977: 123-132 [Ethnography; Tapestry]
Fuhrman, I.: "Die Halsschnur von Bunsol", OFTA 6, Kiel 1941 [Analysis; Archaeology; Mesh Fabric]
Fukuni, S.: Kulturgeschichte von Ikat in Japan. Kyoto 1973 [Ethnography; Ornamentation with Liquid Material(s)]
Fung-Pineda, R.: "Análisis tecnológico de encajes del Antiguo Perú", Ravines (ed.) Tecnología Andina. Lima 1978: 333-345 [Archaeology; Ornamentation with Solid Material(s)]
Furger, A. & Hartmann, F.: Vor 5000 Jahren. Bern 1983 [Analysis; Archaeology; Threads; Plaiting; Weaving]
Futagami, Y. & Plötz, R.: Tsutsugaki-Aizome-Momen. Kevelaer 1983 [Ethnography; Ornamentation with Liquid Material(s)]

Gabric, P.: "Kosare an technici spiralnih strukoneva", Narodne Umjetnosti, Gabric 1, Zagreb 1962 [Folk Art; Plaiting]
Gabric, P.: "Jalba u seln trg kod ozlja", Jugoslavenska Akademija zna nosti 4 Ungebnosti, Zagreb 1962: 151-160 [Folk Art; Warp Fabric]
Gaitzsch, W.: Antike Korb- und Seilerwaren. Stuttgart 1986 [Analysis; Archaeology; Threads; Mesh Fabric; Plaiting]
Galestin, T.P. et al.: Lamak and Malat in Bali and a Sumba Loom. Amsterdam 1956 [Ethnography; Weaving]
Galhano, F.: see also Veiga de Oliveira, E.
Gallinger-Tod, O. & Benson, H.O.: Weaving with reeds and fibres. New York 1975 [Working Instruction; Plaiting; Weaving; Borders]
Gallinger-Tod, O. & Couch del Deo, J.: Designing and making handwoven rugs. New York 1976 [Analysis; Working Instruction; Weaving; Pile Fabric]
Gandert, A.: Tragkörbe in Hessen. Kassel 1963 [Folk Art; Plaiting]
Gans-Ruedin, E.: Handbuch der orientalischen und afrikanischen

Teppiche. München 1971 [General, Historical; Warp Fabric; Pile Fabric; Tapestry]
Garaventa, D.M.: "Chincha Textiles of the Late Intermediate Period, Epoch 8", The J.B.Bird Precolumbian Textile Conf. 1973, Washington 1979: 219-232 [Archaeology; Warp Fabric; Weaving]
Garaventa, D.M.: "A discontinuous warp and weft textile of early horizon date", Nawpa Pacha N°19, Berkeley 1981: 167-177 [Archaeology; Tapestry]
Gardi, B.: Die Weberei der Maabuube-Peul. Basel 1976 [Ethnography; Threads; Weaving]
Gardi, B.: Ein Markt wie Mopti: Handwerkerkasten und traditionelle Techniken in Mali. Basler Beiträge zur Ethnologie Band 25, Basel 1985 [Ethnography; Weaving]
Gardi, B. & Seydou, C.: ""Arkilla kerka": La tenture de mariage chez les Peuls du Mali", Basler Beiträge zur Ethnologie Band 30, Basel 1989: 83-106 [Ethnography; Weaving]
Gardi, R.: "Plangi und Tritik: Vom Färben mit Indigo in Nordkamerun", Atlantis Heft 8, Zürich 1957: 369-373 [Ethnography; Ornamentation with Liquid Material(s)]
Gardi, R.: "Färben und Weaving in Nord-Kamerun", Kosmos 12, Stuttgart 1958: 508-514 [Ethnography; Weaving; Ornamentation with Liquid Material(s)]
Gardner, J.S.: "Textiles precolombinos del Ecuador", Miscel. Antropológica Ecuatoriana 2, Quito 1982: 9-30 [Archaeology; Weaving; Ornamentation with Liquid Material(s)]
Gardner, J.S.: see also King, M.E.
Gass, S. & Lozado, J.H.A.& Dunkelberg, K.: Bambus / Bamboo: Bauen mit pflanzlichen Stäben / Building with vegetal rods. Mitteil. des Inst. für leichte Flächentragwerke 31, Stuttgart 1985 [Analysis; Ethnography; Plaiting; Borders]
Gaworski, M.: see also Warming, W.
Gayet, M.A.: Le Costume en Egypte du IIe au XIIIe siècle. Paris 1900 [General, Historical; Weaving]
Gayton, A.H.: Yokuts and Western Mono-Ethnography. Anthrop. Records 10 (1), Berkeley 1948 [Ethnography; Mesh Fabric; Warp Fabric]
Gayton, A.H.: see also Riesenberg, S.H.
Gazda, K. et al. (ed.): The Art of the Ancient Weaver: Textiles from Egypt. Ann Arbor 1980 [Archaeology; General, Historical; Warp Fabric; Weaving; Tapestry]
Geary, C.: "Basketry in the Aghem-Fungom Area of the Cameroon Grassfields", African Arts Vol.20 N°3, Los Angeles 1987: 42-53 [Ethnography; Plaiting; Ornamentation with Solid Material(s)]
Gehret, E.J. & Keyser, A.G.: The homespun textile tradition of the Pennsylvanian Germans. Harrisburg 1976 [Folk Art; General, Historical; Weaving]
Geijer, A.: "Oriental textiles in Scandinavian versions", Festschrift für Ernst Kühnel, n.p., n.d.: 323-335 [Mesh Fabric]
Geijer, A.: Birka 3, die Textilfunde aus den Gräbern. Uppsala 1938 [Archaeology; Plaiting; Warp Fabric]
Geijer, A.: Oriental textiles in Sweden. Kopenhagen 1951 [Weaving]
Geijer, A.: "Chinese silks exported to Russia in the 17th century", Bull. Mus. Far Eastern Antiq. 25, Stockholm 1953 [Weaving]
Geijer, A.: Engelska Broderier av Romanske Typ. Arbok 1956 [Archaeology]
Geijer, A.: "A silk from Antinoe and the Sasamian Textile Art", Orientalia Suecana 12, 1963, Uppsala 1964 [Archaeology; Weaving]
Geijer, A.: Treasures of Uppsala Cathedral. Uppsala 1964 [Folk Art; Weaving]
Geijer, A.: "Textiler och Arkeologie", Sartyck Svenske Naturvetenskp, 1967: 393-404 [Archaeology; Weaving]
Geijer, A.: Ur textilkonstens historia. Lund 1972 [Folk Art; Weaving; Pile Fabric; Tapestry]
Geijer, A.: A History of Textile Art. London 1979 [Analysis; Threads; Plaiting; Weaving; Pile Fabric; Borders; Tapestry]
Geijer, A.: A History of Textile Art: A Selective Account. Totowa, N.J. 1982 [Analysis; Folk Art; Weaving; Ornamentation with Solid Material(s)]
Geijer, A. & Franzen, A.M.: Textila Gravfynd fran Trondheims Domkrypta. Arbok 1956 [Archaeology; Weaving]
Geijer, A. & Hoffmann, M.: Nordisk Textilteknisk Terminologi. Oslo 1974 [Classification]
Geijer, A. & Lamm, C.: "Orientalische Briefumschläge in schwedischem Besitz", Kung. Vitterhets Hist. o. Antikv. Akad. Handlingar 58 (1), Stockholm 1944 [General, Historical; Weaving]
Geirnaert, D.: "Textiles of West Sumba: lively renaissance of an old tradition", Gittinger, M. (ed.) To Speak with Cloth. Los Angeles 1989: 56-79 [Ethnography; Weaving; Ornamentation with Solid Material(s); Ornamentation with Liquid Material(s)]
Geirnaert, D. & Heringa, R.: The A.E.D.T.A. batik collection. Paris 1989 [Ethnography; Ornamentation with Liquid Material(s)]
Geirnaert-Martin, D.: "Ask lurik why batik: A structural analysis of textiles and classification (Java)", Oosten, J. & Ruiter, de, A. (ed.) The Future of Structuralism. Amsterdam 1981 [Ethnography; Ornamentation with Liquid Material(s)]
Gellermann, N.L.: see also Patterson, N.
Genoud, J.: Vannerie traditionelle d'Afrique et d'Asie et "nouvelle vannerie". Los Angeles 1981 [Collections; Plaiting]
Georgens, D. & Von Gayette Georgens, J.M.: The Ladies' Book Needle Work. Berlin, London n.d. [Working Instruction; Plaiting; Ornamentation with Solid Material(s)]
Gerhards, E. (ed.): Weber und Schnitzer in Westafrika. Freiburg 1987 [Ethnography; Weaving]
Gerhardt-Wentzky, H.: "Sprang, eine alte textile Technik neu entdeckt", Stuttgart 1984 [Working Instruction; Warp Fabric]
Gerhardt-Wenzky, H.: Sprang. Topp Reihe 943, Stuttgart n.d. [Working Instruction; Warp Fabric]
Germann, P.: Spinnen (Gbande, Nordliberia). Encyclopaedia Cinematographica C 70, Göttingen 1963 [Ethnography; Films; Threads]
Gervers, V.: "An early christian curtain in the Royal Ontario Museum", Gervers, V. (ed.) Studies in Textile History. Toronto 1977: 56-81 [Analysis; Archaeology; Ornamentation with Liquid Material(s); Tapestry]
Gervers, V. (ed.): Studies in Textile History. Toronto 1977 [Analysis; Ethnography; Folk Art; Archaeology; Warp Fabric; Weaving; Ornamentation with Solid Material(s)]
Gervers, V.: see also Golombek, L.
Gettys, M. (ed.): Basketry of Southeastern Indians.Museum of the Red River, Idabel, Oklahoma 1984 [Ethnography; Plaiting]
Getzwiller, S.: The Fine Art of Navajo Weaving. Tucson 1984 [Ethnography; Tapestry]
Gewerbemuseum Basel: Textilkunst der Steppen- und Bergvölker Zentralasiens. Basel 1974 [Ethnography; Pile Fabric; Ornamentation with Solid Material(s); Ornamentation with Liquid Material(s)]
Ghose, A.: "Figured Fabrics of old Bengal", Marg Vol.3 N°1, Bombay 1948: 38-62 [Ethnography; Weaving]
Gibson, G.D. & Mc Gurk, C.R.: "High-status caps of the Kongo and Mbundu peoples", Textile Museum Journal 4 (4), Washington 1977: 71-96 [Analysis; Ethnography; Mesh Fabric]
Gifford, E.W.: "The Northfork Mono", UCLA Publ. Am. Arch. and Ethnol. Vol. 31, Berkeley 1931-33: 15-65 [Ethnography; Threads; Mesh Fabric; Plaiting]
Gil del Pozo, A.: Awar: tejidos en telar. La Cantuta 1974 [Ethno-

graphy; Working Instruction; Weaving; Pile Fabric]
Gilbert, K.R.: "Rope-Making", Singer, C. et al. (ed.) History of Technology 1, Oxford 1954: 451-455 [Threads]
Gilfoy, P.: "West African Looms", I.Emery Roundtable on Mus. Textiles 1977, Washington 1979: 43-53 [Ethnography; Weaving]
Gilfoy, P.S.: see also Vollmer, J.E.
Gill, H.S.: A phulkari from Bhatinda. Patiala 1977 [Ethnography; Ornamentation with Solid Material(s)]
Gimbatas, M.: Lithauian Folk Art. Los Angeles 1966 [Folk Art; Collections; Weaving]
Girault, L.: Textiles boliviens: Région de Charazani. Paris 1969 [Ethnography; Weaving]
Gisbert, T.: El Arte Textil en los Andes Bolivianos. n.p., n.d. [Ethnography; Collections; Weaving]
Gisbert, T. & Arze, S.& Cajias, M.: Arte textil y mundo andino. La Paz 1987 [Ethnography; Weaving; Tapestry]
Gittinger, M.S.: Splendid Symbols: Textiles and Traditions in Indonesia. The Textile Museum Washington, Washington 1971 [Analysis; Ethnography; Warp Fabric; Weaving; Ornamentation with Solid Material(s); Ornamentation with Liquid Material(s)]
Gittinger, M.S.: A study of the ship cloths of South Sumatra. Columbia Univ. Thesis, New York 1972 [Ethnography; Weaving]
Gittinger, M.S.: "South Sumatran ship cloths", The Bull. of the Needle and Bobbin Club Vol.57 N°1-2, New York 1974 [Ethnography; Weaving]
Gittinger, M.S.: "Additional Batak cloths that frequently enter into the gift exchange", Textile Museum Journal 4 (2), Washington 1975 [Ethnography; Warp Fabric]
Gittinger, M.S.: "Selected Batak textiles: Technique and function", Textile Museum Journal 4 (2), Washington 1975: 13-29 [Analysis; Ethnography]
Gittinger, M.S.: "Additions to the Indonesian collection", Textile Museum Journal 4 (3), Washington 1976: 43-48 [Collections; Ornamentation with Liquid Material(s)]
Gittinger, M.S.: Selections from the Textile Museum: Indonesia. Washington 1976 [Ethnography; Ornamentation with Liquid Material(s)]
Gittinger, M.S.: "The ship textiles of South Sumatra", Bijdragen tot de Taal-Land en Volkenkunde 132, s'-Gravenhage 1976: 207-227 [Ethnography; Ornamentation with Liquid Material(s)]
Gittinger, M.S.: "An Introduction to the Body-tension Loom and simple Frame Looms of Southeast Asia", I.Emery Roundtable on Mus. Textiles 1977, Washington 1979: 54-68 [Ethnography; Weaving]
Gittinger, M.S.: "Conversations with a Batik Master", Textile Museum Journal 18, Washington 1979: 25-32 [Ethnography; Ornamentation with Liquid Material(s)]
Gittinger, M.S.: "Symposium on Indonesian Textiles", I.Emery Roundtable on Mus. Textiles 1978, Washington 1979 [Ethnography; Ornamentation with Liquid Material(s)]
Gittinger, M.S.: "Indonesian Textiles", Arts of Asia, Sep.-Oct. Hong Kong 1980: 108-123 [Ethnography; Ornamentation with Liquid Material(s)]
Gittinger, M.S.: Master dyers to the World: Technique and trade in early Indian dyed cotton textiles. Washington 1982 [Ethnography; Ornamentation with Liquid Material(s)]
Gittinger, M.S. (ed.): To Speak with Cloth: Studies in Indonesian Textiles. Los Angeles 1989 [Analysis; Ethnography; Warp Fabric; Weaving; Borders; Ornamentation with Solid Material(s); Ornamentation with Liquid Material(s)]
Gittinger, M.S.: "Ingenious techniques in early Indian dyed cotton", Riboud, K. (ed.) In Quest of Themes and Skills. Bombay 1989: 4-15 [Ethnography; Ornamentation with Liquid Material(s)]
Gittinger, M.S.: "A Reassessment of the Tampan of South Sumatra", Gittinger, M. S. (ed.) To Speak with Cloth. Los Angeles 1989 [Ethnography; Weaving]
Glashauser, S. & Westfall, C.: Plaiting, Step-by-Step. New York 1976 [Working Instruction; Plaiting]
Glassmann, J.: Menschen und Maschinen: Industriegeschichtlicher Tatsachenbericht. Chemnitz 1935 [General, Historical; Mesh Fabric]
Glazier, R.: Historic textile fabrics. London 1923 [General, Historical; Weaving]
Gloor, V.: see also Churcher, E.
Gluck, J. & Gluck, S.H.: A survey of Persian Handicrafts. Teheran 1974 [Ethnography; Plaiting; Weaving; Pile Fabric; Ornamentation with Solid Material(s); Ornamentation with Liquid Material(s); Tapestry]
Gluck, S.H.: see also Gluck, J.
Gluckman, D.C.: see also Smart, E.S.
Gockerell, N.: Stickmustertücher. München 1980 [Folk Art; Ornamentation with Solid Material(s)]
Goddard, P.E.: Indians of the Southwest. Am. Mus. Nat. Hist. Handbook Series N°2, New York 1931 [Ethnography; Plaiting; Weaving]
Goddard, P.E.: Indians of the Northwest Coast. Am. Mus. Nat. Hist. Handbook Series N°10, New York 1934 [Ethnography; Plaiting]
Godon, R.: "Les formes du Batik dans l'Aurès", Revue Africaine 83 N°1 & 2, Alger 1944 [Ethnography; Ornamentation with Liquid Material(s)]
Goetz, H.: The Calico Museum of Textiles. Ahmedabad 1952 [Ethnography; Weaving; Tapestry]
Goggin, J.M.: "Plaited Basketry in the New World", Southwest. Journ. of Anthrop. 5 (2), Albuquerque 1949: 165-168 [Ethnography; Plaiting]
Gogol, J.M.: Columbia River Plateau Indian Beadwork. American Indian Basketry 18, Portland 1985 [Collections; Beadwork]
Goitein, S.D.: Portraits of a Yemenite Weaver's Village. Jewish Social Studies, New York 1955 [Ethnography; Weaving]
Golden de Bone, M.: "Patolu and its technique", Textile Museum Journal 4 (3), Washington 1976: 49-62 [Analysis; Ethnography; Ornamentation with Liquid Material(s)]
Golombek, L. & Gervers, V.: "Tiraz fabrics in the Royal Ontario Museum", Gervers, V. (ed.) Studies in Textile History. Toronto 1977: 82-125 [Archaeology]
Gombos, K.: Altorientalische Webteppiche und Stickerei. Sàrvàr 1980 [General, Historical; Ornamentation with Solid Material(s); Tapestry]
Goodell, G.: "A study of Andean Spinning in the Cuzco-Region", Textile Museum Journal 5 (3), Washington 1968 [Ethnography; Threads]
Goodman, F.S.: The embroidery of Mexico and Guatemala. New York 1976 [Analysis; Ethnography; Ornamentation with Solid Material(s)]
Goody, E.N.: "Daboya weavers: relations of production, dependence and reciprocity", Goody, E.N. (ed.) From craft to industry. Cambridge 1982: 50-84 [Ethnography; General, Historical; Weaving]
Gordon, B.: Shaker textile arts. London 1980 [Analysis; Folk Art; Threads; Weaving; Ornamentation with Solid Material(s)]
Goslings, B.M.: see also Couvreur, A.J.L.
Gostelow, M.: Embroidery. London 1977 [Analysis; Working Instruction; Ornamentation with Solid Material(s)]
Gowd, K.V.N.: Selected Crafts of Andhra Pradesh. Census of

India 2 (7A), Delhi 1965 [Ethnography; Mesh Fabric; Plaiting]
Grabowicz, O.: Traditional Designs in Ukrainian Textiles. Ukrainian Mus. New York 1977 [Folk Art; Collections; Weaving; Ornamentation with Solid Material(s)]
Grabowicz, O.: Ukrainian Embroidery Craft. Ukrainian Mus. New York 1980 [Folk Art; Collections; Ornamentation with Solid Material(s)]
Grabowicz, O. & Wolinetz, L.: Rushniky: Ukrainian Ritual cloths. Ukrainian Mus. New York 1981 [Folk Art; Collections; Weaving; Ornamentation with Solid Material(s)]
Gräbner, E.: Die Weberei. Leipzig 1922 [Analysis; Weaving; Pile Fabric]
Gräbner, F.: "Hängematten aus Neuguinea", Ethnologica 1, Leipzig 1909: 223-224 [Ethnography; Mesh Fabric]
Gräbner, F.: "Völkerkunde der Santa-Cruz-Inseln", Ethnologica 1, Leipzig 1909: 71-184 [Ethnography; Threads; Plaiting; Weaving; Pile Fabric]
Gräbner, F.: "Gewirkte Taschen und Spiralwulstkörbe in der Südsee", Ethnologica 2, Leipzig 1913: 25-42 [Ethnography; Mesh Fabric; Plaiting]
Grafton, C.B.: Geometric patchwork patterns. New York 1975 [Working Instruction; Ornamentation with Solid Material(s)]
Grange, R.: see also Bluhm, E.
Grant, J.: "A note on the Materials of ancient textiles and baskets", Singer, C. (ed.) A History of Technology Band 1, Oxford 1954: 447-455 [Analysis; Archaeology; Plaiting]
Graumont, R.: Handbook of Knots. Cambridge 1945 [Analysis; Mesh Fabric]
Graumont, R. & Hensel, J.: Encyclopaedia of Knots and Fancy Rope Work. New York 1942 [Analysis; Mesh Fabric]
Graumont, R. & Wenstrom, E.: Fisherman's Knots and Nets. New York 1948 [Analysis; Mesh Fabric]
Graw, de, I.G. & Kuhn, D.: Secret Splendor of the Chinese Court. Denver 1981 [General, Historical; Weaving]
Green Gigli, J. et al.: Collected Papers on Aboriginal Basketry. Nevada State Mus. Anthrop. Papers 16, Carson City 1974 [Analysis; Ethnography; Plaiting; Borders]
Grieder, T.: "Preceramic and Initial Period Textiles from La Galgada, Peru", Rowe, A.P. (ed.) J.B. Bird Conf. on Andean Textiles 1984, Washington 1986: 19-30 [Analysis; Archaeology; Mesh Fabric; Warp Fabric; Weaving]
Grieder, T. et al.: La Galgada, Peru. Austin 1988 [Analysis; Archaeology; Mesh Fabric; Plaiting; Warp Fabric]
Gross, N.D.: Shisha embroidery: traditional Indian mirror work with instructions and transfer patterns. Dover 1981 [Working Instruction; Ornamentation with Solid Material(s)]
Grosset, J.W.: Zulu Crafts. Pietermaritzburg 1978 [Ethnography; Plaiting; Warp Fabric]
Grossman, E.F.: "An Ancient Peruvian Loom", Handweaver and Craftsman 9 (2), New York 1958: 20-21 [Archaeology; Weaving]
Grossmann, E.F.: "Textiles and Looms from Guatemala and Mexico", Handweaver and Craftsman Vol 7 N°1, 55-56, New York 1955: 6-11 [Ethnography; Warp Fabric]
Grostol, A.: Sprang: med arbeitdsteikningar. Oslo 1932 [Working Instruction; Warp Fabric]
Grote-Hasenbalg, W.: Der Orientteppich. Berlin 1922 [General, Historical; Pile Fabric]
Grothe, H.: Die Construction der Webstühle im Altertum. Berlin 1883 [General, Historical; Weaving]
Grothe, H.: "Der Kalamkar", Orientalisches Archiv N°2, 1911-12, Berlin 1912: 132-138 [General, Historical; Ornamentation with Liquid Material(s)]
Gruber, A.: Chinoiserie. Riggisberg 1984 [General, Historical; Weaving]
Gruber, A. (ed.): Jagdmotive auf Textilien von der Antike bis zum 18. Jahrhundert.Ausstellungskatalog. Abegg-Stiftung Riggisberg, Riggisberg 1990 [Collections; Weaving; Ornamentation with Solid Material(s); Tapestry]
Grünberg, G.& F.: "Die materielle Kultur der Kayabi-Indianer", Archiv für Völkerkunde 21, Wien 1967: 27-88 [Analysis; Ethnography; Collections; Mesh Fabric; Plaiting; Weaving; Pile Fabric; Borders]
Gubser, T.: Die bäuerliche Seilerei: Sterbendes Handwerk 6. Schweiz. Ges. für Volkskunde Heft 6, Basel 1965 [Folk Art; Threads]
Gudjonsson, E.E.: "Icelandic Medieval Embroidery: Terms and Techniques", Gervers, V. (ed.) Studies in Textile History. Toronto 1977: 133-143 [Folk Art; Ornamentation with Solid Material(s)]
Guelton, M.H.: "The ceremonial role of Indonesian textiles as illustrated by those of Sumatra", Riboud, K. (ed.) In Quest of Themes and Skills. Bombay 1989: 100-111 [Ethnography; Weaving; Ornamentation with Solid Material(s); Ornamentation with Liquid Material(s)]
Guernsey, S.J.: see also Kidder, A.V.
Guhr, G.& Neumann, P. (ed.): Ethnographisches Mosaik. Berlin 1982 [Ethnography; Collections; Mesh Fabric; Plaiting; Weaving; Pile Fabric; Beadwork; Ornamentation with Solid Material(s)]
Guiart, J.: "Sacs en fibre d'Australie", Journal de la Société Océan. 1, 2, 1945-6, Paris 1945: 81-89 [Ethnography; Mesh Fabric]
Guicherd, F.: "A propos de la Méchanique Jaquard", Bull. des Soies et Soieries. Août, Lyon 1952 [General, Historical; Weaving]
Gulati, A.N.: The patola of Gujarat. Ahmedabad 1951 [Ethnography; Ornamentation with Liquid Material(s)]
Guliev, G.A.: Aus der Geschichte der Weberei in Aserbeidschan. Nachrichten der Akademie d. Wiss. 7, 1961 [Archaeology; Weaving]
Guliev, G.A.: Über Aserbeidschanische Naboika. Sovetskaja Ethnografia 2, Moskau 1964 [Folk Art]
Gupta, C.S.: Survey of selected crafts: Rajasthan. New Delhi 1966 [Analysis; Ethnography; Pile Fabric]
Gusic, M.: Commentary on the exhibited Material. Zagreb 1955 [Folk Art; Collections; Plaiting; Ornamentation with Solid Material(s)]
Guss, D.M.: To Weave and Sing: Art, Symbol and Narrative in the South American Rain Forest. Berkeley 1989 [Analysis; Ethnography; Plaiting]
Gustafson, P.: Salish weaving. Seattle 1980 [Folk Art; Weaving]
Gwinner, von, S.: Die Geschichte des Patchworkquilts: Ursprünge, Traditionen und Symbolik einer textilen Kunst. München 1987 [Ethnography; Folk Art; Ornamentation with Solid Material(s)]
Gyula, V.: Textilien und Lederstrickwaren aus dem Debrecimen Déri Museum. Debrecim 1984 [Collections; Mesh Fabric]

Haake, A.: Javanische Batik: Methode – Symbole – Geschichte. Hannover 1984 [Analysis; Ethnography; Working Instruction; Ornamentation with Liquid Material(s)]
Haas, S.: "Japanische Papierschablonen für Komon und Chugata Muster", Jahrbuch des Bern. Hist. Mus 43/44, Bern 1966: 515-524 [Ethnography; Ornamentation with Liquid Material(s)]
Haas, S.: Beiträge zur Ethnography der Jainsri (Nordindien). Basel 1970 [Ethnography; Threads; Mesh Fabric; Plaiting; Weaving]
Haas, S. et al.: Götter – Tiere – Blumen: Gelbguss und Stickereien aus Indien. Basel 1987 [Ethnography; Collections; Ornamentation with Solid Material(s)]

Haase, Y.D.: see also Hammel, E.A.
Haberland, E.: Galla Süd-Äthiopiens. Frankfurt 1963 [Ethnography; Threads; Mesh Fabric; Plaiting, Weaving]
Haberland, W.: "Gewebe mit unechtem Plangi von der Zentralperuanischen Küste", Baessler-Archiv NF 12, Berlin 1964: 271-279 [Archaeology; Ornamentation with Liquid Material(s)]
Haberland, W.: Donnervogel und Raubwal. Die indianische Kunst der Nordwestküste Nordamerikas. Hamburg 1979 [Ethnography; Plaiting; Warp Fabric; Ornamentation with Solid Material(s)]
Haberlandt, M.: Textile Volkskunst aus Österreich. Aus den Sammlungen des K.K. Museums für Österr. Volkskunst in Wien. Wien 1912 [Folk Art; Mesh Fabric; Plaiting, Weaving; Beadwork; Ornamentation with Solid Material(s)]
Hacker, K.F.: "Bandha Textiles: India's Ikat and Plangi Expression", Arts of Asia Vol.12 N°4, Hong Kong 1982: 63-71 [Ethnography; Ornamentation with Liquid Material(s)]
Hadaway, W.S.: Cotton Painting and Printing in the Madras Presidency. Madras 1911 [Ethnography; Ornamentation with Liquid Material(s)]
Haddon, A.C. & Start, L.: Iban or Sea Dayak Fabrics. Bedford 1982 [Ethnography; Weaving; Ornamentation with Liquid Material(s)]
Häberlin: Plaiting und Weaving auf Föhr und den Halligen. Braunschweig 1907 [Analysis; Folk Art; Plaiting]
Haeberlin, H.K. & Teit, J.A.: "Coiled Basketry in British Columbia and Surrounding Region", Annual Rep. of the Bur. of Ethnol. 41, 1919-24, Washington 1928: 119-484 [Analysis; Ethnography; Plaiting; Borders]
Haebler, R.: "Die geflochtenen Hängematten der Naturvölker Südamerikas", Zeitschrift für Ethnologie 51, Berlin 1919: 1-18 [Analysis; Ethnography; Warp Fabric]
Haegenbart, H.: Seltene Webtaschen aus dem Orient. München 1982 [Ethnography; Collections; Tapestry]
Hägg, I.: Die Textilfunde aus dem Hafen von Haithabu. Berichte über die Ausgrabungen, Neumünster 1984 [Archaeology; Weaving; Borders; Ornamentation with Liquid Material(s); Fabric Processing]
Hagino, J.P. & Stothert, K.E.: "Weaving a Cotton Saddlebag on the Santa Elena Peninsula Ecuador", Textile Museum Journal 22, Washington 1983: 19-32 [Analysis, Ethnography; Weaving]
Hahn, A.: see also Hissink, K.
Hahn, J.: "Spinnen und Weben im Orient und in Europa", Zeitschrift für Ethnologie 56, Berlin 1924 [General, Historical; Threads; Weaving]
Hahn, R.: see also Brunner-Littmann, B.
Hahn, W.: Die Fachsprache der Textilindustrie im 17. und 18. Jh. Technikgeschichte in Einzeldarstellungen 6538, Düsseldorf 1971 [General, Historical; Weaving]
Hahn-Hissink, K.: Volkskunst aus Guatemala. Frankfurt 1971 [Ethnography; Collections; Weaving]
Hahn-Hissink, K.: see also Hissink, K.
Haidler, M.: see also Rosenberg, A.
Hailey, M.: "Silk industry in the Punjab", The Journal of Indian Art, London 1904 [Ethnography; Weaving]
Hald, M.: Brikvaevning. Copenhagen 1932 [Folk Art; Weaving]
Hald, M.: "Le tissage aux plaques dans les trouvailles préhistoriques du Danemark", Mém. de la Soc. Roy. des Antiqu. du Nord 1931, Copenhague 1933: 389-416 [Archaeology; Weaving]
Hald, M.: "Lundavanten", Särtyck ur Kulturen, Årsbok 1945: 80-83 [Folk Art; Mesh Fabric]
Hald, M.: Olddanske Textiler. Copenhagen 1950 [Analysis; Archaeology; Mesh Fabric; Plaiting, Warp Fabric, Weaving; Borders; Ornamentation with Solid Material(s)]
Hald, M.: An unfinished tubular fabric from the Chiriguano Indians, Bolivia. Ethnogr. Museum of Sweden Mon. 7, Stockholm 1962 [Analysis; Ethnography; Plaiting]
Hald, M.: "Pits, looms and loom pits: Waevning over Gruber", Kuml, Aarhus 1963: 88-107 [Archaeology; Weaving]
Hald, M.: Oldtidsvaeve: Forhistorik Museum. Aarhus 1967 [Collections; Weaving]
Hald, M.: Flettede baand og snore. Gyldendal 1975 [Analysis; Working Instruction; Mesh Fabric; Plaiting]
Hald, M.: Ancient Danish textiles from Bogs and Burials. Publ. Nat. Mus. Arch. Hist. Series 21, Kopenhagen 1980 [Analysis; Archaeology; Threads; Mesh Fabric; Weaving; Borders; Fabric Processing]
Hald, M.: see also Broholm, H.C.
Hali. From 1978 on. London]
Hall, M. & Irwin, J.: Indian painted and printed fabrics. Ahmedabad 1971 [Ethnography; Collections; Ornamentation with Liquid Material(s)]
Hambruch, P.: "Ikatgewebe in Guatemala", Tagungsbericht dt. Anthr. Ges. Hamburg 1929: 61-65 [Ethnography; General, Historical; Ornamentation with Liquid Material(s)]
Hames, R.& I.: "Ye'kwana basketry", Antropológica 44, Carácas 1976: 3-58 [Ethnography; Plaiting]
Hamilton, B. & Hamilton, D.: Alte und neue amerikanische Quilts. Linz 1976 [Folk Art; Ornamentation with Solid Material(s)]
Hamilton, D.: see also Hamilton, B.
Hamilton, S.: "Some Rug Looms of the near and middle East", I.Emery Roundtable on Mus. Textiles 1977, Washington 1979: 33-42 [Ethnography; Weaving]
Hammel, E.A. & Haase, Y.D.: A survey of Peruvian fishing communities. Anthrop. Records 21 (2), Berkeley 1962 [Ethnography; Mesh Fabric]
Hänsel, V.: Kreuzstichmuster: aus der Sammlung des Landschaftmuseum Schloss Trautenfels. Liezen 1983 [Folk Art; Working Instruction; Ornamentation with Solid Material(s)]
Hansen, E.: Tablet Weaving: History, Techniques, Colours, Patterns. Højbjerg 1990 [Analysis; Working Instruction; Weaving]
Hansen, H.H.: "Some Costumes of Highland Burma", Etnologiska Studier 24, Göteborg 1960 [Ethnography; Weaving]
Hardjonagoro, K.R.T.: "The place of batik in the history and the philosophy of Javanese textiles: a personal view", I.Emery Roundtable on Mus. Textiles 1979, Washington 1980: 223-242 [Ethnography; Ornamentation with Liquid Material(s)]
Hardouin, G.: Album de broderie et de filet. Paris n.d. [Working Instruction; Ornamentation with Solid Material(s)]
Harmsen, W.D. (ed.): Patterns and Sources of Navajo weaving. n.p. 1977 [Collections; Weaving; Tapestry]
Harner, S.D.: "An early intermediate period textile sequence from Ancón, Peru", Rowe, A.P. et al. (ed.) The J.B.Bird Precolumbian Textile Conf. 1973, Washington 1979: 151-164 [Archaeology, Mesh Fabric; Plaiting; Weaving]
Harries, J.: see also Forelli, S.
Harrington, M.R.: see also Loud, L.L.
Harris, M.F.: The royal cloth of Cameroon. Ann Arbor 1986 [Ethnography; Ornamentation with Liquid Material(s)]
Hartkamp-Jonxis, E.: "Indian export chintzes", Riboud, K. (ed.) In Quest of Themes and Skills. Bombay 1989: 80-91 [Ethnography; Weaving; Ornamentation with Liquid Material(s)]
Hartkopf, M.: "Webkunst und Trachten der bolivianischen Hochlandindios", Baessler-Archiv NF 19, Berlin 1971: 97-114 [Ethnography; Weaving]
Hartland-Rowe, M.: "The Textile Prints of the Phuthadikobo Museum", African Arts Vol.18 N°3, Los Angeles 1985: 84-86 [Ethnography; Collections; Ornamentation with Liquid

Material(s)]
Hartmann, F.: see also Furger, A.
Hartmann, G.: "Die materielle Kultur der Xikrin, Zentralbrasilien", Baessler-Archiv NF 13, Berlin 1966: 103-124 [Ethnography; Plaiting]
Hartmann, G.: "Die materielle Kultur der Wayaná /]
Nordostbrasilien", Baessler-Archiv NF 19, Berlin 1971: 379-420 [Ethnography; Plaiting; Pile Fabric]
Hartmann, G.: Zwischen Amazonas und Orinoko. Berlin 1972 [Ethnography; Plaiting; Warp Fabric]
Hartmann, G.: Molakana: Volkskunst der Cuna, Panama. Veröff. des Mus. für Völkerkunde NF 37, Berlin 1980 [Ethnography; Collections; Ornamentation with Solid Material(s)]
Hartmann, H.: Indonesien: Kunst und Handwerk. Celle 1952 [Collections; Plaiting; Ornamentation with Liquid Material(s)]
Hartmann, U.: "Klassische Molakana im durchbrochenen Silhouettenstil bei den Kuna, Panama", Zeitschrift für Ethnologie 110, 1985, Berlin 1985: 99-110 [Ethnography; Ornamentation with Solid Material(s)]
Hartmann, U.: "Stilrichtungen bei den Molakana der Kuna-Indianerinnen Panamas am Beispiel der Schildkrötendarstellung", Zeitschrift für Ethnologie 111, Berlin 1986: 259-269 [Ethnography; Ornamentation with Solid Material(s)]
Hartung, R.: Textiles Werken: Das Spiel mit den bildnerischen Mitteln. Band 4, Ravensburg 1963 [Working Instruction; Mesh Fabric; Plaiting; Warp Fabric; Pile Fabric]
Harvey, A.E.: "Archaeological Fabrics from the lower Missouri Valley", I.Emery Roundtable on Mus. Textiles 1974, Washington 1975: 133-140 [Archaeology, Plaiting]
Harvey, M.R. & Kelly, I.: "The Totonac", Handbook of Middle Am. Indians 8, Austin 1969: 638-681 [Ethnography; Threads; Plaiting; Weaving]
Harvey, V.I.: Split-ply twining. Threads in Action, Monograph Series, Freeland 1976 [Classification; Analysis; Plaiting]
Harvey, V.I.: "Derivative work based on porcupine quill embroidery", Rogers, N. (ed.) In Celebration of the Curious Mind. Loveland 1983: 55-61 [Folk Art; Working Instruction; Ornamentation with Solid Material(s)]
Harvey, V.I.: The techniques of basketry. Seattle 1986 [Analysis; Plaiting; Borders]
Haselberger, H.: "Bemerkungen zum Kunsthandwerk im Podo (Republik Mali)", Baessler-Archiv NF 13, Berlin 1965: 433-499 [Ethnography; Ornamentation with Liquid Material(s)]
Hasenfratz, A.: see also Winiger, J.
Hathaway, S.: see also Mailey, J.E.
Haug, P.: Indianische Perlenarbeit. Das deutsche Beadwork-Handbuch: Geschichte, Materialien, Techniken. Wyk auf Föhr 1988 [Ethnography; Beadwork]
Hauser-Schäublin, B.: Leben in Linie, Muster und Farbe. Basel 1989 [Ethnography; Collections; Mesh Fabric; Plaiting]
Hauser-Schäublin, B. & Nabholz-Kartaschoff, M.L.& Ramseyer, U.: Textilien in Bali. Singapore, Basel 1991 [Ethnography; Weaving; Ornamentation with Liquid Material(s)]
Hauser-Schäublin, B. & Nabholz-Kartaschoff, M.L.& Ramseyer, U.: Textiles in Bali. Singapore, Basel 1991 [Ethnography; Weaving; Ornamentation with Liquid Material(s)]
Hausner, W.: "S and Z twist", Handweaver and Craftsman 14, New York 1963 [General, Historical; Threads]
Haussmann, A.: "Impression sur tissus de coton en Chine", Bull. Soc. Ind. de Mulhouse 20, Mulhouse 1847 [Ethnography; Ornamentation with Liquid Material(s)]
Heathcote, D.: "Hausa women's dress in the light of two recent finds", Savanna Vol.2 N°2, 1973: 201-217 [Ethnography; Ornamentation with Solid Material(s)]
Heathcote, D.: "Hausa Embroidery Stitches", The Nigerian Field Vol.39 N°4, London 1974: 163-168 [Ethnography; Ornamentation with Solid Material(s)]
Heathcote, D.: "Hausa hand-embroidered caps", The Nigerian Field Vol.40 N°2, London 1975: 54-73 [Ethnography; Ornamentation with Solid Material(s)]
Heathcote, D.: The Arts of the Hausa. London 1976 [Ethnography; Collections; Plaiting; Weaving; Ornamentation with Solid Material(s)]
Heathcote, D.: The Embroidery of Hausa Dress. Zaria 1979 [Ethnography; Ornamentation with Solid Material(s)]
Hecht, A.: The Art of the Loom: Weaving, Spinning and Dyeing across the World. British Museum Publications, London 1989 [Analysis; Ethnography; Archaeology; Threads; Warp Fabric; Weaving; Ornamentation with Solid Material(s); Ornamentation with Liquid Material(s)]
Heermann, I.: Südsee-Abteilung. Linden-Museum, Stuttgart 1989 [Ethnography; Collections; Mesh Fabric; Plaiting; Beadwork]
Heiden, M.: Handwörterbuch der Textilkunde aller Zeiten und Völker. Stuttgart 1904 [General, Historical]
Heikinmäki, M.C.: Die Gaben der Braut bei den Finnen und Esten. Kanstieteelinen Arkisto 21, Helsinki 1970 [Folk Art; Mesh Fabric; Weaving]
Heine-Geldern, von, R.: Indonesian Art. The Art Institute, Chicago 1949 [Collections; Ornamentation with Liquid Material(s)]
Heinze, S.: Art Teaching for Secondary Schools. Kuching 1969 [Working Instruction; Plaiting; Beadwork; Ornamentation with Liquid Material(s)]
Heissig, W. & Müller, C.C.: "Der Gebrauch der Applikationstechnik bei der Thanka Herstellung", Chabrol, K. (ed.) Die Mongolen. Innsbruck 1989: 184-186 [Analysis; Ethnography; Plaiting; Weaving; Beadwork; Ornamentation with Solid Material(s)]
Heizer, R.F. (ed.): California.Handbook of North Am. Indians 8, Washington 1987 [Ethnography; Mesh Fabric; Plaiting; Warp Fabric; Pile Fabric; Beadwork]
Heizer, R.F. & Weitlaner-Johnson, I.: "A prehistoric sling from Lovelock Cave Nevada", American Antiquity 18, 1952-53, Salt Lake City 1953: 139-147 [Archaeology; Warp Fabric]
Held, S.E.: Weaving. New York 1973 [Weaving]
Helford, W.: "Some problems concerning the "art of war" tapestries", Cieta 41-42, 1-2, Lyon 1975: 100-118 [Threads]
Hellervik, G.: Paracas-Nascatextilier fran södra Peru. Uppsala 1977 [Archaeology; Warp Fabric; Weaving; Pile Fabric; Borders; Ornamentation with Solid Material(s); Fabric Processing]
Hemert, van, M.: "De handwerken op het eiland Marken", Monograph. van het Rijksmuseum v. Volk. Arnhem 1967 [Analysis; Folk Art; Ornamentation with Solid Material(s)]
Henking, K.H.: "Ein Königsornat von Hawaii im Bernischen Historischen Museum", Jahrbuch Hist. Mus. Bern Band 34 1954, Bern 1955: 231-244 [Ethnography; Mesh Fabric; Pile Fabric]
Henking, K.H.: "Die Südsee- und Alaskasammlung Johann Wäber", Jahrbuch Hist. Mus. Bern Band 35 & 36 1955-56, Bern 1957 [Ethnography; Plaiting; Warp Fabric; Beadwork]
Henley, P. & Mattei-Muller, M.C.: "Panare Basketry: Means of commercial exchange and artistic experience", Antropológica 49, Caracas 1978: 29-131 [Ethnography; Plaiting]
Henneberg, von, A.: "Die altägyptischen Gewebe des Ethnographischen Museums im Trocadéro", Bull. du Musée d'Ethnography N°4, Paris 1932 [Archaeology; Weaving; Borders]
Hennemann, D.: Iko-Buschmänner (Südafrika, Kalahari): Herstellen eines Seiles für die Schlingfalle. Encyclopaedia Cinematographica E 2118, Göttingen 1975 [Ethnography; Films; Threads]
Henninger, J.: "Ein Beitrag zur Kenntnis der Herstellungsweise

feiner Matten", Baessler-Archiv NF 19, Berlin 1971: 29-46 [Ethnography; Plaiting]
Henriksen, M.A.: "A Preliminanary Note on Some Northern Thai Woven Patterns", Scand. Inst. of Asian Stud. Kopenhagen 1978: 137-159 [Ethnography; Weaving]
Henschen, I.: Tygtryck i Sverige. Nordiska Museets Handlingar N°14, Stockholm 1942 [Folk Art, Ornamentation with Liquid Material(s)]
Henschen, I.: Sventska vävnander. Stockholm 1943 [Folk Art; Weaving]
Henschen, I.: Handicrafts in Sweden. Stockholm 1951 [Folk Art; Weaving; Pile Fabric]
Hensel, J.: see also Graumont, R.
Henshall, A.: "Textiles and Weaving Appliances in Prehistoric Britain", Proc.of the Prehistoric Soc. 10, Cambridge 1950: 130-162 [Analysis; Archaeology; Threads; Plaiting; Weaving]
Hentschel, K.: "Herstellung der peruanischen und mexikanischen zwei- bis dreischichtigen Hohlgewebe", Baessler-Archiv 20, Berlin 1937: 97-112 [Analysis; Archaeology; Working Instruction; Weaving]
Hentschel, K.: Wolle spinnen mit Herz und Hand. Frankfurt 1949 [Folk Art; Threads]
Hentschel, K.: Der Weg zu den Hohlgeweben. n.p. 1962 [Working Instruction]
Heringa, R.: "Dye process and life sequence: the coloring of textiles in a Javanese village", Gittinger, M. (ed.) To Speak with Cloth. Los Angeles 1989: 106-130 [Ethnography; Weaving; Ornamentation with Liquid Material(s)]
Heringa, R.: see also Geirnaert, D. [Herle, A.: "Traditional Body Ornaments from the Naga Hills", Arts of Asia Vol.20 N°2, Hong Kong 1990: 154-166 [Ethnography; Plaiting]
Herrli, H.: Indische Durri. Band 3, o.O. 1985 [Ethnography; Collections; Tapestry]
Hersh, P.A.: see also Berry, G.M.
Herzog, M.: Kulturgeschichtliche Beispiele zum Thema Fussbekleidung. Dortmunder Reihe: didakt. Mat. für den Textilunt. 2(1), Schalksmühle 1985 [Ethnography; Folk Art; Plaiting; Warp Fabric; Ornamentation with Solid Material(s)]
Heuermann, L.: Bildbatiken. Wien 1972 [Analysis; Ornamentation with Liquid Material(s)]
Hicks, S.: Führer durch die Galerie Alice Pauli. Los Angeles 1975 [General, Historical]
Hicks, S.: Tapisserie mise en liberté. Fuhrer durch das "Maison de la culture de Rennes". Rennes 1976 [Folk Art; Weaving; Tapestry]
Higuera, D.: Los Guajibo de Coromoto. Algunos Aspectos Culturales. Vicariato Apostólico, Monografía N°3, Pt. Ayacucho 1987 [Ethnography; Plaiting]
Hill, J.S.: see also Wassermann, T.E.
Hinderling, P.: "Stoffbildendes Schnurverschlingen", Baessler-Archiv NF 7, Berlin 1959: 1-79 [Classification; Threads; Mesh Fabric]
Hinderling, P.: "Schnüre und Seile, Methode zur technischen Bestimmung für volkskundlichen Gebrauch", Bull. der Sch. Ges. f. Anthr. u. Ethnol. Zürich 1960 [Classification; Threads]
Hinderling, P.: "Über die Herstellung von Schnur- und Ledertaschen in Nord Kamerun", Festschrift A. Bühler Basel 1965: 183-186 [Ethnography; Mesh Fabric]
Hirsch, U.: see also Mellaart, J.
Hissink, K.: Gewebe aus Alt-Peru. Ausstellung Arena und Tor, Frankfurt 1965 [Archaeology; Weaving]
Hissink, K. & Hahn, A.: Die Tacana. Wiesbaden 1984 [Analysis, Ethnography; Plaiting; Warp Fabric; Weaving]
Hissink, K. & Hahn, A.: Chimane: Notizen und Zeichnungen aus Nordost-Bolivien. Stuttgart 1989 [Analysis; Ethnography; Threads; Plaiting; Warp Fabric; Weaving]
Hitchcock, M.: Indonesian Textiles Techniques. Aylesbury 1985 [Ethnography; Weaving; Ornamentation with Liquid Material(s)]
Hitkari, S.S.: Phulkari. New Delhi 1980 [Ethnography; Ornamentation with Solid Material(s)]
Hitkari, S.S.: Ganesha-Sthapana: The folk art of Gujarat. New Delhi 1981 [Ethnography]
Hitkari, S.S.: "Embroidering gardens when dreams flower into marriage", The India Magazin Vol.5 N°1, 1981, Bombay 1985: 28-35 [Ethnography; Ornamentation with Solid Material(s)]
Hitkari, S.S.: "Stickereien für Ganesch", Schmitt-Moser, E. et al. (ed.) Indische Frauenkunst. Bayreuth 1989: 16-19 [Ethnography; Ornamentation with Solid Material(s)]
Hobi, F.: Flechtkunst aus Afrika, Asien und Lateinamerika. Winterthur 1982 [Ethnography; Collections; Plaiting]
Hochberg, B.: Handspindles. Santa Cruz 1980 [Threads]
Hochfelden, B.: Frivolitäten-Arbeiten. Berlin n.d. [Working Instruction; Mesh Fabric]
Hodge, A.: Nigeria's traditional crafts: a survey. London 1982 [Ethnography; Plaiting; Weaving; Ornamentation with Liquid Material(s)]
Hodges, H.: Artifacts. London 1965 [Analysis; Threads; Plaiting; Warp Fabric; Weaving; Pile Fabric; Borders]
Högl, P.: "Ein bucharisches Zelt", Baessler-Archiv NF 28, Berlin 1980: 61-72 [Ethnography; Weaving]
Hörlèn, M.: "Prydnadsvävar: Kuddar – Löpane – Dubar", Mönsterblad 4, Stockholm 1948 [Folk Art; Working Instruction; Weaving]
Hörlèn, M.: "Transmattor och sängöverkast", Mönsterblad 6, Stockholm 1950 [Folk Art; Working Instruction; Weaving]
Hoffmann, M.: En gruppe vevstoler på Vestlandet: Noen synpunkter i diskusjonen om billedvev i Norge. Oslo 1958 [Folk Art; Weaving]
Hoffmann, M.: The warp-weighted loom. Studies in the history and technology of an ancient implement. Studia Norvegica N°14, Oslo 1964 [Analysis; Folk Art; Weaving]
Hoffmann, M.: "Der isländische Gewichtswebstuhl in neuer Deutung", Festschrift A. Bühler. Basel 1965: 187-196 [Folk Art; Weaving]
Hoffmann, M.: Manndalen revisited: Traditional weaving in an old lappish community in transition. Gervers, V. (ed.) Studies in Textile History. Toronto 1977: 149-159 [Folk Art; General, Historical]
Hoffmann, M.: "Looms and their Products", I.Emery Roundtable on Mus. Textiles 1977, Washington 1979: 7-9 [Weaving]
Hoffmann, M.: "Old European Looms", I.Emery Roundtable on Mus. Textiles 1977, Washington 1979: 19-24 [Folk Art; Weaving]
Hoffmann, M.: "The Looms of the Old World", I.Emery Roundtable on Mus. Textiles 1977, Washington 1979: 13-18 [Folk Art; Weaving]
Hoffmann, M.: "Lebende Tradition als Quelle für Erkenntnis des Gebrauchs obsoleter Geräte", Textilsymposium Neumünster, Neumünster 1982: 97-108 [Folk Art; Archaeology]
Hoffmann, M. & Burnham, H.B.: Prehistory of Textiles in the Old World. Viking Fund Publications in Anthropology 50, New York 1973 [Archaeology; Threads; Warp Fabric; Weaving; Borders]
Hoffmann, M. & Traetteberg, R.: "Teglefunnet", Saertykk av Stavanger Museum, Årsbok 1959: 41-60 [Archaeology; Warp Fabric; Weaving; Borders]
Hoffmann, M.: see also Geijer, A.
Holland, B.S.: see also Mc Lendon, S.
Holm, B. & Reid, W.: Form and Freedom: A Dialogue on North-

west Coast Indian Art. Houston 1975 [Ethnography; Plaiting; Warp Fabric; Ornamentation with Solid Material(s)]
Holm, O.: "Jaile: Cordillería rural en la costa del Ecuador", Hartmann, R. (ed.) Amerikanistische Studien. St. Augustin 1978: 261-267 [Folk Art; Threads]
Holmes, W.H.: "Prehistoric textile fabrics of the United States", Annual Report Bur. Ethn. 3, 1881-1882, Washington 1884: 397-425 [Archaeology; Mesh Fabric]
Holmes, W.H.: "A study of the Textile Art in its relation to the development of From and Ornament", Annual Report Smiths. Inst. 6, 1884-1885, Washington 1888: 195-252 [Analysis]
Holmes, W.H.: "Textile Fabrics of Ancient Peru", Bull. of the Bur. of Am. Ethno. 6-10, 1888-1889, Washington 1889: 189-252 [Archaeology; Plaiting; Warp Fabric]
Holmes, W.H.: "Prehistoric textile art of Eastern United States", Annual Report Bur. of Ethn. 13, 1891-92, Washington 1896: 9-46 [Archaeology; Mesh Fabric]
Holmgren, R.J. & Spertus, A.E.: "Tampan pasisir: Pictorial documents of an ancient Indonesian coastal culture", I.Emery Roundtable on Mus. Textiles 1979, Washington 1980: 157-200 [Ethnography; Weaving]
Holt, J.D.: The Art of Featherwork in Old Hawai. Honolulu 1985 [Ethnography; Pile Fabric]
Holter, U.: "Craft techniques used by Uahria women of Darfur", Folk 25, Kopenhagen 1983: 97-128 [Ethnography; Plaiting]
Holz, I.: Javanische Batikmuster auf Kupferstempel. Hamburg 1980 [Ethnography; General, Historical; Ornamentation with Liquid Material(s)]
Holzklau, E.: Brettchenweberei: Tips und Tricks für den Anfang. Stuttgart 1977 [Working Instruction; Weaving]
Hongsermeier, H. (ed.): Tibeter-Teppiche. Innsbruck 1987 [Analysis; Ethnography; Pile Fabric]
Hooper, L.: "Loom and Spindle", Ann. Rep. Smith. Inst. for 1914, Washington 1915: 629-679 [Ethnography; Archaeology; Threads; Weaving]
Horn, P.: "Textilien aus biblischer Zeit", Ciba Rundschau 2, Basel 1968 [Archaeology; General, Historical; Warp Fabric]
Horvàth, A.B. & Werder, M.: Macramé. Schriftenreihe des Rät. Museum 22, Chur 1978 [Folk Art; Plaiting]
Horwitz, H.T.: "Die Drehbewegung in ihrer Bedeutung für die Entwicklung der materiellen Kultur", Anthropos 29, Freiburg 1934: 99-127 [General, Historical; Threads]
Houck, C.: see also Nelson, C.I.
Houlihan, P. et al.: Harmony by Hand; Art of the Southwest Indians: Basketry, Weaving, Pottery. Chronicle Books, San Francicso 1987 [Ethnography; Plaiting; Weaving]
Housego, J.: Tribal rugs: An introduction to the weaving of the tribes of Iran. London 1978 [Ethnography; Pile Fabric; Tapestry]
Houston, J.: Batik with Noel Dyrenforth. London 1975 [Working Instruction; Ornamentation with Liquid Material(s)]
Houwald, von, G.: Mayanga = Wir. Zur Geschichte der Sumu-Indianer in Mittel-Amerika. Beitr. z. mittelam. Völkerkunde 19, Hamburg 1990 [Ethnography; Mesh Fabric; Plaiting; Beadwork]
Hsian, N.: New finds of ancient silk fabrics in Sinkiang. Kaogu Xuebao 1, Peking 1963 [Archaeology; Weaving]
Huang, S. & Wenzhao, L.: Brocades of Guangxi. Chinese Arts and Crafts Vol. 5, Kyoto 1982 [Ethnography; General, Historical; Weaving]
Hubel, R.G.: Orientteppiche und Nomadenknüpfarbeiten vergangener Jahrhunderte. München 1967 [Collections; Pile Fabric]
Hubel, R.G.: Ullstein Teppichbuch. Frankfurt 1972 [General, Historical; Pile Fabric; Tapestry]
Huber, H. & Stöcklin, D.: Korbflechten. Basel 1977 [Working Instruction; Plaiting]
Hugger, P.: Der Korbflechter. Schweiz. Gesell. f. Volkskunde, Abt. Film, Basel 1967 [Analysis; Folk Art; Films; Plaiting]
Hundt, H.J.: "Vorgeschichtliche Gewebe aus dem Hallstädter Salzberg", Jahrbuch d. Röm.-Germ. Zentralmuseums 7. Jahrgang, Mainz 1960 [Archaeology; Weaving; Fabric Processing]
Hundt, H.J.: "Eine leinenumwickelte Schwertscheide der Hallstattzeit", Mainfränkisches Jahrbuch f. Geschichte u. Kunst 15, Frankfurt 1963: 180-185 [Archaeology; Weaving]
Hundt, H.J.: "Die verkohlten Reste von Geweben, Geflechten, Seilen, Schnüren und Holzgeräten aus Grab 200 von El Cigarralejo", Madrider Mitteilungen 9, 1968, Madrid 1969: 187-205 [Analysis; Archaeology; Threads; Plaiting; Weaving]
Hundt, H.J.: "Gewebefunde aus Hallstatt. Webkunst und Tracht in der Hallstattzeit", Ausstellungskataloge Röm.-Germ. Zenralmuseum 4, Mainz 1970: 53-71 [Archaeology; Weaving]
Hundt, H.J.: "Vorgeschichtliche Gewebe aus dem Hallstätter Salzberg", Jahrbuch des Röm.-Germ. Zentralmuseums 14, 1967, Mainz 1970: 38-67 [Archaeology; Weaving]
Hundt, H.J.: "Zu einigen frühgeschichtlichen Webgeräten", Archäologisches Korrespondenzblatt 4, 1974: 177-180 [Archaeology; Weaving]
Hundt, H.J.: Die Textil- und Schnurreste aus der frühgeschichtlichen Wurt Elisenhof. Frankfurt 1980 [Analysis; Archaeology; Threads; Mesh Fabric; Plaiting; Weaving; Borders]
Hunter, N.E.: Rug Analysis: Discussion of Method. Workshop Notes, Textile Museum 7, Washington 1953 [Analysis; Pile Fabric]
Hurwitz, J.: Batikkunst van Java. Rotterdam 1962 [Ethnography; Collections; Ornamentation with Liquid Material(s)]
Hussak von Velthem, L.: "Plumaria Tukano", Boletim do Museu Paraense E.G. 57, Belém 1975: 1-29 [Ethnography; Pile Fabric]
Hutapea, I.: see also Mangkdilaga, I.H.
Hwa, H.D.: Cha su: die Kunst der koreanischen Stickerei: Sammlung Huh Dong Hwa. Köln 1987 [Collections; General, Historical; Ornamentation with Solid Material(s)]
Hyslop, J.S. & Bird, J.B.: The preceramic excavations at the Huaca Prieta, Chicama Valley, Peru. Am.Mus. Nat. Hist. Anth. Papers Vol. 62, Washington 1985 [Analysis; Archaeology; Threads; Mesh Fabric; Warp Fabric; Weaving; Borders]

Icke-Schwalbe, L.: Textile Techniken aus dem westlichen Indien. Wittenberg 1989 [Ethnography; Collections; Ornamentation with Solid Material(s); Ornamentation with Liquid Material(s)]
Idiens, D.: Cook Island Art. Shire Ethnography, Haverfordwest 1990 [Ethnography; Plaiting]
Iklé, C.: "Ikat Technique and Dutch East Indian Ikats", Bull. Needle and Bobbin Club 15 (1-2), New York 1931: 2-59 [Ethnography; Ornamentation with Liquid Material(s)]
Iklé, C.: "The Plangi Technique", Bull. Needle and Bobbin Club Vol.25 N°2, New York 1941: 3-25 [Analysis; Ethnography; Ornamentation with Liquid Material(s)]
Iklé, F.: "Über Flammentücher", Festschrift M.A. Eysen. Dresden 1928: 117-124 [Analysis; Ornamentation with Liquid Material(s)]
Iklé, F.: "Über Altperuanische Stickereien des Trocadéro, Paris", Mitteil. d. Ostschw. Geo.-Com. Ges. St.Gallen 1930 [Analysis; Archaeology; Ornamentation with Solid Material(s)]
Iklé, F.: Primäre textile Techniken. Gewerbemuseum Basel, Basel 1935 [Collections; Mesh Fabric; Plaiting]
Iklé, F.: "Über das Stricken", Schweiz. Arbeitslehrerinnen Zeitung

N°8, 19. Jahrg. Biel 1963: 134-140 [Analysis; Mesh Fabric]
Iklé, F. & Vogt, E.: Primäre textile Techniken. Kunstgewerbe Museum, Zürich 1935 [Collections; Mesh Fabric; Plaiting]
Imanaga, S.: Illustrationen von Jimbaori. Tokyo n.d.
Imperato, P.J.: "Blankets and Covers from the Niger Bend", African Arts Vol.12I N°4, Los Angeles 1979: 38-43 [Ethnography; Weaving]
Indianapolis Museum of Art: Between Traditions: Navajo weaving towards the end of the 19 th Century. Exhibition Catalogue. Indianapolis 1976 [Ethnography; Warp Fabric; Weaving]
Ingers, G.: see also Lundbäck, M.
Ingstad, A.S.: "The functional textiles from the Oseberg Ship", Textilsymposium Neumünster, Neumünster 1982: 85-96 [Archaeology; Weaving]
Innes, R.A.: Non-European Looms in the collections at Bankfield Museum. Halifax 1959 [Analysis; Collections; Weaving; Pile Fabric]
Irwin, J.: "Indian textile trade in the 17th century", Journal of Indian Textile History Vol.1-3, 1955-57, Ahmebadad 1957 [General, Historical]
Irwin, J.: The Kashmir Shawl. London 1973 [Ethnography; General, Historical; Weaving]
Irwin, J.: "The Significance of Chintz", Marg, Bombay 1978: 67-73 [Ethnography; Weaving]
Irwin, J. & Jayakar, P.: Textiles and Ornaments of India. New York 1956 [Ethnography; Collections; Ornamentation with Solid Material(s)]
Irwin, J. & Schwartz, P.R.: Studies in Indo-European textile history. Bombay 1966 [Ethnography; General, Historical]
Irwin, J.: see also Hall, M.
Ito, T.: Tsujigahana. London 1981 [Analysis; Ethnography; Ornamentation with Liquid Material(s)]
Izikowitz, K.G.: "Une coiffure d'apparat d'Ica (Pérou)", Rev. del Inst. Nac. de Etnología 2 (2), Tucumán 1932: 317-45 [Ethnography; Archaeology; Mesh Fabric; Pile Fabric]
Izikowitz, K.G.: "L'origine probable de la technique du simili velours Péruvien", Journal de la Soc. des Améric. n.s. 25, Paris 1933: 9-16 [Analysis; Archaeology; Pile Fabric]

Jacob, A.: see also Bernès, J.P.
Jacobs, J.: Weefkunst van de Hamba. Liber memorialis 1, Gent 1983 [Ethnography; Weaving]
Jaekel-Greifswald, O.: "Zur Urgeschichte der orientalischen Teppiche", Orientalisches Archiv 2, Leipzig 1911-12: 167-173 [Archaeology; Pile Fabric; Tapestry]
Jager-Gerlings, J.H.: Sprekende Weefsels. Koninglijke Instituut v.d. Tropen, Amsterdam 1952 [Analysis; Ethnography; Plaiting; Weaving; Ornamentation with Liquid Material(s); Tapestry]
Jain, J.: see also Dhamija, J.
Jain, J.: see also Fischer, E.
Jaitly, J.: Crafts of Gujarat. New York 1985 [Ethnography; Ornamentation with Solid Material(s)]
James, G.W.: Indian Basketry. Pasadena 1903 [Ethnography; Plaiting]
James, G.W.: Indian Blankets and their Makers: Reprint of the 1892 edition. Beautiful Rio Grande Classics Ser. n.p. 1971 [Ethnography; Warp Fabric; Weaving; Tapestry]
James, G.W.: Indian Blankets and their Makers. New York 1974 [Ethnography; Warp Fabric; Weaving; Tapestry]
James, H.L.: Rugs and Posts: the Story of Navajo Weaving and the Indian Trader. Westchester 1988 [Ethnography; Weaving; Tapestry]
James, M.: The Quiltmaker's Handbook. Englewood Cliffs 1978 [Working Instruction; Ornamentation with Solid Material(s)]
James, M.: The Second Quiltmaker's Handbook. Englewood Cliffs 1981 [Working Instruction; Ornamentation with Solid Material(s)]
Janata, A.: "Ikat in Afghanistan", Afghanistan Journal Jg. 5 Heft 4, Graz 1978: 130-139 [Ethnography; Ornamentation with Liquid Material(s)]
Janata, A. & Jawad, N.: "Ya Ali! Ya Hasan! Ya Husayal: Ein Aspekt religiöser Volkskunst der Hazara", Textilhandwerk in Afghanistan. Liestal 1983: 161-175 [Ethnography; Ornamentation with Solid Material(s)]
Jannes, E.: Från Ceylon till Sri Lanka: Historia i Batik. Vi N°15, 14/4, Stockholm 1973: 1-8 [Ethnography; Ornamentation with Liquid Material(s)]
Jaques, R.: Alte Gewebe in Krefeld. Krefeld 1949 [Archaeology; Collections]
Jaques, R.: Mittelalterlicher Textildruck am Rhein. Kevelaer 1950 [General, Historical; Ornamentation with Liquid Material(s)]
Jaques, R.: Neuerwerbungen aus zehn Jahren. Krefeld 1963 [Collections]
Jaques, R.: Textilkunst des frühen Christentums: Koptische Gewebe vom 2.-12. Jh. Krefeld 1963 [Archaeology; Collections; Tapestry]
Jaques, R.: "Jourtextilien aus dem Chancaytal in der Sammlung Amano in Lima", Verhandlungen des Int. Amerikan. Kongr. 38 (1), Stuttgart 1968: 357-368 [Archaeology; Collections; Mesh Fabric; Weaving; Ornamentation with Solid Material(s); Ornamentation with Liquid Material(s)]
Jaques, R. & Wencker, R.: Die Textilien im Besitz der Schatzkammer der Kirche St. Servatius in Siegburg. Siegburg 1967 [Analysis; Collections; Weaving; Ornamentation with Solid Material(s)]
Jaquet, P. (ed.): Le Musée de l'Impression sur Etoffes de Mulhouse. Mulhouse 1975 [Collections; Ornamentation with Liquid Material(s)]
Jarry, M.: "L'exotisme au temps de Louis XIV", Bull. Cieta 43-44, Lyon 1976: 124-128 [General, Historical; Tapestry]
Jasper, J. & Pirngadie, M.: De Inlandsche Kunstnijverheid in Nederlandsch Indië. Band 1-3, Den Haag 1912-16 [Analysis; Plaiting; Weaving; Ornamentation with Liquid Material(s)]
Jawad, N.: see also Janata, A.
Jayakar, P.: Indian printed textiles. All Indian Handicrafts Board, Bombay n.d. [Ethnography; Ornamentation with Liquid Material(s)]
Jayakar, P.: "The dyed fabrics of India", Marg Vol.2 N°1, Bombay 1947: 93-102 [Ethnography; Ornamentation with Liquid Material(s)]
Jayakar, P.: "Traditional textiles of India", Marg Vol.15 N°1, Bombay 1962 [Ethnography; Weaving]
Jayakar, P.: "Nakshi Bandha of Banaras", Journal of Ind. Textile History 7, Ahmedabad 1967: 21-44 [Ethnography; Weaving]
Jayakar, P.: "Gaiety in Colour and Form: Painted and Printed Cloth", Marg, Bombay 1978: 23-36 [Ethnography; Weaving]
Jayakar, P.: see also Bhagwat, D. Jayakar, P.: see also Irwin, J.
Jeanneret, A.: "A propos de toiles imprimées et peintes destinées à la chasse aux perdrix en Afghanistan", Baessler-Archiv NF 13, Berlin 1965: 115-125 [Ethnography; Ornamentation with Liquid Material(s)]
Jeannin, R.: see also Cresson, J
Jean-Richard, A.: Kattundrucke der Schweiz im 18.Jh. Basel 1968 [General, Historical; Ornamentation with Liquid Material(s)]
Jelmini, J.P. & Clerc-Junier, C.: La soie: receuil d'articles sur l'art de la soie. Neuchâtel 1986 [Analysis; Weaving]
Jenkins, I. & Williams, D.: "A Bronze Portrait Head and its Hair Net", Record of the Art Museum Vol.42 N°2, Princeton Univ. 1987: 9-16 [Archaeology; Warp Fabric]

Jenny, A.: Aus der Entwicklungsgeschichte des Zeugdrucks: Batik. Wegleitungen des Kunstgewerbemuseums 27, Zürich 1919 [Ethnography; General, Historical; Ornamentation with Liquid Material(s)]

Jensen, J.: "Der Korb Ekibbo in Bugunda", Baessler-Archiv NF 19, Berlin 1971: 167-187 [Ethnography; Plaiting]

Jéquier, G.: see also Van Gennep, A.

Jerusalimskaia, A.A.: Über die nordkaukasische "Seidenstrasse" im Frühmittelalter. Sowjetskaia Archeologia 2, 1967, Moskau 1967 [Archaeology; Weaving]

Jessen, E.: Ancient Peruvian textile design in modern stitchery. London 1972 [Working Instruction, Ornamentation with Solid Material(s)]

Jingshan, J.: "Dyeing, weaving and embroidery of the Li People of Guangdong", Chinese Arts and Crafts Vol. 4, Kyoto 1982 [Ethnography; Weaving; Ornamentation with Liquid Material(s)]

Johl, C.H.: Die Webstühle der Griechen und Römer. Leipzig 1917 [Archaeology, Weaving]

Johl, C.H.: Altägyptische Webstühle und Brettchenweberei in Altägypten. Leipzig 1924 [Analysis, Archaeology; Weaving]

Johnson, G.N.: "It's a sin to waste a rag: rug-weaving in western Maryland", Jordan, R.A. Kalcik, S.J. (ed.) Women's Folklore, Women's Culture. Philadelphia 1985: 65-98 [Folk Art; Fabric Processing]

Johnson, N.S.: Weaving on the Hearthside Loom. Detroit 1942 [Working Instruction; Weaving]

Johnson, N.S.: Learn to Weave. Detroit 1949 [Working Instruction; Warp Fabric; Weaving]

Johnson, P.: Turkish embroidery. London 1985 [Collections; Ornamentation with Solid Material(s)]

Johnstone, P.: Greek Island Embroidery. London 1961 [Folk Art; Ornamentation with Solid Material(s)]

Joliet van der Berg, M.& H.: BrettchenWeaving. Bern 1975 [Working Instruction; Weaving]

Jones, S.: Pacific basket makers: a living tradition. Honolulu 1983 [Analysis; Ethnography; Plaiting]

Jones, S.M.: Hawaiian Quilts. Honolulu 1973 [Collections; Ornamentation with Solid Material(s)]

Jones, V.H.: "Notes on the Manufacture of Cedar-Bark Mats by the Chippewa Indians of the Great Lakes", Papers. Michigan Acad. Science, Arts & Letters 32, o.J.: 341-363 [Ethnography; Plaiting]

Jongh, de, D.: "Les moyens de façonnage et leurs charactéristiques", Assoc. pour l'Etude et la Doc. des Textiles d'Asie. Paris 1985: 7-25 [Analysis; Weaving]

Joplin, C.F.: "Yalalag weaving: Its aesthetic, technological and economic nexus", Lechtmann, H.& R. (ed.) Material Culture. St. Paul 1977: 211-236 [Ethnography, Weaving]

Joseph, M.B.: "West African Indigo Cloth", African Arts Vol.11 N°2, Los Angeles 1978: 34-37 [Ethnography; Weaving; Ornamentation with Solid Material(s), Ornamentation with Liquid Material(s)]

Joseph, R.M.: "Batik making and the royal Javanese cemetery at Imogiri", Textile Museum Journal 24, 1985, Washington 1986 [Ethnography; Ornamentation with Liquid Material(s)]

Joyce, T.A.: "The Peruvian Loom in the Proto-Chimu Period", Man 21 (12), London 1921: 177-80 [Archaeology; Weaving]

Joyce, T.A.: "Note on a Peruvian Loom of the Chimu Period", Man 22, London 1922: 1-2 [Archaeology; Weaving]

Juel, A.: Japanske Textiler, Japanese Textiles. Stockholm 1984 [Ethnography; Ornamentation with Liquid Material(s)]

Juhasz, E. (ed.): Sephardi Jews in the Ottoman Empire. Jerusalem 1990 [Folk Art; Weaving, Pile Fabric, Ornamentation with Solid Material(s)]

Justin, V.S.: Flat woven rugs of the World. New York 1980 [Analysis; Ethnography; Threads; Weaving; Pile Fabric; Tapestry]

Jusuf, S. et al.: Pameran tenun ikat indonesia: Indonesische Ikatgewebe. Jakarta 1984 [Ethnography; Collections; Ornamentation with Liquid Material(s)]

Kadow, E.: "Wandteppiche in Mischtechnik", Ciba Rundschau 3, Basel 1973 [General, Historical; Weaving; Tapestry]

Kaeppler, A.: Artificial curiosities, being an exposition of native manufactures collected on the three Pacific voyages of Capt. James Cook. R. N. Bernice P. Bishop Mus. Spec. Publ. 65, Honolulu 1978 [Ethnography; Warp Fabric; Pile Fabric]

Kaeppler, A. et al.: Cook voyage artifacts in Leningrad, Berne and Florence Museum. Bernice P. Bishop Museum Spec. Publ. 66, Honolulu 1978 [Ethnography; Pile Fabric]

Kahlenberg, M.H.: Führer durch das L.A. County Museum of Art. Los Angeles 1976 [Collections; Plaiting]

Kahlenberg, M.H.: Textile Tradition of Indonesia. Los Angeles 1977 [Ethnography; Ornamentation with Liquid Material(s)]

Kahlenberg, M.H.: "The influence of the European herbal on Indonesian Batik", I.Emery Roundtable on Mus. Textiles 1979, Washington 1980: 243-247 [Ethnography; Ornamentation with Liquid Material(s)]

Kahlenberg, M.H. & Berlant, A.: The Navajo Blanket. Los Angeles 1972 [Ethnography; Weaving; Tapestry]

Kahlenberg, M.H. & Berlant, A.: Navajo Blankets. Wegleitungen des Kunstgewerbemuseums 305, Zürich 1976 [Ethnography; Warp Fabric; Tapestry]

Kahlenberg, M.H. & Berlant, A.: The navajo's blanket. New York 1976 [Analysis; Collections; Weaving; Tapestry]

Kahmann, I.: Patchwork und Quilten. München,Wien 1985 [Working Instruction; Ornamentation with Solid Material(s)]

Kaippler, A.: Artificial Curiosities. Honolulu 1978 [Plaiting; Warp Fabric; Pile Fabric]

Kajitani, N.: see also Sonday, M.

Kalter, J.: Aus Steppe und Oase: Bilder turkestanischer Kulturen. Katalog Linden-Museum, Stuttgart 1983 [Analysis; Ethnography; Weaving; Pile Fabric; Ornamentation with Solid Material(s); Ornamentation with Liquid Material(s)]

Kann, P.: "Trachten bolivianischer Hochlandindianer", Archiv fur Völkerkunde 36, Wien 1982: 37-58 [Ethnography; Weaving]

Karmasch, K.: Handbuch der mechanischen Technologie. Band 2, Hannover 1858 [General, Historical; Threads]

Karsten, D.: The economics of handicrafts in traditional societies: South Ethiopia. München 1972 [Ethnography; Weaving]

Kartiwa, S.: Kain tenun donggala. Penerbit 1963 [Ethnography; Ornamentation with Liquid Material(s)]

Kartiwa, S.: "The Kain Songket Minangkabau", I.Emery Roundtable on Mus. Textiles 1979, Washington 1980: 56-80 [Ethnography; Weaving]

Kartiwa, S.: Songket indonesia. Jakarta 1982 [Ethnography; Weaving; Ornamentation with Liquid Material(s)]

Kartiwa, S.: Kain songket indonesia: Songket-weaving in Indonesia. Jakarta 1986 [Ethnography; Weaving]

Kasten, E.: Maskentänze der Kwakiutl: Tradition und Wandel in einem indianischen Dorf. Veröff. des Museums für Völkerkunde Neue Folge 49, Berlin 1990 [Ethnography; Plaiting; Ornamentation with Solid Material(s)]

Katara, S.K.: "Tie-dye industry: the art of dyeing and printing in ancient India", Hasthakala 1.1, Bombay 1972 [Archaeology; Ornamentation with Liquid Material(s)]

Kaudern, W.: "Notes on Plaited Anklets in Central Celebes", Ethnological Studies, Göteborg 1935 [Analysis; Ethnography; Plaiting]

Kauffmann, H.E.: "Das Weben in den Naga-Bergen Assam", Zeitschrift für Ethnologie 69, Berlin 1937 [Analysis; Ethnography; Weaving]
Kauffmann, H.E.: Karen (Hinterindien, Nordthailand): Spinnen und Weaving. Encyclopaedia Cinematographica E 527, Göttingen 1963 [Ethnography; Films; Threads; Weaving]
Kauffmann, H.E.: "Spinnen und Weben: Karen: Hinterindien, Nord Thailand", Encyclopaedia Cinematographica Band 2, 4, Göttingen 1967: 323-333 [Ethnography; Films; Threads; Weaving]
Kaufmann, C.: "Herstellen einer Tragtasche in Maschenstofftechnik", Encyclopaedia Cinematographica Serie 10 N°26, Göttingen 1980: 3-40 [Analysis; Ethnography; Films; Mesh Fabric]
Kaufmann, C.: "Maschenstoffe und ihre gesellschaftliche Funktion am Beispiel der Kwoma von Papua-Neuguinea", Tribus 35, Stuttgart 1986: 127-175 [Analysis; Ethnography; Threads; Mesh Fabric]
Kaufmann, C.: "Ein Federmantel der Maori im Museum für Völkerkunde Basel: Versuch einer textilkundlichen Annäherung", Basler Beiträge zur Ethnologie Band 30, Basel 1989: 391-406 [Ethnography; Warp Fabric; Pile Fabric]
Kaukonen, T.I.: "Ausvaipat eli Villalakamt", Kansatieteelinen Arkisto N° 15 (2), Helsinki 1961 [Folk Art; Weaving]
Keller, J.D.: "Woven World: Neotraditional Symbols of Unity in Vanuatu", Mankind 18 (1), New South Wales 1988: 1-13 [Ethnography; Plaiting]
Kelly, I.: see also Harvey, M.R.
Kelly, I.T.: "Yuki Basketry", UCLA Publ. Am. Arch. and Ethnol. 24, Berkeley 1930: 422-443 [Ethnography; Plaiting]
Kelly, I.T.: "Ethnography of the Surprise Valley Paiute", UCLA Publ. Am. Arch. and Ethnol. 31, Berkeley 1932: 67-260 [Analysis; Ethnography; Plaiting; Borders]
Kelly, I.T. & Fowler, C.S.: "Southern Paiute", Handbook of North Am. Indians 11, Washington 1986: 368-397 [Ethnography; Mesh Fabric; Plaiting]
Kelsey, V. & Osborne, de Jongh, L.: Four keys to Guatemala. New York 1939 [General, Historical; Threads; Plaiting; Weaving]
Kemp, W.B.: "Baffinland Eskimo", Handbook of North Am. Indians 5, Washington 1984: 463-475 [Ethnography; Mesh Fabric]
Kenagy, S. et al. (ed.): Native cultures of the Americas. Southwest Mus. Masterkey 61 (2-3), Los Angeles 1987 [Ethnography; Plaiting; Warp Fabric; Tapestry]
Kendrick, A.E.: Catalogue of textiles from burying grounds in Egypt. Vol. 3, London 1922 [Archaeology; Tapestry]
Kendrick, A.E.: Catalogue of Muhammadan textiles of the medieval period. London 1924 [Archaeology; Collections; Tapestry]
Kensinger, K.: The Cashinahaua of Eastern Peru. Haffenreffer Mus. Anth. Studies 1, Boston 1975 [Ethnography; Plaiting; Weaving; Pile Fabric]
Kent Peck, K.: "Braiding of a Hopi Wedding Sash", Plateau 12 (3), Flagstaff 1940: 46-52 [Ethnography; Warp Fabric; Weaving]
Kent Peck, K.: "Notes on the weaving of Prehistoric Pueblo textiles", Plateau Vol.14 N°1, Flagstaff 1941 [Analysis; Ethnography; Weaving]
Kent Peck, K.: Montezuma Castle Archaeology 2, Textiles. Southwest. Monument Ass. Tech. Vol.3 N°2, Arizona 1954 [Analysis; Archaeology; Plaiting; Warp Fabric; Weaving]
Kent Peck, K.: The Cultivation and Weaving of Cotton in the Prehistoric Southwestern USA. Transactions Am. Philos. Soc. 47, Philadelphia 1957 [Analysis; Archaeology; Threads; Mesh Fabric; Plaiting; Warp Fabric; Half-weaving; Weaving; Borders; Ornamentation with Liquid Material(s); Fabric Processing]
Kent Peck, K.: The Story of Navajo Weaving. Phoenix 1961 [Ethnography; Warp Fabric; Tapestry]
Kent Peck, K.: Introducing West African Cloth. Denver 1971 [Analysis; Ethnography; Pile Fabric; Ornamentation with Liquid Material(s)]
Kent Peck, K.: "Mesoamerican and North American Textiles", I.Emery Roundtable on Mus. Textiles, Washington 1974: 31-36 [Archaeology; General, Historical]
Kent Peck, K.: "The indigenous Southwestern textile tradition in historic times: weaving among the Pima, Papago, Moricopa and Pueblo Indians", I.Emery Roundtable on Mus. Textiles 1976, Washington 1977: 407-412 [Ethnography; Weaving]
Kent Peck, K.: Prehistoric textiles of the Southwest. Santa Fe 1983 [Analysis; Archaeology; Mesh Fabric; Plaiting; Half-weaving; Borders; Ornamentation with Solid Material(s); Ornamentation with Liquid Material(s); Fabric Processing]
Kent Peck, K.: Navajo Weaving: Three Centuries of Change. Santa Fe 1985 [Ethnography; Weaving; Tapestry]
Kent Peck, K.: "Reconstructing Three Centuries of Change in Pueblo Indian Textiles", Basler Beiträge zur Ethnologie Band 30, Basel 1989: 407-420 [Ethnography; Weaving]
Keppel, S.: Primaire textiele technieken van de Mentawai-Eilanden. Antropologische Studies VU 7, Amsterdam 1984 [Analysis; Ethnography; Threads; Mesh Fabric; Plaiting; Borders]
Kerajinan, S.: see also Leigh, B.
Kerkhoff-Hader, B. (ed.): Textilarbeit.Rheinisches Jahrbuch für Volkskunde 27, 1987/88, Bonn 1989 [Folk Art; Weaving]
Keyser, A.G.: see also Gehret, E.J.
Khan Majlis, B.: Technik, Geschichte und Muster indischer Brokatstoffe. Köln 1977 [Ethnography; Weaving]
Khan Majlis, B.: Indonesische Textilien. Ethnologica NF 10, Köln 1984 [Ethnography; Weaving; Ornamentation with Solid Material(s); Ornamentation with Liquid Material(s)]
Khan Majlis, B.: Indonesische Textilien: Wege zu Göttern und Ahnen. Köln 1985 [Ethnography; Weaving; Ornamentation with Liquid Material(s)]
Kichihei, T.: Yuki Tsumugi. Tokyo n.d. [Kidder, A.V.: Textile Arts of Guatemalan Natives. Carnegie Institution of Wash. Vol.3 N°20, Washington 1935 [Ethnography; Warp Fabric; Weaving; Ornamentation with Liquid Material(s)]
Kidder, A.V. & Guernsey, S.J.: Archaeological Exploration in Northeastern Arizona. Bull. of the Bur. Am. Ethn. 65, Washington 1919 [Archaeology; Mesh Fabric; Plaiting; Warp Fabric]
Kidder, A.V. & Guernsey, S.J.: Basket Maker Caves of Northeastern Arizona. Pap. Peabody Mus. Am. Arch. and Ethnol. N°2 (8), Cambridge 1921 [Analysis; Archaeology; Mesh Fabric; Plaiting]
Kiewe, H.E.: Ancient Berber Tapestries and Rugs and Ancient Morrocan Embroideries. London 1952 [Ethnography; Collections; Ornamentation with Solid Material(s); Tapestry]
Kiewe, H.E.: "Traditional Embroideries from the Holy Land and from Norway", Craftsman and Designer, Oxford 1954 [Folk Art; General, Historical; Ornamentation with Solid Material(s)]
Kiewe, H.E.: The Sacred History of Knitting. Oxford 1967 [General, Historical; Mesh Fabric]
Kilchenmann, K.: see also Ursin, A.
Kimakowicz-Winnicki, M. von: Spinn- und Webwerkzeuge. Würzburg 1910 [Folk Art; Threads; Weaving]
King, D.: Samplers. Victoria and Albert Museum, London 1977 [Folk Art; Ornamentation with Solid Material(s)]
King, M.: Textiles anciens: Historic textiles. Bulletin du CIETA, Lyon 1988 [Ethnography; Folk Art; Weaving; Ornamentation with Liquid Material(s)]
King, M.E.: "A preliminary Study of a shaped textile from Peru",

Workshop Notes 13, Washington 1956 [Archaeology; Weaving; Fabric Processing]

King, M.E.: "An Unusual Border Construction from Peru", Bulletin of the Needle and Bobbin Club 41 (1-2), New York 1957: 23-37 [Archaeology; Borders]

King, M.E.: "A new type of Peruvian Ikat", Workshop Notes 17, Washington 1958 [Archaeology; Ornamentation with Liquid Material(s)]

King, M.E.: "Associated early Nazca textiles in the Whyte Collection", Archaeology Vol.15 N°3, New York 1962: 160-162 [Archaeology; Mesh Fabric; Weaving]

King, M.E.: Textiles and basketry of the Paracas period, Ica Valley Peru. Ann Arbor 1965 [Analysis, Archaeology; Threads; Mesh Fabric; Plaiting; Warp Fabric; Weaving; Pile Fabric; Borders; Ornamentation with Solid Material(s), Ornamentation with Liquid Material(s); Tapestry]

King, M.E.: "Textile Fragments from the Riverside Site, Menominee, Michigan", Verh. Int. Amerikanisten Kong. 38.1, Stuttgart 1968 [Archaeology; Warp Fabric; Pile Fabric]

King, M.E.: "Some new Paracas Techniques from Ocucaje, Peru", Verh. des Int. Amerikanisten Kong. 38.1, Stuttgart 1969: 369-377 [Archaeology; Warp Fabric; Pile Fabric]

King, M.E.: "A new textile Technique from Oaxaca", Atti del XL Cong. Americanisti Roma 1972 40. Band 1, Genova 1974: 173-177 [Ethnography; Archaeology; Weaving]

King, M.E.: The Salt Cave Textiles: A Preliminary Account. Archaeology of the Mammoth Cave, New York 1974 [Archaeology; Weaving]

King, M.E.: "North American Ethnographic Textiles", I.Emery Roundtable on Mus. Textiles 1976, Washington 1977: 479-504 [Ethnography; Warp Fabric, Tapestry]

King, M.E.: "The Distribution of Aboriginal Looms and Frames in North America", I.Emery Roundtable on Mus. Textiles 1977, Washington 1979: 127-134 [Analysis; Ethnography; Weaving]

King, M.E.: "The Prehistoric Textile Industry of Mesoamerica", The J.B.Bird Precolumbian Textile Conf. 1973, Washington 1979: 265-278 [Archaeology; Mesh Fabric, Plaiting; Weaving]

King, M.E.: "Sprang in the Paracas period of Peru", Rogers, N. (ed.) In Celebration of the curious Mind. Loveland 1983: 61-67 [Archaeology; Warp Fabric]

King, M.E. & Gardner, J.S.: The analysis of textiles from Spiro mound, Oklahoma. Annals NY Ac. of Sciences Vol. 376, New York 1981 [Archaeology; Warp Fabric]

King, M.E.: see also Emery, I.

King, V.T.: see also Ave, J.B.

Kissel, M.L.: Aboriginal American Weaving. Boston 1910 [Ethnography; Weaving]

Kissel, M.L.: "Basketry of the Papago and Pima", Anthro. Pap. Am. Mus. of Nat. Hist. 17, New York 1916: 115-264 [Analysis; Ethnography; Mesh Fabric, Plaiting]

Kissel, M.L.: "A new Type of Spinning in North America", Am. Anthrop. 18, Menasha 1916: 264-270 [Ethnography; Threads]

Kissel, M.L.: "The Early Geometric Patterned Chilkat", Am. Anthrop. 30 (1), Menasha 1928: 116-120 [Ethnography; Warp Fabric]

Kissling, H.J.: Südost-Europa, Jugoslawien, Kosovo: Knüpfen eines Gebetsteppichs. Encyclopaedia Cinematographica E 2412, Göttingen 1982 [Folk Art; Films, Pile Fabric]

Kitley, P.: "Batik Painting", Craft Australia, Autumn, 1981: 9-26 [Ethnography; Ornamentation with Liquid Material(s)]

Kjellberg, A.: "Medieval Textiles from the Excavations in the Old Town of Oslo", Textilsymposium Neumünster, Neumünster 1982: 136-162 [Archaeology, Weaving; Borders]

Klausen, A.M.: "Basket-work ornamentation among the Dayaks", Stud. Honor. Centen. Uni. Ethn. 3, Oslo 1957 [Ethnography; Plaiting]

Klein, A.: "Tesig-Bandweberei mit Gold- und Silberfäden", Baessler-Archiv NF 22, Berlin 1974: 225-244 [Ethnography; Weaving]

Klein, A.: "Tablet weaving by the Jews of San'a", World Anthropology 86, Den Haag 1979: 425-447 [Ethnography; Weaving]

Klein, O.: "Textile Techniken der Araukaner", Ciba Rundschau 6, Basel 1961 [Analysis; Ethnography; Weaving; Pile Fabric; Ornamentation with Liquid Material(s)]

Klimburg, M. & Pinto, S.: Tessuti ikat dell'Asia Centrale di collezioni italiane. Torino 1986 [Collections; Ornamentation with Liquid Material(s)]

Klingmüller, G. & Münch, F.: Textilkunst: Ein Studienschwerpunkt des Faches Textilgestaltung. Köln 1989 [Ethnography; Folk Art; Weaving; Beadwork; Ornamentation with Solid Material(s); Tapestry]

Klopfer, B.: Das Batikgewebe von Kandy. Institut für Völkerkunde, Köln 1988 [Ethnography; Ornamentation with Liquid Material(s)]

Knauer, T. & Steger-Völkel, R.: Handweberei. Berlin n.d. [Weaving]

Knorr, T.: see also Lindahl, D. [Knottenbelt, M.: "Warping and weaving Mitla cloth on the backstrap lôom", Textile Museum Journal 22, Washington 1983 [Analysis; Ethnography; Weaving]

Knudsen, L.: see also Ottenberg, S.

Kobel-Streiff, R.: "Reservemusterung und Bemalung auf Altperuanischen Geweben", Ethnologische Zeitschrift Zürich 1, Zürich 1972: 233-242 [Archaeology; Ornamentation with Liquid Material(s)]

Koch, G.: Die materielle Kultur der Ellice-Inseln. Berlin 1961 [Ethnography; Plaiting]

Koch, G.: Polynesier (Niutao, Ellice-Archipel): Herstellen von Kokosfaserschnur. Encyclopaedia Cinematographica E 411, Göttingen 1961 [Ethnography; Films; Threads]

Koch, G.: Mikronesier (Gilbert-Inseln, Nonouti): Herstellen von Kokosfaserschnur. Encyclopaedia Cinematographica E 825, Göttingen 1965 [Ethnography; Films; Threads]

Koch, G.: Mikronesier (Gilbert-Inseln, Nonouti): Herstellen eines Kokosfaserseiles. Encyclopaedia Cinematographica E 826, Göttingen 1965 [Ethnography; Films; Threads]

Koch, G.: Kultur der Gilbert-Inseln: Herstellen eines Keschers. Encyclopaedia Cinematographica Eb 1, E 829, Göttingen 1969 [Ethnography; Films; Threads; Mesh Fabric; Plaiting; Pile Fabric]

Koch, G.: "Kultur der Gilbert Inseln: Flechten des Fischkorbes "kurubaene"", Encyclopaedia Cinematographica Band 1, Göttingen 1969: 136-139 [Ethnography; Films; Plaiting]

Koch, G.: Melanesier (Santa-Cruz-Inseln, Riff-Inseln): Weben. Encyclopaedia Cinematographica Eb 4, E 1429, Göttingen 1973 [Ethnography; Films; Weaving]

Koch, G. & König, G.: "Tonganische Flecht- und Knüpfarbeiten", Baessler-Archiv NF 3(4), 1955-56, Berlin 1956: 233-259 [Ethnography; Plaiting]

Koch-Grünberg, T.: Zwei Jahre unter den Indianern Nordwest-Brasiliens. Berlin 1909 [Ethnography; Plaiting; Weaving]

Koch-Grünberg, T.: Vom Roroima zum Orinoco. Band 1, Stuttgart 1923 [Analysis; Ethnography; Threads; Mesh Fabric; Plaiting; Warp Fabric; Pile Fabric; Beadwork]

König, G.: see also Koch, G.

Kogan, P.: Navajo school of Indian Basketry. London 1985 [Analysis; Ethnography; Plaiting]

Kok, R.: Ifugao basketry. Amsterdam 1979 [Analysis; General,

Historical; Plaiting]
Konieczny, M.G.: Textiles of Baluchistan. London 1979 [Analysis; Ethnography; Threads; Warp Fabric; Weaving; Borders]
Koob, K.: "How the Drawloom Works", I Emery Roundtable on Mus. Textiles 1977, Washington 1979: 231-141 [Analysis; Weaving]
Kooijman, S.: "Material Aspects of the Star Mountains Culture", Nova Guinea Vol. 2, 1962, Leiden 1959 [Ethnography; Mesh Fabric; Plaiting; Warp Fabric]
Kooijman, S.: "Traditional handicraft in a changing society: Manufacture and function of stenciled tapa on Moa Island", Mead, S.M. (ed.) Exploring the visual art of Oceania. Honolulu 1974 [Ethnography; Ornamentation with Liquid Material(s)]
Korea-Britain Centennial Committee: Classical Korean Embroideries. n.p., n.d. [Ethnography; Ornamentation with Solid Material(s)]
Korsching, F.: Beduinen im Negev. Mainz 1980 [Ethnography; Threads; Weaving]
Kosswig, L.: "Über Brettchenweberei insbesondere in Anatolien", Baessler-Archiv NF 15, Berlin 1967: 71-133 [Ethnography; Weaving]
Krämer, A.: "Anfänge und Unterschiede des Flechtens und Webens und Besprechung einiger alter Webstühle", Zeitschrift für Ethnologie 59, Berlin 1927 [Plaiting; Warp Fabric; Weaving]
Krafft, S.: Pictorial Weaving from the Viking Age. Oslo 1956 [Archaeology; Weaving; Tapestry]
Krause, F.: "Schleiergewebe aus Alt Peru", Jahrbuch des Städt. Mus. für Völkerk. 8, Leipzig 1921: 30-37 [Archaeology; Weaving]
Krehl-Eschler, E.: see also Nabholz-Kartaschoff, M.L.
Kreischer, L.: Verslag noyens de Pasar Gambir gehonden op het Koningsplein te Weltevreden. Batavia 1907 [Ethnography; General, Historical; Weaving; Ornamentation with Liquid Material(s)]
Kremser, M. & Westhart, K.R.: "Research in Ethnography and Ethnohistory of St.Lucia", Wiener Beiträge zur Ethno. und Anth. N°3, Wien 1986 [Ethnography; Plaiting; Fabric Processing]
Krishna, K.: see also Mohanty, B.C.
Krishna, K.: see also Talwar, K.
Krishna, V.: Banares brocades: Living weavers at work. New Delhi 1966 [Analysis; Ethnography; Weaving]
Kroeber, A.L: "Archaeological explorations in Peru: Cañete Valley", Mem. Field Mus. of Nat. History Vol.2 N°4, Chicago 1937: 221-268 [Archaeology; Plaiting, Weaving]
Kroeber, A.L: "Peruvian Archeology in 1942", Viking Fund Publ. in Anthropology N°4, New York 1944: 5-143 [Archaeology; Mesh Fabric; Plaiting; Weaving, Ornamentation with Liquid Material(s)]
Kroeber, A.L.: "Basket designs of the Indians of North West California", Univ. of Cal. Publ. Nr 4 (2), 1904-07, Berkeley 1905: 105-164 [Ethnography; Plaiting, Ornamentation with Solid Material(s)]
Kroeber, A.L. & Wallace, D.T.: Proto Lima. Field Mus. of Nat. History 44, Chicago 1954 [Analysis; Archaeology; Mesh Fabric; Weaving; Borders; Tapestry]
Kroeber, A.L.: see also O'Neale, L.M.
Kronenberg, A.: Masakin (Ostafrika, Kordofan): Herstellen von Schürzen aus Rindenstoff. Encyclopaedia Cinematographica, Göttingen 1976 [Ethnography; Films]
Kron-Steinhardt, C.: Textilien und Weberei der Bergbewohner Luzons: Indizien einer handelsintensiven, jungen Vergangenheit. Freiburg 1989 [Ethnography; Threads; Weaving; Ornamentation with Solid Material(s); Ornamentation with Liquid Material(s)]
Krucker, H.: "Westafrikanische Mattengeflechte", Mitt. Ostschweiz. Geo. Comm. Ges. 1940-41, St.Gallen 1941: 29-48 [Ethnography; Plaiting; Borders]
Kühnel, E.: see also Bellinger, L.
Kümpers, H.: Kunst auf Baumwolle. Dortmund 1961 [Analysis; Ethnography; Weaving; Ornamentation with Solid Material(s); Ornamentation with Liquid Material(s); Tapestry]
Kûava, P.: see also Svobodová, V.
Kuhar, B.: Klekljane Čipke. Slovenski Ethnografski Muzej, Lublijana 1970 [Folk Art; Plaiting]
Kuhn, D.: Die Webstühle des Tzu-en ichih aus der Hüan Zeit. Sinologica Coloniensa 44 Band 5, Wiesbaden 1977 [General, Historical; Weaving]
Kuhn, D.: Literaturverzeichnis zur Textilkunst Chinas und zur allgemeinen Webtechnologie. Wiesbaden 1977 [Ethnography; Weaving]
Kuhn, D.: Chinese baskets and mats. Wiesbaden 1980 [Analysis; Ethnography; Plaiting]
Kuhn, D.: see also Graw, de, I.G.
Kundegraber, M.: Zur Ausstellung "Körbe und Korbflechten". Steiermärkisches Landesmuseum Joanneum, Stainz 1976 [Collections; Plaiting]
Kunz, H.: PeddigrohrPlaiting. Bern 1980 [Working Instruction; Plaiting; Borders]
Kurrick, H.: Kolavoo Eestis. Eesti Rahwa Museumi Aastaraama, Tartu 1932 [Folk Art; Mesh Fabric; Plaiting; Weaving]
Kurup, K.C.N.: see also Nambiar, P.K.
Kussmaul, F. & Moos, von, I.: Tadschiken (Afghanistan, Badakhshan): Weben eines Teppichs. Encyclopaedia Cinematographica Serie 11, 18, Göttingen 1981 [Ethnography; Films; Weaving]
Kussmaul, F. & Snoy, P.: Tadschiken (Afghanistan, Badakhshan): Lockern und Spinnen von Yak-Wolle. Encyclopaedia Cinematographica E 680, Göttingen 1964 [Ethnography; Films; Threads]
Kussmaul, F. & Snoy, P.: Tadschiken (Afghanistan, Badakhshan): Korbflechten. Encyclopaedia Cinematographica 19, Göttingen 1980 [Ethnography; Films; Plaiting]

La Baume, W.: Die Entwicklung des Textilhandwerks in Alteuropa. Bonn 1955 [Analysis; Mesh Fabric; Warp Fabric; Weaving; Pile Fabric; Borders; Fabric Processing]
La Baume, W.: "Der Gebrauch der Handspindel vom Altertum bis zur Neuzeit.", Studien zur europ. Vor- und Frühges. Neumünster 1968: 421-438 [Archaeology; Threads]
La Pierre, S.: "Modern Baskets of China", Arts of Asia Vol.14 N°3, Hong Kong 1984: 123-130 [Ethnography; Plaiting]
La Plantz, S.: Plaited Basketry: The Woven Form. Bayside 1982 [Working Instruction; Threads; Plaiting]
Labin, B.: "Batik Traditions in the Live of the Javanese", Fischer, J. (ed.) Threads of Tradition. Berkeley 1979: 41-52 [Ethnography; Threads; Weaving; Ornamentation with Liquid Material(s)]
Laczko, G.: "The Weavers: The Aracaunians of Chile", Roosevelt, A. (ed.) The Ancestors. New York 1979: 132-157 [Analysis; Ethnography; Weaving; Ornamentation with Liquid Material(s)]
Lakwete, A.: "Salish Blankets", I Emery Roundtable on Mus. Textiles 1976, Washington 1977: 505-518 [Ethnography; Threads; Weaving]
Lamb, A.: see also Lamb, V.
Lamb, V.: West African Weaving. London 1975 [Analysis; Ethnography; Weaving]

Lamb, V.: Nigerian weaving. Roxford 1980 [Ethnography; Ornamentation with Solid Material(s);]
Ornamentation with Liquid Material(s)]
Lamb, V.: Sierra Leone weaving. Herlingsford 1984 [Analysis; Ethnography; Threads; Mesh Fabric; Half-weaving; Weaving; Pile Fabric]
Lamb, V. & Lamb, A.: The Lamb Collection of West African narrow strip weaving. Washington 1975 [Analysis; Ethnography; Collections; Weaving]
Lamb, V. & Lamb, A.: Au Cameroun. Weaving – Tissage. Roxford 1981 [Ethnography; Threads; Weaving; Pile Fabric; Ornamentation with Solid Material(s); Ornamentation with Liquid Material(s)]
Lambert, M.F. & Ambler, R.: A Survey and Excavation of Caves in Hidalgo County New Mexico. School Am. Res. Monograph. Series 25, Santa Fe 1961 [Archaeology; Plaiting]
Lambrecht, D.J: "New Basketry in Kenya", African Arts Vol.15 N°1, Los Angeles 1981: 63-66 [Ethnography; Plaiting]
Lambrecht, D.J.: see also Lambrecht, F.L.
Lambrecht, F.L. & Lambrecht, D.J.: "Leather and Beads in N'gamiland", African Arts Vol. 10 N°2, Los Angeles 1977: 34-36 [Ethnography; Beadwork]
Lamm, C.: see also Geijer, A.
Lamm, C.J.: "Coptic Wool Embroideries", Bull. de la Soc. d'Arch. Copte 9, Kairo 1938: 23-28 [Archaeology; Ornamentation with Solid Material(s)]
Lammèr, J.: Das grosse Ravensburger Werk-Buch. Ravensburg 1975 [Working Instruction; Mesh Fabric; Plaiting; Weaving; Pile Fabric,]
Beadwork; Ornamentation with Solid Material(s); Ornamentation with Liquid Material(s)]
Lamster, J.C.: Verspreiding van enkele vlechtsystemen in den Nederl. Indischen Archipel. Gedenkschrift Koninkl. Inst. v. d. Taal-Land-en Volkenkunde, s'-Gravenhage 1926 [Analysis; Ethnography; Mesh Fabric; Plaiting]
Lamster, J.C.: "Ikat doeken", Onze Aarde N°4, Amsterdam 1930: 146-154 [Analysis; Ethnography; Ornamentation with Liquid Material(s)]
Lancet-Müller, A.: Bokhara: Führer durch das Israel Museum. Jerusalem 1967 [General, Historical; Ornamentation with Solid Material(s); Ornamentation with Liquid Material(s)]
Lancet-Müller, A.: see also Wilbush, Z.
Landolt-Tüller, A & H.: "Qualamkar-Druck in Isfahan: Beiträge zur Kenntnis traditioneller Textilfärbertechniken", Verhandl. Nat. Forsch. Ges. 87/88, Basel 1976/77: 47-80 [Ethnography; Ornamentation with Liquid Material(s)]
Landreau, A.N.: "Kurdish kilim weaving in the Van Hakkari District of Eastern Turkey", Textile Museum Journal 3 (4), Washington 1973: 27-42 [Ethnography; Warp Fabric; Tapestry]
Landreau, A.N.: Yörük: The nomadic weaving tradition of the Middle East. Pittsburgh 1978 [Ethnography; Collections; Warp Fabric; Weaving; Pile Fabric; Ornamentation with Solid Material(s); Tapestry]
Landreau, A.N. & Pickering, W.R.: Flat Woven Rugs. Washington 1969 [Analysis; Ethnography; Collections; Warp Fabric; Weaving; Ornamentation with Solid Material(s); Tapestry]
Landreau, A.N. & Yoke, R.S.: Flowers of the Yayla: Yörük Weaving of the Toros Mountains. The Textile Museum, Washington 1983 [Ethnography; Threads; Warp Fabric; Weaving]
Lane, B.S.: "The Cowichan knitting industry", Anthropology in British Columbia N°2 1951, Victoria 1952: 14-27 [Ethnography; Threads; Mesh Fabric]
Lane, R.B.: "Chilcotin", Handbook of North Am. Indians 6, Washington 1981: 402-412 [Analysis; Ethnography; Plaiting]
Lane, R.F.: Philippine basketry: an appreciation. Manila 1986 [Analysis; Ethnography; Plaiting]
Lang, W.: see also Lavalle, de, J.A.
Langewis, J.: "Geometric Patterns on Japanese Ikats", Kultuurpatronen Deel 2, Delft 1960: 74-83 [Ethnography; Ornamentation with Liquid Material(s)]
Langewis, J.: "Japanse ikatweefsels", Kultuurpatronen 5-6, Delft 1963: 40-83 [Ethnography; Ornamentation with Liquid Material(s)]
Langewis, L.: "Lamak: A woven Balinese Lamak", Galestin, Th. P. (ed.) Lamak and Malat in Bali and a Sumba Loom. Amsterdam 1956: 31-47 [Ethnography; Weaving]
Langewis, L. & Wagner, F.A.: Decorative Art in Indonesian Textiles. Amsterdam 1964 [Ethnography; Weaving; Ornamentation with Liquid Material(s)]
Lang-Meyer, M. & Nabholz-Kartaschoff, M.L.: "Stickereien der Banjara", Götter, Tiere, Blumen. Führer durch das Mus. f. Völkerkunde, Basel 1987: 83-103 [Analysis; Ethnography; Ornamentation with Solid Material(s)]
Lantis, M.: "Nunivak Eskimo", Handbook of North Am. Indians 5, Washington 1984: 209-223 [Ethnography; Mesh Fabric; Plaiting]
Lantis, M.: "Aleut", Handbook of North Am. Indians 5, Washington 1984: 161-184 [Ethnography; Plaiting]
Lantz, S.P.: "Jebba Island Embroidery", Nigeria N°14, Lagos 1938: 130-133 [Ethnography; Ornamentation with Solid Material(s)]
Lapiner, A.: Pre-Columbian Art of South America. New York 1976 [Archaeology; Plaiting; Weaving; Pile Fabric; Ornamentation with Solid Material(s); Ornamentation with Liquid Material(s); Tapestry]
Laquist, B.: "Observations concerning the band-weaving of the Swedish Lapps", Ethnos 12 (3), Stockholm 1947: 123-126 [Ethnography; Weaving]
Larsen, J.L.: Interlacing: the Elementary Fabric. Tokyo 1986 [Classification; Analysis; Mesh Fabric; Plaiting; Warp Fabric; Weaving]
Larsen, J.L. et al.: The Dyer's Art: Ikat, Batik, Plangi. New York 1976 [Analysis; Ornamentation with Liquid Material(s)]
Laufer, B.: Chinese baskets. Field Mus. Nat. Hist. Anthr. Dep. 3, Chicago 1925 [General, Historical; Plaiting]
Laurencich-Minelli, L. & Bagli, M.: Antichi tessuti Peruviani. Milano 1984 [Analysis; Archaeology; Collections; Pile Fabric]
Laurencich-Minelli, L. & Ciruzzi, S.: Antichi oggetti americani nelle collezioni del Museo Nazionale di Antropologia e Etnologia di Firenze. Archivo per l'Antropol. la Ethn. Vol. 111, Firenze 1981: 121-142 [Archaeology; Collections; Plaiting; Warp Fabric; Weaving; Pile Fabric; Ornamentation with Solid Material(s); Ornamentation with Liquid Material(s)]
Lautz, G.: "Verfahren der verschränkten Masche: ein Problem der Terminologie bestimmter Textilien des Präkolumbischen Peru", Baessler-Archiv NF 30, Berlin 1982: 223-232 [Archaeology; Mesh Fabric; Ornamentation with Solid Material(s)]
Lavalle, de, J.A. & Lang, W.: Arte Precolombina. Arte y tesoros del Perú: Arte textil y adornos. Museo Nacional d. Antropolo. y Arqueol. Vol. 1, Lima 1980 [Archaeology; Collections; Plaiting; Weaving; Pile Fabric; Beadwork; Ornamentation with Solid Material(s); Ornamentation with Liquid Material(s); Tapestry]
Leach, E.R.: "A Melanau (Sarawak) Twine-Making Device", Journal of the Royal Anthr. Inst. Vol.79, 1949, London 1951: 79-87 [Ethnography; Threads]
Leacock, E.: see also Rogers, E.S.
Lechner, Z.: Turskeamije. Osijek 1958 [Folk Art; Weaving]
Lechuga, R.: Una investigación entre los Otomies de Queretaro sobre las técnicas Plangi. Mexico 1979 [Working Instruction;

Ornamentation with Liquid Material(s)]
Lehmann, E. & Bültzingslöwen, von, R.: Nichtgewebte Textilien vor 1400. Wirkerei und Stricktechnik Band 2, Coburg 1954 [Archaeology; Mesh Fabric; Warp Fabric]
Lehmann, E.: see also Bültzingslöwen, von, R.
Lehmann, H.: "Vêtement et tissage des indiens de la Cordillère centrale dans la région de Popayan, Colombie.", Revue de l'Inst. Français d'Amérique Latine, Mexico 1945 [Ethnography; Weaving]
Lehmann, J.: Classification und geographische Verbreitung der Geflechtsarten. Zool. und Anthrop.-Ethnol. Mus. Vol. 10, Leipzig 1907 [Ethnography; Mesh Fabric; Plaiting]
Lehmann, J.: Über Knoten aus Westindien. Frankfurt 1908 [Analysis; Ethnography; Mesh Fabric]
Lehmann, J.: Flechtwerke aus dem malayischen Archipel. Veröff. aus dem Städt. Völkerkundemus. 540 (4), Frankfurt 1912 [Analysis; Ethnography; Plaiting]
Lehmann, J.: Die Ornamente der Natur- und Halbkulturvölker. Frankfurt 1920 [Ethnography]
Lehmann, J.: Ein seltenes Gewebe aus Alt Peru: Zugleich eine Einführung in die Technik des Webens. Erläuterungen zu den Sammlungen N° 3, Frankfurt a.M. 1920 [Archaeology; Weaving]
Lehmann, J.: Forschungsmaterial Knotensystematik. (Manus), Frankfurt n.d. [Classification; Mesh Fabric]
Lehmann-Filhes, M.: Über Brettchenweberei. Berlin 1901 [Analysis; Weaving]
Leib, E. & Romano, R.: "Reign of the Leopard: Ngbe Ritual", African Arts Vol.18 N°1, Los Angeles 1984: 48-57 [Ethnography; Mesh Fabric; Ornamentation with Liquid Material(s)]
Leigh, B. & Kerajinan, S.: Tangan-Tangan Trampil: Hands of Time, the Crafts of Aceh. Jakarta 1989 [Ethnography; Plaiting; Weaving; Ornamentation with Solid Material(s)]
Leigh-Theisen, H.: "Plaiting bei den Murat", Archiv für Völkerkunde N°42, Wien 1988 [Analysis; Ethnography; Plaiting; Borders]
Lemaire, M.L.J.: Kralen, pitten – schelpen. Amsterdam 1953 [Ethnography; Collections; Beadwork]
Lemaire, M.L.J.: "Techniken bei der Herstellung von Perlarbeiten", Baessler-Archiv NF 8, Berlin 1960: 215-234 [Classification; Beadwork]
Lemberg, M.: "Opening of the discussion about the Buyid silks", Cieta 38 (2), Lyon 1973 [Weaving]
Lemberg, M.: "Les soieries Bouyides de la Fondation Abegg à Berne", Cieta 37, 1973, 1, Lyon 1973 [Collections; Weaving]
Lemberg, M. & Schmedding, B.: Abegg-Stiftung Bern in Riggisberg. Bern 1973 [Collections; General, Historical]
Lenser, G.: Tibeter (Zentralasien, Nepal): Spinnen und Färben von Wolle. Encyclopaedia Cinematographica E 707, Göttingen 1964 [Ethnography; Films; Threads]
Leontidi, T.: Ta Kritika Kalathia. Mus. Kritikis Ethnologias Vori 5, Athen 1986 [Analysis; Folk Art; Plaiting; Borders]
Leroi-Gourhan, A.: L'homme et la matière. Paris 1943 [Classification; Threads; Mesh Fabric; Plaiting; Warp Fabric; Weaving; Pile Fabric; Borders]
Leroi-Gourhan, A.: Milieu et techniques. Paris 1945 [Ethnography]
Lestrange, de, M.: Les Sarankole de Badyar: Technique de teinture. Etudes Guinéennes N°6, 1950 [Ethnography; Ornamentation with Liquid Material(s)]
Lettenmair, J.G.: Das grosse Orientteppich-Buch. München 1962 [General, Historical; Pile Fabric]
Levillier, J.: Paracas: A Contribution to the study of Pre-Incaic Textiles in ancient Peru. Paris 1928 [Archaeology; Mesh Fabric]
Levinsohn, R.: Basketry: A renaissance in South Africa. Cleveland 1979 [Ethnography; Plaiting]
Levinsohn, R.: "Rural Kwazulu Basketry", African Arts Vol.14 N°1, Los Angeles 1980: 52-57 [Ethnography; Plaiting]
Levinsohn, R.: "Lesotho Silkscreens and Block Prints", African Arts Vol.18 N°4, Los Angeles 1980: 56-59 [Ethnography; Ornamentation with Liquid Material(s)]
Levinsohn, R.: "Amacunu Beverage Containers", African Arts Vol.16 N°3, Los Angeles 1983: 53-55 [Ethnography; Plaiting]
Lévi-Strauss, M.: Le châle cachemire en France au XIXe siècle. Lyon 1983 [Weaving]
Lévi-Strauss, M.: Les Etoffes Tissées en Fibres de Bananièrs dans l'Ile d'Okinawa, Bashofer. Assoc. pour l'Etude et la Doc. des Textiles d'Asie. Paris 1984 [Ethnography; Weaving]
Lévi-Strauss, M.: Cashmere: Tradition einer Textilkunst. Frankfurt 1987 [General, Historical; Threads; Weaving]
Lewis, A.B.: Block Prints from India for Textiles. Field Mus. of Nat. Hist 3 (179), Chicago 1924 [General, Historical; Ornamentation with Liquid Material(s)]
Lewis, E.: The Romance of Textiles. New York 1953 [General, Historical; Weaving]
Lewis, E.: see also Lewis, P.
Lewis, P. & Lewis, E.: Peuples du Triangle d'Or. Genf/Paris 1984 [Analysis; Ethnography; Threads; Plaiting; Weaving; Ornamentation with Solid Material(s); Ornamentation with Liquid Material(s)]
Ley, H. & Ramisch, E.: Technologie und Wirtschaft der Seide. Herzog, R.O. (ed.) Technologie der Textilfasern Band IV, 2.Teil, Berlin 1929 [General, Historical]
Liebert, E.: Schiffchen-Arbeit. Leipzig 1916 [Working Instruction; Mesh Fabric]
Lin, L.C.: Fabric Impression of Old Lampung Culture. Singapore 1987 [Ethnography; Collections; Weaving]
Lindahl, D. & Knorr, T.: Uzbek. The textiles and life of the nomadic and sedentary Uzbek tribes of Central Asia. Basel 1975 [Ethnography; Collections; Weaving; Pile Fabric; Ornamentation with Solid Material(s); Ornamentation with Liquid Material(s)]
Lindberg, I.: "Tejidos y adornos de los cementerios Quitor de San Pedro de Atacama", Revista Universitaria 48, 1963, Santigao d.Chile 1964: 195-201 [Archaeology; Mesh Fabric; Warp Fabric; Pile Fabric; Ornamentation with Liquid Material(s)]
Lindblom, K.G.: "The use of the hammock in Africa", Riksmuseets Etnografiska Avdelning Smärre Meddelanden N°7, Stockholm 1928: 5-39 [Ethnography; Warp Fabric; Weaving]
Linden-Museum Stuttgart: Abteilungsführer Afrika. Linden-Museum (ed.), Stuttgart 1989 [Ethnography; Folk Art; Collections; Plaiting; Pile Fabric; Beadwork; Ornamentation with Liquid Material(s)]
Linder, A.: Spinnen und Weben, einst und jetzt. Luzern 1967 [Analysis; Folk Art; Threads; Weaving]
Lindström, M.: "Medieval Textile Finds in Lund", Textilsymposium Neumünster, Archäologische Textilfunde, Neumünster 1981: 179-192 [Archaeology; Weaving; Pile Fabric]
Ling Roth, H.: "A Loom from Iquitos", Man 20, N°62, London 1920: 123-125 [Ethnography; Half-weaving; Weaving]
Ling Roth, H.: Studies in primitive looms. Halifax 1934 [Classification; Ethnography; Weaving]
Ling Roth, H.: Ancient Egyptian and Greek Looms. Bankfield Mus. Notes 2. Serie 2, Halifax 1951 [Archaeology; Weaving]
Ling Roth, H.: see also Crowfoot, G.M.
Linné, S.: "Prehistoric Peruvian Painting", Ethnos 18 (1-2), Stockholm 1953: 110-23 [Archaeology; Ornamentation with Liquid Material(s)]
Lippuner, R.: Vannerie traditionelle d'Afrique et d'Asie et "nouvelle" vannerie. Lausanne 1981 [Ethnography; Folk Art; Plaiting]
Lips, J.E.: "Notes on Montagnais – Naskapi economy", Ethnos

12 (1-2), Stockholm 1947: 1-78 [Ethnography; Mesh Fabric; Plaiting]
Lipton, M. (ed.): Tigerteppiche aus Tibet. Stuttgart 1978 [Ethnography; General, Historical; Pile Fabric]
Lipton, M. (ed.): Tigerteppiche aus Tibet. Stuttgart 1989 [Analysis; Ethnography; Collections; Weaving; Pile Fabric]
Lismer, M.: Seneca split basketry. Indian Handicrafts N°4, Chilocco 1941 [Analysis; Ethnography; Plaiting; Borders]
Little, F.: Early American Textiles. New York 1931 [General, Historical; Threads; Weaving; Ornamentation with Solid Material(s)]
Littlefield, A.: La industria de las hamacas en Yucatán, México. Inst. Nacional Indigenista. Mexico 1976 [Ethnography; Threads; Mesh Fabric]
Littleton, C.: see also Amar, A.B.
Lobera, A.: see also Barendse, R.
Loeb, B.E.: Classic Intermontane Beadwork Art of the Crow and Plateau Tribes. Thesis University of Washington, Washington 1983 [Ethnography; Beadwork]
Loebèr, J.A.: Het Vlechtwerk in den Indischen Archipel. Haarlem 1902 [Ethnography; Plaiting]
Loebèr, J.A.: Het "Ikatten" in Nederlandsch-Indië. Onze Kunst, Amsterdam 1902 [Ethnography; Ornamentation with Liquid Material(s)]
Loebèr, J.A.: Het weven in Nederlandsch-Indië: Indische Kunstnijverheid. Bull. van het Kolon. Mus. te Haarlem 29, Amsterdam 1903 [Ethnography; Weaving; Ornamentation with Liquid Material(s)]
Loebèr, J.A.: "Textile Verzierungstechniken bei] aussereuropäischen Völkern", Schmidt, C.W. (ed.) Moderne weibl. Handarbeiten und verwandte Künste. Dresden 1908: 266-281 [Analysis; Ornamentation with Liquid Material(s)]
Loebèr, J.A.: "Bamboe in Nederlandsch-Indië", Bull. van het Kol. Mus. te Haarlem, Amsterdam 1909 [Ethnography; Plaiting]
Loebèr, J.A.: Het schelpen- en kralenwerk in Nederlandsch-Indië. Bull. van het Kol. Mus. te Haarlem, Amsterdam 1913 [Ethnography; Beadwork]
Loebèr, J.A.: Het bladwerk en zijn versiering in Nederlandsch-Indië: Indisch Kunstnijverheid. Koloniaal Institut, Amsterdam 1914 [Ethnography; Plaiting]
Loebèr, J.A.: Textiele Versieringen in Nederlandsch-Indië: Indische Kunstnijverheid. Koloniaal Institut, Amsterdam 1914 [Ethnography; Ornamentation with Liquid Material(s)]
Loebèr, J.A.: Been-, Hoorn- en Schildpadbewerking en het Vlechtwerk in Nederlandsch-Indië. Koloniaal Institut, Amsterdam 1916 [Ethnography; Plaiting]
Loebèr, J.A.: Das Batiken. Oldenburg 1926 [Ethnography; Ornamentation with Liquid Material(s)]
Löffler, L.G.: see also Brauns, C.D. [Lonnqvist, B.: "Dräkt och mode", Kansatieteellinen Arkisto N°24, Helsingfor 1972 [Folk Art; Weaving]
Loir, H.: Le tissage au Raphia du Congo Belge. Annal. d.Mus. du Congo Belge 3 (1), Tervueren 1935 [Analysis; Ethnography; Weaving]
Lombard, M.: Les Textiles dans le Monde Musulman, VII-XIIe siècle: Civilisation et Société. Etudes d'Économie Médiévale 3 (61), Paris 1978 [General, Historical; Threads; Weaving; Pile Fabric]
Lopez, R.: see also Altman, B.
Lorenz, C.: Spinnen und Weben. Bauernarbeit im Rheinwald. Schweiz. Gesell. f. Volkskunde, Abt. Film, Basel 1980 [Analysis; Folk Art; Films; Threads; Weaving]
Lorenzo, F.X.: Notas Etnográficas da Terra de Lobeira: O Liño e a Lá. Arquivos d. Sem. d. Estudos Galegos N°6, Sant-lago 1933 [Analysis; Folk Art; Threads; Weaving; Ornamentation with Solid Material(s)]
Lorm, de, A.J.: "Weefkunst in Nederlandsch Oost-Indië", Natuur en Mens N°4, 1938: 85-90 [Ethnography; Weaving; Ornamentation with Liquid Material(s)]
Lothrop, S.K.: The Indians of Tierra del Fuego. Contr. Mus. Am. Indian 10, New York 1928 [Analysis; Ethnography; Mesh Fabric; Plaiting; Weaving]
Lothrop, S.K. & Mahler, J.: Late Nazca burials in Chaviña, Peru. Pap. of the Peabody Mus. Vol. 50 N°2, Cambridge 1957 [Analysis; Archaeology; Threads; Warp Fabric; Weaving; Tapestry; Fabric Processing]
Lothrop, S.K. & Mahler, J.: A Chancay Style Grave at Zapallán, Perú. Pap. of the Peabody Mus. Arch. and Ethn. Vol.50 N°1, Cambridge 1957 [Analysis; Archaeology; Threads; Plaiting; Weaving; Pile Fabric]
Louber, J.A.: Indonesische Frauenkunst. Wuppertal 1937 [Collections; Ornamentation with Liquid Material(s)]
Loud, L.L. & Harrington, M.R.: Lovelock Cave. UCLA Publ. Am. Arch. Ethnol. 25, Berkeley 1929 [Archaeology; Plaiting; Beadwork; Borders]
Loveless, C.: see also Black, D.
Lozado, J.H.A.: see also Gass, S.
Lucas, A.: Ancient Egyptian Materials and Industries. London 1948 [Archaeology; Plaiting; Weaving]
Lübke, A.: Der Bambus. Ciba Rundschau 3, Basel 1969 [General, Historical; Plaiting]
Lühning, A.: Mitteleuropa, Holstein: Bäuerliches Reepschlagen (Seilerei). Encyclopaedia Cinematographica E 539, Göttingen 1963 [Folk Art; Films; Threads]
Lühning, A.: Mitteleuropa, Schleswig: Drehen von Hartgras-Stricken zum Reetdachdecken. Encyclopaedia Cinematographica E 540, Göttingen 1963 [Folk Art; Films; Threads]
Lühning, A.: Mitteleuropa, Schleswig: Drehen von Garbenbändern. Encyclopaedia Cinematographica E 541, Göttingen 1963 [Folk Art; Films; Threads]
Lühning, A.: Mitteleuropa, Holstein: Tauherstellung mit dem Slingholt. Encyclopaedia Cinematographica E 1460, Göttingen 1971 [Folk Art; Films; Borders]
Lühning, A.: Mitteleuropa, Holstein: Spinnen mit dem Spinnhaken. Encyclopaedia Cinematographica E 1461, Göttingen 1971 [Folk Art; Films; Threads]
Lühning, A.: Mitteleuropa, Holstein: Herstellen einer Leine. Encyclopaedia Cinematographica E 1458, Göttingen 1980 [Folk Art; Films; Threads]
Lühning, A.: Mitteleuropa, Holstein: Herstellen einer Trosse. Encyclopaedia Cinematographica E 1457, Göttingen 1981 [Folk Art; Films; Threads]
Lumholtz, C.: Decorative Art of the Huichol Indians. Mem. Am. Mus. of Nat. History 3 (3), New York 1904 [Ethnography; Plaiting; Ornamentation with Solid Material(s)]
Lundbäck, M. & Ingers, G.: Henslöjden Handarbeten. Stockholm 1952 [Folk Art; Working Instruction; Ornamentation with Solid Material(s)]
Lunt, M.: see also Baker, M.
Luz, D. & Schlenker, H.: "Dogon (Westsudan, mittlerer Niger): Herstellen eines Seiles", Encyclopaedia Cinematographica E 1222, Göttingen 1967: 151-153 [Ethnography; Films; Threads]
Luz, D. & Schlenker, H.: "Dogon (Westsudan, Mittlerer Niger): Flechten einer Schlafmatte", Encyclopaedia Cinematografica E 1223, Band 4, Göttingen 1974: 153-155 [Ethnography; Films; Plaiting]
Luz, H.: Fulbe (Westafrika, Futa Dyalo): Spinnen eines Baumwollfadens. Encyclopaedia Cinematographica E 389, Göttingen 1961 [Ethnography; Films; Threads]

Lyford, C.A.: Quill and Beadwork of the Western Sioux. Indian Handicrafts N°1, Los Angeles 1940 [Analysis; Ethnography; Beadwork; Ornamentation with Solid Material(s)]
Lyford, C.A.: Ojibwa Crafts. Los Angeles 1943 [Ethnography; Plaiting; Warp Fabric; Ornamentation with Solid Material(s)]
Lyford, C.A.: Iroquois Crafts. Indian Handicrafts N°6, Los Angeles 1945 [Ethnography]
Lyman, L.P.: "Knitting: a little field for collectors", Antiques 41 (4), Burlington 1925: 240-242 [General, Historical]
Lyman, T.A.: "The weaving technique of the Green Miao", Ethnos 27 (1-4), Stockholm 1962: 35-39 [Ethnography; Weaving]
Lynch, T.: Early man in the Andes. New York 1980 [Archaeology; Mesh Fabric; Plaiting; Warp Fabric; Weaving]

Ma, Z. & Zhan, H.: Embroidery of the Miao people of Guizho. Chinese Arts and Crafts N°1, Kyoto 1981 [Ethnography; Ornamentation with Solid Material(s)]
Mc Clellan, C. & Denniston, G.: "Environment and Culture in the Cordillera", Handbook of North Am. Indians 6, Washington 1981: 372-386 [Analysis; Ethnography; Plaiting]
Mc Creary, C.F.: The Traditional Maroccan Loom, its Construction and Use. Santa Rosa 1975 [Ethnography; Weaving]
Macdonald, D.K.: Fibres, Spindles and Spinning-Wheels. Toronto 1950 [Threads]
Mac Dougall, T.: see also Weitlaner-Johnson, I.
Mc Gurk, C.R.: see also Gibson, G.D. [Mc Kelvy Bird, R. & Mendizábal Losak, E.: "Textiles, Weaving, and Ethnic Groups of Highland Huánuco, Peru", Rowe, A.P. (ed.) J.B. Bird Conf. on Andean Textiles 1984, Washington 1986: 339-362 [Ethnography; General, Historical; Weaving]
Machschefes, A.: Die Kunst des Doppelwebens. Hannover 1983 [Working Instruction; Weaving]
Mack, J.: Weaving, women and the ancestors in Madagaskar. Indonesian Circle 42, London 1987 [Ethnography; Weaving]
Mack, J.: Malagasy Textiles. Shire Ethnography N°14, Dyfed 1989 [Ethnography; Weaving; Ornamentation with Solid Material(s); Ornamentation with Liquid Material(s)]
Mack, J.: see also Picton, J.
MacKenzie, M.A.: The Bilum is the Mother of us all: an interpretative analysis of the social value of the Telefol looped string bag. Canberra 1986 [Analysis; Ethnography; Threads; Mesh Fabric]
Mackie, L.W.: Weaving through Spanish History. Washington 1969 [Collections; Pile Fabric]
Mackie, L.W. & Rowe, A.P.: Masterpieces in the Textile Museum. Washington 1976 [Collections; Weaving; Pile Fabric]
Mackie, L.W. & Thomson, J.: Turkmen tribal carpets and tradition. Washington 1980 [Ethnography, Pile Fabric]
Mackie, L.W.: see also Straka, J.A.
Mc Kinnon, S.: Flags and Half-Moons: Tanimbrese Textiles in an "Engendered" System of Valuables. Los Angeles 1989 [Ethnography; Ornamentation with Liquid Material(s)]
Mac Laren, PI.R.: "Netting knots and needles", Man 55, London 1955: 85-89 [Analysis, Mesh Fabric]
Mac Leish, K.: "Notes on Hopi Belt-Weaving of Moenkopi", Am. Anthrop. 42, Menasha 1940: 291-310 [Ethnography; Threads; Weaving]
Mc Lendon, S.: "Preparing Museum Collections for use as Primary Data in Ethnographic Researches", Annals of the N.Y. Acad. of Scien. 376. New York 1981: 201-227 [Ethnography; Plaiting]
Mc Lendon, S. & Holland, B.S.: "The Basketmakers: The Pomoans of California", Roosevelt (ed.) The Ancestors. New York 1979: 104-129 [Analysis, Ethnography; Plaiting]
Mc Mullan, J.V. & Sylvester, D.& Beattie, M.H.: Islamic carpets from the Joseph V. McMullan collection. London 1972 [Collections; General, Historical; Pile Fabric]
Mc Neish, R. et al.: The prehistory of the Tehuacán Valley. Band 2, Austin 1967 [Analysis; Archaeology; Threads; Mesh Fabric; Plaiting; Warp Fabric; Weaving; Borders]
Mc Reynolds, P.J.: "Sacred Cloth of Plant and Palm", Arts of Asia Vol.12 N°4, Hong Kong 1982: 94-100 [Ethnography; Weaving]
Magalhaes Calvet de, M.M.: Bordados e Rendas de Portugal. n.p., n.d]
Folk Art; Ornamentation with Solid Material(s)]
Magnus, B.: "A Chieftain's Costume: New Light on an old grave find from West Norway", Textilsymposium Neumünster, Neumünster 1982: 63-74 [Archaeology; Weaving]
Mahapatra, S.: see also Fischer, E.
Mahler, J.: see also Bird, J.B.
Mahler, J.: see also Lothrop, S.K.
Maile, A.: Tie and Dye as present day craft. London 1963 [Analysis; Working Instruction; Ornamentation with Liquid Material(s)]
Mailey, J.: Chinese silk tapestry: K'o-ssu from private and museum collections. New York 1971 [Tapestry]
Mailey, J.: Embroidery of Imperial China. New York 1978 [Archaeology; Ornamentation with Solid Material(s)]
Mailey, J.E. & Hathaway, S.: "A Bonnet and a Pair of Mitts from Ch' ang-Sha", Chronicle of the Museum for Arts of Decoration 2 (10), New York 1958: 315-346 [Archaeology; Weaving]
Majmudar, M.R.: Gujarat: Its Art Heritage. Bombay 1968 [Ethnography; Ornamentation with Solid Material(s); Ornamentation with Liquid Material(s)]
Malhano, H.B.: see also Fenelon-Costa, M.H.
Malkin, B.: "Noanamá Fishing Dip Net", Ethnol. Zeitschrift Zürich 1, Zürich 1974: 283-285 [Ethnography; Mesh Fabric]
Malkin, B.: Noanamá (West Colombia, Pacific Coast): Plaiting a fire fan. Encyclopaedia Cinematographica E 2094, Göttingen 1975: 3-11 [Ethnography; Films; Plaiting]
Malkin, B.: Cofán (South Colombia, Montaña): Plaiting a manioc press "tipiti". Encyclopaedia Cinematographica E 1944, Göttingen 1975: 3-12 [Ethnography; Films; Plaiting]
Malkin, B.: Witoto (East Peru, Selva): Plaiting a manioc press "tipiti". Encyclopaedia Cinematographica E 1997, Göttingen 1975: 3-10 [Ethnography; Films; Plaiting]
Malkin, B.: Shuara (Jivaro): Making a feather headdress. Encyclopaedia Cinematographica E 1948, Göttingen 1976 [Ethnography; Films; Plaiting]
Mallin, H.: Kreuzstichstickereien. Vobachs Handarbeitsbücher Band 17, Berlin, Leipzig n.d. [Working Instruction; Ornamentation with Solid Material(s)]
Malon, M.: 120 Patterns for Traditional Patchwork Quilts. New York n.d. [Working Instruction; Ornamentation with Solid Material(s)]
Mancinelli, F.: "La chasuble du pape Saint-Marc à Abbadia San Salvatore", Cieta 41-42, 1-2, Lyon 1975 [Weaving]
Manderloot, G.F.: "Een Afghaans reisjournal", Tijdstroom 1971: 169-179 [Ethnography; Weaving]
Mangkdilaga, I.H. & Hutapea, I.: Batik: pameran koleksi terpilig Museum Tekstil Jakarta danmuseum Badik Yogyakarta. Jakarta 1980 [Collections; Ornamentation with Liquid Material(s)]
Manndorff, H. & Scholz, F.: Akha (Thailand, Chiang Rai-Provinz): Schären einer Baumwollwebkette. Encyclopaedia Cinematographica E 1244, Göttingen 1967 [Ethnography; Films; Weaving]
Manndorff, H. & Scholz, F.: Akha (Thailand, Chieng Rai-Provinz): Spinnen von Baumwolle. Encyclopaedia Cinematographica

E 1243, Göttingen 1967 [Ethnography; Films; Threads]
Manndorff, H. & Scholz, F.: Miao (Thailand, Tak-Provinz): Herstellen von Hanfgarn zum Weben. Encyclopaedia Cinematographica E 1242, Göttingen 1967 [Ethnography; Films; Threads]
Manndorff, H. & Scholz, F.: Akha (Thailand, Rai-Provinz): Weben von Baumwolle auf dem Trittwebstuhl. Encyclopaedia Cinematographica E 1245, Göttingen 1968 [Ethnography; Films; Weaving]
Mannová, M.: Vysivky. Prag 1972 [Analysis; Folk Art; Weaving; Ornamentation with Solid Material(s)]
Manrique, L.C.: "The Otomi", Handbook of Middle Am. Indians 8, Austin 1969: 682-722 [Ethnography; Threads; Plaiting; Weaving]
Mantscharowa, N.D.: Ukrainische Volkskunst: Textilien und Teppiche. Kiew 1960 [Folk Art; Pile Fabric; Ornamentation with Liquid Material(s)]
Mantuba-Ngoma, M.: Flechtwerke der Mbole. Verlag Galerie Fred Jahn, Berlin n.d. [Analysis; Ethnography; Plaiting]
Mapelli Mozzi, C. & Castello Yturbide, T.: La Tejedora de vida. Mexico 1987 [Ethnography; Collections; Plaiting; Weaving; Ornamentation with Solid Material(s)]
March, K.S.: "Weaving, writing and gender", Man n.s. 18, London 1983: 729-744 [Ethnography; Weaving]
Marcos, J.G.: "Woven textiles in a late Valdivia context", The J.B.Bird Precolumbian Textile Conf. 1973, Washington 1979: 19-26 [Archaeology; Weaving]
Marková, E.: Slovenské Cibky. Bratislava 1962 [Analysis; Folk Art; Plaiting]
Marková, E.: "La production des "Gomba" (manteau à long poil) en Slovaquie", Slovensky Narodopis Vol. 12, Bratislava 1964 [Folk Art; Pile Fabric]
Marková, E.: "Myjavské Plátenká apytliky: Beuteltuch und Beutelgeschirr aus Majava.", Slovensky Narodopis, Bratislava 1967: 555-570 [Folk Art; Threads; Weaving]
Markrich, L.: Principles of the Stitch. Chicago 1976 [Analysis; Working Instruction; Ornamentation with Solid Material(s)]
Markus, B.& K.: Handspinnen: Wolle, die man selber macht. Ravensburg 1974 [Working Instruction; Threads; Weaving]
Marschall, W.: "Weberei auf Nias, Indonesien", Basler Beiträge zur Ethnologie Band 30, Basel 1989: 325-335 [Ethnography; Weaving]
Martin, A.: Sächsische Korbmacherkunst. Dresden 1984 [Folk Art; Plaiting]
Martin, C.: Kumihimo. Japanese silk braiding techniques. Hatfield 1986 [Analysis; Ethnography; Working Instruction; Plaiting]
Martin, J.: see also Breguet, G.
Martin, P. et al.: Caves of the Reserve Area. Fieldiana Anthrop. 42, Chicago 1954 [Archaeology; Mesh Fabric; Plaiting]
Martínez, F.: see also Mirambell, L.
Martinez del Rio, de, R.: see also Castello Yturbide, T.
Marzouk, M.A.: History of textile industry in Alexandria. Alexandria 1955 [General, Historical]
Mas, L.: Exposició antològica del macramé. Granollers 1978 [Working Instruction; Plaiting]
Maslowski, R.F.: see also Adovasio, J.M.
Mason, J.A.: "The Ethnology of the Salinan Indians", Uni. Cal. Pub. Am. Arch. and Ethnol. 10, Berkeley 1912: 99-241 [Ethnography; Plaiting]
Mason, O.T.: Basket-Work of the North American Aborigines. Ann. Rep. Smiths. Inst. 1883-84, Washington 1890 [Analysis; Ethnography; Plaiting]
Mason, O.T.: "Woven basketry: a study in distribution", American Anthropologist 2 (4), Menasha 1900: 771-773 [Ethnography; Plaiting]
Mason, O.T.: "A primitive frame for weaving narrow fabrics", Annual Rep. US Nat. Mus. Smithsonian Inst. 1899, Washington 1901: 487-510 [Analysis; Plaiting; Weaving]
Mason, O.T.: "The technique of aboriginal American basketry", American Anthropologist 3, Menasha 1901: 109-128 [Analysis; Plaiting]
Mason, O.T.: "Directions for collectors of American basketry", Bull. US Nat. Museum Smith. Inst. 39 (190), Washington 1902 [Classification; Plaiting]
Mason, O.T.: "Aboriginal American Basketry", Ann. Rep. Smithon. Instit. 1902, Washington 1904: 171-548 [Analysis; Ethnography; Plaiting]
Mason, O.T.: "Basketry", Handbook of North Am. Indians N°1, Washington 1907: 132-134 [Analysis; Plaiting]
Mason, O.T.: Vocabulary of Malaysian Basket-Work. Proceedings of the US Nat. Mus. 35, Washington 1908 [Analysis; Ethnography; Plaiting; Borders]
Mason, O.T.: "Weaving", Handbook of North Am. Indians, Washington 1910: 928-929 [Ethnography; Weaving]
Massey, W. & Osborne, C.M.: "A burial cave in Baja California", Anthrop. Rec. 16 (8), Los Angeles 1961: 338-363 [Archaeology; Plaiting; Pile Fabric]
Mastache, G.: Técnicas prehispánicas del tejido. Mexico 1971 [Archaeology; Weaving]
Mastache, G.: "Dos fragmentos de tejidos decorados con la técnica de Plangi", Anales INAH N°52, 1972-73, Mexico 1973: 251-262 [Archaeology; Ornamentation with Liquid Material(s)]
Mathews, Z.P.: Color and Shape in American Indian Art. The Metropolitan Museum of Art, New York 1983 [Ethnography; Plaiting; Beadwork]
Mathey, F.: see also Singh, P.
Matley, J.F.: see also Fowler, D. [Matsumoto, K.: 7th. and 8th. Century Textiles in Japan from the Shōsō-in and Hōryu-ji. Kyoto 1984 [Ethnography; Plaiting; Ornamentation with Solid Material(s); Ornamentation with Liquid Material(s); Tapestry]
Mattei-Muller, M.C.: see also Henley, P.
Matterna, J.: The Quiltmaker's Art. Asheville 1982 [Folk Art; Ornamentation with Solid Material(s)]
Mattern-Pabel, P.: Patchwork – Quilt: Geschichte und Entwicklung. Hannover 1981 [Analysis; Folk Art; Ornamentation with Solid Material(s); Fabric Processing]
Matthews, W.: "Navajo Weavers", 13th Ann. Rep. Bur. of Ethnol. Washington 1891-92: 371-391 [Ethnography; Weaving]
Matthews, W.: "The Basket Drum", American Anthropologist 7, Menasha 1894: 202-208 [Ethnography; Plaiting]
Mauldin, B.: Traditions in Transition: Contemporary Basket Weaving of the Southwestern Indians. Albuquerque 1977 [Ethnography; Plaiting]
Maurer, D.P.: Tapicería del Perú Antiguo. Tesis. Lima 1951 [Archaeology; Tapestry]
Maxwell, J.: "Textiles of the Kapuas Basin", I.Emery Roundtable on Mus. Textiles 1979, Washington 1980: 127-140 [Ethnography; Beadwork; Ornamentation with Solid Material(s)]
Maxwell, R.: Textiles of Southeast Asia: Tradition, Trade and Transformation. Australian National Gallery, Oxford 1990 [Ethnography; Weaving; Beadwork; Ornamentation with Solid Material(s); Ornamentation with Liquid Material(s)]
Maxwell, R.J.: "Textile and ethnic configurations in Flores and the Solar archipelago", I.Emery Roundtable on Mus. Textiles 1979, Washington 1980: 141-154 [Ethnography; Ornamentation with Liquid Material(s)]
Maxwell, R.J.: Textiles and tusks: some observation on the social dimension of weaving in East Flores. Clayton 1984 [Ethnography; Ornamentation with Liquid Material(s)]

Mayer, C.C.: Masterpieces of Western textiles. The Art Insitute of Chicago, Chicago 1969 [Folk Art; Collections; Weaving; Pile Fabric; Ornamentation with Solid Material(s)]

Mayer Stinchecum, A.: Kosode: 16th.-19th. Century Textiles from the Nomura Collection. New York 1984 [Ethnography; Collections; Weaving; Ornamentation with Solid Material(s)]

Mayer Thurman, C.C. & Williams, B.: Ancient Textiles from Nubia. Chicago 1979 [Archaeology; Threads]

Mead, C.W.: "Technique of some South American Featherwork", Anthr. Pap. Am. Mus. Nat. Hist 1, New York 1908: 5-17 [Analysis; Ethnography; Pile Fabric; Borders]

Mead, S.M: The Maoris and their Arts. American Museum of Natural History Guide Leaflet 71, New York 1945 [Ethnography; Warp Fabric; Pile Fabric]

Mead, S.M.: The Art of Taaniko Weaving. Washington 1968 [Analysis; Ethnography; Working Instruction; Warp Fabric; Pile Fabric; Borders; Ornamentation with Solid Material(s)]

Mead, S.M.: Traditional Maori Clothing. A study of technological and functional change. Wellington 1969 [Ethnography; Warp Fabric]

Means, P.A.: "A Series of Ancient Andean Textiles", Bull. Needle and Bobbin Club Vol.9 N°1, New York 1925: 3-28 [Analysis; Archaeology; Weaving; Tapestry]

Means, P.A.: "A Group of Ancient Peruvian Fabrics", Bull. Needle and Bobbin Club Vol.11 N°1, New York 1927: 10-26 [Archaeology; Collections; Weaving; Ornamentation with Solid Material(s); Tapestry]

Means, P.A.: "The Origin of the Tapestry Technique in Pre-Spanish Peru", Metropolitan Museum Studies 3 (1), New York 1930: 22-37 [Archaeology; Tapestry]

Means, P.A.: A study of Peruvian Textiles. Boston 1932 [Archaeology; Warp Fabric]

Medlin, M.A.: Awayqa sumaj calchapi: weaving, social organisation and identity in Calcha, Bolivia. Thesis Univ. North Carolina, 1983 [Ethnography; Weaving]

Medlin, M.A.: "Learning to Weave in Calcha, Bolivia", Rowe, A.P. (ed.) J.B. Bird Conf. on Andean Textiles 1984, Washington 1986: 275-288 [Ethnography; Weaving]

Mege Rosso, P.: Arte textil Mapuche. Santiago (Chile) 1990 [Ethnography; Collections; Weaving; Pile Fabric; Ornamentation with Liquid Material(s)]

Meisch, L-A.: "Costume and Weaving in Saraguro, Ecuador", Textile Museum Journal 19-20, 1980-81, Washington 1981: 55-64 [Ethnography; Weaving]

Meisch, L.A.: "Weaving styles in Tarabuco, Bolivia", Rowe, A.P. (ed.) J.B. Bird Conf. on Andean Textiles 1984, Washington 1986: 243-274 [Analysis; Ethnography; General, Historical; Weaving]

Mellaart, J. & Hirsch, U. & Balpinar, B.: The Goddess from Anatolia. Milano 1989 [Analysis; Ethnography; Archaeology; Pile Fabric; Tapestry]

Melo Taveira, E.: "Etnografia da cesta Karajá", Revista do Museu Paulista NS Vol. 27, São Paulo 1980: 227-258 [Ethnography; Plaiting]

Mendizábal Losak, E.: see also Mc Kelvy Bird, R.

Menzel, B.: Textilien aus Westafrika. Band 1-3, Berlin 1973 [Analysis; Ethnography; Threads; Weaving]

Merlange, G.: "The Group of Egypto-Arabic Embroideries of the Elsberg Coll.", Bull. Needle and Bobbin Club Vol.12 N°1, New York 1928: 3-30 [Archaeology; Collections; Ornamentation with Solid Material(s)]

Merritt, J.: "Gardens and poetic images: the woven silks of Persia", Riboud, K. (ed.) In Quest of Themes and Skills. Bombay 1989: 52-60 [Ethnography; Weaving]

Mersich, B.: Volkstümliche Stickereien aus Südosteuropa: Katalog, Sonderausstellung Kittsee. Kittsee 1982 [Analysis; Folk Art; Ornamentation with Solid Material(s)]

Metha, R.J.: The Handicrafts and Industrial Arts of India. Bombay 1960 [Ethnography; General, Historical]

Metha, R.N.: "Patolas", Bull. of the Baroda Museum Vol.7, 1949-50, Baroda 1951: 67-75 [General, Historical; Ornamentation with Liquid Material(s)]

Metha, R.N.: "Bandhas of Orissa", Ahmedabad 1961: 62-73 [General, Historical; Ornamentation with Liquid Material(s)]

Metha, R.N.: Masterpieces of Indian textiles: Hand-spun, hand-woven-traditional. Bombay 1970 [Ethnography; Weaving; Ornamentation with Solid Material(s); Ornamentation with Liquid Material(s)]

Métraux, A.: La civilisation materielle des tribus Tupi-Guarani. Paris 1928 [Ethnography; Threads; Plaiting; Weaving; Pile Fabric]

Meurant, G.: Dessin Shoowa. Brüssel 1986 [Ethnography; Weaving; Ornamentation with Solid Material(s)]

Meurant, G. & Tunis, A.: Traumzeichen: Raphiagewebe des Königreiches Bakuba. München 1989 [Analysis; Ethnography; Weaving; Pile Fabric]

Meurant, G.: see also Tunis, A.

Meyer, R.: Alt-Peru: Leben-Hoffen-Sterben. Detmold 1987 [Archaeology; Collections; Plaiting; Weaving]

Meyers, G.& Co. (ed.): Straw braid manufacturers, Wohlèn, Switzerland. Basel n.d. [Analysis; Folk Art; Plaiting]

Meyer- Heisig, E.: Weberei-Nadelwerk-Zeugdruck. München 1956 [Folk Art; Plaiting; Warp Fabric; Weaving; Pile Fabric; Ornamentation with Solid Material(s); Ornamentation with Liquid Material(s)]

Michell, G.: Islamic heritage of the Deccan. Marg Publications, Bombay 1986 [Ethnography; Pile Fabric; Ornamentation with Solid Material(s)]

Mijer, P.: Batiks and how to make them. New York 1928 [Working Instruction; Ornamentation with Liquid Material(s)]

Mikosch, E.: "The Scent of Flowers: Catalogue of Kashmir Shawls in the Textile Museum", Textile Museum Journal 24, Washington 1985: 7-54 [Collections; General, Historical; Weaving]

Miles, C. & Bovis, P.: American Indian and Eskimo basketry: a key to identification. 3rd printing, New Mexico 1977 [Ethnography; Plaiting]

Milhofer, S.A.: Teppich Atlas: Türkei, Kaukasus. Hannover 1979 [Ethnography; General, Historical; Pile Fabric]

Millán de Palavecino, M.D.: "Notas sobre algunas técnicas nuevas o poco conocidas en el arte textil peruano", Actas y trabajos Mus. Argent. de Ciencias Naturales 1, Buenos Aires 1941: 289-296 [Archaeology; Weaving; Tapestry]

Millán de Palavecino, M.D.: "O Nhanduti no litoral Argentino", Bol. Trimestr. Comm. Catarinense de Folclore 4 (15), Florianópolis 1952: 3-15 [Folk Art; Warp Fabric]

Millán de Palavecino, M.D.: "La cestería decorativa de Río Hondo", Runa Vol.9 Partes 1-2, Buenos Aires 1957: 207-214 [Archaeology; Plaiting]

Millán de Palavecino, M.D.: Il Poncio. Roma 1957 [Folk Art; Weaving; Tapestry]

Millán de Palavecino, M.D.: "Antiguas Técnicas Textiles en el Territorio Argentino", Jornadas de Arqueología y Etnología 2, Buenos Aires 1960 [Analysis; Archaeology; Threads; Mesh Fabric; Warp Fabric; Weaving; Pile Fabric]

Millán de Palavecino, M.D.: "Vestimenta Argentina", Cuadernos del Inst Nac. de Investig. Folcloricas 1 & 2, 1960-61, Buenos Aires 1961: 95-127 [Folk Art; Weaving]

Millán de Palavecino, M.D.: "Descripción de Material Arqueológico Proveniente de Yacimientos de Alta Montana en el Area de Puna", Anales de Arqueología y Etnología 21,

Mendoza 1966: 81-100 [Archaeology; Plaiting; Weaving]
Millán de Palavecino, M.D.: "La indumentaria aborigen", Rel. Soc. Argentina de Antr. 5 (1), Buenos Aires 1970: 3-31 [Mesh Fabric; Plaiting; Weaving]
Miller, D.: "The Jibata: A Japanese Loom", I.Emery Roundtable on Mus. Textiles 1977, Washington 1979: 90-99 [Ethnography; Weaving]
Miller, L.: Cornhusk Bags of the Plateau Indians. Maryhill Mus. of Art Collection, Goldendale 1988 [Ethnography; Warp Fabric; Weaving; Ornamentation with Solid Material(s)]
Miner, H.: "The Importance of Textiles in the Archaeology of the Eastern USA", American Antiquity 1, 1935-36, Salt Lake City 1936: 181-196 [Analysis; Mesh Fabric; Plaiting]
Mirambell, L. & Martínez, F.: Materiales arqueológicos de origen orgánico: textiles. México 1986 [Analysis; Archaeology; Threads; Warp Fabric; Weaving; Pile Fabric; Tapestry]
Mirza, M.: "Zardozi", Traditional Arts of Hyderabad, n.p., n.d.: 41-42 [Ethnography; Ornamentation with Solid Material(s)]
Moes, R. & Tay Pike, A.: Mingei. New York 1985 [Ethnography; Collections; Ornamentation with Solid Material(s); Ornamentation with Liquid Material(s)]
Mohanty, B.C.: Appliqué craft of Orissa. Study of contemporary textiles. Ahmedabad 1980 [Ethnography; Ornamentation with Solid Material(s)]
Mohanty, B.C. & Krishna, K.: Ikat Fabrics of Orissa and Andrah Pradesh. Ahmedabad 1974 [Analysis; Ethnography; Ornamentation with Liquid Material(s)]
Mohanty, B.C. & Mohanty, J.P.: Block Printing and Dyeing of Bagru, Rajasthan. Ahmedabad 1983 [Analysis; Ethnography; Ornamentation with Liquid Material(s)]
Mohanty, J.P.: see also Mohanty, B.C.
Mohr, A. & Sample, L.L.: Twined water bottles of the Cuyana Area. American Antiquity Vol.20, 1954-55, Salt Lake City 1955: 345-354 [Archaeology; Plaiting]
Mollet, J.: Indische Textilien: Volkskunst aus Gujarat und Rajasthan. Olten 1976 [Ethnography; Ornamentation with Solid Material(s); Ornamentation with Liquid Material(s)]
Moltke, H.: "Vom Land und Volk der Kurden", Atlantis 10, Zürich 1959 [Ethnography]
Mom Dusdi, P.: The Thai heritage of weaving and embroidery. The Bhirasri Inst. of Modern Art, Bangkok 1975 [Ethnography; Weaving; Ornamentation with Solid Material(s)]
Montandon, G.: Traité d'Ethnography culturelle: l'ologénèse culturelle. Paris 1934 [Ethnography; Weaving]
Monteiro, D.: see also Costa Fénelon, M.H.
Montell, G.: "Le vrai poncho, son origine post-colombienne", Journal de la Soc. des Américanistes 17, Paris 1925: 173-83 [Ethnography; Folk Art; Weaving; Tapestry]
Mooi, H.: 350 Knoten: Für Makramee-Knüpfer, Seebären und Landratten. Gütersloh 1974 [Analysis; Working Instruction; Mesh Fabric; Plaiting]
Moore, D.R.: Arts and Crafts of Torres Strait. Shire Ethnography, Aylesbury 1989 [Ethnography; Plaiting]
Moore, H.C.: see also Taylor, D. [Moos, von, I.: "Wollweberei im Munjatal", Textilhandwerk in Afghanistan. Liestal 1983: 59-73 [Ethnography; Threads; Weaving]
Moos, von, I.: see also Kussmaul, F.
Mora de Jaramillo, Y.: "Clasificación y Notas sobre Técnicas y el Desarollo Historico de las Artesanías Colombianas", Rev. Col. de Anthrop. N°16, Bogotá 1974 [Threads; Mesh Fabric; Plaiting]
Morris, E.A.: "Seventh Century Basketmaker Textiles from Northern Arizona", I.Emery Roundtable on Mus. Textiles 1974, Washington 1975: 125-132 [Archaeology; Plaiting]
Morris, W.F.: Luchetik: el lenguaje textil de los altos de Chiapas. Chiapas 1980 [Ethnography; Weaving]
Morrison, H.: "Craftsmen in a Harsh Environment", Arts of Asia Vol.12 N°2, Hong Kong 1982: 87-95 [Ethnography; Plaiting; Beadwork]
Morton, E.: In the Name of Ixchel. Crafts N°48, London 1981 [Ethnography; Working Instruction; Weaving]
Morton, W.E.: Introduction to the Study of Spinning. London 1952 [Threads]
Moschner, I.: "Die Wiener Cook-Sammlung, Südsee-Teil", Archiv für Völkerkunde 10, Wien 1955: 136-253 [Ethnography; Warp Fabric; Pile Fabric]
Moseley, M. & Barrett, L.K.: "Change in Preceramic Twined Textiles from the Central Peruvian Coast", American Antiquity 34, Salt Lake City 1969: 162-165 [Archaeology; Warp Fabric]
Moseley, M.E.: see also Stephens, S.G.
Moser, R.J.: Die Ikattechnik in Alleppo. Basler Beiträge zur Ethnologie N°15, Basel 1974 [Analysis; Ethnography; Ornamentation with Liquid Material(s)]
Moshkova, V.G.: Carpets of the peoples of Central Asia. Taschkent 1970 [Ethnography; Weaving; Pile Fabric]
Moss, G.: Embroidered samples in the collection of the Cooper-Hewitt-Museum. New York 1984 [Collections; Ornamentation with Solid Material(s)]
Moss, L.A.G.: "Cloths in the Cultures of the Lesser Sunda Islands", Fischer, J. (ed.) Threads of Tradition. Berkeley 1979: 63-72 [Ethnography; General, Historical; Ornamentation with Liquid Material(s)]
Mostafa, M.: Turkish prayer rugs. Collections of the Mus. Islam. Art N°1, Cairo 1953 [Collections; General, Historical; Pile Fabric]
Mowat, L.: Cassava and Chicha. Shire Ethnography, Haverfordwest 1989 [Ethnography; Plaiting]
Mozes, T.: Portul popular din Bazinul bisulin. Oradea 1975 [Folk Art; Ornamentation with Solid Material(s)]
Muelle, J.C.: see also Vreeland, J.M.
Müller, C.C.: see also Heissig, W.
Müller, E. & Brendler, E.: Unsere Textilien. Zürich 1958 [General, Historical; Threads; Plaiting; Weaving; Pile Fabric; Ornamentation with Solid Material(s)]
Müller, G.: Dintle, eine alte halbvergessene Volkskunst. Liestal 1948 [Folk Art; Mesh Fabric; Plaiting]
Müller, I.: Die primären Textiltechniken auf Sumba, Rote und Timor. München 1967 [Classification; Analysis; Ethnography; Mesh Fabric; Plaiting; Borders]
Müller, I.: see also Müller-Peter, I. und Peter, I.
Müller, I.: see also Boser-Sarivaxévanis, R.
Müller, M.: Amish quilts. Genf 1957 [Folk Art; Fabric Processing]
Mueller, J.: Molas. Art of the Cuna Indians. Washington 1973 [Ethnography; Ornamentation with Solid Material(s)]
Müllers, R.: Blau mit weissen Blumen: Geschichte und Technologie des Blaudrucks. Münster 1977 [Folk Art; Ornamentation with Liquid Material(s)]
Müller-Christensen, S.: Die Gräber im Königschor. Die Kunstdenkmäler Rheinland-Pfalz Band 5, 1972 [Archaeology; Weaving]
Müller-Christensen, S.: "Zwei Seidengewebe als Zeugnisse der Wechselwirkung von Byzanz und Islam", Artes Maiores. Bern 1973: 9-25 [General, Historical; Weaving]
Müller-Christensen, S.: "A silk tapestry in the cathedral of Bamberg", Cieta Bull. 41/42, Lyon 1975: 64-66 [Folk Art; Weaving]
Müller-Christensen, S.: "Eine "Künsteley" des 18. Jh.", Reber, H. & A. (ed.) Festschrift P.W. Meister. Hamburg 1975 [Folk Art]
Müller-Christensen, S.: "Examples of Medieval Tablet-woven Bands", Gervers, V. (ed.) Studies in Textile History. Toronto 1977: 232-237 [Archaeology; Weaving]

Müller-Peter, I.: Seidenband in Basel. Basel 1983 [Folk Art; Weaving]
Münch, F.: see also Klingmüller, G.
Mukharji, T.N.: Art manufactures of India. Reprint New Dehli 1974. Calcutta 1888 [Ethnography; Plaiting; Weaving; Ornamentation with Liquid Material(s)]
Munan, M.: Sarawak Crafts. Singapore 1989 [Ethnography; Plaiting; Weaving; Beadwork; Ornamentation with Liquid Material(s)]
Munan-Oettli, A.: "Blue Beads to trade with the Natives", Arts of Asia Vol.17 N°2, Hong Kong 1987: 88-95 [Ethnography; Beadwork]
Munch-Petersen, N.F.: see also Ottovar, A.
Munksgaard, E.: "The gallic coat from Ronberg", Textilsymposium Neumünster, Neumünster 1982: 41-62 [Archaeology; Weaving]
Munksgaard, J.H.: Kurver. Oslo 1980 [Folk Art; Plaiting]
Muraoka, K. & Okamura, K.: Folk Arts and Crafts of Japan. Tokyo 1973 [Ethnography; Weaving; Ornamentation with Liquid Material(s)]
Muraoka, K.: see also Okamura, K.
Murnane, B.: see also Wass, B.
Murphy, V. & Crill, R.: Tie-dyed Textiles of India: Tradition and Change. n.p. 1989 [Analysis; Ethnography; Ornamentation with Liquid Material(s)]
Murra, J.: "Cloth and its Function in the Inca State", Am. Anthropologist 64 (4), Menasha 1962: 710-728 [Archaeology; Weaving; Tapestry]
Murray, K.C.: "Weaving in Nigeria: A General Survey", Nigeria N°14, London 1938: 118-120 [Ethnography; Weaving]
Musée d'Art et d'Essai: L'art du vannier: Catalogue. Paris 1984 [Folk Art; Plaiting]
Museo Chileno de Arte Precolombino: A Noble Andean Art. Santiago (Chile) 1989 [Analysis; Archaeology; Collections; Mesh Fabric; Weaving; Pile Fabric; Borders; Ornamentation with Solid Material(s); Ornamentation with Liquid Material(s); Tapestry]
Museo Etnografico Barcelona: Manuskript. Barcelona 1976 [Classification; Plaiting]
Museum für Völkerkunde Basel: Ethnographische Kostbarkeiten aus den Sammlungen von Alfred Bühler im Basler Museum für Völkerkunde. Basel 1970 [Collections; Plaiting; Ornamentation with Solid Material(s); Ornamentation with Liquid Material(s)]
Muthmann, F.: Eine Peruanische Wirkerei der Spanischen Kolonialzeit. Bern 1977 [General, Historical; Warp Fabric; Tapestry]
Myers, D.K.: Temple, Household, Horseback: Rugs of the Tibetan Plateau. Washington 1984 [Ethnography; General, Historical; Pile Fabric]
Myers, M.: "Silk furnishings of the Ming and Quing dynasties", Riboud, K. (ed.) In Quest of Themes and Skills. Bombay 1989: 126-140 [Ethnography; Weaving; Tapestry]
Mylius, N.: Ait-Haddidou (Nordafrika, Hoher Atlas): Färben eines Tuches in Plangi-Technik. Encyclopaedia Cinematographica E 1759, Göttingen 1979 [Ethnography; Films; Ornamentation with Liquid Material(s)]
M'hari, C.: "Gold und Silberfadenstickereien in Constantine, Algerien", Abhandl. Staatl. Mus. f.Völkerkunde 34, Dresden 1975 [Analysis; Ornamentation with Solid Material(s)]

Nabholz-Kartaschoff, M.L.: "Ikatgewebe aus Südeuropa", Palette N°30, Basel 1968: 2-13 [Folk Art; Ornamentation with Liquid Material(s)]
Nabholz-Kartaschoff, M.L.: Ikatgewebe aus Nord- und Südeuropa. Basler Beiträge zur Ethnologie 6, Basel 1969 [Folk Art; Ornamentation with Liquid Material(s)]
Nabholz-Kartaschoff, M.L.: Batik. Museum für Völkerkunde, Basel 1970 [Ethnography; Collections; Ornamentation with Liquid Material(s)]
Nabholz-Kartaschoff, M.L.: "Tibeter (Zentralasien, Nepal): Knüpfen eines Teppichs", Encyclopaedia Cinematographica 4(4), 1974 E 708, Göttingen 1972: 402-417 [Ethnography; Films; Pile Fabric]
Nabholz-Kartaschoff, M.L.: "Textilien", Kulturen, Handwerk, Kunst. Basel 1979: 213-228 [Analysis; Ethnography; Warp Fabric; Weaving; Ornamentation with Solid Material(s); Ornamentation with Liquid Material(s)]
Nabholz-Kartaschoff, M.L.: "Bandha Textilien", Fischer, E. (ed.) Orissa. Zürich 1980 [Ethnography; Ornamentation with Liquid Material(s)]
Nabholz-Kartaschoff, M.L.: "Bandha Textiles in India", Journ. Orissa Res. Soc. 1 (2), Orissa 1982 [Ethnography; Ornamentation with Liquid Material(s)]
Nabholz-Kartaschoff, M.L.: Golden sprays and scarlet flowers. Kyoto 1986 [Collections; Weaving; Ornamentation with Solid Material(s); Ornamentation with Liquid Material(s)]
Nabholz-Kartaschoff, M.L.: "Geflechte aus Asien", Schweiz. Arbeitslehrerinnen Zeitung 9 N°69, Biel 1986: 2-5 [Analysis; Ethnography; Plaiting]
Nabholz-Kartaschoff, M.L.: "Volkstümliche Stickereien aus Indien", Haas, S. et al. (ed.) Götter, Tiere Blumen. Basel 1987: 57-81 [Ethnography; Ornamentation with Solid Material(s)]
Nabholz-Kartaschoff, M.L.: "From Telia rumal to Pochampalli tie and dye: old and new ikats from Andhra Pradesh", Riboud, K. (ed.) In Quest of Themes and Skills. Bombay 1989: 62-71 [Ethnography; Ornamentation with Liquid Material(s)]
Nabholz-Kartaschoff, M.L.: "Indian patola: their use in Indonesia and their influence on Indonesian textiles", Riboud, K. (ed.) In Quest of Themes and Skills. Bombay 1989: 92-98 [Ethnography; Ornamentation with Liquid Material(s)]
Nabholz-Kartaschoff, M.L.: "A sacred cloth of Rangda: Kamben cepuk of Bali and Nusa Penida", Gittinger, M. (ed.) To speak with cloth: studies in Indon. textiles. Los Angeles 1989 [Ethnography; Ornamentation with Liquid Material(s)]
Nabholz-Kartaschoff, M.L. & Krehl-Eschler, E.: "Ikat in Andhra Pradesh", Ethnologische Zeitschrift Zürich 2, Zürich 1980: 69-122 [Ethnography; Ornamentation with Liquid Material(s)]
Nabholz-Kartaschoff, M.L. & Näf, G.: "Zur Technik von Flachgeweben und Knüpfteppichen", Alte Teppiche aus dem Orient. Basel 1980: 14-29 [Analysis; Warp Fabric; Pile Fabric; Borders; Tapestry]
Nabholz-Kartaschoff, M.L.: see also Hauser-Schäublin, B.
Nabholz-Kartaschoff, M.L.: see also Lang-Meyer, M.
Nachtigall, H.: Tierradentro: Archaeologie und Ethnologie einer kolumbianischen Landschaft. Zürich 1955 [Analysis; Ethnography; Threads; Mesh Fabric; Plaiting; Weaving]
Nachtigall, H.: Atacameños, Nordargentinien (Puna de Atacama): Weben am Trittwebstuhl. Encyclopaedia Cinematographica Band 1 B 1963-65, Göttingen 1963 [Ethnography; Films; Weaving]
Nachtigall, H.: "Zelt und Haus bei den Beni Mguild-Berbern (Marokko)", Baessler-Archiv NF 14, Berlin 1966: 269-330 [Ethnography; Weaving; Ornamentation with Solid Material(s)]
Nachtigall, H.: "Beni Mguild (Nordafrika, Mittlerer Atlas): Weben einer Zeltbahn am waagrechten Griffwebgerät", Encyclopaedia Cinematographica 2 (5), Göttingen 1969 [Ethnography; Films; Weaving]
Näf, G.: see also Nabholz-Kartaschoff, M.L.

Nakamo, E.: Japanese stencil dyeing. Tokyo 1982 [Working Instruction; Ornamentation with Liquid Material(s)]
Nambiar, P.K.: Silkweaving of Kanchipuram: Handicrafts and artisans of Madras state. Census of India Vol.9 Part 7, Madras 1961 [Ethnography; Weaving]
Nambiar, P.K.: Handicrafts and artisans of Madras state. Census of India, Delhi 1964 [Ethnography; Weaving]
Nambiar, P.K.: Druggets and carpets of Walajapet: Handicrafts and artisans of Madras State. Census of India 1961 Vol.9 Part7, Delhi 1965 [Ethnography; Pile Fabric]
Nambiar, P.K.: Kosa silk weaving at Ganeshpur: Handicrafts in Maharastra. Census of India, New Delhi 1966 [Ethnography; Threads; Weaving]
Nambiar, P.K. & Kurup, K.C.N.: Handicrafts and artisans of Pondicherry state. Census of India 1961 Vol. 25 Part 5, Bombay 1961 [Ethnography; General, Historical]
Nana, S.F.: "Embroidery Blocks of the Sind Region of Pakistan, and some Embroidery", Baessler-Archiv NF 23, Berlin 1975: 399-416 [Ethnography; Ornamentation with Solid Material(s)]
Nanavati, J.M. & Vora, M.P.& Dhaky, M.A: The Embroidery and Beadwork of Kutch and Saurashtra. Baroda 1966 [Ethnography; Beadwork; Ornamentation with Solid Material(s)]
Nardi, R.L.: "Los tejidos tradicionales", El Arte 22, n.p. 1975 [Warp Fabric; Weaving; Pile Fabric; Ornamentation with Liquid Material(s)]
Nardi, R.L.: "Importancia de los tejidos para el diagnóstico cronológico y cultural", Folklore Americano 26, Mexico 1978: 37-47 [Mesh Fabric; Warp Fabric; Weaving]
Nardi, R.L.J.: see also Chertudi, S.
Nath, A.: see also Wacziarg, F.
Nauerth, C.: Koptische Textilkunst im spätantiken Aegypten. Band 2, Trier 1978 [Archaeology; Collections; Tapestry]
Naumova, O.B.: see also Basilov, V.N.
Naupert, A.: "Textilfachkunde. Teil I: Vom Spinnen zum Faden", Teubners Berufs- und Fachbücher 87, 1938 [General, Historical; Threads]
Navajo School of Indian Basketry: Indian Basket Weaving. New York 1949 [Ethnography; Working Instruction; Plaiting; Pile Fabric]
Neal, A.: see also Parker, A.
Neich, R.: Material Culture of Western Samoa. Nat. Mus. New Zealand Bull. 23, Wellington 1985 [Plaiting; Ornamentation with Solid Material(s)]
Nel, R.: Kleines Lexikon der Stickerei. Hannover 1980 [Working Instruction; Ornamentation with Solid Material(s)]
Nelson, C.I.: The quilt engagement calendar. New York 1977 [Folk Art; Ornamentation with Solid Material(s)]
Nelson, C.I. & Houck, C.: Treasury of American Quilts. New York 1984 [Folk Art; Working Instruction; Ornamentation with Solid Material(s)]
Nestor, S.: "The woven spirit", Collings (ed.) Harmony by Hand. San Francisco 1987: 51-73 [Ethnography; Warp Fabric; Weaving]
Nettinga Arnheim, M.R.J.: Basketry and Basketry Techniques. Groningen 1977 [Ethnography; Plaiting; Borders]
Nettleship, M.A.: "A Unique Southeast Asian Loom", Man 5 (4), London 1970: 686-698 [Ethnography; Weaving]
Neugebauer, R. & Orendi, J.: Handbuch der orientalischen Teppichkunde. Leipzig 1923 [General, Historical; Pile Fabric]
Neumann, P.: see also Guhr, G.
Neuwirth, L.: "The Theory of Knots", Scientific American Vol.240 N°6, San Francisco 1979: 110-126 [Classification; Mesh Fabric]
Nevermann, H.: "Die sogenannten Partialgewebe aus Ica und Pachacamac und ihre Herstellung", Rev. Inst. de Ethnol. Tucuman 2, Tucumán 1932: 293-296 [Analysis; Archaeology; Warp Fabric; Tapestry]
Nevermann, H.: Die Indo-Ozeanische Weberei. Mitteilungen d. Mus. für Völkerkunde 20, Hamburg 1938 [Analysis; Ethnography; Threads; Warp Fabric; Weaving; Ornamentation with Liquid Material(s)]
Nevermann, H.: "Völkerkundliches aus Aoba", Ethnologica Band 2, Köln 1960: 189-219 [Ethnography; General, Historical; Plaiting]
Newman, T.R.: Contemporary African arts and crafts. London 1974 [Analysis; Ethnography; Plaiting; Weaving; Ornamentation with Solid Material(s); Ornamentation with Liquid Material(s)]
Newman, T.R.: Contemporary southeast Asian arts and crafts. New York 1977 [Analysis; Ethnography; Plaiting; Weaving; Beadwork; Ornamentation with Liquid Material(s)]
Newton, D.: "The Timbira Hammock as a Cultural Indicator of Social Boundaries", The Human Mirror. Lousiana 1974: 231-251 [Ethnography; Warp Fabric]
Newton, D.: "The Individual in Ethnographic Collections", Annals of the NY Acad. Science Vol. 376, New York 1981: 267-287 [Ethnography; Plaiting]
Nicola, N. & Dorta, S.F.: Aroméri: Arte plumaria do indigena brasileiro: Brazilian Indian feather art. Mercedes-Benz do Brasil, São Bernardo d.C 1986 [Analysis; Ethnography; Pile Fabric]
Niedner, M.: Tüll-Arbeiten. Beyers Handarbeitsbücher Band 43 Heft 2, Leipzig 1921 [Working Instruction; Ornamentation with Solid Material(s)]
Niedner, M.: Filet-Arbeiten. Leipzig 1924 [Working Instruction; Ornamentation with Solid Material(s)]
Niedner, M. & Weber, H.: Sonnenspitzen. Leipzig 1915 [Working Instruction; Warp Fabric]
Niessen, S.A.: "Exchanging Warp in the Batak Ragidup and Bulang", Textile Museum Journal 27/28, Washington 1989: 40-55 [Analysis; Ethnography; Weaving]
Nieuwenhuis, A.W.: Die Veranlagung der Malaischen Völker des Ost-Indischen Archipels. Suppl. Intern. Arch. f. Ethnogr. 21, Leiden 1913 [Ethnography; Plaiting; Ornamentation with Liquid Material(s)]
Niggemeyer, H.: "Baumwollweberei auf Ceram", Ciba Rundschau 106, Basel 1952: 3870-97 [Ethnography; Weaving]
Niggemeyer, H.: "Ein merkwürdiges Seidengewebe aus Sumatra", Tribus 4-5, 1954-55, Stuttgart 1955: 233-236 [Ethnography; Weaving]
Niggemeyer, H.: "Sariweberei und Ikatarbeit im Gebiete von Baudh (Mittel-Orrissa, Indien)", Basler Beiträge zur Ethnologie 2, Basel 1965: 303-318 [Ethnography; Ornamentation with Liquid Material(s)]
Niggemeyer, H.: Baststoffe und Gewebe. Frankfurt 1966 [Ethnography; Collections; Weaving]
Nilsson, K.: Mönster till Pinnbandsspetsar. Oestersund 1928 [Working Instruction; Warp Fabric]
Nistor, F.: Creati si creatori populari din zona etnografica Maramures. Maramures 1967 [Folk Art]
Nistoroaia, G.: Sergare populare. Bucuresti 1975 [Folk Art; Ornamentation with Solid Material(s)]
Nixdorff, H.: Europäische Volkstrachten: Tschechoslowakei. Berlin 1977 [Folk Art; Collections; Mesh Fabric; Plaiting; Warp Fabric; Weaving; Ornamentation with Solid Material(s); Fabric Processing]
Nixdorff, H.: Klöppelspitzen für Volkstrachten in der Teschechoslowakei: Sonderausstellung Festlicher Volkstrachten, Abt. Europa,. Mus. f. Volkskunde Berlin Blatt 5A, Berlin 1977 [Analysis; Folk Art; Plaiting]

Noma, S.: Japanese Costume and Textile Arts. Tokyo 1977 [General, Historical; Ornamentation with Liquid Material(s)]
Nooteboom, C.: "Quelques Techniques de Tissage des Petites Iles de la Sonde", Meded. van het Rijksmus v. Volkek. N°3, Leiden 1948: 1-10 [Analysis; Ethnography; Warp Fabric]
Nooteboom, C.: Aziatische Weefsels in de Collectie Bierens de Haan, van technische zijde bezien. Bull. Mus. Boymans 9 (1), Rotterdam 1958: 15-33 [Ethnography; Collections; Weaving]
Nooteboom, C.: De kleurenpracht van Soemba-Weefsels: Gids van de tentoonstelling. Textiel Museum Tilburg, Tilburg 1958 [Ethnography; Ornamentation with Liquid Material(s)]
Nooy-Palm, H.: "The role of the sacred cloths in the mythology and ritual of the Sa'dan-Toraja of Sulawesi, Indonesia", I. Emery Roundtable on Mus. Textiles 1979, Washington 1980: 81-95 [Ethnography; Weaving]
Noppe, C. & Castillon, du, M.F.: La Chine au fil de la soie: techniques, styles et société du 19e siècle. Marcemont 1988 [Analysis; Ethnography; Weaving; Ornamentation with Solid Material(s)]
Nordenskiöld, E.: An Ethno-geographical Analysis of the Material Culture of two Indian Tribes in the Gran Chaco. Comp. Ethno. Stud. Göteborg 1, Göteborg 1919 [Analysis; Ethnography; Mesh Fabric; Plaiting; Warp Fabric]
Nordenskiöld, E.: The changes in the Material culture of two indian tribes under the influence of new surroundings. Comp. Ethno. Stud. 2, Göteborg 1920 [Analysis; Ethnography; Mesh Fabric; Plaiting; Warp Fabric; Weaving]
Nordenskiöld, E.: The Ethnography of South-America seen from Mojos in Bolivia. Comp. Ethnogr. Stud. 3, Göteborg 1924 [Analysis; Ethnography; Threads; Plaiting; Warp Fabric; Half-weaving; Pile Fabric]
Nordenskiöld, E.: see also Frödin, O.
Nordiska Museet: Hedvig Ulfsparre och Gästriklands textila slöjd. Stockholm 1984 [Folk Art; Plaiting; Weaving; Ornamentation with Solid Material(s)]
Nordland, O.: Primitive Scandinavian textiles in knotless netting. Studia Norvegica N°10, Oslo 1961 [Classification; Analysis; Folk Art; Mesh Fabric]
Nordquist, B.K. & Aradeon, S.B.: Traditional African Dress and Textiles. Washington 1975 [Ethnography; Threads; Weaving; Ornamentation with Solid Material(s); Ornamentation with Liquid Material(s)]
Noss, A.: "Bandlading", By of Bygd 19, Oslo 1966: 111-142 [Folk Art; Weaving]
Nylén, A.: Hemslöjd. Lund 1969 [Analysis; Folk Art; Mesh Fabric; Weaving; Pile Fabric; Ornamentation with Solid Material(s); Tapestry]

Oakland, A.: "Tiahuanaco Tapestry Tunics and Mantles from San Pedro de Atacama, Chile", Rowe, A.P. (ed.) J.B. Bird Conf. on Andean Textiles 1984, Washington 1986: 101-122 [Archaeology; Tapestry]
O'Bannon, G.: Tulu: traditional 20th century pelt-like rugs from Central Anatolia. Philadelphia 1987 [General, Historical]
Oei, L.: Ikat in katoen. Amsterdam 1982 [Ethnography; Ornamentation with Liquid Material(s)]
Oei, L. (ed.): Indigo. Amsterdam 1985 [Ethnography; Ornamentation with Liquid Material(s)]
Oez, T.: Türk Kumas Kdi felerj. Istanbul 1951 [Ethnography]
Oezbel, K.: Chaussettes-Bas-Yazma: Artisanat et tissage turcs. Paris 1967 [Ethnography; Mesh Fabric]
Oezbel, K.: Türk Köylü Coraplari. Istanbul 1976 [Analysis; Ethnography; Mesh Fabric]
Oezbel, K.: Knitted stockings from Turkish villages. Istanbul 1981 [General, Historical; Mesh Fabric]
Ohnemus, S.: "Eipo (West-Neuguinea, Zentrales Hochland): Herstellen eines Perlenbandes in Halbwebtechnik", Encyclopaedia Cinematographica E 2595, Göttingen 1989: 225-236 [Ethnography; Films; Half-weaving; Beadwork]
Ohnemus, S.: see also Seiler-Baldinger, A.
Oka, H.: Wie verpacke ich fünf Eier: Kunst des Verpackens in Japan. Tokio 1982 [General, Historical; Mesh Fabric; Plaiting]
Okada, Y.: History of Japanese Textiles and Lacquer. Tokyo 1958 [Collections; General, Historical; Plaiting; Ornamentation with Solid Material(s); Ornamentation with Liquid Material(s)]
Okamura, K. & Muraoka, K.: Folk Art and Crafts of Japan. New York 1973 [Ethnography; Ornamentation with Liquid Material(s)]
Okamura, K.: see also Muraoka, K.
Olagniers-Riottot, M.: "Six "brocards"-ceintures de femmes Fès-Tétoun 16e-18e siècle", Cieta 1, Lyon 1972 [Ethnography; Weaving]
Olschak, B.C.: "L'art du tissage du Bhutan.", Palette 24, Basel 1966: 3-8 [Ethnography; Weaving]
Olsen Bruhns, K.: "Prehispanic Weaving and Spinning Implements from Southern Ecuador", Textile Museum Journal 27/28, Washington 1989: 71-77 [Archaeology; Threads; Weaving]
Olson, R.L.: "The possible Middle American Origin of Northwest Coast Weaving", American Anthropologist Vol.31 N°1, Menasha 1929: 114-121 [General, Historical; Weaving]
Omar, A.: Traditional Palestinian Embroidery and Jewelery. London 1987 [Ethnography; Ornamentation with Solid Material(s)]
O'Neale, L.M.: "Wide-Loom Fabrics of the Early Nazca Period", Essays in Anthrop. in Honor of A.L. Kroeber. Berkeley 1930: 215-228 [Archaeology; Weaving]
O'Neale, L.M.: Yurok-Karok basket weavers. Uni. Cal. Publ. 32, Berkeley 1932 [Ethnography; Plaiting]
O'Neale, L.M.: "A Peruvian Multicolored Patchwork", Am. Anthropologist N.S. 35 (1), Menasha 1933: 87-94 [Archaeology; Tapestry]
O'Neale, L.M.: "Peruvian Needle-Knitting", Am. Anthropologist 36 (3), Menasha 1934: 405-430 [Archaeology; Mesh Fabric; Ornamentation with Solid Material(s)]
O'Neale, L.M.: "Archaeological Explorations in Peru: Part IV: Middle Cañete Textiles", The Field Museum of Nat. Hist. Anth. M. 2 (4), Chicago 1937: 268-73 [Archaeology; Weaving]
O'Neale, L.M.: "Textile Periods in Ancient Peru. 2", Uni. of Cal. Publ. Am. Arch. and Ethnol. 39, Berkeley 1942: 143-202 [Analysis; Archaeology; Mesh Fabric; Plaiting; Warp Fabric; Weaving; Ornamentation with Solid Material(s); Fabric Processing]
O'Neale, L.M.: "The Paracas Mantle", Cong. Int. de Science Antr. et Ethnol. London 1943: 262-3 [Archaeology; Weaving; Ornamentation with Solid Material(s)]
O'Neale, L.M.: "Mochica (Early Chimu) and Other Peruvian Twill Fabrics", Southwestern. Journal of Anthropology 2 (3), Albuquerque 1943: 269-294 [Archaeology; Weaving]
O'Neale, L.M.: Textiles of Highland Guatemala. Washington 1945 [Analysis; Ethnography; Mesh Fabric; Plaiting; Warp Fabric; Weaving; Pile Fabric; Ornamentation with Solid Material(s)]
O'Neale, L.M.: "Basketry S.:69-96, Weaving S.:105-137", Handbook of South American Indians 5, Washington 1946 [Analysis; Ethnography; Threads; Plaiting; Weaving]
O'Neale, L.M.: "A Note on Certain Mochica (Early Chimu) Textiles", American Antiquity 12 (4), Salt Lake City 1947: 239-45

[Archaeology; Weaving]
O'Neale, L.M.: "Cestaria", Suma Etnologica Brasileira 2, Petrópolis 1986: 323-349 [Analysis; Ethnography; Plaiting]
O'Neale, L.M.: "Tecelagem", Suma Etnologica Brasileira 2, Petrópolis 1986: 397-429 [Analysis; Ethnography; Mesh Fabric]
O'Neale, L.M. & Bacon, E.: Chincha Plain-Weave Cloths. Anthropological Records 9 (2), Los Angeles 1949 [Archaeology; Mesh Fabric; Plaiting; Weaving]
O'Neale, L.M. & Clark, B.: "Textile Periods in Ancient Peru. 3: Gauze Weavers", UCLA Publ. Am. Arch. and Ethnol. 40, Berkeley 1948: 143-222 [Analysis; Archaeology; Weaving]
O'Neale, L.M. & Kroeber, A.L.: "Textile Periods in Ancient Peru. 1", Univ. Calif. Publ. Am. Arch. and Ethnol. 28 (12), Berkeley 1930: 23-56 [Analysis; Archaeology; Mesh Fabric; Weaving; Tapestry]
O'Neale, L.M. & Kroeber, A.L.: "Archaeological Explorations in Peru. 3", Field Mus. Nat. Hist. Anthrop. 2 (3), Chicago 1937: 121-215 [Analysis; Plaiting; Warp Fabric; Weaving; Borders; Ornamentation with Solid Material(s); Tapestry]
O'Neale, L.M. & Whitaker, T.W.: "Embroideries of the Early Nazca Period and the Crop Plants Depicted on them", Southwestern Journal of Anthropology 8 (4), Albuquerque 1947: 294-321 [Archaeology; Ornamentation with Solid Material(s)]
O'Neil, D.: "Manufacturing Techniques of Chibcha Spindle Whorls", Man, Ns. Vol.9 N°3, London 1974: 480-484 [Archaeology; Threads]
Ong, C.: Patterns and pattern-making techniques in the traditional textiles of Southeast Asia. Singapore 1970 [Ethnography; Ornamentation with Liquid Material(s)]
Opie, J.: The Tribal Road: Persian Tribal Rugs. Hali N°29, New York 1986: 33-39 [Ethnography; Pile Fabric]
Oppenheim, K.: Die primären textilen Techniken der Neu-Kaledonier und Loyality-Insulaner. Supplement zu Int. Archiv für Ethnographie 41, Leiden 1942 [Classification; Analysis; Mesh Fabric; Plaiting; Warp Fabric; Half-weaving; Weaving; Borders; Ornamentation with Solid Material(s)]
Oppenheim, K.: see also Bühler-Oppenheim, K.
Opt'land, C.: "Een merkwaardige "Tampun pengantar" van Zuid-Sumatra", Kultuurpatronen Deel 10-11, Delft 1969: 100-117 [General, Historical; Weaving]
Orazbaeva, N.A.: Kazakh decorative and applied art. Leningrad 1970 [Folk Art; Ornamentation with Solid Material(s)]
Orchard, W.C.: Beads and Beadwork of American Indians. Contr. Mus. Am. Indians Heye Found. 11, New York 1929 [Classification; Ethnography; Beadwork; Ornamentation with Solid Material(s)]
Orel, J. & Stanková, J.: The Winding and Sewing Batique Technique. Umeni Aremesla 4, Praha 1960 [Folk Art; Ornamentation with Liquid Material(s)]
Orel, J.: see also Václavik, A.
Orendi, J.: see also Neugebauer, R.
Orr, A.: Cross-stitch and crochet. Pawtucket 1922 [Mesh Fabric]
Ortiz, A. (ed.): Southwest Handbook of North Am. Indians 9, Washington 1979 [Ethnography; Archaeology; Threads; Mesh Fabric; Plaiting; Weaving; Ornamentation with Solid Material(s)]
Ortiz, A. (ed.): Southwest Handbook of North Am. Indians 10, Washington 1983 [Ethnography; Mesh Fabric; Plaiting; Weaving]
Osborne, C.M.: "Shaped breechcloths from Peru", Anthropological Records Band 13 N°2, Berkeley 1950: 157-186 [Archaeology; Weaving]
Osborne, C.M.: "The preparation of Yucca Fibres: An experimental Study", American Antiquity Vol.31 N°2 (2), Salt Lake City 1965: 45-50 [Analysis; Threads; Weaving]
Osborne, C.M.: see also Massey, W.
Osborne, D.& C.: "Twines and Terminologies", American Anthropologist 56, Menasha 1954: 1093-1101 [Classification; Threads]
Osborne, de Jongh, L.: Guatemala Textiles. New Orleans 1935 [Ethnography; Threads; Weaving]
Osborne, de Jongh, L.: "Breves apuntes de la indumentaria indígena de Guatemala", Revista "Folklore Americano" N°11-12, 1963-4, Lima 1964: 22-45 [Ethnography; Weaving; Tapestry]
Osborne, de Jongh, L.: Indian Crafts of Guatemala and El Salvador. Norman 1965 [Ethnography; Weaving]
Osborne, de Jongh, L.: see also Kelsey, V.
Osornio Lopez, M.A.: Al tranco. 20 N°11, Buenos Aires 1938 [Working Instruction; Plaiting]
Osumi, T.: Printed cottons of Asia. Tokyo 1963 [General, Historical; Ornamentation with Liquid Material(s)]
Ota, N.: see also Yanagi, S.
Otavsky, K.: Alte Gewebe und ihre Geschichte: Ein Lese- und Bilderbuch. Riggisberg 1987 [General, Historical; Weaving]
Ottaviano de, I.: Métodos del Tejido Tacana. Inst. Ling. de Verano, Riberalta 1974 [Ethnography; Threads; Warp Fabric]
Ottenberg, S. & Knudsen, L.: "Leopard Society Masquerades: Symbolism and Diffusion", African Arts Vol.18 N°2, Los Angeles 1985: 37-44 [Ethnography; Mesh Fabric]
Ottovar, A. & Munch-Petersen, N.F.: Maldiverne:] Kunstindustrimuseet. København 1980 [Ethnography; Threads; Plaiting; Weaving]
Ovalle Fernandez, I.: Grupos étnicos de México. Inst. Nac. Indigenista, Mexico 1982 [Ethnography; Mesh Fabric; Plaiting; Weaving; Ornamentation with Solid Material(s)]
Overhage-Baader, H.: "Symbole auf alten Orientteppichen", Image 24, Basel 1967 [Warp Fabric; Pile Fabric]
Ötric, O.: Izložba: Folk weaving in northern Dalmatia. Zadar 1981 [Folk Art; Collections; Weaving; Pile Fabric]

Paine, S.: Chikan Embroidery: The Floral Whitework of India. Shire Ethnography N°12, Dyfed 1989 [Analysis; Ethnography; Ornamentation with Solid Material(s)]
Palm, H.: Ancient Art of the Menahasa. Madjalah, Djilid 86, Bandung 1958 [Ethnography; Plaiting; Weaving]
Palmieri, M. & Ferentinos, F.: "The Iban Textiles of Sarawak", Fischer, J. (ed.) Threads of Tradition. Berkeley 1979: 73-78 [Ethnography; Ornamentation with Liquid Material(s)]
Palotay, G.: Sárközi "rostkötes" -ek. Néprajzi Ertesitö 28, 1-4, Budapest n.d. [Folk Art; Plaiting]
Palotay, G. & Ferenc, K.: Magyar adatok a Fonással Készült Isipe-Fökötökhöz. Néprajzi Ertesitö 3-4, 1933, Budapest 1934 [Folk Art; Warp Fabric]
Palotay, G. & Szabó, T.A.: Ismeretlenebb Erdély Magyar Himzéstipusok: Einige ungarische Stickereien aus Siebenbürgen. Néprajzi Ertesitö 33, Budapest 1940 [Folk Art; Ornamentation with Solid Material(s)]
Palotay, G.: see also Ferenc, K.
Pancake, C.M. & Baizerman, S.: "Guatemalan gauze weaves: a description and key to identification", Textile Museum Journal 19-20, 1980-81, Washington 1981: 1-26 [Analysis; Ethnography; Weaving]
Pandit, S.: Indian embroidery: Its variegated charms. Baroda 1976 [Analysis; Ethnography; Ornamentation with Solid Material(s)]
Pangemanan, S.: Keradjinan orang Minahasa. Pelbagai, Batavia 1919 [Ethnography; Threads; Weaving]
Paravicini, E.: Batik und Ikat: Indonesische Färbekunst. Basel 1924 [Ethnography; Ornamentation with Liquid Material(s)]

Parker, A. & Neal, A.: "Outside Influences on the Design of San Blas Indian Molas", I. Emery Roundtable on Mus. Textiles 1976, Washington 1977: 373-385 [Ethnography; Ornamentation with Solid Material(s)]
Parker, A. & Neal, A.: Molas: Folk art of the Cuna Indians. Barre 1977 [Ethnography; Ornamentation with Solid Material(s)]
Pathy, D.: see also Fischer, E.
Patterson, N.: "Spinning and Weaving Part I", Singer, C. et al. (ed.) A History of Technology Band 2, Oxford 1956: 191-220 [Archaeology; Threads; Weaving]
Patterson, N.: "Spinning and Weaving, Part II", Singer, C. et al. (ed.) A History of Technology Band 3, Oxford 1957: 151-181 [General, Historical; Threads; Weaving]
Patterson, N. & Gellermann, N.L.: Swiss-German and Dutch-German Mennonite traditional art in the Waterloo Region Ontario. Mercury Series 27, Ottawa 1979 [Folk Art; Ornamentation with Solid Material(s)]
Paul, A.: Paracas Textiles. Etnografiska Mus. 34, Göteborg 1979 [Archaeology; Weaving; Ornamentation with Solid Material(s)]
Paul, A.: "Re-establishing provenience of two Paracas mantles", Textile Museum Journal 19-20, 1980-81, Washington 1980: 35-40 [Archaeology; Weaving; Ornamentation with Solid Material(s)]
Paul, A.: "Continuity in Paracas Textile Iconography and its Implications for the Meaning of Linear Style Images", Rowe, A.P. (ed.) J.B. Bird Conf. on Andean Tex. 1984, Washington 1986: 81-100 [Archaeology; General, Historical; Weaving; Ornamentation with Solid Material(s)]
Paul, F.: Spruce root basketry of the Alaska Tlingit. Indian Handicrafts 8, Lawrence 1944 [Ethnography; Plaiting; Borders]
Paulis, L.: "Le Drochel", Bull. Needle and Bobbin Club Vol.7 N°2, New York 1923: 3-13 [Analysis; Folk Art; Plaiting]
Pauly, S.B. & Corrie, R.W.: The Kashmir shawl. New Haven 1975 [Ethnography; Collections; Weaving]
Payne Hatcher, E.: Visual Metaphors: a Formal Analysis of Navajo Art. St. Paul 1967 [Ethnography; Weaving; Tapestry]
Pazaurek, G.E.: Glasperlen und Perlenarbeiten in alter und neuer Zeit. Darmstadt 1911 [General, Historical; Beadwork]
Peacock, A.V.: Batik, ikat, plangi and other traditional textiles from Malaysia. Hong Kong 1977 [Ethnography; Collections; Ornamentation with Liquid Material(s)]
Pearson's, M.: Traditional Knitting. London 1984 [Folk Art; Mesh Fabric]
Pedersen, I.R.: "The Analysis of the Textiles from Evebo Eide, Gloppe, Norway", Textilsymposium Neumünster, Neumünster 1982: 75-84 [Archaeology; Weaving; Fabric Processing]
Peebles, M.A.: Court and village: India's textile traditions. Santa Barbara 1982 [Collections; Weaving; Ornamentation with Solid Material(s); Ornamentation with Liquid Material(s)]
Peebles, M.A.: Dressed in splendor: Japanese costume, 1700-1926. Santa Barbara 1987 [Ethnography; Collections]
Pelanzy, A. & Català, R.: Spanish folk crafts. Barcelona 1978 [Folk Art; Plaiting; Weaving; Pile Fabric; Ornamentation with Solid Material(s)]
Pellaton-Chable, B.: "Les dessous du panier: les vanneries de la collection Amoudruz", Bul. Ann. Musée d'Ethnograph. de Genève N°307, Genève 1987: 116-129 [Folk Art; Plaiting]
Pelletier, G.: Abenaki basketry. Nat. Mus. of Man 85, Ottawa 1982 [Ethnography; Plaiting]
Pelras, C.: "Tissages Balinais", Objects et Mondes Tome 2, Fasc. 1, Paris 1962: 215-239 [Ethnography; Weaving]
Pelras, C.: "Contribution à la Géographie et à l'Ethnolgie du Métier à Tisser en Indonésie", Langues et Technique, Nature et Société 2, Paris 1972: 81-97 [Ethnography; Weaving]
Pemberton, J.: Yoruba Beadwork: Art of Nigeria. New York 1980 [Ethnography; Collections; Beadwork]
Pemberton, J.: see also Drewal, H.J.
Pence Britton, N.: Some early Islamic Textiles in the Museum of Fine Arts, Boston. Boston 1938 [Collections; Weaving; Ornamentation with Liquid Material(s)]
Pendelton, M.: Navajo and Hopi weaving techniques. London 1974 [Ethnography; Working Instruction; Tapestry]
Pendergast, M.: Raranga whakairo: Maori plaiting patterns. Auckland 1982 [Analysis; Ethnography; Plaiting]
Pendergast, M.: The Aho Tapu: The Sacred Thread. Honolulu 1987 [Analysis; Ethnography; Plaiting; Warp Fabric; Pile Fabric; Borders]
Perani, J.: "Nupe Costume Crafts", African Arts Vol.12 N°3, Los Angeles 1979: 52-57 [Ethnography; Weaving; Ornamentation with Solid Material(s)]
Perani, J.: "Northern Nigerian Prestige Textiles: Production, Trade, Patronage and Use", Basler Beiträge zur Ethnologie Band 30, Basel 1989: 65-82 [Ethnography; Weaving]
Pérez de Micou, C.: "Aprovechamiento de la Flora Local en la Porción enterriana del Area del Paraná Medio", Instituto Nacional de Antropología, Buenos Aires 1984: 93-118 [Ethnography; Plaiting]
Perini, R.: "Manufatti in legno dell'Età del Bronzo nel territorio delle Alpi meridionali", CH-Landesmuseum (ed.) Die ersten Bauern. Pfahlbaufunde Europas Vol. 2, Zürich 1990: 253-265 [Archaeology; Plaiting]
Pestalozzianum Zürich; Pfahlbauland: Werkverfahren in den Ufer- und Moordörfern. Zürich 1990 [Analysis; Archaeology; Working Instruction; Plaiting; Warp Fabric; Weaving]
Peter, I.: Deux textiles de provenance inconnue. Cieta 41 (42), Lyon 1975 [Weaving]
Peter, I.: Textilien aus Aegypten im Museum Rietberg. Zürich 1976 [Archaeology; Collections; Warp Fabric; Tapestry]
Peter-Müller, I.: "Ein rätselhaftes Bischofsgrab", Jahresbericht des Histor. Museums 1975, Basel 1978: 33-57 [Archaeology; Weaving]
Petersen, K.D.: "Chippewa Mat-Weaving Techniques", Bull. Bur. Am. Ethnol. 186, Washington 1963: 211-286 [Analysis; Ethnography; Plaiting; Borders]
Petersen, K.S.: "Techniques applied to some feather garments from the Tupinamba indians, Brasil", Folk 21-22, 1979-80, Kopenhagen 1980 [Analysis; Ethnography; Pile Fabric]
Petrasch, E.: Die Türkenbeute: eine Auswahl aus der türkischen Trophäensammlung des Markgrafen Ludwig Wilhelm von Baden. Bildhefte des Badischen Landesmus. 20, Karlsruhe 1970 [Folk Art; Plaiting; Weaving; Pile Fabric; Tapestry]
Petrescu, P.: "Roumanian carpets from the collection of the Art Museum of the Academy of the Socialist Republic of Roumania", Revue Roumaine d'Histoire et de l'Art 4, Bukarest 1967 [Folk Art; Tapestry]
Petrucci, V.: Simbolo e Tecnica nei Tessuti dell' Antico Perù. Rom 1982 [Archaeology; Collections; Threads; Mesh Fabric; Plaiting; Weaving]
Petsopoulos, Y.: Der Kelim. Ein Handbuch. München 1980 [Analysis; Ethnography; Tapestry]
Pfister, R.: "Etudes textiles", Revue des Arts Asiatiques Tome 8, Paris 1934: 77-94 [Archaeology; Warp Fabric; Weaving; Ornamentation with Solid Material(s)]
Pfister, R.: "Tissus du Yémen", Revue des Arts Asiatiques Tome 10, Paris 1936: 78-81 [Ethnography; Ornamentation with Solid Material(s); Ornamentation with Liquid Material(s)]
Pfister, R.: Nouveaux textiles de Palmyre. Paris 1937 [Archaeology; Weaving]
Pfister, R.: Textiles de Palmyre. Band 1-3, Paris 1937-40 [Archae-

ology; Weaving]
Pfister, R.: "Coqs sassanides", Revue des Arts Asiatiques Tome 12, Fasc. 1, Paris 1938: 40-47 [Archaeology; Weaving]
Pfister, R.: Les Toiles imprimées de Fostat et l'Hindoustan. Paris 1938 [Archaeology; Ornamentation with Liquid Material(s)]
Pfister, R.: The Indian Art of Calico Printing in the Middle Ages: Characteristics and Influences. Indian Art Vol. 13 N°1, London 1939 [Ethnography; General, Historical; Ornamentation with Liquid Material(s)]
Pfister, R.: "Toiles à inscriptions Abbasides et Fatimides", Bull. d'Études Orientales 11, Paris 1946: 47-90 [Archaeology; General, Historical; Weaving]
Pfister, R.: "Le Rôle de l'Iran dans les Textiles d'Antinoé", Ars Islamica Vol. 13, Ann Arbor 1948: 46-74 [General, Historical; Weaving]
Pfister, R.: Les tissus orientaux de la Bible de Théodule. Boston 1950 [Archaeology; General, Historical; Weaving]
Pfister, R.: Textiles de Halabiyeh. Inst. Franç. Arch. de Beyrouth, Bibl. Archéol. Hist. 48, Paris 1951 [Archaeology; Weaving]
Pfister, R. & Bellinger, L.: Excavations at Dura Europos: Part II: The Textiles. New Haven 1945 [Archaeology; Weaving]
Pfluger-Schindlbeck, I.: see also Dombrowski, G.
Philip Stoller, I.: "The Revival Period in Navajo Weaving", I.Emery Roundtable on Mus. Textiles 1976, Washington 1977: 453-466 [Ethnography; Weaving; Tapestry]
Phillips, J.: European printed fabrics of the 19th century. Bull. Metrop. Mus. of Art Vol.27 N°3, New York 1932 [Folk Art; Ornamentation with Liquid Material(s)]
Phillips, M.W.: Creative Knitting: A New Art Form. New York 1971 [Working Instruction; Mesh Fabric]
Pianzola, M. & Coffinet, J.: La tapisserie. Genève 1971 [General, Historical; Tapestry]
Pickering, W.R.: see also Landreau, A.N.
Picton, J. & Mack, J.: African Textiles. British Museum, London 1979 [Ethnography; Threads; Weaving; Beadwork; Ornamentation with Solid Material(s); Ornamentation with Liquid Material(s)]
Pilar de, M.: Lisières et Franges de Toiles Egyptiennes. Bulletin de Liaison Tex. Anc. N°28, Lyon 1968 [Analysis; Ethnography; Folk Art; Borders]
Pinault, M.: see also Viatte, F.
Pinto, S.: see also Klimburg, M.
Pirngadie, M.: see also Jasper, J.
Pittard, E.: "Les plus anciens tissus européens: Age de la Pierre Polie", Hyphé N°1, Genève 1946: 19-21 [Archaeology; Warp Fabric]
Plá, J.: Ñanduti: Encrucijada de dos mundos. Asunción 1990 [Folk Art; Warp Fabric]
Plazas de Nieto, C.: "Orfebrería Prehispánica del Altiplano Nariñense, Colombia", Revista Colombiana de Antropología Vol.21, 1977-78, Bogotá 1987: 197-244 [Archaeology; Plaiting]
Pleyte, C.M.: De Inlandsche Nijverheid in West-Java als Sociaal-ethnologisch Verschnijnsel. Batavia 1912 [Ethnography; Threads; Weaving; Ornamentation with Liquid Material(s)]
Pleyte, W.: Antiquités coptes. Leiden 1900 [Archaeology; Tapestry]
Plötz, R.: see also Futagami, Y.
Ploier, H.: Textilkunst der Bakuba. Katalog z. Ausst. i. Landesmus. Joanneum, Graz, Graz 1988 [Ethnography; Collections; Weaving; Pile Fabric]
Plumer, C.: African Textiles. Michigan 1971 [Ethnography; Weaving]
Pocius, G.L.: Textile traditions of Eastern Newfoundland. Mercury Series 29, Ottawa 1979 [Folk Art; Threads; Mesh Fabric; Weaving; Pile Fabric; Ornamentation with Solid Material(s)]
Pokornowsky, I.: "Beads and personal adornment", Fabrics of Culture. World Anthropology 86. The Hague 1979: 103-117 [Ethnography; Beadwork]
Polakoff, C.: Into indigo: African textiles and dyeing techniques. New York 1980 [Analysis; Ethnography; Ornamentation with Liquid Material(s)]
Polakoff, C.: African Textiles and Dyeing Techniques. London 1982 [Ethnography; Weaving; Ornamentation with Liquid Material(s)]
Pongnoi, N.: see also Campbell, M.
Ponting, K.G.& Chapman, S.D. (ed.): Textile History 11. Bath 1980 [Analysis; Ethnography; Weaving; Ornamentation with Liquid Material(s)]
Porter, F.W. (ed.): Native American Basketry: An Annotated Bibliography.Art Reference Collection, London 1988 [Ethnography; Plaiting]
Portillo, M.F.: "Equivalencias de las "técnicas de telar" prehispánicas del Perú", Cuadernos Prehispánicos 4, Madrid 1976: 41-60 [Archaeology; Weaving]
Pottinger, D.: Quilts from the Indiana Amish. New York 1983 [Folk Art; Collections; Working Instruction; Ornamentation with Solid Material(s)]
Powell, R.J.: "African Art at the Field Museum", African Arts Vol.18 N°, Los Angeles 1985: 24-36 [Ethnography; Collections; Weaving]
Powers, W.K.: "Bessie Cornelius, star quilter of the Sioux", Archiv für Völkerkunde 39, 1985, Wien 1987: 117-126 [Folk Art; General, Historical; Ornamentation with Solid Material(s)]
Pownall, G.: New Zealand Maori Arts and Crafts. Wellington 1976 [Analysis; Ethnography; Working Instruction; Threads; Plaiting; Warp Fabric; Pile Fabric]
Poynor, R.: "Traditional Textiles in Owo, Nigeria", African Arts Vol.14 N°1, Los Angeles 1980: 47-51 [Ethnography; Weaving]
Praeger, C.E.: "Mathematics and Weaving." The H. Neumann lectures at the Int. Conf. of Math. Educ. Adelaide 1984. Notes on Pure Math. 13, Canberra 1986: 61-74 [Classification; Weaving]
Prangwatthanakun, S. & Cheesman, P.: Lan Na textiles: Yuan Lue Loa. Bangkok 1987 [Ethnography; Weaving; Ornamentation with Liquid Material(s)]
Preysing, M.: Spitzen. Bilderhefte d. Mus. f. Kunst u. Gewerbe N°20, Hamburg 1987 [Folk Art; Collections; Warp Fabric; Ornamentation with Solid Material(s)]
Price, C.: Made in the South Pacific: Arts of the Sea People. New York 1979 [Ethnography; Pile Fabric]
Priest, A. & Simmons, P.: Chinese Textiles. New York 1934 [General, Historical]
Proud, N.: Textile printing and dyeing. London 1965 [Working Instruction; Ornamentation with Liquid Material(s)]
Provence, M.: Le Musée des Tapisseries à Aix-en-Provence. Hyphé N°1, Genf 1946: 31-46 [Collections; Pile Fabric]
Prümers, H.: Präkolumbische Textilien von der mittleren Küste Perus aus der Sammlung des Römer Museums, Hildesheim. Bonn 1983 [Archaeology; Threads; Mesh Fabric; Warp Fabric; Weaving; Borders; Ornamentation with Liquid Material(s)]
Prümers, H.: Der Fundort "El Castillo" im Huarmeytal, Peru: Ein Beitrag zum Problem des Moche-Huari-Textilstils. Bonn 1989 [Analysis; Archaeology; Mesh Fabric; Plaiting; Warp Fabric; Weaving; Borders; Ornamentation with Solid Material(s)]
Prümers, H.: Der Fundort "El Castillo" im Huarmeytal, Peru. Mundus Reihe Alt-Amerikanistik 4, Bonn 1990 [Analysis; Archaeology; Threads; Mesh Fabric; Plaiting; Weaving;

Borders; Ornamentation with Solid Material(s); Ornamentation with Liquid Material(s); Tapestry]
Prunner, G.: Kunsthandwerk aus Guizhou. Hamburg 1983 [Ethnography]
Puls, H.: Textiles of the Kuna Indian. Shire Ethnography, Aylesbury 1988 [Analysis; Ethnography; Ornamentation with Solid Material(s)]
Pupareli, de, D.J.: see also Rolandi, D.S.
Pylkkanen, R.: The use and traditions of Medieval rugs and coverlets in Finnland. Helsinki 1974 [Folk Art; Pile Fabric]

Quadiri, M.A.: "Carpetweaving", Trad. Arts of Hyderabad, n.p., n.d.: 34-36 [Ethnography; Pile Fabric]
Quick, B. & Stein, J.A.: Ply-split camel girths of west India. Museum of Cultural History Vol. 1 N°7, Los Angeles 1982 [Classification; Analysis; Ethnography; Plaiting]

Raadt-Apel, M.J.: "Van Zuylen Batik, Pekalongam, Central Java", Textile Museum Journal 19-20, 1980-81, Washington 1981: 75-92 [Ethnography; Ornamentation with Liquid Material(s)]
Raaschou, D.: "Un document danois sur la fabrication des toiles peintes à Tranquebar, aux Indes, à la fin du XVIIe siècle", Bull. de la Soc. Industrielle N°729, 4, Mulhouse 1967 [General, Historical; Ornamentation with Liquid Material(s)]
Rabineau, P.: "Catalogue of the Cashinahua Collection", Dwyer, J.P. (ed.) The Cashinahua of Eastern Peru. Boston 1975 [Collections; Plaiting; Weaving; Pile Fabric]
Rabineau, P.: Feather arts. Beauty, wealth and spirits from five continents. Chicago 1980 [Collections; Pile Fabric]
Rachman, A.: Pelajaran seni batik modern. n.p., n.d. [Working Instruction; Ornamentation with Liquid Material(s)]
Radin, P.: "Zur Netztechnik der südamerikanischen Indianer", Zeitschrift für Ethnologie 38, Berlin 1906: 926-938 [Ethnography; Mesh Fabric]
Rajab, J.S.: "Some Towels and Other Turkish Embroideries", Arts of Asia Vol. 14 N°3, Hong Kong 1984: 83-87 [Ethnography; Ornamentation with Solid Material(s)]
Rajab, J.S.: "The Road to Medina", Arts of Asia Vol. 17 N°1, Hong Kong 1987: 52-64 [Ethnography; Ornamentation with Solid Material(s); Ornamentation with Liquid Material(s)]
Ramisch, E.: see also Ley, H.
Ramos, L.J. & Blasco, M.C.: "Técnicas textiles del Perú prehispánico utilizadas en los tejidos del Museo de América de Madrid", Cuadernos Prehispánicos 4, Valladolid 1976: 19-40 [Collections; Warp Fabric; Weaving; Ornamentation with Solid Material(s); Tapestry]
Ramos, L.J. & Blasco, M.C.: Los tejidos y las técnicas textiles en el Perú prehispánico. Valladolid 1977 [Analysis; Archaeology; Weaving; Borders; Ornamentation with Solid Material(s); Tapestry]
Ramseyer, U.: "Kamben geringsing" in Tenganan Pegeringsingan. Tenganan 1980 [Ethnography; Ornamentation with Liquid Material(s)]
Ramseyer, U.: "Clothing, Ritual and Society in Tenganan Pegeringsingan, Bali", Verh. Nat. Forsch. Ges. Band 95, Basel 1984 [Ethnography; Ornamentation with Liquid Material(s)]
Ramseyer, U.: "The traditional textile craft and textile workshops of Sidemen, Bali", Indonesian Circle 42, London 1987: 3-15 [Ethnography; Weaving; Ornamentation with Liquid Material(s)]
Ramseyer, U. & Ramseyer-Gygi, N.: Bali, Distrikt Karangasem: Doppelikat in Tenganan Pegeringsingan. Encyclopaedia Cinematographica Serie 9, N°11-14, Göttingen 1979 [Ethnography; Films; Ornamentation with Liquid Material(s)]
Ramseyer-Gygi, N.: see also Ramseyer, U.
Ramseyer-Gygi, U.& N.: see also Bühler, A.
Rangkuty, R.: Peadjaran membatik. Medan n.d. [Working Instruction; Ornamentation with Liquid Material(s)]
Rangnekar, D.V.: Himroo weaving: Handicrafts in Maharastra. Census of India, Bombay 1966 [Ethnography; Weaving]
Ranjan, M.P. & Yier, N.& Pandya, G.: Bamboo and Cane Crafts of Northeast India. New Delhi 1986 [Analysis; Ethnography; Plaiting; Borders]
Rapp, A.: Schweizerische Mustertücher. Bern 1976 [Folk Art; Collections; Ornamentation with Solid Material(s)]
Rapp, A. & Stucky, M.: Zahm und Wild (Basler und Strassburger Bildteppiche des 15. Jahrhunderts). Mainz 1990 [Analysis; Pile Fabric; Tapestry]
Rast, A.: "Die Verarbeitung von Bast", Schweiz. Landesmuseum (ed.) Die ersten Bauern. Pfahlbaufunde Europas Vol. 1, Zürich 1990: 119-122 [Archaeology; Threads; Mesh Fabric; Plaiting; Warp Fabric]
Rast, A.: "Jungsteinzeitliche Kleidung", Schweiz. Landesmuseum (ed.) Die ersten Bauern. Pfahlbaufunde Europas Vol. 1, Zürich 1990: 123-126 [Archaeology; Pile Fabric]
Rast, A.: Neolithische Textilien im Raum Zürich. Ber. der Zürcher Denkmalpflege Monografien, Zürich 1991 [Archaeology; Threads; Mesh Fabric; Plaiting; Warp Fabric; Pile Fabric; Borders]
Rau, C.: "Prehistoric Fishing in Europe and North America", Smith. Contr. to Knowledge 25 (1), Washington 1884: 1-342 [Archaeology; Mesh Fabric]
Rau, W.: Weaving und Plaiting im Vedischen Indien. Akad. d. Wiss. und Lit. 11, Mainz 1970: 649-683 [Ethnography; General, Historical; Weaving]
Rauter, W.: Mitteleuropa. Tirol: Weaving eines Bandes. Encyclopaedia Cinematographica 2 (6), Göttingen 1969 [Folk Art; Films; Weaving]
Ravicz, R. & Romney, K.A.: "The Amuzgo", Handbook of Middle Am. Indians 7, Austin 1969: 417-433 [Ethnography; Weaving]
Ravines, R. (ed.): Tecnología Andina. Lima 1978 [Weaving]
Ravines, R.: "Tintes y diseños textiles actuales de Cajamarca", Tecnología Andina. Lima 1978 [Ethnography; Weaving]
Rawlings, S.: see also Specht, S.
Ray, A.: "The Baluchari saris of Bengal during the Nawabi period", Riboud, K. (ed.) In Quest of Themes and Skills. Bombay 1989: 72-78 [Ethnography; Weaving]
Ray, D.J.: "Bering Strait Eskimo", Handbook of North Am. Indians 5, Washington 1984: 285-302 [Ethnography; Plaiting]
Raymond, P. & Bayona, B.: "Vida y muerte del algodón y de los tejidos santandereanos", Cuadernos de Agroindústria Javeriana N°9, Bogotá 1982 [Archaeology; Weaving]
Réal, D.: Les Batiks de Java. Paris 1923 [General, Historical; Ornamentation with Liquid Material(s)]
Réal, D.: Tissus des Indes Néerlandaises. Paris 1977 [General, Historical; Ornamentation with Liquid Material(s)]
Reath, N.A. & Sachs, E.B.: Persian textiles and their technique from the 6th to the 18th century. New Haven 1937 [Analysis; Collections; Warp Fabric; Weaving]
Redwood: Backstrap weaving of northern Ecuador. Santa Cruz 1974 [Ethnography; Working Instruction; Weaving]
Reed, C.D.: Turkoman Rugs. Cambridge 1966 [Collections; Pile Fabric]
Reichard, G.: Navajo Shepherd and Weaver. New York 1936 [Ethnography; Weaving; Tapestry]
Reichard, G.: Weaving a Navajo Blanket: Reprint from the 1936

edition. New York 1974 [Ethnography; Working Instruction; Weaving; Tapestry]
Reichelt, R.: Das Textilornament: Ein Formenschatz für die Flächengestaltung. Dt. Bauakademie, Berlin 1956 [Folk Art; Plaiting; Weaving; Ornamentation with Solid Material(s); Ornamentation with Liquid Material(s); Fabric Processing]
Reichel-Dolmatoff, G.: "Etnografía Chimila", Boletín de Arqueología 2 (2), Bogotá 1946 [Ethnography; Mesh Fabric; Warp Fabric]
Reichel-Dolmatoff, G.: "Notas etnográficas sobre los Indios del Chocó", Revista Col. Antropología 9, Bogotá 1960 [Ethnography; Plaiting]
Reichel-Dolmatoff, G.: Basketry as Metaphor. Occ. Papers. Mus. Cult. Hist. 5, Los Angeles 1985 [Ethnography; Plaiting]
Reichert, E.: Batiken mit Naturfarben. Bern 1984 [Working Instruction; Ornamentation with Liquid Material(s)]
Reichlen, H.: "Dos telas pintadas del Norte del Perú", Revista Peruana de Cultura N°5, Lima 1965: 5-16 [Archaeology; Ornamentation with Liquid Material(s)]
Reid, W.: see also Holm, B.
Reidemeister, K.: Knotentheorie. Zentralblatt für Mathematik 1, Berlin 1932 [Classification; Mesh Fabric]
Reijnders-Baas, C.: "Sprang: Eine alte Flechttechnik mit zeitgenössischen Möglichkeiten.", Ornamente N°1, 1988: 47-54 [Working Instruction; Warp Fabric]
Reijnders-Baas, C.: "Intertwining. Eine weitere Sprangtechnik", Ornamente N°2, 1988: 31-36 [Working Instruction]
Reindel, M.: Textiles prehispánicos del "Museo de América", Madrid. Bonn 1987 [Archaeology; Mesh Fabric; Weaving]
Reinhard, U.& V.: "Notizen über türkische Webteppiche", Baessler-Archiv NF 22, Berlin 1974: 165-223 [Ethnography; Warp Fabric; Tapestry]
Reinisch, H.: Satteltaschen. Graz 1985 [Warp Fabric; Pile Fabric; Tapestry]
Reitz, G.: see also Bachmann, M.
Rendall, J.& Tuohy, D.R. (ed.): Collected Papers on Aboriginal Basketry. Nevada State Mus. Anthr. Papers 16, Carson City 1974 [Analysis; Ethnography; Plaiting; Pile Fabric; Borders]
Rengifo, A.: Las artesanías rurales de hoy y de ayer. Perú Agrario 3, N°3, Lima 1979 [Ethnography; Folk Art]
Renne, E.P.: "The Thierry Collection of Hausa Artifacts at the Field Museum", African Arts Vol.19 N°4, Los Angeles 1986: 54-59 [Ethnography; Collections; Weaving; Tapestry]
Renner, D.: Die koptischen Stoffe im Martin von Wagner Museum der Universität Würzburg. Wiesbaden 1974 [Archaeology; Collections; Tapestry]
Renner, D.: Die spätantiken und koptischen Textilien im Hessischen Landesmuseum in Darmstadt. Wiesbaden 1985 [Archaeology; Collections; Weaving; Tapestry]
Renner-Volbach, D.: Die koptischen Textilien im Museo Missionario Etnologico der Vatikanischen Museen. Wiesbaden 1988 [Archaeology; Collections; Weaving; Tapestry; Fabric Processing]
Restrepo, V.: Los Chibchas antes de la conquista española. Biblioteca Banco Popular Vol. 26, Bogotá 1972 [Archaeology; Weaving]
Reswick, I.: "Traditional Textiles of Tunisia". African Arts Vol.14 N°3, Los Angeles 1981: 56-65 [Ethnography; Threads; Weaving; Pile Fabric; Tapestry]
Reswick, I.: Traditional textiles of Tunisia and related North African weavings. Los Angeles 1985 [Analysis; Ethnography; Threads; Warp Fabric; Weaving; Pile Fabric; Tapestry]
Revault, J.: Designs and patterns from north African carpets and textiles. New York 1973 [General, Historical; Pile Fabric]
Ribeiro, B.G.: "Bases para uma classificação dos adornos plumários dos Indios do Brasil", Archivo do Mus. Nac. 43, Rio de Janeiro 1957: 59-125 [Classification; Ethnography; Pile Fabric]
Ribeiro, B.G.: "Tupi Indian weavers of the Xingu-River", Nat. Geo.Soc. Research Reports 21, Washington 1978: 411-419 [Ethnography; Plaiting; Warp Fabric; Weaving]
Ribeiro, B.G.: A Civilização da Palha: a Arte do Trançado dos Indios do Brasil: Tecnicas e formas, um estudo taxonômico. São Paulo 1980 [Ethnography; Mesh Fabric; Warp Fabric; Weaving; Borders]
Ribeiro, B.G.: A tecnologia do tecido com tear indígena. Rio de Janeiro 1980 [Ethnography; Plaiting; Weaving]
Ribeiro, B.G.: "Possibilidade de aplicação do criterio de forma no estudo de contatos intertribais, pelo exame de tecnica de remate", Revista de Antropologia 23, São Paulo 1980: 31-67 [Analysis; Ethnography; Plaiting; Borders]
Ribeiro, B.G.: "Visual categories and ethnic identity: The symbolism of Kayabi Indian Basketry", Archeology and Anthropology 5 (1), 1982 [Ethnography; Plaiting]
Ribeiro, B.G.: "A oleira e a tecelã: o papel social da mulher na sociedade Asurini", Revista de Antropologia 25, São Paulo 1982: 25-61 [Ethnography; Threads; Plaiting]
Ribeiro, B.G.: "Araweté: a india vestida", Revista de Antropologia 26, São Paulo 1983: 1-38 [Ethnography; Threads; Warp Fabric]
Ribeiro, B.G.: "La vannerie et l'art décoratif des Indiens du Haut Xingu, Brésil", Objects et Mondes 24 (12), Paris 1984: 57-68 [Ethnography; Plaiting]
Ribeiro, B.G.: "Tecelas Tupi do Xingu", Rev. de Antrop. 27-28, São Paulo 1985: 355-402 [Ethnography; Threads; Mesh Fabric; Plaiting; Warp Fabric; Weaving]
Ribeiro, B.G.: A arte do trançado dos índios do Brasil. Mus. Goeldi, Belém 1985 [Classification; Analysis; Ethnography; Plaiting; Borders]
Ribeiro, B.G.: "Bases para uma classificação dos adornos plumarios dos índios do Brasil", Suma Etnológica Brasileira 3, Petrópolis 1986: 189-226 [Classification; Mesh Fabric; Plaiting; Warp Fabric; Weaving; Pile Fabric; Borders]
Ribeiro, B.G.: "A Arte de trançar: Dois macroestilos, dois modos de vida", Suma Etnológica Brasileira 2, Petrópolis 1986: 283-321 [Analysis; Ethnography; Warp Fabric; Weaving]
Ribeiro, B.G.: "Glossário dos trançados", Suma Etnológica Brasileira 2, Petrópolis 1986: 314-321 [Classification; Ethnography; Mesh Fabric; Plaiting; Weaving]
Ribeiro, B.G.: "Artes têxteis indígenas do Brasil", Suma Etnológica Brasileira 2, Petrópolis 1986: 351-395 [Analysis; Ethnography; Mesh Fabric; Plaiting; Warp Fabric; Weaving]
Ribeiro, B.G.: "Glossário dos tecidos", Suma Etnológica Brasileira 2, Petrópolis 1986: 390-396 [Classification]
Ribeiro, B.G.: "Desenhos semânticos e identidade étnica: o caso Kayabí", Suma Etnológica Brasileira 3, Petrópolis 1986: 265-289 [Ethnography; Plaiting]
Ribeiro, B.G.: Dicionário do artesanato indígena. São Paulo 1988 [Ethnography; Threads; Mesh Fabric; Plaiting; Weaving; Pile Fabric; Beadwork; Borders]
Ribeiro, B.G.: "Semantische Zeichnungen und ethnische Identität: Das Beispiel der Kayabi", Münzel, M. (ed.) Die Mythen Sehen. Roter Faden z. Austellung. Mus. f. Völkerk. 14, Frankfurt 1988: 392-439 [Ethnography; Plaiting]
Ribeiro, B.G.: Arte Indígena: Linguagem Visual: Indigenous Art, Visual Language. São Paulo 1989 [Ethnography; Plaiting; Warp Fabric; Pile Fabric]
Ribeiro, D.&B.G: Arte plumaria dos índios Kaapor. Rio de Janeiro 1957 [Ethnography; Pile Fabric]
Riboud, K.: "A reappraisal of Han-Dynasty monochrome Figured-silks", Cieta 38, 2, Lyon 1973 [Archaeology; Weaving]

Riboud, K.: "Further indication of changing techniques in figured silks of the post-Han period", Cieta 41-42, 1-2, Lyon 1975 [Archaeology; Weaving]
Riboud, K.: "Techniques and problems encountered in certain Han and T'an Specimens", I. Emery Roundtable on Mus. Textiles 1974, Washington 1975: 153-159 [Archaeology; Weaving]
Riboud, K.: "A Closer View of Early Chinese Silks", Gervers, V. (ed.) Studies in Textile History. Toronto 1977: 252-280 [Archaeology; Weaving]
Riboud, K. (ed.): In Quest of Themes and Skills – Asian Textiles. Marg Publications, Bombay 1989 [Ethnography; Archaeology; Weaving; Pile Fabric; Ornamentation with Solid Material(s); Ornamentation with Liquid Material(s); Tapestry]
Riboud, K. & Vial, G.: "Les Soieries Han", Arts Asiatiques Tome 17, Paris 1968: 93-141 [Archaeology; Weaving]
Riboud, K. & Vial, G.: "Tissus de Tonen-Houang conservés au Musée Guimet et à la Bibliothèque Nationale", Mission Paul Pelliot Vol. 13, Paris 1970 [Analysis; Collections; Weaving]
Ricard, P.: "Le Batik Berbère", Hespéris 4, Paris 1925: 411-426 [Ethnography; Ornamentation with Liquid Material(s)]
Ricard, P.: Tapis du Moyen Atlas. Corpus des tapis marocains Vol. 4, Paris 1926 [General, Historical; Pile Fabric]
Ricard, P.: see also Bel, A.
Richman, R.: "Decorative Household Objects in Indonesia", Arts of Asia Vol.10 N°5, Hong Kong 1980: 129-135 [Ethnography; Plaiting; Beadwork]
Rickenbach, W.: Lexikon mit Schwergewicht auf industrielles Weaving. Fachworterbuch der Textilkunde, Zürich 1944 [General, Historical; Weaving]
Riddell, F.A.: "Maidu and Konkow", Handbook of North Am. Indians 8, Washington 1978: 370-386 [Analysis; Ethnography; Mesh Fabric; Plaiting; Pile Fabric]
Riedinger, H.: see also Riedinger, R.
Riedinger, R. & Riedinger, H.: Einfaches Weaving. Stuttgart 1980 [Ethnography; Working Instruction; Weaving]
Riefstahl, R.M.: Persian and Indian textiles. New York 1923 [Ethnography; Weaving]
Riesenberg, S.H. & Gayton, A.H.: "Caroline Island Belt Weaving", Southwestern Journal of Anthro. Vol.8 N°3, Albuquerque 1952: 342-375 [Analysis; Ethnography; Weaving; Beadwork]
Riester, J.: "Die materielle Kultur der Chiquitano Indianer (Ostbolivien)", Archiv fur Völkerkunde 25, Wien 1971: 143-230 [Analysis; Ethnography; Collections; Threads; Mesh Fabric; Plaiting; Warp Fabric; Weaving]
Riester, J.: Die Pauserna-Guarasug'wä. Collectana Inst. Anthropos 3, St. Augustin 1972 [Ethnography; Threads; Mesh Fabric; Plaiting; Warp Fabric]
Ritch, D. & Wada, Y.: Ikat: an introduction. Berkeley 1975 [Analysis; Ethnography; Ornamentation with Liquid Material(s)]
Rivera, A.: see also Villegas, L.
Roberts, H.H.: Basketry of the San Carlos Apache Indians. n.p. 1929 [Ethnography; Plaiting]
Robinson, N.V.: "Mantones de Manila: Their Role in China's Silk Trade", Arts of Asia Vol 17 N°1, Hong Kong 1987: 65-75 [Folk Art; Ornamentation with Solid Material(s)]
Robinson, S.: A history of dyed textiles. London 1969 [Ethnography; Ornamentation with Liquid Material(s)]
Robyn, J.: "Political motives: the batiks of Mohamad Hadi of Solo", Gittinger, M. (ed.) To Speak with Cloth. Los Angeles 1989: 131-150 [Ethnography; Ornamentation with Liquid Material(s)]
Rodee, M.E.: Weaving of the Southwest: from the Maxwell Museum of Anthropology. West Chester 1987 [Analysis; Ethnography; Warp Fabric; Weaving; Pile Fabric]
Rodee, M.E.: Southwestern weaving. Albuquerque 1977 [Ethnography; Collections; Weaving; Tapestry]
Rodee, M.E.: Old Navajo Rugs: Their Development from 1900 to 1940. Albuquerque 1981 [Ethnography; Weaving; Tapestry]
Rodel, G.: Die Technik in der Freiämter, Seetaler und Obwaldner Strohflechterei. Bern 1949 [Analysis; Folk Art; Plaiting]
Rodgers, S.: Power of Gold. Geneva 1985 [Ethnography; Weaving; Ornamentation with Liquid Material(s)]
Rodgers-Siregar, S.: "Blessing shawls: The Social Meaning of Sipirok Batak Ulos", I. Emery Roundtable on Mus. Textiles 1979, Washington 1980: 96-114 [Ethnography; Weaving]
Roessel, R.: "Navajo Arts and Crafts", Handbook of North Am. Indians 10, Washington 1983: 592-604 [Ethnography; Threads; Plaiting; Weaving; Tapestry]
Rogers, E.S.: The Material culture of the Mistassinis. Bull. Anthr. Series Nat. Mus. 218, Ottawa 1967 [Ethnography; General, Historical; Mesh Fabric]
Rogers, E.S. & Leacock, E.: "Montagnais – Naskapi", Handbook of North Am. Indians 6, Washington 1981: 169-189 [Ethnography; Plaiting]
Rogers, E.S. & Smith, J.G.: "Environment and Culture in the Shield and Mackenzie Borderlands", Handbook of North Am. Indians 6, Washington 1981: 130-145 [Ethnography; Mesh Fabric; Plaiting; Pile Fabric]
Rogers, J.M.: Topkapi Textilien: Sarayi-Museum. Zürich 1986 [Analysis; Collections; Ornamentation with Liquid Material(s)]
Rogers, N.: "Some rush mats with warp movement as patterning", Rogers, N. (ed.) In Celebration of the Curious Mind. Loveland 1983: 9-20 [Ethnography; Warp Fabric]
Rohrer, E.F.: "Die Flechterei der Amhara", Jahrbuch des Bern. Hist. Museum 1927, Bern 1928: 17-31 [Ethnography; Plaiting]
Rol, N.: Kleines Lexikon der Stickerei. Hannover 1980 [Analysis; Working Instruction; Ornamentation with Solid Material(s)]
Rolandi, D.S.: "Los tejidos de Río Doncellas, Dep. Cochinoca, Provincia de Jujuy", Actas Jornadas de Arqueología 2, Buenos Aires 1979: 22-73 [Archaeology; Weaving]
Rolandi, D.S.: "Los Gorros de Santa Rosa de Tastil, Prov. de Salta", Relaciones 5 (2), Buenos Aires 1971 [Archaeology; Mesh Fabric; Pile Fabric]
Rolandi, D.S.: "Análisis de la cestería de Alero del Dique, Dep. Prov. de Neuquen", Trabajos de Prehistoria 1, Buenos Aires 1981 [Archaeology; Plaiting]
Rolandi, D.S.: "Los Materiales textiles y cesteros de Huachichocana III: Dep. de Tumbaya, Jujuy", Paleoetnología 9, Buenos Aires 1985 [Archaeology; Mesh Fabric; Plaiting]
Rolandi, D.S. & Pupareli, de, D.J.: "La tejedura tradicional de la Puna Argentino-Boliviana", Cuad. Inst. Nac. Antrop. 5 (10), 1983-85, Buenos Aires 1985 [Ethnography; Threads; Weaving; Ornamentation with Liquid Material(s)]
Roma, J.: Etnografià de Filipines. Barcelona 1986 [Ethnography; Collections; General, Historical]
Romano, R.: see also Leib, E.
Romney, K.A.: see also Ravicz, R.
Ronge, V.: "Das Handwerkertum", Müller, C.C. (ed.) Der Weg zum Dach der Welt. München 1982: 153-201 [Ethnography; Plaiting; Weaving; Pile Fabric; Ornamentation with Liquid Material(s)]
Roquette-Pinto, E.: Rondonia: Eine Reise in das Herzstück Südamerikas. Veröff. zum Archiv für Völkerkunde Band 1, Wien 1954 [Analysis; Ethnography; Plaiting; Warp Fabric]
Rose, E.: "The Master Weavers", Festival of India in the USA 1985-1986, New York 1985: 178-186 [Ethnography; Ornamentation with Solid Material(s); Ornamentation with Liquid

Material(s)]
Rose, R.G.: Symbols of sovereignty: Feather girdles of Tahiti and Hawaii. Pacific Anthropological Recor. 28, Honolulu 1978 [Ethnography; General, Historical; Pile Fabric]
Rosenberg, A. & Haidler, M.& van Rosevelt,A.: The art of the ancient weaver: Textiles from Egypt. Ann Arbor 1980 [Archaeology; Threads, Warp Fabric; Pile Fabric]
Rosengarten, D.: Row upon Row: Sea Grass Baskets of the South Carolina Lowcountry. Mc Kissik Mus. Univ. South Carolina 1986 [Folk Art; Plaiting]
Ross, D.H.: see also Cole, H.M.
Ross, M.: The Essentials of Handspinning. Malvern 1980 [Threads]
Ross, M.: Encyclopaedia of Handspinning. London 1988 [Ethnography; Threads]
Rossbach, E.: Baskets as textile art. New York 1973 [Ethnography; Folk Art; Plaiting; Pile Fabric; Beadwork]
Rossbach, E.: The Art of Paisley. New York 1980 [General, Historical; Weaving]
Rossie, J.P. & Claus, G.J.M. "Imitation de la vie feminine dans les jeux des filles Glirib (Sahara, Tunisie)", Liber Memorialis. Gent 1983: 331-347 [Ethnography; Threads; Plaiting; Weaving]
Roth, W.E.: "Some Technological Notes from the Pomeroon Distr. British Guiana", Journal of the Royal Anthrop. Inst. 40, London 1910: 23-38 [Analysis; Ethnography; Threads; Mesh Fabric; Plaiting, Warp Fabric]
Roth, W.E.: An Introductory Study of the Arts, Crafts and Customs of the Guiana Indians. Annual Rep. Bureau Am. Ethn. 38, 1916-17, Washington 1918 [Analysis; Ethnography; Mesh Fabric; Plaiting, Warp Fabric; Weaving; Beadwork; Borders]
Roth, W.E.: Additional Studies of the Arts, Crafts and Customs of the Guiana Indians. Bull. Bureau Am. Ethnology 91, Washington 1929 [Analysis, Ethnography; Mesh Fabric; Plaiting; Beadwork]
Rouffaer, G.P.: Catalogus der Oostindische Weefsels, Javaansche Batiks en Oud Indische Meubelen. Oost en West, s'-Gravenhage 1901 [Collections; Weaving; Ornamentation with Liquid Material(s)]
Rouffaer, G.P.: Over ikats, tjinde's patola's en chiné's. Kolonial Weekblad 22, 1901, s'-Gravenhage 1902 [Analysis; Ornamentation with Liquid Material(s)]
Rouffaer, G.P.: Weefsels. Museum voor Land- en Volkenkunde, Amsterdam 1902 [Ethnography; Collections; Weaving]
Rouffaer, G.P.: Die Batik-Kunst in Niederländisch-Indien und ihre Geschichte. Utrecht 1914 [Ethnography; Ornamentation with Liquid Material(s)]
Rowe, A.P.: "Interlocking Warp and Weft in the Nasca 2 Style", Textile Museum Journal 3 (3), Washington 1972: 67-78 [Archaeology; Warp Fabric, Tapestry]
Rowe, A.P.: "Weaving processes in the Cuzco area of Peru", Textile Museum Journal 4 (2), Washington 1975: 30-46 [Analysis; Ethnography, Weaving]
Rowe, A.P.: Warp patterned weaves of the Andes. Washington 1977 [Ethnography, Archaeology; Warp Fabric; Weaving; Ornamentation with Liquid Material(s)]
Rowe, A.P.: "Weaving styles in the Cuzco Area", I.Emery Roundtable on Mus. Textiles 1976, Washington 1977: 61-84 [Ethnography, Weaving]
Rowe, A.P.: "Prácticas textiles en el área del Cuzco", Ravines (ed.) Tecnología Andina. Lima 1978: 369-400 [Ethnography; Weaving]
Rowe, A.P.: "Technical features of Inca tapestry tunics", Textile Museum Journal 17, Washington 1978: 5-28 [Archaeology; Tapestry]
Rowe, A.P.: "Seriation of an Ica-Style Garment Type", The J.B. Bird Precolumbian Textile Conf. 1973, Washington 1979: 185-218 [Archaeology; Warp Fabric; Weaving]
Rowe, A.P.: "Textile Evidence for Huari-Music", Textile Museum Journal 18, Washington 1979: 5-24 [Archaeology; General, Historical]
Rowe, A.P.: "A late Nazca – Derived Textile with Tapestry Medallions", Bull. of the Detroit Inst. of Arts Vol.57 N°3, Detroit 1979: 114-123 [Archaeology; Weaving; Tapestry]
Rowe, A.P.: A Century of Change in Guatemalan Textiles. New York 1981 [Ethnography; Weaving]
Rowe, A.P.: Costumes and Featherwork of the Lords of Chimor. Washington 1984 [Analysis; Archaeology; Warp Fabric; Weaving; Borders; Ornamentation with Solid Material(s), Pile Fabric; Beadwork]
Rowe, A.P.: "After Emery: further considerations of fabric classification and terminology", Textile Museum Journal 23, Washington 1984: 53-71 [Classification; Analysis; Weaving; Plaiting, Warp Fabric]
Rowe, A.P.: "The woven structures of European shawls in the Textile Museum collection", Textile Museum Journal 24, Washington 1985: 55-60 [General, Historical; Weaving; Ornamentation with Liquid Material(s)]
Rowe, A.P.: "Textiles from the Nasca Valley at the Time of the Fall of the Huari Empire", Rowe, A.P. (ed.) J.B. Bird Conf. on Andean Textiles 1984, Washington 1986: 151-183 [Archaeology; General, Historical; Pile Fabric]
Rowe, A.P. & Bird, J.B.: "The Ancient Peruvian Gauze Looms", Textile Museum Journal 19-20, 1980-81, Washington 1981: 27-33 [Archaeology; Weaving]
Rowe, A.P.: see also Mackie, L.W.
Rowe, J.H.: "Standardization in Inca Tapestry Tunics", The J.B.Bird Precolumbian Textile Conf. 1973, Washington 1979: 239-264 [Archaeology; Tapestry]
Rowe, M.T.J.: "Textiles", Bull.of the Assoc. In Fine Arts Vol.16 N°2, Yale 1948 [Collections; Weaving]
Foy, C.D.: "Mossi Weaving", African Arts Vol.15 N°3, Los Angeles 1982: 48-53 [Ethnography; Threads; Weaving; Ornamentation with Solid Material(s)]
Roy, N.: Art of Manipur. New Delhi 1979 [Analysis; Ethnography; Weaving]
Roze, U.: The North American Porcupine. Washington 1989 [Ethnography; Ornamentation with Solid Material(s)]
Rubinstein, D.H.: see also Feldman, J.
Rural Industries Bureau, London: Hand-Spinnen und Weben in England. Übersetzt und mit Anmerk. f. schweiz. Verhält. v. d. Heimarbeitsst. d. s. Bauernver. N°7, Zürich 1930 [Folk Art; Threads; Weaving]
Rutt, R.: A History of Hand Knitting. London 1987 [Analysis; Ethnography; Folk Art; Archaeology; Mesh Fabric; Warp Fabric; Weaving]
Rydén, S.: "Notes on a knitting technique from the Tukuna Indians Brazil", Man 34.35.1934, London 1935: 161-163 [Ethnography; Mesh Fabric]
Rydén, S.: "A Basketry Technique from the Lake Titicaca, Peru", Antiquity and Survival N°1, Den Haag 1955: 57-63 [Analysis; Archaeology; Plaiting]
Ryder, M.L.: "The Origin of Felt making and Spinning", American Antiquity 36, Salt Lake City 1962 [Archaeology; Threads]
Ryder, M.L.: "The Origin of Spinning", American Antiquity 38, Salt Lake City 1964 [Archaeology; Threads]
Ryesky, D.: "Wrap-Around skirts from Pinotepa de Don Luis, Oaxaca", I.Emery Roundtable on Mus. Textiles 1976, Washington 1977: 256-269 [Ethnography; Weaving]
Ryesky, D.: World of the weaver: an ethnographic study of textile production in a Mexican village. New York 1977 [Ethnography; Weaving]

Sachs, E.B.: see also Reath, N.A.
Safford, L. & Bishops, R.: America's Quilts and Coverlets. New York 1980 [Folk Art; Ornamentation with Solid Material(s)]
Sahashi, K.: Exquisite. The World of Japanese Kumihimo Braiding. Tokyo 1988 [Analysis; Ethnography; Plaiting]
Salomon, F.: "Weavers of Otavalo", Gross, D. (ed.) Peoples and Cultures of Native South America. New York 1977: 463-493 [Ethnography; Weaving]
Salvador, M.L.: "The Clothing Arts of the Cuna of San Blas, Panama", Graburn, N. (ed.) Ethnic and Tourist Arts. Berkeley 1976: 166-180 [Ethnography; Ornamentation with Solid Material(s)]
Salzer, R.: "Central Algonkin Beadwork", Am. Indian Tradition 7 (5), Illinois 1961: 166-178 [Ethnography; Beadwork]
Sample, L.L.: see also Mohr, A.
Samuel, C.: The Chilkat Dancing Blanket. Washington 1982 [Ethnography; Warp Fabric]
Sanoja Obediente, M.: Tejedores del Valle de Quibor. o.O. 1979 [Analysis; Folk Art; Threads; Weaving]
Sanoja-Obediente, M.: "Dos Elementos de la Cestería Indígena Venezolana", Folia Antropológica N°1, Carácas 1960: 55-69 [Ethnography; Plaiting; Borders]
Sanoja-Obediente, M.: "Cestería encordada del Territorio Federal Amazonas", Folia Antropológica 2, Carácas 1961: 55-69 [Ethnography; Threads; Plaiting; Warp Fabric]
Sanyal, A.: see also Chishti, R.K.
Saraf, D.N.: Arts and crafts: Jammu and Kashmir: Land, people, culture. New Delhi 1987 [Ethnography; Mesh Fabric; Plaiting; Weaving; Ornamentation with Solid Material(s); Ornamentation with Liquid Material(s)]
Saugy, C.: "Artesanía del Tejido (Sur Argentino)", Artesanías Folklóricas Argentinas 2 (4), Buenos Aires 1973: 1-8 [Ethnography; Weaving; Ornamentation with Liquid Material(s)]
Saugy, C.: Artesanías de Misiones. Informes del Instituto Nac. Antrop. Buenos Aires 1974 [Ethnography]
Saugy de Kliauga, C.: "Aspectos Sociales de la Pesca en el Paraná Medio, Entre Ríos, Argentina", Cultura Tradicional del Area Paraná Medio. Buenos Aires 1984: 23-45 [Ethnography; Mesh Fabric]
Saward, B.C.: see also Caulfeild, S.T.A.
Sawyer, A.R.: Paracas Necropolis Headdress and Face Ornaments. Workshop Notes 21, Washington 1960 [Archaeology; Ornamentation with Solid Material(s)]
Sawyer, A.R.: Tiahuanaco Tapestry Design. Mus. of Primitive Art, New York 1963 [Archaeology; Tapestry]
Sawyer, A.R.: Ancient peruvian textiles. Washington 1966 [Archaeology; Weaving; Tapestry]
Sawyer, A.R.: "Painted Nasca textiles", The J.B. Bird Pre-Colombian Textiles Conf. 1973, Washington 1979: 129-150 [Archaeology; Ornamentation with Liquid Material(s)]
Sayer, C.: Mexican Costume. London 1985 [Ethnography; Threads; Mesh Fabric; Plaiting; Warp Fabric; Weaving; Borders; Ornamentation with Solid Material(s); Ornamentation with Liquid Material(s)]
Sayer, C.: Mexican textile techniques. Aylesbury 1988 [Analysis; Ethnography; Threads; Mesh Fabric; Warp Fabric; Weaving; Ornamentation with Solid Material(s); Ornamentation with Liquid Material(s)]
Sayles, E.B.: "Three Mexican Crafts", American Anthropologist 57, Menasha 1955: 953-973 [Ethnography; Weaving]
Scarce, J.: "The Persian Shawl Industry", Textile Mus. Journal, 27/28, Washington 1988/89: 23-39 [Ethnography; Threads; Weaving]
Scarin, E. et al.: La Tradizione del Buratto All' Antella. Le Gualchiere. Ricerche sull'agro fiorentino N°8, Florenz 1989 [Folk Art; Weaving; Ornamentation with Solid Material(s)]
Schaar, E. & Delz, S.: Prähistorisches Weben. Hannover 1983 [Analysis; Archaeology; Plaiting; Warp Fabric; Half-weaving; Weaving; Tapestry]
Schachenmayr: Lehrbuch der Handarbeiten aus Wolle. Göppingen 1934 [Working Instruction; Mesh Fabric]
Schaedler, K.F.: Die Weberei in Afrika südlich der Sahara. München 1987 [Analysis; Ethnography; Threads; Weaving; Pile Fabric; Ornamentation with Solid Material(s); Ornamentation with Liquid Material(s)]
Schaefer, G.: "Der Webstuhl", Ciba Rundschau 16, Basel 1937 [General, Historical; Weaving]
Schäpper, L.: A Modern Approach to Patchwork. London 1984 [Working Instruction; Ornamentation with Solid Material(s)]
Schams: Bindungstechnik gewebter Stoffe. Berlin n.d. [Classification; Weaving]
Scheller, A.: "Seidene Tücher in Doppel-Ikat-Technik: Ihre Herstellung in Deutschland und ihre Verbreitung", Ethnologica Band 5, Leipzig 1941: 172-270 [Folk Art; Ornamentation with Liquid Material(s)]
Schermann, C.H.: see also Schermann, L.
Schermann, L.: Die javanische Batik-Technik und ihre vorderindischen Parallelen. Kunst und Handwerk 60 (10), München 1910 [Ethnography; Ornamentation with Liquid Material(s)]
Schermann, L.: "Brettchenweberei aus Birma und den Himalaya-Ländern", Münchner Jahrbuch d. bildenden Kunst 4, München 1913: 223-242 [Ethnography; Weaving]
Schermann, L. & Schermann, C.H.: Im Stromgebiet des Irrawadi. München 1922 [General, Historical; Weaving]
Schevill, M.B.: Costume as communication: Ethnographic costumes and textiles from Middle America and the central Andes of South America. Seattle 1986 [Ethnography; Mesh Fabric; Weaving; Ornamentation with Solid Material(s); Ornamentation with Liquid Material(s); Tapestry]
Schevill, M.B.: Evolution in textile design from the highlands of Guatemala. Berkeley 1986 [Analysis; Ethnography; Ornamentation with Liquid Material(s)]
Schier, B.: Das Flechten im Lichte der historischen Volkskunde. Frankfurt 1951 [Analysis; Folk Art; Plaiting]
Schier, B. & Simon, I.: Mitteleuropa, Westfalen: Flechten eines Bienenkorbes. Encyclopaedia Cinematographica E 394, Göttingen 1975 [Folk Art; Films; Plaiting]
Schindler, H.: Bauern und Reiterkrieger: Die Mapuche-Indianer im Süden Amerikas. München 1990 [Ethnography; Plaiting; Weaving; Pile Fabric; Ornamentation with Liquid Material(s)]
Schinnerer, L.: Antike Handarbeiten. Wien 1891 [Archaeology; Mesh Fabric; Warp Fabric; Weaving]
Schinnerer, L.: "Einiges über die bosnisch herzegowinischen Strick- und Häkel Arbeiten", Zeitschrift für österr. Volkskunde Heft 1, 3, Wien 1897: 13-18 [Folk Art; Mesh Fabric]
Schlabow, K.: "Der Thorsberger Prachtsmantel, der Schlüssel zum altgermanischen Webstuhl", Festschrift für G. Schwantes. Neumünster 1951 [Archaeology; Weaving]
Schlabow, K.: Die Kunst des Brettchenwebens. Veröff. Förderver. Textil Museum 1, Neumünster 1957 [Analysis; Weaving]
Schlabow, K.: "Vergleich jungsteinzeitlicher Textilfunde mit Webarbeiten der Bronzezeit", Germania 36, 1958 [Archaeology; Warp Fabric; Weaving]
Schlabow, K.: Der Moorleichenfund von Peiting. Veröff. d. Förderver. Textil Museum Heft 2, Neumünster 1961 [Archaeology; General, Historical; Weaving]
Schlabow, K.: Führer durch das Textilmuseum Neumünster: Rundgang durch die Schausammlungen. Veröff. Förderver. Tex. Museum 4, Neumünster 1962 [Collections]

Schlabow, K.: Der Thorsberger Prachtmantel: Schlüssel zum altgermanischen Webstuhl. Veröff. des Förderver. Textil Museum 5, Neumünster 1965 [Archaeology; Weaving]
Schlabow, K.: "Ein Beitrag zum Stand der Leinengewebeforschung vorgeschichtlicher Zeit", Nieders. Landesmuseum Hannover NF 23, Hannover 1972 [Archaeology; Weaving]
Schlabow, K.: Textilfunde der Eisenzeit in Norddeutschland. Neumünster 1976 [Analysis, Archaeology; Collections; Threads; Mesh Fabric, Plaiting; Warp Fabric; Weaving; Borders; Fabric Processing]
Schlabow, K.: Gewebe und Gewand zur Bronzezeit. Veröff. des Förderver. Textil Museum 3, Neumünster 1983 [Archaeology; Mesh Fabric; Warp Fabric; Weaving]
Schlenker, H.: Arhuaco (Kolumbien, Sierra Nevada de Santa Marta): Gewinnung von Agavefasern, Drehen von Schnur. Encyclopaedia Cinematographica E 1885, Göttingen 1973 [Ethnography; Films, Threads]
Schlenker, H.: Makiritare (Venezuela, Orinoco-Quellgebiet): Ernten und Spinnen von Baumwolle. Encyclopaedia Cinematographica E 1781, Göttingen 1974 [Ethnography; Films; Threads]
Schlenker, H.: Waika (Venezuela, Orinoco-Quellgebiet): Spinnen von Baumwolle. Encyclopaedia Cinematographica E 1801, Göttingen 1975 [Ethnography; Films; Threads]
Schlenker, H.: see also Luz, D.
Schlesier, E.: "Me'udama (Neuguinea, Normamby – Island): Plaiting einer Schlafmatte", Encyclopaedia Cinematographica E 533, Göttingen 1967: 247-254 [Ethnography; Films; Plaiting]
Schlichtherle, H.: see also Feldtkeller, A.
Schlosser, I.: Der schone Teppich im Orient und Okzident. Heidelberg 1960 [General, Historical; Pile Fabric]
Schmalenbach, W.: Der Textildruck. Basel 1950 [Folk Art; Ornamentation with Liquid Material(s)]
Schmedding, B.: Mittelalterliche Textilien in Kirchen und Klöstern der Schweiz. Bern 1978 [Collections, Mesh Fabric; Weaving]
Schmedding, B.: see also Lemberg, M.
Schmidt, M.: Indianerstudien in Zentralbrasilien. Berlin 1905 [Analysis, Ethnography, Plaiting, Warp Fabric]
Schmidt, M.: "Besondere Geflechtsart der Indianer im Ucayaligebiet", Archiv für Anthropologie N.S. 6 (4), Braunschweig 1907: 270-281 [Ethnography, Half-weaving]
Schmidt, M.: "Szenenhafte Darstellungen auf altperuanischen Geweben", Zeitschrift für Ethnologie 42, Berlin 1910: 154-164 [Archaeology, Weaving, Tapestry]
Schmidt, M.: "Über altperuanische Gewebe mit szenenhaften Darstellungen", Baessler-Archiv 1, Berlin 1911: 1-61 [Archaeology; Weaving, Tapestry]
Schmidt, M.: Von der Faser zum Stoff. Koln 1975 [Collections; Weaving]
Schmidt-Thome, M. & Tsering, T.: Materielle Kultur und Kunst der Sherpa. Innsbruck 1975 [Ethnography; Weaving]
Schnebel, C.: see also Donner, M.
Schneebaum, T.: Asmat Images. Asmat Museum of Culture and Progress, 1985 [Ethnography, General, Historical; Plaiting]
Schnegelsberg, G.: Classification der Textilien. München 1971 [Classification; Threads; Weaving; Pile Fabric]
Schnegelsberg, G.: "Methoden zur Entwicklung einer textilspezifischen Fachsprache", Z. z. Pflege u. Erforsch. dt. Mutterspr. Jg. 84, N°5, Wiesbaden 1974: 329-345 [Classification; General, Historical]
Schnegelsberg, G.: Textilspezifische Benennungen und Termini. Z. z. Pflege u. Erforsch. dt. Mutterspr. Jg. 87, N°4, Wiesbaden 1977: 245-258 [Classification; General, Historical]
Schneider, J.: Textilien: Katalog der Sammlung des Schweizerischen Landesmuseum. Zürich 1975 [Folk Art; Collections; Mesh Fabric; Plaiting; Warp Fabric; Weaving; Ornamentation with Solid Material(s); Ornamentation with Liquid Material(s)]
Schneider, J.: "The Anthropology of Cloth", Annual Review of Anthropology Vol.16, Palo Alto 1987: 409-478 [Ethnography; General, Historical; Weaving; Ornamentation with Solid Material(s); Ornamentation with Liquid Material(s)]
Schneider, J.: see also Weiner, A.B.
Schneider, K.: "Matten- und Korbherstellung: Bemerkungen zum dominierenden Frauenhandwerk der Birifor in Burkina Faso", Paideuma 34, Wiesbaden 1988: 165-183 [Analysis; Ethnography; Plaiting]
Schoch, W.: "Textilreste", Högl, L. (ed.) Schweiz. Beitrag z. Kulturgesch. u. Archä. Vol. 12, Olten 1985: 90-96 [Archaeology; Threads; Mesh Fabric; Warp Fabric; Weaving]
Schoepf, D.: "Essai sur la plumasserie des Indiens Kayapo, Wayana et Urubu Brésil", Bull. Annuel N°14, Genf 1971: 15-68 [Classification; Ethnography; Pile Fabric]
Schoepf, D.: L'art de la plume Brésil. Genf 1985 [Analysis; Ethnography; Collections; Pile Fabric]
Scholz, F.: Akha (Thailand, Chieng Rai-Provinz): Spinnen von Baumwolle. Encyclopaedia Cinematographica E 1243, Göttingen 1967 [Ethnography; Films; Threads]
Scholz, F.: Akha (Thailand, Chieng Rai-Provinz): Schären einer Baumwoll-Webkette. Encyclopaedia Cinematographica E 1244, Göttingen 1967 [Ethnography; Films; Weaving]
Scholz, F.: Akha (Thailand, Chieng Rai-Provinz): Binden einer Dachmatte. Encyclopaedia Cinematographica E 1247, Göttingen 1967 [Ethnography; Films; Plaiting]
Scholz, F.: Akha (Thailand, Chieng Rai-Provinz): Kettflechten einer Zierschnur aus Baumwolle und Samenkörnern. Encyclopaedia Cinematographica E 1285, Göttingen 1967 [Ethnography; Films; Warp Fabric]
Scholz, F.: Akha (Thailand, Chieng Rai-Provinz): Weben von Baumwolle auf dem Trittwebstuhl. Encyclopaedia Cinematographica E 1245, Göttingen 1968 [Ethnography; Films; Weaving]
Scholz, F.: Akha (Thailand, Chieng Rai-Provinz): Herstellen einer Bastmatte. Encyclopaedia Cinematographica E 1246, Göttingen 1968 [Ethnography; Films; Plaiting]
Scholz, F.: Akha (Thailand, Chieng Rai-Provinz): Flechten eines Deckelkorbes. Encyclopaedia Cinematographica E 1252, Göttingen 1968 [Ethnography; Films; Plaiting]
Scholz, F.: Batiken eines Kindertragtuches: Miao (Thailand, Tak-Provinz). Encyclopaedia Cinematographica 1270, Göttingen 1974 [Ethnography; Films; Ornamentation with Liquid Material(s)]
Scholz, F.: Miao (Thailand, Tak-Provinz): Herrichten einer Kette beim Hanfweben. Encyclopaedia Cinematographica E 1273, Göttingen 1974 [Ethnography; Films; Threads; Weaving; Ornamentation with Liquid Material(s)]
Scholz, F.: Miao (Thailand, Tak-Provinz): Hanfweben auf dem Trittwebstuhl. Encyclopaedia Cinematographica E 1274, Göttingen 1974 [Ethnography; Films; Weaving]
Scholz, F.: Miao (Thailand, Tak-Provinz): Herstellen von Hanfgarn zum Weben. Encyclopaedia Cinematographica E 1272, Göttingen 1974 [Ethnography; Films; Threads]
Scholz, F.: Schwarze Lahu (Thailand, Tak-Provinz): Weben von Tragbändern für Schultertaschen. Encyclopaedia Cinematographica E 1271, Göttingen 1977 [Ethnography; Films; Weaving]
Scholz, F.: see also Manndorff, H.
Scholz-Peter, R.: Indian bead stringing and weaving. New York 1975 [Working Instruction; Beadwork]
Schottelius, J.W.: "Arqueología de la Mesa de los Santos", Boletín

de Arqueología 3, Bogotá 1946 [Archaeology; Weaving]
Schürmann, U.: Teppiche aus dem Kaukasus. Braunschweig n.d. [Collections; General, Historical; Warp Fabric; Pile Fabric]
Schuette, M.: Alte Spitzen. Braunschweig 1963 [General, Historical; Mesh Fabric; Plaiting]
Schultz, H.: Krahó (Brasilien, Tocantinsgebiet): Spinnen eines Baumwollfadens. Encyclopaedia Cinematographica E 430, Göttingen 1962 [Ethnography; Films; Threads]
Schultz, H.: Krahó (Brasilien): Weben eines Kindertraggurtes. Encyclopaedia Cinematographica E 431, Göttingen 1963 [Ethnography, Films; Warp Fabric]
Schultz, H.: "Javahé (Brasilien): Häkeln von Beinbinden", Encyclopaedia Cinematographica E 441, Göttingen 1963: 364-368 [Ethnography, Films; Mesh Fabric]
Schultz, H.: "Flechten einer Kokrit Maske", Encyclopaedia Cinematographica I E 433, Göttingen 1963-65 [Ethnography; Films; Plaiting]
Schultz, H.: "Informações etnograficas sobre os Erigpagtsa do alto Juruena", Rev. Mus. Paulista N.S. 153, São Paulo 1964: 213-314 [Ethnography, Warp Fabric]
Schultz, H.: "Karajá (Brasilien): Knüpfen einer grossen Matte", Encyclopaedia Cinematographica 1, 1963-65, Göttingen 1965: 351-354 [Ethnography; Films, Plaiting]
Schultz, V.C.: "Krahó (Brasilien): Flechten eines Korbes", Encyclopaedia Cinematographica E 1175, Göttingen 1981 [Ethnography; Films; Plaiting]
Schulz, I.: Indianische Textilkunst. Dülmen 1988 [Collections; Weaving; Ornamentation with Solid Material(s); Ornamentation with Liquid Material(s)]
Schulze-Thulin, A.: Amerika-Abteilung. Linden Museum, Stuttgart 1989 [Ethnography; Archaeology; Collections; Plaiting; Warp Fabric; Weaving; Pile Fabric; Beadwork; Ornamentation with Solid Material(s); Tapestry]
Schuster, C.: "Stitch-resist dyed fabrics of Western China", Bull. Needle and Bobbin Club Vol.32 N°1 & 2, New York 1948: 11-29 [Ethnography, Ornamentation with Liquid Material(s)]
Schuster, C.: "Remarks on the Design of an Early Ikat Textile in Japan", Festschrift A. Bühler. Basel 1965: 339-368 [General, Historical; Ornamentation with Liquid Material(s)]
Schuster, G.: "Netztaschen der Zentral-Iatmul im Museum für Völkerkunde Basel", Basler Beiträge zur Ethnologie Band 30, Basel 1989: 335-390 [Analysis; Ethnography; Mesh Fabric; Borders]
Schuster, G.: see also Schuster, M.
Schuster, M.: Waika – Südamerika (Venezuela): Herstellung einer Hängematte u. KorbFlechten aus Lianen. Encyclopaedia Cinematographica D 743, 1957, Göttingen 1962 [Ethnography; Films; Plaiting; Warp Fabric]
Schuster, M.: Waika – Südamerika (Venezuela): Herstellung einer Hängematte (Baumwolle). Encyclopaedia Cinematographica D 744, 1957, Göttingen 1962 [Ethnography; Films; Threads; Warp Fabric]
Schuster, M.: Dekuana. München 1976 [Analysis; Ethnography; Mesh Fabric; Plaiting; Warp Fabric; Beadwork]
Schuster, M. & Schuster, G.: Aibom: Herstellen eines Frauenschurzes. Encyclopaedia Cinematographica E 1732, Göttingen 1980 [Ethnography, Films, Plaiting]
Schuster, M. & Schuster, G.: Aibom (Neuguinea, Mittlerer Sepik) – Gewinnen u. Färben von: Palmstreifen für einen Frauen-Schurz (Reservierungstechnik). Encyclopaedia Cinematographica E 1731, Göttingen 1980 [Ethnography; Films; Ornamentation with Liquid Material(s)]
Schuster, M. & Schuster, G.: Aibom. Gewinnen und Färben von Palmbaststreifen für einen Frauenschurz. Encyclopaedia Cinematographica E 1373, Göttingen 1981 [Ethnography; Films; Threads]
Schuster, M. & Schuster, G.: Aibom (Neuguinea, Mittlerer Sepik): Flechten einer Frauen-Haube. Encyclopaedia Cinematographica E 1374, Göttingen 1981 [Ethnography; Films; Plaiting]
Schuster, M.: see also Zerries, O.
Schwartz, O.: "Jewish weaving in Kurdistan", Journal of Jewish Art 3 (4), Chicago 1977 [Ethnography; Ornamentation with Liquid Material(s)]
Schwartz, P.R.: Contribution à l'histoire de l'application du bleu d'indigo dans l'indiennage européen. Bull. Soc. Indust. 11, Mulhouse 1952 [Ornamentation with Liquid Material(s)]
Schwartz, P.R.: French documents on Indian cotton painting. Journal of Indian Textile History 2-3, Ahmebadad 1956-57 [Ornamentation with Liquid Material(s)]
Schwartz, P.R.: Exposition de toiles peintes anciennes des Indes. Mulhouse 1962 [Ethnography; Ornamentation with Liquid Material(s)]
Schwartz, P.R.: "Les toiles peintes indiennes", Bull. de la Soc. Industrielle, Mulhouse 1962: 37-52 [General, Historical; Ornamentation with Liquid Material(s)]
Schwartz, P.R.: "L'impression sur coton à Ahmedabad en 1678", Bull. Soc. Industrielle 726, 1, Mulhouse 1967 [General, Historical; Ornamentation with Liquid Material(s)]
Schwartz, P.R.: see also Irwin, J.
Schwarz, A.: "Der Haspel", Ciba Rundschau 64, Basel 1945 [Folk Art; Threads]
Schweeger-Hefel, A.: "Dogon (Westsudan): Flechten einer Schlafmatte", Encyclopaedia Cinematographica E 1223, Vol.4, Göttingen 1973/74: 148-151 [Ethnography; Films; Plaiting]
Schweeger-Hefel, A.: Dogon (Westsudan): Herstellen eines Seiles. Encyclopaedia Cinematographica E 1222, Vol.4, Göttingen 1973/74: 151-155 [Ethnography; Films; Threads]
Schweeger-Hefel, A.: "Dogon (Westsudan): Herstellen einer Dachbedeckung", Encyclopaedia Cinematographica E 1224, Vol.4, Göttingen 1973/74: 155-161 [Ethnography; Plaiting]
Scott, D.: "Dressed with Dragons: Chinese Textiles", Antique Collector Vol. 52, 1981: 49-53 [Ethnography; Ornamentation with Solid Material(s)]
Scoville, A.B.: "The indian belt", Bull. Needle and Bobbin Club Vol.6 N°2, New York 1922: 8-13 [Ethnography; Beadwork]
Searle, K.: see also Baizerman, S.
Sebba, A.: Samplers: Five centuries of a gentle craft. London 1979 [Folk Art; Ornamentation with Solid Material(s)]
Sedlak, L.: Cultural patterns in Huichol art. Ann Arbor 1987 [Ethnography; Plaiting; Weaving; Beadwork; Ornamentation with Solid Material(s); Fabric Processing]
Seeberger, M.: "Hutmacherinnen im Lötschental (Wallis)", Altes Handwerk 56, Basel 1987 [Folk Art; Plaiting]
Segal, W.C. et al. (ed.): Encyclopaedia of textiles. Englewood Cliffs 1973 [Analysis; Archaeology; Threads; Mesh Fabric; Weaving; Pile Fabric; Ornamentation with Solid Material(s); Ornamentation with Liquid Material(s); Tapestry]
Segal Brandford, J.: "The Old Saltillo Sarape", I.Emery Roundtable on Mus. Textiles 1976, Washington 1977: 271-292 [Ethnography; Tapestry]
Segawa, S.: Japanese Quilt Art. Kyoto 1985 [Ethnography; Ornamentation with Solid Material(s)]
Seiler-Baldinger, A.: "Zum Problem der Maschenstoffe in Südamerika", Verh. des XXXVIII. Int. Amerikan. Kongr. Band 2, Stuttgart 1968: 531-535 [Classification; Ethnography; Mesh Fabric]
Seiler-Baldinger, A.: Maschenstoffe in Süd- und Mittelamerika. Basler Beiträge zur Ethnologie 9, Basel 1971 [Classification; Ethnography; Archaeology; Threads; Mesh Fabric; Borders]

Seiler-Baldinger, A.: Arhuaco (Kolumbien, Sierra Nevada de Santa Marta): Gewinnung von Agave Fasern. Drehen von Schnur. Encyclopaedia Cinematographica E 1885, Göttingen 1973 [Ethnography; Films; Threads]

Seiler-Baldinger, A.: "Ein seltener Hängemattentypus und seine Verbreitung in Amerika", Atti del XL Cong. Int. degli American. Roma-Genova 1972, Vol. 2, Genova 1974: 349-355 [Ethnography; Mesh Fabric]

Seiler-Baldinger, A.: "Der Federmantel der Tupinamba im Museum für Völkerkunde Basel", Atti del XL Cong. Int. degli American. Roma-Genova 1972, Vol. 2, Genova 1974: 433-438 [Classification; Analysis; Ethnography; Pile Fabric]

Seiler-Baldinger, A.: "General Introduction to the Literature on South American Ethnographic Textiles since 1950", I.Emery Roundtable on Mus. Textiles 1976, Washington 1977: 17-34 [Ethnography]

Seiler-Baldinger, A.: "Meshwork Manufacture in South America. An Example of applied Technology", I.Emery Roundtable on Mus. Textiles 1976, Washington 1977: 35-43 [Classification, Ethnography; Mesh Fabric]

Seiler-Baldinger, A.: "Problems of Textile Classification", I.Emery Roundtable on Mus. Textiles 1976, Washington 1977: 85-86 [Classification]

Seiler-Baldinger, A.: Classification of Textile Techniques. Calico Museum of Textiles, Ahmedabad 1979 [Classification, Threads; Mesh Fabric; Plaiting; Warp Fabric; Half-weaving; Weaving; Pile Fabric; Beadwork; Borders; Ornamentation with Solid Material(s); Ornamentation with Liquid Material(s); Fabric Processing]

Seiler-Baldinger, A.: "Hängematten-Kunst. Textile Ausdrucksform bei Yagua und Ticuna-Indianern Nordwestamazoniens", Verh. Nat. Forsch. Ges. 90 (1979), Basel 1981: 61-130 [Analysis, Ethnography; Threads; Mesh Fabric]

Seiler-Baldinger, A.: "Le confort sauvage", Stoffe und Räume. Langenthal Ausstellungskatalog, Bern 1986: 9-25 [General, Historical; Mesh Fabric; Plaiting; Warp Fabric; Weaving; Ornamentation with Solid Material(s); Ornamentation with Liquid Material(s)]

Seiler-Baldinger, A.: "Träume in der Schwebe: Die Hängematte, ein indianischer Beitrag zur Wohnkultur", Bauen und Wohnen. Basel 1987: 67-76 [Ethnography]

Seiler-Baldinger, A.: Indianer im Tiefland Südamerikas. Basel 1987 [Analysis; Ethnography; Collections; Mesh Fabric; Plaiting; Weaving; Pile Fabric; Beadwork]

Seiler-Baldinger, A.: "Systematik der Textilen Techniken". Basler Beiträge zur Ethnologie 32, Basel 1991 [Classification; Threads, Mesh Fabric; Plaiting; Warp Fabrics; Tapestry; Half-weaving, Weaving; Pile Fabric; Beadwork; Borders; Ornamentation with Solid and Liquid Materials; Fabric Processing]

Seiler-Baldinger, A. & Ohnemus, S.: "Zum Problem des Halbwebens", Verh. Nat.Forsch. Ges. 96, Basel 1986: 85-97 [Classification; Ethnography; Half-weaving]

Seiler-Baldinger, A.: see also Baer, G.

Seipel, W.: Aegypten: Götter, Gräber und die Kunst. Band 1, Lins 1989 [Archaeology; Plaiting; Weaving; Beadwork]

Sekhar, A.C.: Selected crafts of Andrha Pradesh. Census of India Vol.2 Part 7a, New Delhi 1964 [Ethnography, Pile Fabric, Ornamentation with Solid Material(s)]

Sekido, M. & Aoki, M.: Sanshoku dyeing. Shibata Shoten n.d. [Ornamentation with Liquid Material(s)]

Selvanayagam, G.I.: Songket: Malaysia's Woven Treasure. Singapore 1990 [Analysis; Ethnography; Weaving; Ornamentation with Liquid Material(s)]

Senthna, N.H.: Kalamkari. New York 1985 [Ethnography; Ornamentation with Liquid Material(s)]

Seydou, C.: see also Gardi, B.

Shah, H.: see also Fischer, E.

Sharma, L.C.: Himachal Pradesh. Rural craft survey: The Art of weaving. Census of India Vol.20 Part 7A,2, Delhi 1968 [Analysis; Ethnography; Threads; Weaving; Ornamentation with Solid Material(s)]

Sharma, R.C.: Woolen carpet and blanket industry in Uttar Pradesh. Census of India Vol. 15 (1961), Allahabad 1964 [Ethnography; Threads; Weaving; Pile Fabric]

Sheares, C.: Batik in Singapore. Singapore 1975 [Analysis; Ethnography; Ornamentation with Liquid Material(s)]

Sheares, C.: "Southeast Asian Ceremonial Textiles in the National Museum", Arts of Asia Vol 17 N°3, Hong Kong 1987: 100-107 [Ethnography; Collections; Ornamentation with Solid Material(s); Ornamentation with Liquid Material(s)]

Sheltman, C.: "Demirdash and Broussa Weaving", Bull. Needle and Bobbin Club Vol.6 N°2, New York 1922: 4 [Folk Art; Warp Fabric]

Shenai, V.A.: History of textile design. Bombay 1974 [General, Historical; Weaving]

Shepherd, D.G.: The Hispano-Islamic Textiles in the Cooper Union Collection. Chronicle of the Mus. for Arts and Decorations Vol.1 N°10, New York 1943: 357-401 [Folk Art; Weaving]

Shepherd, D.G.: "En defense des soieries persianes", Cieta 37, 1973, 1, Lyon 1973 [Ethnography, Weaving]

Shepherd, D.G.: The Archaeology of the Benjid Textiles. Fiske, K. (ed.) Traditional Arts of Hyderabad. Washington 1974: 175-190 [Archaeology, Weaving]

Shinkoka, K.B.: Traditional handicrafts of Japan: An Exhibition of Contemporary Works. Mus. voor Land- en Volkenkunde, Rotterdam 1963 [Ethnography, Collections]

Shiroishi Miyagi Prefecture: Shifu Fabric. Shiroishi 1946 [Ethnography, Threads, Weaving]

Shivo, P.: Tradition und Volkskunst in Finnland. Helsinki 1978 [Folk Art; Threads; Weaving; Pile Fabric; Ornamentation with Solid Material(s)]

Shurinova, R.: Coptic Textiles. Moskau 1967 [Archaeology; Tapestry]

Sibeth, A.: Batak. Stuttgart 1990 [Ethnography; Plaiting; Weaving; Beadwork; Ornamentation with Solid Material(s); Ornamentation with Liquid Material(s)]

Siderenko, A.I.: Gold embroidery of Bukhara. Tashkent 1981 [Ethnography; Ornamentation with Solid Material(s)]

Sieber, R.: African textiles and decorative arts. Museum of Modern Art, New York 1972 [Ethnography, Plaiting, Weaving, Pile Fabric, Beadwork, Ornamentation with Solid Material(s); Ornamentation with Liquid Material(s)]

Sieber, R.: African furniture and household objects. London 1981 [Ethnography, Plaiting]

Sieber, R.: "Opening September 1987 – The National Museum of African Art", African Arts Vol 20 N°4, Los Angeles 1987: 28-37 [Ethnography; Mesh Fabric; Weaving]

Siegenthaler, F.: Nepalesische Shifu-Herstellung. Basel 1989 [Ethnography; Threads, Weaving]

Sievers, von, C.: Die Batiktechnik. Leipzig 1911 [Ethnography; Ornamentation with Liquid Material(s)]

Siewertsz van Reesema, E.: Egyptisch vlechtwerk. Amsterdam n.d. [Analysis, Archaeology, Warp Fabric]

Siewertsz van Reesema, E.: "Old Egyptian Lace", Bull. Needle and Bobbin Club Vol 4 N°1, New York 1920: 13-19 [Archaeology, Warp Fabric]

Siewertsz van Reseema, E.: Contributions to the Early History of Textile Techniques. Verhandelingen der Koninklijke Akademie van Wettschappen, 16 (2), Amsterdam 1926 [Analysis, Archaeology, Mesh Fabric]

Sigerus, E. (ed.): Siebenbürgisch-Sachsische Leinenstickereien. Sibiu 1922 [General, Historical; Ornamentation with Solid Material(s)]
Signi, A.: Arte & Vida: Catálogo del Museo Etnológico "Mons. Enzo Ceccarelli". Pt. Ayacucho 1988 [Ethnography; Collections; Threads; Plaiting; Warp Fabric; Pile Fabric; Beadwork]
Signorini, I.: Los Huaves de San Mateo del Mar. Mexico 1979 [Analysis; Ethnography; Mesh Fabric; Weaving]
Sillitoe, P.: Made in Niuguini: Technology in the Highlands of Papua New Guinea. London 1988 [Analysis, Ethnography, Threads; Mesh Fabric; Plaiting; Warp Fabric; Pile Fabric; Beadwork; Borders]
Silva Celis, E.: "Elementos arqueológicos procedentes de las montañas de Pisba", Bol. Museo del Oro 1, Bogotá 1978: 22-29 [Archaeology; Mesh Fabric; Weaving]
Silverman-Proust, G.: "Representación gráfica del mito Inkarrí en los tejidos Q'ero", Boletín de Lima 8(48), Lima 1986: 75-80 [Ethnography; Weaving]
Silverman-Proust, G.: "Weaving technique and the registration of knowledge in the Cuzco area of Peru", Journ. of Latin Am. Lore 14 (2), Los Angeles 1988: 207-241 [Ethnography; Weaving]
Silverman-Proust, G.: "Los motivos textiles", Fries, A.M. (ed.) Puna, Qheswa, Yunga. El hombre y su medio en Q'ero. Lima 1989: 75-80 [Ethnography; Weaving]
Simeon, M.: The history of lace. London 1979 [General, Historical; Ornamentation with Solid Material(s)]
Simmonds, D.: see also Barbour, J.
Simmons, P.: see also Priest, A.
Simon, F.: Mitteleuropa, Tirol: Flachsverarbeitung: Spinnen. Encyclopaedia Cinematographica E 791, Göttingen 1965 [Folk Art; Films; Threads]
Simon, F.: Eipo (West-Neuguinea, Zentrales Hochland): Herstellen eines Perlenbandes in Halbwebtechnik. Encyclopaedia Cinematographica E 2595, 7 N°14, Göttingen 1989 [Ethnography; Films; Half-weaving; Beadwork]
Simon, I.: see also Schier, B.
Simpson, L.E. & Weir, M.: The Weaver's Craft. Leicester 1932 [Analysis; Folk Art; Working Instruction; Weaving]
Singer, C. et al. (ed.): A History of Technology. 3 Bände, Oxford 1954-57 [Archaeology; Threads; Plaiting; Weaving]
Singer, P.P.: "Una investigación sobre tejidos de punto precolombino", Revista del Museo Nacional 16, Lima 1947: 171-192 [Archaeology; Mesh Fabric]
Singer Wieder, E.: Analysis and Distribution of Netting Techniques among the South American Indians. Philadelphia 1935 [Classification; Ethnography; Mesh Fabric]
Singer Wieder, E.: "The Techniques of Peruvian Hairnets", Revista del Museo Nacional 5 (1), Lima 1936: 15-24 [Archaeology, Mesh Fabric]
Singer Wieder, E.: "The Looping Technique in Netting", American Antiquity 2, 1936-37, Salt Lake City 1937: 141-142 [General, Historical; Mesh Fabric]
Singh, C.: Textiles and costumes from the Maharaha Swai Man Singh II Museum. Jaipur 1979 [Collections; Weaving; Pile Fabric; Ornamentation with Solid Material(s); Ornamentation with Liquid Material(s)]
Singh, C.: Woollen textiles and costumes from Bharat Kala Bhavan. Varanasi 1981 [General, Historical; Weaving]
Singh, P. & Mathey, F.: Les textiles de l'Inde et les modèles crées par Isey Miyake. Paris 1985 [Collections; Weaving; Ornamentation with Solid Material(s); Ornamentation with Liquid Material(s)]
Siskin, B.: "Changes in the Woven Design from Santo Tomas Chichicastenango", I.Emery Roundtable on Mus. Textiles 1976, Washington 1977: 154-165 [Ethnography, Weaving]
Skinner, M.D.: "The Archaeological looms from Perú in the Museum of Natural History Collection", I.Emery Roundtable on Mus. Textiles, Washington 1974: 67-76 [Archaeology, Weaving]
Skinner, M.D.: "Three Textiles from Huaca Prieta, Chicama Valley, Peru", Rowe, A.P. (ed.) J.B. Bird Conf. on Andean Textiles 1984, Washington 1986: 11-18 [Analysis, Archaeology; Warp Fabric]
Skinner-Dimitrijevic, M.: see also Bird, J.B., Skinner, M.D. [Skyring, F. & Bogle, M.: "Ikats of Southeast Asia", Craft Australia, summer, 1982: 26-29 [Ethnography, Ornamentation with Liquid Material(s)]
Smart, E.S. & Gluckman, D.C.: "Cloth of luxury: velvet in Mughal India", Riboud, K. (ed.) In Quest of Themes and Skills. Bombay 1989: 36-47 [Archaeology, Weaving, Pile Fabric]
Smith, A.D.H.: Brief Guide to the Western painted, dyed and printed Textiles. Victoria and Albert Museum, London 1924 [Collections; Ornamentation with Liquid Material(s)]
Smith, A.D.H.: Brief Guide to the Oriental painted, dyed and printed textiles. Victoria and Albert Museum, London 1924 [Collections; Ornamentation with Liquid Material(s)]
Smith, A.D.H.: Brief Guide to the Chinese woven fabrics. Victoria and Albert Museum, London 1925 [Collections, Weaving]
Smith, A.D.H.: Brief Guide to the Peruvian textiles. Victoria and Albert Museum, London 1926 [Archaeology, Collections]
Smith, A.D.H.: Brief Guide to the Turkish woven Fabrics. Victoria and Albert Museum, London 1931 [Collections; Weaving]
Smith, F.T.: "Gurensi Basketry and Pottery", African Arts Vol.12 N°1, Los Angeles 1978: 78-81 [Ethnography, Plaiting]
Smith, J.G.: see also Rogers, E.S.
Smith, J.R.: Tissage Maori sans métier. Paris 1975 [Analysis, Ethnography, Working Instruction, Warp Fabric]
Smith, M.: The Technique of North American Indian Beadwork. Odgen 1983 [Ethnography, Beadwork]
Smolková, M.A.: O starobylém pletení na "Krosierakách". Prag 1904 [Folk Art; Warp Fabric]
Snethlage, E.H.: "Form und Ornamentik altperuanischer Spindeln", Baessler-Archiv 14, Berlin 1930: 77-95 [Archaeology; Threads]
Snethlage, E.H.: "Ein figurliches Ikat-Gewebe aus Peru", Der Weltkreis 2 (3-4), Berlin 1931: 49-51 [Archaeology, Ornamentation with Liquid Material(s)]
Snoddy-Cuellar, E.: "San Agustin Tlacotepec, Mixteca Alta Belt Weaving Village", I.Emery Roundtable on Mus. Textiles 1976, Washington 1977: 310-319 [Ethnography, Weaving]
Snow, M. & Snow, W.: Step-by-step tablet weaving. New York 1973 [Analysis, Working Instruction, Weaving, Borders, Fabric Processing]
Snow, W.: see also Snow, M.
Snoy, P.: see also Kussmaul, F.
Soekawati,, T.G.R.: Nijverheid en kunstnijverheid op Bali. Mededeelingen van de Kirtya I. 15, Jogjakarta 1941 [Ethnography; Ornamentation with Liquid Material(s)]
Solyom, B. & Solyom, G.: "Notes and Observations on Indonesian Textiles", Fischer, J. (ed.) Threads of Tradition. Berkeley 1979: 15-33 [Ethnography, Weaving, Ornamentation with Liquid Material(s)]
Solyom, B. & Solyom, G.: Fabric traditions of Indonesia. Washington 1984 [Ethnography, Plaiting, Weaving, Ornamentation with Solid Material(s); Ornamentation with Liquid Material(s)]
Solyom, B.: see also Solyom, G.
Solyom, G. & Solyom, B.: Textiles of the Indonesian Archipelago. Asian Studies at Hawaii N°10, Honolulu 1973 [Ethnography; Collections, Ornamentation with Liquid Material(s)]

Solyom, G. & Solyom, B.: Rites de passage. San Diego 1979 [Colections; Ornamentation with Liquid Material(s)]
Solyom, G. & Solyom, B.: "A note on some rare Central Javanese Textiles", I.Emery Roundtable on Mus. Textiles 1979, Washington 1980: 275-281 [Ethnography; Ornamentation with Liquid Material(s)]
Solyom, G. & Solyom, B.: "Cosmic symbolism in semen and alasalasan patterns in Javanese textiles", I.Emery Roundtable on Mus. Textiles 1979, Washington 1980: 248-271 [Ethnography; Ornamentation with Liquid Material(s)]
Solyom, G.: see also Solyom, B.
Sonday, M.: "What can we learn from a fabric about the loom on which it might have been woven?", I.Emery Roundtable on Mus. Textiles 1977, Washington 1979: 242-256 [Analysis, Weaving]
Sonday, M.: Lace in the collection of the Cooper-Hewitt Museum. New York 1982 [Folk Art; General, Historical; Ornamentation with Solid Material(s)]
Sonday, M. & Kajitani, N.: "A second type of Mughal sash", Textile Museum Journal 3 (2), Washington 1971: 6-12 [Analysis; Weaving]
Sonday, M.: see also Coleman, E.A.
Sorber, F.: "Batiks en Afrikadruk in de Gentse Katoendrukkerij Voortman", Liber Memorialis 1, Gent, Belgien 1983: 365-373 [Ethnography; Ornamentation with Liquid Material(s)]
Spahni, J.C.: "Recherches archéologiques à l'embochure du Río Loa (Côte du Pacifique-Chili)", Journ. Soc. Améric. 56 (1), Paris 1967 [Archaeology; Mesh Fabric, Plaiting, Weaving]
Specht, S. & Rawlings, S.: Creating with card-weaving. New York 1973 [Working Instruction; Weaving]
Spée, M.: Traditionele en moderne batik: Ontwikkeling, techniek en methoden. De Bilt 1977 [Analysis, Ethnography, Working Instruction; Ornamentation with Liquid Material(s)]
Speiser, F.: Flechtarbeiten. Gewerbemuseum Basel, Basel 1925 [Ethnography; Plaiting]
Speiser, N.: "Neue Entwicklungen der Sprang-Technik", Heimatwerk 3, Zürich 1971 [Warp Fabric]
Speiser, N.: "Le Kago-Uchi", Cieta 36 (2), Lyon 1972: 9-24 [Ethnography; Plaiting]
Speiser, N.: "Sprang", Schweiz. Arbeitslehrerinnen Zeitung N°5, Biel 1974 [Analysis; Working Instruction; Warp Fabric]
Speiser, N.: The Manual of Braiding. Basel 1983 [Analysis, Working Instruction; Mesh Fabric; Plaiting, Warp Fabric]
Speiser, N.: "The Kago-Uchi", Ars Textrina Vol.4, Dec. Winnipeg 1985: 23-41 [Ethnography, Plaiting, Ornamentation with Liquid Material(s)]
Spencer, R.F.: "North Alaska Coast Eskimo", Handbook of North Am. Indians 5, Washington 1984: 320-337 [Ethnography, Plaiting]
Sperlich, E.: see also Sperlich, N.
Sperlich, N. & Sperlich, E.: Guatemalan Backstrap Weaving. Norman 1980 [Ethnography; Weaving]
Spertus, A.E.: see also Holmgren, R.J.
Spier, L.: "Zuñi Weaving Technique", Am. Anthrop. 16 (1), Menasha 1924: 64-85 [Ethnography; Weaving]
Spirito, O.: Voiles de Gènes. Mulhouse 1964 [Folk Art; Weaving]
Spring, C.: African Textiles. African Coll. Museum of Mankind, London 1989 [Ethnography, Weaving, Pile Fabric, Ornamentation with Solid Material(s); Ornamentation with Liquid Material(s)]
Spuhler, F.: Islamic Carpets and Textiles in the Keir Collection. London 1978 [Archaeology; Collections; Weaving, Pile Fabric]
Stafford, C.E.: Paracas Embroideries. A Study of Repeated Patterns. New York 1941 [Archaeology, Ornamentation with Solid Material(s)]
Standigel, O.: "Tablet-weaving and the technique of the Ramses-girdle", Cieta 41-42, 1-2, Lyon 1975 [Analysis, Archaeology, Weaving]
Stanfiled, N. & Barbour, J.: Adire Cloth in Nigeria. Nigeria: Inst. Afr. Studies, Ibadan 1971 [Analysis; Ethnography; Ornamentation with Liquid Material(s)]
Stanislaw, M.A.: Kalagas: the wall hangings of Southeast Asia. Singapore 1987 [Ethnography, Ornamentation with Solid Material(s)]
Stanková, J.: "Les techniques textiles dans la culture populaire tchéchoslovaque", Cieta 36, 2, Lyon 1972: 29-67 [Folk Art, General, Historical]
Stanková, J.: "Vortucher, genannt "Predaky" aus dem Gebiet Dondleby", Beitrag zum Studium bohm. Gewebe. n.p. 1975: 86-99 [Folk Art, Weaving]
Stanková, J.: "A chapter in the history of woven lace", Textile History Vol.16 N°2, Newton Abbot 1985 [Folk Art, Ornamentation with Solid Material(s)]
Stanková, J.: Ceské lidové tkaniny. Praha 1989 [Analysis, Folk Art; Threads; Weaving, Ornamentation with Liquid Material(s)]
Stanková, J.: see also Orel, J.
Stanley, M.: "The bedouin saha weave and its double cloth cousin", Rogers, N. (ed.) In Celebration of the Curious Mind. Loveland 1983: 68-79 [Analysis, Ethnography, Weaving]
Stapeley, M.B.: Popular Weaving and Embroidery in Spain. Madrid 1924 [Folk Art, Weaving, Ornamentation with Solid Material(s)]
Start, L.: see also Haddon, A.C.
Start, L.E.: Burmese textiles from the Shan and Kachin districts. Bankfield Museum Notes Series 2 N°7, Halifax 1917 [Ethnography, Weaving]
Start, L.E.: The Durham Collection of Garments and Embroideries from Albania and Yugoslavia. Bankfield Museum Notes Series 3 N°4, Halifax 1939 [Folk Art; Collections, Borders; Ornamentation with Solid Material(s)]
Start, L.E.: The McDougall Collection of Indian Textiles from Guatemala and Mexico. Occ. Pap. on Technology 2, Oxford 1948 [Collections, Plaiting, Weaving, Ornamentation with Liquid Material(s)]
Staub, J.: Beiträge zur Kenntnis der materiellen Kultur der Mendi in der Sierra Leone. Solothurn 1936 [Ethnography; Plaiting]
Steffensen, H.: Nålebinding. København 1975 [Archaeology, Working Instruction, Mesh Fabric]
Steffensen, H.: Lardig nålbinding. København 1978 [Archaeology, Working Instruction, Mesh Fabric]
Steffensen, H.: Naaldbinding. Amsterdam 1978 [Archaeology, Working Instruction, Mesh Fabric]
Steger-Volkel, R.: see also Knauer, T.
Stein, J.A.: see also Quick, B.
Steinman, A.: "Tissus à jonques du sud de Sumatra", Revue des Arts Asiatiques Vol.2 N°3, Paris 1937 [Ethnography, Weaving]
Steinmann, A.: Die Ornamente der Ikat-Gewebe von Sumba. n.p., n.d. [Ethnography; General, Historical; Ornamentation with Liquid Material(s)]
Steinmann, A.: Javanisches Kunstgewerbe. Kunstgesellschaft in Luzern, Luzern 1925 [Ethnography; Collections]
Steinmann, A.: Webereien und Batiktücher aus Niederländisch Indien. Wegleitungen des Kunstgewerbemus. Zürich 1925 [Collections, Ornamentation with Liquid Material(s)]
Steinmann, A.: "Enkele opmerkingen aangaande de z.g. Scheepjesdoeken van Zuid-Sumatra", Cultureel Indie Jg. 1, Leiden 1939: 252-256 [General, Historical, Ornamentation with Solid Material(s)]
Steinmann, A.: "Die Ornamentik der Ikat-Gewebe", Ciba Rundschau N°51 Sept. Basel 1941: 1876-82 [Ethnography, Orna-

mentation with Liquid Material(s)]
Steinmann, A.: "Batiken", Ciba Rundschau N°69 Jan. Basel 1947: 2528-63 [Analysis; Ethnography, Ornamentation with Liquid Material(s)]
Steinmann, A.: "Das Batiken in China", Sinologica 2 (2), Basel 1949: 105-126 [Ethnography; Ornamentation with Liquid Material(s)]
Steinmann, A.: "Die Batikgeräte in Asien und Indonesien", Bull. Schweiz. Ges. Anthr. Eth. 1952-53, Bern 1953 [Analysis, Ethnography; Ornamentation with Liquid Material(s)]
Steinmann, A.: Batik: A survey of batik designs. Leigh-on-Sea 1958 [General, Historical; Ornamentation with Liquid Material(s)]
Sonderausstellung des Steirischen Bauernmuseums: Korbe und KorbPlaiting. Stainz 1976 [Folk Art; Collections; Plaiting]
Stephani, L. & Tolmachoff, E.: "Some ancient Greek Textiles found in South Russia", Bull. Needle and Bobbin Club Vol.26 N°2, New York 1942: 17-58 [Archaeology; Ornamentation with Liquid Material(s)]
Stephens, S.G. & Moseley, M.E.: "Early domesticated cottons from archaeological sites in Central Coastal Peru", American Antiquity 39 (1), Salt Lake City 1974: 109-122 [Archaeology]
Stettiner, R.: "Brettchenweberei in den Moorfunden von Damendorf, Daetzen und Torsberg", Mitt. Anthrop. Vereins Schles. Holst. Heft 19, Kiel 1911: 26-56 [Archaeology; Weaving]
Steven, G.A.: Nets: how to make, mend and preserve them. London 1950 [Working Instruction; Mesh Fabric]
Steward, J.H.: Ancient caves of the Great Salt Lake Region. Bull. Bur. Am. Ethn. 116, Washington 1937 [Archaeology, Mesh Fabric; Plaiting]
Stirling, M.W.: Historical and Ethnographical Material on the Jivaro Indians. Bull. Bur. Am. Ethnol. 117, Washington 1938 [General, Historical; Threads; Mesh Fabric, Weaving]
Stoeckel, J.: "Etude sur le tissage au Cambodge", Arts et Archéologie Khmers 1 (4), Paris 1921-23: 387-402 [Ethnography; Weaving]
Stöcklin, D.: see also Huber, H.
Stojanovic, A.: Brnestra (Spanischer Ginster): I Zuka – spartium junceum. Publikacije Etnolokoga Zadova N°4, Zagreb 1962 [Folk Art; Weaving]
Stokar, W.: Spinnen und Weben bei den Germanen. Leipzig 1938 [Archaeology; Threads; Weaving]
Stokes, J.F.: "Nets and Netting", Mem. Bernice Bishop Mus. 2 (1), Honolulu 1906: 105-162 [Ethnography; Mesh Fabric]
Stoltz Gilfoy, P.: Patterns of life: West African strip-weaving traditions. Washington 1987 [Analysis, Ethnography, Collections; Warp Fabric; Weaving]
Stone, R.R.: Technique and form in Huari-style tapestry tunics. The Andean Artist, A.D. 500-800. Thesis Yale University, Yale 1987 [Archaeology; Warp Fabric, Tapestry]
Storey, J.: The Thames and Hudson Manual of Textile Printing. London 1974 [General, Historical; Ornamentation with Liquid Material(s)]
Stothert, K.E.: see also Hagino, J.P.
Stout, C.: Weavers of the jade needle: Textiles in Highland Guatemala. Maxwell Museum, Albuquerque 1976 [Analysis; Ethnography; Weaving]
Straka, J.A. & Mackie, L.W.: The oriental rug collection of Jerome and Mary Jane Straka. New York 1978 [Collections; General, Historical; Warp Fabric; Pile Fabric]
Streiff, R.: "La collection Urubu (Brésil) du Musée d'Ethnography de Genève", Bull. Soc. Suisse des Américanistes 31, Genève 1967: 35-58 [Ethnography, Collections; Plaiting, Pile Fabric]
Strelow, R.: see also Eisleb, D. [Strickler-Streiff, H.: Zur Ausstellung echt javanischer Batiks und anderen malaiischen Textilerzeugnissen. Glarus 1925 [General, Historical, Ornamentation with Liquid Material(s)]
Stritz, A.: "Raffiaplusch aus dem Konigreich Kongo", Wiener Ethnohistorische Blatter 3, Wien 1971: 37-56 [Analysis, Ethnography, Pile Fabric]
Stromberg, E. & Arbman, H.: "Aslevantern Teknik", Fataburen, Stockholm 1934: 73-82 [Folk Art, Working Instruction, Mesh Fabric]
Strupp-Green, J.: "Archaelogical Chihuahuan textiles and modern Tarahumara weaving", Ethnos 1-4, Stockholm 1971: 115-130 [Ethnography, Archaeology; Weaving]
Strupp-Green, J.: "A Synoptic View of Research on Mexican Ethnographic Textiles", I Emery Roundtable on Mus. Textiles 1976, Washington 1977: 159-171 [Ethnography, General, Historical]
Strupp-Green, J. & Fisk, L.L.: "A Bibliography of Mexican Ethnographic Fabrics: Textiles and Costumes", I Emery Roundtable on Mus. Textiles 1976, Washington 1977: 172-237 [Ethnography, General, Historical]
Stuart-Fox, D.: see also Fenton, R.
Stucky, M.: see also Rapp, A.
Sturtevant, W.C.: "The Hole and Slot Heddle", I Emery Roundtable on Mus. Textiles 1976, Washington 1977: 235 [Folk Art, Weaving]
Sucharewa, O.A.: Posch, e feodalni y gorod Buchara. Taschkent 1962 [Ethnography]
Sugimura, T. & Suzuki, H.: Living Crafts of Okinawa. New York 1973 [Ethnography, Ornamentation with Liquid Material(s)]
Sumadio, B.: Pameran seni tenun tradisionil indonesia. Jakarta 1976 [Ethnography, Collections, Ornamentation with Liquid Material(s)]
Supakar, J.N.: "Music of the weave", The India Magazine, Fabric Vol.5 N°1, New Delhi 1985: 70-75 [Ethnography, Weaving, Ornamentation with Liquid Material(s)]
Susnik, B.: Artesanía indígena. Ensayo analítico. Asociación Indigenista del Paraguay, Asunción 1986 [Ethnography, Threads, Mesh Fabric, Plaiting; Warp Fabric; Weaving; Pile Fabric, Beadwork, Borders, Ornamentation with Solid Material(s)]
Suter, P.: Die letzten Heimposamenter, Kanton Basel-Landschaft. Schweiz. Ges. f. Volksk.: altes Handwerk 43, Basel 1978 [Folk Art; Films, Plaiting]
Suttles, W. (ed.): Northwest Coast Handbook of North Am. Indians 7, Washington 1990 [Ethnography, Plaiting, Warp Fabric]
Suwati, K.: Songket indonesia. Jakarta 1982 [Ethnography, Weaving]
Suzuki, H.: see also Sugimura, T.
Svobodová, V.: Mitteleuropa/ West-Mahren: Bandweben mit dem Webgitter. Encyclopaedia Cinematographica E 1810, 5 (2), Gottingen 1975 [Folk Art, Films, Weaving]
Svobodová, V.: Mitteleuropa/ West-Mahren: Teppichweben am Trittwebstuhl. Encyclopaedia Cinematographica E 1811, 5 (3), Gottingen 1975 [Folk Art, Films, Weaving]
Svobodová, V. & Kûava, P.: Mitteleuropa/ West-Mahren: Flachsernte und Flachsverarbeitung (Riffeln, Brechen, Hecheln, Spinnen). Encyclopaedia Cinematographica E 1809, 5 (2), Gottingen 1975 [Folk Art, Films, Threads]
Swallow, D.A.: "Javanese batiks: Meaning, interpretation and change", Indonesian Circle 42, London 1987 [Ethnography, General, Historical; Ornamentation with Liquid Material(s)]
Swanson, E. & Bryon, A.: "An Archaeological Survey of Caves in Washington", American Antiquity Vol.19 N°4, Salt Lake City 1954: 387-389 [Archaeology, Threads]
Swartz, B.K.: A Study of the Material Aspect of Northeastern Maidu Basketry. Kroeber Anthrop. Soc. Papers 19, Berkeley 1958

[Ethnography; Plaiting]
Swiezy, J.: Stroj podlaski: nadbuzanski. Atlas polskich strojow ludowych Vol.4 N°5, Wroclaw 1958 [Folk Art; Weaving]
Sylvester, D.: see also Mc Mullan, J.V.
Sylwan, V.: "Dekorative Wirkereien und Webereien im mittelalterlichen Schweden.", Zeitschrift für bildende Kunst, Leipzig 1928: 92-100 [General, Historical; Warp Fabric; Tapestry]
Sylwan, V.: Svenska Ryor. Stockholm 1934 [Analysis; Folk Art, Pile Fabric]
Sylwan, V.: Woollen Textilies of the Lou-lan People. The Sino-Swedish Expedition Publ. 15 (7,2), Stockholm 1941 [Analysis, Archaeology; Threads; Plaiting; Warp Fabric, Weaving; Borders]
Sylwan, V.: Investigation of Silk from Edsen-Gol and Lop-Nor. The Sino-Swedish Expedition Publ. 32 (7), Vol.6, Stockholm 1949 [Archaeology; Weaving]
Szabó, T.A.: see also Palotay, G.

Taber, B. & Anderson, M.: Backstrap weaving. New York 1975 [General, Historical; Weaving]
Tada, M.: Kumihimo: Silk Braids of Japan. Washington 1986 [Ethnography; Plaiting]
Talwar, K. & Krishna, K.: Indian pigment paintings on cloth. Hist. Textiles of India, Calico Vol. 3, Bombay 1979 [General, Historical; Ornamentation with Liquid Material(s)]
Tanavoli, P.: Lion rugs from Fars from the collection of Parviz and Manijeh. Oshkosh 1974 [Ethnography; Collections; Pile Fabric]
Tanavoli, P.: Lion Rugs from Fars. Kashani 1978 [Ethnography, Collections; Pile Fabric]
Tanavoli, P.: Shahsavan. Fribourg 1985 [Classification; Analysis; Ethnography; Threads; Warp Fabric; Weaving; Pile Fabric; Borders]
Tanavoli, P.: Lion Rugs: The Lion in the Art and Culture of Iran. Basel 1985 [Analysis, Ethnography; Collections; Pile Fabric]
Tanner, C.L.: Southwest Indian Craft Arts. Tucson 1968 [Analysis, Ethnography; Plaiting; Warp Fabric; Borders]
Tanner, C.L.: Prehistoric Southwestern Craft Arts. Tucson 1976 [Threads; Mesh Fabric; Plaiting; Warp Fabric, Weaving; Borders; Ornamentation with Liquid Material(s)]
Tanner, C.L.: Apache Indian Baskets. Tucson 1982 [Ethnography, Plaiting]
Tanner, C.L.: Indian Baskets of the Southwest. Tucson 1983 [Ethnography; Plaiting]
Tanner, H.: "Cashinahua Weaving", Dwyer, J.P. (ed.) The Cashinahua of Eastern Peru. Boston 1975: 111-124 [Ethnography; Weaving]
Targonska, A.: Wzornik rzeszowskich haftow ludowych. Rzenzów 1985 [General, Historical; Ornamentation with Solid Material(s)]
Taszycka, M.: Ceintures et costumes polonais. Mulhouse 1972 [Folk Art; Collections; Weaving]
Tattersall, C.E.C.: Notes on carpet-knotting and weaving. Victoria and Albert Museum, London 1927 [Analysis; Collections; Warp Fabric; Pile Fabric; Borders]
Taullard, A.: Tejidos y ponchos indígenas de Sudamérica. Buenos Aires 1949 [Analysis; Ethnography; Archaeology; Threads; Mesh Fabric; Warp Fabric; Weaving; Pile Fabric; Ornamentation with Solid Material(s); Ornamentation with Liquid Material(s); Tapestry]
Tay Pike, A.: see also Moes, R.
Taylor, D. & Moore, H.C.: "A note on Dominican Basketry and its analogues", Southwest Journ. of Anthrop. 4 (3), Albuquerque 1948: 328-343 [Ethnography, Plaiting]
Taylor, G.J.: "Historical Ethnography of the Labrador Coast", Handbook of North Am. Indians 5, Washington 1984: 508-521 [Ethnography; Plaiting]
Taylor, W.W.: "Archaic Cultures Adjacent to the Northeastern Frontiers of Mesoamerica", Handbook of Middle Am. Indians 4, Austin 1966: 59-94 [Archaeology, Mesh Fabric, Plaiting]
Teit, J.A.: see also Haeberlin, H.K.
Teleki, G.: The Baskets of Rural America. New York 1975 [Folk Art; Plaiting]
Tenri Sankokan Museum: Yamato cotton textiles. Handbook of the Tenri Sankokan Museum N°20, Tenri 1981 [Collections, Plaiting, Weaving, Ornamentation with Liquid Material(s)]
Textilmuseum Krefeld: Osmanische Samte und Seiden. Krefeld 1978 [Analysis, Threads, Weaving, Pile Fabric]
Theisen, H.: "Herstellung eines Batak-Tuches (ulos sibolang sitolun tuho)", Archiv für Völkerkunde 36, Wien 1982 [Analysis, Ethnography, Ornamentation with Liquid Material(s)]
Therik, J.A.: Ikat in Eastern Archipelago. Jakarta 1989 [Ethnography, Weaving, Ornamentation with Liquid Material(s)]
Thomas, E.: "Netting without a Knot", Man 26, London 1926: 8-10 [General, Historical; Mesh Fabric]
Thomas, E.: "Notes on a knitting technique", Man 36, London 1936: 72 [General, Historical; Mesh Fabric]
Thomas, M.: Knitting Book. New York 1972 [Working Instruction, Mesh Fabric]
Thomas, M.: Book of knitting patterns. New York 1972 [Working Instruction, Mesh Fabric]
Thompson, G.H.: Spinning Wheels. Ulster Museum, Belfast 1964 [Folk Art, Collections, Threads]
Thompson, R.F.: Flash of the Spirit. New York 1983 [Ethnography, Weaving]
Thomson, J.: see also Mackie, L.W.
Thorpe, H.G.: "Its in the Cards", Handweaver and Craftsman 3, New York 1952: 17-19 [Working Instruction; Weaving]
Thummel, A.: Knüpf-Arbeiten. Leipzig n.d. [Working Instruction, Plaiting]
Thurmann, C.C.M. & Williams, B.: Ancient textiles from Nubia. Chicago 1979 [Archaeology, Threads; Warp Fabric, Weaving]
Tidball, H.: "Jaspé", Shuttle Craft 1, Monterey 1957 [Working Instruction; Ornamentation with Liquid Material(s)]
Tidhar, A.: see also Bajinski, A.
Tidow, K.: Die Wollweberei im 15. bis 17. Jh. Veroff. des Forderver. Tex. Museums 6, Neumunster 1978 [Folk Art, Weaving]
Tidow, K.: "Untersuchungen an Wollgeweben aus Schleswig und Lübeck", Textilsymposium Neumünster, Neumünster 1982: 163-178 [Archaeology, Weaving]
Tidow, K.: Textilfunde aus dem Bergkloster und dem Heiligen Geist Hospital in Lubeck. Bonn 1982 [Archaeology, Mesh Fabric; Weaving]
Tidow, K.: Untersuchungen an WollgeWeben aus einem Brunnen auf dem Schrangen in Lubeck. Bonn 1983 [Archaeology; Weaving]
Tidow, K.: see also Bender-Jorgensen, L.
Tidow, K.: see also Ullemeyer, R.
Tiesler, E.: Doppeldurchbruch. Handarbeitstechnik Band 3, Leipzig 1977 [Working Instruction; Ornamentation with Solid Material(s)]
Tiesler, E.: Grundmuster. Stricken, Hakeln. Handarbeitstechnik Band 11, Leipzig 1980 [Working Instruction, Mesh Fabric]
Tiesler, E.: Knüpfen – Kloppeln. Handarbeitstechnik Band 6, Leipzig 1980 [Analysis, Working Instruction, Plaiting]
Tietze, K.: Sitten und Gebrauche beim Saen, Ernten, Spinnen, Ikatten, Farben und Weben der Baumwolle im Sikka-Gebiet.

Ethnologica Band 3, Köln 1941 [Ethnography; Threads; Weaving; Ornamentation with Liquid Material(s)]
Tikhonov, N.P.: see also Voskresensky, A.A.
Timmerman, I.: Seide, Purpur und Gold: Untersuchungen zu den Gewebefragmenten aus dem Schrein der Heiligen Drei Könige im Dom zu Köln. Köln 1982 [Archaeology; Weaving]
Timmermann, I.: "Studie zum Batik auf Java", Baessler-Archiv NF 32, Berlin 1984: 69-112 [General, Historical; Ornamentation with Liquid Material(s)]
Timmermann, I.: Die Seide Chinas. Eine Kulturgeschichte am seidenen Faden. Köln 1986 [General, Historical; Weaving]
Timmins, A.: Patchwork. Stoffmosaike und Applikationen. Ravensburg 1968 [Working Instruction; Ornamentation with Solid Material(s)]
Tirta, I.: Batik: the magic cloth. Hong-Kong 1974 [Ethnography; Ornamentation with Liquid Material(s)]
Tirtaamidjaja, N. & Anderson, B.R.O.: Batik, Pola and Tjorak-pattern and motif. Djakarta 1966 [Ethnography; Ornamentation with Liquid Material(s)]
Tkalcic, V.: Selzacko cilimarstvo u Jugoslaviji. Etnoloska Biblioteka Band 5, Zagreb 1929 [Folk Art; Warp Fabric; Weaving; Pile Fabric]
Tolmachoff, E.: see also Stephani, L.
Tomita, J.: Japanese ikat weaving: the technique of kasuri. London 1982 [Analysis; Ornamentation with Liquid Material(s)]
Tomoyuki, Y.: "Dyeing through the Ages", Japan Quarterly Vol.13 N°2, Tokyo 1966: 207-213 [Ethnography; Ornamentation with Liquid Material(s)]
Topham, J.: Traditional crafts of Saudi Arabia. London 1981 [Analysis; Ethnography; Warp Fabric; Weaving]
Torella Nuibò, F.: Breve Historia del Tejido artistico a través de una visita al Museo. Las Colecciones del Museo Textil, Tarasa 1949 [Folk Art; Collections; Weaving]
Torres, R.M.: El Arte de los Huicholes. Guadalajara 1980 [Ethnography; Plaiting; Weaving; Beadwork; Ornamentation with Solid Material(s)]
Tovey, J.: The Technique of Weaving. London 1965 [Working Instruction; Weaving]
Tracht, A.: see also Adelson, L.
Traetteberg, R.: see also Hoffmann, M.
Treiber-Netoliczka, L.: "Das Nachleben der bronzezeitlichen Frauenhäubchen und der Stäbchenflechterei in Siebenbürgen", Festschrift für H. Reinerth. Singen 1970 [Analysis; Folk Art; Warp Fabric]
Trigger, B.G. (ed.): Northeast Handbook of North Am. Indians 15, Washington 1978 [Ethnography; Plaiting; Beadwork]
Trilling, J.: Aegean crossroads: Greek island embroideries. Washington 1983 [Folk Art; Ornamentation with Solid Material(s)]
Trivedi, R.K. (ed.): Selected Crafts of Gujarat. Census of India Vol. 5 Part 7a 69, Dehli 1961 [Ethnography; Plaiting]
Trivedi, R.K.: Selected Crafts of Gujarat: Sujani weaving of Broach. Census of India 1961, Ahmedabad 1967 [Ethnography; Threads; Weaving]
Trivedi, R.K.: Selected Crafts of Gujarat. Census of India 1961 Vol.5 Part 7a, Ahmedabad 1969 [Ethnography; Ornamentation with Liquid Material(s)]
Trivedi, R.K.: Selected Crafts of Gujarat: Block engraving at Pethapur. Census of India 1961 Vol.5 Part 7A, Ahmedabad 1970 [Ethnography]
Trnka, Z.: "Zariecska a Páchovská Farbiaren Morddotlace: Blaudruckfärberei in Zariecie und in Púchov", Slovensky Narodopis 7 (1), Bratislava 1959: 55-88 [Folk Art; Ornamentation with Liquid Material(s)]
Trudel, V.: Schweizer Leinenstickerei des Mittelalters und der Renaissance. Bern 1954 [Folk Art; Ornamentation with Solid Material(s)]
Trupp, F.: Maku (Südost-Kolumbien, Provinz Vaupes): Flechten eines Sammelkorbes. Encyclopaedia Cinematographica E 2548, 10 N°12, Göttingen 1980 [Ethnography; Films; Plaiting]
Tschopik, H.: "Navaho Basketry: a Study of Culture Change", Am. Anthrop. N. S. 42, Menasha 1940: 444-462 [Ethnography; Plaiting]
Tsering, T.: see also Schmidt-Thome, M.
Tsevan, C.T.: Batikmuster bei den nationalen Minderheiten der Provinz Kweichow. Peking 1956 [Ethnography; Ornamentation with Liquid Material(s)]
Tsunoyama, Y.: Pre-Inca textiles in color. Tokio 1966 [Archaeology; Collections; Warp Fabric; Weaving; Ornamentation with Liquid Material(s)]
Tsunoyama, Y.: Textiles of the Andes: Catalogue of the Amano collection. San Francisco 1980 [Analysis; Collections; Mesh Fabric; Warp Fabric; Weaving; Pile Fabric; Ornamentation with Solid Material(s); Ornamentation with Liquid Material(s), Tapestry]
Tsunoyama, Y.: see also Amano, Y.
Tucci, G.: "Old and New Handicrafts in Sardinia", Kultuurpatronen 5-6, Delft 1963: 161-194 [Folk Art; Plaiting; Weaving]
Tuchscherer, J.M. & Vial, G.: Le musée historique des tissus de Lyon. Lyon 1977 [General, Historical]
Tunis, A. & Meurant, G.: Traumzeichen: Raphiagewebe des Königreiches Bakuba. Haus der Kulturen der Welt, München 1989 [Analysis; Ethnography; Weaving; Pile Fabric; Ornamentation with Solid Material(s)]
Tunis, A.: see also Meurant, G.
Tuohy, D.R.: see also Rendall, J.
Turnbaugh, S. & Turnbaugh, W.A.: Indian Baskets. West Chester 1986 [Analysis; Ethnography; Archaeology; Plaiting; Pile Fabric; Beadwork; Borders]
Turnbaugh, W.A.: see also Turnbaugh, S.
Turnbull, K.J.: "Recollections: Elizabeth Bayley Willis and her Collections", Arts of Asia Vol.12 N°4, Hong Kong 1982: 106-119 [Ethnography; Collections; Weaving; Ornamentation with Solid Material(s); Ornamentation with Liquid Material(s)]
Turner, A.: "Fragment: Pre-Columbian cloth found in Utah", Handweaver and Craftsman Vol.22 N°1, New York 1971: 20-21 [Archaeology; Tapestry]
Turner, G.: Hair Embroidery in Sibiria and North America. Pitt-Rivers Mus. Occ. Pap. in Technology 7, Oxford 1955 [Analysis; Ethnography; Ornamentation with Solid Material(s)]

Ullemeyer, R. & Tidow, K.: Die Textil- und Lederfunde der Grabung Feddersen Wierde. Hildesheim 1973 [Analysis; Archaeology; Threads; Warp Fabric; Weaving; Fabric Processing]
Ulloa, L.: Vestimientas y Adornos Prehispánicos en Arica. Santiago (Chile) 1985 [Archaeology; Mesh Fabric; Plaiting; Warp Fabric; Weaving; Pile Fabric]
Underhill, R.: Workaday Life of the Pueblos. Indian Life and Customs N°4, Phoenix n.d. [Ethnography; General, Historical; Weaving]
Underhill, R.: Indians of Southern California. Sherman Pamphlets N°2A, Los Angeles 1941 [Ethnography; General, Historical; Plaiting]
Underhill, R.: The northern Paiute Indians. Sherman Pamphlets N°1B, Los Angeles 1941 [Ethnography; General, Historical; Plaiting]
Underhill, R.: Indians of the Pacific Northwest. Riverside 1945

[Analysis; Ethnography, Plaiting; Weaving; Borders]
Underhill, R.: Pueblo Crafts. Indian Handicrafts 7, Los Angeles 1948 [Analysis, Ethnography; Threads; Plaiting; Warp Fabric; Weaving; Borders]
Ungricht, F.: "Das Schnurweben im Bezirk Andelfingen", Schweiz. Archiv für Volkskunde 21, Basel 1917: 28-30 [Folk Art; Threads; Weaving]
University of Singapore Art Museum: Indian Textiles. Singapore 1964 [Ethnography; Weaving; Ornamentation with Solid Material(s); Ornamentation with Liquid Material(s)]
Upitis, L.: Latvian mittens. Traditional designs and techniques. St. Paul 1981 [Folk Art; Working Instruction; Mesh Fabric]
Uplegger, H.: "Zur Korbflechterei in Marokko", Zeitschrift für Ethnologie 94, Berlin 1969 [Ethnography; Plaiting]
Ursin, A. & Kilchenmann, K.: Batik. Harmonie mit Wachs und Farbe. Bern 1979 [Working Instruction; Ornamentation with Liquid Material(s)]
Usher, A.P.: A History of Mechanical Invention. Boston 1959: 258-303 [General, Historical, Weaving]

Václavík, A.: Volkskunst und Gewebe: Stickereien des tschechischen Volkes. Prag 1956 [Folk Art; Mesh Fabric; Plaiting; Weaving; Ornamentation with Solid Material(s)]
Václavík, A. & Orel, J.: Textile Folk Art. London n.d. [Folk Art; Mesh Fabric, Weaving, Ornamentation with Solid Material(s)]
Vahter, T.: "Ikat- eli flammurai taisia kaukaiten", Suomen Museo N°63, Helsinki 1951: 21-34 [Folk Art, Ornamentation with Liquid Material(s)]
Valansot, O.: "Du métier Bouchon à la mécanique Jacquard", Jelmini, J.-P. et al. (ed.) La soie. Neuchâtel 1986: 103-108 [Folk Art; Weaving]
Valentin, P.: "Raffia im Kameruner Grasland", Ethnologische Zeitschrift 1, Zürich 1970: 67-73 [Ethnography; Plaiting; Pile Fabric]
Valette, M.: "Note sur la teinture des tissus précolombiens du Bas-Pérou", Journal de la Soc. Américanistes N.S. 10, Paris 1913: 43-46 [Archaeology, Ornamentation with Liquid Material(s)]
Vallinheimo, V.: Das Spinnen in Finnland. Kansatieteellinen Arkisto N°11, Helsinki 1956 [Folk Art; Threads]
Valonen, N.: Geflechte und andere Arbeiten aus Birkenrindenstreifen, unter Berücksichtigung finnischer Tradition. Kansatieteellinen Arkisto N°9, Vammala 1952 [Analysis; Folk Art; Plaiting]
Van Gelder, L.: "Indonesian ikat fabrics and their techniques", Fischer, J. (ed.) Threads of Tradition, Berkeley 1979: 35-39 [Ethnography, Ornamentation with Liquid Material(s)]
Van Gelder, L.: Ikat. New York 1980 [Analysis; Ethnography; Working Instruction, Ornamentation with Liquid Material(s)]
Van Gennep, A.: "Netting without a knot", Man 9 N°20, London 1909: 38-39 [Ethnography; Mesh Fabric]
Van Gennep, A.: "Note sur le tissage aux cartons en Chine", T'Oung-pao 13, Leiden 1912 [Ethnography; Weaving]
Van Gennep, A.: "Etudes d'Ethnography sudaméricaine", Journal de la Soc. des Américanistes 11 (1), Paris 1914: 121-133 [Ethnography, Weaving]
Van Gennep, A. & Jéquier, G.: Le tissage aux cartons et son utilisation décorative dans l' Egypte ancienne. Neuchâtel 1916 [Archaeology, Weaving]
Van Stan, I.: Peruvian Domestic Fabrics form Supe: A Study of the Uhle Collection of Painted Cloths. Florida State Univ. Dep. of Anthr. and Arch. Vol. 1 N°3, Talahassee 1955 [Archaeology; Ornamentation with Liquid Material(s)]
Van Stan, I.: "A Peruvian Ikat from Pachacamac", American Antiquity 23 (2), Salt Lake City 1957: 105-159 [Archaeology; Ornamentation with Liquid Material(s)]
Van Stan, I.: Problems in Pre-Columbian Textile Classification. Florida State University Studies N°29, Tallahasse 1958 [Analysis; Archaeology; Threads; Tapestry]
Van Stan, I.: "A Peruvian Tasseled Fabric", Florida State Univ. Dep. of Anthrop. and Arch. Vol. 3, Talahassee 1958 [Archaeology; Borders]
Van Stan, I.: "Three Feather Ornaments from Peru", Archaeology, N.Y. 2, New York 1959: 190-193 [Archaeology; Plaiting; Pile Fabric]
Van Stan, I.: "Miniature Peruvian Shirts with Horizontal Neck Openings", American Antiquity 26 (4), Salt Lake City 1961: 524-31 [Archaeology; Tapestry]
Van Stan, I.: "Ancient Painted Textile Arts: Patchwork and Tie-Dye from Pachacamac", Expedition: Bull. Uni. Mus. Pennsylvania 3 (4), Philadelphia 1961: 34-37 [Archaeology; Ornamentation with Solid Material(s); Ornamentation with Liquid Material(s)]
Van Stan, I.: "A Problematic Example of Peruvian Resist-Dyeing", American Antiquity 29 (2), Salt Lake City 1963: 166-173 [Archaeology; Ornamentation with Liquid Material(s)]
Van Stan, I.: "Ancient Peruvian tapestries with reed warps", Archaeology, N.Y. 17, New York 1964: 251-261 [Archaeology; Warp Fabric; Tapestry]
Van Stan, I.: "A Peruvian Tapestry with Reed Warps", Bull. of the Needle and Bobbin Club 44 (1-2), New York 1964: 13-14 [Archaeology; Mesh Fabric; Tapestry]
Van Stan, I.: "A Triangular Scarf-like Cloth from Pachacamac, Peru", American Antiquity 30 (4), Salt Lake City 1965: 428-433 [Archaeology; Weaving]
Van Stan, I.: Textiles from beneath the Temple of Pachacamac, Peru. Philadelphia 1967 [Analysis; Archaeology; Collections; Weaving; Borders; Ornamentation with Solid Material(s); Ornamentation with Liquid Material(s); Tapestry]
Van Stan, I.: "Brocades or Embroideries? Seventeen Textiles from Pachacamac, Peru", Bull. of the Needle and Bobbin Club 50 (1-2), New York 1967: 5-30 [Archaeology; Weaving; Ornamentation with Solid Material(s)]
Van Stan, I.: "Six bags with woven pockets from Pre-Columbian Peru", Nawpa Pacha 7-8, 1969, Berkeley 1970: 17-28 [Archaeology; Weaving]
Van Stan, I.: "Did Inca weavers use an upright loom?", The J.B. Bird Precolumbian Textile Conf. 1973, Washington 1979: 233-238 [Archaeology; Weaving]
Vanstone, J.W.: "Mainland Southwest Alaska Eskimo", Handbook of North Am. Indians 5, Washington 1984: 224-246 [Ethnography; Plaiting]
Varadarajan, L.: "Towards a Definition of Kalamkari", Marg, Bombay 1978: 19-21 [Ethnography; Ornamentation with Liquid Material(s)]
Varadarajan, L.: South Indian Tradition of Kalamkari. Ahmedabad 1982 [Ethnography; Ornamentation with Liquid Material(s)]
Varadarajan, L.: Ajrakh and related techniques. Ahmedabad 1983 [Ethnography]
Varadarajan, L.: Traditions of Textile printing in Kutch. Ahmedabad 1983 [Ethnography; Ornamentation with Liquid Material(s)]
Vargas, E.P.: "El Enigma del Pallay", Boletín de Lima N°41, Lima 1985: 39-56 [Ethnography; Weaving]
Vasco Uribe, L.G.: Semejantes a los Dioses. Bogotá 1987 [Ethnography; Plaiting]
Veiga de Oliveira, E. & Galhano, F.: Tecnologia tradicional portuguesa. Lisboa 1978 [Analysis; Folk Art; Threads; Weaving]
Veldhuisen-Djajasoebrata, A.: Batik op Java. Rotterdam 1972

[Ethnography; Ornamentation with Liquid Material(s)]
Veldhuisen- Djajasoebrata, A.: Bloemen van het heelal: de kleurrijke wereld van de textiel op Java. Amsterdam 1984 [Ethnography; Ornamentation with Liquid Material(s)]
Veldhuisen-Djajasoebrata, A.: "On the origin and nature of Larangan: forbidden batik patterns from the Central Javanese Principalities", I.Emery Roundtable on Mus. Textiles 1979, Washington 1980: 201-222 [Ethnography; Ornamentation with Liquid Material(s)]
Veldhuisen-Djajasoebrata, A.: Weavings of power and might: the glory of Java. Museum voor Volkenkunde, Rotterdam 1988 [Ethnography, Ornamentation with Liquid Material(s)]
Veltman, T.J. & Fischer, H.W.: "De atjèhsche Zijdeindustrie", Int. Archiv für Ethnographie 20, Leiden 1912: 15-58 [Analysis; Ethnography; Weaving, Ornamentation with Liquid Material(s)]
Venegas, F.P.: El archipélago de los Roques y la Orchilla. Carácas 1956 [Ethnography, Mesh Fabric]
Vergara Wilson, M.: "New Mexican Textiles: A Contemporary Weaver Unravels Historic Threads", The Clarion Vol.13 N°14, New York 1988: 33-40 [Folk Art; Weaving; Ornamentation with Liquid Material(s), Tapestry]
Verma, R.J.: Basket industry in Uttar Pradesh. Allahabad 1961 [Ethnography; Plaiting]
Verma, R.J.: Cotton textiles industry in Uttar Pradesh with special reference to Mau Nath Bhanjan, Azamgarh. Census of India Vol.15 Part 7A, Allahabad 1965 [Ethnography; Weaving]
Verswijver, G.: "Essai sur l'usage de la parure chez les Indiens Kaiapó du Brésil Central", Bull. Ann. Mus. d'Ethnogr. 25-26, Genève 1983: 23-62 [Ethnography; Collections; Plaiting; Pile Fabric; Beadwork]
Verswijver, G.: "Analyse comparative des parures Nahua: Similitudes et différences", Musée d'Ethnography, Bull. Ann. N°29, 1986, Genève 1987: 25-67 [Ethnography; Pile Fabric]
Vesper, C.: Batik. Wittenberg 1922 [Working Instruction; Ornamentation with Liquid Material(s)]
Vial, G.: "Les soieries persanes de la Fondation Abegg", Bull. d. Liaison du Cieta 43/44, Lyon 1976: 26-100 [Analysis; Archaeology; Weaving]
Vial, G.: Treize ceintures de femmes marrocaines du 16e au 19e siècle. Riggisberg 1980 [Analysis; Ethnography; Collections; Weaving]
Vial, G.: "Presentation de deux tissus executés aux baguettes", Assoc. pour l'Etude et la Doc. des Textiles d'Asie, Paris 1985: 32-39 [Ethnography, Weaving]
Vial, G.: "Le Textil, les Tissus", Jelmini, J.P. et al. (ed.) La Soie. Neuenburg 1986: 71-101 [Classification; Analysis; Weaving]
Vial, G.: "Le Lampas", Assoc. pour l'Etude et la Doc. des Textiles d'Asie N°5, Paris 1986: 5-23 [Analysis; Ethnography; Weaving; Pile Fabric]
Vial, G.: see also Riboud, K.
Vial, G.: see also Tuchscherer, J.M.
Viatte, F. & Pinault, M.: Sublime Indigo. Marseille 1987 [Ethnography; Ornamentation with Liquid Material(s)]
Victoria and Albert Museum: Brief Guide to the Persian woven Fabrics. London 1928 [Ethnography; Collections; Weaving]
Victoria and Albert Museum: Guide to the Collection of Carpets. London 1931 [General, Historical; Warp Fabric; Pile Fabric; Tapestry]
Victoria and Albert Museum: Brief Guide to the Chinese Embroideries. London 1931 [Ethnography; Collections; Ornamentation with Solid Material(s)]
Victoria and Albert Museum: Fifty Masterpieces of Textiles. London 1951 [Collections]
Villegas, L. & Rivera, A.: Iwouya: la Guajira a través del tejido. Bogotá 1982 [Analysis; Ethnography; Mesh Fabric; Plaiting; Warp Fabric; Weaving]
Völger, G. & Weck, K.: Pracht und Geheimnis. Ethnologica N. F. 13, Köln 1987 [Ethnography; Archaeology; Collections; Weaving; Ornamentation with Solid Material(s); Ornamentation with Liquid Material(s)]
Vogelsanger, C.: "A sight for the gods", I. Emery Roundtable on Mus. Textiles 1979, Washington 1980: 115-126 [Ethnography; Weaving; Ornamentation with Liquid Material(s)]
Vogt, E.: Primäre textile Techniken. Wegleitungen des Kunstgewerbemuseums 128, Zürich 1935 [Classification; Analysis; Mesh Fabric; Warp Fabric]
Vogt, E.: Geflechte und Gewebe der Steinzeit. Basel 1937 [Analysis; Archaeology; Mesh Fabric; Plaiting; Warp Fabric; Weaving; Pile Fabric]
Vogt, E.: "Frühmittelalterliche Seidenstoffe aus dem Hochaltar der Kathedrale Chur", Zs. für Schweiz. Archäol. u. Kunstgesch. Band 13 Heft 1, Basel 1952 [Archaeology; Weaving]
Vogt, E.: "Frühmittelalterliche Stoffe aus der Abtei St. Maurice", Zs. für Schweiz. Archäol. u. Kunstgesch. Band 18 Heft 3, Basel 1958: 110-140 [Archaeology; Weaving]
Vogt, E.: "Die Textilreste aus dem Reliquienbehälter des Altars in der Kirche St.Lorenz bei Paspels", Zs. für Schweiz. Archeol. u. Kunstgesch. Band 23 Heft 2, Basel 1964: 83-93 [Archaeology; Weaving]
Vogt, E.: see also Iklé, F.
Volbach, W.F.: Spätantike und frühmittelalterliche Stoffe. Röm. Germ. Zentralmuseum Band 10, Mainz 1932 [Collections; General, Historical; Weaving]
Volkart, H.: "Die Brettchen- und Kammweberei", Mitt. d. ostschw. Geo.-Commer. Ges Heft 1, St.Gallen 1907: 1-17 [Folk Art; Weaving]
Volkart, H.: Schriftbänder in Brettchenweberei. St. Gallen 1915 [Folk Art; Weaving]
Volkart, H.: Schweizerische Webegitter. Neuchâtel 1916 [Folk Art; Weaving]
Vollmer, J.E.: "Archaeological and Ethnological Considerations of the Foot-Braced Body-Tension Loom", Gervers, V. (ed.) Studies in Textile History. Toronto 1977: 343-354 [Analysis; Ethnography; Archaeology; Weaving]
Vollmer, J.E.: "Archaeological Evidence for Looms from Yunnan", I.Emery Roundtable on Mus. Textiles 1977, Washington 1979: 78-79 [Archaeology; Weaving]
Vollmer, J.E.: "Oriental Textiles", Arts of Asia 11 (2), Hongkong 1981: 126-137 [Ethnography; Ornamentation with Solid Material(s)]
Vollmer, J.E. & Gilfoy, P.S.: "The Indianapolis Museum of Art – The Oriental Collection: Oriental Textiles", Arts of Asia Vol.11 N°2, Hong Kong 1981: 126-137 [Ethnography; Collections; Ornamentation with Solid Material(s); Ornamentation with Liquid Material(s)]
Von Bayern, T.: Reisestudien aus dem westlichen Südamerika. Berlin 1908 [Ethnography; Mesh Fabric]
Von Gayette Georgens, J.M.: see also Georgens, D.
Von Schorn, O.: Die Textilkunst. Leipzig 1885 [General, Historical; Weaving; Ornamentation with Solid Material(s)]
Vora, M.P.: see also Nanavati, J.M.
Voshage, A.: Das Spitzenklöppeln. Leipzig 1910 [Working Instruction; Plaiting]
Voskresensky, A.A. & Tikhonov, N.P.: "Technical Study of Textiles from the Burial Mounds of Noin-Ula", Bull. Needle and Bobbin Club Vol.20 N°1 & 2, New York 1936: 3-73 [Analysis; Archaeology; Weaving]
Vreeland, J.M.: "Procedimiento para la evaluación y clasificación del Material textil andino", Arqueológicas 15, Lima 1974: 70-

96 [Ethnography, Archaeology; Mesh Fabric; Warp Fabric]
Vreeland, J.M.: "Ancient Andean Textiles", Archaelology Vol.30 N°3, New York 1977 167-178 [Archaeology; Warp Fabric]
Vreeland, J.M.: "The Vertical Loom in the Andes, Past and Present", I.Emery Roundtable on Mus. Textiles 1977, Washington 1979 189-211 [Ethnography; Weaving]
Vreeland, J.M.: "Cotton Spinning and Processing on the Peruvian North Coast", Rowe, A.P (ed.) J.B. Bird Conf. on Andean Textile 1984, Washington 1986 363-373 [Ethnography; Threads]
Vreeland, J.M. & Muelle, J.C.: "Breve glosario de terminología textil andina", Boletín Sem. Arqu. Inst. Riva Aguero 17-18, Lima 1977: 7-21 [General, Historical]
Vromen, J.H.: "Multicolor application in African print work", The Tex. Journ. of Australia 45, Sydney 1970 [Ethnography; Ornamentation with Liquid Material(s)]
Vromen, J.H.: "Primitive prints for fashion fabrics", The Tex. Journ. of Australia 45, Sydney 1970 [Ethnography; Ornamentation with Liquid Material(s)]
Vrydagh, P.A.: "Makisi of Zambia", African Arts Vol.10 N°4, Los Angeles 1977 12-19 [Ethnography; Mesh Fabric]
Vuia, R.: "Flechterei mit Stabchen bei den Rumänen", Zeitschrift für Ethnologie 46, Berlin 1914 [Folk Art; Warp Fabric]
Vuldy, C.: "Pekalongan: Batik et Islam dans une ville du Nord de Java", Etudes Insulindiennes / Archipel N°8, Paris 1987 [Ethnography; General, Historical; Ornamentation with Liquid Material(s)]
Vydra, J.: Der Blaudruck in der slowakischen Volkskunst. Prag 1954 [Folk Art; Ornamentation with Liquid Material(s)]

Wace, A.J.B.: Egyptian Textiles III-VIII Century. Société d'Archéologie Copte, Caire 1944 [Archaeology; Collections; Weaving; Tapestry]
Wace, A.J.B.: "Preliminary Historical Study: A late Roman Tapestry from Egypt", Workshop Notes 9, Washington 1954 [Archaeology; Tapestry]
Wace, A.J.B.: see also Ashton, L.
Wacziarg, F. & Nath, A.: Arts and crafts of Rajasthan. London 1987 [Ethnography, Weaving; Pile Fabric; Ornamentation with Solid Material(s); Ornamentation with Liquid Material(s)]
Wada, Y.: Shibori: the inventive art of Japanese shaped resist dyeing: Tradition, techniques, innovation. New York 1983 [Classification, Analysis, Ornamentation with Liquid Material(s)]
Wada, Y.: see also Ritch, D. [Wagner, F.A.: Sierkunst in Indonesie. Insulinde N 6, Groningen 1949 [Ethnography; Plaiting; Ornamentation with Liquid Material(s)]
Wagner, F.A.: see also Langewis, L.
Wahlman, M.S.: "African Symbolism in Afro-American Quilts", African Arts Vol 20 N°1, Los Angeles 1986: 68-76 [Folk Art; Ornamentation with Solid Material(s)]
Waite, D.B.: Artefacts from the Solomon Islands in the Julius L. Brenchley Collection. London 1987 [Ethnography; Collections; Mesh Fabric; Plaiting]
Walker, M.: Quiltmaking in Patchwork and Appliqué. London 1985 [Folk Art, Working Instruction; Ornamentation with Solid Material(s)]
Wallace, D.T.: "Early Paracas Textile Techniques", American Antiquity 26, Salt Lake City 1960: 279-281 [Archaeology; Ornamentation with Solid Material(s)]
Wallace, D.T.: "A warp set-up from the south coast of Peru", American Antiquity 32, Salt Lake City 1967: 401-402 [Archaeology; Weaving]
Wallace, D.T.: "The analysis of weaving patterns examples from the Early Periods in Peru", I.Emery Roundtable on Mus. Textiles 1974, Washington 1975 101-116 [Archaeology; Weaving]
Wallace, D.T.: "The Process of Weaving Development on the Peruvian Coast", The J.B.Bird Precolumbian Textile Conf. 1973, Washington 1979: 27-50 [Archaeology; Weaving; Borders]
Wallace, D.T.: see also Kroeber, A.L.
Wallace, J.: Batik, à travers l' expérience de Jérome Wallace. Paris 1972 [Folk Art; Ornamentation with Liquid Material(s)]
Wallace, W.J.: "Southern Valley Yokuts", Handbook of North Am. Indians 8, Washington 1978: 448-461 [Ethnography; Mesh Fabric; Plaiting; Ornamentation with Solid Material(s)]
Wallach, E.: see also Zschorsch, G.
Walpole, U.: see also Ellis, F.
Walton, P.: "Textiles, Cordage and Raw Fibre from Coppergate", The Archaeology of York: The Small Finds Vol.17 N°5, London 1989: 16-22 [Analysis; Archaeology; Threads; Mesh Fabric; Plaiting; Weaving; Borders]
Wang, L.H.: The Chinese purse. Taiwan 1986 [Ethnography; Ornamentation with Solid Material(s)]
Wanner, A.: Bündner Trachten. Chur 1979: 348-354 [Folk Art; Threads; Ornamentation with Solid Material(s)]
Wanner, A.: Kunstwerke in Weiss: Stickereien aus St. Gallen und Appenzell. St.Gallen 1983 [Analysis; Collections; Ornamentation with Solid Material(s)]
Warburg, L. & Friis, L.: Spind og tvind. Kunstindustrimuseet og Herning Museum, Herning 1975 [General, Historical; Threads]
Wardle, H.N.: "Certain rare West-Coast baskets", American Anthropologist 14, Menasha 1912: 287-313 [Ethnography; Plaiting; Borders]
Wardle, H.N.: "An Ancient Paracas Mantle", Bull. of the Uni. Mus. Pennsylvania 7 (4), Philadelphia 1939: 20-25 [Archaeology; Ornamentation with Solid Material(s)]
Wardle, H.N.: "Triple Cloth: New Types of Ancient Peruvian Techniques", American Anthropologist Vol.46 N°3, Menasha 1944: 416-448 [Archaeology; Weaving]
Wark, E.: The Craft of Patchwork. London 1984 [Working Instruction; Ornamentation with Solid Material(s)]
Warming, W. & Gaworski, M.: The World of Indonesian Textiles. London 1981 [Ethnography; Weaving; Ornamentation with Liquid Material(s)]
Washburn, D.K. & Crowe, D.W.: Symmetries of culture: theory and practice of plane pattern analysis. University of Washington Press, Seattle, London 1988 [Ethnography; Archaeology; Mesh Fabric; Plaiting; Warp Fabric; Weaving; Beadwork; Ornamentation with Solid Material(s); Ornamentation with Liquid Material(s); Tapestry]
Wass, B. & Murnane, B.: African Textiles. Madison 1978 [Ethnography; Weaving; Ornamentation with Solid Material(s); Ornamentation with Liquid Material(s)]
Wasseff, W.W.: see also Forman, M.
Wassén, H.S.: "Some words on the Cuna Indians and especially their "Mola"- Garments", Revista do Museu Paulista N°15, São Paulo 1964: 329-357 [Ethnography; Ornamentation with Solid Material(s)]
Wassén, S.H.: Mola: Cuna-Indiansk textilkonst. Göteborg 1962 [Ethnography; Ornamentation with Solid Material(s)]
Wassén, S.H.: A Medicine-man's Implements and Plants in a Tiahuanacoid Tomb in Highland Bolivia. Etnologiska Studier 32. Göteborg 1972 [Archaeology; Mesh Fabric; Plaiting; Weaving; Ornamentation with Solid Material(s); Tapestry]
Wassermann, T.E. & Hill, J.S.: Bolivian Indian Textiles. New York 1981 [Ethnography; Weaving]
Wassing-Visser, R.: Weefsels en Adatkostums uit Indonesie. Volkenkundig Museum Nusantara, Delft 1982 [Ethnography; Weaving; Beadwork; Ornamentation with Liquid Material(s)]
Wastraprema, H.: Kain Adat: Traditional textiles. Jakarta 1976

[Ethnography; Ornamentation with Solid Material(s)]
Watkins, F.E.: The Native Weaving of Mexico and Guatemala. Los Angeles 1939 [Ethnography; Weaving]
Watson-Franke, M.B. "A woman's profession in Guajiro culture: Weavers", Antropologica 37, Caracas 1974: 24-40 [Ethnography; Weaving]
Watt, G.: Indian Art at Delhi, 1903. Delhi 1903 [Ethnography; Collections; Pile Fabric; Ornamentation with Solid Material(s); Ornamentation with Liquid Material(s)]
Wattal, H.K.: Technical survey of the carpet industry in India. Marg Vol.18 N°4, Bombay 1965 [Analysis; Ethnography; Pile Fabric]
Weber, F.: Indonesische Gewebe. Wegleitung Kunstgewerbemuseum, Zürich 1935 [Ethnography; Weaving]
Weber, H.: see also Niedner, M.
Weber, M.: Timor und seine Textiltechniken (Mimeo). Basel 1977 [Ethnography; Threads; Weaving; Ornamentation with Liquid Material(s)]
Weber, M.: Eleganz in Schwarz. Katalog zur Ausstellung "Spitzen vom 18.Jh. bis heute". Industrie- und Gewerbemuseum, St. Gallen 1979 [Folk Art; Plaiting]
Weber, R.L.: Emmon's notes on Field Museum's collection of Northwest Coast basketry. Fieldiana Anthropology 9, Chicago 1986 [Ethnography; Collections; Plaiting]
Webster, M.D.: Quilts: their story and how to make them. New York 1948 [General, Historical; Ornamentation with Solid Material(s)]
Weck, K.: see also Volger, G.
Wegner, B.& D.: "Stickereien in Afghanistan", Textilhandwerk in Afghanistan. Liestal 1983: 133-159 [Ethnography; Ornamentation with Solid Material(s)]
Wegner, D.: "Nomaden- und Bauernteppiche in Afghanistan", Baessler-Archiv NF 12, Berlin 1964: 141-179 [Ethnography; Pile Fabric]
Wegner, D.H.G.: Textilkunst der Steppen- und Bergvölker Zentralasiens. Gewerbemuseum Basel, Basel 1974 [Ethnography; Pile Fabric; Ornamentation with Solid Material(s); Ornamentation with Liquid Material(s); Tapestry]
Wegner, D.H.G.: "Der Knupfteppich bei den Belutschen und ihren Nachbarn", Tribus 29, Stuttgart 1980: 57-105 [General, Historical; Pile Fabric]
Wehmeyer, E.: Das unterhaltsame Textil Buch. Braunschweig 1949 [General, Historical; Threads; Mesh Fabric; Weaving]
Weigand, de, C.G. & Weigand, de, P.C.: "Contemporary Huichol Textiles: Patterns of Change", I.Emery Roundtable on Mus. Textiles 1976, Washington 1977: 293-297 [Ethnography; Weaving]
Weigand, de, P.C.: see also Weigand, de, C.G.
Weiner, A.B.& Schneider, J. (ed.): Cloth and Human Experience. Washington 1989 [Ethnography; Folk Art; Archaeology; Threads; Plaiting; Weaving; Ornamentation with Solid Material(s)]
Weir, M.: see also Simpson, L.E.
Weir, S.: Palestinian embroidery. A village arab craft. London 1970 [Ethnography; Ornamentation with Solid Material(s)]
Weir, S.: Spinning and Weaving in Palestine. London 1970 [Ethnography; Threads; Weaving]
Weir, S.: The Bedouin. London 1976 [Ethnography; Threads; Weaving; Tapestry]
Weir, S.: Palestinian Costume. London 1989 [Ethnography; Plaiting; Ornamentation with Solid Material(s); Ornamentation with Liquid Material(s)]
Weisswange, K.: Kpelle (Westafrica, Liberia): Knüpfen eines kleinen Fischnetzes. Encyclopaedia Cinematographica E 736, Göttingen 1966 [Ethnography; Films; Mesh Fabric]
Weisswange, K.: Loma (Westafrika, Liberia): Weben eines Vorratsbeutels mit Hilfe eines Litzenbündels. Encyclopaedia Cinematographica, Göttingen 1975 [Ethnography; Films; Weaving]
Weitlaner-Johnson, I.: Twine-Plaiting: a Historical, Technical and Comparative Study. Thesis UCL, Berkeley 1950 [Analysis; Ethnography; Archaeology; Warp Fabric]
Weitlaner-Johnson, I.: "Twine-Plaiting in the New World", Int. Congr. of Americanist 32, Kopenhagen 1956: 198-213 [Ethnography; Warp Fabric]
Weitlaner-Johnson, I.: "Miniature Garments found in Mixteca Alta Caves Mexico", Folk 8-9, 1966-67, Kopenhagen 1967: 179-190 [Archaeology; Warp Fabric; Borders]
Weitlaner-Johnson, I.: "A painted textile from Tenancingó", Archiv f. Völkerkunde 24, Wien 1970: 265-272 [Archaeology; Ornamentation with Liquid Material(s)]
Weitlaner-Johnson, I.: "Basketry and Textiles", Handbook of Middle Am. Indians, Univ. Texas 10 (1), Austin 1971: 297-321 [Archaeology; Plaiting; Weaving; Ornamentation with Liquid Material(s)]
Weitlaner-Johnson, I.: "Weft-wrap openwork techniques in arquaeological and contemporary textiles of Mexico", Textile Museum Journal 4.3, Washington 1976 [Analysis; Ethnography; Archaeology; Threads; Warp Fabric; Weaving; Ornamentation with Solid Material(s)]
Weitlaner-Johnson, I.: Design motifs on Mexican Indian textiles. Graz 1976 [General, Historical; Weaving]
Weitlaner-Johnson, I.: Los textiles de la Cueva de la Candelaria, Coahuila. Colección científica Arqueología 51, México 1977 [Archaeology; Weaving; Fabric Processing]
Weitlaner-Johnson, I.: "Old-Style Wrap Around Skirts Woven by Zapotec Indians of Mitla, Oaxaca", I.Emery Roundtable on Mus. Textiles 1976, Washington 1977: 238-255 [Ethnography; Mesh Fabric; Warp Fabric; Weaving]
Weitlaner-Johnson, I.: "The ring-warp loom in Mexico", I.Emery Roundtable on Mus. Textiles 1977, Washington 1979: 135-159 [Analysis; Ethnography; Weaving]
Weitlaner-Johnson, I. & Mac Dougall, T.: "Chichicaztli Fibre; the spinning and weaving of it in Southern Mexico", Archiv für Völkerkunde 20, Wien 1966 [Ethnography; Threads; Mesh Fabric]
Weitlaner-Johnson, I.: see also Heizer, R.F.
Weldon's Encyclopaedia: Weldon's Encyclopaedia of Needlework. London [Working Instruction; Mesh Fabric; Ornamentation with Solid Material(s)]
Wells, M.D.: Micronesian Handicraft Book of the Trust Territory of the Pacific Islands. New York 1982 [Ethnography; Plaiting; Beadwork]
Wells, O.: Salish Weaving: Primitive and Modern. Sardis 1969 [Ethnography; Weaving; Tapestry]
Weltfish, G.: Coiled Gambling Baskets of the Pawnee and other Plain Tribes. Indian Notes Vol.7 N°3, New York 1930 [Ethnography; Plaiting]
Weltfish, G.: "Prehistoric North American Basketry Techniques and Modern Distributions", American Anthrop. N. S. 32, Menasha 1930: 454-495 [Ethnography; Archaeology; Plaiting]
Weltfish, G.: "Problems in the Study of Ancient and Modern Basketmakers", American Anthropologist 34, Menasha 1932: 108-117 [Archaeology; Plaiting]
Wencker, R.: Zur Webtechnik: Gebilddamast. Krefeld 1968 [Folk Art; Collections; Weaving]
Wencker, R.: see also Jaques, R.
Wenstrom, E.: see also Graumont, R.
Wenzhao, L.: see also Huang, S.

Werder, M.: see also Horvàth, A B
Wertime, J.T.: "Flat-woven structures found in nomadic and village weavings from the near East and Central Asia", Textile Museum Journal 18, Washington 1979: 33-54 [Analysis; Ethnography; Warp Fabric; Weaving]
West, A.: Australian Aboriginal Cordage and Single-Element Fabric Structures (Thesis). Sidney 1980 [Analysis; Ethnography; Threads, Mesh Fabric, Borders; Fabric Processing]
Westfall, C.: see also Glashauser, S.
Westfall, C.D.: The web of India: a diary. Univ. Montclair 1981 [Ethnography; Threads; Weaving, Beadwork; Ornamentation with Solid Material(s); Ornamentation with Liquid Material(s)]
Westfall, C.D. & Desai, D.: Gujurati embroidery. Winnipeg 1987 [Ethnography, Ornamentation with Solid Material(s)]
Westfall, C.D. & Desai, D.: "Bandhani (tie dye)", Ars Textrina Vol. 8, Winnipeg 1987 [Ethnography; Ornamentation with Liquid Material(s)]
Westfall, C.D. & Desai, D.: "Kantha", Ars Textrina Vol. 7, Winnipeg 1987: 162-177 [Ethnography, Working Instruction; Ornamentation with Solid Material(s)]
Westhart, K.R.: see also Kremser, M.
Westphal-Hellbusch, S.: "Einige Besonderheiten der Kleidung der Jat im unteren Sind (Indus-Delta) und im Kutch", Baessler-Archiv NF 13, Berlin 1965: 402-430 [Ethnography; Ornamentation with Solid Material(s)]
Westphal-Hellbusch, S.: "Randgruppen im Nahen und Mittleren Osten", Baessler-Archiv NF 28, Berlin 1980: 1-60 [Ethnography; Plaiting]
Wey, O.: "Seeufersiedlungen am Sempachersee", Schweiz. Landesmuseum (ed.) Die ersten Bauern. Pfahlbaufunde Europas Vol. 1, Zurich 1990: 281-284 [Archaeology; Warp Fabric]
Wheat, J.B.: "Documentary Basis for Material Changes and Design Styles in Navajo Blanket Weaving", I. Emery Roundtable on Mus. Textiles 1976, Washington 1977: 420-444 [Ethnography, Warp Fabric, Weaving; Tapestry]
Wheat, J.B.: The Gift of Spiderwoman. Southwestern Textiles: The Navajo Tradition. Philadelphia 1984 [Ethnography; Weaving; Tapestry]
Whitaker, K.: Navajo Weaving Design: 1750-1900: Thesis of the University of California. Los Angeles 1986 [Ethnography; Weaving; Tapestry]
Whitaker, T.W.: see also O'Neale, L.M.
White, V.: Pa Ndan. The needle work of the Hmong. Cheney 1982 [Ethnography; General, Historical; Ornamentation with Solid Material(s)]
Whiteford, A.H.: Southwestern Indian Baskets: their History and their Makers: With a Catalogue of the School of American Research Coll. Santa Fe 1988 [Ethnography; Plaiting]
Whitford, A.C.: "Fibreplants of the North American Aborigines", Journal of the NY Botanical Garden Feb Vol.44 N°518, New York 1943: 25-48 [Archaeology; Threads; Mesh Fabric; Plaiting; Warp Fabric]
Whiting, A.: "Hopi Textiles", I Emery Roundtable on Mus. Textiles 1976, Washington 1977: 413-419 [Ethnography; Weaving]
Whiting, G.: "Netted Feather Robes", Bull. Needle and Bobbin Club Vol.9 N°1, New York 1925: 36-44 [Ethnography; Pile Fabric]
Wiasmitinow, A.: "Aus der Geschichte des Zeugdruckes seit Beginn bis Perkin", Sandoz Bull 17 N°1, Basel 1963 [Folk Art; Ornamentation with Liquid Material(s)]
Widmer, M.: Knupfen heute. n.p., n.d. [Analysis; Working Instruction; Plaiting]
Wiedemann, I.: "Coca Pouches from Colombia", Kutscher,G. (ed.) Indiana 3, Berlin 1975: 111-118 [Analysis; Ethnography; Mesh Fabric; Plaiting; Borders]
Wiedemann, I.: "The Folklore of Coca in the South-American Andes: Coca Pouches, Lime Calabashes and Rituals", Zeitschrift für Ethnologie Band 104 N°2, Braunschweig 1979: 278-304 [Ethnography; Weaving]
Wiedemann, I.: "Brazilian hammocks", Zeitschrift für Ethnologie Band 104 N°1, Braunschweig 1979: 105-133 [Ethnography; Mesh Fabric; Warp Fabric]
Wiet, G.: Tissus et Tapisseries du Musée Arabe au Caire. Syria 16, Paris 1935 [Ethnography; Weaving; Tapestry]
Wilbert, J.: The Thread of Life. Stud. Pre-Col. Art + Arch. 12, Washington 1974 [Ethnography; Archaeology; Threads]
Wilbert, J.: Warao Basketry: Form and Function. Occ. Pap. Mus. Cultural Hist. 3, Los Angeles 1975 [Analysis; Ethnography; Plaiting]
Wilbush, Z.: "Arab Women's Dress in Judea and Southern Israel", Ethnologische Zeitschrift 1, Zürich 1976: 5-29 [Ethnography; Ornamentation with Solid Material(s)]
Wilbush, Z. & Lancet-Müller, A.: Bokhara. Jerusalem 1967 [Ethnography]
Wild, J.P.: "Textiles", Strong, D. (ed.) Roman Crafts. New York 1976 [Archaeology; Threads; Weaving]
Wildschut, W. & Ewers, J.C.: Crow Indian Beadwork: A descriptive and historical study. Ogden 1985 [Ethnography; Beadwork]
Will, C.: Die Korbflechterei. Schönheit und Reichtum eines alten Handwerks. Material, Technik, Anwendung. München 1978 [Analysis; Folk Art; Working Instruction; Plaiting]
Willey, G. & Corbett, J.M.: Early Ancón and Early Supe Culture. Columbia Studies in Arch. and Ethnol. Vol. 3, New York 1954 [Analysis; Archaeology; Threads; Mesh Fabric; Plaiting; Warp Fabric; Weaving; Borders; Tapestry]
Williams, B.: see also Mayer Thurman, C.C.
Williams, B.: see also Thurmann, C.C.M.
Williams, D.: see also Jenkins, I.
Willoughby, C.C.: "Textile Fabrics of the New England Indians", Am. Anthropol. 7, Menasha 1905: 85-93 [Ethnography; Plaiting]
Willoughby, C.C.: "A new type of ceremonial blanket from the Northwest Coast", Am. Anthro. 12, Menasha 1910: 1-10 [Analysis; Ethnography; Warp Fabric]
Wilson, K.: A history of textiles. Boulder 1979 [Analysis; Ethnography; Folk Art; Archaeology; Threads; Mesh Fabric; Warp Fabric; Weaving; Ornamentation with Liquid Material(s)]
Winiger, J. & Hasenfratz, A.: Die Ufersiedlungen am Bodensee: Archäologische Untersuchungen im Kt. Thurgau 1981-83. Antiqua 10, Basel 1985 [Archaeology]
Wirz, P.: "Die magischen Gewebe von Bali und Lombok", Jahrbuch d. Bern. Hist. Museum 11, 1931, Bern 1932: 39-49 [Ethnography; Ornamentation with Liquid Material(s)]
Wirz, P.: "Die Gemeinde der Gogodara", Nova Guinea 16 (4), Leiden 1934: 371-490 [Ethnography; Mesh Fabric]
Wirz, P.: Die Ainu: Sterbende Menschen im Fernen Osten. Basel 1955 [General, Historical; Plaiting; Weaving]
Wissa, R.: Bildteppiche aus Harrania. Hanau 1972 [Ethnography; Tapestry]
Wissler, C.: Indian Beadwork. Am. Mus. of Nat. Hist. Guide N°50, New York 1919 [Ethnography; Beadwork]
Wolinetz, L.: see also Grabowicz, O.
Wollard, L.: Knotting and Netting. London 1953 [Mesh Fabric; Plaiting]
Woolley, G.C.: "Some notes on Murut basket work and patterns", J. o. t. Malayan Branch o. t. Royal Asiat Soc. 7 (2). 1929: 291-315 [Ethnography; Plaiting]
Woolley, G.C.: "Murut Basketwork", J. o. t. Malayan Branch o. t. Roy. Asiat. Soc. 10 (1), 1932: 23-28 [Ethnography; Plaiting]

Wright, D.: The Complete Book of Baskets and Basketry. New York 1977 [Ethnography, Folk Art, Working Instruction; Plaiting]
Wroth, W.: Hispanic crafts of the Southwest. Colorado 1977 [General, Historical, Weaving, Ornamentation with Solid Material(s)]
Wullf, H.E.: The traditional crafts of Persia. Cambridge 1966 [Analysis, Ethnography, Threads, Weaving; Pile Fabric]
Wyss, R.: "Ein Netzbeutel zur Thematik des Fernhandels", Schweiz. Landesmuseum (ed.) Die ersten Bauern. Pfahlbaufunde Europas Vol. 1, Zurich 1990: 131-133 [Archaeology; Warp Fabric]

Yamamoto, Y.: A sense of tradition. An ethnographic approach to Nias Material Culture. Ann Arbor 1986 [Ethnography; Plaiting]
Yamanobe, T.: Cotton fabrics with splashed patterns. n.p. 1960 [Ornamentation with Liquid Material(s)]
Yamanobe, T.: "Dyeing through the ages", Japan Quarterly 13.2, Tokyo 1966: 207-213 [Ethnography, Ornamentation with Liquid Material(s)]
Yanagi, S. & Ota, N.: Zwei Artikel über Bilder-Kasuri. Tokyo 1932 [Ethnography; Ornamentation with Liquid Material(s)]
Yde, J.: Material Culture of the Waiwái. Copenhagen 1965 [Ethnography; Threads, Mesh Fabric; Plaiting; Pile Fabric]
Yier, N.: see also Ranjan, M.P.
Yoffe, M.L.: "Botswana Basketry", African Arts Vol.12 N°1, Los Angeles 1978: 42-47 [Ethnography; Plaiting]
Yogi, O.: "Lurik, a traditional textile in Central Java", I.Emery Roundtable on Mus. Textiles 1979, Washington 1980: 282-288 [Ethnography, Ornamentation with Liquid Material(s)]
Yoke, R.S.: see also Landreau, A.N.
Yorke, R. & Allen, M.: Woven images: Bolivian weaving from the 19. and 20. centuries. Halifax 1980 [Ethnography; Collections; Weaving]
Yoshida, E.: Sashiko. n.p. 1977 [Ethnography]
Yoshida, H.: Njara Mwatu (boat shaped wooden sledge), and traditional textiles ethnographical Materials from Sumba and surrounding islands. Handbook of the Tenri Sankokan Mus. Coll. 19, Peking 1980 [Ethnography; Ornamentation with Liquid Material(s)]
Yoshimoto, S.: Kain perada. Hirayama collection: The gold-printed textiles of Indonesia. Kodansha 1988 [Analysis; Ethnography; Collections, Ornamentation with Solid Material(s)]
Yoshimoto, S.: see also Yoshioka, T.
Yoshioka, T. & Yoshimoto, S.: Sarasa of the world: Indian chintz, European print, batik, Japanese stencil. Tokyo 1980 [Ethnography; Ornamentation with Liquid Material(s)]
Young, D.M.D.: "Der amerikanische Patchwork Quilt", Sandoz Bull. 35, Basel 1974: 2-19 [Folk Art; Ornamentation with Solid Material(s)]
Young, S.: see also Bryan, N.G.
Yturbide, M.T. & Castello, C.M.: El traje indígena de México. 2, Mexico 1965 [Ethnography, General, Historical]

Zaldivar, M.L.L.: La cestería en México. México 1982 [Ethnography; Plaiting]
Zaloscer, H.: Ägyptische Wirkereien. Bern 1962 [Archaeology; Tapestry]
Zaman, N.: The art of Kantha embroidery. Dacca 1981 [General, Historical; Ornamentation with Solid Material(s)]
Zebrowski, M.: "The Hindu and Muslim elements of Mughal art with reference to textiles", Riboud, K. (ed.) In Quest of Themes and Skills. Bombay 1989: 26-35 [Ethnography; Archaeology; Weaving; Ornamentation with Solid Material(s); Ornamentation with Liquid Material(s)]
Zechlin, R.: Werkbuch für Mädchen. Ravensburg 1966 [Analysis; Working Instruction; Mesh Fabric; Plaiting; Weaving; Pile Fabric; Borders; Ornamentation with Solid Material(s); Ornamentation with Liquid Material(s); Fabric Processing]
Zeller, R.: "Über die Batiksammlung des Berner Museums", Jahresbericht des Hist. Museums, Bern 1907 [Ethnography; Collections; Ornamentation with Liquid Material(s)]
Zeller, R.: Malayanische Handweberei. Gewerbemus. Bern Wegleitung N°3, Bern 1926 [Ethnography; Ornamentation with Liquid Material(s)]
Zerries, O.: Altamerikanische Kunst: Mexico-Peru. München 1968 [Archaeology; Collections; Weaving; Pile Fabric; Ornamentation with Solid Material(s)]
Zerries, O.: Makiritare (Venezuela, Orinoco-Quellgebiet): Flechten einer Schale. Encyclopaedia Cinematographica E 1782, Göttingen 1974 [Ethnography; Films; Plaiting]
Zerries, O.: Makiritare (Venezuela): Ernten und Spinnen von Baumwolle. Encyclopaedia Cinematographica E 1781, Göttingen 1976 [Ethnography; Films; Threads]
Zerries, O.: Waika (Venezuela, Orinoco-Quellgebiet): Spinnen von Baumwolle. Encyclopaedia Cinematographica E 1801, Göttingen 1976 [Ethnography; Films; Threads]
Zerries, O.: Unter Indianern Brasiliens: Sammlung Spix und Martius 1817-1820. Sammlungen a. d. Staatl. Mus. f. Völkerk. Band I, München 1980 [Analysis; Ethnography; Collections; Plaiting; Pile Fabric]
Zerries, O. & Schuster, M.: Mahekodotedi. München 1974 [Ethnography; Mesh Fabric; Plaiting; Warp Fabric]
Zhan, H.: see also Ma, Z.
Zick-Nissen, J.: Nomadenkunst aus Balutschistan. Berlin 1968 [Ethnography; Collections; Tapestry]
Ziemba, W.T. & Abdulkadir, A.& Schwartz, S.L.: Turkish flat weaves (Anatolia). London 1979 [Analysis; Ethnography; Warp Fabric; Tapestry]
Zigmond, M.L.: "Kawaiisu", Handbook of North Am. Indians 11, Washington 1986: 398-411 [Ethnography; Plaiting]
Zimmermann, W.H.: "Archäologische Befunde]
frühmittelalterlicher Webhäuser", Textilsymposium Neumünster, Neumünster 1981 [Archaeology; Weaving]
Zimmermann, W.H.: "Archaeologische Befunde frühmittelalterlicher Webbäume: Ein Beitrag zum Gewichtswebstuhl", Textilsymposium Neumünster, Neumünster 1982: 109-134 [Archaeology; Weaving]
Zimmermann, W.H.: "Frühe Darstellung vom Gewichtswebstuhl auf Felszeichnungen in der Val Camonica (Lombardei)", Archaeological Textiles 2. NESAT Symposium, Kopenhagen 1984 [Archaeology; Weaving]
Zimmern, N.H.: Introduction to Peruvian Costume. The Brooklin Museum, New York 1949 [Archaeology; Collections; Weaving; Pile Fabric; Ornamentation with Solid Material(s)]
Zolles, M.: Nordische Handweberei. Plauern 1942 [Working Instruction; Weaving]
Zoras, P.: Broderies et ornements du costume Grec. Athenes 1966 [Folk Art; Ornamentation with Solid Material(s)]
Zorn, E.: "Warping and Weaving on a Four Stake Ground Loom in the Lake Titicaca Basin Community of Taquile, Peru", I.Emery Roundtable on Mus. Textiles 1977, Washington 1979: 212-227 [Ethnography; Weaving]
Zorn, E.: "Sling Braiding in the Macusani Area", Textile Museum Journal 19-20.1980-81, Washington 1980: 41-54 [Analysis; Ethnography; Working Instruction; Plaiting]
Zorn, E.: "Textiles in Herders' Ritual Bundles of Macusani, Peru",

Rowe, A.P. (ed.) J.B. Bird Conf. on Andean Textiles 1984, Washington 1986: 289-308 [General, Historical; Weaving]
Zschorsch, G. & Wallach, E & Lang, M.: Das Klöppeln. Berlin 1923 [Working Instruction; Plaiting]
Zumbühl, H.: Manual de construcción de un telar de pedal y sus auxiliares. Huancayo 1981 [Working Instruction; Weaving]
Zumbühl, H.: "Die Bandweberinnen von Viques, Peru", Ethnologica Helvetica 12, Basel 1988: 15-52 [Analysis; Ethnography; Weaving]

Index

Page numbers in **bold type** indicate primary references.

English

German

French

Italian

Portuguese, Spanish